DICTIONARY OF BANKING AND FINANCE

SECOND EDITION

Titles in the series

English Dictionary for Students	1-901659-06-2
Dictionary of Accounting	0-948549-27-0
Dictionary of Agriculture, 2nd ed	0-948549-78-5
Dictionary of American Business	0-948549-11-4
Dictionary of Automobile Engineering	0-948549-66-1
Dictionary of Banking & Finance, 2nd ed	1-901659-30-5
Dictionary of Business, 2nd ed	0-948549-51-3
Dictionary of Computing, 3rd ed	1-901659-04-6
Dictionary of Ecology & Environment, 3rd ed	0-948549-74-2
Dictionary of Government & Politics, 2nd ed	0-948549-89-0
Dictionary of Hotels, Tourism, Catering Management	0-948549-40-8
Dictionary of Human Resources & Personnel, 2nd ed	0-948549-79-3
Dictionary of Information Technology, 2nd ed	0-948549-88-2
Dictionary of Law, 2nd ed	0-948549-33-5
Dictionary of Library & Information Management	0-948549-68-8
Dictionary of Marketing, 2nd ed	0-948549-73-4
Dictionary of Medicine, 2nd ed	0-948549-36-X
Dictionary of Military	1-901659-24-0
Dictionary of Printing & Publishing, 2nd ed	0-948549-99-8
Dictionary of Science & Technology	0-948549-67-X
Professional Series	
Dictionary of Astronomy	0-948549-43-2
Dictionary of Multimedia, 2nd ed	1-901659-01-1
Dictionary of PC & the Internet, 2nd ed	1-901659-12-7

Workbooks

Check your:	
Vocabulary for Banking & Finance	0-948549-96-3
Vocabulary for Business, 2nd ed	1-901659-27-5
Vocabulary for Colloquial English	0-948549-97-1
Vocabulary for Computing	0-948549-72-6
Vocabulary for Hotels, Tourism	0-948549-75-0
Vocabulary for Law, 2nd ed	1-901659-21-6
Vocabulary for Medicine	0-948549-59-9

DICTIONARY OF BANKING AND FINANCE

SECOND EDITION

P.H. Collin

PETER COLLIN PUBLISHING

First published in Great Britain 1991
Second edition published 1999

Reprinted 2000

Published by Peter Collin Publishing Ltd
1 Cambridge Road, Teddington, Middlesex, TW11 8DT

British Library Cataloguing-in-Publication Data

A catalogue record for this book is available from the British Library

ISBN 1-901659-30-5

Text computer typeset by PCP
Printed and bound in Finland by WS Bookwell
Cover artwork by Gary Weston

Preface to the first edition

This dictionary provides a basic vocabulary of terms used in the fields of banking, investment, the Stock Exchange, and general finance. It covers both British and American usage.

The main words and phrases are defined in simple English, and many examples are given to show how the words may be used in context. In some cases, the definitions are expanded by explanatory comments. We also give quotations from newspapers and financial magazines from various parts of the world.

The supplement at the back gives additional information in the form of tables.

Preface to the second edition

The vocabulary of banking and finance, like that of so many modern disciplines, moves forward rapidly, and we have expanded and edited the text of the dictionary to keep pace with current changes. We have also made a further selection of recent quotations from newspapers and magazines.

At the same time, to make the dictionary more useful to students, we now give phonetic transcriptions for all the headwords.

Aa

Schedule A ['ʃedju:l 'eɪ] schedule to the Finance Acts under which tax is charged on income from land or buildings

Table A ['teɪbl 'eɪ] model articles of association of a limited company set out in the Companies Act, 1985

A, AA, AAA ['eɪ *or* 'dʌbl 'eɪ *or* 'trɪpl 'eɪ] letters indicating that a share or bond or bank has a certain rating for reliability; ***these bonds have a AAA rating***

> COMMENT: the AAA rating is given by Standard & Poor's or by Moody's, and indicates a very high level of reliability for a corporate or municipal bond in the US

> the rating concern lowered its rating to single-A from double-A, and its senior debt rating to triple-B from single-A
>
> *Wall Street Journal*

> the troubled retailer, which posted a shock profit warning last week, has lost its triple-A credit rating and been warned that the rating will be slashed again if a clear recovery strategy does not emerge
>
> *Sunday Business*

'A' shares ['eɪ 'ʃeəz] *plural noun* ordinary shares with limited voting rights or no right to vote at all

AAD = ARAB ACCOUNTING DINAR unit of account used between member states of the Arab Monetary Fund

ABA ['eɪ 'bi: 'eɪ] = AMERICAN BANKERS ASSOCIATION; **ABA transit number** = number allocated to an American financial institution, such as a bank (it appears on American cheques in the top right-hand corner, above the 'check routing symbol')

abandonment [ə'bændənmənt] *noun* act of giving something up voluntarily (such as an option or the right to a property)

abatement [ə'beɪtmənt] *noun* act of reducing; **tax abatement** = reduction of tax

ABI = ASSOCIATION OF BRITISH INSURERS

above par ['əbʌv 'pɑ:] *phrase* (share) with a market price higher than its par value

above-the-line [ə'bʌv ðə 'laɪn] *adjective & adverb* **(a)** *(companies)* income and expenditure before tax; ***exceptional items are noted above-the-line in company accounts*** **(b)** revenue items in a government budget dealing with taxes and government expenditure **(c)** *(advertising)* advertising for which a payment is made (such as an ad in a magazine or a stand at a trade fair) and for which a commission is paid to the advertising agency; *compare* BELOW-THE-LINE

absolute ['æbsəlu:t] *adjective* complete, total; **absolute monopoly** = situation where only one producer or supplier produces or supplies something; ***the company has an absolute monopoly of imports of French wine***; **absolute title** = land registered with the Land Registry, where the owner has a guaranteed title to the land (absolute title also exists to leasehold land, giving the proprietor a guaranteed valid lease)

absorb [əb'sɔ:b] *verb* **(a)** to take in a small item so as to form part of a larger one; **to absorb a surplus** = to take back surplus stock so that it does not affect a business; **overheads have absorbed all our profits** = all our profits have gone in paying overhead expenses; **to absorb a loss by a subsidiary** = to write a subsidiary company's loss into the main accounts **(b) business which has been absorbed by a competitor** = a small business which has been acquired by a larger one

absorption [əb'sɔ:pʃən] *noun* **(a)** making a smaller business part of a larger one **(b) absorption costing** = costing a product to include both the direct costs of production and the overhead costs which are absorbed as well; **absorption rate** = rate at which production costs are increased to absorb higher overhead costs

abstract ['æbstrækt] *noun* short form of a report or document; ***to make an abstract of the company accounts***

a/c *or* **acc** = ACCOUNT

accelerate [ək'seləreɪt] *verb* to make something go faster; to make a maturity date become closer

> in a separate development, the Geneva-based bank confirmed that it has accelerated the six Swiss bond issues. Acceleration means the bonds become payable immediately and allows bondholders to rank alongside the company's other creditors
>
> *Times*

accelerated depreciation [ək'seləreɪtɪd diprisi'eɪʃn] *noun* system of depreciation which reduces the value of assets at a high rate in the early years to encourage companies, because of tax advantages, to invest in new equipment; *compare* STRAIGHT-LINE DEPRECIATION

> COMMENT: this applied in the UK until 1984; companies could depreciate new equipment at 100% in the first year. The system still applies in the USA

acceleration [əkselə'reɪʃn] *noun* making an unpaid balance or bond repayment become payable immediately

accept [ək'sept] *verb* **(a)** to take something which is being offered; **to accept a bill** = to sign a bill of exchange to indicate that the drawee promises to pay it; **to accept delivery of a shipment** = to take goods into the warehouse officially when they are delivered **(b)** to say yes, or to agree to something; ***60% of shareholders have accepted the offer***

acceptable [ək'septəbl] *adjective* which can be accepted; ***the offer is not acceptable to the shareholders***

acceptance [ək'septəns] *noun* **(a)** (i) act of signing a bill of exchange to show that you agree to pay it; (ii) a bill which has been accepted; **to present a bill for acceptance** = to present a bill for payment by the person who has accepted it; **acceptance credit** = arrangement of credit from a bank, where the bank accepts bills of exchange drawn on the bank by the debtor: the bank then discounts the bills and is responsible for paying them when they mature; the debtor owes the bank for the bills but these are covered by letters of credit; **acceptance house** *US* **acceptance bank** = ACCEPTING HOUSE; *see also* DOCUMENTS AGAINST ACCEPTANCE **(b)** act of accepting an offer of new shares for which you have applied **(c) acceptance of an offer** = agreeing to an offer; **to give an offer a conditional acceptance** = to accept an offer provided that certain things happen or that certain terms apply; **we have his letter of acceptance** = we have received a letter from him accepting the offer

accepting house *or* **acceptance house** [ək'septɪŋ or ə'septəns 'haʊs] *noun* firm (usually a merchant bank) which accepts bills of exchange (i.e. promises to pay them) and is paid a commission for this; **Accepting Houses Committee** = the main London merchant banks, which organize lending of money with the Bank of England; they receive slightly better discount rates from the Bank

acceptor [ə'septə] *noun* person or company that signs a bill of exchange, and so undertakes to pay it

access ['ækses] **1** noun **to have access to something** = to be able to obtain or reach something; ***he has access to large amounts of venture capital***; ***she has access to the company's deposit account*** **2** *verb* to call up (data) which is stored in a computer; ***she accessed the address file on the computer***; **access time** = time taken by a computer to find data stored in it

Access ['ækses] British credit card organization, linked to the MasterCard system, run by three High Street banks

accommodation [əkɒmə'deɪʃən] *noun* **(a)** money lent for a short time **(b) to reach an accommodation with creditors** = to agree terms for settlement with creditors **(c) accommodation bill** = bill of exchange where the drawee who signs it is helping another company (the drawer) to raise a loan; it is given on the basis of trade debts owed to the borrower **(d) accommodation address** = address used for receiving messages but which is not the real address of the company

accordance [ə'kɔːdəns] noun **in accordance with** = in agreement with, according to, as someone says or writes; ***in accordance with your instructions we have deposited the money in your current account***; ***I am submitting the claim for damages in accordance with the advice of our legal advisers***

accord and satisfaction [ə'kɔːd ənd sætɪs'fækʃn] *noun* (i) payment by a debtor of (part of) a debt; (ii) the performing by a debtor of some act or service which is accepted by the creditor in full settlement, so that the debtor can no longer be sued

accordingly [ə'kɔːdɪŋli] *adverb* in agreement with what has been decided; ***we***

have received your letter and have altered the contract accordingly

according to [ə'kɔːdɪŋ 'tʊ] *preposition* as someone says or writes; ***the shares were bought according to written instructions from the client***

> the budget targets for employment and growth are within reach according to the latest figures
>
> *Australian Financial Review*

account [ə'kaʊnt] **1** *noun* **(a)** record of money paid or owed; ***please send me your account; the company asked for a detailed*** *or* ***an itemized account or costs incurred***; **expense account** = money which a businessman is allowed by his company to spend on travelling and entertaining clients in connection with his business; ***he charged his hotel bill to his expense account*** **(b)** *(in a shop)* arrangement which a customer has to buy goods and pay for them at a later date (usually the end of the month); ***to have an account*** *or* ***a charge account*** *or* ***a credit account with Harrods; put it on my account*** *or* ***charge it to my account***; *(of a customer)* **to open an account** = to ask a shop to supply goods which you will pay at a later date; *(of a shop)* **to open an account** *or* **to close an account** = to start or to stop supplying a customer on credit; **to settle an account** = to pay all the money owed on an account; **to stop an account** = to stop supplying a customer until he has paid what he owes **(c)** **on account** = as part of a total bill; **to pay money on account** = to pay to settle part of a bill; **advance on account** = money paid as a part payment **(d)** customer who regularly does a large amount of business with a firm and has an account with them; ***he is one of our largest accounts; our salesmen call on their best accounts twice a month***; **account executive** = employee who looks after certain customers or who is the link between certain customers and his company **(e)** **the accounts of a business** *or* **a company's accounts** = detailed record of a company's financial affairs; **to keep the accounts** = to write each sum of money in the account book; ***the accountant's job is to enter all the money received in the accounts***; **annual accounts** = accounts prepared at the end of a financial year; **management accounts** = financial information (sales, expenditure, credit, and profitability) prepared for a manager so that he can take decisions; **period of account** = period usually covered by a firm's accounts; **profit and loss account (P&L account)** = accounts for a company showing expenditure and income over a period of time, almost always one calendar year, balanced to show a final profit or loss (the balance sheet shows the state of a company's finances at a certain date; the profit and loss account shows the movements which have taken place since the last balance sheet) (NOTE: the American equivalent is the **profit and loss statement** or **income statement**); **accounts department** = department in a company which deals with money paid, received, borrowed or owed; **accounts manager** = manager of an accounts department; **accounts payable** = money owed by a company; **accounts receivable** = money owed to a company **(f)** **bank account** *US* **banking account** = arrangement to keep money in a bank; ***she has a building society account; he put the money into his bank account; he has an account with Lloyds; I have an account with the Woolwich; to put money in(to) your account; to take money out of your account*** *or* ***to withdraw money from your account***; **budget account** = account where you plan income and expenditure to allow for periods when expenditure is high, by paying a set amount each month; **current account** *or* **cheque account** *US* **checking account** = account which pays little or no interest but from which the customer can withdraw money when he wants by writing cheques; **deposit account** = account which pays interest but on which notice usually has to be given to withdraw money; **external account** = account in a British bank of someone who is living in another country; **frozen account** = account where the money cannot by used or moved because of a court order; **instant (access) account** = account which pays interest, but from which you can withdraw money when you need it; **joint account** = account for two people; ***most married people have joint accounts so that they can each take money out when they want it***; **offshore account** = account in a tax haven; **overdrawn account** = account where you have taken out more money than you have put in (i.e. where the bank is lending you money); **postal account** = account where all dealings are done by post, so reducing overhead costs and allowing a higher interest to be paid; **savings account** = account where you put money in regularly and which pays interest, often at a higher rate than a deposit account; **term account** = account where money is invested for a fixed period at a higher rate of interest; **to open an account** = to start an account by putting money in; ***she opened an account with the Halifax Building Society***; **to close an**

account = to take all money out of a bank account and stop the account; ***he closed his account with Lloyds*** **(g)** *(Stock Exchange)* period during which shares are traded for credit, and at the end of which the shares bought must be paid for (on the London Stock Exchange, there are twenty-four accounts during the year, each running usually for ten working days); **account day** = day on which shares which have been bought must be paid for (usually a Monday ten days after the end of an account) (also called 'settlement day'); ***share prices rose at the end of the account*** *or* ***at the account end***; **trading for the account** *or* **dealing for the account** *or* **account trading** = buying shares and selling the same shares during an account, which means that the dealer has only to pay the difference between the price of the shares bought and the price obtained for them when they are sold; *US* **rolling account** = system where there are no fixed account days, but stock exchange transactions are paid at a fixed period after each transaction has taken place (as opposed to the British system, where an account day is fixed each month) **(h)** *(balance of payments)* **current account balance of payments** = record of imports and exports, payments for services, and invisibles, etc.; **capital account** = items in a country's balance of payments which do not refer to the buying and selling of merchandise, but to investments made in other countries **(i)** notice; **to take account of inflation** *or* **to take inflation into account** = to assume that there will be a certain percentage inflation when making calculations **2** verb **to account for** = to explain and record a money deal; ***to account for a loss*** *or* ***a discrepancy***; ***the reps have to account for all their expenses to the sales manager***

accountancy [ə'kaʊntənsi] *noun* work of an accountant; ***he is studying accountancy*** *or* ***he is an accountancy student*** (NOTE: American English uses **accounting** in this meaning)

accountant [ə'kaʊntənt] *noun* person who keeps a company's accounts and prepares financial statements; person who advises a company on its finances; person who examines accounts; ***the chief accountant of a manufacturing group***; ***I send all my income tax queries to my accountant***; **certified accountant** = accountant who has passed the professional examinations and is a member of the Association of Certified Accountants: *US* **certified public accountant** = accountant who has passed professional examinations; **chartered accountant** = accountant who has passed the professional examinations and is a member of the Institute of Chartered Accountants; **cost accountant** = accountant who gives managers information about their business costs; **management accountant** = accountant who prepares financial information for managers so that they can take decisions; *US* **accountant's opinion** = report of the audit of a company's books, carried out by a certified public accountant

accounting [ə'kaʊntɪŋ] *noun* work of recording money paid, received, borrowed or owed; ***the auditors have introduced a new accounting system***; **accounting period** = period usually covered by a firm's accounts; **cost accounting** = preparing special accounts of manufacturing and sales costs; **current cost accounting** = method of accounting which notes the cost of replacing assets at current prices, rather than valuing assets at their original cost; **Accounting Standards Board** = committee set up by British accounting institutions to monitor methods used in accounting (NOTE: the word **accounting** is used in American English to mean the subject as a course of study, where British English uses **accountancy**)

> applicants will be professionally qualified and have a degree in Commerce or Accounting
>
> *Australian Financial Review*

accrete [ə'kri:t] *verb* to add to, especially to add interest to a fund

accretion [ə'kri:ʃn] *noun* adding interest to a fund over a period of time

accrual [ə'kru:əl] *noun* **(a)** noting financial transactions when they take place and not when payment is actually made; **accruals basis** *or* **accruals concept** = concept that accounts are prepared with financial transactions accrued (revenue and costs are both reported during the period to which they refer and not during the period when payments are received or made) **(b)** gradual increase by addition; **accrual of interest** = automatic addition of interest to capital

accrue [ə'kru:] *verb* to increase and be due for payment at a later date; ***interest accrues from the beginning of the month***; ***accrued interest is added quarterly***; **accrued dividend** = dividend earned since the last dividend was paid; **accrued interest** = interest which has been earned by an interest-bearing investment

acct [ə'kaʊnt] = ACCOUNT

accumulate [əˈkjuːmjʊleɪt] *verb* to grow larger by adding; ***to allow dividends to accumulate***; **accumulated depreciation** = total amount by which an asset has been depreciated since it was purchased; **accumulated profit** = profit which is not paid as dividend but is taken over into the accounts of the following year; **accumulated reserves** = reserves which a company has put aside over a period of years

accumulation [əkjuːmjəˈleɪʃn] *noun* growing larger by adding; **accumulation units** = type of units in a unit trust, where dividends accumulate and form more units (as opposed to income units, where the investor receives the dividends as income)

ACD = AUTHORIZED CORPORATE DIRECTOR

ACH *US* = AUTOMATED CLEARING HOUSE

achieve [əˈtʃiːv] *verb* to succeed in doing something, to do something successfully; ***the company has achieved great success in the Far East***; ***we achieved all our objectives in 1998***

> the company expects to move to profits of FFr 2m for 1990 and achieve equally rapid growth in following years
>
> *Financial Times*

acid test ratio [ˈæsɪd ˈtest ˈreɪʃiəʊ] *noun* ratio of liquid assets (that is, current assets less stock) to current liabilities, giving an indication of a company's solvency (NOTE: also called **quick ratio**)

ACP states [ˈeɪ ˈsiː piː ˈsteɪts] *noun* African, Caribbean and Pacific states which are linked to the European Community through the LomeacConvention (1985)

acquire [əˈkwaɪə] *verb* to buy; ***to acquire a company***

acquirer [əˈkwaɪərə] *noun* person or company that buys something (such as another company)

acquisition [ækwɪˈzɪʃən] *noun* (i) thing bought; (ii) act of getting or buying something; (iii) takeover of a company; ***the chocolate factory is his latest acquisition***; ***the company has a record of making profitable acquisitions of traders in the retail sector***; **acquisition accounting** *US* **purchase acquisition** = full consolidation, where the assets of a subsidiary company which has been purchased are included into the parent company's balance sheet, and the premium paid for the goodwill is written off against the year's earnings

across-the-board [əˈkrɒs ðə ˈbɔːd] *adjective* applying to everything or everyone; ***an across-the-board price increase***; **across-the-board tariff increase** = increase in duty which applies to a whole range of items

ACT [ˈeɪ ˈsiː ˈtiː] = ADVANCE CORPORATION TAX

act [ækt] **1** *noun* **(a)** law passed by a parliament which must be obeyed by the people *GB*; **Companies Act** = Act which rules how companies should do their business; **Finance Act** = annual Act of Parliament which gives the government power to raise taxes as proposed in the budget; **Financial Services Act** = Act of the British Parliament which regulates the offering of financial services to the public **(b)** **act of God** = something you do not expect to happen, and which cannot be avoided, such as storms or floods (acts of God are not usually covered by insurance policies) **2** *verb* **(a)** to work; ***to act as an agent for an American company***; ***to act for someone*** *or* ***to act on someone's behalf*** **(b)** to do something; ***the board will have to act quickly if the company's losses are going to be reduced***; ***the lawyers are acting on our instructions***; **to act on a letter** = to do what a letter asks to be done; *(of several people)* **to act in concert** = to work together to achieve an aim, such as to take over a company, especially is such a way as to defraud other investors; *see also* CONCERT PARTY

action [ˈækʃən] *noun* **(a)** thing which has been done; **to take action** = to do something; ***you must take action if you want to stop people cheating you*** **(b)** **direct action** = strike or go-slow by the workforce; **to take industrial action** = to do something (usually to go on strike) to show that you are not happy with conditions at work **(c)** case in a law court where a person or company sues another person or company; **to take legal action** = to sue someone; ***action for libel*** *or* ***libel action***; ***to bring an action for damages against someone***; **civil action** = case brought by a person or company against someone who has done them wrong; **criminal action** = case brought by the state against someone who is charged with a crime **(d)** *(French)* share

active [ˈæktɪv] *adjective* busy; **active account** = account, such as a bank account or investment account, which is used (i.e., money is deposited and withdrawn) frequently (NOTE: the opposite, an account which is not used, is a **dormant account** or **inactive account**); **active partner** = partner who works in the company; ***an active demand for oil shares***; ***oil shares are very active***; ***an active day on the Stock Exchange***; ***business is active***

activity [æk'tɪvəti] *noun* being active or busy; ***a low level of business activity***; ***there was a lot of activity on the Stock Exchange during the morning session***; **activity chart** = plan showing work which has been done so that it can be compared to the plan of work to be done; **monthly activity report** = report by a department on what has been done during the past month

> preliminary indications of the level of business investment and activity during the March quarter will provide a good picture of economic activity in 1990
>
> *Australian Financial Review*

actual ['æktʃuəl] **1** *adjective* real or correct; ***what is the actual cost of one unit? the actual figures for directors' expenses are not shown to the shareholders***; **actual price** = price for a commodity which is for immediate delivery (NOTE: also called **cash price, physical price, spot price**) **2** *noun* **(a)** **actuals** = real figures; ***these figures are the actuals for 1998*** **(b)** physical commodity which is ready for delivery (as opposed to futures) (NOTE: also called **cash, physical** or **spot**)

actuarial [æktjʊ'eərɪəl] *adjective* calculated by an actuary; ***the premiums are worked out according to actuarial calculations***; **actuarial tables** = lists showing how long people of certain ages are likely to live, used to calculate life assurance premiums

actuary ['æktjʊəri] *noun* person employed by an insurance company or other organization to calculate the risk involved in an insurance, and therefore the premiums payable by persons taking out insurance; **consulting actuary** = independent actuary who advises large pension funds

> COMMENT: in the UK, actuaries are qualified after passing the examinations of the Institute of Actuaries

ADB ['eɪ 'di: 'bi:] = AFRICAN DEVELOPMENT BANK, ASIAN DEVELOPMENT BANK

add [æd] *verb* to put figures together to make a total; ***to add interest to the capital***; ***interest is added to the account monthly***; **added value** = amount added to the value of a product or service, being the difference between its cost and the amount received when it is sold; *see also* VALUE ADDED

adding machine ['ædɪŋ mə'ʃi:n] *noun* machine which makes additions automatically

addition [ə'dɪʃən] *noun* putting numbers together; ***you don't need a calculator to do simple addition***

additional [ə'dɪʃənl] *adjective* extra which is added; ***additional costs***; ***additional charges***; ***additional clauses to a contract***; ***additional duty will have to be paid***; **additional voluntary contributions (AVCs)** = extra money paid by an individual into a company pension scheme to improve the benefits he will receive on retirement; **free-standing additional voluntary contributions plan (FSAVC)** = separate pension plan taken out by an individual in addition to a company pension scheme

address [ə'dres] **1** *noun* details of number, street and town where an office is or a person lives; ***my business address and phone number are printed on the card***; **accommodation address** = address used for receiving messages but which is not the real address of the company; **cable address** = short address for sending cables; **forwarding address** = address to which a person's mail can be sent on; **home address** = address of a house or flat where someone lives; ***please send the documents to my home address***; **address list** = list of addresses; ***we keep an address list of two thousand addresses in Europe*** **2** *verb* to write the details of an address on an envelope, etc.; ***to address a letter*** *or* ***a parcel***; ***please address your enquiries to the manager***; ***a letter addressed to the managing director***; ***an incorrectly addressed package***

addressee [ædre'si:] *noun* person to whom a letter or package is addressed

addressing machine [ə'dresɪŋ mə'ʃi:n] *noun* machine which puts addresses on envelopes automatically

add up ['æd 'ʌp] *verb* to put several figures together to make a total; ***to add up a column of figures***; **the figures do not add up** = the total given is not correct

add up to ['æd 'ʌp 'tʊ] *verb* to make a total; ***the total expenditure adds up to more than £1,000***

adequacy ['ædɪkwəsi] *noun* having enough of something; **capital adequacy ratio** = amount of money which a bank has to have in the form of shareholders' capital, shown as a percentage of its assets (this has been agreed internationally at 8%)

adequate ['ædɪkwət] *adjective* large enough; **to operate without adequate cover** = to act without being completely protected by insurance

adjudicate [ə'dʒu:dɪkeɪt] *verb* to give a judgement between two parties in law; to decide a legal problem; ***to adjudicate a claim***; ***to adjudicate in a dispute***; **he was adjudicated bankrupt** = he was declared legally bankrupt

adjudication [ədʒu:dɪ'keɪʃən] *noun* act of giving a judgement or of deciding a legal problem; **adjudication order** *or* **adjudication of bankruptcy** = order by a court making someone bankrupt; **adjudication tribunal** = group which adjudicates in industrial disputes

adjudicator [ə'dʒu:dɪkeɪtə] *noun* person who gives a decision on a problem; ***an adjudicator in an industrial dispute***

adjust [ə'dʒʌst] *verb* to change something to fit new conditions; ***to adjust prices to take account of inflation***; ***prices are adjusted for inflation***

> inflation-adjusted GNP moved up at a 1.3% annual rate
>
> *Fortune*

> Saudi Arabia will no longer adjust its production to match short-term supply with demand
>
> *Economist*

adjustable [ə'dʒʌstəbl] *adjective* which can be adjusted; **adjustable peg** = currency which is pegged to another, but with the possibility of adjusting the exchange rate from time to time; *US* **adjustable rate mortgage (ARM)** = mortgage where the interest rate changes according to the current market rates; *US* **adjustable rate preferred stock (ARPS)** = preference shares on which dividends are paid in line with the interest rate on Treasury bills

adjuster [ə'dʒʌstə] *noun* **(a)** person who calculates losses for an insurance company; **average adjuster** = person who calculates how much of an insurance is to be borne by each party **(b) market value adjuster (MVA)** = method of calculating loss in market value of a bond or insurance when it is being surrendered

> another deterrent to an early surrender of with-profit bonds is the so-called market value adjuster (MVA). This allows life offices to reduce the sum paid to a bondholder if market values are temporarily depressed to protect the interests of long-term investors
>
> *Sunday Times*

adjustment [ə'dʒʌsmənt] *noun* **(a)** act of adjusting; slight change; ***tax adjustment***; ***wage adjustment***; ***to make an adjustment to salaries***; ***an adjustment of prices to take account of rising costs***; **average adjustment** = calculation of the share of cost of damage or loss of a ship; *US* **adjustment credit** = short-term loan from the Federal Reserve to a commercial bank **(b)** entry in accounts which does not represent a receipt or payment, but which is made to make the accounts correct **(c)** change in the exchange rates to correct a balance of payment deficit; **adjustment trigger** = factor (such as a certain level of inflation) which triggers an adjustment in exchange rates

adjustor [ə'dʒʌstə] *noun* = ADJUSTER

administer [əd'mɪnɪstə] *verb* to organize or to manage; ***he administers a large pension fund***; *US* **administered price** = price fixed by a manufacturer which cannot be varied by a retailer (NOTE: in British English, this is called **resale price maintenance**)

administration [ədmɪnɪ'streɪʃən] *noun* **(a)** action of organizing, controlling or managing a company; **administration costs** *or* **expenses of the administration** *or* **administration expenses** = costs of management, not including production, marketing or distribution costs **(b)** appointment by a court of a person to manage the affairs of a company; **administration order** = (i) order by a court, by which a debtor repays his debts in instalments; (ii) order by a court to appoint an administrator for a company; **letters of administration** = letter given by a court to allow someone to deal with the estate of a person who has died

> his repeated failure to get any of the money paid to the UK finally exhausted the patience of bank creditors, which have been pressing for the company to put itself into administration since the end of last week. Administration involves the appointment of an outside administrator by the court to oversee a reorganization of the company's affairs and orderly

disposal of its assets for the benefit of all its creditors

Financial Times

administrative receiver [əd'mɪnɪstrətɪv rɪ'si:və] *noun* person appointed by a court to administer the affairs of a company

administrator [əd'mɪnɪstreɪtə] *noun* **(a)** person who directs the work of other employees in a business **(b)** (i) person or bank appointed by a court to manage the affairs of someone who dies without leaving a will; (ii) person appointed by a court to administer the affairs of a company

ADR ['eɪ 'di: 'ɑ:] = AMERICAN DEPOSITARY RECEIPT

ad valorem ['æd və'lɔ:rəm] *Latin phrase* meaning 'according to value', showing that a tax is calculated as a percentage of the value of the goods taxed; ***ad valorem duty***; ***ad valorem tax***

advance [əd'vɑ:ns] **1** *noun* **(a)** money paid as a loan or as a part of a payment to be made later; ***a cash advance***; ***to receive an advance from the bank***; ***an advance on account***; ***to make an advance of £100 to someone***; ***to pay someone an advance against a security***; ***can I have an advance of £50 against next month's salary?*** **(b) in advance** = early, before something happens; ***to pay in advance***; ***freight payable in advance***; ***price fixed in advance*** **(c)** early; ***advance booking***; ***advance payment***; ***you must give seven days' advance notice of withdrawals from the account***; **Advance Corporation Tax (ACT)** = tax paid by a company in advance of its main corporation tax payments; it is paid when dividends are paid to shareholders and is deducted from the main tax payment when that falls due; it appears on the tax voucher attached to a dividend warrant **(d)** increase; ***advance in trade***; ***advance in prices*** **2** *verb* **(a)** to lend; ***the bank advanced him £10,000 against the security of his house*** **(b)** to increase; ***prices generally advanced on the stock market*** **(c)** to make something happen earlier; ***the date of the AGM has been advanced to May 10th***; ***the meeting with the German distributors has been advanced from 11.00 to 09.30***

adverse ['ædvə:s] *adjective* bad, not helpful; **adverse action** = action of refusing someone credit; **adverse balance of trade** = situation when a country imports more than it exports; **adverse trading conditions** = bad conditions for trade

advice [əd'vaɪs] *noun* **(a) advice note** = written notice to a customer giving details of goods ordered and shipped but not yet delivered; **as per advice** = (i) according to what is written on the advice note; (ii) advising that a bill of exchange has been drawn **(b)** opinion as to what action to take; **to take legal advice** = to ask a lawyer to say what should be done; ***the accountant's advice was to send the documents to the police***; ***we sent the documents to the police on the advice of the accountant*** *or* ***we took the accountant's advice and sent the documents to the police***

advise [əd'vaɪz] *verb* **(a)** to tell someone what has happened; ***we are advised that the shipment will arrive next week*** **(b)** to suggest to someone what should be done; ***we are advised to take the shipping company to court***; ***the accountant advised us to send the documents to the police***

advise against [əd'vaɪz ə'genst] *verb* to suggest that something should not be done; ***the bank manager advised against closing the account***; ***my stockbroker has advised against buying those shares***

adviser *or* **advisor** [əd'vaɪzə] *noun* person who suggests what should be done; ***he is consulting the company's legal adviser***; **financial adviser** = person or company that gives advice on financial problems for a fee

advisory [əd'vaɪzərɪ] *adjective* as an adviser; ***he is acting in an advisory capacity***; **an advisory board** = a group of advisers; **advisory funds** = funds placed with a financial institution to invest on behalf of a client, the institution investing them at its own discretion

AER = ANNUAL EQUIVALENT RATE

AEX = AMSTERDAM STOCK EXCHANGE

AFBD = ASSOCIATION OF FUTURES BROKERS AND DEALERS

Affõrsvõrlden General Index index of prices on the Stockholm Stock Exchange

affect [ə'fekt] *verb* to change, to have a bad effect on (something); ***the new government regulations do not affect us***; ***the company's sales in the Far East were seriously affected by the embargo***

the dollar depreciation has yet to affect the underlying inflation rate

Australian Financial Review

affiliate [ə'fɪlɪət] *noun* company which partly owns another company, or is partly owned by the same holding company as another

affiliated [ə'fɪlieɪtɪd] *adjective* connected with or partly owned by another company; ***one of our affiliated companies***

affinity card [ə'fɪnɪti 'kɑ:d] *noun* credit card which is sponsored by a charity or educational institution to which a percentage of each purchase made is given by the credit card company

affluent ['æfluənt] *adjective* very rich; ***we live in an affluent society***

afford [ə'fɔ:d] *verb* to be able to pay or buy; ***we could not afford the cost of two telephones***; ***the company cannot afford the time to train new staff***

afghani [æf'gɑ:ni] currency used in Afghanistan

African Development Bank (ADB) ['æfrɪkən dɪ'veləpmənt 'bæŋk] bank set up by African countries to provide long-term loans to help agricultural development and improvement of the infrastructure (the bank now has non-African members)

afterdate ['ɑ:ftədeɪt] *noun* bill of exchange payable at a date later than that on the bill

after-hours ['ɑ:ftə'aʊəz] *adjective* **after-hours buying** *or* **selling** *or* **dealing** *or* **trading** = buying, selling or dealing in shares after the Stock Exchange has officially closed for the day, such deals being subject to normal Stock Exchange rules (in this way, dealers can take advantage of the fact that because of time differences, the various stock exchanges round the world are open almost all twenty-four hours of the day)

aftermarket ['ɑ:ftəmɑ:kɪt] *noun* market in new shares, which starts immediately after trading in the shares begins (i.e., a secondary market)

after tax ['ɑ:ftə 'tæks] *phrase* after tax has been paid; **real return after tax** = return calculated after deducting tax and inflation; **after-tax profit** = profit after tax has been deducted

AG = AKTIENGESELLSCHAFT

against [ə'genst] *preposition* relating to or part of; compared with; ***to pay an advance against a security***; ***can I have an advance against next month's salary? the bank advanced him £10,000 against the security of his house***

> investment can be written off against the marginal rate of tax
>
> *Investors Chronicle*

aged debtors analysis *US* **aging schedule** ['eɪdʒd 'detəz ə'næləsɪs *or* 'eɪdʒɪŋ 'skedju:l] *noun* list which analyses a company's debtors, showing the number of days their payments are overdue

agency ['eɪdʒənsi] *noun* **(a)** office or job of representing another company in an area; ***they signed an agency agreement*** *or* ***an agency contract***; **sole agency** = agreement to be the only person to represent a company or to sell a product in a certain area; ***he has the sole agency for Nissan cars*** **(b)** office or business which arranges things for other companies; *US* **agency bank** = bank which does not accept deposits, but acts as an agent for another (usually foreign) bank; **agency bill** = bill of exchange drawn on the local branch of a foreign bank; **agency broker** = dealer who acts for a client, buying and selling shares for a commission; **advertising agency** = office which plans or designs and manages advertising for companies; **employment agency** = office which finds jobs for staff; **news agency** = office which distributes news to newspapers and television stations **(c)** *US* security issued by a government agency, such as a Federal Home Loan Bank

agent ['eɪdʒənt] *noun* **(a)** person who represents a company or another person in an area; ***to be the agent for IBM***; **sole agent** = person who has the sole agency for a company in an area; ***he is the sole agent for Nissan cars***; **agent's commission** = money (often a percentage of sales) paid to an agent **(b)** person in charge of an agency; ***advertising agent***; ***estate agent***; ***travel agent***; **commission agent** = agent who is paid by commission, not by fee; **forwarding agent** = person or company that arranges shipping and customs documents; **insurance agent** = person who arranges insurance for clients; **land agent** = person who runs a farm or a large area of land for the owner; **managing agent** = person who runs the day-to-day activities of a Lloyd's syndicate **(c)** *US* **(business) agent** = chief local official of a trade union **(d)** *US* **agent bank** = bank which uses the credit card system set up by another bank

agent de change *French* = *STOCKBROKER*

agente de cambio y bolsa *Spanish* = *STOCKBROKER*

agente di cambio *Italian* = *STOCKBROKER*

aggregate ['ægrɪgət] *adjective* total, with everything added together; ***aggregate output***; **aggregate demand** = total demand for goods and services from all sectors of the economy (from individuals, companies and the government); **aggregate risk** = risk which a bank runs in lending to a customer; **aggregate supply** = total supply of goods and services to meet the aggregate demand

AGI = ANNUAL GROSS INCOME

> individuals covered by an employer-sponsored retirement plans can contribute the maximum amount to a tax-deductible IRA only if their AGI falls below $25,000 ($40,000 for married couples filing jointly)
>
> *Fortune*

> eligibility to fund an Education IRA phases out for singles with AGIs of $95,000 to $110,000 and for married couples filing jointly with AGIs of $150,000 to $160,000
>
> *Fortune*

agio ['ædʒiəʊ] *noun* **(a)** charge made for changing money of one currency into another, or for changing banknotes into cash **(b)** difference between two values, such as between the interest charged on loans made by a bank and the interest paid by the bank on deposits, or the difference between the values of two currencies, or between a gold coin and paper currency of the same face value

AGM ['eɪ 'dʒi: 'em] = ANNUAL GENERAL MEETING

agree [ə'gri:] *verb* **(a)** to approve; ***the auditors have agreed the accounts; the figures were agreed between the two parties; we have agreed the budgets for next year; terms of the contract are still to be agreed; he has agreed your prices*** **(b)** to say yes, or to accept; ***it has been agreed that the lease will run for 25 years; after some discussion he agreed to our plan; we all agreed on the plan*** (NOTE: to agree **to** *or* **on** a plan); **(c) to agree to do something** = to say that you will do something; ***she agreed to be chairman; will the finance director agree to resign? the bank will never agree to lend the company £250,000***

agreed [ə'gri:d] *adjective* which has been accepted by everyone; ***an agreed amount; on agreed terms***; **agreed takeover bid** = takeover bid which is accepted by the target company and recommended by the directors to the shareholders

agreement [ə'gri:mənt] *noun* contract between two parties which explains how they will act; ***written agreement; unwritten*** *or* ***verbal agreement; to draw up*** *or* ***to draft an agreement; to break an agreement; to sign an agreement; to witness an agreement; an agreement has been reached*** *or* ***concluded*** *or* ***come to; to reach an agreement*** *or* ***to come to an agreement on prices*** *or* ***salaries; an international agreement on trade; A collective wage agreement; an agency agreement; a marketing agreement***; **blanket agreement** = agreement which covers many different items; **exclusive agreement** = agreement where a company is appointed sole agent for a product in a market; **gentleman's agreement** *US* **gentlemen's agreement** = verbal agreement between two parties who trust each other; *US* **agreement among underwriters** = document which forms a syndicate of underwriters, linking them to the issuer of a new share issue

> after three days of tough negotiations the company has reached agreement with its 1,200 unionized workers
>
> *Toronto Star*

agree with [ə'gri: wɪð] *verb* **(a)** to say that your opinions are the same as someone else's; ***I agree with the chairman that the figures are lower than normal*** **(b)** to be the same as; ***the auditors' figures do not agree with those of the accounts department***

AICPA = AMERICAN INSTITUTE OF CERTIFIED PUBLIC ACCOUNTANTS

AIM = AMSTERDAM INTERPROFESSIONAL MARKET, ALTERNATIVE INVESTMENT MARKET

AIMA = ALTERNATIVE INVESTMENT MANAGEMENT ASSOCIATION

airmail ['eəmeɪl] **1** *noun* way of sending letters or parcels by air; ***to send a package by airmail; airmail charges have risen by 15%***; **airmail envelope** = very light envelope for sending airmail letters; **airmail sticker** = blue sticker with the words 'by air mail' *or* 'par avion' which can be stuck to an envelope or packet to show it is being sent by air **2** *verb* to send letters or parcels by air; ***to airmail a document to New York***

Aktie *German* = *SHARE*

Aktiengesellschaft (AG) *German* = *PUBLIC LIMITED COMPANY (PLC)*

alien corporation ['eɪliən kɔ:pə'reɪʃn] *noun US* company which is incorporated in a foreign country

all or none (AON) ['ɔ:l ɔ: 'nʌn] *noun* buying order which stipulates that the whole order has to be bought at a certain price and no parts of the order can be executed separately

allocate ['æləkeɪt] *verb* to divide (a sum of money) in various ways and share it out; ***we allocate 10% of revenue to publicity***; ***$2,500 was allocated to office furniture***

allocation [ælə'keɪʃən] *noun* **(a)** dividing a sum of money in various ways; ***allocation of capital***; ***allocation of funds to a project*** **(b)** **share allocation** *or* **allocation of shares** = spreading the number of shares available among a large group of people who have applied for them

allonge [ə'lɒnʒ] *noun* piece of paper attached to a bill of exchange, so that more endorsements can be written on it

All Ordinaries Index (AO Index) ['ɔ:l 'ɔ:dnəriz 'ɪndeks] index of prices on the Australian Stock Exchange

allot [ə'lɒt] *verb* to share out; **to allot shares** = to give a certain number of shares to people who have applied for them (NOTE: **allotting - allotted**)

allotment [ə'lɒtmənt] *noun* **(a)** sharing out funds by giving money to various departments; ***allotment of funds to a project*** **(b)** giving shares in a new company to people who have applied for them; ***share allotment***; ***payment in full on allotment***; **letter of allotment** *or* **allotment letter** = letter which tells someone who has applied for shares in a new company how many shares he has been allotted (the letter acts as a temporary share certificate)

allow [ə'laʊ] *verb* **(a)** to say that someone can do something; ***junior members of staff are not allowed to use the chairman's lift***; ***the company allows all members of staff to take six days' holiday at Christmas*** **(b)** to give; ***to allow someone a discount***; ***to allow 5% discount to members of staff***; ***to allow 10% interest on large sums of money*** **(c)** to agree or to accept legally; ***to allow a claim*** *or* ***an appeal***

allowable [ə'laʊəbl] *adjective* legally accepted; **allowable expenses** = expenses which can be claimed against tax

allowance [ə'laʊəns] *noun* **(a)** money which is given for a special reason; ***travel allowance*** *or* ***travelling allowance***; ***foreign currency allowance***; **cost-of-living allowance** = addition to normal salary to cover increases in the cost of living; **entertainment allowance** = money which a manager is allowed to spend each month on meals with visitors **(b)** **allowances against tax** *or* **tax allowances** *or* **personal allowances** = part of someone's income which is not taxed; **annual depreciation allowance** *or* **write-down allowance** = allowance for the depreciation of an asset over a period of years; **capital allowances** = allowances against tax for purchase of capital assets, such as machinery; **allowance for bad debt** = provision made in a company's accounts for debts which may never be paid **(c)** money removed in the form of a discount; ***allowance for depreciation***; ***allowance for exchange loss***

---

most airlines give business class the same baggage allowance as first class

Business Traveller

---

the compensation plan includes base, incentive and car allowance totalling $50,000+

Globe and Mail (Toronto)

---

allow for [ə'laʊ 'fɔ:] *verb* to give a discount for, to add an extra sum to cover something; ***to allow for money paid in advance***; ***to allow 10% for packing***; **delivery is not allowed for** = delivery charges are not included; **allow 28 days for delivery** = calculate that delivery will take at least 28 days

All-Share Index ['ɔ:l 'ʃeə 'ɪndeks] index based on the market price of about 700 companies listed on the London Stock Exchange (NOTE: the full name is **Financial Times Actuaries All-Share Index**)

all-time ['ɔ:l'taɪm] *adjective* **all-time high** *or* **all-time low** = highest or lowest point ever reached; ***sales have fallen from their all-time high of last year***

alpha ['ælfə] *noun* **(a)** anticipated performance of a share, compared to the market in general **(b)** rate of return on a unit trust or mutual fund, compare with typical returns for that category of trust; *see also* BETA

alpha shares *or* **alpha securities** *or* **alpha stocks** ['ælfə 'ʃeəz] *noun* shares in the main companies listed on the London Stock Exchange (about 130 companies, whose shares are frequently traded, normally in parcels of 1000 shares; transactions in alpha stocks are listed on SEAQ); *see also* BETA, DELTA, GAMMA

Alternative Investment Market (AIM) [ɒlt'tɜ:nətɪv ɪn'vesmənt 'mɑ:kɪt] London stock market, regulated by the London Stock

Exchange, dealing in shares in smaller companies which are not listed on the main London Stock Exchange (the AIM is a way in which smaller companies can sell shares to the investing public without going to the expense of obtaining a full share listing)

> the Group was floated on AIM in 1996
>
> *Money Observer*

Alternative Minimum Tax (AMT) [ɒlˈtɜːnətɪv ˈmɪnɪməm ˈtæks] *US* federal tax on certain capital gains and other income above normal taxable income

alternative order [ɒlˈtɜːnətɪv ˈɔːdə] *noun* order to do one of two things (such as buy or sell stock at certain prices)

aluminium *US* **aluminum** [æljuːˈmɪniəm *US* əˈluːmɪnəm] *noun* metal which is frequently traded on commodity exchanges such as the London Metal Exchange

American Bankers Association (ABA) [əˈmerɪkən ˈbæŋkəz əsəʊsiˈeɪʃn] association which represents US banks and promotes good practice

American Depositary Receipt (ADR) [əˈmerɪkən diˈpɒzɪtəri rɪˈsiːt] document issued by an American bank to US citizens, making them unregistered shareholders of companies in foreign countries; the document allows them to receive dividends from their investments, and ADRs can themselves be bought or sold

> COMMENT: buying and selling ADRs is easier for American investors than buying or selling the actual shares themselves, as it avoids stamp duty and can be carried out in dollars without incurring exchange costs

> we constantly stare at the idea of having an ADR facility, but I am not sure it would be worthwhile. We could get a NASDAQ quote as a service to institutions in the US, but when it comes to dealing they usually just pick up the phone and deal through London. There was a trend for British companies to get the Big Board listing, but I don't go for that. We get some institutional interest in our shares in the US without having an ADR
>
> *Money Observer*

American Express (AmEx) [əˈmerɪkən ɪkˈspres] **American Express card** = plastic card which is used to make purchases (the sums charged have to be repaid within a short period of time)

> COMMENT: there are several cards in the American Express system: the basic card (which is green), the gold card, platinum card and blue card, all of which have different criteria for joining

> the AmEx card is worth its weight in platinum - anybody who travels and doesn't have it is playing Russian roulette
>
> *Smart Money*

American Institute of Banking (AIB) [əˈmerɪkən ˈɪnstitjuːt əv ˈbæŋkɪŋ] part of the ABA which organizes training for bank staff

American Institute of Certified Public Accountants (AICPA) [əˈmerɪkən ˈɪnstitjuːt əv ˈsɜːtɪfaɪd ˈpʌblɪk əˈkaʊntənts] official organization representing CPAs

American Stock Exchange (Amex) [əˈmerɪkən ˈstɒk ɪksˈtʃeɪndʒ] the smaller of the two Stock Exchanges based in New York (the other is the New York Stock Exchange or NYSE) (NOTE: also called **Curb Exchange** or **Little Board,** as opposed to the **Big Board,** or **NYSE**)

Amex [ˈæmeks] *noun (informal)* = AMERICAN STOCK EXCHANGE

AmEx [ˈæmeks] *noun (informal)* = AMERICAN EXPRESS

amortizable [æmɔːˈtaɪzəbəl] *adjective* which can be amortized; ***the capital cost is amortizable over a period of ten years***

amortization [əmɔːtaɪˈzeɪʃn] *noun* act of amortizing; ***amortization of a debt***

amortize [ˈæmɔːtaɪz] *verb* **(a)** to pay off (a debt) by repaying it or by putting money aside regularly over a period of time; ***the capital cost is amortized over five years***; *see also* SINKING FUND **(b)** to depreciate or to write down the capital value of an asset over a period of time in a company's accounts

amount [əˈmaʊnt] **1** *noun* quantity of money; ***only part of the amount owing has been paid***; ***most of the bad debts have been recovered, leaving only a small amount to be written off***; ***what is the amount outstanding?***; ***she has a small amount invested in gilt-edged stock*** **2** *verb* **to amount to** = to make a total of; ***their debts amount to over £1m***

Amsterdam Stock Exchange (AEX) [æmstəˈdæm ˈstɒk ɪksˈtʃeɪndʒ] the main stock exchange in the Netherlands; business is transacted by 'hoekmen' (marketmakers) or directly between banks on the Amsterdam Interprofessional Market (AIM)

analog computer ['ænəlɒg kəm'pju:tə] *noun* computer which works on the basis of electrical impulses representing numbers

analysis [ə'næləsɪs] *noun* detailed examination and report; ***job analysis***; ***market analysis***; ***sales analysis***; ***to carry out an analysis of the market potential***; ***to write an analysis of the sales position***; **cost analysis** = examination in advance of the costs of a new product; **systems analysis** = using a computer to suggest how a company can work more efficiently by analysing the way in which it works at present (NOTE: plural is **analyses**)

analyst ['ænəlɪst] *noun* person who analyzes; **City analyst** = person who studies the London stock market; **market analyst** = person who studies the stock market in general; **investment analyst** = person working for a stockbroking firm, who analyzes the performance of companies in certain sectors of the market, or the performance of a market sector as a whole, or economic trends in general

> unlike City analysts, who must produce instant reaction to the statistics, the MPC has weeks to ponder the facts behind the figures
>
> *The Times*

analyze *or* **analyse** ['ænəlaɪz] *verb* to examine in detail; ***to analyze a statement of account***; ***to analyze the market potential***

angel ['eɪndʒəl] *noun* **(a)** person who provides backing for a stage performance, such as a play or musical, and receives a percentage dividend when the start-up costs have been covered **(b)** **(business) angel** = backer, person who backs new projects with money; **angel network** = network of backers, organized through a central office which keeps a database of suitable investors and puts them in touch with entrepreneurs who need financial backing; ***the expansion of the business angel network means that entrepreneurs with sound business plans should now be able to raise the necessary finance for their projects*** **(c)** **fallen angel** = share that was once in favour, but whose attraction has slipped and whose share price is on the way down

> those other investors, who have been providing even more dollars to startup companies than the VCs do, include private, individual 'angel' investors, state and local organizations trying to spur their economies, and large corporations. The angels, usually wealthy professionals and retired entrepreneurs, contribute about $20 billion a year to startup companies. The best way to find these folks is through angel networks like those run out of MIT and the Small Business Administration
>
> *Fortune*

> the struggle to find an angel can be one hell of a business
>
> *Evening Standard*

announce [ə'naʊns] *verb* to tell something to the public; ***to announce the results for 1998***; ***to announce a programme of investment***

announcement [ə'naʊnsmənt] *noun* telling something in public; ***announcement of a cutback in expenditure***; ***announcement of the appointment of a new managing director***; ***the managing director made an announcement to the staff***

annual ['ænjuəl] *adjective* for one year; ***annual statement of income***; ***he has six weeks' annual leave***; ***the annual accounts***; ***annual growth of 5%***; **annual depreciation allowance** *or* **annual write-down allowance** = allowance for the depreciation of an asset over a period of years; *US* **annual gross income (AGI)** = total annual income before any deductions or exclusions; **annual report** = report of a company's financial situation at the end of a year, sent to all the shareholders; **annual rest system** = system by which extra payments or overpayments made to reduce the amount borrowed on a mortgage are credited to the account only once a year; **annual return** = official report which a registered company has to make each year to the Registrar of Companies; **on an annual basis** = each year; ***the figures are revised on an annual basis***

> real wages have risen at an annual rate of only 1% in the last two years
>
> *Sunday Times*

> the remuneration package will include an attractive salary, profit sharing and a company car together with four weeks annual holiday
>
> *Times*

Annual Equivalent Rate (AER) ['ænjʊəl ɪ'kwɪvələnt 'reɪt] *noun* figure which shows what the interest rate on an account would be if interest was paid for a full year and compounded

annual general meeting (AGM) ['ænjʊəl 'dʒenərəl 'mi:tɪŋ] *noun* annual meeting of all the shareholders of a company, when the company's financial situation is presented by and discussed with the directors, when the accounts for the past year are approved, when auditors are appointed, etc. (NOTE: the American term is **annual meeting** or **annual stockholders' meeting**)

annualized ['ænjʊəlaɪzd] *adjective* shown on an annual basis; **annualized percentage rate** = yearly percentage rate, calculated by multiplying the monthly rate by twelve (not as accurate as the APR, which includes fees and other charges)

annually ['ænjʊəli] *adverb* each year; ***the figures are updated annually***

Annual Percentage Rate (APR) ['ænjʊəl pə'sentɪdʒ 'reɪt] *noun* rate of interest (such as on a hire-purchase agreement) shown on an annual compound basis, including fees and charges

> COMMENT: because hire purchase agreements quote a flat rate of interest covering the whole amount borrowed or a monthly repayment figure, the Consumer Credit Act, 1974, forces lenders to show the APR on documentation concerning hire purchase agreements, so as to give an accurate figure of the real rate of interest as opposed to the nominal rate. The APR includes various fees charged (such as the valuation of a house for mortgage); it may also vary according to the sum borrowed - a credit card company will quote a lower APR if the borrower's credit limit is low

> ever since October, when the banks' base rate climbed to 15 per cent, the main credit card issuers have faced the prospect of having to push interest rates above 30 per cent APR. Though store cards have charged interest at much higher rates than this for some years, 30 per cent APR is something the banks fight shy of
>
> *Financial Times Review*

annuitant [ə'nju:ɪtənt] *noun* person who receives an annuity

annuity [ə'nju:əti] *noun* money paid each year to a retired person, usually in return for a lump-sum payment; the value of the annuity depends on how long the person lives, as it usually cannot be passed on to another person; annuities are fixed payments, and lose their value with inflation, whereas a pension can be index-linked; ***to buy*** *or* ***to take out an annuity***; **annuity for life** *or* **life annuity** = annual payments made to someone as long as he is alive; **reversionary annuity** = annuity paid to someone on the death of another person; *US* **variable annuity** = annuity based on funds invested in common stock, which varies with the value of the stock, as opposed to a fixed annuity

> COMMENT: when a person retires, he or she is required by law to purchase a 'compulsory purchase annuity' with the funds accumulated in his or her pension fund. This gives them a taxable income for the rest of their life, but usually it is a fixed income which does not change with inflation

> variable annuities are essential baskets of mutual-fund-like vehicles called sub-accounts which come with insurance features
>
> *Wall Street Journal*

antedate ['æntɪdeɪt] *verb* to put an earlier date on a document; ***the invoice was antedated to January 1st***

anti- ['ænti] *prefix* against

anticipate [æn'tɪsɪpeɪt] *verb* to expect something to happen; **anticipated balance** = balance which is forecast from a deposit when it matures

anti-dumping ['ænti'dʌmpɪŋ] *adjective* which protects a country against dumping; ***anti-dumping legislation***

anti-inflationary ['æntiɪn'fleɪʃnəri] *adjective* which tries to restrict inflation; ***anti-inflationary measures***

anti-trust ['ænti'trʌst] *adjective* which attacks monopolies and encourages competition; **anti-trust laws** *or* **legislation** = laws in the US which prevent the formation of monopolies

AO = ALL-ORDINARIES INDEX

AOB = ANY OTHER BUSINESS

AON = ALL OR NONE

APACS = ASSOCIATION FOR PAYMENT CLEARING SERVICES

applicant ['æplɪkənt] *noun* person who applies for something; ***applicant for a job*** *or* ***job applicant***; ***there were thousands of applicants for shares in the new company***

application [æplɪ'keɪʃən] *noun* asking for something, usually in writing; ***application for shares***; ***shares payable on application***; ***application for a job*** *or* ***job application***; **application form** = form to be filled in when applying for a new issue of shares or for a job; ***to fill in an application (form) for an issue of shares*** *or* ***a share application (form) attach the cheque to the share application form***

apply [ə'plaɪ] *verb* **(a)** to ask for something, usually in writing; ***to apply for a job***; ***to apply for shares***; ***to apply in writing***; ***to apply in person*** **(b)** to affect or to touch; ***this clause applies only to deals outside the EU***

appoint [ə'pɔɪnt] *verb* to choose someone to do a job; ***to appoint an official receiver***

appointment [ə'pɔɪntmənt] *noun* being appointed to a job; **on his appointment as receiver** = when he was made receiver of the company

apportion [ə'pɔ:ʃən] *verb* to share out (costs); ***costs are apportioned according to projected revenue***

apportionment [ə'pɔ:ʃənmənt] *noun* sharing out of (costs)

appraisal [ə'preɪzəl] *noun* calculation of the value of someone or something; **staff appraisals** = reports on how well each member of staff is working

appraise [ə'preɪz] *verb* to assess, to calculate the value of something

appreciate [ə'pri:ʃɪeɪt] *verb* **(a)** *(of currency, stock)* to increase in value; ***the dollar has appreciated in terms of the yen***; ***these shares have appreciated by 5%*** **(b)** to notice how good something is; ***the customer always appreciates efficient service***; ***tourists do not appreciate long delays at banks***

appreciation [əpri:ʃɪ'eɪʃən] *noun* **(a)** *(of currency, stock)* increase in value; ***these shares show an appreciation of 10%***; ***the appreciation of the dollar against the peseta*** **(b)** valuing something highly; ***he was given a rise in appreciation of his excellent work***

appro ['æprəʊ] *noun* = *APPROVAL*; **to buy something on appro** = to buy something which you will only pay for if it is satisfactory

appropriate [ə'prəʊprɪeɪt] *verb* to put a sum of money aside for a special purpose; ***to appropriate a sum of money for a capital project***

appropriation [əprəʊprɪ'eɪʃən] *noun* act of putting money aside for a special purpose; ***appropriation of funds to the reserve***; **appropriation account** = part of a profit and loss account which shows how the profit has been dealt with (i.e. how much has been given to the shareholders as dividends, how much is being put into the reserves, etc.)

approval [ə'pru:vəl] *noun* **(a)** agreement; ***to submit a budget for approval***; **certificate of approval** = document showing that an item has been approved officially **(b) on approval** = sale where the buyer only pays for goods if they are satisfactory; ***to buy a photocopier on approval***

approve [ə'pru:v] *verb* **(a) to approve of** = to think something is good; ***the chairman approves of the new company letter heading***; ***the sales staff do not approve of interference from the accounts division*** **(b)** to agree to something officially; ***to approve the terms of a contract***; ***the proposal was approved by the board***; *US* **approved securities** = state bonds which can be held by banks to form part of their reserves (the list of these bonds is the 'approved list')

approximate [ə'prɒksɪmət] *adjective* not exact, but almost correct; ***the sales division has made an approximate forecast of expenditure***

approximately [ə'prɒksɪmətli] *adverb* almost correctly; ***expenditure is approximately 10% down on the previous quarter***

approximation [əprɒksɪ'meɪʃən] *noun* rough calculation; ***approximation of expenditure***; ***the final figure is only an approximation***

APR ['eɪ 'pi: 'ɑ:] = ANNUAL PERCENTAGE RATE

arb [ɑ:b] *(informal)* = ARBITRAGEUR

arbitrage ['ɑ:bɪtreɪdʒ] *noun* **(a)** making a profit from the difference in value of various assets, such as: selling foreign currencies or commodities on one market and buying on another at almost the same time to profit from different exchange rates; buying currencies forward and selling them forward at a later date, to benefit from a difference in prices; buying a security and selling another security to the same buyer with the intention of forcing up the value of both securities; **arbitrage fund** = fund which tries to take advantage of price discrepancies for the same asset in different markets; **index arbitrage** = buying or selling a basket of stocks against an index option or future; *see also* PROGRAM **(b)** **risk arbitrage** = buying shares in companies which are likely to be taken over and so rise in price; **arbitrage syndicate** = group of people formed to raise the capital to invest in arbitrage deals

arbitrager *or* **arbitrageur** [ˈɑːbɪtreɪdʒə or ɑːbɪtrɑːˈʒɜː] *noun* person whose business is risk arbitrage

> COMMENT: arbitrageurs buy shares in companies which are potential takeover targets, either to force up the price of the shares before the takeover bid, or simply as a position while waiting for the takeover bid to take place. They also sell shares in the company which is expected to make the takeover bid, since one of the consequences of a takeover bid is usually that the price of the target company rises while that of the bidding company falls. Arbitrageurs may then sell the shares in the target company at a profit, either to one of the parties making the takeover bid, or back to the company itself. See also GREENMAIL

arbitration [ɑːbɪˈtreɪʃən] *noun* settlement of a dispute by the two parties concerned, using an arbitrator, an outside person chosen by both sides; ***to submit a dispute to arbitration***; ***to refer a question to arbitration***; ***to take a dispute to arbitration***; ***to go to arbitration***; **arbitration board** *or* **arbitration tribunal** = group which arbitrates; **industrial arbitration tribunal** = court which decides in industrial disputes

ARM = ADJUSTABLE RATE MORTGAGE

arm's length [ˈɑːmz ˈleŋθ] *phrase* **to deal with someone at arm's length** = to deal as if there were no financial link between the two parties (as when a company buys a service from one of its own subsidiaries); **arm's length transaction** = transaction which is carried out by two parties with no connection between them (resulting in a fair market value for the item sold)

> it is desirable that all dealing should be done at arm's length, but there are a number of grey areas; for example the so-called 'soft' commissions, whereby fund managers can pay commission out of the fund to stockbrokers, and themselves receive back services as a form of rebate on these commissions
>
> *Financial Times Review*

around [əˈraʊnd] *preposition* **(a)** approximately; ***the office costs around £2,000 a year to heat***; ***his salary is around $85,000*** **(b)** *(in foreign exchange dealings)* with a premium or discount; **5 points around** = with a 5-point premium and a 5-point discount, both calculated on the spot price

ARPS = ADJUSTABLE RATE PREFERRED STOCK

arrangement fee [əˈreɪndʒmənt ˈfiː] *noun* charge made by a bank to a client for arranging credit facilities; **scheme of arrangement** = scheme drawn up by an individual or company to offer ways of paying debts, so as to avoid bankruptcy proceedings

> on the upside scenario the outlook is reasonably optimistic, bankers say, the worst scenario being that a scheme of arrangement cannot be achieved, resulting in liquidation
>
> *Irish Times*

arrears [əˈrɪəz] *plural noun* money which is owed, but which has not been paid at the right time; ***arrears of interest***; ***to allow mortgage repayments to fall into arrears***; ***salary with arrears effective from January 1st***; **in arrears** = owing money which should have been paid earlier; ***the payments are six months in arrears***; ***he is six weeks in arrears with his rent***

arrive [əˈraɪv] *noun* **(a)** to reach a place; ***the consignment has still not arrived***; ***the shipment arrived without any documentation***; ***the plane arrives in Sydney at 04.00*** **(b) to arrive at** = to calculate and agree; ***to arrive at a price***; ***after some discussion we arrived at a compromise***

article [ˈɑːtɪkl] *noun* **(a)** product, thing for sale; ***to launch a new article on the market***; ***a black market in luxury articles*** **(b)** section of a legal agreement; ***see article 10 of the contract***; **article 8 currency** = strong convertible currency (according to the IMF) **(c) articles of association** = document which lays down the rules for a company regarding meetings, the appointment of directors, etc. (NOTE: in American English these are called **bylaws**); ***director appointed under the articles of the company***; ***this procedure is not allowed under the articles of association of the company;*** US **articles of incorporation**

= document which sets up a company and lays down the relationship between the shareholders and the company (NOTE: in British English called **Memorandum of Association**); **Memorandum (and articles) of Association** = legal document setting up a limited company and giving details of its aims, directors, and registered office; **articles of partnership** = document setting up a partnership, giving the details of the business and the amount each partner is contributing to it

asap ['æsæp or 'eɪ 'es 'eɪ 'piː] = AS SOON AS POSSIBLE

ascending tops [ə'sendɪŋ 'tɒps] *noun* term used by chartists to refer to an upward trend in the market, where each peak is higher than the preceding one

ASEAN = ASSOCIATION OF SOUTHEAST ASIAN NATIONS

Asian ['eɪʒn] *adjective* referring to Asia; **Asian Currency Unit** = unit of account for dollar deposits held in Singapore and other Asian markets; **Asian dollar** = American dollar deposited in Singapore and other Asian markets, and traded in Singapore; **Asian dollar bonds** = bonds issued in Asian dollars; *compare* EURODOLLAR; **Asian monetary unit** = unit used in financial dealings between members of the Asian Clearing Union

Asian Development Bank (ADB) ['eɪʒn dɪ'veləpmənt 'bæŋk] bank set up by various Asian countries, with other outside members, to assist countries in the region with money and technical advice

ask [ɑːsk] *verb* **(a)** to put a question to someone; ***he asked the information office for details of companies exhibiting at the motor show***; ***ask the salesgirl if the bill includes VAT*** **(b)** to tell someone to do something; ***he asked the switchboard operator to get him a number in Germany***; ***she asked her secretary to fetch a file from the managing director's office***; ***the customs officials asked him to open his case***

asked price ['ɑːskt 'praɪs] *noun* price at which a commodity or stock is offered for sale by a seller (also called 'offer price' in the UK)

ask for ['ɑːsk 'fɔː] *verb* **(a)** to say that you want or need something; ***he asked for the file on current debtors***; ***they asked for more time to repay the loan***; ***there is a man in reception asking for Mr Smith*** **(b)** to put a price on something for sale; ***they are asking £24,000 for the car***

asking price ['ɑːskɪŋ 'praɪs] *noun* price at which a seller wishes to sell an item; ***the asking price is £24,000***

assay mark [ə'seɪ 'mɑːk] *noun* mark put on gold or silver items to show that the metal is of the correct quality

assess [ə'ses] *verb* to calculate the value of something; ***to assess damages at £1,000***; ***to assess a property for the purposes of insurance***

assessment [ə'sesmənt] *noun* calculation of value; ***assessment of damages***; ***assessment of property***; **tax assessment** = calculation by a tax inspector of the amount of tax a person owes; **staff assessments** = reports on how well members of staff are working

asset ['æset] *noun* thing which belongs to company or person, and which has a value; ***he has an excess of assets over liabilities***; ***her assets are only £640 as against liabilities of £24,000***; **capital assets** *or* **fixed assets** = property or machinery which a company owns and uses, but which the company does not buy or sell as part of its regular trade; **current assets** = assets used by a company in its ordinary work (such as materials, finished products, monies owed by customers, cash); **frozen assets** = assets of a company which by law cannot be sold because someone has a claim against them; **intangible assets** = assets which have a value, but which cannot be seen (such as goodwill, or a patent, or a trademark); **liquid assets** = cash, or bills which can be quickly converted into cash; **personal assets** = moveable assets which belong to a person; **tangible assets** = assets which are solid (such as machinery, furniture or jewels or cash); **asset allocation** = deciding how much money should be spent on the purchase of different types of investment, such as growth units or income units, depending on the particular needs of the individual investor (NOTE: the counterpart, deciding which shares to buy, is **stockpicking**); **asset backing** = support for a share price provided by the value of the company's assets; **asset play** = share which seems to be undervalued based on its asset value and so is an attractive buy; **asset-rich company** = company with valuable tangible assets, such as property, which provide firm backing for its shares; **asset stripper** = person who buys a company to sell its assets; **asset stripping** = buying a company at a lower price than its asset value, and then selling its assets; **asset value** = value of a company calculated by adding together all its assets

> COMMENT: a company's balance sheet will show assets in various forms: current assets, fixed assets, intangible assets, etc.

last year and over the past three years his superior stock picking overcame the failure of his asset allocation

Smart Money

according to academic research, decisions about asset allocation account for over 90% of investment performance over time as reported by the Financial Analyst Journal

Fortune

many companies are discovering that a well-recognised brand name can be a priceless asset that lessens the risk of introducing a new product

Duns Business Month

asset-backed ['æsɪt'bækt] *adjective* **asset-backed securities** = shares which are backed by the security of assets

it accounted for nearly a quarter of the entire European market in asset-backed securities in the first three months of this year

Wall Street Journal

assign [ə'saɪn] *verb* **(a)** to give legally; ***to assign a right to someone***; ***to assign shares to someone*** **(b)** to give someone a job of work; ***he was assigned the job of checking the sales figures***

assignation [æsɪg'neɪʃən] *noun* legal transfer; ***assignation of shares to someone***; ***assignation of a patent***

assignee [æsaɪ'ni:] *noun* person who receives something which has been assigned to him

assignment [ə'saɪnmənt] *noun* **(a)** legal transfer of a property or of a right to someone else in return for a payment; ***assignment of a patent*** *or* ***of a copyright***; ***to sign a deed of assignment*** **(b)** particular job of work; ***he was appointed managing director with the assignment to improve the company's profits***; ***the oil team is on an assignment in the North Sea***

assignor [æsaɪ'nɔ:] *noun* person who assigns a right to someone

assigns [ə'saɪnz] *plural noun* people to whom property has been assigned; **his heirs and assigns** = people who have inherited his property and had it transferred to them

associate [ə'səʊsɪət] **1** *adjective* linked; **associate bank** = bank which is part of a group such as Visa or MasterCard; **associate company** = company which is partly owned by another (though less than 50%), and where the share-owning company exerts some management control or has a close trading relationship with the associate; **associate director** = director who attends board meetings, but has not been elected by the shareholders **2** *noun* **(a)** person who works in the same business as someone; ***she is a business associate of mine*** **(b)** = ASSOCIATE COMPANY **(c)** person or company linked to another in a takeover bid

associated company [ə'səʊsɪeɪtɪd 'kʌmpni] *noun* = *ASSOCIATE COMPANY*; ***Smith Ltd and its associated company, Jones Brothers***

association [əsəʊsɪ'eɪʃən] *noun* **(a)** group of people or of companies with the same interest; ***trade association***; ***employers' association***; ***manufacturers' association***; **Association of Chartered Certified Accountants (ACCA)** = organization whose members are certified accountants; **Association of Futures Brokers and Dealers (AFBD)** = self-regulating organization which regulates the activities of dealers in futures and options; *see also* BANKER, BUILDING SOCIETY, FINANCE, INSURER **(b) Memorandum of Association** = document drawn up at the same time as the articles of association of a company, in which the company's objects are defined, the details of the share capital, directors, registered office, etc., are set out, etc. (NOTE: in American English called **articles of incorporation**)

Association for Payment Clearing Services (APACS) organization which deals with the clearing of payments in the UK

> COMMENT: APACS has three sections: BACS which deals with electronic payments such as direct debits and salary cheques; CHAPS which deals with electronic transfer of large amounts of money; and the Cheque & Credit Clearing Company, which deals with paper transactions such as cheques

Association of Southeast Asian Nations (ASEAN) organization formed originally in 1967 to promote economic growth, social and educational development and general stability in Southeast Asia (the current members are: Brunei, Indonesia,

Laos, Malaysia, Myanmar, Philippines, Singapore, Thailand and Vietnam

assumable mortgage [ə'sju:məbl 'mɔ:gɪdʒ] *noun US* mortgage which can be passed to another person, such as a person buying the property from the mortgagor

assume [ə'sju:m] *verb* to take; ***to assume all risks***; ***he has assumed responsibility for marketing***

assumption [ə'sʌmpʃən] *noun* **(a)** taking; ***assumption of risks*** **(b)** *US* transfer of the rest of a mortgage to someone

assure [ə'ʃʊə] *verb* to insure, to have a contract with a company where if regular payments are made, the company will pay compensation if you die; ***to assure someone's life***; ***he has paid the premiums to have his wife's life assured***; **the life assured** = the person whose life has been covered by the life assurance

assurance [ə'ʃʊərəns] *noun* insurance, agreement that in return for regular payments, a company will pay compensation for loss of life; ***assurance company***; ***assurance policy***; **life assurance** = insurance which pays a sum of money when someone dies

assurer *or* **assuror** [ə'ʃʊərə] *noun* insurer, company which insures (NOTE: **assure, assurer,** and **assurance** are used in Britain for insurance policies relating to something which will certainly happen (such as death); for other types of policy (i.e., those against something which may or may not happen, such as an accident) use the terms **insure, insurer,** and **insurance**)

AST = AUTOMATED SCREEN TRADING

ASX = AUSTRALIAN STOCK EXCHANGE

at best ['æt 'best] *phrase* **sell at best** *or* **sell at the market** = instruction to a stockbroker to sell shares at the best price possible

at call ['æt 'kɔ:l] *phrase* immediately available; **money at call** = loans which the lender can ask to be repaid at any time

ATM ['eɪ 'ti: 'em] = AUTOMATED TELLER MACHINE

> Swiss banks are issuing new Eurocheque cards which will guarantee Eurocheque cash operations but will also allow cash withdrawals from ATMs in Belgium, Denmark, Spain, France, the Netherlands, Portugal and Germany
>
> *Banking Technology*

at par ['æt 'pɑ:] *phrase* **share at par** = share whose value on the stock market is the same as its face value

at sight ['æt 'saɪt] *phrase* bill of exchange which is payable when it is presented

attaché [ə'tæʃeɪ] *noun* junior diplomat who does special work; **commercial attaché** = diplomat whose job is to promote the commercial interests of his country

attachment order [ə'tætʃmənt 'ɔ:də] *noun* order from a court to hold a debtor's property to prevent it being sold until debts are paid

attract [ə'trækt] *verb* to make something or someone come; ***the deposits attract interest at 15%***

> airlines offer special stopover rates and hotel packages to attract customers and to encourage customer loyalty
>
> *Business Traveller*

attractive [ə'træktɪv] *adjective* which attracts; **attractive prices** = prices which are cheap enough to make buyers want to buy; **attractive salary** = good salary to make high-quality applicants apply for the job

attributable profit [ə'trɪbjʊtəbl 'prɒfɪt] *noun* profits which can be shown to come from a particular area of a company's operations

auction ['ɔ:kʃən] **1** *noun* **(a)** selling of goods where people offer bids, and the item is sold to the person who makes the highest offer; ***sale by auction***; ***auction rooms***; ***to sell goods by auction US at auction***; **to put something up for auction** = to offer an item for sale at an auction; **Dutch auction** = auction where the auctioneer offers an item for sale at a high price and gradually reduces the price until someone makes a bid **(b)** method of selling government stock, where all stock on issue will be sold, and the highest price offered will be accepted (as opposed to tendering, where not all the stock may be sold if the tender prices are too low); *(Stock Exchange)* **auction system** = system where prices are struck as the result of marketmakers offering stock for sale on the trading floor (as opposed to a quote system, where prices are quoted on a computerized screen) **2** *verb* to sell at an auction; ***the factory was closed and the machinery was auctioned off***

> the Canadian government auctioned $1.3 billion in two-year bonds due March 5, 1993, at an average yield of 9.292 per cent
>
> *Toronto Globe & Mail*

auctioneer [ɔːkʃəˈnɪə] *noun* person who conducts an auction

audit [ˈɔːdɪt] **1** *noun* examination of the books and accounts of a company; ***to carry out the annual audit***; **external audit** *or* **independent audit** = audit carried out by an independent auditor; **internal audit** = audit carried out by a department inside the company; ***he is the manager of the internal audit department***; **lifestyle audit** = study of a person's living standards to see if it is consistent with his reported income; **audit trail** = (i) series of checks showing how a final figure in audited accounts was arrived at; (ii) checking a series of computer transactions for errors or irregularities (one of the ways of detecting fraud on a Stock Exchange) **2** *verb* to examine the books and accounts of a company; ***to audit the accounts***; ***the books have not yet been audited***

> the IRS audits about 1 to 2 percent of individual income-tax returns filed each year, and roughly a quarter of those files are subjected to lifestyle audits
>
> *Smart Money*

auditing [ˈɔːdɪtɪŋ] *noun* action of examining the books and accounts

auditor [ˈɔːdɪtə] *noun* person who audits; **external auditor** = independent person who audits the company's accounts; **internal auditor** = member of staff who audits a company's accounts; **auditors' fees** = fees paid to a company's auditors, which are approved by the shareholders at an AGM; **auditors' report** = report written by a company's auditors after they have examined the accounts of the company (the report certifies that in the opinion of the auditors, the accounts give a true picture of the company's financial position)

> COMMENT: auditors are appointed by the company's directors and voted by the AGM. In the USA, audited accounts are only required by corporations which are registered with the SEC, but in the UK all limited companies must provide audited annual accounts

austral [ˈɔːstræl] currency used in Argentina

Australian Stock Exchange (ASX) [ɒsˈtreɪliən ˈstɒk ɪksˈtʃeɪndʒ] the national stock exchange of Australia, formed of six exchanges (in Adelaide, Brisbane, Hobart, Melbourne, Perth and Sydney)

AUT = AUTHORIZED UNIT TRUST

authenticate [ɔːˈθentɪkeɪt] *verb* to say that something is true, especially when stating that gold is of a correct quality

authentication [ɔːθentɪˈkeɪʃn] *noun* **(a)** action of checking that something is true, such as an instruction sent to a bank by email **(b)** method of proving the identity of a person or company; **certificate of authentication** = unique number supplied to a company by an independent source (an 'authenticator') to prove that the company is who they claim to be

> COMMENT: authentication is particularly important on the internet where you do not actually see the person or premises of a company when making a purchase. If CompanyX wants to prove to internet customers that they are really CompanyX and not an fraudster, they must ask an independent authenticator to issue them with a unique certificate of authentication. A visitor to the CompanyX web site can ask to see this certificate and will be shown the unique number supplied by the trustworthy independent authenticator. Authentication is normally only used on commercial web sites that are selling goods.

authenticator [ɔːˈθentɪkeɪtə] *noun* **independent authenticator** = company that has the authority (from the government or the internet controlling body) to issue certificates of authentication when they are sure that a company is who it claims to be

authority [ɔːˈθɒrəti] *noun* **(a)** power to do something; ***he has no authority to act on our behalf***; **authority to purchase** = bill drawn up and presented with shipping documentation to the purchaser's bank, allowing the bank to purchase the bill **(b)** **local authority** = elected section of government which runs a small area of a country; **the authorities** = the government, the people in control

authorization [ɔːθəraɪˈzeɪʃən] *noun* permission, power to do something; ***do you have authorization for this expenditure? he has no authorization to act on our behalf***

authorize [ˈɔːθəraɪz] *verb* **(a)** to give permission for something to be done; ***to authorize payment of £10,000*** **(b)** to give someone the authority to do something; ***to***

authorize someone to act on the company's behalf

> in 1934 Congress authorized President Franklin D. Roosevelt to seek lower tariffs with any country willing to reciprocate
>
> *Duns Business Month*

authorized [ˈɔːθəraɪzd] *adjective* permitted; **authorized capital** *or* **authorized (capital) stock** = amount of capital in the form of shares which a company is allowed to issue, as stated in the memorandum of association (not all the shares need to be issued); **authorized corporate director (ACD)** = person who is in charge of an Oeic; **authorized dealer** = person or company (such as a bank) that is allowed by the country's central bank to buy and sell foreign currency; **authorized unit trusts (AUTs)** = official name for unit trusts which have to be managed according to EU directives

AUTIF = ASSOCIATION OF UNIT TRUSTS AND INVESTMENT TRUSTS

automaker [ˈɔːtəʊmeɪkə] *noun US* company that manufactures cars (NOTE: British English is **car maker**)

> Detroit's automakers have a mountain of cash. They've expanded their operations around the world, and now they are buying back their stock
>
> *Fortune*

automated [ˈɔːtəmeɪtɪd] *adjective* worked automatically by machines; **Automated Screen Trading (AST)** = system where securities are bought, sold and matched automatically by computer; *US* **Automated Clearing House (ACH)** = organization set up by the federal authorities to settle transactions carried out by computer, such as automatic mortgage payments, and trade payments between businesses; **Automated Teller Machine (ATM)** = machine which gives out cash when a special card is inserted and special instructions given; *see also* PIN, SEAQ

automatic [ɔːtəˈmætɪk] *adjective* which works or takes place without any person making it happen; ***there is an automatic increase in salaries on January 1st***; **automatic data processing** = data processing done by a computer; **automatic telling machine** = AUTOMATED TELLER MACHINE (ATM) **automatic vending machine** = machine which provides drinks, cigarettes, etc., when a coin is put in

automatically [ɔːtəˈmætɪkəli] *adverb* working without a person giving any instructions; ***the invoices are sent out automatically***; ***a demand note is sent automatically when the account is overdue***

automation [ɔːtəˈmeɪʃən] *noun* use of machines to do work with very little supervision by people

availability [əveɪləˈbɪləti] *noun* being easily obtained; **offer subject to availability** = the offer is valid only if the goods are available

available [əˈveɪləbl] *adjective* which can be obtained or bought; ***funds which are made available for investment in small businesses***; **available capital** = capital which is ready to be used; **available funds** = funds held by a bank which it can use for loans or other investments

aval [ˈævæl] *noun* term used in Europe to refer to a bill or promissory note which is guaranteed by a third party

AVC [ˈeɪ ˈviː ˈsiː] = ADDITIONAL VOLUNTARY CONTRIBUTION

average [ˈævərɪdʒ] **1** *noun* **(a)** number calculated by adding together several figures and dividing by the number of figures added; ***the average for the last three months*** *or* ***the last three months' average***; ***sales average*** *or* ***average of sales***; **moving average** = average of share prices on a stock market, where the calculation is made over a period which moves forward regularly (the commonest are 100-day or 200-day averages, or 10- or 40-week moving averages; the average is calculated as the average figure for the whole period, and moves forward one day or week at a a time (these averages are often used by chartists); **weighted average** = average which is calculated taking several factors into account, giving some more value than others **(b) on an average** = in general; ***on an average, £15 worth of goods are stolen every day*** **(c)** sharing of the cost of damage or loss of a ship between the insurers and the owners; **average adjuster** = person who calculates how much of an insurance is to be borne by each party; **general average** = sharing of the cost of lost goods by all parties to an insurance (where some goods have been lost in an attempt to save the rest of the cargo); **particular average** = situation where part of a shipment is lost or damaged and the insurance costs are borne by the owner of the lost goods (he receives no compensation from the other owners of the shipment) **2** *adjective* middle (figure); ***average cost per unit***; ***average sales per representative***; ***the average***

figures for the last three months; ***the average increase in prices***; **average balance** = the balance in an account calculated over a period **3** *verb* to produce as an average figure; ***price increases have averaged 10% per annum***; ***days lost through sickness have averaged twenty-two over the last four years***

> a share with an average rating might yield 5 per cent and have a PER of about 10
>
> *Investors Chronicle*

> the average price per kilogram for this season to the end of April has been 300 cents
>
> *Australian Financial Review*

average due date ['ævərɪdʒ 'dju: 'deɪt] *noun* date when several payments (due at different dates) are settled in one payment

average out ['ævərɪdʒ 'aʊt] *verb* to come to a figure as an average; ***it averages out at 10% per annum***; ***sales increases have averaged out at 15%***

averager ['ævərɪdʒə] *noun* person who buys the same share at various times and at various prices to give an average price

average-sized ['ævərɪdʒ'saɪzd] *adjective* not large or small; ***they are an average-sized company***; ***he has an average-sized office***

averaging ['ævərɪdʒɪŋ] *noun* **(a)** buying or selling shares at different times and at different prices to establish an average price **(b)** **pound-cost averaging** = buying securities at different times, but always spending the same amount of money (NOTE: in American English, this is called **dollar-cost averaging**)

avoid [ə'vɔɪd] *verb* to try not to do something; ***the company is trying to avoid bankruptcy***; ***my aim is to avoid paying too much tax***; ***we want to avoid direct competition with Smith Ltd*** (NOTE: you avoid something or avoid **doing** something)

avoidance [ə'vɔɪdəns] *noun* trying not to do something; ***avoidance of an agreement*** *or* ***of a contract***; **tax avoidance** = trying (legally) to pay as little tax as possible

avoirdupois [ævədə'pɔɪz] *noun* non-metric system of weights used in the UK, the USA and other countries (the basic units are the ounce, the pound, the hundredweight and the ton)

> COMMENT: avoirdupois weight is divided into drams (16 drams = 1 ounce); ounces (14 ounces = one pound); pounds (100 pounds = 1 hundredweight); hundredweight (20 hundredweight = 1 ton). Avoirdupois weights are heavier than troy weights with the same names: the avoirdupois pound equals 0.45kg, whereas the troy pound equals 0.37kg

award [ə'wɔ:d] **1** *noun* decision which settles a dispute; ***an award by an industrial tribunal***; ***the arbitrator's award was set aside on appeal*** **2** *verb* to decide the amount of money to be given to someone; ***to award someone a salary increase***; ***to award damages***; ***the judge awarded costs to the defendant***; **to award a contract to someone** = to decide that someone will have the contract to do work

away [ə'weɪ] *preposition* US **the bid is away from the market** = the bid is lower than the quoted market level

ax [æks] *noun* US *(informal)* the financial adviser who is the current expert on a particular stock or market sector

Bb

Schedule B ['ʃedju:l 'bi:] schedule to the Finance Acts under which tax is charged on income from woodlands

Table B ['teɪbl 'bi:] model memorandum of association of a limited company set out in the Companies Act, 1985

'B' shares ['bi: 'ʃeəz] *plural noun* ordinary shares with special voting rights (often owned by the founder of a company and his family)

baby bonds ['beɪbi 'bɒndz] *plural noun US* bonds in small denominations (i.e. $100) which the small investor can afford to buy

baby boomer ['beɪbi 'bu:mə] *see* BOOMER

back [bæk] **1** *noun* opposite side to the front; ***the conditions of sale are printed on the back of the invoice; please endorse the cheque on the back*** **2** *adjective* referring to the past; **back interest** = interest not yet paid; **back orders** = orders received in the past and not fulfilled (usually because the item is out of stock); ***after the strike it took the factory six weeks to clear all the accumulated back orders***; **back payment** = paying money which is owed; ***the salesmen are claiming for back payment of unpaid commission***; **back payments** = payments which are due; **back rent** = rent owed; ***the company owes £100,000 in back rent*** **3** *adverb* as things were before; ***he will pay back the money in monthly instalments; the store sent back the cheque because the date was wrong*** **4** *verb* **(a) to back someone** = to help someone financially; ***the bank is backing him to the tune of £100,000; he is looking for someone to back his project*** **(b) to back a bill** = to sign a bill promising to pay it if the person it is addressed to is not able to do so

> the businesses we back range from start-up ventures to established companies in need of further capital for expansion
>
> *The Times*

back and filling ['bæk ən 'fɪlɪŋ] *adjective* (market) where prices rise and fall slightly

backdate ['bækdeɪt] *verb* to put an earlier date on a cheque or an invoice; ***backdate your invoice to April 1st; the pay increase is backdated to January 1st***

backdoor ['bækdɔ:] *noun* **by the backdoor** = acquiring a listing on a Stock Exchange by buying a listed company (which is cheaper than applying for a new listing)

back-end loaded ['bækend 'ləʊdɪd] *adjective* (insurance or investment scheme) where commission is charged when the investor withdraws his money from the scheme; *compare* FRONT-END

backer ['bækə] *noun* **(a)** person who backs someone; ***he has an Australian backer; one of the company's backers has withdrawn*** **(b) backer of a bill** = person who backs a bill

backhander ['bækhændə] *noun (informal)* bribe, money given to someone to get him to help you

backing ['bækɪŋ] *noun* **(a)** financial support; ***he has the backing of an Australian bank; the company will succeed only if it has sufficient backing; who is providing the backing for the project*** *or* ***where does the backing for the project come from?*** **(b) asset backing** = support for a share price provided by the value of the company's assets; **currency backing** = gold or government securities which maintain the strength of a currency

> the company has received the backing of a number of oil companies who are willing to pay for the results of the survey
>
> *Lloyd's List*

backlog ['bæklɒg] *noun* work (such as orders or letters) which has piled up waiting to be done; ***the office is trying to cope with a backlog of share deals; my secretary can't cope with the backlog of paperwork***

back office ['bæk 'ɒfɪs] *noun* **(a)** the part of a broking firm where the paperwork involved in buying and selling shares is processed **(b)** *US* part of a bank where cheques are processed, statements of account drawn up, etc. **(c)** *US* general administration department of a company (NOTE: also called **operations department**)

> last year she consolidated the back-office operations of the company's two book publishers
>
> *Fortune*

back out ['bæk 'aʊt] *verb* to stop being part of a deal or an agreement; ***the bank backed out of the contract***; ***we had to cancel the project when our German partners backed out***

back to back ['bæk tə 'bæk] *adjective* **back to back credit** = (i) credit facilities for the purchase of goods (the credit is asked for by the purchaser, but is granted to a middleman, who buys the goods, then sells them on to the final purchaser, and uses the credit as a basis for obtaining further credit facilities); (ii) credit in a currency allowed to a foreign trader on the basis of credit which has been granted by a bank in the trader's own country; **back to back loan** = loan from one company to another in one currency arranged against a loan from the second company to the first in another currency (used by international companies to get round exchange controls)

back up ['bæk 'ʌp] *verb* **(a)** to support or to help; ***he brought along a file of documents to back up his claim***; ***the finance director said the managing director had refused to back him up in his argument with the VAT office*** **(b)** US *(of a market)* to go into reverse; **to back up a portfolio** = to sell long-term bonds and replace them by short-term bonds

backup ['bækʌp] *adjective* supporting or helping; ***we offer a free backup service to customers***; ***after a series of sales tours by representatives, the sales director sends backup letters to all the contacts***; **backup copy** = copy of a computer disk to be kept in case the original disk is damaged; **backup credit** = credit provided by banks for a eurocurrency note; **backup line** = credit provided by banks against the security of commercial bills of exchange which are about to mature

backwardation [bækwə'deɪʃən] *noun* **(a)** penalty paid by the seller when postponing delivery of shares to the buyer **(b)** (i) situation where the spot price of a commodity or currency is higher than the futures price; (ii) difference between the spot and futures prices (NOTE: the opposite is **forwardation** or **contango**)

BACS [bæks] = BANKERS AUTOMATED CLEARING SERVICES company set up to organize the payment of direct debits, standing orders, salary cheques and other payments generated by computers; it operates for all the British clearing banks and several building societies; it forms part of APACS; *compare* CHAPS

bad [bæd] *adjective* not good; **bad bargain** = item which is not worth the price asked; **bad buy** = thing bought which was not worth the money paid for it; **bad cheque** = cheque which is returned to drawer for any reason; **bad debt** = debt which will not be paid (usually because the debtor has gone out of business) and which has to be written off in the accounts; **bad debt provision** = money put aside in accounts to cover potential bad debts; ***the company has written off £30,000 in bad debts***

> bad loans to businesses are the principal cause of Japan's banking difficulties
>
> *The Banker*

baht [bɑːt] currency used in Thailand

bailee [beɪ'liː] *noun* person who receives property by way of bailment

bailment ['beɪlmənt] *noun* transfer of goods by someone (the bailor) to someone (the bailee) who then holds them until they have to be returned to the bailor (such as putting jewels in a bank's safe deposit box)

bailor ['beɪlə] *noun* person who transfers property by way of bailment

bail out ['beɪl 'aʊt] *verb* **(a)** to rescue a company which is in financial difficulties **(b)** to sell your holdings in a company **(c) to bail someone out** = to pay money to a court as a guarantee that someone will return to face charges; ***she paid $3,000 to bail him out***

> the government has decided to bail out the bank which has suffered losses to the extent that its capital has been wiped out
>
> *South China Morning Post*

> investors who are already in environmental stocks might reconsider if they're thinking of bailing out
>
> *Wall Street Journal*

> the Japanese government has not yet recognised the substantial cost of bailing out Japan's banks, insurance companies, and

```
other entities whose creditors
the government will protect
against loss
```

The Banker

bail-out ['beɪlaʊt] *noun* rescue of a company in financial difficulties

balance ['bæləns] **1** *noun* **(a)** amount to be put in one of the columns of an account to make the total debits and credits equal; **credit balance** = balance in an account showing that more money has been received than is owed; **debit balance** = balance in an account showing that more money is owed than has been received; ***the account has a credit balance of £100***; ***because of large payments to suppliers, the account has a debit balance of £1,000***; **balance in hand** = cash held to pay small debts; **balance brought down** = amount entered in an account at the end of a period to balance income and expenditure; **balance brought forward** *or* **balance carried forward** = amount entered in an account at the beginning a period, after it has been brought down at the end of the previous period **(b)** rest of an amount owed; ***you can pay £100 deposit and the balance within 60 days***; **balance due to us** = amount owed to us which is due to be paid; **balance certificate** = share certificate given to an investor who has sold part of his shareholding (the certificate refers to the balance of the shares he has retained) **(c) balance of trade** *or* **trade balance** = record of the international trading position of a country in merchandise, excluding invisible trade; **adverse** *or* **unfavourable balance of trade** = situation where a country imports more than it exports; **favourable trade balance** = situation where a country exports more than it imports; ***the country has had an adverse balance of trade for the second month running*** **(d) bank balance** = state of an account at a bank at a particular time **2** *verb* **(a)** to calculate the amount needed to make the two sides of an account equal; ***I have finished balancing the accounts for March***; **the February accounts do not balance** = the two sides of the accounts for February are not equal; **to balance off the accounts** = to make the two sides of an account balance at the end of an accounting period, by entering a debit balance in the credit side or a credit balance in the debit side, and carrying the balance forward into the next period; **balancing item** *or* **balancing figure** = item introduced into a balance sheet to make the two sides balance **(b)** to plan a budget so that expenditure and income are equal; **balanced budget** = budget where expenditure and income are equal

balance of payments (BOP) ['bæləns əv 'peɪmənts] *noun* (i) the international financial position of a country, including invisible as well as visible trade; (ii) all trade and movements of money between countries worldwide; **capital account balance of payments** = items in a country's balance of payments which do not refer to the buying and selling of merchandise, but to investments made in other countries; **current account balance of payments** = record of imports and exports, payments for services, and invisibles, etc.; **long-term balance of payments** = record of movements of capital relating to overseas investments and the purchase of companies overseas; **overall balance of payments** = the total of current and long-term balance of payments; **balance of payments deficit** = situation where a country buys more from other countries than it sells as exports; **balance of payments surplus** = situation where a country sells more to other countries than it buys from them

balance sheet ['bæləns 'ʃiːt] *noun* statement of the financial position of a company at a particular time, such as the end of the financial year or the end of a quarter, showing the company's assets and liabilities; ***the company balance sheet for 1998 shows a substantial loss***; ***the accountant has prepared the balance sheet for the first half-year***

> COMMENT: the balance sheet shows the state of a company's finances at a certain date; the profit and loss account shows the movements which have taken place since the last balance sheet

balboa [bæl'bəʊə] currency used in Panama

balloon [bə'luːn] *noun* (i) loan where the last repayment is larger than the others; (ii) large final payment on a loan, after a number of periodic smaller loans; *US* **balloon mortgage** = mortgage where the final payment (called a 'balloon payment') is larger than the others

ballot ['bælət] **1** *noun* **(a)** election where people vote for someone by marking a cross on a paper with a list of names (as opposed to a 'show of hands', where people lift their hands to vote); **ballot paper** = paper on which the voter marks a cross to show who he wants to vote for; **ballot box** = sealed box into which ballot papers are put; **postal ballot** = election where the voters send their ballot papers by post; **secret ballot** = election where the voters vote in secret **(b)** selecting by taking papers at random out of a box; *the*

share issue was oversubscribed, so there was a ballot for the shares **2** *verb* to take a vote by ballot; ***the union is balloting for the post of president***

Baltic Futures Exchange (BFE) ['bɒltɪk 'fju:tʃəz ɪks'tʃeɪndʒ] institution in London specializing in the chartering of shipping for sea freight and planes for airfreight, and also in commodity futures, such as wheat, barley, potatoes and pigs

banca ['bænkæ] *Italian* bank

Banca d'Italia ['bænkæ dɪ'tæliə] the central bank of Italy

banco ['bænkəʊ] *Spanish & Portuguese* bank

Banco de España ['bænkəʊ deɪ es'pænjæ] the central bank of Spain

Banco de Portugal ['bænkəʊ deɪ pɔ:tu'gæl] the central bank of Portugal

band [bænd] *noun* range of figures between low and high, within which a figure can move (used for the range of movement which a currency is allowed to make against other currencies)

bank [bæŋk] **1** *noun* **(a)** business which holds money for its clients, which lends money at interest, and trades generally in money; ***he put all his earnings into his bank***; ***I have had a letter from my bank telling me my account is overdrawn***; **bank loans** *or* **bank advances** = loans from a bank; ***he asked for a bank loan to start his business***; **bank borrowing** = money borrowed from a bank; ***the new factory was financed by bank borrowing***; **bank borrowings have increased** = loans given by banks have increased; **bank deposits** = all money placed in banks by private or corporate customers; **bank return** = statement of the financial position of a central bank **(b) central bank** = main government-controlled bank in a country, which controls the financial affairs of the country by fixing main interest rates, issuing currency and controlling the foreign exchange rate; **the Federal Reserve Banks** = central banks in the USA which are owned by the state, and directed by the Federal Reserve Board; **the World Bank** = central bank, controlled by the United Nations, whose funds come from the member states of the UN and which lends money to member states; *US* **national bank** = bank which is chartered by the federal government and is part of the Federal Reserve system (as opposed to a 'state bank'); **state bank** = commercial bank licensed by the authorities of a state, and not necessarily a member of the Federal Reserve system (as opposed to a 'national bank') **(c) savings bank** = bank where you can deposit money and receive interest on it; **merchant bank** = bank which lends money to companies and deals in international finance; **the High Street banks** = main British banks which accept deposits from and allow withdrawals by individuals **2** *verb* to deposit money into a bank or to have an account with a bank; ***he banked the cheque as soon as he received it***; **where do you bank?** = where do you have a bank account?; ***I bank at*** *or* ***with Barclays***

Bank [bænk] *German* bank

bankable ['bæŋkəbl] *adjective* which a bank will accept as security for a loan; ***a bankable paper***

bank account ['bæŋk ə'kaʊnt] *noun* account which a customer has with a bank, where the customer can deposit and withdraw money; ***to open a bank account***; ***to close a bank account***; ***how much money do you have in your bank account? she has £100 in her savings bank account***; ***if you let the balance in your bank account fall below £100, you have to pay bank charges***

bank balance ['bæŋk 'bæləns] *noun* state of a bank account at any particular time; ***our bank balance went into the red last month***

bank bill ['bæŋkbɪl] *noun* **(a)** *GB* bill of exchange by one bank telling another bank (usually in another country) to pay money to someone (bank bills are more secure than trade bills, which are issued by companies) **(b)** *US* piece of printed paper money (NOTE: British English is **bank note**)

bank book ['bæŋk 'bʊk] *noun* book, given by a bank, which shows the amount of money which you deposit or withdraw from your savings account

bank card ['bæŋk 'kɑ:d] *noun* *US* card issued by a bank to a customer, used to withdraw money from a cash dispenser or as a cheque guarantee card

bank charges ['bæŋk 'tʃɑ:dʒɪz] *plural noun* charges which a bank makes for carrying out work for a customer

bank clerk ['bæŋk 'klɑ:k] *noun* person who works in a bank, but not a manager

bank discount rate ['bæŋk 'dɪskɒnt 'reɪt] *noun* rate charged by a bank for a loan where the interest charges are deducted when the loan is made

bank draft ['bæŋk 'drɑ:ft] *noun* order by one bank telling another bank (usually in another country) to pay money to someone

banker ['bæŋkə] *noun* **(a)** person who is in an important position in a bank; **merchant banker** = person who has a high position in a merchant bank **(b)** generally, a bank; *US* **banker's acceptance** = bill of exchange guaranteed by a bank; **banker's bill** = order by one bank telling another bank (usually in another country) to pay money to someone; **banker's draft** = draft payable by a bank in cash on presentation; **banker's lien** = right of a bank to hold some property of a customer as security against payment of a debt; **banker's order** = order written by a customer asking a bank to make a regular payment; ***he pays his subscription by banker's order***; **banker's reference** = details of a company's bank, account number, etc., supplied so that a client can check if the company is a risk; **British Bankers' Association (BBA)** = organization representing British banks

Bank for International Settlements (BIS) ['bæŋk fə ɪntə'næʃənl 'setlmənts] bank (based in Basle) which acts as a clearing bank for the central banks of various countries, through which they settle their currency transactions and also acts on behalf of the IMF

bank giro ['bæŋk 'dʒaɪrəʊ] *noun GB* method used by clearing banks to transfer money rapidly from one account to another (used by individuals when paying bills); *see also* GIRO

bank holiday ['bæŋk 'hɒlədi] *noun* a weekday which is a public holiday when the banks are closed; ***New Year's Day is a bank holiday***

bank identification number (BIN) ['bæŋk aɪdentɪfɪ'keɪʃn 'nʌmbə] internationally organized six-digit number which identifies a bank for charge card purposes

banking ['bæŋkɪŋ] *noun* the business of banks; ***he is studying banking***; ***she has gone into banking;*** *US* **banking account** = account which a customer has with a bank; **a banking crisis** = crisis affecting the banks; **banking hours** = hours when a bank is open for its customers; ***you cannot get money out of the bank after banking hours***; **Banking Ombudsman** = official whose duty is to investigate complaints by members of the public against banks which are members of the Banking Ombudsman scheme; **basic banking services** = basic services offered by banks to their customers, in connection with operating their accounts; *see also* CODE

bank manager ['bæŋk 'mænɪdʒə] *noun* person in charge of a branch of a bank; ***he asked his bank manager for a loan***

bank note *or* **banknote** ['bæŋknəʊt] *noun* **(a)** piece of printed paper money (in England, issued by the Bank of England; in Scotland, commercial banks can issue notes); ***he pulled out a pile of used bank notes*** (NOTE: American English is **bank bill**) **(b)** *US* interest-bearing certificate issued by a bank

Bank of England ['bæŋk əv 'ɪŋlənd] central British bank, owned by the state, which, together with the Treasury, regulates the nation's finances

> COMMENT: the Bank of England issues banknotes which carry the signatures of its officials. It is the lender of last resort to commercial banks and supervises banking institutions in the UK. Its Monetary Policy Committee is independent of the government, and sets interest rates. The Governor of the Bank of England is appointed by the government

Bank of Japan ['bæŋk əv dʒə'pæn] the central bank of Japan

bank on ['bæŋk 'ɒn] *verb* to do something because you are sure something will happen; ***he is banking on getting a loan from his father to set up in business***; ***do not bank on the sale of your house***

bank rate ['bæŋk 'reɪt] *noun* discount rate of a central bank; formerly, the rate at which the Bank of England lent to other banks (then called the Minimum Lending Rate (MLR), and now the 'base rate')

bankroll ['bæŋkrəʊl] *verb (informal)* to pay for, to finance (a project)

bankrupt ['bæŋkrʌpt] **1** *adjective & noun* (person) who has been declared by a court not to be capable of paying his debts and whose affairs are put into the hands of a receiver; ***he was adjudicated*** *or* ***declared bankrupt***; ***a bankrupt property developer***; ***he went bankrupt after two years in business***; **certificated bankrupt** = bankrupt who has been discharged from bankruptcy with a certificate to show he was not at fault; **discharged bankrupt** = person who has been released from being bankrupt because he has paid his debts; **undischarged bankrupt** = person who has been declared bankrupt and has not been released from that state **2** *verb* to make someone become bankrupt; ***the recession bankrupted my father***

bankruptcy ['bæŋkrəptsi] *noun* state of being bankrupt; ***the recession has caused thousands of bankruptcies***; **adjudication of**

bankruptcy *or* **declaration of bankruptcy** *or* **bankruptcy order** = legal order making someone bankrupt; **discharge in bankruptcy** = being released from bankruptcy after paying debts; **to file a petition in bankruptcy** *or* **to file for bankruptcy** = to apply officially to be made bankrupt or to ask officially for someone else to be made bankrupt; ***two of their competitors recently filed for bankruptcy***; *see also* CHAPTER 11

COMMENT: in the UK, 'bankruptcy' is applied only to individual persons, but in the USA the term is also applied to corporations. In the UK, a bankrupt cannot hold public office (for example, he cannot be elected an MP) and cannot be the director of a company. He also cannot borrow money. In the USA, there are two types of bankruptcy: 'involuntary', where the creditors ask for a person or corporation to be made bankrupt; and 'voluntary', where a person or corporation applies to be made bankrupt (in the UK, this is called 'voluntary liquidation')

> Pan Am didn't file for bankruptcy protection - but its two main airline units did
>
> *Barron's*

bank statement ['bæŋk 'steɪtmənt] *noun* written statement from a bank showing the balance of an account

banque [bɒŋk] *French* bank

banque d'affaires ['bɒŋk dæ'feə] *French* merchant bank

Banque de France ['bɒŋk də 'frɒns] the Central Bank of France

bar [bɑ:] *noun* thing which stops you doing something; ***government legislation is a bar to foreign trade***

bar-bell ['bɑ:'bel] *noun US* portfolio which concentrates on very long-term and very short-term bonds only; *compare* LADDER

bar chart ['bɑ: 'tʃɑ:t] *noun* chart where values or quantities are shown as thick columns of different heights

bar code ['bɑ: 'kəʊd] *noun* system of lines printed on a product which when read by a computer give a reference number or price

Barclays Index ['bɑ:klɪz 'ɪndeks] index of prices on the New Zealand Stock Exchange

bargain ['bɑ:gɪn] **1** *noun* **(a)** agreement on the price of something; **to drive a hard bargain** = to be a difficult negotiator, to agree a deal which is favourable to you; **it is a bad bargain** = it is not worth the price **(b)** thing which is cheaper than usual; ***that car is a (real) bargain at £500***; **bargain hunter** = person who looks for cheap deals; **bargain hunting** = looking for cheap shares, which no one has noticed **(c)** sale and purchase of one lot of shares on the Stock Exchange; **bargains done** = number of deals made on the Stock Exchange during a day **2** *verb* to discuss a price for something; ***you will have to bargain with the dealer if you want a discount***; ***they spent two hours bargaining about*** *or* ***over the price***

bargaining ['bɑ:gɪnɪŋ] *noun* act of discussing a price, usually wage increases for workers; **(free) collective bargaining** = negotiations between employers and workers' representatives over wage increases and conditions; **bargaining power** = strength of one person or group when discussing prices or wage settlements; **bargaining position** = statement of position by one group during negotiations

barren ['bærn] *adjective* (money) which is not earning any interest

barrier ['bærɪə] *noun* **(a)** thing which stops someone doing something, especially sending goods from one place to another; **customs barriers** *or* **tariff barriers** = customs duty intended to make trade more difficult; **to impose trade barriers on certain goods** = to restrict the import of certain goods by charging high duty; **to lift trade barriers from imports** = to remove restrictions on imports **(b)** *(economics)* **barriers to entry** = things which make it difficult for a firm to enter a market and compete with firms already in that market

> a senior European Community official has denounced Japanese trade barriers, saying they cost European producers $3 billion a year
>
> *The Times*

> to create a single market out of the EC member states, physical, technical and tax barriers to free movement of trade between member states must be removed. Imposing VAT on importation of goods from other member states is seen as one such tax barrier
>
> *Accountancy*

barter ['bɑ:tə] **1** *noun* system where goods are exchanged for other goods and not sold for money; **barter agreement** *or* **barter arrangement** *or* **barter deal** = agreement to exchange goods by barter; ***the company has***

agreed a barter deal with Bulgaria **2** *verb* to exchange goods for other goods, but not buy them for money; ***they agreed a deal to barter tractors for barrels of wine***

> under the barter agreements, Nigeria will export 175,000 barrels a day of crude oil in exchange for trucks, food, planes and chemicals
>
> *Wall Street Journal*

bartering ['bɑːtərɪŋ] *noun* act of exchanging goods for other goods and not for money

base [beɪs] **1** *noun* **(a)** lowest or first position; ***turnover increased by 200%, but starting from a low base***; **base currency** = currency against which exchange rates of other currencies are quoted; **base-weighted index** = index which is weighted according to the base year; **base year** = first year of an index, against which later years' changes are measured; **(bank) base rate** = basic rate of interest on which the actual rate a bank charges on loans to its customers is calculated; *see also* DATABASE **(b)** place where a company has its main office or factory, a place where a businessman has his office; ***the company has its base in London and branches in all European countries***; ***he has an office in Madrid which he uses as a base while he is travelling in Southern Europe*** **2** *verb* **(a)** to start to calculate or to negotiate from a position; ***we based our calculations on the forecast turnover***; **based on** = calculating from; ***based on last year's figures***; ***based on population forecasts*** **(b)** to set up a company or a person in a place; ***the European manager is based in our London office***; ***our overseas branch is based in the Bahamas***; ***a London-based bank***

> the base lending rate, or prime rate, is the rate at which banks lend to their top corporate borrowers
>
> *Wall Street Journal*

> other investments include a large stake in the Chicago-based insurance company
>
> *Lloyd's List*

basic ['beɪsɪk] **1** *adjective* **(a)** normal; **basic pay** *or* **basic salary** *or* **basic wage** = normal salary without extra payments; **basic balance** = balance of current account and long-term capital accounts in a country's balance of payments; **basic discount** = normal discount without extra percentages; ***our basic discount is 20%, but we offer 5% extra for rapid settlement***; **basic rate of income tax** = the main or first rate of tax, levied on most salaries **(b)** most important; **basic commodities** = ordinary farm produce, produced in large quantities (such as corn, rice, sugar, etc.) **(c)** simple, from which everything starts; ***he has a basic knowledge of the market***; ***to work at the cash desk, you need a basic qualification in maths***

basics ['beɪsɪks] *plural noun* simple and important facts; ***he has studied the basics of foreign exchange dealing***; **to get back to basics** = to consider the basic facts again

basis ['beɪsɪs] *noun* **(a)** point or number from which calculations are made; ***we forecast the turnover on the basis of a 6% price increase***; **basis point** = one hundredth of a percentage point (0.01%), the basic unit used in measuring market movements or interest rates; **basis price** = (i) price agreed between buyer and seller on the over-the-counter market; (ii) price of a bond shown as its annual percentage yield to maturity; **basis swap** = exchange of two financial instruments, each with a variable interest calculated on a different rate **(b)** *US* the difference between the cash price and futures price for a commodity **(c)** term of days used to calculate interest; **money market basis** = calculated on a year of 365 days **(d)** general terms of an agreement; **on a short-term** *or* **long-term basis** = for a short or long period; ***he has been appointed on a short-term basis***; ***we have three people working on a freelance basis*** (NOTE: the plural is **bases**)

basket ['bɑːskɪt] *noun* **(a)** container made of thin pieces of wood, metal or plastic; **filing basket** = container kept on a desk for documents which have to be filed; **shopping basket** *US* **market basket** = basket used for carrying shopping (its imaginary contents are used to calculate a consumer price index); ***the price of the average shopping basket*** *US* ***the market basket has risen by 6%*** **(b) currency basket** *or* **basket of currencies** = group of currencies, each of which is weighted, calculated together as a single unit against which another currency can be measured; ***the pound has fallen against a basket of European currencies***

batch [bætʃ] **1** *noun* **(a)** group of items which are made at one time; ***this batch of shoes has the serial number 25-02*** **(b)** group of documents which are processed at the same time; ***a batch of invoices***; ***today's batch of orders***; ***the accountant signed a batch of cheques***; ***we deal with the orders in batches of fifty***; **batch processing** = system of data processing where information is collected into batches before being loaded into the computer **2** *verb* to put items together in groups; ***to batch invoices** or **cheques***

batch number ['bætʃ 'nʌmbə] *noun* number attached to a batch; ***when making a complaint always quote the batch number on the packet***

BBA = BRITISH BANKERS' ASSOCIATION

bear [beə] **1** *noun (Stock Exchange)* person who sells shares (or commodities or currency) because he thinks the price will fall and he will be able to buy again more cheaply later; **covered bear** = bear who holds the stock which he is selling; **uncovered bear** = person who sells stock which he does not hold, hoping to be able to buy stock later at a lower price when he needs to settle; **bear covering** = point in a market where dealers who sold stock short, now buy back (at lower prices) to cover their positions; **bear market** = period when share prices fall because shareholders are selling since they believe the market will fall further; **bear position** = short position, that is, selling shares which you do not own (you will buy them later at a lower price so as to be able to settle); **taking a bear position** = acting on the assumption that the market is likely to fall; **bear raid** = selling large amounts of stock (which the seller does not hold), in order to depress the market so as to be able to pick up stock again later at lower prices; **bear squeeze** = (i) action by banks to raise exchange rates, forcing currency bear sellers to buy back currency at a loss (i.e., at a higher price); (ii) operation by marketmakers to increase the price of shares, so as to force bears to buy at higher prices than they intended (NOTE: the opposite is **bull**) **2** *verb* **(a)** to give interest; ***government bonds which bear 5% interest*** **(b)** to have (a name); to have something written on it; ***the cheque bears the signature of the company secretary***; ***envelope which bears a London postmark***; ***a letter bearing yesterday's date***; ***the share certificate bears his name*** **(c)** to pay costs; ***the costs of the exhibition will be borne by the company***; ***the company bore the legal costs of both parties*** (NOTE: **bearing - bore - has borne**)

bearer ['beərə] *noun* person who holds a cheque or certificate; **the cheque is payable to bearer** = the cheque will be paid to the person who holds it, not to any particular name written on it

bearer bond *or* **bearer security** ['beərə 'bɒnd or sɪ'kjʊərəti] *noun* bond which is payable to the bearer and does not have a name written on it (useful if the owner wishes to avoid being identified by the income tax authorities)

bearing ['beərɪŋ] *adjective* which bears, which produces; ***certificate bearing interest at 5%***; **an interest-bearing account** = bank account which gives interest

bearish ['beərɪʃ] *adjective* (i) (factor) which tends to make market prices fall; (ii) (investor) who believes that market prices will fall

bed-and-breakfast deal ['bed ənd 'brekfəst 'di:l] *noun* formerly, an arrangement where shares are sold one day and bought back the following day, in order to establish a profit or loss for tax declaration

> COMMENT: this is no longer possible, since a period of thirty days has to elapse between the sale and repurchase of the same shares to allow a new price to be established

bed-pepping ['bed'pepɪŋ] *noun* arrangement by which you sell existing investments and put the resulting cash into a PEP. This establishes any gains on the investments, so that you can calculate whether you should pay capital gains tax

behavioural finance [bɪ'heɪvjərəl 'faɪnæns] *noun* psychological view of the way people take financial decisions

> a new field called behavioral finance, which focuses on the way investor psychology rewards contrarian stock picking and causes over- or underreaction to things like dividends, spinoffs, splits and new issues
>
> *Smart Money*

Beige Book ['beɪʒ 'bʊk] *noun US* report on the financial position prepared by the district banks for the Federal Reserve Board; *see also* BLUE BOOK, GREEN BOOK

bellwether ['belwðə] *noun* leading share which is thought of as an indicator of market trends as a whole (such as Lloyds in the UK)

> the Treasury's bellwether 30-year bond declined 3/32 to 98 20/32, yielding 7.99 per cent
>
> *Toronto Globe & Mail*

> Monday seemed to whet investors' appetite for the technology bellwether
>
> *Barron's*

> more than 24 hours before semiconductor giant and market

bellwether Intel will report its quarterly earnings

Wall Street Journal

belly up ['beli 'ʌp] *phrase (informal)* **to go belly up** = to fail, to go into liquidation

below par [bɪ'ləʊ 'pɑː] *phrase* (share) with a market price lower than its par value

below-the-line [bɪ'ləʊðə'laɪn] **1** *adjective* **below-the-line expenditure** = exceptional payments which are separated from a company's normal accounts **2** *noun* (i) part of a budget referring to receipts from redeemed debts and expenditure covered by borrowings; (ii) extraordinary items which are set against net profits after tax (as opposed to exceptional items which are set against profits before tax); *compare* ABOVE-THE-LINE

belt and braces *US* **belt and suspenders** ['belt ənd 'breɪsɪz] *noun (informal)* **a belt and braces man** = a very cautious lender, one who asks for extra collateral as well as guarantees for a loan

benchmark ['bentʃmɑːk] *noun* point in an index which is important, and can be used to compare with other figures

the US bank announced a cut in its prime, the benchmark corporate lending rate, from 10+% to 10%

Financial Times

the dollar dropped below three German marks - a benchmark with more psychological than economic significance - for the first time since October

Fortune

the benchmark 113/4 due 2003/2007 was quoted at 107 11/32, down 13/32 from Monday

Wall Street Journal

the benchmark March potato futures contract on Liffe surged to more than £310 in November after the wet weather hit the crops in the UK and Europe

Financial Times

beneficial [benɪ'fɪʃəl] *adjective* **beneficial occupier** = person who occupies a property but does not own it fully; **beneficial owner** = person who owns a property which is being used by someone else; **beneficial interest** = interest which allows someone to occupy or receive rent from a property, but not to own it

beneficiary [benɪ'fɪʃəri] *noun* person who gains money from something; ***the beneficiaries of a will***

the pound sterling was the main beneficiary of the dollar's weakness

Business Times (Lagos)

benefit ['benɪfɪt] **1** *noun* **(a)** payments which are made to someone under a national or private insurance scheme; ***she receives £60 a week as unemployment benefit***; ***the sickness benefit is paid monthly***; ***the insurance office sends out benefit cheques each week***; **death benefit** = money paid to the family of someone who dies in an accident at work **(b) fringe benefits** = extra items given by a company to workers in addition to their salaries (such as company cars, private health insurance) **2** *verb* **(a)** to make better or to improve; ***a fall in inflation benefits the exchange rate*** **(b) to benefit from** *or* **by something** = to be improved by something, to gain more money because of something; ***exports have benefited from the fall in the exchange rate***; ***the employees have benefited from the profit-sharing scheme***

the retail sector will also benefit from the expected influx of tourists

Australian Financial Review

what benefits does the executive derive from his directorship? Compensation has increased sharply in recent years and fringe benefits for directors have proliferated

Duns Business Month

salary is negotiable to £30,000, plus car and a benefits package appropriate to this senior post

Financial Times

California is the latest state to enact a program forcing welfare recipients to work for their benefits

Fortune

bequest [bɪ'kwest] *noun* personal property, money, etc., given to someone in a will (but not real estate); ***he made several bequests to his staff***; *compare* DEVISE

berhad [bɜː'hæd] *(in Malaysia)* limited company; *see also* SDN

at best ['æt 'best] *phrase* **sell at best** *or* **sell at the market** = instruction to stockbroker to sell shares at the best price possible

best-selling ['best'selɪŋ] *adjective* which sells very well; ***these CDs are our best-selling line***

bet [bet] **1** *noun* amount deposited when you risk money on the result of a race *or* of a game **2** *verb* to risk money on the result of something; ***he bet £100 on the result of the election***; ***I bet you £25 the dollar will rise against the pound***; **betting tax** = tax levied on betting on horses, dogs, etc. (NOTE: **betting - bet - has bet**)

beta ['bi:tə] **1** *noun* measurement of the return on investment in a certain stock compared against a one percentage point return on the stock market in general: it shows the volatility in the price of the share compared to the FTSE All-Share Index **2** *adjective* **beta shares** *or* **beta securities** *or* **beta stocks** = group of about 500 shares which are traded on the London Stock Exchange, but not as frequently as the alpha shares (prices of beta shares are quoted on SEAQ, but not the share transactions); *see also* ALPHA, DELTA, GAMMA

b/f = BROUGHT FORWARD

BFE = BALTIC FUTURES EXCHANGE

bi- [baɪ] *prefix* twice; **bi-monthly** = twice a month; **bi-annually** = twice a year

bid [bɪd] **1** *noun* **(a)** offer to buy something (such as a share, currency, commodity, or a unit in a unit trust) at a certain price; **to make a bid for something** = to offer to buy something; ***the company made a bid for its rival***; **to make a cash bid** = to offer to pay cash for something; **to put in a bid for something** *or* **to enter a bid for something** = to offer (usually in writing) to buy something; **bid basis** = pricing of unit trusts at a lower bid price to encourage buyers; **bid market** = market where there are more bids to buy than offers to sell (the opposite is an 'offered' market); **bid price** = (i) price at which an marketmaker will buy shares on the Stock Exchange; (ii) price at which units in a unit trust are sold back to the trust by an investor (the opposite, i.e. the price offered by the purchaser, is called the 'offer' price; the difference between the two is the 'spread'); *(on the Stock Exchange)* **bid-offer spread** = difference between buying and selling prices (i.e. between the bid and offer prices); **bid-offer price** = price charged by unit trusts to buyers and sellers of units, based on the bid-offer spread; **bid rate** = rate of interest offered on deposits **(b)** *(at an auction)* **opening bid** = first bid; **closing bid** = last bid at an auction, the bid which is successful **(c)** offer to do some work at a certain price; ***he made the lowest bid for the job*** **(d)** *US* offer to sell something at a certain price; ***they asked for bids for the supply of spare parts*** **(e)** **takeover bid** = offer to buy all or a majority of shares in a company so as to control it; ***to withdraw a takeover bid***; **the company rejected the takeover bid** = the directors recommended that the shareholders should not accept it; *see also* AGREED, CONTESTED, HOSTILE **2** *verb* **(a)** *(at an auction)* **to bid for something** = to offer to buy something; **he bid £1,000 for the jewels** = he offered to pay £1,000 for the jewels **(b)** to offer to buy; ***investors bid up equities to record heights*** (NOTE: **bidding - bid - has bid**)

---

if initial fees, exit fees and annual management charges were not enough, conventional unit trusts charge buyers and sellers of units a difference price - known as bid-offer price

The Times

---

bidder ['bɪdə] *noun* person who makes a bid (usually at an auction); ***several bidders made offers for the house***; **the property was sold to the highest bidder** = to the person who had made the highest bid or who offered the most money; **the tender will go to the lowest bidder** = to the person who offers the best terms or the lowest price for services

bidding ['bɪdɪŋ] *noun* action of making offers to buy (usually at an auction); **the bidding started at £1,000** = the first and lowest bid was £1,000; **the bidding stopped at £250,000** = the last bid (and the successful bid) was for £250,000; **the auctioneer started the bidding at £100** = he suggested that the first bid should be £100

Big Bang ['bɪg 'bæŋ] *noun* **(a)** the change in practices on the London Stock Exchange, culminating in the introduction of electronic trading on October 27th 1986; the changes included the abolition of stock jobbers and the removal of the system of fixed commissions; the Stock Exchange trading floor closed and deals are now done by phone or computer (NOTE: the American equivalent was **May Day**) **(b)** similar changes in financial practices in other countries

---

1 December was a key date when a series of Big Bang measures took effect. Among them was the fact that Japanese banks and other institutions became free to

begin direct marketing of investment trusts

The Banker

Big Blue ['bɪg 'blu:] *informal name for* IBM

Big Board ['bɪg 'bɔ:d] *noun US (informal)* = NEW YORK STOCK EXCHANGE (in fact, it is the display system of the NYSE); *compare* LITTLE BOARD

at the close, the Dow Jones Industrial Average was up 24.25 at 2,559.65, while New York S.E. volume totalled 180m shares. Away from the Big Board, the American S.E. Composite climbed 2.31 to 297.87

Financial Times

Big Four ['bɪg 'fɔ:] *noun* **(a)** the four large British commercial banks: Barclays, LloydsTSB, Midland and Natwest (now joined by several former building societies that have become banks) **(b)** the four largest Japanese securities houses: Daiwa, Nikko, Nomura, Yamaichi

Big Three ['bɪg 'θri:] *US (informal)* name for the three big car makers in Detroit, i.e., General Motors (GM), Chrysler and Ford

the Big Three could buy a number of struggling overseas automakers that would give them strong ties to developing markets

Fortune

bilateral [baɪ'lætərəl] *adjective* between two parties or countries; ***the minister signed a bilateral trade agreement***; **bilateral clearing** = the system of annual settlements of accounts between certain countries, where accounts are settled by the central banks; **bilateral credit** = credit allowed by banks to other banks in a clearing system (to cover the period while cheques are being cleared)

bill [bɪl] **1** *noun* **(a)** written list of charges to be paid; ***the salesman wrote out the bill; does the bill include VAT? the bill is made out to Smith Ltd; the builder sent in his bill; he left the country without paying his bills***; **to foot the bill** = to pay the costs **(b)** list of charges in a restaurant; ***can I have the bill please? the bill comes to £20 including service; does the bill include service? the waiter has added 10% to the bill for service*** **(c)** written paper promising to pay money; **bills payable** = bills which a debtor will have to pay; **bills receivable** = bills which a creditor will receive in the end; **due bills** = bills which are owed but not yet paid; *see also* BILL OF EXCHANGE (below), TREASURY **(d) bill of lading** = list of goods being shipped, which the transporter gives to the person sending the goods to show that the goods have been loaded **(e)** *US* piece of paper money; ***a $5 bill*** (NOTE: British English is a **note**) **(f) bill of sale** = document which the seller gives to the buyer to show that the sale has taken place **(g)** draft of a new law which will be discussed in Parliament **2** *verb* to present a bill to someone so that it can be paid; ***the builders billed him for the repairs to his neighbour's house***

billing ['bɪlɪŋ] *noun* writing of invoices or bills; **billing error** = mistake in charging a sum to a credit card

bill of exchange ['bɪl əv ɪks'tʃeɪnʒ] *noun* document signed by the person authorizing it, which tells another to pay money unconditionally to a named person on a certain date (usually used in payments in foreign currency); **accommodation bill** = bill of exchange where the person signing is helping someone else to raise a loan; **Treasury Bill** *US* **T Bill** = short-term bill of exchange which does not give any interest and is sold by the government at a discount through the central bank; **bank bill** = bill of exchange endorsed by a bank; **bill broker** = discount house, a firm which buys and sells bills of exchange for a fee; **demand bill** = bill of exchange which must be paid when payment is asked for; **trade bill** = bill of exchange between two companies who are trading partners (it is issued by one company and endorsed by the other); **to accept a bill** = to sign a bill of exchange to show that you promise to pay it; **to discount a bill** = to buy a bill of exchange at a lower price than that written on it in order to cash it later

COMMENT: a bill of exchange is a document raised by a seller and signed by a purchaser, stating that the purchaser accepts that he owes the seller money, and promises to pay it at a later date. The person raising the bill is the 'drawer', the person who accepts it is the 'drawee'. The seller can then sell the bill at a discount to raise cash. This is called a 'trade bill'. A bill can also be accepted (i.e. guaranteed) by a bank, and in this case it is called a 'bank bill'

billion ['bɪljən] number one thousand million (NOTE: in American English it has always meant one thousand million, but in British English it formerly meant one million million, and it is still sometimes used with this meaning. With figures it is usually written **bn: $5bn** say 'five billion dollars')

```
gross wool receipts for the
selling season to end June 30
appear likely to top $2 billion
```

Australian Financial Review

```
at its last traded price the
bank was capitalized at around
$1.05 billion
```

South China Morning Post

BIN = BANK IDENTIFICATION NUMBER

bind [baɪnd] *verb* to tie or to attach; ***the company is bound by its articles of association***; ***he does not consider himself bound by the agreement which was signed by his predecessor*** (NOTE: **binding - bound**)

binder ['baɪndə] *noun* **(a)** stiff cardboard cover for papers; **ring binder** = cover with rings in it which fit into special holes made in sheets of paper **(b)** *US* temporary agreement for insurance sent before the insurance policy is issued (NOTE: British English for this is **cover note**)

binding ['baɪndɪŋ] *adjective* which legally forces someone to do something; ***a binding contract***; ***this document is not legally binding***; **the agreement is binding on all parties** = all parties signing it must do what is agreed

birr [bɜ:] currency used in Ethiopia

BIS = BANK FOR INTERNATIONAL SETTLEMENTS

black [blæk] **1** *adjective* **(a) black economy** = goods and services which are paid for in cash, and therefore not declared for tax **(b) in the black** = in credit; ***the company has moved into the black***; ***my bank account is still in the black*** **2** *verb* to forbid trading in certain goods or with certain suppliers; ***three firms were blacked by the government***; ***the union has blacked a trucking firm***

Black Friday ['blæk 'fraɪdeɪ] *noun* any sudden collapse on a stock market (called after the first major collapse of the US stock market on 24th September, 1869)

blackleg ['blækleg] *noun* worker who goes on working when there is a strike

black list ['blæk 'lɪst] *noun* list of goods, people or companies which have been blacked

blacklist ['blæklɪst] *verb* to put goods, people or a company on a black list; ***his firm was blacklisted by the government***

black market *noun* buying and selling goods or currency in a way which is not allowed by law (as in a time of rationing); ***there is a flourishing black market in spare parts for cars***; ***you can buy gold coins on the black market***; **to pay black market prices** = to pay high prices to get items which are not easily available

Black Monday ['blæk 'mʌndeɪ] Monday, 19th October, 1987, when world stock markets crashed

Black Tuesday ['blæk 'tju:zdeɪ] Tuesday, 29th October, 1929, when the US stock market crashed

Black Wednesday ['blæk 'wenzdeɪ] Wednesday, 16th September, 1992, when the pound sterling left the ERM and was devalued against other currencies

> COMMENT: not always seen as 'black', since many people believe it was a good thing that the pound left the ERM

blank [blæŋk] **1** *adjective* with nothing written; **a blank cheque** = a cheque with no amount of money or name written on it, but signed by the drawer **2** *noun* space on a form which has to be completed; ***fill in the blanks and return the form to your local office***

blanket lien ['blæŋkɪt 'li:n] *noun US* lien on a person's property (including personal effects)

blind trust ['blaɪnd 'trʌst] *noun* trust set up to run a person's affairs without the details of any transaction being known to the person concerned (set up by politicians to avoid potential conflicts of interest)

blip [blɪp] *noun* bad economic figures (higher inflation rate, lower exports, etc.), which only have a short-term effect

block [blɒk] **1** *noun* **(a)** series of items grouped together; ***he bought a block of 6,000 shares***; **block booking** = booking of several seats or rooms at the same time; ***the company has a block booking for twenty seats on the plane*** *or* ***for ten rooms at the hotel***; **block trading** = trading in very large numbers of shares **(b)** series of buildings forming a square with streets on all sides; ***they want to redevelop a block in the centre of the town***; **a block of offices** *or* **an office block** = a large building which only contains offices **2** *verb* to stop something taking place; ***he used his casting vote to block the motion***; ***the planning committee blocked the redevelopment plan***; **blocked account** = bank account which cannot be used, usually because a government has forbidden its use; **blocked currency** = currency which cannot be taken out of a country because of government exchange controls; ***the company has a large account in blocked roubles***

blowout ['bləʊaʊt] *noun* US rapid sale of the whole of a new stock issue

blue [blu:] *adjective* **blue-chip investment** *or* **blue-chip share** *or* **blue chip** = risk-free stock of a good company, with a good record of dividends; US **blue sky laws** = state laws to protect investors against fraudulent traders in securities

Blue Book ['blu: 'bʊk] *noun* **(a)** US document reviewing monetary policy, prepared for the Federal Reserve **(b)** GB annual publication of national statistics of personal incomes and spending patterns

blue-collar ['blu:'kɒlə] *adjective* **blue-collar worker** = manual worker in a factory; **blue-collar union** = trade union formed mainly of blue-collar workers

Blue list ['blu: 'lɪst] *noun* US daily list of municipal bonds and their ratings, issued by Standard & Poor's

bn ['bɪljən] = BILLION

board [bɔ:d] **1** *noun* **(a)** *see* BOARD OF DIRECTORS (below) **(b)** US *(informal)* the board of governors of the Federal Reserve **(c)** group of people who run a trust or a society; **advisory board** = group of advisors; **editorial board** = group of editors **(d) on board** = on a ship or plane or train; **free on board (f.o.b.)** = price includes all the seller's costs until the goods are on the ship for transportation **(e)** screen on which share prices are posted (on the wall of the trading floor in a Stock Exchange); **board order** = order to a stockbroker to buy or sell at a particular price; **Big Board** = New York Stock Exchange; **Little Board** = American Stock Exchange **2** *verb* to go on to a ship or plane or train; ***customs officials boarded the ship in the harbour***

boardroom ['bɔ:drʊm] *noun* room where the directors of a company meet; **boardroom battles** = arguments between directors

board of directors ['bɔ:d əv daɪ'rektəz] *noun* **(a)** GB group of directors elected by the shareholders to run a company; ***the bank has two representatives on the board***; ***he sits on the board as a representative of the bank***; ***two directors were removed from the board at the AGM***; **she was asked to join the board** = she was asked to become a director; **board meeting** = meeting of the directors of a company **(b)** US group of people elected by the shareholders to draw up company policy and to appoint the president and other executive officers who are responsible for managing the company

COMMENT: directors are elected by shareholders at the AGM, though they are usually chosen by the chairman or chief executive. A board will consist of a chairman (who may be non-executive), a chief executive or managing director, and a series of specialist directors in charge of various activities of the company (such as production director or sales director). The company secretary will attend board meetings, but is not a director. Apart from the executive directors, who are in fact employees of the company, there may be several non-executive directors, appointed either for their expertise and contacts, or as representatives of important shareholders such as banks. These non-executive directors are paid fees. The board of an American company may be made up of a large number of non-executive directors and only one or two executive officers; a British board has more executive directors

a proxy is the written authorization an investor sends to a stockholder meeting conveying his vote on a corporate resolution or the election of a company's board of directors

Barrons

CEOs, with their wealth of practical experience, are in great demand and can pick and choose the boards they want to serve on

Duns Business Month

boiler room ['bɔɪlə 'ru:m] *noun* room in which telephone sales executives try to sell securities to potential investors

BOJ = BANK OF JAPAN

bolivar ['bɒlɪvɑ:] *noun* currency used in Venezuela

boliviano [bɒlɪvi'ɑ:nəʊ] currency used in Bolivia (also called the Bolivian peso)

Bombay Stock Exchange (BSE) the main stock exchange in India

bona fide ['bəʊnə 'faɪdi] *adjective* trustworthy, which can be trusted; **a bona fide offer** = an offer which is made honestly

> the bank, exposed to false accusations in the media, suffered an immediate loss of goodwill from many long-standing bona fide clients
>
> *Financial World*

bonanza [bəˈnænzə] *noun* great wealth; very profitable business; ***the oil well was a bonanza for the company; 1995 was a bonanza year for the computer industry***

bona vacantia [ˈbəunə vəˈkænsiə] *noun* property with no owner, or which does not have an obvious owner, and which usually passes to the Crown

bond [bɒnd] *noun* **(a)** contract document promising to repay money borrowed by a company or by the government at a certain date, and paying a fixed interest at regular intervals; **government bonds** *or* **treasury bonds** = bonds issued by the central government; **municipal bond** *or* **local authority bond** = bond issued by a town or district; **bond market** = market in which government or municipal bonds are traded; **bearer bond** = bond which is payable to the bearer and does not have a name written on it; **catastrophe bond** = bond with very high interest rate but, which may be worth less or give a lower rate of interest if a disaster such as an earthquake occurs; **corporate bond** = loan stock officially issued by a company to raise capital, usually against the security of some of its assets (the company promises to pay a certain amount of interest on a set date every year until the redemption date, when it repays the loan); **debenture bond** = certificate showing that a debenture has been issued; *US* **general obligation bond (GO bond)** = a municipal or state bond issued to finance public undertakings such as roads, etc., but which is repaid out of general funds; **mortgage bond** = certificate showing that a mortgage exists and that property is security for it; *GB* **premium bond** = government bond, part of the National Savings scheme, which pays no interest, but gives the owner the chance to win a monthly prize; *see also* JUNK BONDS; **bond rating** = rating of the reliability of a company or government or local authority which has issued a bond (the highest rating is AAA); *see also* MOODY, STANDARD & POOR; **bond yield** = income produced by a bond, shown as a percentage of its purchase price **(b)** form of insurance fund which is linked to a unit trust (there is no yield because the income is automatically added to the fund) **(c) goods (held) in bond** = goods held by the customs until duty has been paid; **entry of goods under bond** = bringing goods into a country in bond; **to take goods out of bond** = to pay duty on goods so that they can be released by the customs

> COMMENT: bonds are in effect another form of long-term borrowing by a company or government. They can carry a fixed interest or a floating interest, but the yield varies according to the price at which they are bought; bond prices go up and down in the same way as share prices. Note that in the USA, only the word 'bonds' is used of government borrowings, while in the UK, these are also referred to as 'stocks': see the note at STOCK

> the sector has recently been thrown into further turmoil by the introduction of so-called catastrophe bonds
>
> *The Times*

> New York City GO bonds have rallied strongly, both in absolute terms and relative to the rest of the market
>
> *Barron's*

> sovereign bonds got hit in the fourth quarter as the Asian crisis intensified
>
> *Barron's*

> it was also a good time to adopt a more cautious investment stance by shifting into defensive investments, such as government gilts and corporate bonds
>
> *Sunday Times*

> both corporate bonds and gilts are interest-rate sensitive, neither security is risk-free and corporate bonds will always be riskier than gilts
>
> *Money Observer*

> what might be termed 'pure' corporate bonds are conventional loan stock - debentures which are secured against a company's assets are the least risky
>
> *Money Observer*

bonded [ˈbɒndɪd] *adjective* held in bond; **bonded warehouse** = warehouse where goods are stored in bond until duty is paid

bondholder [ˈbɒndhəuldə] *noun* person who holds bonds

bondized ['bɒndaɪzd] *adjective* (insurance fund) linked to a unit trust

bond-washing ['bɒnd'wɒʃɪŋ] *noun* selling securities cum dividend and buying them back later ex dividend, or selling US Treasury bonds with the interest coupon, and buying them back ex-coupon, so as to reduce tax

bonus ['bəʊnəs] *noun* **(a)** extra payment; **capital bonus** = extra payment by an insurance company which is produced by a capital gain; **cost-of-living bonus** = money paid to meet the increase in the cost of living; **Christmas bonus** = extra payment made to staff at Christmas; **incentive bonus** = extra pay offered to a worker to encourage him to work harder; **productivity bonus** = extra payment made because of increased productivity **(b) bonus issue** = scrip issue or capitalization issue, where a company transfers money from reserves to share capital and issues free extra shares to the shareholders (the value of the company remains the same, and the total market value of shareholders' shares remains the same, the market price being adjusted to account for the new shares (also called 'share split') (NOTE: the American equivalent is **stock split** or **stock dividend**); **bonus share** = extra share given to an existing shareholder **(c) no-claims bonus** = reduction of premiums on an insurance because no claims have been made

book [bʊk] *noun* **(a)** set of sheets of paper attached together; **a company's books** = the financial records of a company; **account book** *or* **book of account** = book which records sales and purchases; **cash book** = record of cash; **order book** = record of orders; **the company has a full order book** = it has sufficient orders to keep the workforce occupied; **purchase book** = records of purchases; **sales book** = records of sales; **book debts** = trade debts as recorded in a company's accounts; **book sales** = sales as recorded in the sales book; **book value** = value of an asset as recorded in the company's balance sheet **(b) bank book** = book which shows money which you have deposited or withdrawn from a bank account; **cheque book** = book of new cheques **(c)** *(of a marketmaker)* **to make a book** = to have a list of shares which he is prepared to buy or sell on behalf of clients **(d)** *(in foreign exchange dealing)* statement of a dealer's exposure to the market (i.e. the amount which he is due to pay or has borrowed); **book-squaring** = reducing the dealer's exposure to the market to nil

COMMENT: the books of account record a company's financial transactions. These are: sales (sales day book and sales returns book); purchases (purchases day book and purchases returns book); cash payments and receipts (cash book) and adjustments (journal). These books are commonly known as the 'books of prime entry', but in addition, a company's accounting records usually include the ledger accounts (nominal ledger, sales ledger and purchases ledger) which may also be referred to as 'books of account'

Sure, new issues perform poorly. But that's because they tend to be high-book value companies, not because investors are too optimistic about their prospects

Smart Money

bookkeeper ['bʊkki:pə] *noun* person who keeps the financial records of a company

bookkeeping ['bʊkki:pɪŋ] *noun* keeping of the financial records of a company or an organization; **single-entry bookkeeping** = recording a transaction with only one entry, as in a cash book; **double-entry bookkeeping** = method of bookkeeping, where both debit and credit entries are recorded in the accounts at the same time (e.g. as a sale is credited to the sales account the purchaser's debt is debited to the debtors account); **bookkeeping transaction** = transaction (such as the issue of bonus shares) which involves changes to a company's books of accounts, but does not alter the value of the company in any way

bookwork ['bʊkwɜ:k] *noun* keeping of financial records

boom [bu:m] **1** *noun* **(a)** time when sales or production or business activity are increasing; ***a period of economic boom; the boom of the 1980s***; **boom industry** = industry which is expanding rapidly; **a boom share** = share in a company which is expanding; **the boom years** = years when there is an economic boom **(b)** time when anything is increasing; **baby boom** = period, such as after a war, when more children are born than usual **2** *verb* to expand, to become prosperous; ***business is booming; sales are booming***

boomer *or* **baby boomer** ['beɪbi 'bu:mə] *noun* person born during a baby boom; ***most boomers have not saved enough money for retirement; another boomer turns 50 every seven seconds***

booming ['bu:mɪŋ] *adjective* which is expanding or becoming prosperous; ***a***

booming industry** or **company**; **technology is a booming sector of the economy

boost [bu:st] **1** *noun* help to increase; ***this publicity will give sales a boost***; ***the government hopes to give a boost to industrial development*** **2** *verb* to make something increase; ***we expect our publicity campaign to boost sales by 25%***; ***the company hopes to boost its market share***; ***incentive schemes are boosting production***

> the company expects to boost turnover this year to FFr 16bn from FFr 13.6bn last year
>
> *Financial Times*

BOP = BALANCE OF PAYMENTS

border ['bɔ:də] *noun* frontier between two countries; **border tax adjustment** = deduction of indirect tax paid on goods being exported or imposition of local indirect tax on goods being imported

borrow ['bɒrəʊ] *verb* **(a)** to take money from someone for a time, possibly paying interest for it, and repaying it at the end of the period; ***he borrowed £1,000 from the bank***; ***the company had to borrow heavily to repay its debts***; ***they borrowed £25,000 against the security of the factory***; **to borrow short** *or* **long** = to borrow for a short or long period **(b)** *(on a commodity market)* to buy at spot prices and sell forward at the same time

borrower ['bɒrəʊə] *noun* person who borrows; ***borrowers from the bank pay 12% interest***

borrowing ['bɒrəʊɪŋ] *noun* **(a)** action of borrowing money; ***the new factory was financed by bank borrowing***; **borrowing costs** *or* **cost of borrowing** = the interest and other charges paid on money borrowed; **borrowing power** = amount of money which a company can borrow; **Public Sector Borrowing Requirement (PSBR)** = amount of money which a government has to borrow to pay for its own spending **(b) borrowings** = money borrowed; ***the company's borrowings have doubled***; **bank borrowings** = money borrowed from banks; **gross borrowings** = total of all monies borrowed by a company (such as overdrafts, long-term loans, etc.) but without deducting cash in bank accounts and on deposit; **net borrowings** = total of all borrowings less the cash in bank accounts and on deposit

> COMMENT: borrowings are sometimes shown as a percentage of shareholders' funds (i.e. capital and money in reserves); this gives a percentage which is the 'gearing' of the company

borsa ['bɔ:sə] *Italian* stock exchange

Börse ['bɜ:sə] *German* stock exchange

bottom ['bɒtəm] **1** *noun* lowest part or point; **sales have reached rock bottom** = the very lowest point of all; **the bottom has fallen out of the market** = sales have fallen below what previously seemed to be the lowest point possible; **rock-bottom price** = lowest price of all **2** *verb* **to bottom (out)** = to reach the lowest point; **the market has bottomed out** = has reached the lowest point and does not seem likely to fall further

bottom feeder ['bɒtəm 'fi:də] *noun (informal)* someone who tries to buy shares when they are falling or have fallen substantially, in the hope that they will rise again

bottom line ['bɒtəm 'laɪn] *noun* final result, the last line in accounts indicating total profit or loss; **the boss is interested only in the bottom line** = he is only interested in the final profit

bought [bɔ:t] **(a) bought deal** = method of selling shares in a new company or selling an issue of new shares in an existing company, where securities houses guarantee to buy all the shares on offer at a fixed price **(b) bought ledger** = book in which expenditure is noted; **bought ledger clerk** = office worker who deals with the bought ledger **(c)** *see also* BUY

bounce [baʊns] **1** *verb (of a cheque)* to be returned to the person who has tried to cash it, because there is not enough money in the payer's account to pay it; ***he paid for the car with a cheque that bounced*** **2** *noun see also* DEAD-CAT

bounty ['baʊnti] *noun* government subsidy made to help an industry

bourse ['bu:əs] *French* stock exchange (NOTE: in English, the word is used of European stock exchanges in general)

boutique [bu:'ti:k] *noun* small financial institution offering specialist advice or services

boycott ['bɔɪkɒt] **1** *noun* refusal to buy or to deal in certain products; ***the union organized a boycott against*** *or* ***of imported cars*** **2** *verb* to refuse to buy or to deal in a certain product; ***we are boycotting all imports from that***

***country*; the management has boycotted the meeting** = has refused to attend the meeting

bracket ['brækɪt] **1** *noun* (i) group of items or people taken together; (ii) one of the various groups of underwriters underwriting a loan; **people in the middle-income bracket** = people with average incomes, not high or low; **he is in the top tax bracket** = he pays the highest level of tax **2** *verb* **to bracket together** = to treat several items together in the same way; ***in the sales reports, all the European countries are bracketed together***

branch [brɑːntʃ] *noun* local office of a bank or large business; local shop of a large chain of shops; ***the bank has branches in most towns in the south of the country***; ***the insurance company has closed its branches in South America***; ***he is the manager of our local branch of Lloyds bank***; ***we have decided to open a branch office in Chicago***; ***the manager of our branch in Lagos*** *or* ***of our Lagos branch***; **branch manager** = manager of a branch

> a leading manufacturer of business, industrial and commercial products requires a branch manager to head up its mid-western Canada operations based in Winnipeg
>
> *Globe and Mail (Toronto)*

breach [briːtʃ] *noun* failure to carry out the terms of an agreement; **breach of contract** = failing to do something which is in a contract; **the company is in breach of contract** = it has failed to carry out the duties of the contract; **breach of warranty** = supplying goods which do not meet the standards of the warranty applied to them

break [breɪk] **1** *noun* **(a)** sharp fall in share prices **(b)** lucky deal, good opportunity; *see also* TAX BREAK **2** *verb* **(a)** to fail to carry out the duties of a contract; **to break an engagement to do something** = not to do what has been agreed **(b)** to cancel (a contract); ***the company is hoping to be able to break the contract*** (NOTE: **breaking - broke - has broken**)

break down ['breɪk 'daʊn] *verb* **(a)** to stop working because of mechanical failure; ***the fax machine has broken down***; ***what do you do when your photocopier breaks down?*** **(b)** to stop; ***negotiations broke down after six hours*** **(c)** to show all the items in a total list of costs or expenditure; ***we broke the expenditure down into fixed and variable costs***; ***can you break down this invoice into spare parts and labour?***

breakdown ['breɪkdaʊn] *noun* **(a)** stopping work because of mechanical failure; ***we cannot communicate with our Nigerian office because of the breakdown of the telex lines*** **(b)** stopping talking; ***a breakdown in wage negotiations*** **(c)** showing details item by item; ***please give me a breakdown of investment costs***

break even ['breɪk 'iːvən] *verb* to balance costs and receipts, but not make a profit; ***last year the company only just broke even***; ***we broke even in our first two months of trading***

breakeven point [breɪk'iːvn 'pɔɪnt] *noun* (i) point at which sales cover costs, but do not show a profit; (ii) *(Stock Exchange)* transaction which does not show a profit or loss

break-out ['breɪkaʊt] *noun* movement of a share price above or below its previous trading level

breakpoint ['breɪkpɔɪnt] *noun* level of deposits in an account that triggers a new higher level of interest

break up ['breɪk 'ʌp] *verb* to split something large into small sections; ***the company was broken up and separate divisions sold off***

> market sharks have frequently pointed out that the company's break-up value per share exceeds the company's share price by an enticing margin
>
> *Fortune*

break-up value ['breɪkʌp 'væljuː] *noun* value of a company if split into its different divisions which are sold separately

Bretton Woods Agreement ['bretən 'wʊdz ə'griːmənt] *noun* international agreement reached in 1944, setting up the International Monetary Fund and the World Bank, and a system of fixed exchange rates between currencies

bribe [braɪb] **1** *noun* money given to someone in authority to get him to help; ***the minister was dismissed for taking bribes*** **2** *verb* to pay someone money to get him to do something for you; ***we had to bribe the minister's secretary before she would let us meet her boss***

bricks and mortar ['brɪks ən 'mɔːtə] *noun* fixed assets of a company, especially its buildings

bridge finance ['brɪdʒ 'faɪnæns] *noun* loans to cover short-term needs

bridging loan *US* **bridge loan** ['brɪdʒɪŋ 'ləʊn *or* 'brɪdʒ 'ləʊn] *noun* short-term loan to help someone buy a new house when he has not yet sold his old one

bring down ['brɪŋ 'daʊn] *verb* **(a)** to reduce; ***petrol companies have brought down the price of oil*** **(b)** = BRING FORWARD (b)

bring forward ['brɪŋ 'fɔːwəd] *verb* **(a)** to make earlier; ***to bring forward the date of repayment***; ***the date of the next meeting has been brought forward to March*** **(b)** to take an account balance from the end of the previous period as the starting point for the current period; ***balance brought down*** *or* ***forward: £365.15***

bring in ['brɪŋ 'ɪn] *verb* to earn (an interest); ***these shares only bring in a small amount***

brisk [brɪsk] *adjective* selling actively; ***sales are brisk***; ***the market in oil shares is particularly brisk***; ***a brisk market in oil shares***

broad tape ['brɔːd 'teɪp] *noun US* news service giving general information about securities and commodities

broker ['brəʊkə] *noun* **(a)** person who acts as a middleman between a seller and a buyer; **foreign exchange broker** = person who buys and sells foreign currency on behalf of other people; **insurance broker** = person who arranges insurance for clients; **ship broker** = person who sells shipping or transport of goods to clients **(b)** **(stock)broker** = person or firm that buys and sells shares or bonds on behalf of clients; **agency broker** = dealer who acts as the agent for an investor, buying and selling for a commission; **discount broker** = broker who charges a lower commission than other brokers; **broker-dealer** = dealer who makes a market in shares (i.e. buys shares and holds them for resale) and also deals on behalf of investor clients; **broker's commission** = payment to a broker for a deal carried out (formerly, the commission charged by brokers on the London Stock Exchange was fixed, but since 1986, commissions are variable); **dealing-only (stock)broker** *or* **execution-only (stock)broker** = broker who buys and sells shares for clients, but does not provide any advice and does not manage portfolios (as opposed to a full-service broker); **full-service broker** = broker who manages portfolios for clients, and gives advice on shares and financial questions in general (as opposed to an execution-only broker or discount broker)

> even an execution-only broker should be able to advise you on whether the market is experiencing acute Sets problems
>
> *Investors Chronicle*

> call three or four brokers and ask how they would price a certain bond in the amount you have to invest. If they can't find your bonds, you know you've got a stock-broker not a full-service broker
>
> *Fortune*

---

brokerage ['brəʊkərɪdʒ] *noun* **(a)** broker's commission, the payment to a broker for a deal carried out **(b)** = BROKING; **brokerage (firm** *or* **house)** = firm which buys and sells shares for clients

---

> it also means that your brokerage makes its money by tacking on a markup when you buy or a markdown when you sell
>
> *Fortune*

---

broking ['brəʊkɪŋ] *noun* dealing in stocks and shares

BSA = THE BUILDING SOCIETIES ASSOCIATION

BSE Index = BOMBAY STOCK EXCHANGE INDEX index of prices on the Indian Stock Exchange

buck [bʌk] **1** *noun US (informal)* dollar; **to make a quick buck** = to make a profit very quickly **2** *verb* **to buck the trend** = to go against the trend

bucket shop ['bʌkɪt 'ʃɒp] *noun* **(a)** *GB* travel agency which specializes in selling cut-price air tickets **(b)** *US* brokerage firm which tries to push the sale of certain securities

budget ['bʌdʒɪt] **1** *noun* **(a)** plan of expected spending and income (usually for one year); ***to draw up a budget***; ***we have agreed the budgets for next year***; **advertising budget** = money planned for spending on advertising; **cash budget** = plan of cash income and expenditure; **overhead budget** = plan of probable overhead costs; **publicity budget** = money allowed for expected expenditure on publicity; **sales budget** = plan of probable sales **(b)** **the Budget** = the annual plan of taxes and government spending proposed by a finance minister; ***the minister put forward a budget aimed at boosting the economy***; **to balance the budget** = to plan income and expenditure so that they balance; ***the president is planning for a balanced budget***; **budget deficit** = deficit in a country's planned budget, where income from taxation will not be sufficient to pay for the government's expenditure **(c)** *US* **Office of Management and Budget (OMB)** = government department which prepares the US federal budget; **Director of the Budget** = member of the government in charge of the preparation of the budget (the equivalents in the UK are the **Chief Secretary to the Treasury** and the **Financial Secretary**) **(d)** *(in a bank)* **budget account** = bank account where you plan income and expenditure to allow for periods when expenditure is high, by paying a set amount each month **(e)** *(in shops)* cheap; **budget department** = cheaper department; **budget prices** = low prices **2** *verb* to plan probable income and expenditure; ***we are budgeting for £10,000 of sales next year***

> he budgeted for further growth of 150,000 jobs (or 2.5 per cent) in the current financial year
>
> *Sydney Morning Herald*

> the minister is persuading the oil, gas, electricity and coal industries to target their advertising budgets towards energy efficiency
>
> *The Times*

> the Federal government's budget targets for employment and growth are within reach according to the latest figures
>
> *Australian Financial Review*

budgetary ['bʌdʒɪtəri] *adjective* referring to a budget; **budgetary policy** = policy of planning income and expenditure; **budgetary control** = keeping check on spending; **budgetary requirements** = spending or income required to meet the budget forecasts

budgeting ['bʌdʒɪtɪŋ] *noun* preparing of budgets to help plan expenditure and income

buffer stocks ['bʌfə 'stɒks] *noun* stocks of a commodity bought by an international body when prices are low and held for resale at a time when prices have risen, with the intention of reducing sharp fluctuations in world prices of the commodity

building and loan association ['bɪldɪŋ ənd 'ləʊn əsəʊsi'eɪʃən] *noun* *US* = SAVINGS AND LOAN ASSOCIATION

building society ['bɪldɪŋ sə'saɪəti] *noun* *GB* financial institution which accepts and pays interest on deposits and lends money to people who are buying property against the security of the property; ***he put his savings into a building society*** *or* ***into a building society account***; ***I saw the building society manager to ask for a mortgage***; **The Building Societies Association (BSA)** = organization representing building societies; **the Building Societies Ombudsman** = official whose duty is to investigate complaints by members of the public against building societies (all building societies belong to the Building Societies Ombudsman Scheme)

> COMMENT: building societies mainly invest the money deposited with them as mortgages on properties, but a percentage is invested in government securities. Societies can now offer a range of banking services, such as cheque books, standing orders, overdrafts, etc., and now operate in much the same way as banks; indeed, many building societies have changed from 'mutual status' where the owners of the society are its investors and borrowers, to become publicly-owned banks. The comparable US institutions are the Savings & Loan Associations, or 'thrifts'

build into ['bɪld 'ɪntʊ] *verb* to add something to something being set up; ***you must build all the forecasts into the budget***; **we have built 10% for contingencies into our cost forecast** = we have added 10% to our basic forecast to allow for items which may appear suddenly

build up ['bɪld 'ʌp] *verb* **(a)** to create something by adding pieces together; ***he bought several shoe shops and gradually built up a chain*** **(b)** to expand something gradually; ***to build up a profitable business***; ***to build up a team of salesmen***

buildup ['bɪldʌp] *noun* gradual increase; ***a buildup in sales*** *or* ***a sales buildup***; ***there will be a big publicity buildup before the launch of the new model***

bull [bʊl] *noun (Stock Exchange)* person who believes the market will rise, and therefore buys shares (or commodities or currency) to sell at a higher price later; **bull market** = period when share prices rise because people are optimistic and buy shares; **bull position** = buying shares in the hope that they will rise; **stale bull** = investor who bought shares hoping that they would rise, and now finds that they have not risen and wants to sell them (NOTE: the opposite is **bear**)

> lower interest rates are always a bull factor for the stock market
>
> *Financial Times*

bulldog bond ['bʊldɒg 'bɒnd] *noun* bond issued in sterling in the UK market by a non-British corporation; *compare* SAMURAI, YANKEE

bullet ['bʊlɪt] *noun US* repayment of the capital of a loan when it matures; **bullet bond** = eurobond which is only redeemed when it is mature (it is used in payments between central banks and also acts as currency backing); **bullet loan** = loan which is repaid in a single payment

bullion ['bʊljən] *noun* gold or silver bars; ***the price of bullion is fixed daily***; ***to fix the bullion price for silver***; **bullion bank** = bank which hold bullion for customers

> some bankers have turned to lending some of their gold to so-called bullion banks for annual interest between 1% and 2%
>
> *Fortune*

bullish ['bʊlɪʃ] *adjective* which feels that the markets are likely to rise

> another factor behind the currency market's bullish mood may be the growing realisation that Japan stands to benefit from the current combination of high domestic interest rates and a steadily rising exchange rate
>
> *Far Eastern Economic Review*

> if stock markets remain continuously bullish, this can encourage higher business investment, faster economic growth, lower unemployment
>
> *The Times*

bumping ['bʌmpɪŋ] *noun US* situation where a senior employee takes the place of a junior (in a restaurant, in a job)

Bund [bʊnt] *noun* German government bond

> in London, the March Bund-futures contract finished 0.03 point higher at 83.73. The German-based March Bund contract eased 0.01 point to 83.72
>
> *Wall Street Journal*

> in the flight to quality, investors bought so many bund futures that even if only a third of them had requested delivery, there did not exist enough bonds in the market to satisfy the potential demand
>
> *Financial Times*

Bundesbank ['bʊndəzbæŋk] *noun* **the Deutsches Bundesbank** = the German central bank, based in Frankfurt

Bundesobligation ['bʊndəzɒblɪgætsi'əʊn] *noun* German medium-term note (which cannot be bought by non-German buyers)

bundle ['bʌndl] *noun (informal)* **to make a bundle** = to make a lot of money

> a CEO who made a bundle selling when the stock was at its high can certainly afford to pick up a few shares when the same stock plummets
>
> *Smart Money*

bundling ['bʌndlɪŋ] *noun* action of selling various financial services together as a package, such as a mortgage and house insurance

buoyant ['bɔɪənt] *adjective* (market) where share prices are rising continuously

bureau de change ['bjʊrəʊ də 'ʃɒnʒ] *noun* office where currencies can be exchanged

business

business agent ['bɪznəs 'eɪdʒənt] *noun US* chief local official of a trade union

businessman *or* **businesswoman** ['bɪznɪsmæn or 'bɪznɪswʊmən] *noun* man or woman engaged in business; **she's a good businesswoman** = she is good at commercial deals; **a small businessman** = man who owns a small business

bust [bʌst] *adjective (informal)* **to go bust** = to become bankrupt

busted bonds ['bʌstɪd 'bɒndz] *noun* old shares or bonds which are no longer marketable, but the certificates may still have a value as collectors' items

butterfly ['bʌtəflaɪ] *noun* **butterfly spread** = buying two call options and selling two call options, with different dates and prices, all at the same time

buy [baɪ] **1** *verb* to get something by paying money; ***he bought 10,000 shares***; ***the company has been bought by its leading supplier***; ***to buy wholesale and sell retail***; ***he buys old clocks for cash***; **to buy at best** = to buy securities at the best price available, even if it is high; **to buy forward** = to buy foreign currency before you need it, in order to be sure of the exchange rate (NOTE: **buying - bought**) **2** *noun* **good buy** *or* **bad buy** = thing bought which is or is not worth the money paid for it; ***that watch was a good buy***; ***this car was a bad buy***

buy back ['baɪ 'bæk] *verb* **(a)** to buy something which you have sold; ***he sold the shop last year and is now trying to buy it back*** **(b)** *(of a company)* to buy its own shares

buyback ['baɪbæk] *noun* **(a)** type of loan agreement to repurchase bonds or securities at a later date for the same price as they are being sold (NOTE: also called **repurchase agreement** or **repo**) **(b)** international trading agreement where a company builds a factory in a foreign country and agrees to buy all its production **(c)** **share buyback** *US* **stock buyback** = arrangement where a company buys its own shares on the stock market

> with so many unknowns surrounding big cash expenditures, the Big Three naturally look at buybacks as a less risky alternative
>
> *Fortune*

> buybacks are appealing because investors pay attention
>
> *Fortune*

> the company continued its stock-buyback program, one of the industry's most aggressive
>
> *Barron's*

buyer ['baɪə] *noun* **(a)** person who buys; **there were no buyers** = no one wanted to buy; **a buyers' market** = market where shares or commodities or products are sold cheaply because there are few buyers (NOTE: the opposite is a **seller's market**); **impulse buyer** = person who buys something when he sees it, not because he was planning to buy it **(b)** person who buys a certain type of goods wholesale, which are then stocked by a large store; **head buyer** = most important buyer in a store; ***she is the shoe buyer for a London department store***

buy in ['baɪ 'ɪn] *verb* **(a)** *(of a seller at an auction)* to buy the thing which you are trying to sell because no one will pay the price you want **(b)** *(Stock Exchange)* to buy stock to cover a position **(c)** *(of a company)* to buy its own shares

buyin ['baɪɪn] noun **management buyin** = purchase of a company by a group of outside executives

buying ['baɪɪŋ] *noun* getting something for money; **bulk buying** = getting large quantities of goods at low prices; **forward buying** *or* **buying forward** = buying shares or commodities or currency for delivery at a later date; **impulse buying** = buying items which you have just seen, not because you had planned to buy them; **panic buying** = rush to buy something at any price because stocks may run out; **buying department** = department in a company which buys raw materials or goods for use in the company; **buying power** = ability to buy; ***the buying power of the pound has fallen over the last years***

buyout ['baɪaʊt] *noun* purchase of a controlling interest in a company; **employee buyout** = purchase of a company by its employees; **institutional buyout (IBO)** = takeover of a company by a financial institution, which backs a group of managers who will run it; **leveraged buyout (LBO)** = buying all the shares in a company by borrowing money against the security of the shares to be bought; **management buyout (MBO)** = takeover of a company by a group of employees (usually senior managers and directors)

> we also invest in companies whose growth and profitability could be improved by a management buyout
>
> *The Times*

> in a normal leveraged buyout, the acquirer raises money by borrowing against the assets or cash flow of the target company
>
> *Fortune*

BV = BESLOTEN VENOOTSCHAP Dutch public limited company

bylaws ['baɪlɔːz] *noun* *US* rules governing the internal running of a corporation (the number of meetings, the appointment of officers, etc.) (NOTE: in the UK, called **Articles of Association**)

by-product ['baɪ'prɒdʌkt] *noun* product made as a result of manufacturing a main product

Cc

Schedule C ['ʃedju:l 'si:] schedule to the Finance Acts under which tax is charged on profits from government stock

Table C ['teɪbl 'si:] model memorandum and articles of association set out in the Companies Act 1985 for a company limited by guarantee having no share capital

CA = CHARTERED ACCOUNTANT

CAB = CITIZENS ADVICE BUREAU

cable ['keɪbl] **1** *noun* **(a)** method of sending messages via a telegraphic wire; **cable transfer** = transfer of money by telegraph **(b)** spot exchange rate for the dollar and sterling **2** *verb* to send by telegraph; ***the money was cabled to the Spanish bank***

CAC [kæk] = COMPAGNIE DES AGENTS DE CHANGE

CAC 40 (index) ['kæk 'kærɒnt] index of prices on the Paris Stock Exchange, based on the prices of forty leading shares

CAD = CASH AGAINST DOCUMENTS

caisse d'épargne ['kes deɪ'pɑ:ŋjə] *French* savings bank

cage [keɪdʒ] *noun* *US* **(a)** the part of a broking firm where the paperwork involved in buying and selling shares is processed (NOTE: the British equivalent is the **back office**) **(b)** section of a bank where a teller works (surrounded by glass windows)

caja popular ['kæjæ pɒpu'lɑ:] *Spanish* savings bank

calculate ['kælkjʊleɪt] *verb* **(a)** to find the answer to a problem using numbers; ***the bank clerk calculated the rate of exchange for the dollar*** **(b)** to estimate; ***I calculate that we have six months' stock left***

calculating machine ['kælkjʊleɪtɪŋ mə'ʃi:n] *noun* machine which calculates

calculation [kælkjʊ'leɪʃən] *noun* answer to a problem in mathematics; **rough calculation** = approximate answer; ***I made some rough calculations on the back of an envelope***; ***according to my calculations, we have six months' stock left***; **we are £20,000 out in our calculations** = we have £20,000 more or less than we anticipated

calculator ['kælkjʊleɪtə] *noun* electronic machine which works out the answers to problems in mathematics; ***my pocket calculator needs a new battery***; ***he worked out the discount on his calculator***

calendar ['kæləndə] *noun* **(a)** book, set of sheets of paper showing the days and months in a year, often attached to pictures; **calendar month** = a whole month as on a calendar, from the 1st to the 30th or 31st; **calendar year** = year from the 1st January to 31st December **(b)** list of dates, especially a list of dates of new share issues

call [kɔ:l] **1** *noun* **(a)** demand for repayment of a loan by a lender; **call loan** = bank loan repayable at call; **money at call** *or* **money on call** *or* **call money** = money loaned for which repayment can be demanded without notice (used by commercial banks, placing money on very short- term deposit with discount houses); **call rate** = rate of interest on money at call **(b)** *(Stock Exchange)* (i) demand to pay for new shares, which then become paid up; (ii) price established during a trading session; **at call** = immediately available; **call option** = option to buy shares at a future date and at a certain price (NOTE: the opposite is **put option**); **call price** = price to be paid on redemption of a US bond; **call purchase** *or* **call sale** = transaction where the seller or purchaser can fix the price for future delivery; **call rule** = price fixed on a Stock Exchange at the end of a day's trading and which remains valid until trading starts again the next day **(c)** conversation on the telephone; **local call** = call to a number on the same exchange; **trunk call** *or* **long-distance call** = call to a number in a different zone or area; **overseas call** *or* **international call** = call to another country; **person-to-person call** = call where you ask the operator to connect you with a named person; **transferred charge call** *US* **collect call** = call where the person receiving the call agrees to pay for it; **to make a call** = to dial and speak to someone on the telephone; **to take a call** = to answer the telephone; **to log calls** = to note all details of telephone calls made **(d)** visit; ***the salesmen make six calls a day***; **business call** = visit to talk to someone on business; **cold call** = sales visit where the salesman has no appointment and the client is not an established customer; **call rate** = number of calls (per day or per week) made by a salesman **2** *verb* **(a)** to ask for a loan to be repaid immediately **(b)** to telephone to someone; ***I'll call you at your office tomorrow*** **(c) to call on someone** = to visit; ***our salesmen call on their best accounts twice a month*** **(d)** to ask someone to do something; **the union called a strike** = the union told its members to go on strike

callable [ˈkɔːləbl] *adjective* **callable bond** = bond which can be redeemed before it matures; **callable capital** = the part of a company's capital which has not been called up

call-back pay [ˈkɔːlbæk ˈpeɪ] *noun* pay given to a worker who has been called back to work after his normal working hours

called up capital [ˈkɔːldʌp ˈkæpɪtl] *noun* share capital in a company which has been paid for

call in [ˈkɔːl ˈɪn] *verb* to ask for a debt to be paid

call-over price [ˈkɔːləʊvə ˈpraɪs] *noun (on commodity markets)* price which is applied when selling is conducted by a chairman, and not by open outcry

call up [ˈkɔːl ˈʌp] *verb* to ask for share capital to be paid

calm [kɑːm] *adjective* quiet, not excited; ***the markets were calmer after the government statement on the exchange rate***

cambio [ˈkæmbiəʊ] *Spanish* foreign exchange

cambiste [ˈkɑːmbist] *French* foreign exchange dealer

cancel [ˈkænsəl] *verb* **(a)** to stop something which has been agreed or planned; ***to cancel an appointment*** *or* ***a meeting*** *or* ***a contract***; ***the government has cancelled the order for a fleet of buses*** **(b) to cancel a cheque** = to stop payment of a cheque which has been signed (NOTE: British spelling is **cancelling - cancelled** but American spelling is **canceling - canceled**)

cancellation [kænsəˈleɪʃən] *noun* stopping something which has been agreed or planned; ***cancellation of an appointment***; ***cancellation of an agreement***; **cancellation clause** = clause in a contract which states the terms on which the contract may be cancelled

cancel out [ˈkænsəl ˈaʊt] *verb* to balance and so make invalid or even; ***the two clauses cancel each other out***; ***costs have cancelled out the sales revenue***

cap [kæp] **1** *noun* **(a)** upper limit placed on something, such as an interest rate (the opposite, i.e. a lower limit, is a 'floor'); **cap and collar** = giving both an upper and a lower limit to a loan **(b)** = CAPITALIZATION; ***last year the total market cap of all the world's gold companies fell from $71 billion to $46 billion***; *see also* MEGA-CAP, MICRO-CAP, MIDCAP, SMALL-CAP **2** *verb* to place an upper limit on something; **capped floating rate note** = floating rate note which has an agreed maximum rate

CAP [ˈsiː ˈeɪ ˈpiː] = COMMON AGRICULTURAL POLICY

capacity [kəˈpæsəti] *noun* **(a)** amount which can be produced, amount of work which can be done; ***industrial*** *or* ***manufacturing*** *or* ***production capacity***; **to work at full capacity** = to do as much work as possible; **to use up spare** *or* **excess capacity** = to make use of time or space which is not fully used; **capacity utilization** = output shown as a percentage of capacity **(b)** amount of space; **storage capacity** = space available for storage; **warehouse capacity** = space available in a warehouse **(c)** (i) ability; (ii) *(of a borrower)* ability to pay back a loan; **earning capacity** = amount of money someone is able to earn

> analysts are increasingly convinced that the industry simply has too much capacity
>
> *Fortune*

capita [ˈkæpɪtə] *see* PER CAPITA

capital [ˈkæpɪtl] *noun* **(a)** money, property and assets used in a business; ***company with £10,000 capital*** *or* ***with a capital of £10,000***; **authorized capital** = maximum capital which is permitted by a company's articles of association; **capital adequacy ratio** *or* **capital-to-asset ratio** *or* **capital/asset ratio** = amount of money which a bank has to have in the form of shareholders' capital, shown as a percentage of its assets (internationally agreed at 8%); **capital allowances** = allowances against tax for the purchase of capital assets, such as machinery; **capital assets** = property or machines, etc., which a company owns and uses; **capital base** = the capital structure of a company (shareholders' capital plus certain loans and retained profits) used as a way of assessing the company's worth; **capital bonus** = bonus payment by an insurance company which is produced by capital gain; **capital commitments** = expenditure on assets which has been authorized by directors, but not yet spent at the end of a financial period; **capital employed** = shareholders' funds plus long-term debts of a business; *see also* RETURN ON CAPITAL EMPLOYED; **capital equipment** = equipment which a factory or office uses to work; **capital expenditure** *or* **investment** *or* **outlay** = money spent on fixed assets (property, machines, furniture); **capital goods** = goods used to manufacture other goods (i.e. machinery); **capital levy** = tax on the value of a person's property and possessions; **capital loss** = loss made by selling assets; **capital market** = international market where money can be raised for investment in a business; **capital profit** = profit made by selling an asset; **capital ratio** = CAPITAL ADEQUACY RATIO; **capital reserves** = the share capital of a company which comes from selling assets and not from normal trading; **capital shares** = shares in a unit trust which rise in value as the capital value of the units rises, but do not receive any income (the other form of shares in a split-level investment trust are income shares, which receive income from the investments, but do not rise in value); **capital structure of a company** = way in which a company's capital is set up; **capital transfer tax** = formerly, tax on gifts or bequests of money or property; **circulating capital** = capital required in the form of raw materials, finished products and work in progress for a company to carry on its business; **cost of capital** = interest paid on the capital used in operating a business; **equity capital** = amount of a company's capital which is owned by the shareholders; **fixed capital** = capital in the form of buildings and machinery; **issued capital** = amount of capital issued as shares to the shareholders; **junior capital** = capital in the form of shareholders' equity, which is repaid only after secured loans (senior capital) if the firm goes into liquidation; **paid-up capital** = amount of money paid for the issued capital shares; **risk capital** *or* **venture capital** = capital for investment which may easily be lost in risky projects; **senior capital** = capital in the form of secured loans to a company (it is repaid before junior capital, such as shareholders' equity, in the event of liquidation); **share capital** = value of the assets of a company held as shares, less its debts; **working capital** = capital in cash and stocks needed for a company to be able to work **(b)** money for investment; **capital exports** = movement of capital out of a country (into overseas investments, or into loans to overseas countries); **capital flow** *or* **capital movement** *or* **movements of capital** = movement of investment capital from one country to another; **flight of capital** = rapid movement of capital out of one country because of lack of confidence in that country's economic future; **capital markets** = places where companies can look for long-term investment capital

to prevent capital from crossing the Atlantic in search of high US interest rates and exchange-rate capital gains

Duns Business Month

issued and fully paid capital is $100 million, comprising 2340 preference shares of $100 each and 997,660 ordinary shares of $100 each

Hongkong Standard

the Bank for International Settlements (BIS) has indicated it is considering permitting banks to include funds raised through preference share issues in the requirement that the institutions have an 8% capital-to-asset ratio

Far Eastern Economic Review

the current bank capital/asset ratio of about 6% is much lower than the capital/asset ratio of non-financial companies in Europe

The Banker

on 2 September, the day after Malaysia announced restrictions on foreign capital flows, the FT put forward persuasive arguments in favour of temporary capital controls in times of financial crisis. In particular, it recognised the destabilising influence that short-term capital flows - invariably speculative by nature - have on emerging economies and the millions of people whose lives suffer in the aftermath

Money Observer

capital account ['kæpɪtəl ə'kaʊnt] *noun* **(a)** account of dealings (money invested in the company, or taken out of the company) by the owners of a company **(b)** items in a country's balance of payments which do not refer to the buying and selling merchandise, but refer to investments **(c)** *US* total equity in a business

capital asset pricing model (CAPM) ['kæpɪtəl 'æsɪt 'praɪsɪŋ 'mɒdəl] method of calculating the expected return on a share, by showing what percentage of future return is dependent on the movements of the stock market taken as a whole

capital gains ['kæpɪtl 'geɪnz] *noun* money made by selling a fixed asset or by selling shares (if the asset is sold for less than its purchase price, the result is a capital loss); **capital gains tax (CGT)** = tax paid on capital gains

> COMMENT: in the UK capital gains tax is payable on the sale of assets, in particular shares and properties, above a certain minimum level

> Canadians' principal residences have always been exempt from capital gains tax
>
> *Toronto Star*

capitalism ['kæpɪtəlɪzəm] *noun* economic system where each person has the right to invest money, to work in business, to buy and sell, with no restriction from the state

capitalist ['kæpɪtəlɪst] **1** *noun* person who invests money in a business **2** *adjective* working according to the principles of capitalism; ***a capitalist economy***; ***the capitalist system***; ***the capitalist countries***

capitalization [kæpɪtəlaɪ'zeɪʃən] *noun* **market capitalization** = (i) value of a company calculated by multiplying the price of its shares on the Stock Exchange by the number of shares issued; (ii) value of all the shares listed on a stock market; ***company with a £1m capitalization***; **capitalization issue** = bonus issue, free issue or scrip issue, where a company transfers money from reserves to share capital and issues free extra shares to the shareholders (the value of the company remains the same, and the total market value of shareholders' shares remains the same, the market price being adjusted to account for the new shares); **capitalization of reserves** = issuing free bonus shares to shareholders

> she aimed to double the company's market capitalization
>
> *Fortune*

capitalize ['kæpɪtəlaɪz] *verb* **(a)** to invest money in a working company; **company capitalized at £10,000** = company with a working capital of £10,000 **(b)** to convert reserves or assets into capital

> at its last traded price the bank was capitalized at around $1.05 billion with 60 per cent in the hands of the family
>
> *South China Morning Post*

capitalize on ['kæpɪtəlaɪz 'ɒn] *verb* to make a profit from; ***to capitalize on your market position***

CAPM = CAPITAL ASSET PRICING MODEL

captive market ['kæptɪv 'mɑːkɪt] *noun* market where one supplier has a monopoly and the buyer has no choice over the product which he must purchase

capture ['kæptʃə] *verb* to take or to get control of something; **to capture 10% of the market** = to sell hard, and so take a 10% market share; **to capture 20% of a company's shares** = to buy shares in a company rapidly and so own 20% of it

carat ['kærət] *noun* measurement of the quality of gold; measurement of the quality of precious stones, such as diamonds

> COMMENT: pure gold is 24 carats; most jewellery and other items made from gold are not pure, but between 19 and 22 carats. 22 carat gold has 22 parts of gold to two parts of alloy

card [kɑːd] *noun* small piece of stiff paper or plastic; **business card** = card showing a businessman's name and the address of the company he works for; **cash card** = plastic card used to obtain money from a cash dispenser; **charge card** = credit card for which a fee is payable, but which does not allow the user to take out a loan (he has to pay off the total sum charged at the end of each month); **cheque (guarantee) card** = plastic card from a bank which guarantees payment of a cheque up to a certain amount, even if the user has no money in his account; **credit card** = plastic card which allows you to borrow money or to buy goods without paying for them immediately; **punched card** = card with holes punched in it which a computer can read; **smart card** = credit card with a microchip, used for withdrawing money from ATMs, or for purchases at EFTPOS terminals; **store card** = credit card issued by a large department store, which can only be used for purchases in that store

> ever since October, when the banks' base rate climbed to 15 per cent, the main credit card issuers have faced the prospect of having to push interest rates

> above 30 per cent APR. Though store cards have charged interest at much higher rates than this for some years, 30 per cent APR is something the banks fight shy of
>
> *Financial Times Review*

cardholder ['kɑ:dhəʊldə] *noun* person who holds a credit card or bank cash card

carpetbagger ['kɑ:pɪtbægə] *noun* person who invests in a building society or pension fund, hoping to benefit from eventual windfall payments if the society is demutualized or the fund is bought

> in spite of yesterday's news of yet another building society turning into a bank, the happy days for carpetbaggers are drawing to a close
>
> *The Times*

> in a bid to stop carpetbaggers opening accounts in the hope of gaining a windfall at a later date, smaller building societies have withdrawn to service their local community. They often restrict some, if not all, of their accounts to savers living in their immediate operating area
>
> *Money Observer*

carriage ['kærɪdʒ] *noun* transporting goods from one place to another; cost of transport of goods; ***to pay for carriage***; ***to allow 10% for carriage***; ***carriage is 15% of the total cost***; **carriage free** = deal where the customer does not pay for the shipping; **carriage paid** = deal where the seller has paid for the shipping; **carriage forward** = deal where the customer will pay for the shipping when the goods arrive

carrier ['kæriə] *noun* **(a)** company which transports goods; ***we only use reputable carriers***; **air carrier** = company which sends cargo or passengers by air **(b)** vehicle or ship which transports goods; **bulk carrier** = ship which carries large quantities of loose goods (such as corn)

carry ['kæri] **1** *noun* cost of borrowing to finance a deal; **positive carry** = deal where the cost of the finance is less than the return; **negative carry** = deal where the cost of finance is more than the return on the capital used **2** *verb* **(a)** to take from one place to another; ***to carry goods***; ***a tanker carrying oil from the Gulf***; ***the train was carrying a consignment of cars for export*** **(b)** to vote to approve; **the motion was carried** = the motion was accepted after a vote **(c)** to produce; ***the bonds carry interest at 10%***

carry forward ['kæri 'fɔ:wəd] *verb* to take an account balance at the end of the current period or page as the starting point for the next period or page; **balance carried forward** *or* **balance c/f** = amount entered in an account at the end of a period or page of an account book to balance the debit and credit entries; it is then taken forward to start the next period or page

carry over ['kæri 'əʊvə] *verb* **(a) to carry over a balance** = to take a balance from the end of one page or period to the beginning of the next **(b) to carry over stock** = to hold stock from the end of one stocktaking period to the beginning of the next

carryover ['kæriəʊvə] *noun* **(a)** stock of a commodity held at the beginning of a new financial year **(b)** not paying an account on settlement day, but later; **carryover day** = the first day of trading on a new account on the London Stock Exchange

cartel [kɑ:'tel] *noun* group of companies which try to fix the price or to regulate the supply of a product because they can then profit from this situation

cash [kæʃ] **1** *noun* **(a)** money in coins or notes; **cash in hand** = money and notes in the till, kept to pay small debts; **hard cash** = money in notes and coins, as opposed to cheques or credit cards; **petty cash** = small amounts of money; **ready cash** = money which is immediately available for payment; **cash account** = account which records the money which is received and spent; **cash advance** = loan in cash against a future payment; **cash balance** = balance in cash, as opposed to amounts owed; **cash book** = book in which cash transactions are entered; **cash box** = metal box for keeping cash; **cash budget** = plan of cash income and expenditure; **cash card** = card used to obtain money from a cash dispenser; **cash desk** = place in a store where you pay for the goods bought; **cash dispenser** = machine which gives out money when a special card is inserted and instructions given; **cash dividend** = dividend paid in cash, as opposed to a dividend in the form of bonus shares; **cash economy** = black economy, where goods and services are paid for in cash, and therefore not declared for tax; **cash float** = cash put into the cash box at the beginning of the day or week to allow business to start;

cash limit = maximum amount someone can withdraw from an ATM using a cash card; **cash market** = the gilt-edged securities market (where purchases are paid for almost immediately, as opposed to the futures market); **cash offer** = offer to pay in cash, especially offer to pay cash when buying shares in a takeover bid; **cash payment** = payment in cash; **cash position** = state of the cash which a company currently has available; *(on commodity markets)* **cash price** = price for buying a commodity for immediate delivery, as opposed to the price for future delivery (also called 'actual price' or 'spot price'); **cash purchases** = purchases made in cash; **cash ratio** = (i) ratio of cash or other liquid assets to the current liabilities in a business; (ii) ratio of cash to deposits in a bank (usually a percentage laid down by the central bank); **cash register** *or* **cash till** = machine which shows and adds the prices of items bought, with a drawer for keeping the cash received; **cash reserves** = a company's reserves in cash, deposits or bills, kept in case of urgent need; **cash transfer hatch** = small door in an outside wall, allowing cash to be passed through (as from a supermarket to a security van) **(b)** using money in coins or notes; **cash discount** = discount given to a customer who is paying cash; **to pay cash down** = to pay in cash immediately; **cash price** *or* **cash terms** = lower price or terms which apply if the customer pays cash; **settlement in cash** *or* **cash settlement** = (i) paying a bill in cash; (ii) paying for government securities immediately on purchase; **cash sale** *or* **cash transaction** = transaction paid for in cash; **terms: cash with order** = terms of sale showing that the payment has to be made in cash when the order is placed; **cash against documents (CAD)** = payment in cash when documents are delivered to a bank; **cash on delivery (COD** *or* **c.o.d.)** = payment in cash when goods are delivered; **cash discount** *or* **discount for cash** = discount given for payment in cash **(c) cash basis** = method of preparing the accounts of a business, where receipts and payments are shown at the time when they are made (as opposed to showing debts or credits which are outstanding at the end of the accounting period; also called 'receipts and payments basis') **2** *verb* **to cash a cheque** = to exchange a cheque for cash

cashable ['kæʃəbl] *adjective* which can be cashed; ***a crossed cheque is not cashable at any bank***

cash and carry ['kæʃ ən 'kæri] *noun* **(a)** large store, selling goods at low prices, where the customer pays cash and has to take the goods away himself; ***cash and carry warehouse*** **(b)** buying a commodity for cash and selling the same commodity on the futures market

cash cow ['kæʃ 'kaʊ] *noun* product or subsidiary company that consistently generates good profits but does not provide growth

cash crops ['kæʃ 'krɒps] *noun* agricultural crops grown for sale to other buyers or to other countries, rather than for domestic consumption

cash flow ['kæʃ 'fləʊ] *noun* cash which comes into a company from sales (cash inflow) less the money which goes out in purchases or overhead expenditure (cash outflow); **cash flow forecast** = forecast of when cash will be received or paid out; **cash flow statement** = report which shows cash sales and purchases; **net cash flow** = difference between the money coming in and the money going out; **negative cash flow** = situation where more money is going out of a company than is coming in; **positive cash flow** = situation where more money is coming into a company than is going out; **the company is suffering from cash flow problems** = cash income is not coming in fast enough to pay the expenditure going out

cashier [kæ'ʃɪə] *noun* person who takes money from customers in a shop; person who deals with customers' money in a bank; *US* **cashier's check** = a bank's own cheque, drawn on itself and signed by the cashier or other bank official

cash in ['kæʃ 'ɪn] *verb* to sell (shares) for cash

cash in on ['kæʃ 'ɪn ɒn] *verb* to profit from; ***the company is cashing in on the interest in computer games***

cash in transit ['kæʃ ɪn 'trænzɪt] *noun* cash being moved from one bank or business to another; ***cash-in-transit services are an easy target for robbers***

> 43 attacks on cash-in-transit services took place inside bank and building society premises in 1997
>
> *Financial World*

cashless society ['kæʃləs sə'saɪəti] *noun* society where no one uses cash, all purchases being made by credit cards, charge cards or cheques

cash-strapped ['kæʃstræpt] *adjective* **cash-strapped** *or* **strapped for cash** = short of money

> not surprisingly, cash-strapped Indonesians headed straight to the local pawnshops with their bracelets and rings
>
> *Fortune*

cash up ['kæʃ 'ʌp] *verb* to add up the cash in a shop at the end of the day

casual ['kæʒjʊəl] *adjective* not permanent, not regular; **casual labour** = workers who are hired for a short period; **casual work** = work where the workers are hired for a short period; **casual labourer** *or* **casual worker** = worker who can be hired for a short period

cat [kæt] *see also* FAT CAT, DEAD-CAT BOUNCE

catastrophe [kə'tæstrəfi] *noun* **catastrophe bond** = bond with very high interest rate but, which may be worth less or give a lower rate of interest if a disaster such as an earthquake occurs

caveat ['kæviæt] *noun* warning; **to enter a caveat** = to warn legally that you have an interest in a case, and that no steps can be taken without your permission

caveat emptor ['kæviæt 'emptɔ:] = LET THE BUYER BEWARE phrase meaning that the buyer is himself responsible for checking that what he buys is in good order

caveat venditor ['kæviæt ven'ditɔ:] = LET THE SELLER BEWARE phrase meaning that the seller is legally bound to make sure that the goods he sells are in good order

CBS All-Share, CBS Tendency ['si: 'bi: 'es] indices of prices on the Amsterdam Stock Exchange

CBOT = CHICAGO BOARD OF TRADE

CCA ['si: 'si: 'eɪ] = CURRENT COST ACCOUNTING

CD ['si: 'di:] = CERTIFICATE OF DEPOSIT

cedi ['si:di] *noun* currency used in Ghana

ceiling ['si:lɪŋ] *noun* highest point, such as the highest interest rate, the highest amount of money which a depositor may deposit, etc.; ***there is a ceiling of $100,000 on deposits***; ***to fix a ceiling to a budget***; **ceiling price** *or* **price ceiling** = highest price that can be reached

cent [sent] **(a)** *noun* small coin, one hundredth of a dollar; ***the stores are only a 25-cent bus ride away***; ***they sell oranges at 99 cents each*** (NOTE: **cent** is usually written ø in prices: 25ø, but not when a dollar price is mentioned: **$1.25**) **(b)** *see* PER CENT

central ['sentrəl] *adjective* organized at one main point; **central government** = the main government of a country (as opposed to municipal, local, provincial or state governments); **central office** = main office which controls all smaller offices; **central purchasing** = purchasing organized by a central office for all branches of a company; **central rate** = exchange rate of a currency against the US dollar according to IMF rules

central bank ['sentrl 'bæŋk] *noun* main government-controlled bank in a country, which controls the financial affairs of the country by fixing main interest rates, issuing currency, supervising the commercial banks and controlling the foreign exchange rate; **central bank discount rate** = rate at which a central bank discounts bills, such as treasury bills; **central bank intervention** = action by a central bank to change base interest rates, to impose exchange controls, to buy or sell the country's own currency, in an attempt to influence international money markets

> central bankers in Europe and Japan are reassessing their intervention policy
>
> *Duns Business Month*

centralization [sentrəlaɪ'zeɪʃən] *noun* organization of everything from a central point

centralize ['sentrəlaɪz] *verb* to organize from a central point; ***all purchasing has been centralized in our main office***; ***the group benefits from a highly centralized organizational structure***

centre *US* **center** ['sentə] *noun* **(a)** **business centre** = part of a town where the main banks, shops and offices are **(b)** important town; ***industrial centre***; ***manufacturing centre***; ***the centre for the shoe industry*** **(c)** group of items in an account; **cost centre** = person or group whose costs can be itemized and to which fixed costs can be allocated; **profit centre** = person or department which is considered separately for the purposes of calculating a profit

CEO ['si: 'i: 'əʊ] *US* = CHIEF EXECUTIVE OFFICER

certain ['sɜ:tn] *adjective* **(a)** sure; ***the chairman is certain we will pass last year's total sales*** **(b)** **a certain number** *or* **a certain quantity** = some; **certain annuity** = annuity which will be paid for a certain number of years only

certificate [sə'tɪfɪkət] *noun* official document which shows that something is owned by someone or that something is true; **clearance certificate** = document showing that goods have been passed by customs; **savings certificate** = document showing you have invested money in a government savings scheme; **share certificate** = document proving that you own shares; **certificate of approval** = document showing that an item has been officially approved; **certificate of incorporation** = document issued by Companies House to show that a company has been incorporated; **certificate of origin** = document showing where imported goods come from or were made; **certificate of quality** = certificate showing the grade of a soft commodity; **certificate of registration** = document showing that an item has been registered; **certificate of tax deducted** = document issued by a financial institution showing that tax has been deducted from interest payments on an account

certificated bankrupt [sə'tɪfɪkeɪtɪd 'bæŋkrʌpt] *noun* bankrupt who has been discharged from bankruptcy with a certificate to show that he was not at fault

certificate of deposit (CD) [sə'tɪfɪkət əv dɪ'pɒzɪt] *noun* document from a bank showing that money has been deposited at a certain guaranteed interest rate for a certain period of time

> COMMENT: a CD is a bearer instrument, which can be sold by the bearer. It can be sold at a discount to the value, so that the yield on CDs varies. CDs are traded on the secondary market by discount houses and CD futures are traded on LIFFE

certify ['sɜːtɪfaɪ] *verb* to make an official declaration in writing; ***I certify that this is a true copy***; ***the document is certified as a true copy***; **certified accountant** = accountant who has passed the professional examinations and is a member of the Chartered Association of Certified Accountants; **certified cheque** US **certified check** = cheque which a bank says is good and will be paid out of money put aside from the payer's bank account

cession ['seʃən] *noun* giving up property to someone (especially a creditor)

c/f = CARRIED FORWARD

CFA ['siː 'ef 'eɪ *or* 'seɪ 'ef 'æ] = COMMUNAUTE FINANCIERE AFRICAINE; **CFA franc** = franc with a fixed exchange rate against the euro, used in African countries which were formerly French colonies (Benin, Burkina Faso, Cameroon, C.A.R., Chad, Congo, Equatorial Guinea, Gabon, Ivory Coast, Mali, Niger, Senegal, Togo)

CFO ['siː 'ef 'əʊ] US = CHIEF FINANCIAL OFFICER

CFP ['siː 'ef 'piː *or* 'seɪ 'ef 'peɪ] = COMMUNAUTE FINANCIERE PACIFIQUE; **CFP franc** = franc with a fixed exchange rate against the euro, used in French territories in the Pacific

CGT ['siː 'dʒiː 'tiː] = CAPITAL GAINS TAX

chairman ['tʃeəmən] *noun* person who presides over the board meetings of a company; ***the chairman of the board*** *or* ***the company chairman***; **the chairman's report** *or* **chairman's statement** = annual report from the chairman of a company to the shareholders; *see also* VICE-CHAIRMAN

> COMMENT: Note that in a UK company, the chairman is less important than the managing director, although one person can combine both posts. In the US, a company president is less important than the chairman of the board

> the corporation's entrepreneurial chairman seeks a dedicated but part-time president. The new president will work a three-day week
>
> *Globe and Mail (Toronto)*

Chamber of Commerce ['tʃeɪmbə əv 'kɒməs] *noun* group of local businessmen who meet to discuss problems which they have in common and to promote commerce in their town

Chancellor of the Exchequer ['tʃɑːnsələ əv ðiː ɪks'tʃekə] *noun* GB chief finance minister in the British government

change [tʃeɪndʒ] **1** *noun* **(a)** money in coins or small notes; **small change** = coins; **to give someone change for £10** = to give someone coins or notes in exchange for a ten pound note; **change machine** = machine which gives small change for a larger coin or note **(b)** money given back by the seller, when the buyer can pay only with a larger note or coin than the amount asked; ***he gave me the wrong change***; ***you paid the £5.75 bill with a £10 note, so you should have £4.25 change***; **keep the change** = keep it as a tip (said to waiters, etc.) **2** *verb* **(a) to change a £10 note** = to give change in smaller notes or coins for a £10 note **(b)** to give one type of currency for another; ***to change £1,000 into dollars***; ***we want to***

change some traveller's cheques **(c) to change hands** = to be sold to a new owner; ***the shop changed hands for £100,000***

changer ['tʃeɪndʒə] *noun* **(money-)changer** = person who exchanges money of one currency for that of another

channel ['tʃænl] *verb* to send in a certain direction; ***they are channelling their research funds into developing European communication systems***

CHAPS [tʃæps] = CLEARING HOUSE AUTOMATED PAYMENTS SYSTEM computerized system for clearing cheques organized by the banks; *compare* BACS

chapter ['tʃæptə] *noun US* section of an Act of Congress; **Chapter 11** = section of the US Bankruptcy Reform Act 1978, which allows a corporation to be protected from demands made by its creditors for a period of time, while it is reorganized with a view to paying its debts; the officers of the corporation will negotiate with its creditors as to the best way of reorganizing the business; **Chapter 7** = section of the US Bankruptcy Reform Act 1978, which sets out the rules for the liquidation of an incorporated company

charge [tʃɑːdʒ] **1** *noun* **(a)** money which must be paid; price of a service; ***to make no charge for delivery***; ***to make a small charge for rental***; ***there is no charge for service*** *or* ***no charge is made for service***; **admission charge** *or* **entry charge** = price to be paid before going into an exhibition, etc.; **bank charges** = charges made by a bank for carrying out work for a customer; **handling charge** = money to be paid for packing, invoicing or dealing with goods which are being shipped; **inclusive charge** = charge which includes all items; **interest charges** = money paid as interest on a loan; *(for a PEP, unit trust, etc.)* **(annual) management charge** = charge made by the financial institution which is managing the account; **scale of charges** = list showing various prices; **service charge** = charge added to a bill in a restaurant to pay for service; ***a 10% service charge is added***; ***does the bill include a service charge?***; **charge account** = arrangement which a customer has with a store to buy goods and to pay for them at a later date, usually when the invoice is sent at the end of the month; the customer will make regular monthly payments into the account and is allowed credit of a multiple of those payments; **charge card** = credit card for which a fee is payable, but which does not allow the user to take out a loan (he has to pay off the total sum charged at the end of each month); **charges forward** = charges which will be paid by the customer; **a token charge is made for heating** = a small charge is made which does not cover the real costs at all; **free of charge** = free, with no payment to be made **(b)** guarantee of security for a loan, for which assets are pledged; **fixed charge** = charge linked to certain specified assets; **floating charge** = charge linked to any of the company's assets **(c)** being formally accused in a court; ***he appeared in court on a charge of embezzling*** *or* ***on an embezzlement charge*** **2** *verb* **(a)** to ask someone to pay for services later; **to charge the packing to the customer** *or* **to charge the customer with the packing** = the customer has to pay for packing **(b)** to ask for money to be paid; ***to charge £5 for delivery***; ***how much does he charge?***; **he charges £6 an hour** = he asks to be paid £6 for an hour's work **(c)** to take something as guarantee for a loan **(d)** *(in a court)* to accuse someone formally of having committed a crime; ***he was charged with embezzling his clients' money***

> traveller's cheques cost 1% of their face value - some banks charge more for small amounts
>
> *Sunday Times*

chargeable ['tʃɑːdʒəbl] *adjective* which can be charged; ***repairs chargeable to the occupier***; **sums chargeable to the reserve** = sums which can be debited to a company's reserves; **chargeable gains** = gains made by selling an asset, such as shares, on which capital gains will be charged

chargee [tʃɑː'dʒiː] *noun* person who has the right to force a debtor to pay

charging period ['tʃɑːdʒɪŋ 'pɪːəriəd] *noun* period of time during which charges are made to a credit card before they are charged to the cardholder

> if charges and/or debit interest accumulate to your current or savings account during a charging period you will be given at least 14 days' notice of the amount before it is deducted from your account
>
> *Banking Code*

chart [tʃɑːt] *noun* diagram showing information as a series of lines or blocks, etc.; **bar chart** = diagram where quantities and values are shown as thick columns of different heights or lengths; **flow chart** = diagram showing the arrangement of various work processes in a series; **organization chart** = diagram showing how a company or an office is organized; **pie chart** = diagram where information is shown as a circle cut up into sections of different sizes; **sales chart** = diagram showing how sales vary from month to month

charter ['tʃɑːtə] **1** *noun* **(a) bank charter** = official government document allowing the establishment of a bank; **charter value** = value of a bank being able to continue do business in the future, reflected as part of its share price **(b)** hiring transport for a special purpose; **charter flight** = flight in an aircraft which has been hired for that purpose; **charter plane** = plane which has been chartered **(c) shoppers' charter** = law which protects the rights of shoppers against shopkeepers who are not honest or against manufacturers of defective goods **2** *verb* to hire for a special purpose; ***to charter a plane*** *or* ***a boat*** *or* ***a bus***

chartered ['tʃɑːtəd] *adjective* **(a) chartered accountant** (CA) = accountant who has passed the professional examinations and is a member of the Institute of Chartered Accountants **(b)** (company) which has been set up by charter, and not registered as a company; **chartered bank** = bank which has been set up by government charter (formerly used in England, but now only done in the USA and Canada) **(c) chartered ship** *or* **bus** *or* **plane** = ship, bus or plane which has been hired for a special purpose

Chartered Association of Certified Accountants professional association of accountants in the UK

Chartered Institute of Bankers (CIB) professional association of bankers, providing training, professional examinations, etc., which are recognised worldwide

charting ['tʃɑːtɪŋ] *noun* using charts to analyze stock market trends and forecast future rises or falls

chartist ['tʃɑːtɪst] *noun* person who studies stock market trends and forecasts future rises or falls

chattels ['tʃætlz] *plural noun* goods, moveable property but not real estate; *US* **chattel mortgage** = money lent against the security of an item purchased, but not against real estate

cheap [tʃiːp] *adjective & adverb* not costing a lot of money, not expensive; **cheap labour** = workforce which does not earn much money; ***we have opened a factory in the Far East because of the cheap labour*** *or* ***because labour is cheap***; **cheap money** = money which can be borrowed at low interest; **cheap rate** = rate which is not expensive; **to buy something cheap** = at a low price; ***he bought two companies cheap and sold them again at a profit***; **they work out cheaper by the box** = these items are cheaper per unit if you buy a box of them

cheaply ['tʃiːpli] *adverb* without paying much money; ***the salesman was living cheaply at home and claiming a high hotel bill on his expenses***

cheapness ['tʃiːpnəs] *noun* being cheap; ***the cheapness of the pound means that many more tourists will come to London to do their Christmas shopping***

cheat [tʃiːt] *verb* to trick someone so that he loses money; ***he cheated the income tax out of thousands of pounds***; ***she was accused of cheating clients who came to ask her for advice***

check [tʃek] **1** *noun* **(a)** sudden stop; **to put a check on imports** = to stop some imports coming into a country **(b) check digit** = last digit of a string of computerized reference numbers, used to validate the transaction; **check sample** = sample to be used to see if a consignment is acceptable **(c)** investigation or examination; ***the auditors carried out checks on the petty cash book*** **(d)** *US (in restaurant)* bill **(e)** *US* = CHEQUE; **check card** = card issued by a bank to use in ATMs, but also used in some retail outlets; **check routing symbol** = number shown on an American cheque which identifies the Federal Reserve district through which the cheque will be cleared (similar to the British 'bank sort code'); *compare* ABA TRANSIT NUMBER **(f)** *US* mark on paper to show that something is correct; ***make a check in the box marked 'R'*** (NOTE: British English is **tick**) **2** *verb* **(a)** to stop or to delay; ***to check the entry of contraband into the country*** **(b)** to examine or to investigate; ***to check that an invoice is correct***; ***to check and sign for goods***; **he checked the computer printout against the invoices** = he examined the printout and the invoices to see if the figures were the same **(c)** *US* to mark with a sign to show that something is correct; ***check the box marked 'R'***

checkable ['tʃekəbl] *adjective US* (deposit account) on which checks can be drawn

checking account ['tʃekɪŋ ə'kaʊnt] *noun US* bank account on which you can write cheques

checkoff ['tʃekɒf] *noun US* system where union dues are automatically deducted by the employer from a worker's paycheck

check out ['tʃek 'aʊt] *verb (in a store)* to go through a checkout and pay for the goods bought

> whenever more than two customers are waiting in line to check out, a sales associate opens a new register
>
> *Fortune*

checkout ['tʃekaʊt] *noun (in a supermarket)* place where you pay for the goods you have bought

cheque [tʃek] *noun* note to a bank asking for money to be paid from your account to the account of the person whose name is written on the note; ***a cheque for £10*** *or* ***a £10 cheque***; **cheque account** = bank account which allows the customer to write cheques; **cheque to bearer** = cheque with no name written on it, so that the person who holds it can cash it; **crossed cheque** = cheque with two lines across it showing that it can only be deposited at a bank and not exchanged for cash; **open** *or* **uncrossed cheque** = cheque which can be cashed anywhere; **blank cheque** = cheque with the amount of money and the payee left blank, but signed by the drawer; **pay cheque** *or* **salary cheque** = monthly cheque by which an employee is paid; **traveller's cheques** US **traveler's checks** = cheques taken by a traveller, which can be cashed in a foreign country; **dud cheque** *or* **bouncing cheque** *or* **cheque which bounces** US **rubber check** = cheque which cannot be cashed because the person writing it has not enough money in his account to pay it; *see also* UNPAID **(b)** **to cash a cheque** = to exchange a cheque for cash; **to endorse a cheque** = to sign a cheque on the back to show that you accept it; **to make out a cheque to someone** = to write someone's name on a cheque; ***who shall I make the cheque out to?***; **to pay by cheque** = to pay by writing a cheque, and not using cash or a credit card; **to pay a cheque into your account** = to deposit a cheque; **the bank referred the cheque to drawer** = returned the cheque to the person who wrote it because there was not enough money in the account to pay it; **to sign a cheque** = to sign on the front of a cheque to show that you authorize the bank to pay the money from your account; **to stop a cheque** = to ask a bank not to pay a cheque which has been signed and sent

cheque book US **checkbook** ['tʃekbʊk] *noun* booklet with new cheques

cheque (guarantee) card ['tʃek gærən'ti: 'kɑ:d] *noun* plastic card from a bank which guarantees payment of a cheque up to a certain amount, even if there is no money in the account

Chicago Board of Trade (CBOT) [ʃɪ'kɑ:gəʊ 'bɔ:d əv 'treɪd] commodity market based in Chicago, trading in metals, soft commodities and financial futures

Chicago Mercantile Exchange (CME) [ʃɪ'kɑ:gəʊ 'mɜ:kəntaɪl ɪks'tʃeɪndʒ] commodity market based in Chicago, trading in livestock futures, and in financial futures on the IMM

Chicago school [ʃɪ'kɑ:gəʊ 'sku:l] school of monetarists, based at the University of Chicago, led by Professor Milton Friedman

chickenfeed ['tʃɪkɪnfi:d] *noun (informal)* small amount of money

chief [tʃi:f] *adjective* most important; ***he is the chief accountant of an industrial group***; **chief cashier** = main cashier in a bank (NOTE: the American equivalent is **head teller**); **chief executive** US **chief executive officer (CEO)** = executive in charge of the management of all of a company (often the same person as the managing director); **chief financial officer (CFO)** = executive in charge of a company's financial operations, reporting to the CEO; **chief operating officer (COO)** = director in charge of all a company's operations (same as a 'managing director')

Chinese walls ['tʃaɪni:z 'wɑ:lz] *noun* imaginary barriers between departments in the same organization, set up to avoid insider dealing or conflict of interest (as when a merchant bank is advising on a planned takeover bid, its investment department should not know that the bid is taking place, or they would advise their clients to invest in the company being taken over) (NOTE: also called **firewalls** in American English)

> the ability to put Chinese walls in place has enabled proefessional firms to merge
>
> *The Times*

> the difficulty with Chinese walls, is that while they are well adapted to deal with foreseeable or deliberate disclosure of information, they are not well adapted to deal with disclosure that is accidental or negligent
>
> *The Times*

chip [tʃɪp] *noun* **(a) a computer chip** = a small piece of silicon able to store data, used in computers; **chip card** = SMART CARD **(b) blue chip** = very safe investment, risk-free share in a good company; **Green chips** = samll companies with potential for growth; **Red chips** = good risk-free Chinese companies

> COMMENT: blue chips were originally named after the colour of the highest value poker chip

CHIPS [tʃɪps] = CLEARING HOUSE INTERBANK PAYMENTS SYSTEM the computerized clearing bank system used in the USA

chop [tʃɒp] *noun (in the Far East)* stamp, a mark made on a document to show that it has been agreed, acknowledged, paid, or that payment has been received

churning ['tʃɜːnɪŋ] *noun* **(a)** practice employed by stockbrokers, where they buy and sell on a client's discretionary account in order to earn their commission (the deals are frequently of no advantage to the client) **(b)** practice employed by insurance salesmen where the salesman suggests that a client should change his insurance policy solely in order to earn the salesman a commission

> more small investors lose money through churning than almost any other abuse, yet most people have never heard of it. Churning involves brokers generating income simply by buying and selling investments on behalf of their clients. Constant and needless churning earns them hefty commissions which bites into the investment portfolio
>
> *Guardian*

CIB = CHARTERED INSTITUTE OF BANKERS

c.i.f. *or* **CIF** ['siː 'aɪ 'ef] = COST, INSURANCE AND FREIGHT

circular ['sɜːkjʊlə] **1** *adjective* sent to many people; **circular letter of credit** = letter of credit sent to all branches of the bank which issues it **2** *noun* **(a)** leaflet or letter sent to many people; ***they sent out a circular offering a 10% discount*** **(b)** leaflet sent by a broker to clients, with information about companies and shares

circularize ['sɜːkjʊləraɪz] *verb* to send a circular to; ***the committee has agreed to circularize the members***; ***they circularized all their customers with a new list of prices***

circulate ['sɜːkjʊleɪt] *verb* **(a)** *(of money)* **to circulate freely** = to move about without restriction by the government **(b)** to send or to give out without restrictions; **to circulate money** = to issue money, to make money available to the public and industry **(c)** to send information to; ***they circulated a new list of prices to all their customers***

circulating capital ['sɜːkjʊleɪtɪŋ 'kæpɪtəl] *noun* capital required in cash, raw materials, finished products and work in progress for a company to carry on its business

circulation [sɜːkjʊ'leɪʃən] *noun* **(a)** movement; ***the company is trying to improve the circulation of information between departments***; **circulation of capital** = movement of capital from one investment to another **(b) to put money into circulation** = to issue new notes to business and the public; ***the amount of money in circulation increased more than was expected***

> the level of currency in circulation increased to N4.9 billion in the month of August
>
> *Business Times (Lagos)*

circumstances ['sɜːkəmstænsɪz] *noun* general situation; way in which something happens; *see also* FINANCIAL

Citizens Advice Bureau (CAB) ['sɪtɪzənz əd'vaɪs 'bjuːrəʊ] office where people can go to get free advice on legal and administrative problems

city ['sɪti] *noun* **(a)** large town; ***the largest cities in Europe are linked by hourly flights***; **capital city** = main town in a country, where the government is located; **inter-city** = between cities; ***inter-city train services are often quicker than going by air*** **(b) the City (of London)** = old centre of London, where banks and large companies have their main offices; the British financial centre; ***he works in the City*** *or* ***he is in the City***; **City desk** = section of a British newspaper office which deals with business news; **City editor** = business or finance editor of a British paper; **they say in the City that the company has been sold** = the London business world is saying that the company has been sold

civil ['sɪvl] *adjective* **civil action** = court case brought by a person or a company against someone who has done them wrong; **civil law** = laws relating to people's rights and to agreements between individuals

civil servant ['sɪvl 'sɜːvənt] *noun* person who works in the civil service

civil service ['sɪvl 'sɜːvɪs] *noun* organization and personnel which administer a country; ***you have to pass an examination***

to get a job in the civil service *or* ***to get a civil service job***

claim [kleɪm] **1** *noun* **(a)** asking for money; **wage claim** = asking for an increase in wages; **the union put in a 6% wage claim** = the union asked for a 6% increase in wages for its members **(b) legal claim** = statement that you think you own something legally; ***he has no legal claim to the property*** **(c) insurance claim** = asking an insurance company to pay for damages or for loss; **claims department** = department of an insurance company which deals with claims; **claim form** = form to be filled in when making an insurance claim; **claims manager** = manager of a claims department; **no claims bonus** = lower premium paid because no claims have been made against the insurance policy; **to put in a claim** = to ask the insurance company officially to pay damages; ***to put in a claim for repairs to the car***; ***she put in a claim for £250,000 damages against the driver of the other car***; **to settle a claim** = to agree to pay what is asked for; ***the insurance company refused to settle his claim for storm damage*** **(d) small claims court** = court which deals with claims for small amounts of money **2** *verb* **(a)** to ask for money; ***he claimed £100,000 damages against the cleaning firm***; ***she claimed for repairs to the car against her insurance*** **(b)** to say that something is your property; ***he is claiming possession of the house***; ***no one claimed the umbrella found in my office*** **(c)** to state that something is a fact; ***he claims he never received the goods***; ***she claims that the shares are her property***

claimant ['kleɪmənt] *noun* person who claims; **rightful claimant** = person who has a legal claim to something

claim back ['kleɪm 'bæk] *verb* to ask for money to be paid back

claimer ['kleɪmə] *noun* = *CLAIMANT*

class [klɑ:s] *noun* **(a)** category or group into which things are classified according to quality or price; **first-class** = top quality, most expensive; ***he is a first-class accountant;*** *GB* **first-class mail** = more expensive mail service, designed to be faster; **second-class mail** = less expensive, slower mail service; *see also* FIRST-CLASS, SECOND-CLASS **(b)** *US* type of common stock (Class A stock is similar to the British 'A' Shares); *see also* MEZZANINE

classify ['klæsɪfaɪ] *verb* to put into classes or categories; ***shares are classified as alpha, beta, gamma or delta on the London Stock Exchange***; **classified advertisements** = advertisements listed in a newspaper under special headings (such as 'property for sale' or 'jobs wanted'); **classified directory** = book which lists businesses grouped under various headings (such as computer shops or newsagents)

clause [klɔ:z] **1** *noun* section of a contract; ***there are ten clauses in the contract***; ***according to clause six, payments will not be due until next year***; **exclusion clause** = clause in an insurance policy or warranty which says which items are not covered by the policy; **penalty clause** = clause which lists the penalties which will happen if the contract is not fulfilled; **termination clause** = clause which explains how and when a contract can be terminated **2** *verb* to list details of the relevant parties to a bill of exchange

claw back ['klɔ: 'bæk] *verb* to take back money which has been allocated; ***income tax claws back 25% of pensions paid out by the government***; ***of the £1m allocated to the project, the government clawed back £100,000 in taxes***

clawback ['klɔ:bæk] *noun* **(a)** money taken back, especially money taken back by the government from grants or tax concessions which had previously been made **(b)** allocation of new shares to existing shareholders, so as to maintain the value of their holdings

clean [kli:n] *adjective* with no problems, no record of offences; **clean bill of lading** = bill of lading with no note to say the shipment is faulty or damaged

clean float ['kli:n 'fləʊt] *noun* floating a currency freely on the international markets, without any interference from the government; *compare* DIRTY FLOAT

clear [klɪə] **1** *adjective* **(a) clear profit** = profit after all expenses have been paid; ***we made $6,000 clear profit on the sale***; **clear title** = title to property without any charges or other encumbrances **(b)** free or total period of time; **three clear days** = three whole working days; ***allow three clear days for the cheque to be paid into the bank*** **2** *verb* **(a) to clear goods through customs** = to have all documentation passed by customs so that goods can enter or leave the country **(b)** to sell cheaply in order to get rid of stock; ***'demonstration models to clear'*** **(c) to clear 10%** *or* **$5,000 on the deal** = to make 10% or $5,000 clear profit; **we cleared only our expenses** = the sales revenue only paid for the costs and expenses without making any profit **(d) to clear a cheque** = to pass a cheque through the banking system, so that the money is transferred from the payer's account to another; ***the cheque took ten days to clear*** *or* ***the bank took ten days to clear the cheque***

clearance ['klɪərəns] *noun* **(a) customs clearance** = passing goods through customs so that they can enter or leave the country; **to effect customs clearance** = to clear goods through customs; **clearance certificate** = certificate showing that goods have been passed by customs **(b) clearance sale** = sale of items at low prices to get rid of stock **(c) clearance of a cheque** = passing of a cheque through the banking system, transferring money from one account to another; ***you should allow six days for cheque clearance***

clearing ['klɪərɪŋ] *noun* **(a) clearing of goods through customs** = passing of goods through customs **(b) clearing of a debt** = paying all of a debt **(c)** settling of a banking or stock exchange transaction through a centralized system; **clearing house** = central office where clearing banks exchange cheques, or where stock exchange or commodity exchange transactions are settled; **Clearing House Automated Payments System (CHAPS)** = computerized system for clearing cheques organized by the banks (NOTE: in the USA, the equivalent is the **Clearing House Interbank Payments System or CHIPS**); *compare* BACS; **clearing member** = member firm of a stock exchange which is also a member of the stock exchange clearing house

clearing bank ['kli:rɪŋ 'bæŋk] *noun* bank which clears cheques, one of the major British High Street banks, specializing in normal banking business for ordinary customers (loans, cheques, overdrafts, interest-bearing deposits, etc.)

clear off ['klɪər 'ɒf] *verb* **to clear off a debt** = to pay all of a debt

clerk [klɑ:k *US* klɜ:k] *noun* person who works in an office; **articled clerk** = clerk who is bound by a contract to work in a lawyer's office for some years to learn the trade; **chief clerk** *or* **head clerk** = most important clerk; **bank clerk** = person who works in a bank

client ['klaɪənt] *noun* person with whom business is done, person who pays for a service; **clients' account** = account with a bank for clients of a solicitor

clientele [kli:ən'tel] *noun* all the clients of a business; all the customers of a shop

climb [klaɪm] *verb* to go up; ***the company has climbed to No. 1 position in the market***; ***profits climbed rapidly as the new management cut costs***

close 1 [kləʊz] *noun* end of a day's trading session on a stock or commodity exchange; ***at the close of the day's trading the shares had fallen 20%*** **2** [kləʊs] *adjective* **close to** = very near, almost; ***the company was close to bankruptcy***; ***we are close to meeting our sales targets*** **3** [kləʊz] *verb* to end **(a)** to stop doing business for the day; ***the office closes at 5.30***; ***we close early on Saturdays*** **(b) to close the accounts** = to come to the end of an accounting period and make up the profit and loss account; **to close a position** = to arrange your affairs so that you no longer have any liability to pay (as by selling all your securities or when a purchaser of a futures contract takes on a sales contract for the same amount to offset the risk) **(c) to close an account** = (i) to stop supplying a customer on credit; (ii) to take all the money out of a bank account and stop the account; **he closed his building society account** = he took all the money out and stopped using the account **(d) the shares closed at $15** = at the end of the day's trading the price of the shares was $15

> Toronto stocks closed at an all-time high, posting their fifth straight day of advances in heavy trading
>
> *Financial Times*

> declines in unlisted outpaced the losses of listed stocks, and the NASDAQ composite dropped 13.01 per cent to close August at 381.21
>
> *Financial Times Review*

close company *US* **close(d) corporation** ['kləʊs 'kʌmpənɪ *or* 'kləʊs kɔ:pə'reɪʃən *or* 'kləʊzd kɔ:pə'reɪʃən] *noun* privately owned company controlled by a few shareholders (in the UK, less than five) where the public may own a small number of the shares

closed [kləʊzd] *adjective* **(a)** shut, not open, not doing business; ***the office is closed on Mondays***; ***all the banks are closed on the National Day*** **(b)** restricted; **closed shop** = system where a company agrees to employ only union members in certain jobs; ***a closed shop agreement***; ***the union is asking the management to agree to a closed shop*** **(c) closed economy** = type of economy where trade and financial dealings are tightly controlled by the government; **closed fund** = fund, such as an investment trust, where the investor buys shares in the trust and receives dividends (as opposed to an open-ended trust, such as a unit trust, where the investor buys units, and his investment is used to purchase further securities for the trust); **closed market** = market where a supplier deals only with one agent or distributor and does not supply any others direct; ***they signed a closed market agreement with an Egyptian company***

close down ['kləuz 'daun] *verb* to shut completely and cease trading

> the best thing would be to have a few more plants close down and bring supply more in line with current demand
>
> *Fortune*

close-ended *US* **closed-end** ['kləuz'endɪd or 'kləuzd'end] *adjective* (investment) which has a fixed capital, such as an investment trust; **closed-end mortgage** = mortgage where the borrower cannot use the propoerty as security for other borrowings, such as a second mortgage, and cannot repay the mortgage early either; *see also* CLOSED FUND

> a $30-per-share closed-end mutual fund
>
> *Smart Money*

> more and more closed-end fund managements are considering issuing preferred stock
>
> *Barron's*

closely held ['kləusli 'held] *adjective* (shares in a company) which are controlled by only a few shareholders

close off ['kləuz 'ɒf] *verb* to come to the end of an accounting period and make up the profit and loss account

close out ['kləuz 'aut] *verb* to end a futures contract by selling the relevant commodity or financial instrument

closing ['kləuzɪŋ] **1** *adjective* **(a)** final, coming at the end; **closing bid** = last bid at an auction, the bid which is successful; **closing date** = last date; ***the closing date for tenders to be received is May 1st***; **closing price** = price of a share at the end of a day's trading **(b)** at the end of an accounting period; ***closing balance***; ***closing stock*** **2** *noun* **(a)** shutting of a shop, being shut; **Sunday closing** = not opening a shop on Sundays; **closing time** = time when a shop or office stops work; **early closing day** = weekday (usually Wednesday or Thursday) when shops close in the afternoon **(b) closing bell** = bell which is rung when a Stock Exchange closes for business **(c) closing of an account** = act of stopping supply to a customer on credit **(d)** action of finalizing a deal; *US* **closing statement** = statement of all charges and fees involved in a mortgage, made just before the mortgage is signed

> in 1991, the New York Stock Exchange began allowing individual investors to trade stocks after the 4 p.m. closing bell
>
> *Smart Money*

closing-down sale ['kləuzɪŋdaun 'seɪl] *noun* sale of goods when a shop is closing for ever

closing out ['kləuzɪŋ 'aut] *noun* ending of a futures contract by selling the relevant commodity

closure ['kləuʒə] *noun* act of closing

CMBS = COMMERCIAL MORTGAGE-BACKED SECURITIES; *see* SECURITIES

CME ['si: 'em 'i:] = CHICAGO MERCANTILE EXCHANGE

CML = COUNCIL OF MORTGAGE LENDERS

c/o ['si: 'əu] = CARE OF

Co. [kəu] = COMPANY; ***J. Smith & Co. Ltd***

co- [kəu] *prefix* working or acting together; **co-financing** = arranging finance for a project from a series of sources

COB [kɒb] *French* = *COMMISSION DES OPERATIONS DE BOURSE* (the French equivalent of the SEC or SIB)

co-creditor ['kəu'kredɪtə] *noun* person who is a creditor of the same company as you are

COD *or* **c.o.d.** ['si: 'əu 'di:] = CASH ON DELIVERY

code [kəud] *noun* **(a)** system of signs, numbers or letters which mean something; **area code** = numbers which indicate an area for telephoning; ***what is the code for Edinburgh?***; **bar code** = system of lines printed on a product which can be read by a computer to give a reference number or price; **international dialling code** = numbers used for dialling a phone number in another country; **machine-readable codes** = sets of signs or letters (such as bar codes or post codes) which can be read by computers; **post code** *US* **ZIP code** = letters and numbers used to indicate a town or street in an address on an envelope; **stock code** = numbers and letters which refer to an item of stock **(b)** set of rules; **The Banking Code** = voluntary code of practice adopted by banks and building societies in their dealings with their customers; **code of practice** *US* **code of ethics** = rules drawn up by an association which the members must follow when doing business; **Takeover Code** *or* **City Code on Takeovers and Mergers** = code of practice which regulates how takeovers should take place; it is enforced by the Takeover Panel

> The Code provides valuable safeguards for customers. It should help them understand how banks and building societies are expected to deal with them
>
> *Banking Code*

co-director ['kəʊdɪ'rektə] *noun* person who is a director of the same company as you

cohabit ['kəʊhæbɪt] *verb (of two people)* to live together when not married; ***a woman who cohabits may lose out financially if her partner dies***

cohabitant ['kəʊ'hæbɪtənt] *noun* person who lives with another

> some pensions shcemes make provision for cohabitants but there is no legislation that syas that they have to
>
> *The Times*

cohabitation [kəʊhæbɪ'teɪʃn] *noun (of two people)* living together, when not married; ***most public-sector pension schemes do not recognise cohabitation***

coin [kɔɪn] *noun* piece of metal money; ***this machine takes only 10p coins***; ***he found a £2 coin in the street***; **coins of the realm** = the coins which are legal tender in the UK (these are: 1p, 2p, 5p, 10p, 50p, £1, £2)

co-insurance ['kəʊɪn'ʃʊərəns] *noun* insurance policy where the risk is shared among several insurers

COLA *US* = COST OF LIVING ALLOWANCE

cold [kəʊld] *adjective* without being prepared; **cold start** = starting a new business, opening a new shop where there was none before

cold call ['kəʊl 'kɔːl] **1** *noun* sales call (either a visit or a telephone call) where the salesman has no appointment and the client is not an established customer **2** *verb* to make a cold call; ***the broker cold-called clients***

cold caller ['kəʊld 'kɔːlə] *noun* salesman who makes cold calls

> he knew all about cold callers and their high-pressure push to buy speculative stocks
>
> *Wall Street Journal*

cold calling ['kəʊld 'kɔːlɪŋ] *noun* making cold calls on potential customers

> it a was a classic transaction - so classic it is immortalized on tape for rookie cold-calling stockbrokers to hear
>
> *Wall Street Journal*

> the SIB is considering the introduction of a set of common provisions on unsolicited calls to investors. The SIB is aiming to permit the cold calling of customer agreements for the provision of services relating to listed securities. Cold calling would be allowed when the investor is not a private investor
>
> *Accountancy*

collapse [kə'læps] **1** *noun* **(a)** sudden fall in price; ***the collapse of the market in silver***; ***the collapse of the dollar on the foreign exchange markets*** **(b)** sudden failure of a company; ***investors lost thousands of pounds in the collapse of the company*** **2** *verb* **(a)** to fall suddenly; ***the market collapsed***; ***the yen collapsed on the foreign exchange markets*** **(b)** to fail suddenly; ***the company collapsed with £25,000 in debts***

collar ['kɒlə] *noun* **(a)** *see* BLUE COLLAR, GOLD COLLAR, WHITE COLLAR **(b)** purchasing fixed minimum and maximum rates ('floors' and 'caps') of interest, dividends or repayments at the same time; *see also* CAP

> COMMENT: if a company has money in variable rate investments and wants to protect its income, it will buy a floor; instead of paying the premium for this purchase it will simultaneously sell a cap, so effectively creating a 'collar' round its investments

collateral [kɒ'lætərəl] **1** *noun* security, such as negotiable instruments, shares, or goods, used to provide a guarantee for a loan **2** *adjective* used as a security; **collateral loan** = loan secured on assets

> examiners have come to inspect the collateral that thrifts may use in borrowing from the Fed
>
> *Wall Street Journal*

collateralize [kə'lætərəlaɪz] *verb* to secure a debt on a collateral

collect [kə'lekt] **1** *verb* **(a)** to make someone pay money which is owed; **to collect a debt** = to go and make someone pay a debt **(b)** to take things away from a place; ***we have to collect the stock from the warehouse***; ***can you collect my letters from the typing pool?*** **2** *adverb & adjective US* (phone call) where the person receiving the call agrees to pay for it; ***to make a collect call***; ***he called his office collect***

collectables *or* **collectibles** [kə'lектəbəlz] *noun* things which can be collected as a hobby but can also be considered as an investment (such as stamps, old coins, etc.)

collecting agency [kə'lektɪŋ 'eɪdʒənsi] *noun* agency which collects money owed to other companies for a commission

collection [kə'lekʃən] *noun* **(a)** getting money together; making someone pay money which is owed; ***tax collection*** *or* ***collection of tax***; **debt collection** = collecting money which is owed; **debt collection agency** = company which collects debts for other companies for a commission; **bills for collection** = bills where payment is due **(b)** fetching of goods; ***the stock is in the warehouse awaiting collection***; **collection charges** *or* **collection rates** = charge for collecting something; **to hand something in for collection** = to leave something for someone to come and collect **(c) collections** = money which has been collected

collector [kə'lektə] *noun* person who makes people pay money which is owed; ***collector of taxes*** *or* ***tax collector***; ***debt collector***

colon [kɒ'lɒn] *noun* currency used in Costa Rica, El Salvador

column ['kɒləm] *noun* series of numbers, one under the other; ***to add up a column of figures***; ***put the total at the bottom of the column***; **credit column** = right-hand side in accounts showing money received; **debit column** = left-hand side in accounts showing money paid or owed

combine ['kɒmbaɪn] *noun* large financial or commercial group; ***a German industrial combine***

COMECON ['kɒmɪkɒn] = COUNCIL FOR MUTUAL ECONOMIC ASSISTANCE formerly, an economic alliance of countries in Eastern Europe, including Bulgaria, Czechoslovakia, Hungary, Poland, Romania, the USSR; also including Cuba, Vietnam and Mongolia

COMEX ['kɒmeks] = NEW YORK COMMODITY EXCHANGE

comfort ['kʌmfət] *noun* **letter of comfort** *or* **comfort letter** = (i) letter supporting someone who is trying to get a loan; (ii) letter from a company promising to lend money to a subsidiary

---

comfort letters in the context of a group of companies can take the form of (a) an undertaking by a holding company to provide finance to a subsidiary; (b) an undertaking to meet the debts and liabilities of a subsidiary as they fall due. Comfort letters are encountered in numerous other situations: where a bank is to grant finance to a subsidiary company, it may seek a comfort letter from the parent to the effect that the parent will not dispose of its interest in the subsidiary

Accountancy

COMIT index index of prices on the Milan Stock Exchange

commerce ['kɒmɜːs] *noun* business, buying and selling of goods and services; *see also* CHAMBER OF COMMERCE

commercial [kə'mɜːʃəl] *adjective* **(a)** referring to business; **commercial aircraft** = aircraft used to carry cargo or passengers for payment; **commercial attachÚ** = diplomat who represents and tries to promote his country's business interests; **commercial bank** = bank which offers banking services to the public, as opposed to a merchant bank; **commercial bill** = bill of exchange issued by a company (a trade bill) or accepted by a bank (a bank bill) (as opposed to treasury bills which are issued by the government); **commercial directory** = book which lists all the businesses and business people in a town; **commercial district** = part of a town where offices and shops are; **commercial law** = laws regarding business; **commercial lawyer** = lawyer who specializes in business and company law; **commercial mortgage** = mortgage on commercial property, such as offices, shops, factories, etc.; **commercial mortgage-backed securities (CMBS)** = shares which are backed by the security of a commercial mortgage; ***in the commercial mortgage-backed securities (CMBS) market supply is exploding***; *see also* ASSET-BACKED; **commercial paper (CP)** = IOU issued by a company to raise a short-term loan; **commercial port** = port which has only goods traffic; **commercial property** = building used for offices or shops;

sample only - of no commercial value = not worth anything if sold **(b)** profitable; **not a commercial proposition** = not likely to make a profit

commercialization [kəmɜːʃəlaɪˈzeɪʃn] *noun* making something into a business proposition; ***the commercialization of museums***

commercialize [kəˈmɜːʃəlaɪz] *verb* to make something into a business; ***the holiday town has become so commercialized that it is unpleasant***

commercially [kəˈmɜːʃəli] *adverb* in a business way; **not commercially viable** = not likely to make a profit

commission [kəˈmɪʃən] *noun* **(a)** money paid to a salesman or agent or stockbroker, usually a percentage of the sales made or the business done; ***she gets 10% commission on everything she sells***; **he charges 10% commission** = he asks for 10% of sales as his payment; **commission agent** = agent who is paid a percentage of sales; **broker's commission** *or* **trade commission** = commission paid to a broker who buys or sells for a client; US **commission broker** = stockbroker who works for a commission; **commission house** = firm which buys or sells (usually commodities) for clients, and charges a commission for this service; **commission rep** = representative who is not paid a salary, but receives a commission on sales; **commission sale** *or* **sale on commission** = sale where the salesman is paid a commission; *see also* HALF-COMMISSION **(b)** group of people officially appointed to examine some problem; ***the government has appointed a commission of inquiry to look into the problems of small exporters***; ***he is the chairman of the government commission on export subsidies***; *(France)* **Commission des Opérations de Bourse (COB)** = body which supervises the French Stock Exchanges (the equivalent of the British SIB or the American SEC)

commissioner [kəˈmɪʃənə] *noun* someone who represents authority; **Commissioner of Inland Revenue** = person appointed officially to supervise the collection of taxes, including income tax, capital gains tax and corporation tax, but not VAT; **Special Commissioner** = official appointed by the Treasury to hear cases where a taxpayer is appealing against an income tax assessment

commit [kəˈmɪt] *verb* **to commit oneself to** = to guarantee (a loan issue)

commitment [kəˈmɪtmənt] *noun* agreement by an underwriting syndicate to underwrite a Note Issuance Facility; **commitment fee** = fee paid to a bank which has arranged a line of credit which has not been fully used

commodity [kəˈmɒdəti] *noun* thing sold in very large quantities, especially raw materials and food such as metals or corn; **primary** *or* **basic commodities** = farm produce grown in large quantities, such as corn, rice, cotton; **staple commodity** = basic food or raw material which is most important in a country's economy; **commodity market** *or* **commodity exchange** = place where people buy and sell commodities; **commodity futures** = trading in commodities for delivery at a later date; ***coffee rose 5% on the commodity futures market yesterday***; **commodity trader** = person whose business is buying and selling commodities

> COMMENT: commodities are either traded for immediate delivery (as 'actuals' or 'physicals'), or for delivery in the future (as 'futures'). Commodity markets deal either in metals (aluminium, copper, lead, nickel, silver, zinc) or in 'soft' items, such as cocoa, coffee, sugar and oil. In London the exchanges are the London Metal Exchange and the London Commodity Exchange. Gold is traded on the London Gold Market, petroleum on the International Petroleum Exchange (IPE). In the USA, the New York Commodity Exchange (COMEX) deals in metals, the Chicago Board of Trade (CBOT) in metals, soft commodities and financial futures, and the Chicago Mercantile Exchange (CME) in livestock and livestock futures.

common [ˈkɒmən] *adjective* belonging to several different people or to everyone; **common carrier** = firm which carries goods or passengers, and which anyone can use; US **common dividend** = dividend payable on common stock; **common ownership** = ownership of a company or a property by a group of people; **common pricing** = illegal fixing of prices by several businesses so that they all charge the same price; US **common stock** = ordinary shares in a company, giving shareholders a right to vote at meetings and to receive dividends (NOTE: the British equivalent are **ordinary shares**); *(in the EU)* **Common Agricultural Policy (CAP)** = agreement between members of the EU to protect farmers by paying subsidies to fix prices of farm produce

common law [ˈkɒmən ˈlɔː] *noun* law as laid down in decisions of courts, rather than by statute, used in Great Britain and the United States

Common Market ['kɒmən 'mɑ:kɪt] *noun* **the European Common Market** = formerly the name for the European Community, an organization which links several European countries for the purposes of trade

Communauté française africaine (CFA) *see* CFA

Communauté française pacifique (CFP) *see* CFP

commute [kə'mju:t] *verb* to change a right into cash; ***he decided to commute part of his pension rights into a lump sum payment***

company ['kʌmpəni] *noun* **(a)** business, a group of people organized to buy, sell or provide a service; **to put a company into liquidation** = to close a company by selling its assets for cash; **to set up a company** = to start a company legally **(b)** *(forms of company)* **associate company** = company which is partly owned by another company; **family company** = company where most of the shares are owned by members of a family; **holding company** = company which exists only to own shares in subsidiary companies; **joint-stock company** = company whose shares are held by many people; **limited (liability) company** = company where a shareholder is responsible for repaying the company's debts only to the face value of the shares he owns; **listed company** = company whose shares can be bought or sold on the Stock Exchange; **parent company** = company which owns more than half of another company's shares; **private (limited) company** = company with a small number of shareholders, whose shares are not traded on the Stock Exchange; **public limited company (plc)** = company whose shares can be bought on the Stock Exchange; **subsidiary company** = company which is owned by a parent company **(c) finance company** = company which provides money for hire-purchase; **insurance company** = company whose business is insurance; **shipping company** = company whose business is in transporting goods or passengers in ships; **a tractor** *or* **aircraft** *or* **chocolate company** = company which makes tractors or aircraft or chocolate **(d) company car** = car which belongs to a company and is lent to an employee to use personally; **company doctor** = (i) doctor who works for a company and looks after sick workers; (ii) specialist businessman who advises companies which are in difficulties on methods of becoming profitable again; **company director** = person appointed by the shareholders to help run a company; **company law** = laws which refer to the way companies may work; **company secretary** = person responsible for the company's legal and financial affairs (NOTE: the American equivalent is the **corporate secretary**); *GB* **the Companies Acts** = Acts of Parliament which regulate the workings of companies, stating the legal limits within which companies may do their business; **Companies Registration Office (CRO)** *or* **Companies House** = official organization where the records of companies must be deposited, so that they can be inspected by the public

comparable ['kɒmpərəbl] *adjective* which can be compared; ***the two sets of figures are not comparable***; **which is the nearest company comparable to this one in size?** = which company is of a similar size and can be compared with this one?; **on a comparable-store basis** = when comparing similar stores belonging to different companies; *see also* SAME

> their sales increased 10% on a comparable-store basis for all of last year
>
> *Fortune*

> the company's most mature market posted a 7% increase in comparable-store sales over the Christmas period
>
> *Fortune*

compare with [kəm'peə 'wɪð] *verb* to put two things together to see how they differ; ***how do the sales this year compare with last year's?***; ***compared with 1996, last year was a boom year***

compensate ['kɒmpenseɪt] *verb* to pay for damage done; ***to compensate a salesman for loss of commission*** (NOTE: you compensate someone **for** something)

compensation [kɒmpen'seɪʃən] *noun* **(a) compensation for damage** = payment for damage done; **compensation for loss of office** = payment to a director who is asked to leave a company before his contract ends; **compensation for loss of earnings** = payment to someone who has stopped earning money or who is not able to earn money; **compensation fund** = fund operated by the Stock Exchange to compensate investors for losses suffered when members of the Stock Exchange default **(b) compensation deal** = deal where an exporter is paid (at least in part) in goods from the country to which he is exporting **(c)** *US* salary; **compensation package** = salary, pension and other benefits offered with a job

> it was rumoured that the government was prepared to compensate small depositors
>
> *South China Morning Post*

> golden parachutes are liberal compensation packages given to executives leaving a company
>
> *Publishers Weekly*

compensatory [kɒmpən'seɪtri] *adjective* which compensates; **compensatory financing** = finance from the IMF to help a country in difficulty

compete [kəm'pi:t] *verb* **to compete with someone** *or* **with a company** = to try to do better than another person or another company; ***we have to compete with cheap imports from the Far East***; ***they were competing unsuccessfully with local companies on their home territory***; **the two companies are competing for a market share** *or* **for a contract** = each company is trying to win a larger part of the market or to win the contract

competing [kəm'pi:tɪŋ] *adjective* which competes; **competing firms** = firms which compete with each other; **competing products** = products from different companies which have the same use and are sold in the same markets at similar prices

competition [kɒmpə'tɪʃən] *noun* **(a)** trying to do better than another supplier; **free competition** = being free to compete without government interference; **keen competition** = strong competition; ***we are facing keen competition from European manufacturers*** **(b) the competition** = companies which are trying to compete with your product; ***we have lowered our prices to beat the competition***; ***the competition have brought out a new range of products***

> profit margins in the industries most exposed to foreign competition are worse than usual
>
> *Sunday Times*

> competition is steadily increasing and could affect profit margins as the company tries to retain its market share
>
> *Citizen (Ottawa)*

competitive [kəm'petɪtɪv] *adjective* which competes fairly; *US* **competitive bid** = method of auctioning new securities, where various underwriters offer the stock at competing prices of terms; **competitive devaluation** = devaluation of a currency to make a country's goods more competitive on the international markets; **competitive price** = low price aimed to compete with a rival product; **competitive pricing** = putting low prices on goods so as to compete with other products; **competitive products** = products made to compete with existing products

> the company blamed fiercely competitive market conditions in Europe for a £14m operating loss last year
>
> *Financial Times*

competitiveness [kəm'petɪtɪvnəs] *noun* being competitive

> farmers are increasingly worried by the growing lack of competitiveness for their products on world markets
>
> *Australian Financial Review*

competitor [kəm'petɪtə] *noun* person or company that competes; ***two German firms are our main competitors***

> sterling labour costs continue to rise between 3% and 5% a year faster than in most of our competitor countries
>
> *Sunday Times*

complete [kəm'pli:t] *verb* to sign a contract for the sale of a property and to exchange it with the other party, so making it legal

completion [kəm'pli:ʃən] *noun* act of finishing something; **completion date** = date when something will be finished; **completion of a contract** = signing of a contract for the sale of a property when the buyer pays and the seller passes ownership to the buyer

compliance [kəm'plaɪəns] *noun* (i) agreement to do what is ordered; (ii) doing what has been ordered; **compliance department** = department in a stockbroking firm which makes sure that the Stock Exchange rules are followed and that confidentiality is maintained in cases where the same firm represents rival clients; **compliance officer** = person working in the compliance department of a stockbroking firm

comply [kəm'plaɪ] *verb* **to comply with a court order** = to obey an order given by a court

composite ['kɒmpəzɪt] *adjective* made up a various parts joined together; **composite index** = index made from various indices; ***New York Stock Exchange composite transactions***

> at the end of August the DJIA had dropped 10.01 per cent to 2614.36, while Standard & Poor's Composite was down 9.43 per cent to 322.56
>
> *Financial Times Review*

composition [kɒmpə'zɪʃən] *noun* agreement between a debtor and creditors to settle a debt by repaying only part of it

compound 1 ['kɒmpaʊnd] *adjective* **compound interest** = interest which is added to the capital and then earns interest itself **2** [kəm'paʊnd] *verb* **(a)** to agree with creditors to settle a debt by paying part of what is owed **(b)** to add to; ***the interest is compounded daily***

> that means that in 20 years, after the annual fee is compounded, the extra half a percentage point could take a 10% bite out of the investor's accumulated earnings
>
> *Wall Street Journal*

compounded [kəm'paʊndɪd] *adjective* added together; **compounded annual return** = net return on an investment, calculated after adding interest and deducting tax; **compounded interest rate** = interest rate showing the effect of adding the interest to the capital

> employees can watch their savings soar over a period of years, thanks to the benefits of compounded interest
>
> *Fortune*

comprehensive insurance [kɒmprɪ'hensɪv] *noun* insurance policy which covers you against all risks which are likely to happen

compromise ['kɒmprəmaɪz] **1** *noun* agreement between two sides, where each side gives way a little; ***management offered £5 an hour, the union asked for £9, and a compromise of £7.50 was reached*** **2** *verb* to reach an agreement by giving way a little; ***he asked £15 for it, I offered £7 and we compromised on £10***

comptroller [kən'trəʊlə] *noun* financial controller; *US* **Comptroller of the Currency** = official of the US government responsible for the regulation of US national banks (that is, banks which are members of the Federal Reserve)

compulsory liquidation *or* **compulsory winding up** [kəm'pʌlsəri lɪkwɪ'deɪʃn] *noun* liquidation which is ordered by a court

computable [kəm'pju:təbl] *adjective* which can be calculated

computation [kɒmpjʊ'teɪʃən] *noun* calculation

computational [kɒmpjʊ'teɪʃənl] *adjective* **computational error** = mistake made in calculating

compute [kəm'pju:t] *verb* to calculate, to do calculations

computer [kəm'pju:tə] *noun* electronic machine which calculates, stores information and processes it automatically; **computer bureau** = office which offers to do work on its computers for companies which do not have their own computers; **computer department** = department in a company which manages the company's computers; **computer error** = mistake made by a computer; **computer file** = section of information on a computer (such as the payroll, list of addresses, customer accounts); **computer language** = system of signs, letters and words used to instruct a computer; **computer listing** = printout of a list of items taken from data stored in a computer; **computer manager** = person in charge of a computer department; **computer program** = instructions to a computer, telling it to do a particular piece of work; **computer programmer** = person who writes computer programs; **computer services** = work using a computer, done by a computer bureau; **computer time** = time when a computer is being used (paid for at an hourly rate); ***running all those sales reports costs a lot in computer time***; **business computer** = powerful small computer which is programmed for special business uses; **personal computer** *or* **home computer** = small computer which can be used in the home

computerize [kəm'pju:təraɪz] *verb* to change from a manual system to one using computers; ***our stock control has been completely computerized***

computerized [kəm'pju:təraɪzd] *adjective* worked by computers; ***a computerized invoicing system***

computer-readable [kəm'pju:tə'ri:dəbl] *adjective* which can be read and understood by a computer; ***computer-readable codes***

computing [kəm'pju:tıŋ] *noun* referring to computers; **computing speed** = speed at which a computer calculates

concealment of assets [kən'si:lmənt əv 'æsıts] *noun* hiding assets so that creditors do not know they exist

concentration [kɒnsən'treıʃn] *noun* **(a)** action of grouping a large number of things together **(b)** *US* action of a bank in lending too much to one single sector of the economy (banks should not lend more than 10% of loans to a single sector)

concern [kən'sɜ:n] *noun* business or company; **his business is a going concern** = the company is working (and making a profit); **sold as a going concern** = sold as an actively trading company

concert ['kɒnsət] *noun (of several people)* **to act in concert** = to work together to achieve an aim (this is illegal if the aim is to influence a share price by all selling or buying together)

concert party ['kɒnsət 'pɑ:ti] *noun* arrangement where several people or companies work together in secret (usually to acquire another company through a takeover bid)

concession [kən'seʃn] *noun* **(a)** right to use someone else's property for business purposes; **mining concession** = right to dig a mine on a piece of land **(b)** right to be the only seller of a product in a place; ***she runs a jewellery concession in a department store*** **(c)** allowance; **tax concession** = allowing less tax to be paid

concessionaire [kənseʃə'neə] *noun* person who has the right to be the only seller of a product in a place

concessionary fare [kən'seʃnəri 'feə] *noun* reduced fare for certain types of passenger (such as old age pensioners or employees of the transport company)

conciliation [kənsılı'eıʃən] *noun* bringing together the parties in a dispute so that the dispute can be settled

condition [kən'dıʃən] *noun* **(a)** term of a contract; duties which have to be carried out as part of a contract; something which has to be agreed before a contract becomes valid; **conditions of employment** *or* **conditions of service** = terms of a contract of employment; **conditions of sale** = agreed ways in which a sale takes place (such as discounts or credit terms); **on condition that** = provided that; ***they were granted the lease on condition that they paid the legal costs*** **(b)** general state; ***the union has complained of the bad working conditions in the factory***; ***an item sold in good condition***; ***what was the condition of the car when it was sold?***; ***they blamed their poor sales figures on adverse trading conditions***

conditional [kən'dıʃənl] *adjective* provided that certain things take place; **to give a conditional acceptance** = to accept, provided that certain things happen or that certain terms apply; **the offer is conditional on the board's acceptance** = provided the board accepts; **he made a conditional offer** = he offered to buy, provided that certain terms applied

conditionality [kəndıʃə'nælıti] *noun* state of having conditions attached, such as a loan from the IMF

condominium [kɒndə'mıniəm] *noun US* system of ownership, where a person owns an individual apartment in a building, together with a share of the land and common parts (stairs, roof, etc.)

confirm [kən'fɜ:m] *verb* **(a)** to say that something is true or exact; ***they wrote to confirm the details of the contract*** **(b)** *(of a bank)* to say that letters of credit from foreign purchasers are agreed, and that the sellers will be paid for orders placed

confirmation [kɒnfə'meıʃən] *noun* **(a)** writing to confirm the details of a transaction or agreement; ***he received confirmation from the bank that the deeds had been deposited*** **(b)** agreement that orders from foreign purchasers will be paid

confiscation [kɒnfıs'keıʃn] *noun* taking away someone's possessions as a punishment

> further efforts by the UK government to tighten the penalties for money laundering include extending asset confiscation powers to enable courts to make confiscation orders without the need for a criminal trial
>
> *Financial World*

conflict of interest ['kɒnflıkt əv 'ıntrest] *noun* (i) situation where a person may profit personally from decisions which he takes in his official capacity; (ii) situation where a firm may be recommending a course of action to clients which is not in their best interest, but may well profit the firm, or where different departments of the same firm are acting for rival clients

conglomerate [kən'glɒmərət] *noun* group of subsidiary companies linked together and forming a group making very different types of products

consensus [kən'sensəs] *noun* opinion which most people agree on; **the Wall Street consensus** = the general opinion among analysts on Wall Street

> I looked first for those with most recent quarterly earnings of at least 20 percent above consensus estimates
>
> *Smart Money*

> earnings are in line with the Wall Street consensus
>
> *Barron's*

conservative [kən'sɜːvətɪv] *adjective* careful, not overestimating; ***a conservative estimate of sales***; ***his forecast of expenditure is very conservative***; **at a conservative estimate** = calculation which probably underestimates the final figure; ***their turnover has risen by at least 20% in the last year, and that is probably a conservative estimate***

conservatively [kən'sɜːvətɪvli] *adverb* not overestimating; ***the total sales are conservatively estimated at £2.3m***

conservator [kən'sɜːvətə] *noun US* official appointed by a court to manage a person's affairs

consider [kən'sɪdə] *verb* to think seriously about something; **to consider the terms of a contract** = to examine and discuss if the terms are acceptable

consideration [kənsɪdə'reɪʃən] *noun* **(a)** serious thought; ***we are giving consideration to moving the head office to Scotland*** **(b)** something valuable exchanged as part of a contract (not always money, it could be an issue of shares as part of the purchase price when taking over a company); **for a small consideration** = for a small fee or payment

consign [kən'saɪn] *verb* **to consign goods to someone** = to send goods to someone for him to use or to sell for you

consignation [kɒnsaɪ'neɪʃən] *noun* act of consigning

consignee [kɒnsaɪ'niː] *noun* person who receives goods from someone for his own use or to sell for the sender

consignment [kən'saɪnmənt] *noun* **(a)** sending of goods to someone who will sell them for you; **consignment note** = note saying that goods have been sent; **goods on consignment** = goods kept for another company to be sold on their behalf for a commission **(b)** group of goods sent for sale; ***a consignment of goods has arrived***; ***we are expecting a consignment of cars from Japan***

consignor [kən'saɪnə] *noun* person who consigns goods to someone

consolidate [kən'sɒlɪdeɪt] *verb* **(a)** to put the accounts of several subsidiary companies into the accounts of the main group (if the parent company owns less than 100%, then items in the accounts relating to minority shareholders are shown separately); **consolidated accounts** = accounts where the financial position of several different companies (i.e., a holding company and its subsidiaries) are recorded together; **consolidated balance sheet** = balance sheets of subsidiary companies grouped together into the balance sheet of the parent company; **consolidated profit and loss account** = profit and loss account which groups together the accounts of several companies in a group **(b)** to group goods together for shipping; **consolidated shipment** = goods from different companies grouped together into a single shipment **(c)** *(price on the Stock Exchange)* to remain at the same level for some time, before moving up again **(d)** *GB* **Consolidated fund** = money in the Exchequer which comes from tax revenues and is used to pay for government expenditure

consolidated stock [kən'sɒlɪdeɪtɪd 'stɒk] = CONSOLS

consolidation [kənsɒlɪ'deɪʃən] *noun* **(a)** grouping together of goods for shipping **(b)** taking profits from speculative investments and investing them safely in blue-chip companies

consols ['kɒnsɒlz] *plural noun GB* irredeemable government bonds (they pay an interest but do not have a maturity date)

consortium [kən'sɔːtiəm] *noun* group of companies which are brought together for a special purpose; ***a consortium of Canadian companies*** *or* ***a Canadian consortium***; ***a consortium of French and British companies is planning to construct the new aircraft***

constructive notice [kən'strʌktɪv 'nəʊtɪs] *noun* **(a)** knowledge which the law says a person has of something (whether or not the person actually has it) because certain information is available to him if he makes reasonable inquiry **(b)** *US* printed notice published in a newspaper to inform the public that something has taken place

consular invoice ['kɒnsjʊlə 'ɪnvɔɪs] *noun* invoice stamped by a consul to show that goods being imported have correct documentation and are being shipped legally

consult [kən'sʌlt] *verb* to ask an expert for advice; ***he consulted his accountant about his tax problems***

consultancy [kən'sʌltənsi] *noun* act of giving specialist advice; ***a consultancy firm***; ***he offers a consultancy service***

consultant [kən'sʌltənt] *noun* specialist who gives advice; ***a management consultant***; ***a tax consultant***

consulting [kən'sʌltɪŋ] *adjective* person who gives specialist advice; **consulting actuary** = independent actuary who advises large pension funds

consumable goods *or* **consumables** [kən'sju:məbl 'gʊdz or kən'sju:məblz] *noun* goods which are bought by members of the public and not by companies

consumer [kən'sju:mə] *noun* person or company that buys and uses goods and services; ***gas consumers are protesting at the increase in prices***; ***the factory is a heavy consumer of water***; **consumer council** = group representing the interests of consumers; **consumer credit** = credit given by shops, banks and other financial institutions to consumers so that they can buy goods; lenders have to be licensed under the Consumer Credit Act, 1974 (the American equivalent is also called **installment credit**); **Consumer Credit Act, 1974** = act of Parliament which licenses lenders, and requires them to state clearly the full terms of loans which they make (including the APR); **consumer durables** = items such as washing machines, refrigerators or cookers which are bought and used by the public; **consumer goods** = goods bought by consumers, by members of the public; *US* **consumer lease** = lease for the use or purchase of an item of equipment to be used in the home; **consumer panel** = group of consumers who report on products they have used so that the manufacturers can improve them or use what the panel says about them in advertising; **consumer price index (CPI)** = American index showing how prices of consumer goods have risen over a period of time (the British equivalent is the Retail Prices Index or RPI); **consumer protection** = protecting consumers against unfair or illegal traders; **consumer research** = research into why consumers buy goods and what goods they really want to buy; **consumer resistance** = lack of interest by consumers in buying a product; ***the latest price increases have produced considerable consumer resistance***; **consumer society** = type of society where consumers are encouraged to buy goods; **consumer spending** = spending by private households on goods and services

> analysis of the consumer price index for the first half of 1985 shows that the rate of inflation went down by about 12.9 per cent
>
> *Business Times (Lagos)*

contango [kən'tæŋgəʊ] *noun* **(a)** payment of interest to a stockbroker for permission to carry payment for shares from one account day to the next; **contango day** = formerly, the day when the rate of contango payments was fixed **(b)** *(on commodity markets)* cash price which is lower than the forward price (NOTE: also called **forwardation;** the opposite is **backwardation)**

contested takeover [kən'testɪd 'teɪkəʊvə] *noun* takeover where the board of the company do not recommend it to the shareholders and try to fight it

contingency [kən'tɪndʒənsi] *noun* possible state of emergency when decisions will have to be taken quickly; **contingency fund** *or* **contingency reserve** = money set aside in case it is needed urgently; **contingency plans** = plans which will be put into action if something happens which no one expects; **to add on 10% to provide for contingencies** = to provide for further expenditure which may be incurred; ***we have built 10% for contingencies into our cost forecast***

contingent [kən'tɪndʒənt] *adjective* **(a)** **contingent expenses** = expenses which will be incurred only if something happens; **contingent liability** = liability which may or may not occur, but for which provision is made in a company's accounts (as opposed to 'provisions', where money is set aside for an anticipated expenditure); **contingent reserves** = money set aside to cover unexpected payments **(b)** **contingent policy** = policy which pays out only if something happens (as if the person named in the policy dies before the person due to benefit)

contra ['kɒntrə] **1** *noun* **contra account** = account which offsets another account; **contra entry** = entry made in the opposite side of an account to make an earlier entry worthless (i.e. a debit against a credit); **per contra** *or* **as per contra** = words showing that a contra entry has been made **2** *verb* **to contra an entry** = to enter a similar amount in the opposite side of an account

contract 1 ['kɒntrækt] *noun* **(a)** legal agreement between two parties; ***to draw up a contract***; ***to draft a contract***; ***to sign a contract***; **the contract is binding on both parties** = both parties signing the contract must do what is agreed; **under contract** = bound by the terms of a contract; ***the firm is under contract to deliver the goods by November***; **to void a contract** = to make a contract invalid; **contract of employment** = contract between management and an employee showing all conditions of work; **service contract** = contract between a company and a director showing all conditions of work; **exchange of contracts** = point in the sale of a property when the buyer and seller both sign the contract of sale which then becomes binding; **to exchange contracts** = to sign a contract when buying a property, done by both buyer and seller at the same time, making the sale binding **(b)** **contract law** *or* **law of contract** = laws relating to agreements; **by private contract** = by private legal agreement **(c)** *(Stock Exchange)* deal to buy or sell shares; agreement to purchase options or futures; **contract note** = note showing that shares have been bought or sold but not yet paid for, also including the commission; **futures contract** = contract for the purchase of commodities for delivery at a date in the future; **financial futures contract** = contract for the purchase of gilt-edged securities for delivery at a date in the future (NOTE: a futures contract is a contract to purchase; if an investor is bullish, he will buy a contract, but if he feels the market will go down, he will sell one) **(d)** agreement for supply of a service or goods; ***contract for the supply of spare parts***; ***to enter into a contract to supply spare parts***; ***to sign a contract for £10,000 worth of spare parts***; **to put work out to contract** = to decide that work should be done by another company on a contract, rather than employing members of staff to do it; **to award a contract to a company** *or* **to place a contract with a company** = to decide that a company shall have the contract to do work for you; **to tender for a contract** = to put forward an estimate of cost for work under contract; ***conditions of contract*** *or* ***contract conditions***; **breach of contract** = breaking the terms of a contract; **the company is in breach of contract** = the company has failed to do what was agreed in the contract; **contract work** = work done according to a written agreement **2** ['kɒntrækt or kən'trækt] *verb* to agree to do some work by contract; ***to contract to supply spare parts*** *or* ***to contract for the supply of spare parts***; **the supply of spare parts was contracted out to Smith Ltd** = Smith Ltd was given the contract for supplying spare parts; **to contract out of an agreement** = to withdraw from an agreement with the written permission of the other party

> COMMENT: a contract is an agreement between two or more parties to create legal obligations between them. Some contracts are made 'under seal', i.e. they are signed and sealed by the parties; most contracts are made orally or in writing. The essential elements of a contract are: (a) that an offer made by one party should be accepted by the other; (b) consideration (i.e. payment of money); (c) the intention to create legal relations. The terms of a contract may be express or implied. A breach of contract by one party entitles the other party to sue for damages or to ask for something to be done

contracting party [kən'træktɪŋ] *noun* person or company that signs a contract

contractor [kən'træktə] *noun* person or company that does work according to a written agreement; **haulage contractor** = company which transports goods by contract; **government contractor** = company which supplies the government with goods by contract

contractual [kən'træktjʊəl] *adjective* according to a contract; **contractual liability** = legal responsibility for something as stated in a contract; **to fulfil your contractual obligations** = to do what you have agreed to do in a contract; **he is under no contractual obligation to buy** = he has signed no agreement to buy; **contractual savings** = savings in the form of regular payments into long-term investments such as pension schemes

contractually [kən'træktjʊəli] *adverb* according to a contract; ***the company is contractually bound to pay his expenses***

contrarian [kən'treəriən] *adjective* going against a trend; **contrarian research** = research that shows you should buy shares against the current trend; **contrarian stockpicking** = choosing stocks and shares against the trend of the market

contribute [kən'trɪbju:t] *verb* to give money, to add to money; ***to contribute 10% of the profits***; ***he contributed to the pension fund for 10 years***

contribution [kɒntrɪ'bju:ʃən] *noun* money paid to add to a sum; **contribution of capital** = money paid to a company as additional capital; **employer's contribution** = money paid by an employer towards a worker's pension; **National Insurance contributions (NIC)** = money paid each month by a worker and the company to the National Insurance; **pension contributions** = money paid by a company or worker into a pension fund

contributor [kən'trɪbjutə] *noun* **contributor of capital** = person who contributes capital

contributory [kən'trɪbjutəri] *adjective* **(a)** **contributory pension plan** *or* **scheme** = pension plan where the employee has to contribute a percentage of salary (NOTE: the opposite is a **non-contributory scheme**) **(b)** which helps to cause; ***rising exchange rates have been a contributory factor in** or **to the company's loss of profits***

control [kən'trəul] **1** *noun* **(a)** power; being able to direct something; ***the company is under the control of three shareholders***; ***the family lost control of its business***; **to gain control of a company** = to buy more than 50% of the shares so that you can direct the business; **to lose control of a company** = to find that you have less than 50% of the shares in a company, and so are no longer able to direct it **(b)** restricting or checking something; making sure that something is kept in check; **under control** = kept in check; ***expenses are kept under tight control***; ***the company is trying to bring its overheads back under control***; **out of control** = not kept in check; ***costs have got out of control***; **budgetary control** = keeping check on spending; **credit control** = checking that customers pay on time and do not exceed their credit limits; **quality control** = making sure that the quality of a product is good; **stock control** = making sure that movements of stock are noted **(c)** **exchange controls** = government restrictions on changing the local currency into foreign currency; ***the government has imposed exchange controls***; ***they say the government is going to lift exchange controls***; **price controls** = legal measures to prevent prices rising too fast **2** *verb* **(a)** **to control a company** = to be able to direct the business of a company, because you own more than 50% of the shares; ***the business is controlled by a company based in Luxembourg***; ***the company is controlled by the majority shareholder*** **(b)** to make sure that something is kept in check or is not allowed to develop; ***the government is fighting to control inflation** or **to control the rise in the cost of living***

controlled [kən'trəuld] *adjective* ruled, kept in check; **government-controlled** = ruled by a government; **controlled economy** = economy where the most business activity is directed by orders from the government

controller [kən'trəulə] *noun* **(a)** person who controls (especially the finances of a company); **stock controller** = person who notes movements of stock **(b)** *US* chief accountant in a company

controlling [kən'trəulɪŋ] *adjective* **to have a controlling interest in a company** = to own more than 50% of the shares so that you can direct how the company is run

convergence [kən'vɜːdʒəns] *noun* **(a)** situation where the economic factors applying in two countries move closer together (as when basic interest rates, or budget deficits become more and more similar) **(b)** situation where the price of a commodity on the futures market moves towards the spot price as settlement date approaches

> the lack of European action on budget deficits was likely to make interest rate convergence more difficult before the January start for EMU
>
> *The Times*

> this might appeal to the Chancellor because it promotes both eventual euro-convergence and the coincidence of the British economic and electoral cycles
>
> *The Times*

conversion [kən'vɜːʃən] *noun* change **(a)** **conversion of funds** = using money which does not belong to you for a purpose for which it is not supposed to be used **(b)** **conversion price** *or* **conversion rate** = (i) rate at which a currency is changed into a foreign currency; (ii) price at which preference shares are converted into ordinary shares **(c)** changing convertible loan stock into ordinary shares; **conversion discount** *or* **conversion premium** = difference between the price of convertible stock and the ordinary shares into which they are to be converted (if the convertible stock is cheaper, the difference is a 'conversion premium'; if the stock is dearer, the difference is a 'conversion discount'; **conversion issue** = issue of new bonds (called 'conversion bonds') timed to coincide with the date of maturity of older bonds, with the intention of persuading investors to reinvest; **conversion period** = time during which convertible loan stock may be changed into ordinary shares; **conversion value** = value of convertible stock, including the extra value of the ordinary shares into which they may be converted

convert [kən'vɜːt] *verb* **(a)** to change money of one country for money of another; ***we converted our pounds into Swiss francs*** **(b) to convert funds to your own use** = to use someone else's money for yourself

convertibility [kənvɜːtə'bɪləti] *noun* (i) ability to exchange one currency for another easily; (ii) ability to exchange a currency for gold or SDRs

convertible [kən'vɜːtəbl] **1** adjective **convertible currency** = currency which can be exchanged for another easily; **convertible debentures** *or* **convertible loan stock** = debentures or loan stock which can be exchanged for ordinary shares at a later date **2** noun **convertibles** = corporate bonds or preference shares which can be converted into ordinary shares at a set price on set dates

> the fortunes of convertibles tend to reflect the performance of the share market, because they offer the right to convert into the ordinary shares of the issuing company on a fixed date and at a fixed price
>
> *Money Observer*

conveyance [kən'veɪəns] *noun* legal document which transfers a property from the seller to the buyer

conveyancer [kən'veɪənsə] *noun* person who draws up a conveyance

conveyancing [kən'veɪənsɪŋ] *noun* legally transferring a property from a seller to a buyer; **do-it-yourself conveyancing** = drawing up a legal conveyance without the help of a lawyer

COO = CHIEF OPERATING OFFICER

cooling off period ['kuːlɪŋ 'ɒf 'pɪːriəd] *noun* (i) during an industrial dispute, a period when negotiations have to be carried on and no action can be taken by either side; (ii) period when a person is allowed to think about something which he has agreed to buy on hire-purchase and possibly change his mind; (iii) period of ten days during which a person who has signed a life assurance policy may cancel it

cooperative [kəʊ'ɒpərətɪv] *adjective* where the profits are shared among the workers; **cooperative bank** = bank which is owned by its members, who deposit money or who borrow money as loans; **cooperative society** = organization where customers and workers are partners and share the profits

copper ['kɒpə] *noun* metal which is traded on commodity exchanges such as the London Metal Exchange

coproperty [kəʊ'prɒpəti] *noun* ownership of property by two or more people together

coproprietor [kəʊprə'praɪətə] *noun* person who owns a property with another person or several other people

cordoba ['kɔːdəbə] *noun* currency used in Nicaragua

corner ['kɔːnə] **1** *noun* **(a)** place where two streets or two walls join; **corner shop** = small general store in a town on a street corner **(b)** situation where one person or a group controls the supply of a certain commodity **2** *verb* **to corner the market** = to own most or all of the supply of a certain commodity and so control the price; ***the syndicate tried to corner the market in silver***

corp [kɔːpə'reɪʃn] *US* = CORPORATION

corporate ['kɔːpərət] *adjective* **(a)** referring to a whole company; **corporate bond** = loan stock officially issued by a company to raise capital, usually against the security of some of its assets (the company promises to pay a certain amount of interest on a set date every year until the redemption date, when it repays the loan); **corporate finance** = financing of a company; **corporate image** = idea which a company would like the public to have of it; **corporate loan** = loan issued by a corporation; **corporate plan** = plan for the future work of a whole company; **corporate planning** = planning the future work of a whole company; **corporate profits** = profits of a corporation; **corporate raider** = person or company which buys a stake in another company before making a hostile takeover bid; *US* **corporate resolution** = document signed by the officers of a corporation, naming those persons who can sign cheques, withdraw cash and have access to the corporation's bank account (NOTE: the British equivalent is the **bank mandate**); *US* **corporate secretary** = person responsible for the corporation's legal and financial affairs (NOTE: the British equivalent is the **company secretary**) **(b)** referring to business in general; ***corporate America***; ***corporate Britain***

> the prime rate is the rate at which banks lend to their top corporate borrowers
>
> *Wall Street Journal*

> corporate profits for the first quarter showed a 4 per cent drop from last year
>
> *Financial Times*

if corporate forecasts are met, sales will exceed $50 million

Citizen (Ottawa)

corporation [kɔːpəˈreɪʃən] *noun* **(a)** large company; **finance corporation** = company which provides money for hire purchase; **corporation tax** = tax on profits made by companies, calculated before dividends are paid; **Advance Corporation Tax (ACT)** = tax paid by a company in advance of its main tax payments; it is paid when dividends are paid to shareholders and appears on the tax voucher attached to a dividend warrant; **mainstream corporation tax** = tax paid by a company on its profits (the ACT is set against this) **(b)** *US* company which is incorporated in the United States; **corporation income tax** = tax on profits made by incorporated companies **(c)** *GB* municipal authority; **corporation loan** = loan issued by a local authority

correction [kəˈrekʃən] *noun* making something correct; change which makes something correct; **technical correction** = situation where a share price or a currency moves up or down because it was previously too low or too high, because of technical factors

now the market is having a correction, or a bear market, which is correspondingly worse than others round the world. The bear market is signalled when the index cuts below its 200-day moving average

Money Observer

a correction is commonly defined as a drop of 10% or more in the stock market from its peak, while a bear market is a drop of 20% or more, although many analysts define these events differently

Wall Street Journal

he thinks that beginning last week, blue chips are now joining the smaller stocks in a correction

Wall Street Journal

correspondent [kɒrɪsˈpɒndənt] *noun* **(a)** **correspondent bank** = bank which acts as an agent for a foreign bank **(b)** journalist who writes articles for a newspaper on specialist subjects; ***a financial correspondent***; ***'the Times' business correspondent***; ***he is the Paris correspondent of the 'Telegraph'***

cost [kɒst] **1** *noun* **(a)** amount of money which has to be paid for something; ***what is the cost of a first class ticket to New York? computer costs are falling each year***; ***we cannot afford the cost of two telephones***; **to cover costs** = to produce enough money in sales to pay for the costs of production; ***the sales revenue barely covers the costs of advertising*** *or* ***the manufacturing costs***; **to sell at cost** = to sell at a price which is the same as the cost of manufacture or the wholesale cost; **fixed costs** = business costs which do not rise with the quantity of the product made; **historic(al) cost** = actual cost of purchasing something which was purchased some time ago; **labour costs** = cost of hourly-paid workers employed to make a product; **manufacturing costs** *or* **production costs** = costs of making a product; **operating costs** *or* **running costs** = cost of the day-to-day organization of a company; **variable costs** = production costs which increase with the quantity of the product made (such as wages, raw materials); **cost accountant** = accountant who gives managers information about their business costs; **cost accounting** = specially prepared accounts of manufacturing and sales costs; **cost analysis** = calculating in advance what a new product will cost; **cost centre** = person or group whose costs can be itemized and to which fixed costs can be allocated; **cost, insurance and freight (c.i.f.)** = estimate of a price, which includes the cost of the goods, the insurance and the transport charges; **cost price** = selling price which is the same as the price which the seller paid for the item (i.e. either the manufacturing cost or the wholesale price); **cost of sales** = all the costs of a product sold, including manufacturing costs and the staff costs of the production department, before general overheads are calculated **(b)** **cost of borrowing** *or* **cost of money** = interest rate paid on borrowed money **(c)** **costs** = expenses involved in a court case; **to pay costs** = to pay the expenses of a court case; ***the judge awarded costs to the defendant***; ***costs of the case will be borne by the prosecution*** **2** *verb* **(a)** to have a price; ***how much does the machine cost? this cloth costs £10 a metre*** **(b)** **to cost a product** = to calculate how much money will be needed to make a product, and so work out its selling price

cost-benefit analysis [ˈkɒstˈbenɪfɪt əˈnæləsɪs] *noun* examining the ratio between costs and benefits, especially in comparing different production processes

cost-cutting ['kɒst'kʌtɪŋ] *noun* reducing costs; ***we have taken out the telex as a cost-cutting exercise***

cost-effective ['kɒstɪ'fektɪv] *adjective* which gives value, especially when compared with something else; ***we find advertising in the Sunday newspapers very cost-effective***

cost-effectiveness ['kɒstɪ'fektɪvnəs] *noun* being cost-effective; ***can we calculate the cost-effectiveness of air freight against shipping by sea?***

costing ['kɒstɪŋ] *noun* calculation of the manufacturing costs, and so the selling price of a product; ***the costings give us a retail price of $2.95***; ***we cannot do the costing until we have details of all the production expenditure***

costly ['kɒstli] *adjective* expensive, which costs a lot of money

cost of living ['kɒst əv 'lɪvɪŋ] *noun* money which has to be paid for food, heating, rent etc.; ***to allow for the cost of living in the salaries***; **cost-of-living allowance** = addition to normal salary to cover increases in the cost of living (in the USA, called COLA); **cost-of-living bonus** = extra money paid to meet the increase in the cost of living; **cost-of-living increase** = increase in salary to allow it to keep up with the increased cost of living; **cost-of-living index** = way of measuring the cost of living which is shown as a percentage increase on the figure for the previous year; similar to the consumer price index, but including other items such as the interest on mortgages

cost plus ['kɒst 'plʌs] *noun* system of charging, where the buyer pays the costs plus a percentage commission to the seller; ***we are charging for the work on a cost plus basis***

cost-push inflation ['kɒst'pʊʃ ɪn'fleɪʃən] *noun* inflation caused by increased wage demands and increased raw materials costs, which lead to higher prices and in turn lead to further wage demands (NOTE: the opposite is **demand-pull inflation**)

council ['kaʊnsl] *noun* governing body of an organization, such as the Stock Exchange council

counselling ['kaʊnsəlɪŋ] *noun* **debt counselling** = advising people who are in debt of the best ways to arrange their finances to pay off their debts; **Consumer Credit Counselling Service** = service which advises people about problems with items bought on credit

> we will liaise, wherever possible, with debt counselling organisations that we recognise, for example Citizens Advice Bureaux, money advice centres, etc.
>
> *The Banking Code*

count [kaʊnt] *verb* **(a)** to add figures together to make a total; ***he counted up the sales for the six months to December*** **(b)** to include; ***did you count my trip to New York as part of my sales expenses?***

counter- ['kaʊntə] *prefix* against

counterbid ['kaʊntəbɪd] *noun* higher bid in reply to a previous bid; ***when I bid £20 he put in a counterbid of £25***

counter-claim ['kaʊntəkleɪm] **1** *noun* claim for damages made in reply to a previous claim; ***Jones claimed £25,000 in damages against Smith, and Smith entered a counter-claim of £50,000 for loss of office*** **2** *verb* to put in a counter-claim; ***Jones claimed £25,000 in damages and Smith counter-claimed £50,000 for loss of office***

counterfeit ['kaʊntəfɪt] **1** *adjective* false or imitation (money) **2** *verb* to make imitation money

counterfoil ['kaʊntəfɔɪl] *noun* slip of paper kept after writing a cheque, an invoice or a receipt, as a record of the deal which has taken place; *see also* STUB

countermand [kaʊntə'mɑːnd] *verb* **to countermand an order** = to say that an order must not be carried out

counter-offer ['kaʊntə'ɒfə] *noun* higher offer made in reply to another offer; ***Smith Ltd made an offer of £1m for the property, and Blacks replied with a counter-offer of £1.4m***

> the company set about paring costs and improving the design of its product. It came up with a price cut of 14%, but its counter-offer - for an order that was to have provided 8% of its workload next year - was too late and too expensive
>
> *Wall Street Journal*

counterparty ['kaʊntə'pɑːti] *noun* the other party in a deal

counterpurchase ['kaʊntə'pɜːtʃəs] *noun* international trading deal, where a company agrees to use money received on a sale to purchase goods in the country where the sale was made

countersign ['kaʊntəsaɪn] *verb* to sign a document which has already been signed by someone else; ***all cheques have to be countersigned by the finance director***; ***the purchasing manager countersigns all my orders***

countertrade ['kaʊntətreɪd] *noun* trade which does not involve payment of money, but rather barter, buy-back deals, etc.

countervailing duty ['kaʊntəveɪlɪŋ 'dju:ti] *noun* duty imposed by a country on imported goods, where the price of the goods includes a subsidy from the government in the country of origin

counting house ['kaʊntɪŋ 'haʊs] *noun (old-fashioned)* the department in a firm that dealt with cash

count on ['kaʊnt 'ɒn] *verb* to expect something to happen; ***they are counting on getting a good response from the TV advertising***; ***do not count on a bank loan to start your business***

country bank ['kʌntri 'bæŋk] *noun US* bank based in a town which has no office of the Federal Reserve

country broker ['kʌntri 'brəʊkə] *noun* broking firm which is not based in London (often independently run and charging lower commission than larger London firms)

coupon ['ku:pɒn] *noun* **(a)** piece of paper used in place of money; **gift coupon** = coupon from a store which is given as a gift and which must be exchanged in that store **(b)** (i) slip of paper attached to a government bond certificate which can be cashed to provide the annual interest; (ii) the interest on a government bond; **cum coupon** = with a coupon attached; **ex coupon** = without the interest coupons; **zero-coupon bond** = bond which carries no interest, but which is issued at a deep discount which provides a capital gain; *US* **coupon security** = government security which carries a coupon and pays interest, as opposed to one which pays no interest but is sold at a discount to its face value **(c)** piece of paper which replaces an order form; **coupon ad** = advertisement with a form attached, which is to be cut out and returned to the advertiser with your name and address if you want further information about the product advertised; **reply coupon** = form attached to a coupon ad, which must be filled in and returned to the advertiser

covenant ['kʌvənənt] **1** *noun* legal contract; **deed of covenant** = official signed agreement by which someone agrees to certain conditions, such as the payment of a certain sum of money each year **2** *verb* to agree to pay a sum of money each year by contract; ***to covenant to pay £10 per annum***

cover ['kʌvə] **1** *noun* **(a) insurance cover** = protection guaranteed by an insurance policy; ***do you have cover against theft?***; **to operate without adequate cover** = without being protected by insurance; **to ask for additional cover** = to ask the insurance company to increase the amount for which you are insured; **full cover** = insurance against all risks; **cover note** = letter from an insurance company giving details of an insurance policy and confirming that the policy exists (NOTE: the American English for this is **binder**) **(b)** security to guarantee a loan or future purchases; forward contract which is entered into to protect against exchange rate falls; ***do you have sufficient cover for this loan?*** **(c) dividend cover** = ratio of profits to dividend **2** *verb* **(a)** to have enough money to pay; to take steps to give yourself security against a possible loss; **the damage was covered by the insurance** = the insurance company paid for the damage; **to cover a position** = to have enough money to be able to pay for a forward purchase; **to cover a risk** = to be protected by insurance against a risk; **to be fully covered** = to have insurance against all risks; ***the insurance covers fire, theft and loss of work***; **covered bear** = bear who holds the stock which he sells; *see also* UNCOVERED **(c)** to earn enough money to pay for costs, expenses etc.; ***we do not make enough sales to cover the expense of running the shop***; ***breakeven point is reached when sales cover all costs***; **the dividend is covered four times** = profits are four times the dividend paid out

> three export credit agencies have agreed to provide cover for large projects in Nigeria
>
> *Business Times (Lagos)*

coverage ['kʌvərɪdʒ] *noun US* protection guaranteed by insurance; ***do you have coverage against fire damage?***

covering letter *or* **covering note** ['kʌvərɪŋ 'letə *or* 'kʌvərɪŋ 'nəʊt] *noun* letter or note sent with documents to say why you are sending them

CP = COMMERCIAL PAPER

CPI ['si: 'pi: 'aɪ] = CONSUMER PRICE INDEX

crash [kræʃ] **1** *noun* financial collapse; sudden fall in prices on a stock market; ***he lost all his money in the crash of 1929*** **2** *verb* to collapse financially; ***the company crashed with debts of over £1 million***

crawling peg ['krɔ:lıŋ 'peg] *noun* method of controlling exchange rates, allowing them to move up or down slowly

create [kri'eıt] *verb* to make something new; ***by acquiring small unprofitable companies he soon created a large manufacturing group***; ***the government scheme aims at creating new jobs for young people***

> he insisted that the tax advantages he directed towards small businesses will help create jobs and reduce the unemployment rate
>
> *Toronto Star*

creation [kri'eıʃən] *noun* making; **job creation scheme** = government-backed scheme to make work for the unemployed

creative accountancy *or* **creative accounting** [kri'eıtiv ə'kauntıŋ] *noun* adaptation of a company's figures to present a better picture than is correct (to appear to make a company more attractive to a potential buyer, or for some other reason which may not be strictly legal); **creative financing** = finding methods of financing a commercial project that are different from the normal methods of raising money

credere ['kreıdəri] *see* DEL CREDERE

credit ['kredıt] **1** *noun* **(a)** allowing a customer time before he has to pay for goods or services; ***to give someone six months' credit***; ***to sell on good credit terms***; **extended credit** = credit on very long repayment terms; **interest-free credit** = arrangement to borrow money without paying interest on the loan; **long credit** = terms allowing the borrower a long time to pay; **open credit** = bank credit given to good customers without security; **short credit** = terms allowing the customer only a short time to pay; **trade credit** = credit offered by one company when trading with another; **credit account** = account which a customer has with a shop which allows him to buy goods and pay for them later; **credit (reference) agency** *US* **credit bureau** *or* **mercantile agency** = company which reports on the creditworthiness of customers to show whether they should be allowed credit; **credit bank** = bank which lends money; **credit control** = (i) check that customers pay on time and do not owe more than their credit limit; (ii) limits on bank lending imposed by a government; **credit facilities** = arrangement with a bank or supplier to have credit so as to buy goods; **credit freeze** *or* **credit squeeze** = period when lending by banks is restricted by the government; **credit history** = details of a person's past borrowings; **letter of credit** = letter from a bank, allowing someone credit and promising to repay at a later date; **irrevocable letter of credit** = letter of credit which cannot be cancelled; **credit limit** = fixed amount which is the most a customer can owe on credit; **he has exceeded his credit limit** = he has borrowed more money than he is allowed; **to open a line of credit** *or* **a credit line** = to make credit available to someone; *US* **credit line** = overdraft, the amount by which a person can draw money from an account with no funds, with the agreement of the bank; **credit rating** = amount which a credit agency feels a customer should be allowed to borrow; **credit references** = details of persons, companies or banks who have given credit to a person or company in the past, supplied as references when opening a credit account with a new supplier; **credit refusal** *US* **credit denial** = action of refusing to give someone credit (anyone who has been refused credit can ask to see the reasons for the decision); **credit risk** = risk that a borrower may not be able to repay a loan; **credit scoring** = method of calculating the credit risk of a potential customer using statistical information; **on credit** = without paying immediately; ***to live on credit***; ***we buy everything on sixty days credit***; ***the company exists on credit from its suppliers***; *see also* COUNSELLING **(b)** money received by a person or company and recorded in the accounts; ***to enter £100 to someone's credit***; ***to pay in £100 to the credit of Mr Smith***; **debits and credits** = money which a company owes and which is due to it; **credit balance** = balance in an account showing that more money has been received than is owed by the company; ***the account has a credit balance of £1,000***; **credit column** = right-hand column in accounts showing money received; **credit entry** = entry on the credit side of an account; **credit note** = note showing that money is owed to a customer; ***the company sent the wrong order and so had to issue a credit note***; **credit side** = right-hand side of accounts showing money received; **account in credit** = account where the credits are higher than the debits; *US* **adjustment credit** = short-term loan from the Federal Reserve to a commercial bank; **bank credit** = loans or overdrafts from a bank to a customer; **tax credits** = part of a dividend on which the company has already paid tax, so that the shareholder is not taxed on it **2** *verb* to put money into someone's account; to note money received in an account; ***to credit an account with £100*** *or* ***to credit £100 to an account***

credit card ['kredɪt 'kɑ:d] *noun* plastic card which allows you to borrow money and to buy goods up to a certain limit without paying for them immediately, but only after a period of grace of 25-30 days; *see also* DEBIT CARD

creditor ['kredɪtə] *noun* person or company that is owed money (a company's creditors are its current liabilities); **creditor nation** = country which has lent money to another; **trade creditors** = companies which are owed money by a company (the amount owed to trade creditors figures in the annual accounts); **creditors' meeting** = meeting of all persons to whom an insolvent company owes money, to decide how to obtain the money owed; US **creditors' committee** = group of creditors of a corporation being reorganized under Chapter 11, who meet officials of the corporation to discuss the progress of the reorganization

credit-shelter trust ['kredɪt'ʃeltə 'trʌst] *noun* money put in trust in order to escape federal estate tax

> COMMENT: this type of trust is where someone leaves half his estate to his wife and puts the other half into a trust; after his death, his wife can continue to enjoy the income from the trust, and when she dies her estate and also the trust pass to her heirs tax free

another popular tool is the credit-shelter trust, which also allows some access to assets that have been moved out of your estate

Fortune

Crédit Suisse Index ['kreɪdi 'swi:s 'ɪndeks] index of prices on the Zurich stock exchange

credit union ['kredɪt 'ju:njən] *noun* US group of people who pay in regular deposits or subscriptions which earn interest and are used to loan to other members of the group

creditworthiness ['kredɪt'wɜ:ðɪnəs] *noun* ability of a customer to pay for goods bought on credit

credit-worthy ['kredɪt'wɜ:ði] *adjective* (person or company) trusted to be able to pay for goods supplied on credit

crisis ['kraɪsɪs] *noun* serious economic situation where decisions have to be taken rapidly; ***international crisis***; ***banking crisis***; ***financial crisis***; **crisis management** = management of a business or a country's economy during a period of crisis; **to take crisis measures** = to take severe measures rapidly to stop a crisis developing (NOTE: plural is **crises** ['kraɪsi:z])

CRO = COMPANIES REGISTRATION OFFICE

crore [krɔ:] *noun (in India)* ten million (NOTE: one crore equals 100 lakh)

for the year 1989-90, the company clocked a sales turnover of Rs.7.09 crore and earned a profit after tax of Rs.10.39 lakh on an equity base of Rs.14 lakh

Business India

cross [krɒs] *verb* **to cross a cheque** = to write two lines across a cheque to show that it has to be paid into a bank; **crossed cheque** = cheque which has to be paid into a bank

cross-border ['krɒs'bɔ:də] *adjective* from one country to another, covering several countries; **cross-border capital flows** = movements of capital from one country to another; **cross-border listing** = listing of a security on stock exchanges in more than one country

that became easier when the Japanese Government removed some reporting requirements on cross-border capital flows

Wall Street Journal

cross-holding ['krɒs 'həʊldɪŋ] *noun* situation where two companies hold shares in each other (to prevent each from being taken over)

cross out ['krɒs 'aʊt] *verb* to put a line through something which has been written; ***she crossed out £250 and put in £500***

cross rate ['krɒs 'reɪt] *noun* **exchange cross rates** = rates of exchange for two currencies, shown against each other, but in terms of a third currency, often the US dollar

cross-selling ['krɒs 'selɪŋ] *noun* selling insurance or other financial services at the same time as a mortgage

crowding out ['kraʊdɪŋ 'aʊt] *noun* situation where there is little money for private companies to borrow, because the government's borrowings are very heavy

crown [kraʊn] *noun* word used in English to refer to the currencies of several countries, such as the Czech Republic, Denmark, Norway, Sweden, etc.

crown jewels ['kraʊn 'dʒu:əlz] *noun* most valuable assets of a company (the reason why other companies may want to make takeover bids)

cum [kʌm] *preposition* with; **cum all** = price of a share including all entitlements; **cum dividend** *or* **cum div** = price of a share including the next dividend still to be paid; **cum coupon** = with an interest coupon attached; the price of a bond with the right to receive the next interest payment; **cum rights** = shares sold with the right to purchase new shares in a rights issue; *see also* EX

cumulative [ˈkjuːmjʊlətɪv] *adjective* which is added automatically each year; **cumulative interest** = interest which is added to the capital each year; **cumulative preference share** *US* **cumulative preferred stock** = preference share which will have the dividend paid at a later date even if the company is not able to pay a dividend in the current year

curb exchange [ˈkɜːb ɪksˈtʃeɪndʒ] = AMERICAN STOCK EXCHANGE

currency [ˈkʌrənsi] *noun* **(a)** money in coins and notes which is used in a particular country; **convertible currency** = currency which can easily be exchanged for another; **foreign currency** = currency of another country; **foreign currency account** = bank account in the currency of another country (e.g. a dollar account in the UK); **foreign currency reserves** = a country's reserves held in currencies of other countries; **hard currency** = currency of a country which has a strong economy and which can be changed into other currencies easily; ***to pay for imports in hard currency***; ***to sell raw materials to earn hard currency***; **legal currency** = money which is legally used in a country; **soft currency** = currency of a country with a weak economy, which is cheap to buy and difficult to exchange for other currencies; **currency backing** = gold or securities which maintain the international strength of a currency; **currency basket** *or* **basket of currencies** = group of currencies, each weighted and calculated together as a single unit against which another currency can be measured; **dual currency bond** = bond which is paid for in one currency but which is repayable in another; **currency conversion systems** = computer software used to convert accounts from one currency to another automatically; **currency note** = bank note **(b)** foreign currency, the currency of another country; **currency band** = exchange rate levels between which a currency is allowed to move without full devaluation; **currency clause** = clause in a contract which avoids problems of payment caused by changes in exchange rates, by fixing the exchange rate for the various transactions covered by the contract; **currency futures** = purchases of foreign currency for delivery at a future date; **currency movements** = changes in exchange rates between countries; **currency swap** = agreement to use a certain currency for payments under a contract in exchange for another currency (the two companies involved each can buy one of the currencies at a more favourable rate than the other); *see also* SINGLE (NOTE: currency has no plural when it refers to the money of one country: **he was arrested trying to take currency out of the country**)

---

the strong dollar's inflationary impact on European economies, as national governments struggle to support their sinking currencies and push up interest rates

Duns Business Month

---

today's wide daily variations in exchange rates show the instability of a system based on a single currency, namely the dollar

Economist

---

the level of currency in circulation increased to N4.9 billion in the month of August

Business Times (Lagos)

---

current [ˈkʌrənt] *adjective* referring to the present time; **current assets** = assets used by a company in its ordinary work (such as materials, finished products, monies owed by customers, cash); **current cost accounting (CCA)** = method of accounting which notes the cost of replacing assets at current prices, rather than valuing assets at their original cost; **current liabilities** = debts which a company has to pay within the next accounting period (in a company's annual accounts, these would be debts which must be paid within the year and are usually payments for goods or services received); **current price** = (i) today's price; (ii) price which has been adjusted for inflation; **current rate of exchange** = today's rate of exchange; **current yield** = dividend calculated as a percentage of the current price of a share on the stock market

---

crude oil output plunged during the past month and is likely to remain at its current level for the near future

Wall Street Journal

---

current account ['kʌrənt ə'kaʊnt] *noun* **(a)** account in an bank from which the customer can withdraw money when he wants (current accounts do not always pay interest) (NOTE: the American equivalent is a **checking account**) **(b)** account of the balance of payments of a country relating to the sale or purchase of raw materials, goods and invisibles

> customers' current deposit and current accounts also rose to $655.31 million at the end of December
>
> *Hongkong Standard*

curve [kɜːv] *noun* line which bends round; ***the graph shows an upward curve***; **learning curve** = line on a graph which shows the relationship between experience in doing something and competence at carrying it out; **sales curve** = graph showing how sales increase or decrease; *see also* YIELD

cushion ['kʊʃən] *noun* money which allows a company to pay interest on its borrowings or to survive a loss; ***we have sums on deposit which are a useful cushion when cash flow is tight***

custodial [kʌs'təʊdiəl] *adjective* referring to custody, to holding valuable items for someone

> institutional investors appoint custodial banks to look after trillions of dollars of financial assets around the world
>
> *The Banker*

custodian [kʌs'təʊdiən] *noun* person *or* company that looks after valuable items for someone

custody ['kʌstədi] *noun* control of a thing under the law, as when holding valuables, share certificates, etc., in safekeeping for someone

> the custody agreement is the principal legal contract between the custodian and the client. It sets out the terms governing settlement, safekeeping and related services offered by the custodian
>
> *The Banker*

custom ['kʌstəm] *noun* **(a)** use of a shop by regular shoppers; **to lose someone's custom** = to do something which makes a regular customer go to another shop; **custom-built** *or* **custom-made** = made specially for one customer; ***he drives a custom-built Rolls Royce*** **(b) the customs of the trade** = general way of working in a trade

customer ['kʌstəmə] *noun* person or company that buys goods or services; ***the shop was full of customers***; ***can you serve this customer first please? he is a regular customer of ours***; **customer appeal** = what attracts customers to a product; **customer service department** = department which deals with customers and their complaints and orders; *(of a bank)* **business customer** = company which has an account with a bank; **personal customer** = private individual who has an account with a bank

customize ['kʌstəmaɪz] *verb* to change something to fit the special needs of a customer; ***we used customized computer terminals***

customs ['kʌstəmz] *plural noun* **H.M. Customs and Excise** = (i) British government department which organizes the collection of taxes on imports, excise duty on alcohol, etc., and VAT; (ii) office of this department at a port or airport; **to go through customs** = to pass through the area of a port or airport where customs officials examine goods; **to take something through customs** = to carry something illegal through a customs area without declaring it; ***he was stopped at the customs checkpoint***; ***her car was searched by customs***; **customs barrier** = customs duty intended to prevent imports; **customs broker** = person or company that takes goods through customs for a shipping company; **customs clearance** = document given by customs to a shipper to show that customs duty has been paid and the goods can be shipped; **customs declaration** = statement showing goods being imported on which duty will have to be paid; ***you have to fill in a customs (declaration) form before leaving the aircraft***; **customs duty** = tax paid on goods brought into or taken out of a country; **the crates had to go through a customs examination** = the crates had to be examined by customs officials; **customs formalities** = declaration of goods by the shipper and examination of them by the customs; **customs officers** *or* **customs officials** = people working for the customs; **customs tariff** = list of duties to be paid on imported goods; **customs union** = agreement between several countries that goods can travel between them, without paying duty, while goods from other countries have to pay special duties

cut [kʌt] **1** *noun* **(a)** sudden lowering of a price or salary; ***the store has made a number of price cuts*** *or* ***cuts in prices***; **job cuts** =

reductions in the number of jobs; ***we anticipate more job cuts as the recession gets worse***; **he took a cut in salary** = he accepted a lower salary **(b)** share in a payment; ***he introduces new customers and gets a cut of the salesman's commission*** **2** *verb* **(a)** to lower suddenly; ***we are cutting prices on all our models***; **to cut (back) production** = to reduce the quantity of products made; ***the company has cut back its sales force***; ***we have taken out the photocopier in order to try to cut costs*** **(b)** to reduce the number of something; **to cut jobs** = to reduce the number of jobs by making people redundant; **he cut his losses** = he stopped doing something which was creating a loss (NOTE: **cutting - cut)**

> state-owned banks cut their prime rates a percentage point to 11%
>
> *Wall Street Journal*

> the US bank announced a cut in its prime from 10+ per cent to 10 per cent
>
> *Financial Times*

cutback ['kʌtbæk] *noun* reduction; ***cutbacks in government spending***

cut down (on) ['kʌt 'daʊn ɒn] *verb* to reduce suddenly the amount of something used; ***the government is cutting down on welfare expenditure***; ***the office is trying to cut down on electricity consumption***; ***we have installed a word-processor to cut down on paperwork***

cut in ['kʌt 'ɪn] *verb (informal)* **to cut someone in on a deal** = to give someone a share in the profits of a deal

cutoff date ['kʌtɒf 'deɪt] *noun* date when something is stopped, such as the final date for receiving applications for shares, or the date when the current trading account ends and the next account begins

cut-price [kʌt'praɪs] *adjective* sold at a cheaper price than usual; ***cut-price goods***; ***cut-price petrol***; **cut-price store** = store selling cut-price goods

cut-throat competition ['kʌtθrəʊt kɒmpə'tɪʃn] *noun* sharp competition by cutting prices and offering high discounts

cutting ['kʌtɪŋ] *noun* **cost cutting** = reducing costs; ***we have made three secretaries redundant as part of our cost-cutting programme***; **price cutting** = sudden lowering of prices; **price-cutting war** = competition between companies to get a larger market share by cutting prices

cycle ['saɪkl] *noun* period of time when something leaves its original position and then returns to it; **economic cycle** *or* **trade cycle** *or* **business cycle** = period during which trade expands, then slows down and then expands again; *see also* MARKET

cyclical ['sɪklɪkəl] *adjective* which happens in cycles; **cyclical factors** = way in which a trade cycle affects businesses; **cyclical stocks** = shares in companies which move in a regular pattern (such as shares in a turkey producer might rise in the period before Christmas)

Dd

Schedule D ['ʃedjʊl 'di:] schedule to the Finance Acts under which tax is charged on income from trades, professions, interest and other earnings which do not come from employment

Table D ['teɪbl 'di:] model memorandum and articles of association of a public company with share capital limited by guarantee, set out in the Companies Act, 1985

daily ['deɪli] *adjective* done every day; **daily consumption** = amount used each day; **daily interest** *or* **interest calculated daily** *or* **on a daily basis** = rate of interest calculated each day and added to the principal; **daily production of cars** = number of cars produced each day; **daily sales returns** = reports of sales made each day; **a daily newspaper** *or* **a daily** = newspaper which is produced every day

Daimyo bond ['daɪmjəʊ 'bɒnd] Japanese bearer bond which can be cleared through European clearing houses

dalasi [də'lɑ:si] *noun* currency used in the Gambia

damp down ['dæmp 'daʊn] *verb* to reduce; ***to damp down demand for domestic consumption of oil***

data ['deɪtə] *noun* information (letters or figures) available on computer; **data acquisition** *or* **data capture** = getting information; keyboarding information onto a database; **bank of data** *or* **databank** = store of information in a computer; **data mining** = comparing two sets of data in order to find a connection between them, as by comparing the results of two unconnected companies and basing your investment strategy on them; **data processing** = selecting and examining data in a computer to produce special information (NOTE: **data** is usually singular: **the data is easily available**)

---

a statistical folly called data mining - finding relationships that exist but have no real connection

Smart Money

---

databank ['deɪtəbæŋk] *noun* store of information in a computer

database ['deɪtəbeɪs] *noun* store of information in a large computer from which other types of information can be produced; ***we can extract the lists of potential customers from our database***

Datastream ['deɪtəstri:m] *noun* data system available online, giving information about securities, prices, stock exchange transactions, etc.

date [deɪt] **1** *noun* **(a)** number of day, month and year; ***I have received your letter of yesterday's date***; **date stamp** = rubber stamp for marking the date on letters received; **date of bill** = date when a bill will mature; **maturity date** = date when a government stock will mature; **date of receipt** = date when something is received; **date of record** *or* **record date** = date when a shareholder must be registered to qualify for a dividend; **return date** = date by which a company has to file its annual return with the Companies Registration Office **(b) to date** = up to now; **interest to date** = interest up to the present time; *see also* OUT-OF-DATE **2** *verb* to put a date on a document; ***the cheque was dated March 24th***; ***you forgot to date the cheque***; **to date a cheque forward** = to put a later date than the present one on a cheque

dated ['deɪtɪd] *adjective* with a date written on it; **dated securities** *or* **dated stocks** = securities with a date for redemption (as opposed to undated securities); **long-dated bill** = bill which is payable in more than three months' time now; **long-dated stocks** *or* **longs** = government stocks which mature in over fifteen years' time; **short-dated bill** = bill which is payable within a few days; **short-dated gilts** *or* **shorts** = government stocks which mature in less than five years time

dawn raid ['dɔ:n 'reɪd] *noun* sudden planned purchase of a large number of a company's shares at the beginning of a day's trading (up to 15% of a company's shares may be bought in this way, and the purchaser must wait for seven days before purchasing any more shares; it is assumed that a dawn raid is the first step towards a takeover of the target company)

DAX index ['dæks 'ındeks] = DEUTSCHE AKTIEN INDEX index of prices on the Frankfurt stock exchange

day [deı] *noun* **(a)** period of 24 hours; ***there are thirty days in June***; ***the first day of the month is a public holiday***; **settlement day** = (i) day when accounts have to be settled; (ii) account day, the day on which shares which have been bought must be paid for (usually a Monday ten days after the end of an account); **three clear days** = three whole working days; ***to give ten clear days' notice***; ***allow four clear days for the cheque to be paid into the bank***; *see also* GRACE; **day order** = order to a stockbroker to buy or sell on a certain day; **day trader** = trader who buys and sells the same futures on the same day **(b)** period of work from morning to night; **she took two days off** = she did not come to work for two days; **he works three days on, two days off** = he works for three days, then has two days' holiday; **to work an eight-hour day** = to spend eight hours at work each day; **day shift** = shift which works during the daylight hours such as from 8 a.m. to 5.30 p.m.; ***there are 150 men on the day shift***; ***he works the day shift***; **day release** = arrangement where a company allows a worker to go to college to study for one or two days each week; ***the junior sales manager is attending a day release course***

day book ['deı 'bʊk] *noun* book with an account of sales and purchases made each day

DCF = DISCOUNTED CASH FLOW

dead [ded] *adjective* not working; **dead account** = account which is no longer used; **dead loss** = total loss; ***the car was written off as a dead loss***; **dead money** = money which is not invested to make a profit; **dead season** = time of year when there are few tourists about

dead-cat bounce ['ded 'kæt 'baʊns] *noun* slight rise in a share price after a sharp fall, showing that some investors are still interested in buying the share at the lower price, although further sharp falls will follow

> COMMENT: called this because when dropped from a great height even a dead cat will bounce a little!

deadline ['dedlaın] *noun* date by which something has to be done; **to meet a deadline** = to finish something in time; ***we've missed our October 1st deadline***

deadlock ['dedlɒk] **1** *noun* point where two sides in a dispute cannot agree; ***the negotiations have reached a deadlock***; **to break a deadlock** = to find a way to start discussions again **2** *verb* to be unable to agree to continue discussing; **talks have been deadlocked for ten days** = after ten days the talks have not produced any agreement

deal [di:l] **1** *noun* business agreement or affair or contract; ***to arrange a deal*** *or* ***to set up a deal*** *or* ***to do a deal***; ***to sign a deal***; ***the sales director set up a deal with a Russian bank***; ***the deal will be signed tomorrow***; ***they did a deal with an American airline***; **to call off a deal** = to stop an agreement; ***when the chairman heard about the deal he called it off***; **cash deal** = sale done for cash; **package deal** = agreement where several different items are agreed at the same time; ***they agreed a package deal, which involves the construction of the factory, training of staff and purchase of the product*** **2** *verb* **(a) to deal with** = to organize; ***leave it to the filing clerk - he'll deal with it***; **to deal with an order** = to supply an order **(b)** to trade, to buy and sell; **to deal with someone** = to do business with someone; **to deal in leather** *or* **to deal in options** = to buy and sell leather or options; **he deals on the Stock Exchange** = his work involves buying and selling shares on the Stock Exchange for clients

dealer ['di:lə] *noun* **(a)** person who buys and sells; **foreign exchange dealer** = person who buys and sells foreign currencies; **retail dealer** = person who sells to the general public; **wholesale dealer** = person who sells in bulk to retailers **(b)** *(Stock Exchange)* person or firm that buys or sells on their own account, not on behalf of clients; **broker-dealer** = dealer who makes a market in shares (i.e. buys shares and holds them for resale) and also deals on behalf of investor clients

dealing ['di:lıŋ] *noun* **(a)** buying and selling on a Stock Exchange or commodities exchange; **dealing for the account** *or* **within the account** = buying shares and selling the same shares during an account, which means that the dealer has only to pay the difference between the price of the shares bought and the price obtained for them when they are sold; **fair dealing** = legal trade, legal buying and selling of shares; **foreign exchange dealing** = buying and selling foreign currencies; **forward dealings** = buying or selling commodities forward; **insider dealing** = illegal buying or selling of shares by staff of a company who have secret information about the company's plans; **option dealing** =

buying and selling share options; **dealing floor** *or* **trading floor** = (i) area of a broking house where dealing in securities is carried out by phone, using monitors to display current prices and stock exchange transactions; (ii) part of a stock exchange where dealers trade in securities (NOTE: American English for this is **pit**); **dealing-only broker** = broker who buys and sells shares for clients, but does not provide any advice and does not manage portfolios (as opposed to a full-service broker) **(b)** buying and selling goods; **to have dealings with someone** = to do business with someone

dear [dɪə] *adjective* expensive, costing a lot of money; ***property is very dear in this area***; **dear money** = money which has to be borrowed at a high interest rate, and so restricts expenditure by companies

death [deθ] *noun* act of dying; **death benefit** = insurance benefit paid to the family of someone who dies in an accident at work; **death in service** = insurance benefit or pension paid when someone dies while employed by a company; *US* **death duty** *or* **death taxes** = taxes paid on the property left by a dead person (NOTE: the British equivalent is **estate duty** *or* **inheritance tax**)

debenture [dɪˈbentʃə] *noun* acknowledgement of a debt issued by a limited company (debentures pay a fixed interest and are very long-dated; they use the company's assets as security); ***the bank holds a debenture on the company***; **convertible debenture** = debenture which can be converted into ordinary shares at a certain date; **mortgage debenture** = debenture where the loan is secured against the company's property; **debenture issue** *or* **issue of debentures** = borrowing money against the security of the company's assets; **debenture bond** = (i) certificate showing that a debenture has been issued; (ii) *US* unsecured loan; **debenture capital** = capital borrowed by a company, using its fixed assets as security; **debenture holder** = person who holds a debenture for money lent; **debenture register** *or* **register of debentures** = list of debenture holders of a company; **debenture stock** = stock in a company which is secured on the company's assets

> COMMENT: in the UK, debentures are always secured on the company's assets; in the USA, debenture bonds are not secured

debit [ˈdebɪt] **1** *noun* money which a company owes; **debits and credits** = money which a company owes and money it is due to receive; **debit balance** = balance in an account, showing that the company owes more money than it has received; **debit card** = plastic card, similar to a credit card, but which debits the holder's account immediately through an EPOS system; **debit column** = left-hand column in accounts showing the money paid or owed to others; **debit entry** = entry on the debit side of an account; **debit interest** = interest on debts, such as overdrafts; **debit side** = left-hand side of an account showing the money paid or owed to others; **debit note** = note showing that a customer owes money; ***we undercharged Mr Smith and had to send him a debit note for the extra amount***; **direct debit** = system where a customer allows a company to charge costs to his bank account automatically and where the amount charged can be increased or decreased with the agreement of the customer; ***I pay my electricity bill by direct debit*** **2** *verb* **to debit an account** = to charge an account with a cost; ***his account was debited with the sum of £25***

debitable [ˈdebɪtəbl] *adjective* which can be debited

debt [det] *noun* **(a)** (i) any money owed; (ii) money borrowed by a company to finance its activities; ***the company stopped trading with debts of over £1 million***; **to be in debt** = to owe money; **he is in debt to the tune of £250** = he owes £250; **to get into debt** = to start to borrow more money than you can pay back; **the company is out of debt** = the company does not owe money any more; **to pay back a debt** = to pay all the money owed; **to pay off a debt** = to finish paying money owed; **to reschedule a debt** = to arrange for the repayment of a debt to be put off to a later date; **to service a debt** = to pay interest on a debt; ***the company is having problems in servicing its debts***; **bad debt** = money owed which will never be paid back; ***the company has written off £30,000 in bad debts***; **secured debts** *or* **unsecured debts** = debts which are guaranteed or not guaranteed by assets; **debt collection** = collecting money which is owed; **debt collection agency** = company which collects debts for a commission; **debt collector** = person who collects debts; **debts due** = money owed which is due for repayment; **debt servicing** = payment of interest on a debt; **debt-service ratio** = the debts of a company shown as a percentage of its equity; **debt swap** = method of reducing exposure to a long-term Third World debt by selling it at a discount to another bank; *see also* COUNSELLING **(b)** **funded debt** = (i) short-term debt which has been converted into long-term by selling long-term securities such as debentures to raise the money; (ii) part of the British National Debt which pays interest, but where there is no date for repayment of the principal; **the National Debt** = money borrowed by a government

debt-convertible bond ['detkən'vɜːtəbl 'bɒnd] *noun* floating-rate bond which can be converted to a fixed rate of interest; *see also* DROPLOCK BOND

debtor ['detə] *noun* person who owes money; **debtor side** = debit side of an account; **debtor nation** = country whose foreign debts are larger than money owed to it by other countries

> the United States is now a debtor nation for the first time since 1914, owing more to foreigners than it is owed itself
>
> *Economist*

decelerate [diː'seləreɪt] *verb* to slow down

> certainly the economy is decelerating, but growth is a long way from turning negative
>
> *Investors Chronicle*

> the UK economy is at the uncomfortable stage in the cycle where two years of tight money are having the desired effect on demand: output is falling and unemployment is rising but headline inflation and earnings are showing no signs of decelerating
>
> *Sunday Times*

decile ['desaɪl] *noun* one of a series of nine figures below which one tenth or several tenths of the total fall

decimal ['desɪməl] *noun* **decimal system** = system based on the number 10; **correct to three places of decimals** = correct to three figures after the decimal point (e.g. 3.485)

decimalization [desɪməlaɪ'zeɪʃn] *noun* changing to a decimal system

decimalize ['desɪməlaɪz] *verb* to change to a decimal system

decimal point ['desɪməl 'pɔɪnt] *noun* dot which indicates the division between the whole unit and its smaller parts (such as 4.75)

> COMMENT: the decimal point is used in the UK and USA. In most European countries a comma is used to indicate a decimal, so 4,75% in Germany means 4.75% in the UK

declaration [deklə'reɪʃən] *noun* (i) any official statement; (ii) statement that someone is taking up an option; **declaration of bankruptcy** = official statement that someone is bankrupt; **declaration of income** = statement declaring income to the tax office; **customs declaration** = statement declaring goods brought into a country on which customs duty should be paid; **VAT declaration** = statement declaring VAT income to the VAT office

declare [dɪ'kleə] *verb* to make an official statement or to announce to the public; ***to declare someone bankrupt***; ***to declare a dividend of 10%***; **to declare goods to customs** = to state that you are importing goods which are liable to duty; ***the customs officials asked him if he had anything to declare***; **to declare an interest** = to state in public that you own shares in a company being discussed or that you are related to someone who can benefit from your contacts, etc.

declared [dɪ'kleəd] *adjective* which has been made public or officially stated; **declared value** = value of goods entered on a customs declaration

decline [di'klaɪn] **1** *noun* gradual fall; ***the decline in the value of the dollar***; ***a decline in buying power***; ***the last year has seen a decline in real wages*** **2** *verb* to fall slowly; ***shares declined in a weak market***; ***imports have declined over the last year***; ***the economy declined during the last government***

> Saudi oil production has declined by three quarters to around 2.5m barrels a day
>
> *Economist*

> this gives an average monthly decline of 2.15 per cent during the period
>
> *Business Times (Lagos)*

decrease 1 ['diːkriːs] *noun* fall or reduction; ***decrease in price***; ***decrease in value***; ***decrease in imports***; ***exports have registered a decrease***; ***sales show a 10% decrease on last year*** **2** [dɪ'kriːs] *verb* to fall or to become less; ***imports are decreasing***; ***the value of the pound has decreased by 5%***

deduct [dɪ'dʌkt] *verb* to remove money from a total; ***to deduct £3 from the price***; ***to deduct a sum for expenses***; ***after deducting costs the gross margin is only 23%***; ***expenses***

are still to be deducted; **tax deducted at source** = tax which is removed from a salary, interest payment or dividend payment before the money is paid

deductible [dɪ'dʌktəbl] *adjective* which can be deducted; **tax-deductible** = which can be deducted from an income before tax is paid; **these expenses are not tax-deductible** = tax has to be paid on these expenses

deduction [dɪ'dʌkʃən] *noun* removing of money from a total; money removed from a total; ***net salary is salary after deduction of tax and social security***; **deductions from salary** *or* **salary deductions** *or* **deductions at source** = money which a company removes from salaries to give to the government as tax, national insurance contributions, etc.; **tax deductions** = (i) money removed from a salary to pay tax; (ii) *US* business expenses which can be claimed against tax

deed [di:d] *noun* legal document, written agreement; **deed of arrangement** = document which sets out the agreement between a creditor and a debtor; **deed of assignment** = document which legally transfers a property from a debtor to a creditor; **deed of covenant** = signed legal agreement to pay someone a sum of money every year; **deed of partnership** = agreement which sets up a partnership; **deed of transfer** = document which transfers the ownership of shares; **title deeds** = document showing who owns a property; ***we have deposited the deeds of the house in the bank***

deep discount ['di:p 'dɪskaʊnt] *noun* very large discount; **deep-discount** *or* **deep-discounted bond** = Eurobond which is issued at a very large discount but which does not produce any interest; *compare* ZERO-COUPON; **deep-discounted rights issue** = rights issue where the new shares are priced at a very low price compared to their current market value

---

as the group's shares are already widely held, the listing will be via an introduction. It will also be accompanied by a deeply discounted £25m rights issue, leaving the company cash positive

Sunday Times

---

defalcation [di:fæl'keɪʃən] *noun* illegal use of money by someone who is not the owner but who has been trusted to look after it

default [dɪ'fɔ:lt] **1** *noun* failure to carry out the terms of a contract, especially failure to pay back a debt; **in default of payment** = with no payment made; **the company is in default** = the company has failed to carry out the terms of the contract; **by default** = because no one else will act; **he was elected by default** = he was elected because all the other candidates withdrew **2** *verb* to fail to carry out the terms of a contract, especially to fail to pay back a debt; **to default on payments** = not to make payments which are due under the terms of a contract

defaulter [dɪ'fɔ:ltə] *noun* person who defaults

defeasance [dɪ'fi:zəns] *noun* clause (in a collateral deed) which says that a contract or bond or recognizance will be revoked if something happens or if some act is performed

defence *US* **defense** [dɪ'fens] *noun* **(a)** protecting someone or something against attack, as defending a company against a takeover bid; ***the merchant bank is organizing the company's defence against the takeover bid***; **defence document** = document published by a company which is the subject of a takeover bid, saying why the bid should be rejected **(b)** fighting a lawsuit on behalf of a defendant; **defence counsel** = lawyer who represents the defendant in a lawsuit

defend [dɪ'fend] *verb* to fight to protect someone or something which is being attacked, such a company which is the subject of a takeover bid; ***the company is defending itself against the takeover bid***; ***he hired the best lawyers to defend him against the tax authorities***; **to defend a lawsuit** = to appear in court to state your case when accused of something; **defended takeover** *or* **contested takeover** = takeover where the board of the company do not recommend it to the shareholders and try to fight it

defendant [dɪ'fendənt] *noun* person who is sued or who is accused of doing something to harm someone

defensive shares *or* **defensive stocks** [dɪ'fensɪv 'ʃeəz or 'stɒks] *noun* shares which are not likely to fall in value because they are in stable market sectors, and which are therefore bought as protection against potential losses in more speculative investments

---

it was also a good time to adopt a more cautious investment stance by shifting into defensive investments, such as government gilts and corporate bonds

Sunday Times

defer [dɪ'fɜː] *verb* to put back to a later date, to postpone; ***to defer payment***; ***the decision has been deferred until the next meeting*** (NOTE: **deferring - deferred**)

deferment [dɪ'fɜːmənt] *noun* postponement, putting back to a later date; ***deferment of payment***; ***deferment of a decision***; ***deferment of taxes***

deferral [dɪ'fɜːrəl] *noun* postponement, putting back to a later date; ***tax deferral***

deferred [dɪ'fɜːd] *adjective* put back to a later date; **deferred coupon note** *or* **deferred interest bond** = bond where the interest is not paid immediately, but only after a certain date; **deferred creditor** = person who is owed money by a bankrupt but who is paid only after all other creditors; **deferred equity** = share ownership at a later date (i.e. as part of convertible loan stock); **deferred payment** = payment for goods by instalments over a long period; **deferred ordinary shares** *or* **deferred stock** = shares which receive a dividend after all other dividends have been paid; **deferred tax** = tax which may become payable at some later date

deficiency [dɪ'fɪʃənsi] *noun* lack; money lacking; ***there is a £10 deficiency in the petty cash***; **to make up a deficiency** = to put money into an account to balance it

deficit ['defɪsɪt] *noun* amount by which spending is higher than income; **the accounts show a deficit** = the accounts show a loss; **to make good a deficit** = to put money into an account to balance it; **balance of payments deficit** *or* **trade deficit** = situation when a country imports more than it exports and so pays out more in foreign currency than it earns; **deficit financing** = planning by a government to cover the shortfall between tax income and expenditure by borrowing money

defined [dɪ'faɪnd] *adjective* with specific aims; US **defined benefit plan** *or* **defined contribution plan** = pension plans set up by corporations for their employees

deflate [dɪ'fleɪt] *verb* **to deflate the economy** = to reduce activity in the economy by cutting the supply of money

deflation [dɪ'fleɪʃən] *noun* reduction in economic activity, resulting in falls in output, wages, prices, etc. (the opposite of inflation)

the real economy stands on the verge of deflation, amid wage cuts, layoffs, and a collapse in consumer spending

The Times

deflationary [dɪ'fleɪʃnəri] *adjective* which can cause deflation; ***the government has introduced some deflationary measures in the budget***

the strong dollar's deflationary impact on European economies as national governments push up interest rates

Duns Business Month

deflator [dɪ'fleɪtə] *noun* amount by which a country's GNP is reduced to take inflation into account; **domestic demand deflator** = figure used to remove inflation from the calculations for domestic demand

the domestic demand deflator - a measure which includes the prices of capital goods and government services as well as consumer prices - actually fell in the first quarter of this year

Investors Chronicle

defray [dɪ'freɪ] *verb* to provide money to pay (costs); ***the company agreed to defray the costs of the exhibition***

degearing [diː'gɪərɪŋ] *noun* reduction in gearing, reducing a company's loan capital in relation to the value of its ordinary shares

del credere [del 'kreɪdəri] *noun* amount added to a charge to cover the possibility of not being paid; **del credere agent** = agent who receives a high commission because he guarantees payment by customers

delinquency [dɪ'lɪŋkwənsi] *noun* US being overdue in payment of an account, an interest payment, etc.

delinquent [dɪ'lɪŋkwənt] *adjective* US (account or payment of tax) which is overdue

delist [diː'lɪst] *verb* to remove a company from a Stock Exchange listing (as when a company is 'taken private' when an individual investor buys all the shares)

the corporation said the National Association of Securities Dealers delisted its common stock from the NASDAQ system effective Monday, for failure to submit its annual report on time

Wall Street Journal

delisting [diːˈlɪstɪŋ] *noun* action of removing a company from a Stock Exchange listing

> two key factors fuelling the current delistings are the poor share prices achieved by small companies and a lack of interest from institutional investors
>
> *Accountancy*

deliver [dɪˈlɪvə] *verb* to transport goods to a customer; **goods delivered free** *or* **free delivered goods** = goods transported to the customer's address at a price which includes transport costs; **goods delivered on board** = goods transported free to the ship or plane but not to the customer's warehouse; **delivered price** = price which includes packing and transport

delivery [dɪˈlɪvəri] *noun* **(a) delivery of goods** = transport of goods to a customer's address; ***parcels awaiting delivery***; ***free delivery*** *or* ***delivery free***; ***delivery within 28 days***; ***allow 28 days for delivery***; ***delivery is not allowed for*** *or* ***is not included***; **delivery note** = list of goods being delivered, given to the customer with the goods; **delivery order** = instructions given by the customer to the person holding his goods, to tell him where and when to deliver them; **the store has a delivery service to all parts of the town** = the store will deliver goods to all parts of the town; **delivery time** = number of days before something will be delivered; **delivery van** = goods van for delivering goods to retail customers; **express delivery** = very fast delivery; **recorded delivery** = mail service where the letters are signed for by the person receiving them; ***we sent the documents (by) recorded delivery***; **cash on delivery (c.o.d.)** = payment in cash when the goods are delivered; **to take delivery of goods** = to accept goods when they are delivered; ***we took delivery of the stock into our warehouse on the 25th*** **(b)** goods being delivered; ***we take in three deliveries a day***; ***there were four items missing in the last delivery*** **(c)** transport of a commodity to a purchaser; **delivery month** = month in a futures contract when actual delivery will take place **(d)** transfer of a bill of exchange or other negotiable instrument to the bank which is due to make payment

delta shares *or* **delta securities** *or* **delta stocks** [ˈdeltə] *noun* shares in about 120 companies listed on the London Stock Exchange, but not on the SEAQ system because they are very rarely traded; *see also* ALPHA, BETA, GAMMA

demand [dɪˈmɑːnd] **1** *noun* **(a)** asking for payment; **payable on demand** = which must be paid when payment is asked for; **demand bill** = bill of exchange which must be paid when payment is asked for; **demand deposit** = money in a deposit account which can be taken out when you want it by writing a cheque; **demand draft** = draft which is to be paid immediately; **demand note** = promissory note which must be paid when it is presented; **final demand** = last reminder from a supplier, after which he will sue for payment **(b)** need for goods at a certain price; ***there was an active demand for oil shares on the stock market***; ***the factory had to cut production when demand slackened***; ***the office cleaning company cannot keep up with the demand for its services***; **to meet a demand** *or* **to fill a demand** = to supply what is needed; ***the factory had to increase production to meet the extra demand***; **there is not much demand for this item** = not many people want to buy it; **this book is in great demand** *or* **there is a great demand for this book** = many people want to buy it; **effective demand** = actual demand for a product which can be paid for; **demand price** = price at which a certain quantity of goods will be bought; **supply and demand** = amount of a product which is available and the amount which is wanted by customers; **law of supply and demand** = general rule that the amount of a product which is available is related to the needs of potential customers **2** *verb* to ask for something and expect to get it; ***she demanded a refund***; ***the suppliers are demanding immediate payment of their outstanding invoices***

> spot prices are now relatively stable in the run-up to the winter's peak demand
>
> *Economist*

> the demand for the company's products remained strong throughout the first six months of the year with production and sales showing significant increases
>
> *Business Times (Lagos)*

> growth in demand is still coming from the private rather than the public sector
>
> *Lloyd's List*

demand-led inflation *or* **demand-pull inflation** [dɪˈmɑːndˈled or dɪˈmɑːndˈpʊl ɪnˈfleɪʃn] *noun* inflation caused by rising demand which cannot be met (NOTE: the opposite is **cost-push inflation**)

demerge [diːˈmɜːdʒ] *verb* to separate a company into various separate parts

demerger [diːˈmɜːdʒə] *noun* separation of a company into several separate parts (especially used of a companies which have grown by acquisition)

demise [dɪˈmaɪz] *noun* **(a)** death; ***on his demise the estate passed to his daughter*** **(b)** granting of a property on a lease

demonetize [diːˈmʌnɪtaɪz] *verb* to stop a coin or note being used as money

demonetization [diːmʌnɪtaɪˈzeɪʃn] *noun* stopping a coin or note being used as money

demurrage [dɪˈmʌrɪdʒ] *noun* money paid to a customer when a shipment is delayed at a port or by customs

demutualization [diːmjuːtʃuəlaɪˈzeɪʃn] *noun* action of a mutual society, such as building society, in becoming a publicly owned corporation

> a deal could lead to demutualization benefits for its members
>
> *Investors Chronicle*

> the full effect of the demutualization bonuses cannot yet be determined
>
> *The Times*

demutualize [diːˈmjuːtʃuəlaɪz] *verb* to stop having mutual status, by becoming a Plc and selling shares to the general public on the stock market

> COMMENT: building societies, insurance companies, etc., have mutual status, that is they belong to their members, the people who have deposits with them, who invest in their pensions funds, or who borrow money from them. By floating on the stock exchange and becoming Plcs, they can act like any large company and borrow money to fund development or to acquire other companies. However, when a mutual society becomes a Plc or is bought by a Plc, its structure has to change. Its members become shareholders, and value is returned to them in the form of cash windfalls, free shares, etc.

> the insurer may be forced to demutualize after a warning that it must pay up to £1 billion in guaranteed annuities promised in the 1970s and 1980s
>
> *The Times*

denomination [dɪnɒmɪˈneɪʃən] *noun* unit of money (written on a coin, banknote or stamp); ***coins of all denominations***; ***small denomination notes***

department [dɪˈpɑːtmənt] *noun* **(a)** specialized section of a large company; ***she wrote to the complaints department***; ***he works in the design department***; **accounts department** = section which deals with money paid or received; **new issues department** = section of a bank which deals with issues of new shares; **personnel department** = section of a company dealing with the staff; **head of department** *or* **department head** *or* **department manager** = person in charge of a department **(b)** section of a large store selling one type of product; ***you will find beds in the furniture department***; **budget department** = department in a large store which sells cheaper goods **(c)** section of the British government containing several ministries; **the Department of Trade and Industry (DTI)** = British government department which supervises and regulates commercial dealings and promotes British trade overseas (NOTE: the person in charge of a government department is the **Secretary of State**)

departmental [diːpɑːtˈmentl] *adjective* referring to a department; **departmental manager** = manager of a department

department store [dɪˈpɑːtmənt ˈstɔː] *noun* large store with sections for different types of goods

deposit [dɪˈpɒzɪt] **1** *noun* **(a)** money placed in a bank for safe keeping and to earn interest; **certificate of deposit (CD)** = document from a bank showing that money has been deposited at a certain guaranteed interest rate for a certain period of time; **bank deposits** = all the money placed in banks; ***bank deposits are at an all-time high***; **fixed deposit** = deposit which pays a fixed interest over a fixed period; **deposit account** = bank account which pays interest but on which notice has to be given to withdraw money (NOTE: in the USA, called a **time deposit**); **deposit at 7 days' notice** = money deposited which you can withdraw by giving seven days' notice; **deposit slip** = piece of paper stamped by the cashier to prove that you have paid money into your account; **deposit-taking institution** *or* **licensed deposit-taker (LDT)** = institution such as a building society, bank or friendly society, which is licensed to receive money on deposit from private individuals and to pay interest on it **(b) safe deposit** = bank safe where you can leave jewellery or documents; **safe deposit box** = small box which you can rent, in which you can keep jewellery or documents in a bank's safe **(c)** money given in advance so that the thing which you want to buy will not be sold to someone else; ***to pay a deposit on a watch***; ***to leave £10 as deposit*** **2** *verb* **(a)** to put documents somewhere for safe keeping; ***to deposit shares with a bank***; ***we have deposited the deeds of the house with the bank***; ***he deposited his will with his solicitor*** **(b)** to put money into a bank account; ***to deposit £100 in a current account***

depositary [dɪ'pɒzɪtəri] *noun US* person or corporation which can place money or documents for safekeeping with a depository; *see also* AMERICAN DEPOSITARY RECEIPT (NOTE: do not confuse with **depository**)

depositor [dɪ'pɒzɪtə] *noun* person who deposits money in a bank, building society, etc.

depository [dɪ'pɒzɪtəri] *noun* **(a) furniture depository** = warehouse where you can store household furniture **(b)** bank or company with whom money or documents can be deposited (NOTE: do not confuse with **depositary**)

depreciate [dɪ'pri:ʃɪeɪt] *verb* **(a)** to reduce the value of assets in accounts; ***we depreciate our company cars over three years*** **(b)** to lose value; ***share which has depreciated by 10% over the year***; ***the pound has depreciated by 5% against the dollar***

> this involved reinvesting funds on items which could be depreciated against income for three years
>
> *Australian Financial Review*

> buildings are depreciated at two per cent per annum on the estimated cost of construction
>
> *Hongkong Standard*

depreciation [dɪpri:ʃɪ'eɪʃən] *noun* **(a)** reduction in value, writing down the capital value of an asset over a period of time in a company's accounts; **depreciation rate** = rate at which an asset is depreciated each year in the accounts; **accelerated depreciation** = system of depreciation which reduces the value of assets at a high rate in the early years to encourage companies, as a result of tax advantages, to invest in new equipment; **annual depreciation** = reduction in the book value of an asset at a certain rate per year; **historic cost depreciation** = depreciation based on the original cost of the asset; **replacement cost depreciation** = depreciation based on the actual cost of replacing the asset in the current year; **straight line depreciation** = depreciation calculated by dividing the cost of an asset by the number of years it is likely to be used **(b)** loss of value; ***a share which has shown a depreciation of 10% over the year***; ***the depreciation of the pound against the dollar***

depress [dɪ'pres] *verb* to reduce; ***reducing the money supply has the effect of depressing demand for consumer goods***

depressed [dɪ'prest] *adjective* **depressed area** = part of a country suffering from depression; **depressed market** = market where there are more goods than customers

depression [dɪ'preʃən] *noun* period of economic crisis with high unemployment and loss of trade; **the Great Depression** = the world economic crisis of 1929-1933; *compare* RECESSION

dept [dɪ'pɑ:tmənt] = DEPARTMENT

deregulate [di:'regjuleɪt] *verb* to remove government controls from an industry; ***the US government deregulated the banking sector in the 1980s***

deregulation [di:regju'leɪʃn] *noun* reducing government control over an industry; ***the deregulation of the airlines***

derivative instruments *or* **derivatives** [dɪ'rɪvətɪv 'ɪntrəmənts or dɪ'rɪvətɪvz] *noun* any forms of traded security, such as option contracts, which are derived from ordinary bonds and shares, exchange rates or stock market indices; **fixed-income derivatives** = derivatives which pay a fixed interest at stated dates in the future; **managed derivatives fund** = fund which uses mainly futures and options instead of investing in the underlying securities

> Paul announced that he had just quit his job trading fixed-income derivatives at a big Wall Street firm to go out on his own
>
> *Fortune*

> COMMENT: derivatives traded on stock exchanges or futures exchanges include options on futures or exchange rates or interest rate; while they can be seen as a way of hedging against possible swings in exchange rates or commodity prices, they can also produce huge losses if the market goes against the trader

descending tops [dɪ'sendɪŋ 'tɒps] *noun* term used by chartists to refer to a falling market, where each peak is lower than the one before

designate 1 ['dezɪgneɪt] *verb* to appoint someone to a post; ***she was designated chairman of the meeting*** **2** ['dezɪgnət] *adjective* person who has been appointed to a job but who has not yet started work; ***the chairman designate*** (NOTE: always follows a noun)

desk [desk] *noun* **(a)** writing table in an office, usually with drawers for stationery; ***desk diary***; ***desk drawer***; ***desk light***; **a three-drawer desk** = desk with three drawers; **desk pad** = pad of paper kept on a desk for writing notes **(b) cash desk** *or* **pay desk** = place in a store where you pay for goods bought; ***please pay at the desk*** **(c)** *US* section of a bank dealing with a particular type of business, such as the foreign exchange desk (NOTE: the British equivalent is **department**) **(d)** section of a newspaper; **the City desk** = the department of a British newspaper which deals with business news

destabilize [dɪ'steɪbɪlaɪz] *verb* to make something less stable; ***the comments by the speculators were aimed at destabilizing the country's economy***

destabilizing [dɪ'steɪbɪlaɪzɪŋ] *adjective* which makes something less stable

---

the report recognised the destabilizing influence that short-term capital flows - invariably speculative by nature - have on emerging economies and the millions of people whose lives suffer in the aftermath

Money Observer

---

detailed account ['di:teɪld ə'kaʊnt] *noun* account which lists every item

determine [dɪ'tɜ:mɪn] *verb* to fix, to arrange, to decide; ***to determine prices*** *or* ***quantities***; ***conditions still to be determined***

Deutschmark *or* **mark** ['dɔɪtʃmɑ:k or mɑ:k] *noun* currency used with the euro in Germany (NOTE: also called a **mark;** when used with a figure, usually written **DM** before the figure: **DM250:** say 'two hundred and fifty Deutschmarks')

devalue [di:'vælju:] *verb* to reduce the value of a currency against other currencies; ***the pound has been devalued by 7%***; ***the government has devalued the pound by 7%***

devaluation [di:vælju'eɪʃən] *noun* reduction in value of a currency against other currencies; ***the devaluation of the rouble***

develop [dɪ'veləp] *verb* **(a)** to plan and produce; ***to develop a new product*** **(b)** to plan and build an area; ***to develop an industrial estate***

developer [dɪ'veləpə] *noun* **a property developer** = person who plans and builds a group of new houses or new factories, or who renovates old buildings

developing country *or* **developing nation** [dɪ'veləpɪŋ'kʌntrɪ or dɪ'veləpɪŋ'neɪʃən] *noun* country which is not fully industrialized

development [dɪ'veləpmənt] *noun* **(a)** planning the production of a new product; ***research and development*** **(b) industrial development** = planning and building of new industries in special areas; **property development** = renovating old buildings or building new ones on their sites, seen as a business activity; **development area** *or* **development zone** = area which has been given special help from a government to encourage businesses and factories to be set up there

deviate ['di:vieɪt] *verb* to turn away from what is normal or usual

deviation [di:vi'eɪʃn] *noun* changing from what is normal or usual; **standard deviation** = measure of how much a bond's yield deviates from its average yield; ***the standard deviation of bond yields this year is just 0.08%, compared with a 0.84% deviation so far in the 1990s***

devise [dɪ'vaɪz] *noun* giving freehold land to someone in your will; *compare* BEQUEST

differential [dɪfə'renʃəl] **1** *adjective* which shows a difference; **differential tariffs** = different tariffs for different classes of goods (as, for example, when imports from certain countries are taxed more heavily than similar imports from other countries) **2** *noun* **price differential** = difference in price between products in a range; **wage differentials** = differences in salary between workers in similar types of jobs; **to erode wage differentials** = to reduce differences in salary gradually

difficulty ['dɪfɪkʌlti] *noun see also* FINANCIAL

digit ['dɪdʒɪt] *noun* single number; ***a seven-digit phone number***; **double-digit** = more than 10 and less than 100

---

they look for companies with double-digit earnings increases

Smart Money

---

digital ['dɪdʒɪtl] *adjective* **digital clock** = clock which shows the time as a series of figures (such as 12:05:23); **digital computer**

= computer which calculates on the basis of numbers

diligence ['dɪlɪdʒəns] *noun see* DUE DILIGENCE

dilute [daɪ'lu:t] *verb* to make less valuable; ***conversion of the loan stock will dilute the assets per share by 5%***; **fully diluted shares** = total number of shares which includes convertible shares, stock options, etc.; **fully diluted earnings per share** = earnings per share calculated over the whole number of shares assuming that convertible shares have been converted to ordinary shares

> employees now own or control nearly one-fourth of all fully diluted shares
>
> *Smart Money*

> the net asset value is fully diluted
>
> *Barron's*

dilution [daɪ'lu:ʃən] *noun* **dilution of equity** *or* **of shareholding** = situation where the ordinary share capital of a company has been increased but without an increase in the assets, so that each share is worth less than before; **dilution levy** = extra charge levied by fund managers on investors buying or selling units in a fund, to offset any potential effect on the value of the fund of such sales or purchases

> the company's sky-high price/earnings ratio and the ongoing dilution caused by its huge stock options program haven't deterred investors
>
> *Barron's*

> there are only very few cases when a dilution levy would be required. My concern is that investment companies may believe otherwise
>
> *The Times*

dime [daɪm] *noun US (informal)* ten cent coin

diminish [dɪ'mɪnɪʃ] *verb* to become smaller; ***our share of the market has diminished over the last few years***; **law of diminishing returns** = general rule that as more factors of production (land, labour and capital) are added to the existing factors, so the amount they produce is proportionately smaller

dinar ['di:nɑ:] *noun* unit of currency used in many countries (including Bosnia, Macedonia, Yugoslavia, and many Arabic countries: Algeria, Bahrain, Iraq, Jordan, Kuwait, Libya, Tunisia, South Yemen and Sudan); **Arab accounting dinar (AAD)** = unit used for accounting purposes between member countries of the Arab Monetary Fund

dip [dɪp] **1** *noun* sudden small fall; ***last year saw a dip in the company's performance*** **2** *verb* to fall in price; ***shares dipped sharply in yesterday's trading*** (NOTE: **dipping - dipped**)

direct [daɪ'rekt] **1** *verb* to manage or to organize; ***he directs our South-East Asian operations***; ***she was directing the development unit until last year*** **2** *adjective* straight, with no interference; **direct business** = insurance business transacted between an insurance company and the person taking out the insurance (without going through a broker); **direct cost** = production cost of a product; **direct paper** = financial paper sold direct to investors; **direct selling** = selling a product direct to the customer without going through a shop; **direct share ownership** = ownership of shares by private individuals, buying or selling through brokers, and not via holdings in unit trusts; **direct taxation** = tax, such as income tax, which is paid direct to the government; ***the government raises more money by direct taxation than by indirect*** **3** *adverb* straight, with no third party involved; ***we pay income tax direct to the government***; **to dial direct** = to contact a phone number yourself without asking the operator to do it for you; ***you can dial New York direct from our office if you want***

direct debit ['daɪrekt 'debɪt] *noun* system where a customer allows a company to charge costs to his bank account automatically and where the amount charged can be increased or decreased with the agreement of the customer

direction [daɪ'rekʃən] *noun* **(a)** organizing or managing; ***he took over the direction of a multinational group*** **(b) directions for use** = instructions showing how to use something

directive [də'rektɪv] *noun* order or command to someone to do something (especially an order from the Council of Ministers or the Commission of the European Community referring to a particular problem in certain countries); ***the Commission issued a directive on food prices***; **working-time directive** = directive concerning the maximum number of hours an employee can work in the EU

> the EU has adopted a working-time directive
>
> *Evening Standard*

directly [daɪ'rektli] *adverb* straight, with no third party involved; ***we deal directly with the insurers, without using a broker***

direct mail ['daɪrekt 'meɪl] *noun* selling a product by sending publicity material to possible buyers through the post; ***these calculators are only sold by direct mail***; ***the company runs a successful direct-mail operation***; **direct-mail advertising** = advertising by sending leaflets to people through the post

director [daɪ'rektə] *noun* **(a)** person appointed by the shareholders to help run a company; **managing director** = director who is in charge of the whole company; **chairman and managing director** = managing director who is also chairman of the board of directors; **board of directors** = (i) *GB* group of directors elected by the shareholders to run a company; (ii) *US* group of people elected by the shareholders to draw up company policy and to appoint the president and other executive officers who are responsible for managing the company; **directors' report** = annual report from the board of directors to the shareholders; **directors' salaries** = salaries of directors (which have to be listed in the company's profit and loss account); **associate director** = director who attends board meetings but has not been elected by the shareholders; **executive director** = director who actually works full-time in the company; **non-executive director** = director who attends board meetings only to give advice; **outside director** = director who is not employed by the company **(b)** person who is in charge of a project, an official institute, etc.; ***the director of the government research institute***; ***she was appointed director of the organization***

> COMMENT: directors are elected by shareholders at the AGM, though they are usually chosen by the chairman or chief executive. A board will consist of a chairman (who may be non- executive), a chief executive or managing director, and a series of specialist directors in change of various activities of the company (such as production director or sales director). The company secretary will attend board meetings, but may not be a director. Apart from the executive directors, who are in fact employees of the company, there may be several non-executive directors, appointed either for their expertise and contacts, or as representatives of important shareholders such as banks. The board of an American company may be made up of a large number of non-executive directors and only one or two executive officers; a British board has more executive directors

> the research director will manage and direct a team of business analysts reporting on the latest developments in retail distribution throughout the UK
>
> *Times*

directorate [daɪ'rektərət] *noun* group of directors

directorship [daɪ'rektəʃɪp] *noun* post of director; ***he was offered a directorship with Smith Ltd***

> what benefits does the executive derive from his directorship? In the first place compensation has increased sharply in recent years
>
> *Duns Business Month*

directory [daɪ'rektəri] *noun* list of people or businesses with information about their addresses and telephone numbers; **classified directory** = list of businesses grouped under various headings, such as computer shops or newsagents; **commercial directory** *or* **trade directory** = book which lists all the businesses and business people in a town; **street directory** = list of people living in a street; map of a town which lists all the streets in alphabetical order in an index; **telephone directory** = book which lists all people and businesses in alphabetical order with their phone numbers; ***to look up a number in the telephone directory***; ***his number is in the London directory***

dirham ['dɪəræm] *noun* currency used in Morocco and the United Arab Emirates

dirty float ['dɜ:ti 'fləʊt] *noun* floating a currency, where the government intervenes to regulate the exchange rate; *compare* CLEAN FLOAT (NOTE: also called a **managed float**)

disallow [dɪsə'laʊ] *verb* not to accept a claim for insurance; ***he claimed £2,000 for fire damage, but the claim was disallowed***

disburse [dɪs'bɜ:s] *verb* to pay money

disbursement [dɪs'bɜ:smənt] *noun* payment of money

> dividend amounts are annual disbursements based on the last quarterly, semiannual or annual declared dividend rate
>
> *Barron's*

discharge [dɪs'tʃɑ:dʒ] **1** *noun* **(a)** **discharge in bankruptcy** *US* **discharge of bankruptcy** = being released from bankruptcy after paying your debts **(b)** payment of debt; **in full discharge of a debt** = paying a debt completely; **final discharge** = final payment of what is left of a debt **(c) in discharge of his duties as director** = carrying out his duties as director **2** *verb* **(a) to discharge a bankrupt** = to release someone from bankruptcy because he has paid his debts **(b) to discharge a debt** *or* **to discharge your liabilities** = to pay a debt or your liabilities in full **(c)** to dismiss or to sack; ***to discharge an employee***

disciplinary procedure [dɪsɪˈplɪnəri prəˈsiːdʒə] *noun* way of warning a worker officially that he is breaking rules or that he is working badly

disclaimer [dɪsˈkleɪmə] *noun* legal refusal to accept responsibility

disclose [dɪsˈkləʊz] *verb* to tell details; ***the bank has no right to disclose details of my account to the tax office***

disclosure [dɪsˈkləʊʒə] *noun* act of telling details; ***the disclosure of the takeover bid raised the price of the shares***; **disclosure of shareholding** = making public the fact that someone owns shares in a company (if someone owns or buys 5% of the shares in a listed company, this holding must be declared to the Stock Exchange)

discount [ˈdɪskaʊnt] **1** *noun* **(a)** percentage by which a full price is reduced to a buyer by the seller; ***to give a discount on bulk purchases***; **to sell goods at a discount** *or* **at a discount price** = to sell goods below the normal price; **basic discount** = normal discount without extra percentages; ***we give 25% as a basic discount, but can add 5% for cash payment***; **quantity discount** = discount given to people who buy large quantities; **10% discount for quantity purchases** = you pay 10% less if you buy a large quantity; **10% discount for cash** *or* **10% cash discount** = you pay 10% less if you pay in cash; **trade discount** = discount given to a customer in the same trade **(b) discount broker** = broker who deals for a smaller commission than other brokers; **discount house** = (i) financial company which specializes in buying and selling bills at a discount, using money which has been borrowed short-term from commercial banks to finance the operation; (ii) shop which specializes in selling cheap goods bought at a high discount; **discount market** = market for borrowing and lending money, through Treasury bills, certificates of deposit, etc.; **discount rate** = percentage taken when a bank discounts bills; **discount store** = shop which specializes in cheap goods bought at a high discount; *US* **discount window** = way in which the Federal Reserve grants loans to a bank by giving advances on the security of Treasury bills which the bank is holding **(c)** amount by which something is sold for less than its value; **currency at a discount** = currency whose future value is less than its spot value; **shares which stand at a discount** = shares which are lower in price than their asset value or their par value (NOTE: the opposite are shares which are **at a premium**) **2** *verb* **(a)** to reduce prices to increase sales **(b) to discount bills of exchange** = to buy bills of exchange for less than the value written on them in order to cash them later; **discounted value** = difference between the face value of a share and its lower market price **(c)** to react to something which may happen in the future (such as a possible takeover bid or currency devaluation); **shares are discounting a rise in the dollar** = shares have risen in advance of a rise in the dollar price

---

pressure on the Federal Reserve Board to ease monetary policy and possibly cut its discount rate mounted yesterday

Financial Times

---

banks refrained from quoting forward US/Hongkong dollar exchange rates as premiums of 100 points replaced the previous day's discounts of up to 50 points

South China Morning Post

---

discountable [dɪsˈkaʊntəbl] *adjective* which can be discounted; ***these bills are not discountable***

discounted cash flow (DCF) [dɪsˈkaʊntɪd ˈkæʃ ˈfləʊ] *noun* calculating the forecast return on capital investment by discounting future cash flows from the investment, usually at a rate equivalent to the company's minimum required rate of return

> COMMENT: Discounting is necessary because it is generally accepted that money held today is worth more than money to be received in the future. The effect of discounting is to reduce future income or expenses to their 'present value'. Once discounted, future cash flows can be compared directly with the initial cost of a capital investment which is already stated in present value terms. If the present value of income is greater than the present value of costs the investment can be said to be worthwhile

discounter [dɪs'kaʊntə] *noun* person or company that discounts bills or sells goods at a discount

> The magic of the company is that it combines the cost structure of a discounter and the brands of a department store
>
> *Fortune*

> a 100,000 square-foot warehouse generates ten times the volume of a discount retailer; it can turn its inventory over 18 times a year, more than triple a big discounter's turnover
>
> *Duns Business Month*

discrepancy [dɪs'krepənsi] *noun* situation where totals do not add up correctly in accounts; ***there is a discrepancy in the accounts***; **statistical discrepancy** = amount by which sets of figures differ

discretion [dɪs'kreʃən] *noun* being able to decide correctly what should be done; **I leave it to your discretion** = I leave it for you to decide what to do; **at the discretion of someone** = if someone decides; ***membership is at the discretion of the committee***

discretionary [dɪs'kreʃənəri] *adjective* which can be done if someone wants; **the minister's discretionary powers** = powers which the minister could use if he thought he should do so; **discretionary account** = a client's account with a stockbroker, where the broker invests and sells at his own discretion without the client needing to give him specific instructions; **on a discretionary basis** = way of managing a client's funds, where the fund manager uses his discretion to do as he wants, without the client giving him any specific instructions; **discretionary client** = client whose funds are managed on a discretionary basis; **discretionary funds** = funds managed on a discretionary basis

> churning is most common with portfolios managed on a discretionary basis where clients leave all the investment decisions to their adviser
>
> *Guardian*

diseconomies of scale [dɪsi:'kɒnəmi:z əv 'skeɪl] *noun* situation where increased production actually increases unit cost

> COMMENT: after having increased production using the existing workforce and machinery, giving economies of scale, the company finds that in order to increase production further it has to employ more workers and buy more machinery, leading to an increase in unit cost

disenfranchise [dɪsɪn'fræntʃaɪz] *verb* to take away someone's right to vote; ***the company has tried to disenfranchise the ordinary shareholders***

disequilibrium [dɪsi:kwɪ'lɪbriəm] *noun* situation which is not stable (as when a country's balance of payments is in deficit)

dishonour *US* **dishonor** [dɪs'ɒnə] *verb* **to dishonour a bill** = not to pay a bill; **dishonoured cheque** = cheque which the bank will not pay because there is not enough money in the account to pay it

disinflation [dɪsɪn'fleɪʃən] *noun* reducing inflation in the economy by increasing tax, reducing the level of money supply, etc.

disinflationary [dɪsɪn'fleɪʃənəri] *adjective* which reduces the level of inflation in the economy

> last year was particularly brutal, as central bank gold sales, short-selling, and the disinflationary effects of the Asian crisis combined to knock gold down 20%
>
> *Fortune*

disintermediation [dɪsɪntəmi:di'eɪʃn] *noun* **(a)** cutting out intermediaries, as when lenders lend money direct to a borrower **(b)** situation when investors remove their money from deposit accounts and invest directly in the stock market (NOTE: the opposite is **reintermediation**)

> the resulting new financial environment can be characterized as a process of competition-driven disintermediation from banking systems into securitized money and capital markets
>
> *The Banker*

disinvest [dɪsɪn'vest] *verb* **(a)** to reduce investment by selling shares **(b)** to reduce investment by not replacing capital assets when they wear out

> it is always a good idea to disinvest capital in businesses that produce subpar returns on capital
>
> *Fortune*

disinvestment [dɪsɪn'vestmənt] *noun* **(a)** reducing investments by selling shares **(b)** reduction in capital assets by not replacing them when they wear out

disk [dɪsk] *noun* round flat plate, used to store information in computers; **floppy disk** = small disk for storing information through a computer; **hard disk** = solid disk in a sealed case which will store a large amount of computer information; **disk drive** = part of a computer which makes a disk spin round in order to read it or store information on it

diskette [dɪs'ket] *noun* small floppy disk

disposable [dɪs'pəʊzəbl] *adjective* **disposable personal income** = income left after tax and national insurance have been deducted (also called 'take-home' pay)

disposal [dɪs'pəʊzəl] *noun* sale; ***disposal of securities** or **of property***; **lease** *or* **business for disposal** = lease or business for sale

dispose [dɪs'pəʊz] *verb* **to dispose of** = to get rid of, to sell cheaply; ***to dispose of excess stock***; ***to dispose of your business***

disqualify [dɪs'kwɒlɪfaɪ] *verb* to make a person unqualified to do something, such as to be a director of a company

disqualification [dɪskwɒlɪfɪ'keɪʃn] *noun* making someone disqualified to do something

> Even 'administrative offences' can result in disqualification. A person may be disqualified for up to five years following persistent breach of company legislation in terms of failing to file returns, accounts and other documents with the Registrar
>
> *Accountancy*

dissolve [dɪ'zɒlv] *verb* to bring to an end; ***to dissolve a partnership** or **a company***

dissolution [dɪsə'lu:ʃən] *noun* ending (of a partnership)

distrain [dɪs'treɪn] *verb* to seize goods to pay for debts

distress [dɪ'stres] *noun* **distress merchandise** = goods sold cheaply to pay a company's debts; **distress sale** = sale of goods at low prices to pay a company's debts; **distress securities fund** = type of fund which invests in companies where there may be a major problems

distressed [dɪ'strest] *adjective* **distressed companies** = companies which may go into liquidation, and whose shares are seen as a speculative buy

distributable profits [dɪ'strɪbju:təbl 'prɒfɪts] *noun* profits which can be distributed to shareholders as dividends if the directors decide to do so

distribute [dɪ'strɪbju:t] *verb* **(a)** to share out dividends; **distributed profits** = profits passed to shareholders in the form of dividends **(b)** to send out goods from a manufacturer's warehouse to retail shops; ***Smith Ltd distributes for several smaller companies***

distribution [dɪstrɪ'bju:ʃən] *noun* **(a)** act of sending goods from the manufacturer to the wholesaler and then to retailers; ***distribution costs***; ***distribution manager***; **channels of distribution** *or* **distribution channels** = ways of sending goods from the manufacturer to the retailer; **distribution network** = series of points or small warehouses from which goods are sent all over a country **(b) distribution slip** = paper attached to a document or a magazine showing all the people in an office who should read it **(c) distribution of income** = payment of dividends to shareholders

distributive trades [dɪs'trɪbjʊtɪv 'treɪdz] *noun* businesses involved in the distribution of goods for sale

> the first clue will come with the publication of the CBI distributive trades survey on Thursday, but the official sales figures will not be published until January 21
>
> *The Times*

distributor [dɪ'strɪbjʊtə] *noun* company which sells and sends out goods for another company which makes them; **sole distributor** = retailer who is the only one in an area who is allowed by the manufacturer to sell a certain product; **a network of distributors** = a series of distributors spread all over a country

distributorship [dɪ'strɪbjʊtəʃɪp] *noun* position of being a distributor for a company

diversification [daɪvɜ:sɪfɪ'keɪʃən] *noun* (i) adding another quite different type of business to a firm's existing trade; (ii) placing money in a wide spread of investments; **product diversification** *or* **diversification into new products** = adding new types of products to the range already made

diversify [daɪ'vɜ:sɪfaɪ] *verb* **(a)** to add new types of business to existing ones; ***to diversify into new products*** **(b)** to invest in different types of shares or savings so as to spread the risk of loss

divest [daɪ'vest] *verb* **to divest oneself of something** = to get rid of something; ***the company had divested itself of its US interests***

divestiture [daɪ'vestitʃə] *noun* sale of an asset

dividend ['dɪvɪdend] *noun* part of a company's profits paid to shareholders; **to raise** *or* **to increase the dividend** = to pay out a higher dividend than in the previous year; **to maintain the dividend** = to keep the same dividend as in the previous year; **to pass the dividend** *US* **to omit the dividend** = to pay no dividend; **final dividend** = dividend paid at the end of a year's trading, which has to be approved by the shareholders at an AGM; **gross dividend per share** = dividend per share paid before tax is deducted; **interim dividend** = dividend paid at the end of a half-year; **dividend check;** *see* DIVIDEND WARRANT; **dividend cover** = the ratio of profits to dividends paid to shareholders; **the dividend is covered four times** = the profits are four times the dividend; **dividend forecast** = forecast of the amount of an expected dividend; **forecast dividend** *or* **prospective dividend** = dividend which a company expects to pay at the end of the current year; **dividend per share** = amount of money paid as dividend for each share held; **dividend warrant** = cheque which makes payment of a dividend (NOTE: the American equivalent is **dividend check**); **dividend yield** = dividend expressed as a percentage of the current market price of a share; **cum dividend** = share sold with the dividend still to be paid; **ex dividend** = share sold after the dividend has been paid; **the shares are quoted ex dividend** = the share price does not include the right to the dividend

> a dividend is a cut of the profits given to shareholders on a yearly basis
>
> *The Times*

DM *or* **D-Mark** = DEUTSCHMARK

doctor ['dɒktə] *noun* specialist who examines people when they are sick to see how they can be made well; ***the staff are all sent to see the company doctor once a year***; **doctor's certificate** = document written by a doctor to say that a worker is ill and cannot work; **company doctor** = (i) doctor who works for a company and looks after sick workers; (ii) specialist businessman who rescues businesses which are in difficulties

document ['dɒkjumənt] *noun* paper with writing on it; **documents against acceptance** = note to a bank to instruct that documents attached to a draft should be given to the drawee when the draft is accepted; **formal documents** = documents giving full details of a takeover bid (the official timetable for the bid starts with the sending out of the formal documents); **document image processing** = system for scanning documents, such as cheques, and storing the information in a retrieval system

documentary [dɒkju'mentəri] *adjective* in the form of documents; ***documentary evidence***; ***documentary proof***; **documentary credit** = credit document used in export trade, when a bank issues a letter of credit against shipping documents

documentation [dɒkjumen'teɪʃən] *noun* all documents referring to something; ***please send me the complete documentation concerning the sale***

dollar ['dɒlə] *noun* **(a)** unit of currency used in the USA and other countries, such as Australia, Bahamas, Barbados, Bermuda, Brunei, Canada, Fiji, Hong Kong, Jamaica, New Zealand, Singapore, Zimbabwe; ***the US dollar rose 2%***; ***the book fifty Canadian dollars***; ***they charged my six Australian dollars for a cup of coffee***; **East Caribbean dollar** = currency used in Antigua, Dominica, Grenada, Montserrat, St Lucia and St Vincent **(b)** *(in particular)* the currency used in the USA; **five dollar bill** = banknote for five dollars; **dollar area** = area of the world where the US dollar is the main trading currency; **dollar balances** = a country's trade balances expressed in US dollars; **dollar cost averaging;** *see* AVERAGING; **dollar crisis** = fall in the exchange rate for the US dollar; **dollar gap** *or* **dollar shortage** = situation where the supply of US dollars is not enough to satisfy the demand for them from overseas buyers; **dollar stocks** = shares in US companies (NOTE: usually written $ before a figure: **$250.** The currencies used in different countries can be shown by the initial letter of the country: **C$** (Canadian dollar) **A$** (Australian dollar), etc.))

domestic [də'mestɪk] *adjective* referring to the home market, to the market of the country where the business is situated; ***domestic sales***; ***domestic turnover***; **domestic consumption** = consumption on the home market; ***domestic consumption of oil has fallen sharply***; **domestic interest rates** = interest rates payable in a local currency on deposits placed in that country; **domestic market** = market in the country where a company is based; ***they produce goods for the domestic market***; **domestic production** = production of goods for domestic consumption

domicile ['dɒmɪsaɪl] **1** *noun* place where someone lives or where a company's office is registered **2** *verb* **he is domiciled in Denmark** = he lives in Denmark officially; **bills domiciled in France** = bills of exchange which have to be paid in France

> although hedge funds are mostly domiciled in offshore tax havens such as the Cayman Islands and the British Virgin Islands, London is becoming a major centre for the management companies which advise on fund portfolios
>
> *Money Observer*

dong [dɒŋ] *noun* currency used in Vietnam

dormant ['dɔːmənt] *adjective* not active; **dormant account** = bank account which is not used (NOTE: the opposite, an account which is used, is an **active account**)

double ['dʌbl] **1** *adjective* **(a)** twice as large, two times the size; ***their turnover is double ours***; **to be on double time** = to earn twice the usual wages for working on Sundays or other holidays; **double-entry bookkeeping** = system of bookkeeping where both credit and debit sides of an account are noted; **double option** = option to buy or sell at a certain price in the future (a combination of call and put options); **double taxation** = taxing the same income twice; **double taxation agreement** = agreement between two countries that a person living in one country shall not be taxed in both countries on the income earned in the other country **(b) in double figures** *or* **double-digit** = with two figures, between 10 to 99; ***inflation is in double figures***; ***we have had double-figure*** *or* ***double-digit inflation for some years*** **2** *verb* to become twice as big; to make something twice as big; ***we have doubled our profits this year*** *or* ***our profits have doubled this year***; ***the company's borrowings have doubled***

> the returns on a host of risk-free investments have been well into double figures
>
> *Money Observer*

> they look for companies with double-digit earnings increases
>
> *Smart Money*

doubtful ['daʊtfəl] *adjective* which is not certain; **doubtful loan** = loan which may never be repaid

Dow [ðə 'daʊ] *(informal)* **the Dow** = DOW JONES INDEX, DOW JONES INDUSTRIAL AVERAGE; **the Dow 30** = DOW JONES INUSTRIAL AVERAGE; **Dogs of the Dow** = the ten highest-yielding stocks from the Dow 30 that are supposed to do well over long periods

Dow Jones Index [daʊ 'dʒəʊnz 'ɪndeks] any of several indices published by the Dow Jones Co., based on prices on the New York Stock Exchange

> COMMENT: the main index is the Dow Jones Industrial Average (see below). Other Dow Jones indexes are the Dow Jones 20 Transportation Average; Dow Jones 15 Utility Average; Dow Jones 65 Composite Average (formed of the Industrial average the Transportation Average and the Utility Average taken together and averaged); also the Dow Jones Global-US Index is a capitalization weighted index based on June 30, 1982 = 100. A new European-based index is the Dow Jones Euro Stoxx 50 Index, comprising fifty blue-chip companies from various European countries

Dow Jones Industrial Average (DJIA) [daʊ'dʒəʊnz ɪn'dʌstrɪəl 'ævrɪdʒ] index of share prices on the New York Stock Exchange, based on a group of thirty major corporations; ***the Dow Jones Average rose ten points***; ***general optimism showed in the rise on the Dow Jones Average*** (NOTE: also called the **Dow 30**)

down [daʊn] *adverb & preposition* in a lower position or to a lower position; ***the inflation rate is gradually coming down***; ***shares are slightly down on the day***; ***the price of petrol has gone down***; **to pay money down** = to make a deposit; ***he paid £50 down and the rest in monthly instalments***

downgrade [daʊn'greɪd] *verb* (i) to reduce the forecast for a share; (ii) to reduce the credit rating for a bond

down market ['daʊn 'mɑːkɪt] **1** *adverb & adjective* cheaper, appealing to a less wealthy section of the population; ***the company has adopted a down-market image***; **the company has decided to go down market** = the company has decided to make products which appeal to a wider section of the public **2** *noun* stock market which is falling (NOTE: the opposite is an **up market**)

> how your emerging growth fund performs in a down market is just as important as in an up market
>
> *Smart Money*

down payment ['daʊn 'peɪmənt] *noun* part of a total payment made in advance; ***he made a down payment of $100***

downside ['daʊnsaɪd] *noun* **downside factor** *or* **downside potential** = possibility of making a loss (in an investment); **downside risk** = risk that an investment will fall in value (NOTE: the opposite is **upside**)

> stocks that we believe have limited downside risk
>
> *Smart Money*

> daily trading volumes on the major markets suggest there was no great avalanche of selling; but there was little or no buying either, and hence no support on the downside
>
> *Financial Times Review*

downstream ['daʊnstri:m] *adjective* referring to the operations of a company at the end of a process (as selling petrol through garages as an operation of a petroleum company); *compare* UPSTREAM

downswing ['daʊnswɪŋ] *noun* downward movement of share prices (NOTE: the opposite is **upswing**)

downtick ['daʊntɪk] *noun US* price of stock sold which is lower than the price of the previous sale

down time ['daʊn 'taɪm] *noun* time when a machine is not working because it is broken or being mended, etc.; time when a worker cannot work because machines have broken down, because components are not available, etc.

downtown ['daʊntaʊn] *noun & adverb* in the central business district of a town; ***his office is in downtown Philadelphia***; ***a downtown store***; ***they established a business downtown***

down trend ['daʊn 'trend] *noun* falling trend in prices; ***the price per chip has been in a long-term down trend***

downturn ['daʊntɜ:n] *noun* movement towards lower prices or sales or profits; ***a downturn in the market price***; ***the last quarter saw a downturn in the economy***

dozen ['dʌzn] *noun* twelve; ***to sell in sets of one dozen***; **cheaper by the dozen** = the product is cheaper if you buy twelve at a time

Dr *abbreviation for* drachma

drachma ['drækmə] currency used in Greece (NOTE: usually written **Dr** before a figure: **Dr22bn**)

draft [drɑ:ft] **1** *noun* **(a)** order for money to be paid by a bank; **banker's draft** = draft payable by a bank in cash on presentation; **to make a draft on a bank** = to ask a bank to pay money for you; **sight draft** = bill of exchange which is payable when it is presented **(b)** first rough plan or document which has not been finished; ***draft of a contract*** *or* ***draft contract***; ***he drew up the draft agreement on the back of an envelope***; ***the first draft of the contract was corrected by the managing director***; ***the finance department has passed the final draft of the accounts***; **rough draft** = plan of a document which may have changes made to it before it is complete **2** *verb* to make a first rough plan of a document; ***to draft a letter***; ***to draft a contract***; ***the contract is still being drafted*** *or* ***is still in the drafting stage***

drafter ['drɑ:ftə] *noun* person who makes a draft; ***the drafter of the agreement***

drafting ['drɑ:ftɪŋ] *noun* act of preparing the draft of a document; ***the drafting of the contract took six weeks***

drain [dreɪn] **1** *noun* gradual loss of money flowing away; ***the costs of the London office are a continual drain on our resources*** **2** *verb* to remove something gradually; ***the expansion plan has drained all our profits***; ***the company's capital resources have drained away***

> a sharply higher oil price has drained funds from many high-consuming Western countries and diverted resources towards oil producers
>
> *Financial Times Review*

draw [drɔ:] *verb* **(a)** to take money away; ***to draw money out of an account***; **to draw a salary** = to have a salary paid by the company; ***the chairman does not draw a salary*** **(b)** to write a cheque; ***he paid the invoice with a cheque drawn on an Egyptian bank*** (NOTE: **drawing - drew - has drawn**)

drawback ['drɔ:bæk] *noun* **(a)** thing which is not convenient, which is likely to cause problems; ***one of the main drawbacks of the scheme is that it will take six years to complete*** **(b)** paying back customs duty when imported goods are then re-exported

draw down ['drɔ: 'daʊn] *verb* to draw money which is available under a credit agreement

drawdown ['drɔ:daʊn] *noun* drawing money which is available under a credit agreement; **income drawdown** *or* **pension drawdown** = arrangement by which you take smaller amounts on a regular basis out of money accumulating in the pension fund, instead of taking it all at the same time in a lump sum to pay for an annuity

drawee [drɔː'iː] *noun* person or bank asked to make a payment by a drawer

drawer ['drɔːə] *noun* person who writes a cheque or a bill asking a drawee to pay money to a payee; **the bank returned the cheque to drawer** = the bank would not pay the cheque because the person who wrote it did not have enough money in the account to pay it

drawing ['drɔːɪŋ] *noun* **drawing account** = current account, account from which the customer may take money when he wants; **drawing rights** = right of a member country of the IMF to borrow money from the fund in a foreign currency; *see also* SPECIAL DRAWING RIGHTS

draw up ['drɔː 'ʌp] *verb* to write a legal document; ***to draw up a contract*** *or* ***an agreement***; ***to draw up a company's articles of association***

drift [drɪft] **1** *verb* to move slowly; ***shares drifted lower in a dull market***; ***strikers are drifting back to work*** **2** *noun* slow movement; **post-earnings-announcement drift** = unexplained downward movement of shares in companies following announcements that quarterly earnings have exceeded expectations

> with the market in what I see as a sluggish downward drift, I'm starting this portfolio with 20 percent cash
>
> *Smart Money*

drive [draɪv] **1** *noun* energetic way of working; **sales drive** = vigorous effort to increase sales **2** *verb* **to drive a company out of business** = to force a company into liquidation; ***the company was almost driven out of business a few years ago***

drop [drɒp] **1** *noun* fall; ***drop in sales***; ***sales show a drop of 10%***; ***a drop in prices*** **2** *verb* to fall; ***sales have dropped by 10%*** *or* ***have dropped 10%***; ***the pound dropped three points against the dollar*** (NOTE: **dropping - dropped**)

> while unemployment dropped by 1.6 per cent in the rural areas, it rose by 1.9 per cent in urban areas during the period under review
>
> *Business Times (Lagos)*

> since last summer American interest rates have dropped by between three and four percentage points
>
> *Sunday Times*

droplock bond ['drɒplɒk 'bɒnd] *noun* floating rate bond which will convert to a fixed rate of interest if interest rates fall to a certain point; *see also* DEBT CONVERTIBLE BOND

drop ship ['drɒp 'ʃɪp] *verb* to deliver a large order direct to a customer

drop shipment ['drɒp 'ʃɪpmənt] *noun* delivery of a large order from the manufacturer direct to a customer's shop or warehouse without going through an agent or wholesaler

DTI [diː tiː 'aɪ] = DEPARTMENT OF TRADE AND INDUSTRY

dual ['djuːəl] *adjective* referring to two things at the same time; **dual control** = system where two people have to sign a cheque, or validate a transaction, or have keys to a safe, etc.; **dual currency bond** = bond which is paid for in one currency but which is repayable in another on redemption; **dual listing** = listing a share on two stock exchanges; **dual pricing** = giving different prices to the same product depending on the market in which it is sold

duck [dʌk] *see* LAME DUCK

dud [dʌd] *adjective & noun (informal)* false; not good (coin or banknote); ***the £50 note was a dud***; **dud cheque** = cheque which the bank refuses to pay because the person writing it has not enough money in his account to pay it

due [djuː] *adjective* **(a)** owed; ***sum due from a debtor***; ***bond due for repayment***; **to fall due** *or* **to become due** = to be ready for payment; **bill due on May 1st** = bill which has to be paid on May 1st; **balance due to us** = amount owed to us which should be paid; **due bills** = amounts which are owed but not yet paid **(b)** **in due form** = written in the correct legal form; ***receipt in due form***; ***contract drawn up in due form***; **after due consideration of the problem** = after thinking seriously about the problem

> many expect the US economic indicators for April, due out this Thursday, to show faster economic growth
>
> *Australian Financial Review*

due diligence ['djuː 'dɪlɪdʒəns] *noun* **(a)** examination of the accounts of a company before it is taken over to see if there are any problems which have not been disclosed **(b)**

duty of an official such as a bank manager not to act in an irresponsible way

dues [djuːz] *plural noun* **(a) dock dues** *or* **port dues** *or* **harbour dues** = payment which a ship makes to the harbour authorities for the right to use the harbour **(b)** orders taken but not supplied until new stock arrives; ***we are recording orders for this item while we wait for a stock delivery from our factory in Singapore***

dull [dʌl] *adjective* not exciting, not full of life; **dull market** = market where little business is done

dullness [ˈdʌlnəs] *noun* being dull; ***the dullness of the market***

dump [dʌmp] *verb* **to dump goods on a market** = to get rid of large quantities of excess goods cheaply in an overseas market

> a serious threat lies in the 400,000 tonnes of subsidized beef in EC cold stores. If dumped, this meat will have disastrous effects in Pacific Basin markets
>
> *Australian Financial Review*

dumping [ˈdʌmpɪŋ] *noun* act of getting rid of excess goods cheaply in an overseas market; ***the government has passed anti-dumping legislation***; ***dumping of goods on the European market***; **panic dumping of sterling** = rush to sell sterling at any price because of possible devaluation

Dun & Bradstreet (D&B) [ˈdʌn ən ˈbrædstriːt] organization which produces reports on the financial rating of companies; it also acts as a debt collection agency

duplicate 1 [ˈdjuːplɪkət] *noun* copy; ***he sent me the duplicate of the contract***; **duplicate receipt** *or* **duplicate of a receipt** = copy of a receipt; **in duplicate** = with a copy; **receipt in duplicate** = two copies of a receipt; ***to print an invoice in duplicate*** **2** [ˈdjuːplɪkeɪt] *verb* **(a)** *(of a bookkeeping entry)* **to duplicate with another** = to repeat another entry, to be the same as another entry **(b) to duplicate a letter** = to make a copy of a letter

duplicating [ˈdjuːplɪkeɪtɪŋ] *noun* copying; **duplicating machine** = machine which makes copies of documents; **duplicating paper** = special paper to be used in a duplicating machine

duplication [djuːplɪˈkeɪʃən] *noun* copying of documents; **duplication of work** = work which is done twice without being necessary

duplicator [ˈdjuːplɪkeɪtə] *noun* machine which makes copies of documents

Dutch [dʌtʃ] *adjective* **(a)** referring to the Netherlands **(b) Dutch auction** = auction where the auctioneer offers an item for sale at a high price and then gradually reduces the price until someone makes a bid; **to go Dutch** = to share a bill (as in a restaurant)

> Dutch government bonds: prices were about 0.12 point lower as market participants awaited auction results for the new 10-year 9% state loan. The issue is being sold via a Dutch-style auction, which means that all paper is sold at the lowest accepted price
>
> *Wall Street Journal*

dutiable [ˈdjuːtiəbl] *adjective* **dutiable goods** *or* **dutiable items** = goods on which a customs duty has to be paid

duty [ˈdjuːti] *noun* **(a)** tax which has to be paid; ***to take the duty off alcohol***; ***to put up the duty on cigarettes***; **ad valorem duty** = duty calculated on the sales value of the goods; **customs duty** *or* **import duty** = tax on goods imported into a country; **excise duty** = tax on certain goods (such as alcohol and petrol) which are produced in the country; **goods which are liable to duty** = goods on which customs or excise tax has to be paid; **duty-paid goods** = goods where the duty has been paid; **stamp duty** = tax on legal documents (such as the conveyance of a property to a new owner); **estate duty** *US* **death duty** = tax paid on the property left by a dead person **(b)** responsibility; **duty of care** = duty which every person has not to act in a negligent way

> Canadian and European negotiators agreed to a deal under which Canada could lower its import duties on $150 million worth of European goods
>
> *Globe and Mail (Toronto)*

> the Department of Customs and Excise collected a total of N79m under the new advance duty payment scheme
>
> *Business Times (Lagos)*

duty-free [ˈdjuːtiˈfriː] *adjective & adverb* sold with no duty to be paid; ***he bought a duty-free watch at the airport*** *or* ***he bought the watch duty-free***; **duty-free shop** = shop at an airport *or* on a ship where goods can be bought without paying duty

Ee

e.& o.e. = ERRORS AND OMISSIONS EXCEPTED

Schedule E [ˈʃedjuːl ˈiː] schedule to the Finance Acts under which tax is charged on wages, salaries and pensions

Table E [ˈteɪbl ˈiː] model memorandum and articles of association of an unlimited company with share capital, set out in the Companies Act

early withdrawal [ˈɜːli wɪðˈdrɔːəl] *noun* withdrawing money from a deposit account before due date; ***early withdrawal usually incurs a penalty***

earmark [ˈɪəmɑːk] *verb* to reserve for a special purpose; ***to earmark funds for a project***; ***the grant is earmarked for computer systems development***

earn [ɜːn] *verb* **(a)** to be paid money for working; ***to earn £50 a week***; ***our agent in Paris certainly does not earn his commission***; **earned income** = income from wages, salaries, pensions, etc. (as opposed to 'unearned' income from investments) **(b)** to produce interest or dividends; ***what level of dividend do these shares earn?***; ***an account which earns interest at 10%***

earner [ˈɜːnə] *noun* **(a)** person who earns money; **second earner** = spouse who also earns a salary; ***a lot of second earners have got pay increases or better-paying jobs during the recent expansion, pushing themselves and their spouses into higher tax rates*** **(b)** *(informal)* **a nice little earner** = business that produces a good income

earnest [ˈɜːnɪst] *noun* money paid as a down payment

earning [ˈɜːnɪŋ] *noun* **earning capacity** *or* **earning power** = amount of money someone should be able to earn; ***he is such a fine dress designer that his earning power is very large***; **earning potential** = (i) amount of money a person should be able to earn; (ii) amount of dividend a share should produce; **earning power** = ability of a company to be more profitable and so pay higher dividends

earnings [ˈɜːnɪŋz] *plural noun* **(a)** salary or wages, profits and dividends or interest received; **compensation for loss of earnings** = payment to someone who has stopped earning money or who is not able to earn money; **invisible earnings** = foreign currency earned by a country in providing services (such as banking, tourism), not in selling goods; *US* **earnings credit** = allowance which reduces bank charges on checking accounts; **earnings-related contributions** = contributions to social security which rise as the worker's earnings rise **(b)** money which is earned in interest or dividends; **earnings per share (EPS** *or* **eps)** = money earned in profit per share (the total profits after tax and preference dividends have been paid, divided by the number of shares); ***these shares sell at 7 times earnings***; **earnings growth** = increase in profit per share; ***the company's aim is to sustain 10% a year earnings growth***; **earnings projection** = forecast of earnings per share; **earnings season** = period when all companies declare their dividends; ***the quarterly ritual known as earnings season*** (NOTE: also called the **reporting season**); **earnings yield** = money earned in dividend per share (the last dividend paid divided by the current market price of one share); **gross earnings** = earnings before tax and other deductions; **retained earnings** = profits which are not paid out to shareholders as dividend; *see also* DILUTE, DRIFT, PRICE/EARNINGS RATIO

---

if corporate forecasts are met, sales will exceed $50 million in 1985 and net earnings could exceed $7 million

Citizen (Ottawa)

---

the US now accounts for more than half of our world-wide sales. It has made a huge contribution to our earnings turnaround

Duns Business Month

---

last fiscal year the chain reported a 116% jump in earnings, to $6.4 million or $1.10 a share

Barrons

> its annual earnings growth could slow to about 10 percent this year from the midteens of the past
>
> *Smart Money*

> he and his assistant have worked out a system for handling the 20 or so reports that will come in on an average earnings-report day
>
> *Smart Money*

> January is a pivotal earnings-reporting month, with companies not only revealing how they did for the just-ended fourth quarter but also giving their first glimpse of the year ahead
>
> *Smart Money*

> the four-times-a-year frenzy known as corporate earnings season
>
> *Smart Money*

EASDAQ an independent European stock market, based in Brussels and London, trading in companies with European-wide interests

ease [iːz] **1** *noun* slight fall in prices **2** *verb (of prices, interest rates, etc.)* to fall a little; ***the share index eased slightly today***

East Caribbean dollar ['iːst kærɪ'biːən 'dɒlə] currency used in Antigua, Dominica, Grenada, Montserrat, St Lucia and St Vincent

easy ['iːzi] *adjective* **(a)** not difficult; **easy terms** = terms which are not difficult to accept, price which is easy to pay; ***the shop is let on very easy terms***; **the loan is repayable in easy payments** = with very small sums paid back regularly; **easy money** = (i) money which can be earned with no difficulty; (ii) money available on easy repayment terms; **easy money policy** = government policy of expanding the economy by making money more easily available (lower interest rates, easy access to credit, etc.) **(b) easy market** = market where few people are buying, so prices are lower than they were before; ***the Stock Exchange was easy yesterday***; **share prices are easier** = prices have fallen slightly

EBA = EURO BANKING ASSOCIATION

EBRD = EUROPEAN BANK FOR RECONSTRUCTION AND DEVELOPMENT

e-business ['iː'bɪznəs] = ELECTRONIC BUSINESS general term that refers to any type of business activity on the internet, including marketing, branding and research

> hundreds have built software and hardware targeted specifically at enabling the future of e-business. The products include everything from Web product catalogs to encryption tools to digital certificates that verify the authenticity of documents
>
> *Fortune*

EC ['iː 'siː] = EUROPEAN COMMUNITY

ECB ['iː 'siː 'biː] = EUROPEAN CENTRAL BANK

ECGD ['iː siː 'dʒiː 'diː] = EXPORT CREDIT GUARANTEE DEPARTMENT

e-commerce ['iː'kɒməːs] = ELECTRONIC COMMERCE general term that is normally used to refer to the process of buying and selling goods over the internet

> so existing distributors have a great opportunity to move into e-commerce - provided they're able to deal with the necessary cultural change
>
> *Fortune*

> e-commerce has gifted the world's supplies to the world's buyers - the constraints of traditional trade have disappeared
>
> *Accountancy*

econometrics [iːkənə'metrɪks] *plural noun* study of the statistics of economics, using computers to analyse statistics and make forecasts using mathematical models

economic [iːkə'nɒmɪk] *adjective* **(a)** which provides enough money; ***the flat is let at an economic rent***; ***it is hardly economic for the company to run its own warehouse*** **(b)** referring to the financial state of a country; ***the government's economic policy***; ***the economic situation is looking gloomy***; ***an explanation of the country's economic system***; ***they tried to forecast the economic trends***; **economic crisis** *or* **economic depression** = state where a country is in financial collapse; ***the government has introduced import controls to solve the current economic crisis***; **economic cycle** = period during which trade expands, then slows down, then expands again; **economic development** = expansion of the commercial and financial situation; ***the economic development of the region has totally changed since oil was discovered there***; **economic environment** = general situation of the economy; ***the new economic environment has made pricing an urgent issue***; **economic growth** = increase in the national income; ***the country enjoyed a period of economic growth in the 1980s***; **economic indicators** = statistics which show how the economy is going to perform in the short or long term (unemployment rate, overseas trade, etc.); **economic sanctions** = restrictions on trade with a country in order to make its government change policy; ***the western nations imposed economic sanctions on the country***

> each of the major issues on the agenda at this week's meeting is important to the government's success in overall economic management
>
> *Australian Financial Review*

economical [i:kəˈnɒmɪkəl] *adjective* which saves money or materials, which is cheap; **economical car** = car which does not use much petrol; **economical use of resources** = using resources as carefully as possible

economics [i:kəˈnɒmɪks] *plural noun* **(a)** study of production, distribution, selling and use of goods and services **(b)** study of financial structures to show how a product or service is costed and what returns it produces; ***the economics of town planning***; ***I do not understand the economics of the coal industry***

> believers in free-market economics often find it hard to sort out their views on the issue
>
> *Economist*

economist [ɪˈkɒnəmɪst] *noun* person who specializes in the study of economics; ***agricultural economist***

economy [ɪˈkɒnəmi] *noun* **(a)** being careful not to waste money or materials; **an economy measure** = an action to save money or materials; **to introduce economies** *or* **economy measures into the system** = to start using methods to save money or materials; **economies of scale** = making a product more profitable by manufacturing it in larger quantities; *compare* DISECONOMIES; **economy car** = car which does not use much petrol; **economy class** = cheapest class on a plane; ***to travel economy class***; **economy drive** = campaign to save money or materials; **economy size** = large size, large packet which is a bargain **(b)** financial state of a country, the way in which a country makes and uses its money; ***the country's economy is in ruins***; **black economy** = work which is paid for in cash or goods, but not declared to the tax authorities; **capitalist economy** = system where each person has the right to invest money, to work in business, to buy and sell with no restrictions from the state; **controlled economy** = system where business activity is controlled by orders from the government; **free market economy** = system where the government does not interfere in business activity in any way; **global economy** = economy of the whole world; **mixed economy** = system which contains both nationalized industries and private enterprise; **planned economy** = system where the government plans all business activity

> but economically and politically, the major force on the planet may instead be the global economy - a point the economic crisis in East Asia has driven home in recent months
>
> *Smart Money*

> the European economies are being held back by rigid labor markets and wage structures, huge expenditures on social welfare programs and restrictions on the free movement of goods within the Common Market
>
> *Duns Business Month*

ECP = EUROPEAN COMMERCIAL PAPER

ecu *or* **ECU** [ˈekju:] *noun* = *EUROPEAN CURRENCY UNIT*

COMMENT: the ECU is used for internal accounting purposes within the EU, and for settlements between banks. The value of the ECU is calculated as a composite of various European currencies: currently, it is 0.719DM + 1.31FFr + 3.71BFr + 140L + 0.256fl + 0.14LuxFr + £0.0378 + I£0.00871 + 0.217DKr + dr1.15. These values remain the same, but the actual value of each currency may fluctuate slightly within set limits in the Exchange Rate Mechanism.

> the official use of the ecu remains limited. Since its creation in 1981 the ecu has grown popular because of its stability
>
> *Economist*

EDI ['iː 'diː 'aɪ] = ELECTRONIC DATA INTERCHANGE

EDP ['iː diː 'piː] = ELECTRONIC DATA PROCESSING

EEA ['iː 'iː 'eɪ] = EUROPEAN ECONOMIC AREA

EEC ['iː 'iː 'siː] = EUROPEAN ECONOMIC COMMUNITY; ***the USA was increasing its trade with the EEC*** (NOTE: now called the **European Union or EU**)

effect [ɪ'fekt] **1** *noun* **(a)** result; ***the effect of the pay increase was to raise productivity levels***; **terms of a contract which take effect** *or* **come into effect from January 1st** = terms which start to operate on January 1st; **prices are increased 10% with effect from January 1st** = new prices will apply from January 1st; **to remain in effect** = to continue to be applied **(b)** meaning; **clause to the effect that** = clause which means that; **we have made provision to this effect** = we have put into the contract terms which will make this work **2** *verb* to carry out; **to effect a payment** = to make a payment; **to effect customs clearance** = to clear goods through customs; **to effect a settlement between two parties** = to bring two parties together and make them agree to a settlement

effective [ɪ'fektɪv] *adjective* **(a)** real; **effective control of a company** = situation where someone owns more of a company's shares than anyone else, but less than 50%, and so in effect controls the company because no other single shareholder can outvote him; **effective demand** = actual demand for a product which can be paid for; **effective exchange rate** = rate of exchange for a currency calculated against a basket of currencies; **effective price** = share price which has been adjusted to allow for a rights issue; **effective rate** = real interest rate on a loan or deposit (i.e., the APR); **effective yield** = actual yield shown as a percentage after adjustments have been made **(b) effective date** = date on which a rule or a contract starts to be applied, or on which a transaction takes place; **clause effective as from January 1st** = clause which starts to be applied on January 1st; *see also* COST-EFFECTIVE

effectiveness [ɪ'fektɪvnəs] *noun* working, producing results; ***I doubt the effectiveness of television advertising***; *see* COST-EFFECTIVENESS

effectual [ɪ'fektʃʊəl] *adjective* which produces a correct result

efficiency [ɪ'fɪʃənsi] *noun* ability to work well or to produce the right result or the right work quickly; ***with a high degree of efficiency***; ***a business efficiency exhibition***; ***an efficiency expert***

> increased control means improved efficiency in purchasing, shipping, sales and delivery
>
> *Duns Business Month*

efficient [ɪ'fɪʃənt] *adjective* able to work well or to produce the right result quickly; ***the efficient working of a system***; ***he needs an efficient secretary to look after him***; **efficient-market theory** = theory that the prices operating in a certain market reflect all known information about the market and therefore make it impossible for abnormal profits to be made

> he is among the most militant proponents of the efficient-market theory. He thinks it's impossible to beat the averages over time and that any profit investors earn relates solely to the risk they take
>
> *Smart Money*

efficiently [ɪ'fɪʃəntli] *adverb* in an efficient way; ***she organized the sales conference very efficiently***

efflux ['eflʌks] *noun* flowing out; ***efflux of capital to North America***

EFT ['iː 'ef 'tiː] = ELECTRONIC FUNDS TRANSFER

EFTA ['eftə] = EUROPEAN FREE TRADE ASSOCIATION

EFTPOS ['eft'pɒs] = ELECTRONIC FUNDS TRANSFER AT POINT OF SALE

EGM ['iː 'dʒiː 'em] = EXTRAORDINARY GENERAL MEETING

EIB ['iː 'aɪ 'biː] = EUROPEAN INVESTMENT BANK

EIRIS = ETHICAL INVESTMENT RESEARCH SERVICE

EIS = ENTERPRISE INVESTMENT SCHEME

elastic [ɪ'læstɪk] *adjective* which can expand or contract easily because of small changes in price

elasticity [elæs'tɪsəti] *noun* (i) ability to change easily; (ii) the rate of change in response to a factor which has changed; **elasticity of supply and demand** = changes in supply and demand of an item depending on its market price

elect [ɪ'lekt] *verb* to choose someone by a vote; ***to elect the officers of an association***; ***she was elected president***

-elect [ɪ'lekt] *suffix* person who has been elected but has not yet started the term of office; ***she is the president-elect*** (NOTE: the plural is **presidents-elect**)

election [ɪ'lekʃən] *noun* act of electing; ***the election of officers of an association***; ***the election of directors by the shareholders***

electronic [elek'trɒnɪk] *adjective* referring to or using computers; **electronic banking** = using computers to carry out banking transactions, such as withdrawals through cash dispensers, transfer of funds at point of sale, etc.; **electronic business** *or* **e-business** *or* **electronic commerce** *or* **e-commerce** = doing business via computers, modems, the Internet and e-mail, etc., as when shopping via the internet or using e-mail to buy shares; **electronic data interchange (EDI)** = system of exchange of information between banks using computers; **electronic data processing (EDP)** = selecting and examining data stored in a computer to produce information; **electronic funds transfer (EFT)** = system for transferring money from one account to another electronically (as when using a smart card); **electronic funds transfer at point of sale (EFTPOS)** = system for transferring money directly from the purchaser's account to the seller's, when a sale is made using a plastic card; **electronic mail** *or* **email** = system of sending messages from one computer terminal to another, via telephone lines; **electronic point of sale (EPOS)** = system where sales are charged automatically to a customer's credit card and stock is controlled by the shop's computer

electronics [elek'trɒnɪks] *plural noun* applying the scientific study of electrons to produce manufactured products, such as computers, calculators or telephones; ***the electronics industry***; ***an electronics specialist*** *or* ***expert***; ***electronics engineer***

element ['elɪmənt] *noun* basic part; ***the elements of a settlement***

eligible ['elɪdʒəbl] *adjective* which can be chosen; **eligible bill** *or* **eligible paper** = bill which will be accepted by the Bank of England or the US Federal Reserve, and which can be used as security against a loan; **eligible liabilities** = liabilities which go into the calculation of a bank's reserves

eligibility [elɪdʒə'bɪləti] *noun* being eligible; ***the chairman questioned her eligibility to stand for re-election***

eliminate [ɪ'lɪmɪneɪt] *verb* to remove; ***to eliminate defects in the system***; ***using a computer should eliminate all possibility of error***

elite ['eɪli:t] *noun* group of the best people; **elite stock** = top-quality shares

> at his peak he owned nearly 100 shares of Warren Buffett's elite stock (bought at prices ranging from $900 to $20,000 per share)
>
> *Smart Money*

e-mail *or* **email** ['i:'meɪl] = ELECTRONIC MAIL

embargo [em'bɑ:gəʊ] **1** *noun* government order which stops a type of trade; **to lay** *or* **put an embargo on trade with a country** = to say that trade with a country must not take place; **to lift an embargo** = to allow trade to start again; **to be under an embargo** = to be forbidden (NOTE: plural is **embargoes**) **2** *verb* to stop trade or not to allow trade; ***the government has embargoed trade with the Eastern countries***

> the Commerce Department is planning to loosen export controls for products that have been embargoed but are readily available elsewhere in the West
>
> *Duns Business Month*

embezzle [ɪm'bezl] *verb* to use money which is not yours, or which you are looking after for someone; ***he was sent to prison for six months for embezzling his clients' money***

embezzlement [ɪm'bezlmənt] *noun* act of embezzling; ***he was sent to prison for six months for embezzlement***

embezzler [ɪm'bezlə] *noun* person who embezzles

emergency [ɪ'mɜ:dʒənsi] *noun* critical situation which needs rapid action to control; *US* **emergency credit** = credit given by the Federal Reserve to an organization which has no other means of borrowing

emerging [ɪ'mɜ:dʒɪŋ] *adjective* which is beginning to appear and grow; **emerging country** = country which is developing rapidly; **emerging growth fund** = growth fund that invests in emerging markets; **emerging market** = new market, as in South-East Asia or Eastern Europe, which is developing fast and is seen as potentially profitable to fund managers

> the World Bank reports that the bulk of growth in the world is switching to emerging countries
>
> *Money Observer*

> the particularly volatile emerging markets are targeted by many hedge funds
>
> *Money Observer*

> up until a few months ago, recent history presented a strong bias towards investing in emerging markets such as south China and Indonesia
>
> *Money Observer*

> in October some emerging markets performed strongly, with Indonesia and Russia leading with gains of 55.9% and 48.5% in dollar terms
>
> *The Banker*

emoluments [ɪ'mɒljumənts] *plural noun* pay, salary or fees, or the earnings of directors who are not employees

e-money ['iː'mʌni] *noun* term used to described the various options available to pay for goods over the internet

> COMMENT: this normally refers to either credit card payments or virtual tokens or a virtual credit card or a micropayment.

employ [ɪm'plɔɪ] *verb* to give someone regular paid work; **to employ twenty staff** = to have twenty people working for you; **to employ twenty new staff** = to give work to twenty new people

> 70 per cent of Australia's labour force was employed in service activity
>
> *Australian Financial Review*

employed [ɪm'plɔɪd] **1** *adjective* **(a)** in regular paid work; **he is not gainfully employed** = he has no regular paid work; **self-employed** = working for yourself; ***he worked in a bank for ten years but now is self-employed*** **(b)** (money) used profitably; **return on capital employed (ROCE)** = profit shown as a percentage of shareholders' funds **2** *plural noun* people who are working; ***the employers and the employed***; **the self-employed** = people who work for themselves

employee [emplɔɪ'iː] *noun* worker, person employed by a company or firm; ***employees of the firm are eligible to join a profit-sharing scheme***; ***relations between management and employees have improved***; ***the company has decided to take on new employees***; **employee buyout** = purchase of a company by its employees; **employee share ownership plan** *US* **employee stock ownership plan (ESOP)** = scheme which allows employees to obtain shares in the company for which they work (though tax may be payable if the shares are sold to employees at a price which is lower than the current market price)

> companies introducing robotics think it important to involve individual employees in planning their introduction
>
> *Economist*

employer [ɪm'plɔɪə] *noun* person or company that has regular workers and pays them; **employers' organization** *or* **association** = group of employers with similar interests; **employer's contribution** = money paid by an employer towards a worker's pension

employment [ɪm'plɔɪmənt] *noun* regular paid work; **full employment** = situation where everyone in a country who can work has a job; **full-time employment** = work for all of a working day; **part-time employment** = work for part of a working day; **temporary employment** = work which does not last for more than a few months; **to be without employment** = to have no work; **to find someone alternative employment** = to find another job for someone; **conditions of employment** = terms of a contract where someone is employed; **contract of employment** *or* **employment contract** = contract between employer and an employee stating all the conditions of work; **security of employment** = feeling by a worker that he has the right to keep his job until he retires

> the blue-collar unions are the people who stand to lose most in terms of employment growth
>
> *Sydney Morning Herald*

empower [ɪm'paʊə] *verb* to give someone the power to do something; ***she was empowered by the company to sign the contract***

EMS ['iː 'em 'es] = EUROPEAN MONETARY SYSTEM

EMU ['iː 'em 'juː] = EUROPEAN MONETARY UNION

encash [ɪn'kæʃ] *verb* to cash a cheque, to exchange a cheque for cash

encashable [ɪnˈkæʃəbl] *adjective* which can be cashed

encashment [ɪnˈkæʃmənt] *noun* act of exchanging for cash

encumbrance [ɪnˈkʌmbrəns] *noun* liability, such as a mortgage or charge, which is attached usually to a property or land

end [end] **1** *noun* final point or last part; ***at the end of the contract period***; **at the end of six months** = after six months have passed; **account end** = the end of an accounting period; **month end** = the end of the month, when accounts have to be drawn up; **end product** = manufactured product, made at the end of a production process; **end user** = person who actually uses a product **2** *verb* to finish; ***the account ended on a weak note***

endorse [ɪnˈdɔːs] *verb* **to endorse a bill** *or* **a cheque** = to sign a bill or a cheque on the back to show that you pass ownership of it to someone else

endorsee [endɔːˈsiː] *noun* person whose name is written on a bill or a cheque as having the right to cash it

endorsement [ɪnˈdɔːsmənt] *noun* **(a)** act of endorsing; signature on a document (such as a cheque) which endorses it **(b)** note on an insurance policy which adds conditions to the policy

endorser [ɪnˈdɔːsə] *noun* person who endorses a bill or cheque which then is passed to another person

> COMMENT: by endorsing a cheque (i.e., signing it on the back), a person whose name is on the front of the cheque is passing ownership of it to another party, such as the bank, which can then accept it and pay him cash for it. If a cheque is deposited in an account, it does not need to be endorsed. Cheques can also be endorsed to another person: a cheque made payable to Mr A. Smith can be endorsed by Mr Smith on the back, with the words: 'Pay to Brown Ltd', and then his signature. This has the effect of making the cheque payable to Brown Ltd, and to no one else

endowment [ɪnˈdaʊmənt] *noun* giving money to provide a regular income; **endowment assurance** *or* **endowment insurance** *or* **endowment policy** = insurance policy where a sum of money is paid to the insured person on a certain date, or to his estate if he dies earlier

endowment mortgage [ɪnˈdaʊmənt ˈmɔːɡɪdʒ] *noun* mortgage backed by an endowment policy

> COMMENT: the borrower pays interest on the mortgage in the usual way, but does not repay the capital; the endowment assurance (a life insurance) is taken out to cover the total capital sum borrowed, and when the assurance matures the capital is paid off, and a further lump sum is usually available for payment to the borrower; a mortgage where the borrower repays both interest and capital is called a 'repayment mortgage'

energy [ˈenədʒi] *noun* power from electricity or petrol, etc.; ***we try to save energy by switching off the lights when the rooms are empty***; ***if you reduce the room temperature to eighteen degrees, you will save energy***; **energy shares** = shares in companies (gas, electricity, etc.) which provide energy

enforce [ɪnˈfɔːs] *verb* to make sure something is done or that a rule is obeyed; ***to enforce the terms of a contract***

enforcement [ɪnˈfɔːsmənt] *noun* making sure that something is obeyed; ***enforcement of the terms of a contract***

engage [ɪnˈɡeɪdʒ] *verb* **(a) to engage someone to do something** = to make someone do something legally; ***the contract engages us to a minimum annual purchase*** **(b)** to employ under a contract; ***we have engaged the best commercial lawyer to represent us***; ***the company has engaged twenty new salesmen*** **(c) to be engaged in** = to be busy with; ***he is engaged in work on computers***; ***the company is engaged in trade with Africa***

engagement [ɪnˈɡeɪdʒmənt] *noun* agreement to do something; **to break an engagement to do something** = not to do what you have legally agreed; ***the company broke their engagement not to sell our rivals' products***

entail [ɪnˈteɪl] **1** *noun* legal condition which passes ownership of a property only to certain persons **2** *verb* to involve; ***itemizing the sales figures will entail about ten days' work***

enter [ˈentə] *verb* **(a)** to write; ***to enter a name on a list***; ***the clerk entered the interest in my bank book***; ***to enter up an item in a ledger***; **to enter a bid for something** = to offer (usually in writing) to buy something; **to enter a caveat** = to warn legally that you have an interest in a case, and that no steps can be taken without your permission **(b) to enter into** = to begin; ***to enter into a partnership with a legal friend***; ***to enter into an agreement*** *or* ***a contract***

entering ['entərɪŋ] *noun* act of writing items in a record

enterprise ['entəpraɪz] *noun* **(a)** system of carrying on a business; **free enterprise** = system of business free from government interference; **private enterprise** = businesses which are owned privately, not nationalized; ***the project is completely funded by private enterprise***; **enterprise zone** = area of the country where businesses are encouraged to develop by offering special conditions such as easy planning permission for buildings, reduction in the business rate, etc. **(b)** business; **a small-scale enterprise** = a small business; **a state enterprise** = a state-controlled company; ***bosses of state enterprises are appointed by the government***

entertain [entə'teɪn] *verb* to offer meals, hotel accommodation or theatre tickets, etc., to (business) visitors

entertainment [entə'teɪnmənt] *noun* offering meals, etc., to business visitors; **entertainment allowance** = money which a manager is allowed by his company to spend on meals with visitors; **entertainment expenses** = money spent on giving meals to business visitors

entitle [ɪn'taɪtl] *verb* to give the right to something; **he is entitled to a discount** = he has the right to be given a discount

entitlement [ɪn'taɪtlmənt] *noun* right; **holiday entitlement** = number of days' paid holiday which a worker has the right to take; ***she has not used up all her holiday entitlement***; **pension entitlement** = amount of pension which someone has the right to receive when he retires *(Australia)* **entitlement issue** = rights issue

entrepot ['ɒntrəpəʊ] *noun* **entrepot port** = town with a large international commercial port dealing in re-exports; **entrepot trade** = exporting of imported goods

entrepreneur [ɒntrəprə'nɜː] *noun* person who directs a company and takes commercial risks

entrepreneurial [ɒntrəprə'nɜːriəl] *adjective* taking commercial risks; ***an entrepreneurial decision***

entry ['entri] *noun* **(a)** written information put in an accounts ledger; **credit entry** *or* **debit entry** = entry on the credit or debit side of an account; **single-entry bookkeeping** = noting a deal with only one entry; **double-entry bookkeeping** = noting of both debit and credit sides of an account; **to make an entry in a ledger** = to write in details of a deal; **contra entry** = entry made in the opposite side of an account to make an earlier entry worthless (such as a debit entry against a credit); **to contra an entry** = to enter a similar amount on the opposite side of the account **(b)** act of going in; place where you can go in; ***to pass a customs entry point***; ***entry of goods under bond***; **entry charge** = money which you have to pay before you go in; **entry visa** = visa allowing someone to go into a country; **multiple entry visa** = entry visa which allows someone to enter a country as often as he likes

environmental shares [ɪnvaɪrən'mentl 'ʃeəz] *noun* shares in companies which are seen to be active in the environmental field (stores which sell 'green' produce, waste disposal companies, etc.)

> as the ecological fever spread, even stocks peripherally involved in environmental cleanup activities were getting price-earnings ratios well above the market average. Investors blindly accepted the idea that all environmental stocks were recession-proof
>
> *Wall Street Journal*

epos *or* **EPOS** ['iːpɒs] = ELECTRONIC POINT OF SALE

eps *or* **EPS** ['iː 'piː 'es] = EARNINGS PER SHARE

e-purse ['iː'pɜːs] *noun* = *ELECTRONIC PURSE* concept developed to provide a way of holding a virtual token when shopping on the internet; *see also* VIRTUAL TOKEN

equal ['iːkwəl] **1** *adjective* exactly the same; ***male and female workers have equal pay***; **equal opportunities programme** = programme to avoid discrimination in employment (NOTE: the American equivalent is **affirmative action**) **2** *verb* to be the same as; ***production this month has equalled our best month ever*** (NOTE: British spelling is **equalling - equalled** but American spelling is **equaling - equaled**

equalize ['iːkwəlaɪz] *verb* to make equal; ***to equalize dividends***

equally ['iːkwəli] *adverb* in the same way; ***costs will be shared equally between the two parties***; ***they were both equally responsible for the disastrous launch***

equate [ɪ'kweɪt] *verb* to reduce to a standard value

equation [ɪ'kweɪʃn] *noun* set of mathematical rules applied to solve a problem; ***the basic accounting equation is that assets equal liabilities plus equity***

equilibrium [iːkwɪ'lɪbriəm] *noun* situation where a country's balance of payments is neither in deficit nor in excess; *compare* DISEQUILIBRIUM

equities ['ekwətiz] *plural noun* ordinary shares

> in the past three years commercial property has seriously underperformed equities and dropped out of favour as a result
>
> *Investors Chronicle*

equity ['ekwəti] *noun* **(a)** the value of a company which is the property of its shareholders (the company's assets less its liabilities, not including the ordinary share capital); **equity accounting** = putting part of the profits of a subsidiary into the parent company's books **(b)** the ordinary shares in a company; *US* **common equity** = ordinary shares in a company; ***return on common equity: 16.1%*** (NOTE: British English equivalent is **ordinary shares**); **shareholders' equity** *or* **equity capital** = a company's capital which is invested by shareholders, who thus become owners of the company (note that preference shares are not equity capital, since they involve less risk and do not share in the profitability of the company); **equity earnings** = profits after tax, which are available for distribution to shareholders in the form of dividends, or which can be retained in the company for future development; **equity finance** = finance for a company in the form of ordinary shares paid for by shareholders; **equity fund** *or* **equity investment fund** = fund which is invested in equities, not in government securities or other funds; **equity gearing** = ratio of a company's borrowings to its share capital; *US* **equity REIT** = trust which invests in rented property; **equity sweetener** = incentive to encourage people to lend a company money, in the form of a warrant giving the right to buy shares at a later date and at a certain price (NOTE: the American equivalent is **equity kicker**); *see also* RISK **(c)** the value of an asset, such as a house, less any mortgage on it; ***his plan is to sell his house to release some of the equity tied up in it***; *see also* NEGATIVE EQUITY

> funds that investors craved in any one year fell behind the average equity fund 70 percent of the time over the next few years
>
> *Smart Money*

> the private equity market is showing little sign of slowing down yet, although deals are changing shape
>
> *Investors Chronicle*

> as with most UK regions, the private equity sector has not just matured, but evolved
>
> *Investors Chronicle*

> investment trusts can raise more capital but this has to be done as a company does it, by a rights issue of equity
>
> *Investors Chronicle*

equivalence [ɪ'kwɪvələns] *noun* being equivalent

equivalent [ɪ'kwɪvələnt] **1** *adjective* **to be equivalent to** = to have the same value as or to be the same as; ***the total dividend paid is equivalent to one quarter of the pretax profits***; *see also* ANNUAL EQUIVALENT RATE **2** *noun* thing which has the same value as another; ***shares at £3.00 are the equivalent of £6.00 before the share split***; ***the invoice is for £100, payable in sterling or the dollar equivalent***

ERDF = EUROPEAN REGIONAL DEVELOPMENT FUND

ERM ['iː 'ɑː 'em] = EXCHANGE RATE MECHANISM

error ['erə] *noun* mistake; ***he made an error in calculating the total***; ***the secretary must have made a typing error***; **clerical error** = mistake made in an office; **computer error** = mistake made by a computer; **margin of error** = number of mistakes which can be accepted in a document or in a calculation; **errors and omissions excepted (e. & o.e.)** = words written on an invoice to show that the company has no responsibility for mistakes in the invoice; **error rate** = number of mistakes per thousand entries or per page

escalate ['eskəleɪt] *verb* to increase steadily

escalation [eskə'leɪʃən] *noun* **escalation of prices** = steady increase in prices; **escalation clause** = ESCALATOR CLAUSE

escalator ['eskəleɪtə] *noun* **escalator bond** = fixed-rate bond where the rate rises each year; **escalator clause** = clause in a contract allowing for regular price increases because of increased costs

escape [ɪs'keɪp] *noun* getting away from a difficult situation; **escape clause** = clause in a contract which allows one of the parties to avoid carrying out the terms of the contract under certain conditions

ESCB = EUROPEAN SYSTEM OF CENTRAL BANKS

escrow ['eskrəʊ] *noun* agreement between two parties that something should be held by a third party until certain conditions are fulfilled; **in escrow** = held in safe keeping by a third party; **document held in escrow** = document given to a third party to keep and to pass on to someone when money has been paid; **escrow account** = account where money is held in escrow until a contract is signed or until goods are delivered, etc.

escudo [es'kjʊdəʊ] unit of currency used with the euro in Portugal

ESOP = EMPLOYEE SHARE OWNERSHIP PLAN

establish [ɪs'tæblɪʃ] *verb* to set up or to open; ***the company has established a branch in Australia***; ***the business was established in Scotland in 1823***; ***it is a young company - it has been established for only four years***; **to establish oneself in business** = to become successful in a new business

establishment [ɪs'tæblɪʃmənt] *noun* **(a)** commercial business; ***he runs an important printing establishment*** **(b)** number of people working in a company; **to be on the establishment** = to be a full-time employee; **office with an establishment of fifteen** = office with a budgeted staff of fifteen; **establishment charges** = cost of people and property in a company's accounts

estate [ɪs'teɪt] *noun* **(a) real estate** = property (land or buildings); **estate agency** = office which arranges for the sale of property; **estate agent** = person in charge of an estate agency **(b)** property left by a dead person; **estate duty** = tax on property left by a dead person; *US* **estate tax** = federal tax on property left by a dead person

---

thanks to the recent tax changes, a bigger chunk of your estate should escape federal estate tax

Fortune

---

most of the latest changes to the estate-tax law are tweaks, not bold strokes, but they're welcome nonetheless

Fortune

---

estimate 1 ['estɪmət] *noun* **(a)** calculation of probable cost, size or time of something; **rough estimate** = very approximate calculation; **at a conservative estimate** = calculation which probably underestimates the final figure; ***their turnover has risen by at least 20% in the last year, and that is a conservative estimate***; **these figures are only an estimate** = these are not the final accurate figures; ***can you give me an estimate of how much time was spent on the job?*** **(b)** calculation of how much something is likely to cost in the future, given to a client so as to get him to make an order; ***estimate of costs*** *or* ***of expenditure***; ***before we can give the grant we must have an estimate of the total costs involved***; ***to ask a builder for an estimate for building the warehouse***; **to put in an estimate** = to give someone a written calculation of the probable costs of carrying out a job; ***three firms put in estimates for the job*** **2** ['estɪmeɪt] *verb* **(a)** to calculate the probable cost, size or time of something; ***to estimate that it will cost £1m*** *or* ***to estimate costs at £1m***; ***we estimate current sales at only 60% of last year's*** **(b) to estimate for a job** = to state in writing the future costs of carrying out a piece of work so that a client can make an order; ***three firms estimated for the fitting of the offices***

estimated ['estɪmeɪtɪd] *adjective* calculated approximately; ***estimated sales***; ***estimated figure***

estimation [estɪ'meɪʃən] *noun* approximate calculation

estimator ['estɪmeɪtə] *noun* person whose job is to calculate estimates for carrying out work

estoppel [ɪ'stɒpəl] *noun* rule of evidence whereby someone is prevented from denying or asserting a fact in legal proceedings

ethical ['eθɪkl] *adjective* morally right; **ethical criteria** = standards used to judge if something is morally right or not; **ethical fund** = fund which invests in companies which follow certain moral standards, i.e. companies which do not manufacture weapons, or which do not trade with certain countries or which only use environmentally acceptable sources of raw materials, etc.; ***as far as capital returns compare, ethical funds have done slightly better than average*** (NOTE: also called **socially responsible funds**); **ethical index** = index of shares in companies which follow certain moral standards; **ethical investment** = investing in companies which follow certain moral standards (NOTE: also called **social investing**); **Ethical Investment Research Service (EIRIS)** = organization which does research into companies and recommends those which follow certain standards; **ethical screening** = checking companies against certain moral standards, and removing those which do not conform

> different funds apply different ethical tests: some bar companies because of pollution, while others veto tobacco firms or defence companies
>
> *Sunday Business*

> one or more of the growing number of ethical funds whose purpose is to assemble portfolios of shares that screen out companies engaged in undesirable activities
>
> *Money Observer*

> ethical screening, say the doubters, creates funds that are underweight in multinational companies and overweight in small companies and technology stocks
>
> *Money Observer*

> trustees of pension funds have a reputation for focusing solely on returns, and so far the institutional money in ethical environmental funds comes from charities and local authorities
>
> *Money Observer*

> some people argue that, because of the ethical criteria, the funds have less choice of investments than their conventional counterparts and that is bound to hamper their performance
>
> *Money Observer*

> research by EIRIS suggests that investing according to ethical criteria makes little difference to overall financial performance
>
> *Money Observer*

EU ['iː 'juː] = EUROPEAN UNION

Eurex ['jʊəreks] European derivatives market developed by combining the German Terminb"rse and the Swiss Soffex

EURIBOR = EUROPEAN INTERBANK OFFERED RATE

euro ['jʊərəʊ] *noun* currency adopted as legal tender in several European countries from January 1st, 1999; ***many articles are priced in euros***; ***what's the exchange rate for the euro?***; **euro account** = bank account in euros (NOTE: written € before numbers: **€ 250** say: 'two hundred and fifty euros')

> COMMENT: the countries which are joined together in the European Monetary Union and adopted the euro as their common currency in 1999 are: Austria, Belgium, Finland, France, Germany, Ireland, Italy, Luxembourg, the Netherlands, Portugal, and Spain. The conversion of these currencies to the euro was fixed on 1st January 1999 at the following rates: Austrian schilling: 13.7603; Belgian & Luxembourg franc: 40.3399; Finnish Markka: 5.94573; French franc: 6.55957; German mark: 1.95583; Irish punt: 0.787564; Italian lira: 1936.27; Dutch guilder: 2.20371; Portuguese escudo: 200.482; Spanish peseta: 166.386. The CFA franc and CFP franc were pegged to the euro at the same time

Euro- ['jʊərəʊ] *prefix* referring to Europe or the European Community

Eurobond ['jʊərəʊbɒnd] *noun* long-term bearer bond issued by an international corporation or government outside its country of origin and sold to purchasers who pay in a eurocurrency (sold on the Eurobond market)

Eurocard ['jʊərəʊkɑːd] cheque card used when writing Eurocheques

Eurocheque ['jʊərəʊtʃek] *noun* cheque which can be cashed in any European bank (the Eurocheque system is based in Brussels)

Eurocommercial paper (ECP) [jʊərəʊkə'mɜːʃl 'peɪpə] *noun* form of short-term borrowing in eurocurrencies

eurocredit [jʊərəʊ'kredɪt] *noun* large bank loan in a eurocurrency (usually provided by a group of banks to a large commercial undertaking)

Eurocurrency ['jʊərəʊkʌrənsi] *noun* any currency used for trade within Europe but outside its country of origin, the eurodollar being the most important; ***a eurocurrency loan***; ***the eurocurrency market***

eurodeposit ['jʊərəʊdɪpɒzɪt] *noun* deposit of eurodollars in a bank outside the USA

Eurodollar ['jʊərəʊdɒlə] *noun* US dollar deposited in a bank outside the USA, used mainly for trade within Europe; ***a Eurodollar loan***; ***the Eurodollar markets***

euroequity ['jʊərəʊekwɪti] *noun* share in an international company traded on European stock markets outside its country of origin

Euroland ['jʊərəʊlænd] *noun* the European countries which use the euro as a common currency, seen as a group

Euromarket ['jʊərəʊmɑ:kɪt] *noun* **(a)** the European Community seen as a potential market for sales **(b)** the eurocurrency market, the international market for lending or borrowing in eurocurrencies

euronote ['jʊərəʊnəʊt] *noun* short-term eurocurrency bearer note

euro-option ['jʊərəʊɒpʃn] *noun* option to buy European bonds at a later date

Europe ['jʊərəp] *noun* **(a)** group of countries to the West of Asia and the North of Africa; ***most of the countries of Western Europe are members of the European Union***; ***Canadian exports to Europe have risen by 25%*** **(b)** *used to refer to* the European Union

European [jʊərə'pi:ən] *adjective* referring to Europe; **European Commercial Paper (ECP)** = commercial paper issued in a eurocurrency; **European Economic Area (EEA)** = trading area formed by an agreement on trade between the EU and EFTA in 1993; *US* **European options** = American term for options which can only be exercised on their expiration date (American options can be exercised at any time up to the expiration date); **the European Parliament** = parliament of members (MEPs) elected in each member country of the EU

European Bank for Reconstruction and Development (EBRD) bank, based in London, which channels aid from the EU to Eastern European countries

European Central Bank (ECB) [jʊrə'piən 'sentrəl 'bæŋk] *noun* central bank for most of the countries in the European Union, those which have accepted European Monetary Union and have the euro as their common currency

> the ECB begins with some $300 billion of foreign exchange reserves, far more than any other central bank
>
> *Investors Chronicle*

> any change in the European bank's statutes must be agreed and ratified by all EU member nations
>
> *The Times*

European Commission [jʊərə'pi:ən kə'mɪʃn] *noun* main executive body of the EC, made up of members nominated by each member state (NOTE: also called the **Commission of the European Community**)

European Currency Unit (ECU) [jʊərə'pi:ən 'kərənsi: 'ju:nɪt] monetary unit used within the EU; *see entry at* ECU

European Free Trade Association (EFTA) [jʊərə'pi:ən 'fri: 'treɪd əsəʊsi'eɪʃn] a group of countries (Iceland, Liechtenstein, Norway and Switzerland) formed to encourage freedom of trade between its members; EFTA countries are linked with the EU countries to form the EEA

European Interbank Offered Rate (EURIBOR) [jʊərə'pi:ən 'ɪntəbæŋk 'ɒfəd 'reɪt] rate at which European banks offer to lend funds to other banks

> officials at Liffe had been concerned about the initial success of Euribor, a money market reference rate calculated in Brussels
>
> *Financial Times*

European Investment Bank (EIB) ['jʊrəp'pi:ən ɪn'vestmənt 'bæŋk] international European bank set up to provide loans to European countries

European Monetary System (EMS) ['jʊərəpi:ən 'mʌnɪtərɪ 'sistəm] system of controlled exchange rates between some of the member countries of the European Union

> COMMENT: the EMS now only applies to countries such as Greece which are members of the EU but not part of the EMU

European Monetary Union (EMU) ['jʊərəpi:ən 'mʌnɪtərɪ 'ju:niən] process by which some of the member states of the EU joined together to adopt the euro as their common currency on 1st January 1999

European Regional Development Fund (ERDF) [jʊərə'pi:ən 'ri:dʒənəl di:'veləpmənt 'fʌnd] fund set up to provide grants to underdeveloped parts of Europe

European Social Charter [jʊərə'pi:ən səʊʃl 'tʃɑ:tə] charter for workers, drawn up by the EU in 1989, by which workers have the right to a fair wage, to equal treatment for men and women, a safe work environment, training, freedom of association and collective bargaining, provision for disabled workers, freedom of movement from country to country, guaranteed standards of living both for the working population as well as for retired people, etc. (Note that there is no machinery for enforcing the Social Charter)

European Union [jʊərəʊ'pi:ən 'ju:niən] (formerly called the European Economic Community (EEC) or the Common Market) a group of European countries linked together by the Treaty of Rome, basing their cooperation on the four fundamental freedoms of movement: of goods, capital, people and services

> COMMENT: the European Community was set up in 1957 and changed its name to the European Union when it adopted the Single Market. It has now grown to include fifteen member states. These are: Austria, Belgium, Denmark, Finland, France, Germany, Greece, Ireland, Italy, Luxembourg, the Netherlands, Portugal, Spain, Sweden and the United Kingdom. The member states of the EU are linked together by the Treaty of Rome in such a way that trade is more free, that money can be moved from one country to another freely, that people can move from one country to another more freely, and that people can work more freely in other countries of the group

euroyen [jʊərəʊjen] *noun* Japanese yen deposited in a European bank and used for trade within Europe

Eurozone ['jʊərəʊzəʊn] *noun* the European countries which use the euro as a common currency, seen as a group

> the European Central Bank left the door open yesterday for a cut in Eurozone interest rates
>
> *Financial Times*

EVA = ECONOMIC VALUE ADDED

evade [ɪ'veɪd] *verb* to try to avoid something; **to evade tax** = to try illegally to avoid paying tax

evaluate [ɪ'væljueɪt] *verb* to calculate a value; ***to evaluate costs***

evaluation [ɪvælju'eɪʃən] *noun* calculation of value; **job evaluation** = examining different jobs within a company to see what skills and qualifications are needed to carry them out

evasion [ɪ'veɪʒən] *noun* avoiding; **tax evasion** = illegally trying not to pay tax

event-driven [ɪ'vent'drɪvn] *adjective* activated and designed to profit from a certain event, such as a merger, bankruptcy or takeover

> event-driven funds isolate out the more general effect of market movements. They are the 'special situations' funds
>
> *Money Observer*

ex- [eks] *preposition* **(a)** out of, from; **price ex warehouse** = price for a product which is to be collected from the manufacturer's or agent's warehouse and so does not include delivery; **price ex works** *or* **ex factory** = price not including transport from the maker's factory **(b)** without; **ex-all (xa)** share price where the share is sold without the dividend, rights issue, or any other current issue; **ex-capitalization** *or* **ex cap (xc)** = share price where the share is sold without a recent scrip issue; **ex-coupon** = bond sold without the current interest coupon; **share quoted ex dividend** *or* **ex div (xd)** = share price not including the right to receive the next dividend; ***the shares went ex dividend yesterday***; **ex-rights (xr)** = share price where the share is sold without a recent rights issue (NOTE: the opposite of **ex** is **cum**)

exact [ɪg'zækt] *adjective* very correct; ***the exact time is 10.27***; ***the salesgirl asked me if I had the exact sum, since the shop had no change*** *US* **exact interest** = annual interest calculated on the basis of 365 days (as opposed to ordinary interest, calculated on 360 days)

exactly [ɪg'zæktli] *adverb* very correctly; ***the total cost was exactly £6,500***

examine [ɪg'zæmɪn] *verb* to look at someone or something very carefully to see if it can be accepted; ***the customs officials asked to examine the inside of the car***; ***the police are examining the papers from the managing director's safe***

examination [ɪgzæmɪ'neɪʃən] *noun* **(a)** looking at something very carefully to see if it is acceptable; **customs examination** = looking at goods or baggage by customs officials **(b)** test to see if someone has passed a course; ***he passed his accountancy examinations***; ***she came first in the final examination for the course***; ***he failed his proficiency examination and so had to leave his job***

examiner [ɪg'zæmɪnə] *noun* **(a)** person who examines something to see if it is correct **(b)** *(in Ireland)* court-appointed administrator for a company

> bankers to the group said that the interim report of the examiner held few surprises for them and that they were ready to begin the hard task of negotiation with the examiner and company representatives
>
> *Irish Times*

exceed [ɪk'siːd] *verb* to be more than; ***discount not exceeding 15%***; ***last year costs exceeded 20% of income for the first time***; **he has exceeded his credit limit** = he has borrowed more money than he is allowed

except [ɪk'sept] *preposition & conjunction* not including; ***in Britain, VAT is levied on all goods and services except books, newspapers, food and children's clothes***; ***sales are rising in all markets except the Far East***

excepted [ɪk'septɪd] *adverb* not including; **errors and omissions excepted** = note on an invoice to show that the company has no responsibility for mistakes in the invoice

exceptional [ɪk'sepʃənl] *adjective* not usual or different; **exceptional items** = items in a balance sheet which do not appear there each year and which are included in the accounts before the pre-tax profit is calculated (as opposed to extraordinary items, which are calculated after the pre-tax profit)

excess [ɪk'ses] *noun* amount which is more than what is allowed; ***an excess of expenditure over revenue***; **excess capacity** = spare capacity which is not being used; **excess liquidity** = cash held by a bank above the normal requirement for that bank; **excess profits** = profit which is more than what is thought to be normal; **excess profits tax** = tax on excess profits

> control of materials provides manufacturers with an opportunity to reduce the amount of money tied up in excess materials
>
> *Duns Business Month*

excessive [ɪk'sesɪv] *adjective* too large; ***excessive management charges***

exchange [ɪks'tʃeɪndʒ] **1** *noun* **(a)** giving of one thing for another; **part exchange** = giving an old product as part of the payment for a new one; ***to take a car in part exchange***; **exchange of contracts** = point in the sale of property when the buyer and the seller both sign the contract of sale which then becomes binding **(b) foreign exchange** = (i) exchanging the money of one country for that of another; (ii) money of another country; ***the company has more than £1m in foreign exchange***; **foreign exchange broker** = person who buys and sells foreign currency on behalf of other people; **foreign exchange market** = dealings in foreign currencies; ***he trades on the foreign exchange market***; ***foreign exchange markets were very active after the dollar devalued***; **rate of exchange** *or* **exchange rate** = price at which one currency is exchanged for another; ***the current rate of exchange is 9.35 francs to the pound***; **exchange rate mechanism (ERM)** = method of stabilizing exchange rates within the European Monetary System, where currencies could only move up or down within a narrow band (usually 2.25% either way, but for certain currencies widened to 6%) without involving a realignment of all the currencies in the system; **exchange control** = control by a government of the way in which its currency may be exchanged for foreign currencies; **exchange controls** = government restrictions on changing the local currency into foreign currency; ***the government had to impose exchange controls to stop the rush to buy dollars***; **exchange cross rates** = rates of exchange for various currencies, shown in terms of each other; **exchange dealer** = person who buys and sells foreign currency; **exchange dealings** = buying and selling foreign currency; *GB* **Exchange Equalization Account** = account with the Bank of England used by the government when buying or selling foreign currency to influence the sterling exchange rate (NOTE: the American equivalent is the **Exchange Stabilization Fund**); **exchange premium** = extra cost above the normal rate for buying a foreign currency **(c) bill of exchange** = document which tells a bank to pay a person (usually used in foreign currency payments) **(d)** market for shares, commodities, futures, etc.; **Stock Exchange** = place where stocks and shares are bought and sold; ***the company's shares are traded on the New York Stock Exchange***; ***he works on the Stock Exchange***; **commodity exchange** = place where commodities are bought and sold **2** *verb* **(a) to exchange one article for another** = to give one thing in place of something else; ***he exchanged his motorcycle for a car***; ***if the trousers are too small you can take them back and exchange them for a larger pair***; ***goods can be exchanged only on production of the sales slip*** **(b) to exchange contracts** = to sign a contract when buying a property, done by both buyer and seller at the same time, making the sale binding **(c)** to change money of one country for money of another; ***to exchange francs for pounds***

> under the barter agreements, Nigeria will export crude oil in exchange for trucks, food, planes and chemicals
>
> *Wall Street Journal*

> can free trade be reconciled with a strong dollar resulting from floating exchange rates
>
> *Duns Business Month*

> a draft report on changes in the international monetary system casts doubt on any return to fixed exchange-rate parities
>
> *Wall Street Journal*

exchangeable [ɪks'tʃeɪndʒəbl] *adjective* which can be exchanged

exchanger [ɪks'tʃeɪndʒə] *noun* person who buys and sells foreign currency

Exchequer [ɪks'tʃekə] *noun GB* **the Exchequer** = (i) fund of all money received by the government of the UK from taxes and other revenues; (ii) the British government's account with the Bank of England; (iii) the British government department dealing with public revenue; **the Chancellor of the Exchequer** = the chief British finance minister; **Exchequer stocks** = Treasury stocks, British government stocks used to finance government expenditure

excise ['eksaɪz] *noun* **(a) excise duty** = tax on certain goods produced in a country (such as alcohol or cigarettes) (NOTE: duty on goods imported into a country is **customs duty**) **(b) Customs and Excise** *or* **Excise Department** = government department which deals with taxes on imports and on products such as alcohol produced in the country; it also deals with VAT

exciseman ['eksaɪzmæn] *noun* person who works in the Excise Department

exclude [ɪks'klu:d] *verb* to keep out or not to include; ***the interest charges have been excluded from the document***; ***damage by fire is excluded from the policy***

exclusion [ɪks'klu:ʒən] *noun* **(a)** act of not including; **exclusion clause** = clause in an insurance policy or warranty which says which items or events are not covered **(b)** *US* item reported on the tax return but on which no tax is payable; ***in addition you have a lifetime exclusion for federal gift and estate taxes of $625,000, up from $600,000 in 1997***

> there was also a once-in-a-lifetime $125,000 exclusion on the sale of a principal residence, but only taxpayers age 55 and older could take it
>
> *Fortune*

exclusive [ɪks'klu:sɪv] *adjective* **(a) exclusive agreement** = agreement where a person is made sole agent for a product in a market; **exclusive right to market a product** = right to be the only person to market the product **(b) exclusive of** = not including; ***all payments are exclusive of tax***; ***the invoice is exclusive of VAT***

exclusivity [eksklu:'sɪvɪti] *noun* exclusive right to market a product

execute ['eksɪkju:t] *verb* to carry out (an order)

execution [eksɪ'kju:ʃən] *noun* **(a)** carrying out of a legal order or contract; **stay of execution** = temporary stopping of a legal order; ***the court granted the company a two-week stay of execution*** **(b)** carrying out of a commercial order or contract; **execution-only service** = service which buys and sells shares for clients, but does not provide any advice and does not manage portfolios; **execution-only broker** = broker who buys and sells shares for clients, but does not provide any advice and does not manage portfolios (as opposed to a full-service broker)

executive [ɪg'zekjʊtɪv] **1** *adjective* which puts decisions into action; **executive committee** = committee which runs a society or a club; **executive director** = director who actually works full-time in the company; **executive powers** = right to put decisions into action; ***he was made managing director with full executive powers over the European operation*** **2** *noun* person in a business who takes decisions, a manager or director; ***sales executive***; ***senior*** *or* ***junior executive***; **account executive** = employee who is the link between his company and certain customers; **chief executive** = executive director in charge of a company; **executive share option scheme** = scheme where executives of a company receive options to buy shares in the company at a certain price in the future

executor [ɪg'zekjʊtə] *noun* person or firm that sees that the terms of a will are carried out; ***he was named executor of his brother's will***

exempt [ɪg'zempt] **1** *adjective* not covered by a law; not forced to obey a law; **exempt from tax** *or* **tax-exempt** = not required to pay tax; ***as a non-profit-making organization we are exempt from tax;*** *US* **exempt securities** = securities, such as municipal bonds, which do not need to be registered with the SEC **2** *verb* to free something from having tax paid on it or from having to pay tax;

non-profit-making organizations are exempted from tax; ***food is exempted from sales tax***; ***the government exempted trusts from tax***

exemption [ɪg'zempʃən] *noun* act of exempting something from a contract or from a tax; **exemption from tax** *or* **tax exemption** = being free from having to pay tax; ***as a non-profit-making organization you can claim tax exemption***

exercise ['eksəsaɪz] **1** *noun* **(a)** use of something; **exercise of an option** = using an option, putting an option into action; **exercise date** = date when an option can be put into effect; **exercise price** = price at which an option will be put into effect **(b)** financial year; ***during the current exercise*** **2** *verb* to use; **to exercise an option** = to put an option into action; ***only 25% of the shareholders exercised their option to purchase shares at £1.57p***; ***he exercised his option to acquire sole marketing rights for the product***; ***the chairwoman exercised her veto to block the motion***

ex gratia ['eks 'greɪʃə] *adjective* **an ex gratia payment** = payment made as a gift, with no other obligations

exit ['egzɪt] *noun* going out, leaving; **exit charge** *or* **exit fee** = charge made when selling units in a unit trust (only some trusts apply this charge) or when selling out of a PEP

ex officio ['eks ə'fɪʃɪəʊ] *adjective & adverb* because of an office held; ***the treasurer is ex officio a member*** *or* ***an ex officio member of the finance committee***

expand [ɪk'spænd] *verb* to increase, to get bigger, to make something bigger; ***an expanding economy***; ***the company is expanding fast***; ***we have had to expand our sales force***

expansion [ɪk'spænʃən] *noun* increase in size; ***the expansion of the domestic market***; ***the company had difficulty in financing its current expansion programme***

> inflation-adjusted GNP moved up at a 1.3% annual rate, its worst performance since the economic expansion began
>
> *Fortune*

> the businesses we back range from start-up ventures to established businesses in need of further capital for expansion
>
> *Times*

> the group is undergoing a period of rapid expansion and this has created an exciting opportunity for a qualified accountant
>
> *Financial Times*

expect [ɪk'spekt] *verb* to hope that something is going to happen; ***they are expecting a cheque from their agent next week***; ***the company was sold for more than the expected price***

> he observed that he expected exports to grow faster than imports
>
> *Sydney Morning Herald*

> American business as a whole has seen profits well above the levels normally expected at this stage of the cycle
>
> *Sunday Times*

expectancy [ɪk'spektənsi] *noun* **life expectancy** = number of years a person is likely to live

expenditure [ɪk'spendɪtʃə] *noun* amounts of money spent; **capital expenditure** = money spent on fixed assets (such as property or machinery); **the company's current expenditure programme** = the company's spending according to the current plan; **heavy expenditure on equipment** = spending large sums of money on equipment (NOTE: usually singular, but American English uses the plural **expenditures**)

expense [ɪk'spens] *noun* **(a)** money spent; ***it is not worth the expense***; ***the expense is too much for my bank balance***; **at great expense** = having spent a lot of money; **he furnished the office regardless of expense** = without thinking how much it cost **(b) expense account** = money which a businessman is allowed by his company to spend on travelling and entertaining clients in connection with his business; ***I'll put this lunch on my expense account***; ***expense account lunches form a large part of our current expenditure***

expenses [ɪk'spensɪz] *plural noun* money paid for doing something in the course of business, but not for manufacturing a product or for purchasing stock; ***the salary offered is £10,000 plus expenses***; **all expenses paid** = with all costs paid by the company; ***the company sent him to San Francisco all expenses paid***; **to cut down on expenses** = to try to reduce spending; **allowable expenses** = business expenses which are allowed against tax; **business expenses** = money spent on running a business, not on stock or assets;

entertainment expenses = money spent on giving meals to business visitors; **fixed expenses** = money which is spent regularly (such as rent, electricity, telephone); **incidental expenses** = small amounts of money spent at various times, in addition to larger amounts; **legal expenses** = money spent on fees paid to lawyers; **overhead expenses** *or* **general expenses** *or* **running expenses** = money spent on the day-to-day cost of a business; **travelling expenses** = money spent on travelling and hotels for business purposes

expiration [ekspɪ'reɪʃən] *noun* coming to an end; ***expiration of an insurance policy***; ***to repay before the expiration of the stated period***; **on expiration of the lease** = when the lease comes to an end; **expiration date** = EXPIRY DATE

expire [ɪk'spaɪə] *verb* to come to an end; ***the option expired last Tuesday***; ***our lease expires in 2005***; **his passport has expired** = his passport is no longer valid

expiry [ɪk'spaɪəri] *noun* coming to an end; ***expiry of an option*** *or* ***of an insurance policy***; **expiry date** = (i) date when something will end, such as the last date for exercising an option; (ii) the last date on which a credit card can be used

export 1 ['ekspɔ:t] *noun* **(a) exports** = goods sent to a foreign country to be sold; ***exports to Africa have increased by 25%*** **(b)** action of sending goods to a foreign country to be sold; ***the export trade*** *or* ***the export market***; **export department** = section of a company which deals in sales to foreign countries; **export duty** = tax paid on goods sent out of a country for sale; **export house** = company which specializes in the export of goods made by other manufacturers; **export licence** = government permit allowing something to be exported; ***the government has refused an export licence for computer parts***; **export manager** = person in charge of an export department in a company; **Export Credit Guarantee Department (ECGD)** = British government department which insures sellers of exports sold on credit against the possibility of non-payment by the purchasers **2** [ɪk'spɔ:t] *verb* to send goods to foreign countries for sale; ***50% of our production is exported***; ***the company imports raw materials and exports the finished products***

exportation [ekspɔ:'teɪʃən] *noun* act of sending goods to foreign countries for sale

exporter [eks'pɔ:tə] *noun* person, company or country which sells goods in foreign countries; ***a major furniture exporter***; ***Canada is an important exporter of oil*** *or* ***an important oil exporter***

exporting [eks'pɔ:tɪŋ] *adjective* which exports; **oil exporting countries** = countries which produce oil and sell it to other countries

expose ['ɪk'spəʊz] *verb* **to be exposed to something** = to be in a position where something might harm you; ***the banks are highly exposed to bad debts in Asia***

exposure [ɪk'spəʊʒə] *noun* amount of risk which a lender or investor runs; ***he is trying to cover his exposure in the property market***; *see also* OVEREXPOSURE

> COMMENT: exposure can be the amount of money lent to a customer (a bank's exposure to a foreign country) or the amount of money which an investor may lose if his investments collapse (such as his exposure in the Australian market)

> whether UK investors should increase their exposure to Europe depnds on their attitidue to risk
>
> *Investors Chronicle*

express [ɪk'spres] **1** *adjective* **(a)** rapid or very fast; ***express letter***; ***express delivery*** **(b)** clearly shown in words; ***the contract has an express condition forbidding sale in Africa*** **2** *verb* **(a)** to put into words or diagrams; ***this chart shows home sales expressed as a percentage of total turnover*** **(b)** to send very fast; ***we expressed the order to the customer's warehouse***

expressly [ɪk'spresli] *adverb* clearly in words; ***the contract expressly forbids sales to the United States***

extend [ɪk'stend] *verb* **(a)** to make available or to give; ***to extend credit to a customer*** **(b)** to make longer; ***to extend a contract for two years***

extended credit [ɪk'stendɪd 'kredɪt] *noun* **(a)** credit allowing the borrower a very long time to pay; ***we sell to Australia on extended credit*** **(b)** *US* extra long credit used by commercial banks borrowing from the Federal Reserve

extension [ɪk'stenʃən] *noun* **(a)** allowing longer time; **to get an extension of credit** = to get more time to pay back; **extension of a contract** = continuing the contract for a further period **(b)** *(in an office)* individual telephone linked to the main switchboard; ***can you get me extension 21? extension 21 is engaged***; ***the sales manager is on extension 53***

> the White House refusal to ask for an extension of the auto import quotas
>
> *Duns Business Month*

extensive [ɪk'stensɪv] *adjective* very large, covering a wide area; ***an extensive network of sales outlets***

external [ɪk'stɜ:nl] *adjective* **(a)** outside a country; **external account** = (i) account with a British bank of someone who is living in another country; (ii) a country's balance of payments account with other countries; **external debt** = money owed by foreign countries; **external debts** *or* **external funds** = money which a company has borrowed from outside sources (such as a bank) as opposed to money raised from shareholders; **external trade** = trade with foreign countries **(b)** outside a company; **external audit** = audit carried out by an independent auditor; **external growth** = growth by buying other companies, rather than by expanding existing sales or products

extract ['ekstrækt] *noun* printed document which is part of a larger document; ***he sent me an extract of the accounts***

extraordinary [ɪk'strɔ:dənəri] **1** *adjective* different from normal; **extraordinary items** = large items of income or expenditure which do not arise from normal trading and which do not occur every year - they are shown separately on the profit and loss account, after taxation (as opposed to exceptional items, which are calculated before the pre-tax profit) **2** *noun (informal)* **extraordinaries** = extraordinary items

> certain company costs, like accountancy fees, occur yearly. Extraordinaries are one-off
>
> *The Times*

Extraordinary General Meeting (EGM) [ɪk'strɔ:dənəri 'dʒenrəl 'mi:tɪŋ] *noun* special meeting of shareholders to discuss an important matter which cannot wait until the next AGM (such as a change in the company's articles of association); ***to call an Extraordinary General Meeting***

Ff

Schedule F ['ʃedju:l 'ef] schedule to the Finance Acts under which tax is charged on income from dividends

face value ['feɪs 'vælju:] *noun* value written on a coin, banknote or share certificate

> travellers cheques cost 1% of their face value - some banks charge more for small amounts
>
> *Sunday Times*

facility [fə'sɪləti] *noun* **(a)** being able to do something easily; ***we offer facilities for payment*** **(b)** loan; **credit facilities** = arrangement with a bank or supplier to have credit so as to buy goods; **overdraft facility** = arrangement with a bank to have an overdraft; **facility fee** *or* **arrangement fee** = charge made to a borrower by a bank for arranging credit facilities

factor ['fæktə] **1** *noun* **(a)** thing which is important or which influences; ***the drop in sales is an important factor in the company's lower profits***; **cost factor** = problem of cost; **cyclical factors** = way in which a trade cycle affects businesses; **deciding factor** = most important factor which influences a decision; **load factor** = number of seats in a bus, plane or train which are occupied by passengers who have paid the full fare; **factors of production** = things needed to produce a product (land, labour and capital) **(b) by a factor of ten** = ten times **(c)** (i) person who acts for another and is paid a commission; (ii) person or company that is responsible for collecting debts for companies, by buying debts at a discount to their face value **2** *verb* **(a)** to buy debts from a company at a discount **(b) to factor in** = to add a factor when making calculations

> COMMENT: a factor collects a company's debts when due, and pays the creditor in advance part of the sum to be collected; the debtors are informed of this arrangement, as opposed to invoice discounting, where the debtor is not told

> the market has already factored in the 8p full-year dividend announced yesterday
>
> *The Times*

factoring ['fæktərɪŋ] *noun* business of buying debts at a discount; **factoring charges** = cost of selling debts to a factor for a commission

factory gate prices ['fæktri 'geɪt 'praɪsɪz] *noun* prices of manufactured goods leaving the factory

fail [feɪl] *verb* **(a)** not to do something which you were trying to do; ***the company failed to notify the tax office of its change of address*** **(b)** to be unsuccessful commercially; **the company failed** = the company went bankrupt; ***he lost all his money when the bank failed***

failure ['feɪljə] *noun* **(a)** breaking down, stopping; ***the failure of the negotiations*** **(b) failure to pay a bill** = not paying a bill **(c) commercial failure** = financial collapse or bankruptcy; ***he lost all his money in the bank failure***

fair [feə] **1** *noun* **trade fair** = large exhibition and meeting for advertising and selling a certain type of product; ***the fair is open from 9 a.m. to 5 p.m.***; ***the computer fair runs from April 1st to 6th***; ***there are two trade fairs running in London at the same time - the carpet manufacturers' and the computer dealers'*** **2** *adjective* **(a)** honest or correct; **fair deal** = arrangement where both parties are treated equally; ***the workers feel they did not get a fair deal from the management***; **fair dealing** = legal buying and selling of shares; **fair price** = good price for both buyer and seller; **fair trade** = (i) international business system where countries agree not to charge import duties on certain items imported from their trading partners; (ii) *US* = RESALE PRICE MAINTENANCE; **fair trading** *or* **fair dealing** = way of doing business which is reasonable and does not harm the consumer; *GB* **Office of Fair Trading** = government department which protects consumers against unfair or illegal business; **fair value** *US* **fair market value** = price paid by a buyer who knows the value of what he is buying to a seller who also knows the value of what he is selling (i.e., neither is cheating the other); **fair wear and tear** = acceptable damage caused by normal use; ***the insurance policy covers most damage, but not fair wear and tear to the machine*** **(b) fair copy** = document which is written or typed with no changes or mistakes

fall [fɔːl] **1** *noun* sudden drop, suddenly becoming smaller, loss of value; ***a fall in the exchange rate***; ***a fall in the price of gold***; ***a fall on the Stock Exchange***; ***profits showed a 10% fall*** **2** *verb* **(a)** to drop suddenly to a lower price; ***shares fell on the market today***; ***gold shares fell 10%*** *or* ***fell 45 cents on the Stock Exchange***; ***the price of gold fell for the second day running***; ***the pound fell against other European currencies*** **(b)** to happen, to take place; ***the public holiday falls on a Tuesday***; **payments which fall due** = payments which are now due to be made (NOTE: **falling - fell - has fallen**)

> market analysts described the falls in the second half of last week as a technical correction to the market
>
> *Australian Financial Review*

> for the first time since mortgage rates began falling in March a financial institution has raised charges on homeowner loans
>
> *Globe and Mail (Toronto)*

fall away [ˈfɔːl əˈweɪ] *verb* to become less; ***hotel bookings have fallen away since the tourist season ended***

fall back [ˈfɔːl ˈbæk] *verb* to become lower or cheaper after rising in price; ***shares fell back in light trading***

fall back on [ˈfɔːl ˈbæk ˈɒn] *verb* to have to use something that has been kept for emergencies; ***to fall back on cash reserves***

fall behind [ˈfɔːl bɪˈhaɪnd] *verb* to be late in doing something; ***he fell behind with his mortgage repayments***

falling [ˈfɔːlɪŋ] *adjective* which is growing smaller or dropping in price; **a falling market** = market where prices are coming down; **the falling pound** = the pound which is losing its value against other currencies

> falling profitability means falling share prices
>
> *Investors Chronicle*

fall off [ˈfɔːl ˈɒf] *verb* to become lower or cheaper or less; ***sales have fallen off since the tourist season ended***

fall out [ˈfɔːl ˈaʊt] *verb* **the bottom has fallen out of the market** = sales have fallen below what previously seemed to be their lowest point

fallout [ˈfɔːlaʊt] *noun* bad result, collapse

> a by-product of the fallout in stock markets has been a widening of spreads between buying and selling prices on some unit trusts
>
> *Money Observer*

false [fɔːls] *adjective* not true or not correct; ***to make a false entry in the balance sheet***; **false market** = market in shares caused by persons or companies conspiring to buy or sell and so influence the share price to their advantage; **false pretences** = doing or saying something to cheat someone; ***he was sent to prison for obtaining money by false pretences***; **false weight** = weight on shop scales which is wrong and so cheats customers

falsify [ˈfɔːlsɪfaɪ] *verb* to change something to make it wrong; ***to falsify the accounts***

falsification [fɔːlsɪfɪˈkeɪʃən] *noun* action of making false entries in accounts

family [ˈfæmli] *noun* group of people who are related to each other, especially a mother, father and children; **family firm** *or* **family-run firm** = firm where the shareholders and directors are members of the same family; ***it was a three-store family-run chain***

Fannie Mae [ˈfæni ˈmeɪ] *(informal) US* = FEDERAL NATIONAL MORTGAGE ASSOCIATION

FAS = FEDERAL ACCOUNTING STANDARDS

FASIT = FINANCIAL ASSET SECURITIZATION INVESTMENT TRUST

fat cat [ˈfæt ˈkæt] *noun (informal)* businessman who earns an enormous salary and bonus

favourable *US* **favorable** [ˈfeɪvərəbl] *adjective* which gives an advantage; **favourable balance of trade** = situation where a country's exports are more than the imports; **on favourable terms** = on specially good terms; ***the shop is let on very favourable terms***

fax [fæks] **1** *noun* (i) system for sending facsimile copies of documents via the telephone lines; (ii) document sent by this method; ***we received a fax of the order this morning***; ***can you confirm the booking by fax?*** **2** *verb* to send a message by fax; ***the details of the offer were faxed to the brokers this morning***

> COMMENT: banks will not accept fax messages as binding instructions (as for example, a faxed order for money to be transferred from one account to another)

FAZ index daily index of leading industrial shares on the Frankfurt Stock Exchange (published in the Frankfurter Allgemeine Zeitung)

FD = FINANCIAL DIRECTOR

> some 50% of FDs believed that the economy would weaken
>
> *Accountancy Age*

FDI = FOREIGN DIRECT INVESTMENT

FDIC = FEDERAL DEPOSIT INSURANCE CORPORATION

the Fed [ðə 'fed] *US (informal)* = FEDERAL RESERVE BOARD; **Fed Funds** = FEDERAL FUNDS; **Fed Wire** = = FEDERAL RESERVE WIRE SYSTEM

> indications of weakness in the US economy were contained in figures from the Fed on industrial production for April
>
> *Financial Times*

> the half-point discount rate move gives the Fed room to reduce the federal funds rate further if economic weakness persists. The Fed sets the discount rate directly, but controls the federal funds rate by buying and selling Treasury securities
>
> *Wall Street Journal*

federal ['fedərəl] *adjective* **(a)** referring to a system of government where a group of states are linked together in a federation **(b)** referring to the central government of the United States; ***most federal offices are in Washington***; **federal (credit) agencies** = agencies (such as the Federal Home Loan Banks) which provide credit to individual borrowers and are backed by the federal government; **federal funds** *or* **fed funds** = deposits by commercial banks with the Federal Reserve Banks, which can be used for short-term loans to other banks; **fed funds rate** = the rate charged by banks for lending money deposited with the Federal Reserve to other banks

> federal examiners will determine which of the privately-insured savings and loans qualify for federal insurance
>
> *Wall Street Journal*

> since 1978 America has freed many of its industries from federal rules that set prices and controlled the entry of new companies
>
> *Economist*

Federal Accounting Standards (FAS) ['fedərəl ə'kaʊntɪŋ 'stændədz] the US regulations governing accounting procedures

Federal Deposit Insurance Corporation (FDIC) ['fedərəl dɪ'pɒzɪt ɪnʃʊrəns kɔːpə'reɪʃn] *US* federal agency which manages insurance funds that insure deposits in commercial banks and in savings and loans associations

Federal Home Loan Banks ['fedərəl 'həʊm 'ləʊn 'bæŋks] *US* group of twelve banks which lend to Savings and Loans Associations, and to other institutions which lend money to homeowners against mortgages

Federal Home Loan Mortgage Corporation (FHLMC *or* **Freddie Mac)** ['fedərəl 'həʊm 'ləʊn 'mɔːgɪdʒ kɔːpə'reɪʃn] *US* federal organization which backs mortgages issued by the Savings and Loans Associations

Federal National Mortgage Association (FNMA *or* **Fannie Mae)** ['fedərəl 'næʃnl 'mɔːgɪdʒ əsəʊsi'eɪʃn] *US* privately owned organization which regulates mortgages and helps offer mortgages backed by federal funds

Federal Reserve ['fedərəl rɪ'zɜːv] system of federal government control of the US banks, where the Federal Reserve Board regulates money supply, prints money, fixes the discount rate and issues government bonds

> COMMENT: the Federal Reserve system is the central bank of the USA. The system is run by the Federal Reserve Board, a committee of seven members (or 'governors') who are all appointed by the President. The twelve Federal Reserve Banks act as lenders of last resort to local

commercial banks. Although the board is appointed by the president, the whole system is relatively independent of the US government

Federal Reserve Bank ['fedərəl rɪ'zɜːv 'bæŋk] *US* one of the twelve regional banks in the USA which are owned by the state and directed by the Federal Reserve Board

Federal Reserve Board (FRB) ['fedərəl rɪ'zɜːv 'bɔːd] *US* committee which runs the central banks in the USA

> pressure on the Federal Reserve Board to ease monetary policy mounted yesterday with the release of a set of pessimistic economic statistics
>
> *Financial Times*

Federal Reserve Wire System (Fed Wire) computerized communications system which links the Federal Reserve Board, its banks, and the US Treasury

Federal Trade Commission ['fedrəl 'treɪd kə'mɪʃən] federal agency established to keep business competition free and fair

federation [fedə'reɪʃən] *noun* group of societies, companies or organizations which have a central organization which represents them and looks after their common interests; ***federation of trades unions; employers' federation***

fee [fiː] *noun* **(a)** money paid for work carried out by a professional person (such as an accountant or a doctor or a lawyer); ***we charge a small fee for our services***; **director's fees** = fees paid to a director of a company **(b)** money paid for something; ***entrance fee*** *or* ***admission fee***; ***registration fee*** **(c) exit fee** = charge made when selling units in a unit trust (only some trusts apply this charge) or when selling out of a PEP

fiat money ['fiːæt 'mʌni] *noun* coins or notes which are not worth much as paper or metal, but are said by the government to have a value

FIBOR ['fiːbɔː] = FRANKFURT INTERBANK OFFERED RATE

fictitious assets [fɪk'tɪʃəs 'æsɪts] *noun* assets which do not really exist, but are entered as assets to balance the accounts

fiddle ['fɪdl] **1** *noun (informal)* cheating; ***it's all a fiddle***; **he's on the fiddle** = he is trying to cheat **2** *verb (informal)* to cheat; ***he tried to fiddle his tax returns; the salesman was caught fiddling his expense account***

fide ['faɪdi] *see* BONA FIDE

fiduciary [fɪ'djuːʃjəri] *adjective & noun* (person) acting as trustee for someone else; **fiduciary deposits** = bank deposits which are managed for the depositor by the bank

FIFO ['faɪfəʊ] = FIRST IN FIRST OUT

fifty-fifty ['fɪfti 'fɪfti] *adjective & adverb* half; **to go fifty-fifty** = to share the costs equally; **he has a fifty-fifty chance of making a profit** = he has an equal chance of making a profit or a loss

figure ['fɪgə] *noun* **(a)** number; cost written in numbers; ***the figure in the accounts for heating is very high***; **he put a very low figure on the value of the lease** = he calculated the value of the lease as very low **(b) figures** = written numbers; **sales figures** = total sales; **to work out the figures** = to calculate; **his income runs into five figures** *or* **he has a five-figure income** = his income is more than £10,000; **in round figures** = not totally accurate, but correct to the nearest 10 or 100; ***they have a workforce of 2,500 in round figures***; *see also* DOUBLE FIGURES, SINGLE FIGURES **(c) figures** = results for a company; ***the figures for last year*** *or* ***last year's figures***

file [faɪl] **1** *noun* **(a)** cardboard holder for documents, which can fit in the drawer of a filing cabinet; ***put these letters in the customer file; look in the file marked 'Scottish sales'***; **box file** = cardboard box for holding documents **(b)** documents kept for reference; **to place something on file** = to keep a record of something; **to keep someone's name on file** = to keep someone's name on a list for reference; **file copy** = copy of a document which is kept for reference in an office **(c)** section of data on a computer (such as payroll, address list, customer accounts); ***how can we protect our computer files?*** **2** *verb* **(a) to file documents** = to put documents in order so that they can be found easily; ***the correspondence is filed under 'complaints'*** **(b)** to make an official request; **to file for bankruptcy** *or* **to file a petition in bankruptcy** = (i) to ask officially to be made bankrupt yourself; (ii) to ask officially for someone else to be made bankrupt **(c)** to register something officially; ***to file an application for a patent*** **(d)** *US* **to file a return to the tax office** = to fill in and send a tax return; *(of husband and wife)* **to file jointly** = to make a joint tax declaration; **to file separately** = to file two separate tax returns, one for the husband and one for the wife; **tax-filing program** = computer software to help draw up your income tax return

two of their competitors recently filed for bankruptcy

Fortune

---

filer ['faɪlə] *noun US* person who files an income tax return; **single filer** = unmarried individual who files an income tax return

the IRS audits about 1 to 2 percent of individual income-tax returns filed each year, and roughly a quarter of those filers are subjected to lifestyle audits

Smart Money

the rules have changed for tax filers, mostly for the better

Fortune

---

fill [fɪl] *verb US* to carry out a client's instructions to buy or sell; **fill or kill (FOK)** = carry out a client's order immediately or else the order is cancelled

FIMBRA ['fɪmbrə] = FINANCIAL INTERMEDIARIES, MANAGERS AND BROKERS REGULATORY ASSOCIATION

final ['faɪnl] *adjective* last, coming at the end of a period; ***to pay the final instalment***; ***to make the final payment***; ***to put the final details on a document***; **final date for payment** = last date by which payment should be made; **final closing date** = last date for acceptance of a takeover bid, when the bidder has to announce how many shareholders have accepted his offer; **final demand** = last reminder from a supplier, after which he will sue for payment; **final discharge** = last payment of what is left of a debt; **final dividend** = dividend paid at the end of a year's trading, which has to be approved by the shareholders; **final product** = manufactured product, made at the end of a production process

finalize ['faɪnəlaɪz] *verb* to agree final details; ***we hope to finalize the agreement tomorrow***; ***after six weeks of negotiations the loan was finalized yesterday***

finance 1 ['faɪnæns] *noun* **(a)** money used by a company, provided by the shareholders or by loans; **finance charge** = (i) the cost of borrowing money; (ii) additional charge made to a customer who asks for extended credit; **finance company** *or* **finance corporation** *or* **finance house** = company, usually part of a commercial bank, which provides money for hire-purchase; **finance house deposits** = amount of money deposited by banks with finance houses and used by them to provide hire-purchase loans to clients; **finance market** = place where large sums of money can be lent or borrowed; **high finance** = lending, investing and borrowing of very large sums of money, organized by financiers; **Finance and Leasing Association (FLA)** = organization representing firms engaged in business finance and the leasing of equipment and cars; *see also* BEHAVIORAL FINANCE **(b)** money (of a club, local authority, etc.); ***she is the secretary of the local authority finance committee*** **(c) finances** = money or cash which is available; ***the bad state of the company's finances*** **2** [faɪ'næns] *verb* to provide money to pay for something; ***to finance an operation***

Finance Act ['faɪnæns 'ækt] *noun GB* annual act of parliament which gives the government the power to obtain money from taxes as proposed in the Budget

Finance Bill ['faɪnæns 'bɪl] *noun* **(a)** *GB* bill which lists the proposals in a chancellor's budget and which is debated before being voted into law as the Finance Act **(b)** *US* short-term bill of exchange which provides credit for a corporation so that it can continue trading

Finance Ministry ['faɪnæns 'mɪnɪstri] *noun* government department dealing with a country's finance

> COMMENT: in most countries, the government department dealing with finance is called the Finance Ministry, with a Finance Minister in charge. Both in the UK and the USA, the department is called the Treasury, and the minister in charge is the Chancellor of the Exchequer in the UK, and the Treasury Secretary in the USA

financial [fɪ'nænʃəl] *adjective* concerning money; **financial adviser** = person or company that gives advice on financial matters for a fee; **financial assistance** = help in the form of money; **financial circumstances** = state of someone's finances; ***the more you tell us about your full financial circumstances, the more we may be able to help***; **financial correspondent** = journalist who writes articles on money matters for a newspaper; **financial difficulties** = bad state of someone's finances; ***if you find yourself in financial difficulties go to your bank manager for advice***; **financial futures** = investments in financial instruments, such as gilt-edged stocks, eurodollars, etc., for delivery at a date in the future; **financial institution** = organization such as a building society, pension fund or insurance company, which invests large amounts of money in securities; **financial instrument** = any form of investment in the stock market or in other financial markets, such as shares, government stocks, certificates of deposit, bills of exchange, etc.; **financial intermediary** = institution which takes deposits or loans from individuals and lends money to clients (banks, building societies, hire purchase companies, are all types of financial intermediaries); **financial position** = state of a company's bank balance (assets and debts); **financial resources** = money which is available for investment; ***a company with strong financial resources***; **financial risk** = possibility of losing money; ***there is no financial risk in selling to East European countries on credit***; **financial supermarket** = company which offers a range of financial services (a bank may offer loans, mortgages, pensions, insurance as well as the normal personal banking services) (NOTE: also called **one-stop shopping**); **financial year** = the twelve months' period for a firm's accounts (not necessarily the same as a calendar year)

Financial Asset Securitization Investment Trust (FASIT) *US* investment trust that combines various loans, money outstanding on credit card purchases, etc., into one single fund for an individual

financially [fɪˈnænʃəli] *adverb* regarding money; **company which is financially sound** = company which is profitable and has strong assets

financials [faɪˈnænʃlz] *noun* = *FINANCIAL FUTURES*

Financial Secretary to the Treasury [fɪˈnænʃəl ˈsekrətri] *noun* minister of state in charge of the Treasury, under the Chancellor of the Exchequer; *see also* CHIEF SECRETARY

Financial Services Act [fɪˈnænʃəl ˈsɜːvɪsɪz ˈækt] Act of the British Parliament which regulates the offering of financial services to the general public and to private investors

Financial Services Authority (FSA) [fɪˈnænʃəl ˈsɜːvɪsɪz ɔːˈθɒrɪti] government agency set up to regulate all financial services, such as banks, stockbrokers, unit trusts and Oeics, pension companies, professional bodies, investment exchanges, etc., and to supervise the regulators in each sector (IMRO, SFA, etc., are now all part of the FSA)

> the Financial Services Authority recently announced its intention to allow unit trusts to introduce single pricing and hopes to introduce the new system early next year. The FSA's initiative will prevent the manipulation of bid/offer spreads that result in investors losing out
>
> *Money Observer*

financial statement [faɪˈnænʃəl ˈsteɪtmənt] *noun* **(a)** document which shows the financial situation of a company or individual at a particular moment; ***the accounts department has prepared a financial statement for the shareholders*** **(b) the Financial Statement** = document which sets out the details of the budget presented by the Chancellor of the Exchequer (it is published on Budget Day)

Financial Times (FT) [faɪˈnænʃəl ˈtaɪmz] important British financial daily newspaper (printed on pink paper); **FTSE Actuaries Share Indices** = several indices based on prices on the London Stock Exchange, which are calculated by and published in the Financial Times; **FTSE All-Share Index** = index based on the market price of about 840 companies listed on the London Stock Exchange (it includes the companies on the FTSE 100, the FTSE Mid 250 and the FTSE SmallCap Indices) (NOTE: also simply called the **All-Share Index**); **FTSE Eurotop 300 Index** = index of 300 leading European shares, quoted in euros; **FT Industrial Group Share Index** = index based on the market prices of more than 470 leading industrial companies; **FT-Stock Exchange 100 Share Index (FTSE 100** *or* **Footsie)** = index based on the prices of the one hundred largest companies (this is the main London index); **FTSE Mid 250 Share Index** = index based on the market prices of 250 companies capitalized between £300m and £2.5bn (this is about 16% of the total stock market capitalization); **FTSE SmallCap Index** = index which covers about 500 smaller companies which are too small to be included in the two main indices; **FTSE All-Small Index** = index covering the FTSE SmallCap companies, plus about 750 Fledgling Companies which are too small to be included in the All-Share Index

> directing all of their investments into a FTSE All-Share tracker (an index fund) would be not only acceptable but probably very clever. The index fund would probably grow faster than any trust given time
>
> *Money Observer*

financier [faɪˈnænsiə] *noun* person who organizes deals involving large amounts of money

financing [faɪˈnænsɪŋ] *noun* providing money; ***the financing of the project was done by two international banks***; **deficit financing** = planning by a government to borrow money to cover the shortfall between expenditure and income from taxation

finder's fee [ˈfaɪndəz ˈfiː] *noun* **(a)** fee paid to a person who finds a client for another (as for example, someone who introduces a client to a stockbroking firm) **(b)** fee paid to a person who arranges a loan for someone, finds a property for someone to buy, etc.

fine [faɪn] **1** *noun* money paid because of something wrong which has been done; ***he was asked to pay a $25,000 fine***; ***we had to pay a $10 parking fine*** **2** *verb* to punish someone by making him pay money; ***to fine someone £2,500 for obtaining money by false pretences*** **3** *adjective* very small; **fine rate of discount** = lowest rate of discount on offer **4** *adverb* very thin or very small; **we are cutting our margins very fine** = we are reducing our margins to the smallest possible

fine tune [ˈfaɪn ˈtjuːn] *verb* to make small adjustments to (a plan or the economy) so that it works better

fine-tuning [ˈfaɪn ˈtjuːnɪŋ] *noun* making small adjustments to interest rates, the tax bands, the money supply, etc., to improve a nation's economy

finish [ˈfɪnɪʃ] **1** *noun* end of a day's trading on the Stock Exchange; ***oil shares rallied at the finish*** **2** *verb* to come to an end; ***the market finished the day on a stronger note***

Finnmark [ˈfɪnmɑːk] *noun* name for the currency used with the euro in Finland (NOTE: also called the **marka**)

fire sale [ˈfaɪə ˈseɪl] *noun* (i) sale of fire-damaged goods; (ii) sale of anything at a very low price

firewalls [ˈfaɪəwɔːlz] *noun US* = CHINESE WALLS

firm [fɜːm] **1** *noun* business or partnership; ***he is a partner in a law firm***; ***a manufacturing firm***; ***an important publishing firm*** **2** *adjective* **(a)** which cannot be changed; ***to make a firm offer for something***; ***to place a firm offer for two aircraft***; ***they are quoting a firm price of £1.22 per unit***; **firm order** = (i) confirmed order, which the purchaser cannot withdraw; (ii) order to a broker to sell or buy on a certain date; **firm sale** = sale which does not allow the purchaser to return the goods **(b)** not dropping in price, and possibly going to rise; ***sterling was firmer on the foreign exchange markets***; ***shares remained firm*** **3** *verb (Stock Exchange)* to remain at a price and gradually go up; ***the shares firmed at £1.50***

> COMMENT: strictly speaking, a 'firm' is a partnership or other trading organization which is not a limited company. In practice, it is better to use the term for businesses such as 'a firm of accountants' or 'a firm of stockbrokers', rather than for 'a major aircraft construction firm' which is likely to be a plc

> some profit-taking was noted, but underlying sentiment remained firm
>
> *Financial Times*

firmness [ˈfɜːmnəs] *noun* being steady at a certain price, being likely to rise; ***the firmness of the pound***

> Toronto failed to mirror New York's firmness as a drop in gold shares on a falling bullion price left the market closing on a mixed note
>
> *Financial Times*

firm up [ˈfɜːm ˈʌp] *verb* to finalize, to agree final details; ***we expect to firm up the deal at the next trade fair***

first [fɜːst] *noun* person or thing that is there at the beginning or earlier than others; ***our company was one of the first to sell into the European market***; **first half** *or* **first half-year** = six months' period from January to the end of June; **first in first out (FIFO)** = (i) redundancy policy, where the people who have been working longest are the first to be made redundant; (ii) accounting policy where stock is valued at the price of the oldest purchases; *compare* LIFO; **first mortgage** = mortgage taken out on a property, usually when buying the property (the lender has a lien on the property; if the first mortgage is not sufficient, a second mortgage can be taken out, but the second lender will have less security than the first, and will charge more)

first-class [ˈfɜːsˈklɑːs] *adjective & noun* **(a)** top quality; most expensive; ***he is a first-class accountant*** **(b)** most expensive and comfortable type of travel or type of hotel; ***to travel first-class***; ***first-class travel provides the best service***; ***a first-class ticket***; ***to stay in first-class hotels***; **first-class mail** = (i) *GB* most expensive mail service, designed to be faster; (ii) *US* mail service for letters and postcards; ***a first-class letter should get to Scotland in a day***

first quarter ['fɜ:st 'kwɔ:tə] *noun* three months' period from January to the end of March

fiscal ['fɪskəl] *adjective* referring to tax or to government revenues; ***the government's fiscal policies***; **fiscal agent** = bank which acts as an agent for a eurobond issue; **fiscal drag** = negative effect on an individual's work of higher personal taxation; **fiscal measures** = tax changes made by a government to improve the working of the economy; **fiscal policy** = the policy of a government regarding taxation; **fiscal year** = (i) twelve-month period on which taxes are calculated (in the UK, April 6th to April 5th); (ii) any twelve-month period used by a company as the period for calculating its taxes

> the standard measure of fiscal policy - the public sector borrowing requirement - is kept misleadingly low
>
> *Economist*

fixation [fɪk'seɪʃn] *noun* (i) stating of a price on an options market; (ii) fixing of a price, such as the price of gold

fixed [fɪkst] *adjective* permanent, which cannot be removed; **fixed assets** = property or machinery which a company owns and uses, but which the company does not buy or sell as part of its regular trade; **fixed capital** = capital in the form of buildings and machinery; **fixed charge** = charge linked to certain specified assets, such as a mortgage on a property; **fixed costs** = costs paid to produce a product which do not increase with the amount of product made (such as rent); **fixed deposit** = deposit which pays a stated interest over a set period; **fixed exchange rate** = rate of exchange of one currency against another which cannot fluctuate, and can only be changed by devaluation or revaluation; **fixed expenses** = money which is spent regularly (such as rent, electricity, telephone); **fixed income** = income which does not change (as from an annuity); **fixed-income derivatives** = derivatives which pay a fixed interest at stated dates in the future; **fixed rate** = rate (such as an exchange rate) which does not change; **fixed rate loan** = loan on which the rate of interest stays the same for the duration of the loan; **fixed scale of charges** = rate of charging which cannot be altered

> coupons are fixed by reference to interest rates at the time a gilt is first issued
>
> *Investors Chronicle*

> you must offer shippers and importers fixed rates over a reasonable period of time
>
> *Lloyd's List*

fixed-interest ['fɪkst'ɪntrest] *adjective* (investment) which produces an interest which does not vary; **fixed-interest investments** = investments producing an interest which does not change; **fixed-interest securities** = securities (such as government bonds) which produce an interest which does not change

fixed-price ['fɪkst'praɪs] *noun* which has a price which cannot be changed; **fixed-price agreement** = agreement where a company provides a service or a product at a price which stays the same for the whole period of the agreement; **fixed-price offer for sale** = offer to purchase shares in a new company for a price which has been fixed at flotation (as opposed to tendering)

fixed-term ['fɪksttɜ:m] *adjective* lasting for a fixed number of years; **fixed-term product** = financial product, such as a bond, which runs for a fixed number of years

fixer ['fɪksə] *noun (informal)* person who has a reputation for arranging business deals (often illegally)

fixing ['fɪksɪŋ] *noun* **(a)** arranging; ***fixing of charges***; ***fixing of a mortgage rate*** **(b) price fixing** = illegal agreement between companies to charge the same price for competing products **(c)** regular meeting to set a price; **gold fixing** = system where the world price for gold is set twice a day in US dollars on the London Gold Exchange and in Paris and Zurich

fl *abbreviation for* guilder

FLA = FINANCE AND LEASING ASSOCIATION

flag [flæg] *noun* term used by chartists to refer to a period when prices consolidate a previous advance or fall

flat [flæt] **1** *adjective* **(a)** (market prices) which do not fall or rise because of low demand; ***the market was flat today*** **(b)** fixed, not changing; **flat rate** = charge which always stays the same; ***we pay a flat rate for electricity each quarter***; ***he is paid a flat rate of £2 per thousand***; **flat yield** = interest rate as a percentage of the price paid for fixed-interest stock **2** *noun* set of rooms for one family in a building with other sets of similar rooms; **company flat** = flat owned by a company and used by members of staff from time to time (NOTE: American English is **apartment**)

> the government revised its earlier reports for July and August. Originally reported as flat in July and declining by 0.2% in August, industrial production is now seen to have risen by 0.2% and 0.1% respectively in those months
>
> *Sunday Times*

flat bed imprinter ['flæt 'bed ɪm'prɪntə] *noun US see* IMPRINTER

flat out ['flæt 'aʊt] *adverb* working hard or at full speed; ***the factory worked flat out to complete the order on time***

fledgling companies ['fledʒlɪŋ 'kʌmpniz] *noun* companies which are just starting in business, especially companies listed on the London Stock Exchange with a capitalization which is too small for them to be included in the FTSE All-Share Index

flexible ['fleksəbl] *adjective* which can be altered or changed; ***flexible budget***; ***flexible prices***; ***flexible pricing policy***; **flexible working hours** = system where workers can start or stop work at different hours of the morning or evening provided that they work a certain number of hours per day or week; ***we work flexible hours***

flexibility [fleksə'bɪləti] *noun* being easily changed; ***there is no flexibility in the company's pricing policy***

flight ['flaɪt] *noun* **flight of capital** = rapid movement of capital out of one country because of lack of confidence in that country's economic future; **flight to quality** = tendency of investors to buy safe blue-chip securities when the economic outlook is uncertain

> although just a trickle so far, Japanese capital flight could take off within the next two weeks as Japanese citizens seek a higher return on their savings
>
> *The Banker*

> in the flight to quality, investors bought so many bund futures that even if only a third of them had requested delivery, there did not exist enough bonds in the market to satisfy the potential demand
>
> *Financial Times*

flip side ['flɪp 'saɪd] *noun* negative factors (in a proposal)

float [fləʊt] **1** *noun* **(a)** cash taken from a central supply and used for running expenses; ***the sales reps have a float of £100 each***; **cash float** = cash put into the cash box at the beginning of the day to allow business to start; ***we start the day with a £20 float in the cash desk*** **(b)** starting a new company by selling shares in it on the Stock Exchange; ***the float of the new company was a complete failure*** **(c)** allowing a currency to settle at its own exchange rates, without any government intervention; **dirty float** *or* **managed float** = floating a currency, where the government intervenes to regulate the exchange rate; **clean float** = floating a currency freely on the international markets, without any interference from the government **2** *verb* **(a) to float a company** = to start a new company by selling shares in it on the Stock Exchange; **to float a loan** = to raise a loan on the financial market by asking banks and companies to subscribe to it **(b)** to let a currency find its own exchange rate on the international markets and not be fixed; ***the government has let sterling float***; ***the government has decided to float the pound***

floater ['fləʊtə] *noun US* loan with a variable interest rate

floating ['fləʊtɪŋ] **1** *noun* **(a) floating of a company** = starting a new company by selling shares in it on the Stock Exchange **(b) the floating of the pound** = letting the pound find its own exchange rate on the international market **2** *adjective* which is not fixed; ***floating exchange rates***; ***the floating pound***; **floating charge** = charge linked to any or all of the company's assets; **floating rate** = (i) rate of interest on a loan which is not fixed, but can change with the current bank interest rates; (ii) exchange rate for a currency which can vary according to market demand, and is not fixed by the government; **floating-rate notes (FRNs)** = eurocurrency loans arranged by a bank which are not at a fixed rate of interest (they mature in 5-7 years)

> in a world of floating exchange rates the dollar is strong because of capital inflows rather than weak because of the nation's trade deficit
>
> *Duns Business Month*

floor [flɔː] *noun* **(a)** part of the room which you walk on; **floor space** = area of floor in an office or warehouse; ***we have 3,500 square metres of floor space to let***; **the factory floor** = main works of a factory; **on the shop floor** = in the works or in the factory or among the ordinary workers; ***the feeling on the shop***

floor is that the manager does not know his job **(b)** all rooms on one level in a building; ***the shoe department is on the first floor***; ***her office is on the 26th floor*** **(c) dealing floor** *or* **trading floor** = (i) area of a broking house where dealing in securities is carried out by phone, using monitors to display current prices and stock exchange transactions; (ii) part of a stock exchange where dealers trade in securities (NOTE: American English for this is also **pit**); *US* **floor broker** = stockbroker who is a member of a brokerage house; *US* **floor trader** = independent trader on a Stock Exchange, who buys and sells on his own account **(d)** bottom level of something (such as the lowest exchange rate which a government will accept for its currency or the lower limit imposed on an interest rate; the opposite is the 'ceiling' or 'cap'); **to establish a floor at an auction** = to fix the bottom price below which the seller will not sell; **floor limit** = highest sale through a credit card that a retailer can accept without haveing to get authorization from the bank that issued the card; **floor price** = lowest price, price which cannot go any lower

flop [flɒp] **1** *noun* failure, not being a success; ***the new model was a flop*** **2** *verb* to fail, not to be a success; ***the flotation of the new company flopped badly*** (NOTE: **flopping - flopped**)

florin ['flɒrɪn] *noun* another name for the Dutch guilder (NOTE: the abbreviation for the guilder is **fl**)

flotation [fləʊ'teɪʃən] *noun* **the flotation of a new company** = starting a new company by selling shares in it

flow [fləʊ] **1** *noun* **(a)** movement; **capital flow** = the flow of capital into or out of a country; ***the flow of investments out of Japan***; *see also* INFLOW, OUTFLOW **(b)** **cash flow** = cash which comes into a company from sales and goes out in purchases or overhead expenditure; **discounted cash flow (DCF)** = calculation of forecast sales of a product in current terms with reductions for current interest rates; **the company is suffering from cash flow problems** = cash income is not coming in fast enough to pay for the expenditure going out **(c) flow chart** *or* **flow diagram** = chart which shows the arrangement of work processes in a series **2** *verb* to move smoothly; ***production is now flowing normally after the strike***

> on 2 September, the day after Malaysia announced restrictions on foreign capital flows, the FT put forward persuasive arguments in favour of temporary capital controls in times of financial crisis. In particular, it recognised the destabilizing influence that short-term capital flows - invariably speculative by nature - have on emerging economies and the millions of people whose lives suffer in the aftermath
>
> *Money Observer*

fluctuate ['flʌktjueɪt] *verb* to move up and down; ***prices fluctuate between £1.10 and £1.25***; ***the pound fluctuated all day on the foreign exchange markets***

fluctuating ['flʌktjueɪtɪŋ] *adjective* moving up and down; ***fluctuating dollar prices***

fluctuation [flʌktju'eɪʃən] *noun* up and down movement; ***the fluctuations of the franc***; ***the fluctuations of the exchange rate***

FNMA = FEDERAL NATIONAL MORTGAGE ASSOCIATION

FOB *or* **f.o.b.** ['ef 'əʊ 'bi:] = FREE ON BOARD

FOK = FILL OR KILL

folio ['fəʊlɪəʊ] **1** *noun* page with a number, especially two facing pages in an account book which have the same number **2** *verb* to put a number on a page

foot [fʊt] *verb* **(a) to foot the bill** = to pay the bill; ***the director footed the bill for the department's Christmas party*** **(b)** *US* **to foot up an account** = to add up a column of numbers

footings ['fʊtɪŋz] *noun US (informal)* the bottom line in a bank's balance sheet

Footsie ['fʊtsi:] = FINANCIAL TIMES-STOCK EXCHANGE 100 INDEX an index based on the prices of one hundred leading companies (this is the main London index)

FOR = FREE ON RAIL

'Forbes' 500 ['fɔ:bz 'faɪv 'hʌndrəd] list of the largest US corporations, published each year in 'Forbes' magazine

forbid [fə'bɪd] *verb* to tell someone not to do something or to say that something must not be done; ***the contract forbids resale of the goods to the USA***; ***the staff are forbidden to use the front entrance*** (NOTE: **forbidding - forbade - forbidden**)

force [fɔ:s] **1** *noun* **(a)** strength; **to be in force** = to be operating or working; ***the rules***

have been in force since 1946; **to come into force** = to start to operate or work; ***the new regulations will come into force on January 1st*** **(b)** group of people; **labour force** *or* **workforce** = all the workers in a company or in an area; ***the management has made an increased offer to the labour force***; ***we are opening a new factory in the Far East because of the cheap local labour force***; **sales force** = group of salesmen **(c) force majeure** = something which happens which is out of the control of the parties who have signed a contract (such as strike, war, storm) **2** *verb* to make someone do something; ***competition has forced the company to lower its prices***

forced [fɔ:st] *adjective* **forced sale** = sale which takes place because a court orders it or because it is the only way to avoid a financial crisis

force down ['fɔ:s 'daʊn] *verb* to make something become lower; **to force prices down** = to make prices come down; ***competition has forced prices down***

force up ['fɔ:s 'ʌp] *verb* to make something become higher; **to force prices up** = to make prices go up; ***the war forced up the price of oil***

forecast ['fɔ:kɑ:st] **1** *noun* description or calculation of what will probably happen in the future; ***the chairman did not believe the sales director's forecast of higher turnover***; ***we based our calculations on the forecast of sales***; **cash flow forecast** = forecast of when cash will be received or paid out; **dividend forecast** = forecast of the amount of an expected dividend (NOTE: also called **prospective dividend**); **population forecast** = calculation of how many people will be living in a country or in a town at some point in the future; **sales forecast** = calculation of future sales **2** *verb* to calculate or to say what will probably happen in the future; ***he is forecasting sales of £2m***; ***economists have forecast a fall in the exchange rate***; **forecast dividend** = dividend which a company expects to pay at the end of the current year (NOTE: **forecasting - forecast**)

forecaster ['fɔ:kɑ:stə] *noun* person who says what he thinks will happen in the future; **economic forecaster** = person who says how he thinks a country's economy will perform in the future

forecasting ['fɔ:kɑ:stɪŋ] *noun* calculating what will probably happen in the future; **manpower forecasting** = calculating how many workers will be needed in the future, and how many will actually be available

foreclose [fɔ:'kləʊz] *verb* to acquire a property because the owner cannot repay money which he has borrowed (using the property as security); ***the bank foreclosed on his farm***

foreclosure [fɔ:'kləʊʒə] *noun* act of foreclosing

foreign ['fɒrən] *adjective* not belonging to your own country; ***foreign cars have flooded our market***; ***we are increasing our trade with foreign countries***; **foreign banks** *or* **foreign branches** = banks from other countries which have branches in a country; **foreign currency** = money of another country; **foreign-currency account** = account in a currency which is not the currency of the country in which the account is held; **foreign direct investment (FDI)** = investment in a developing country by foreign companies or governments; **foreign investments** = money invested in other countries; **foreign money order** = money order in a foreign currency which is payable to someone living in a foreign country; **foreign trade** = trade with other countries

> a sharp setback in foreign trade accounted for most of the winter slowdown
>
> *Fortune*

> the treasury says it needs the cash to rebuild its foreign reserves which have fallen from $19 billion when the government took office to $7 billion in August
>
> *Economist*

foreign exchange (forex) ['fɒrən ɪks'tʃeɪndʒ] *noun* **(a)** exchanging the money of one country for that of another; **foreign exchange broker** *or* **dealer** = person who deals on the foreign exchange market; **foreign exchange dealing** = buying and selling foreign currencies; **the foreign exchange markets** = market where people buy and sell foreign currencies **(b)** foreign currencies; **foreign exchange reserves** = foreign money held by a government to support its own currency and pay its debts; **foreign exchange transfer** = sending of money from one country to another

> the dollar recovered a little lost ground on the foreign exchanges yesterday
>
> *Financial Times*

forex *or* **Forex** ['fɔ:reks] = FOREIGN EXCHANGE

> the amount of reserves sold by the authorities were not sufficient to move the $200 billion Forex market permanently
>
> *Duns Business Month*

forfaiting ['fɔ:fɪtɪŋ] *noun* providing finance for exporters, where an agent (the forfaiter) accepts a bill of exchange from an overseas customer; he buys the bill at a discount, and collects the payments from the customer in due course

forfeit ['fɔ:fɪt] **1** *noun* taking something away as a punishment; **forfeit clause** = clause in a contract which says that goods or a deposit will be taken away if the contract is not obeyed; **the goods were declared forfeit** = the court said that the goods had to be taken away from their owner **2** *verb* to have something taken away as a punishment; **to forfeit a patent** = to lose a patent because payments have not been made; **to forfeit a deposit** = to lose a deposit which was left for an item because you have decided not to buy that item

forfeiture ['fɔ:fɪtʃə] *noun* act of forfeiting a property

forint ['fɒrɪnt] *noun* currency used in Hungary

form [fɔ:m] **1** *noun* **(a) form of words** = words correctly laid out for a legal document; **receipt in due form** = correctly written receipt; **form letter** = letter which is sent without any change to several correspondents (such as a letter chasing payment) **(b)** official printed paper with blank spaces which have to be filled in with information; ***you have to fill in form A20***; ***passengers must fill in customs declaration forms***; ***a pad of order forms***; **application form** = form which has to be filled in to apply for something; **claim form** = form which has to be filled in when making an insurance claim **2** *verb* to start or to organize; ***the brothers have formed a new company***

forma ['fɔ:mə] *see* PRO FORMA

formal ['fɔ:məl] *adjective* clearly and legally written; ***to make a formal application***; ***to send a formal order***; **formal documents** = documents giving full details of a takeover bid (the official timetable for the bid starts with the sending out of the formal documents)

formality [fɔ:'mæləti] *noun* something which has to be done to obey the law; **customs formalities** = declaration of goods by the shipper and examination of them by the customs

formation *or* **forming** [fɔ:'meɪʃən or 'fɔ:mɪŋ] *noun* act of organizing; ***the formation of a new company***

formula investing ['fɔ:mjʊlə ɪn'vestɪŋ] *noun* method of investing according to a set plan (such as purchasing a certain value of shares each month, or only investing in shares of companies with a capitalization of less than £25m)

fortune ['fɔ:tʃu:n] *noun* large amount of money; ***he made a fortune from investing in oil shares***; ***she left her fortune to her three children***

'Fortune' 500 ['fɔ:tʃu:n 'faɪv 'hʌndrəd] the 500 largest companies in the USA, as listed annually in 'Fortune' magazine

forward ['fɔ:wəd] **1** *adjective* in advance, to be paid at a later date; **forward buying** *or* **buying forward** = buying shares or currency or commodities at today's price for delivery at a later date; **forward contract** = one-off agreement to buy foreign currency or shares or commodities for delivery at a later date at a certain price; **forward cover** = arrangement to cover the risks on a forward contract; **forward delivery** = delivery at some date in the future which has been agreed between the buyer and seller; **forward margin** = difference between the current (or spot) price and the forward price; **forward market** = market for purchasing foreign currency or oil or commodities for delivery at a later date (these are one-off deals, as opposed to futures contracts which are continuous); **forward (exchange) rate** = rate for purchase of foreign currency at a fixed price for delivery at a later date; ***what are the forward rates for the pound?***; **forward sales** = sales for delivery at a later date **2** *adverb* **(a) to date a cheque forward** = to put a later date than the present one on a cheque; **carriage forward** *or* **freight forward** = deal where the customer pays for transporting the goods; **charges forward** = charges which will be paid by the customer **(b) to buy forward** = to buy foreign currency before you need it, in order to be certain of the exchange rate; **to sell forward** = to sell foreign currency, commodities, etc., for delivery at a later date **(c) balance brought forward** *or* **carried forward** = balance which is entered in an account at the end of a period and is then taken to be the starting point of the next period

forwardation ['fɔ:wə'deɪʃn] *noun (on commodity markets)* cash price which is lower than the forward price (NOTE: also called **contango**; the opposite is **backwardation**)

forwarder *or* **freight forwarder** ['freɪt 'fɔ:wədə] *noun* person or company that arranges shipping and customs documents for several shipments from different companies, putting them together to form one large shipment

forwarding ['fɔ:wədɪŋ] *noun* **(a)** arranging shipping and customs documents; **air forwarding** = arranging for goods to be shipped by air; **forwarding agent** = FORWARDER; **forwarding instructions** *or* **instructions for forwarding** = instructions showing how the goods are to be shipped and delivered **(b) forwarding address** = address to which a person's mail can be sent on

foul [faʊl] *adjective* **foul bill of lading** = bill of lading which says that the goods were in bad condition when received by the shipper

founder ['faʊndə] *noun* person who starts a company; **founder's shares** = special shares issued to the person who starts a company

401(k) plan *US* personal pension plan arranged by an employer for a member of staff, invested in bonds, mutual funds or stock (the employee contributes a proportion of salary, on which tax is deferred; the employer can also make contributions)

fourth market ['fɔ:θ 'mɑ:kɪt] *noun US* trading in securities between financial institutions, without going through the stock market

fourth quarter ['fɔ:θ 'kwɔ:tə] *noun* period of three months from October to the end of the year

fraction ['frækʃən] *noun* very small amount; ***only a fraction of the new share issue was subscribed***

fractional ['frækʃənl] *adjective* very small; **fractional certificate** = certificate for part of a share

fragile ['frædʒaɪl] *adjective* likely to collapse or break

> in a fragile financial system normal functioning can be disrupted by some not unusual event. In this sense a fragile system is more susceptible to future outbreaks of financial disorder and turbulence
>
> *The Banker*

fragility [frə'dʒɪlɪti] *noun* being weak, being likely to collapse; **financial fragility** = being in a weak position financially (NOTE: the opposite is **robustness**)

franc [fræŋk] *noun* **(a)** unit of money used with the euro in France and Belgium, and also in Switzerland and many other countries; ***French francs*** *or* ***Belgian francs*** *or* ***Swiss francs; it costs twenty-five Swiss francs*** **(b)** specifically, the currency used with the euro in France; **franc account** = bank account in francs; **franc zone** = currency area consisting of the former French colonies in Africa or in the Pacific (it uses the CFA franc or the CFP franc as unit of currency) (NOTE: in English usually written **Fr** before the figure: **Fr2,500** (say: 'two thousand, five hundred francs'). Currencies of different countries can be shown by the initial letters of the countries: **FFr** (French francs); **SwFr** (Swiss francs); **BFr** (Belgian francs))

franchise ['fræntʃaɪz] **1** *noun* licence to trade using a brand name and paying a royalty for it; ***he has bought a printing franchise*** *or* ***a hot dog franchise*** **2** *verb* to sell licences for people to trade using a brand name and paying a royalty; ***his sandwich bar was so successful that he decided to franchise it***

franchisee [fræntʃaɪ'zi:] *noun* person who runs a franchise

franchiser ['fræntʃaɪzə] *noun* person who licenses a franchise

franchising ['fræntʃaɪzɪŋ] *noun* act of selling a licence to trade as a franchise; ***he runs his sandwich chain as a franchising operation***

franchisor ['fræntʃaɪzə] *noun* = FRANCHISER

franco ['fræŋkəʊ] *adverb* free

Frankfurt ['fræŋkfɔ:t] main financial centre in Germany; **Frankfurt Interbank Offered Rate (FIBOR)** = rate used for calculating loans on the Frankfurt money markets

Frankfurter Allgemeine Zeitung ['fræŋkfɔ:tə 'ælgemaɪnə 'tsaɪtuŋ] daily paper published in Frankfurt; **FAZ index** = daily index of leading industrial shares on the Frankfurt Stock Exchange

fraud [frɔ:d] *noun* making money by making people believe something which is not true; ***he got possession of the property by fraud; he was accused of frauds relating to foreign currency***; **to obtain money by fraud** = to obtain money by saying or doing something to cheat someone; **fraud squad** = special police department which investigates frauds; **Serious Fraud Office (SFO)** = government department in charge of investigating major fraud in companies

fraudulent ['frɔ:djʊlənt] *adjective* not honest, aiming to cheat people; ***a fraudulent transaction***

fraudulently ['frɔ:djʊləntli] *adverb* not honestly; ***goods obtained fraudulently***; ***the solicitor acted fraudulently***

Freddie Mac ['fredi 'mæk] US *(informal)* = FEDERAL HOME LOAN MORTGAGE CORPORATION

free [fri:] **1** *adjective & adverb* **(a)** not costing any money; ***we were given free tickets to the exhibition***; ***the price includes free delivery***; ***goods are delivered free***; ***catalogue sent free on request***; **carriage free** = the customer does not pay for the shipping; **free gift** = present given by a shop to a customer who buys a certain amount of goods; **free issue** = scrip issue or capitalization issue, an issue of shares, where a company transfers money from reserves to share capital and issues free extra shares to the shareholders (the value of the company remains the same, and the total market value of shareholders' shares remains the same, the market price being adjusted to account for the new shares); **free sample** = sample given free to advertise a product; **free trial** = testing of a machine with no payment involved; ***to send a piece of equipment for two weeks' free trial***; **free of charge** = with no payment to be made; **free on board (FOB)** = (i) price including all the seller's costs until the goods are on the ship for transportation; (ii) US price includes all the seller's costs until the goods are delivered to a certain place; **free on rail (FOR)** = price including all the seller's costs until the goods are delivered to the railway for shipment **(b)** with no restrictions; **free capital** = amount of a company's capital in shares which are available for trading on a Stock Exchange; **free collective bargaining** = negotiations over wage increases and working conditions between the management and the trade unions; **free competition** = being free to compete without government interference; **free currency** = currency which is allowed by the government to be bought and sold without restriction; **free enterprise** = system of business with no interference from the government; **free market** = market which has no restrictions placed on it (either by a government or by a company); **free market economy** = system where the government does not interfere in business activity in any way; **free period** = the period of grace allowed to credit card holders before payment for credit card purchases is demanded; **free port** *or* **free trade zone** = port or area where there are no customs duties; **free reserves** = part of a bank's reserves which are above the statutory level and so can be used for various purposes as the bank wishes; **free trade** = system where goods can go from one country to another without any restrictions; **free trade area** = group of countries practising free trade; **free trader** = person who is in favour of free trade; **free of tax** *or* **tax-free** = with no tax having to be paid; **interest-free credit** *or* **loan** = credit or loan where no interest is paid by the borrower; **free of duty** *or* **duty-free** = with no duty to be paid; ***to import wine free of duty*** *or* ***duty-free*** **2** *verb* to make something available or easy; ***the government's decision has freed millions of pounds for investment***

> American business as a whole is increasingly free from heavy dependence on manufacturing
>
> *Sunday Times*

> can free trade be reconciled with a strong dollar resulting from floating exchange rates?
>
> *Duns Business Month*

> free traders hold that the strong dollar is the primary cause of the nation's trade problems
>
> *Duns Business Month*

freefall ['fri:fɔ:l] *noun* sudden collapse of prices; ***on the news of the devaluation the stock market went into freefall***

freehold property ['fri:həʊld 'prɒpəti] *noun* property which the owner holds for ever and on which he pays no rent

freeholder ['fri:həʊldə] *noun* person who owns a freehold property

freephone ['fri:fəʊn] *noun* GB system where one can telephone to reply to an advertisement or to place an order or to ask for information and the seller pays for the call (the US equivalent is the 800 number)

freepost ['fri:pəʊst] *noun* GB system where one can write to an advertiser or place an order or ask for information to be sent, and the seller pays the postage

free-standing ['fri:'stændɪŋ] *adjective* standing separately, not attached to a wall

> free-standing ATMs pose all sorts of security problems because they must be accessed from the front, often in a public area
>
> *Financial World*

freeze [fri:z] **1** *noun* **credit freeze** = period when lending by banks is restricted by the government; **wages and prices freeze** *or* **freeze on wages and prices** = period when wages and prices are not allowed to be increased **2** *verb* to keep money or costs, etc., at their present level and not allow them to rise; ***we have frozen expenditure at last year's level***; ***to freeze wages and prices***; ***to freeze credits***; ***to freeze company dividends*** (NOTE: **freezing - froze - has frozen**)

freeze out [fri:z 'aʊt] *verb* **to freeze out competition** = to trade successfully and cheaply and so prevent competitors from operating

freight [freɪt] *noun* **(a)** cost of transporting goods by air, sea or land; ***at an auction, the buyer pays the freight***; **freight charges** *or* **freight rates** = money charged for transporting goods; ***freight charges have gone up sharply this year***; **freight costs** = money paid to transport goods; **freight forward** = deal where the customer pays for transporting the goods **(b) air freight** = shipping of goods in an aircraft; ***to send a shipment by air freight***; **air freight charges** *or* **rates** = charge for sending goods by air; **sea freight** = sending goods by sea

freightage ['freɪtɪdʒ] *noun* cost of transporting goods

frequent flier ['fri:kwənt 'flaɪə] *noun* person who flies regularly, usually on business

> don't bother haggling with your credit-card company if you hold a card linked to a frequent-flier or rebate program
>
> *Smart Money*

friendly society ['frendli sə'saɪəti] *noun* group of people who pay regular subscriptions which are used to help members of the group when they are ill or in financial difficulties

fringe benefits ['frɪnʒ 'benɪfɪts] *plural noun* extra items given by a company to workers in addition to a salary, such as company cars, private health insurance (also called 'perks')

FRN = FLOATING RATE NOTE

front [frʌnt] *noun* **(a)** business or person used to hide an illegal trade; ***his restaurant is a front for a drugs organization*** **(b) money up front** *US* **front money** = payment in advance; ***they are asking for £10,000 up front before they will consider the deal***; ***he had to put money up front before he could clinch the deal***

front-end ['frʌnt 'end] *adjective* referring to the start of an investment or insurance; **front-end fee** = initial loading of the management charges into the first premium paid for an insurance; **front-end loaded** = where most of the management charges are incurred in the first year of the investment or insurance, and are not spread out over the whole period

front man ['frʌnt 'mæn] *noun* person who seems honest but is hiding an illegal trade

front-running ['frʌnt'rʌnɪŋ] *noun US* buying shares or options because you have heard of a large order to purchase which in coming; ***they were accused of persistent front-running***

> as to the supposed sin of front-running, a moment's thought will demonstrate that, far from sinister, the action is very much in the public interest
>
> *Barron's*

frozen ['frəʊzn] *adjective* not allowed to be changed or used; **frozen account** = bank account where the money cannot be changed or used because of a court order; **frozen assets** = assets of a company which by law cannot be sold because someone has a claim against them; **frozen credits** = credit in an account which cannot be moved; **his assets have been frozen by the court** = the court does not allow him to sell his assets; *see also* FREEZE

FSA = FINANCIAL SERVICES AUTHORITY

FSAVC = FREE-STANDING ADDITIONAL VOLUNTARY CONTRIBUTION

FT ['ef 'ti:] = FINANCIAL TIMES

FT Actuaries Share Indices several indices based on prices on the London Stock Exchange, which are calculated by and published in the Financial Times in conjunction with the Institute of Actuaries and the Faculty of Actuaries; *see also* FINANCIAL TIMES

FTSE index = FINANCIAL TIMES-STOCK EXCHANGE INDEX

fulfil *US* **fulfill** [fʊl'fɪl] *verb* to complete something in a satisfactory way; ***the clause regarding payments has not been fulfilled***; **to fulfil an order** = to supply the items which have been ordered; ***we are so understaffed that we cannot fulfil any more orders before Christmas***

fulfilment *US* **fulfillment** [fʊl'fɪlmənt] *noun* carrying something out in a satisfactory way; **order fulfilment** = supplying items which have been ordered

full [fʊl] *adjective* **(a)** complete, including everything; **we are working at full capacity** = we are doing as much work as possible; **full costs** = all the costs of manufacturing a product, including both fixed and variable costs; **full cover** = insurance cover against all risks; **in full discharge of a debt** = paying a debt completely; **full employment** = situation where all the people who can work have jobs; **full listing** = listing of a company on the London Stock Exchange (as opposed to trading on the USM market); **full price** = price with no discount; **full-price ticket** = ticket which is sold at full price, with no reductions **(b) in full** = completely; ***he accepted all our conditions in full***; ***full refund*** *or* ***refund paid in full***; **full payment** *or* **payment in full** = paying all money owed

> a tax-free lump sum can be taken partly in lieu of a full pension
>
> *Investors Chronicle*

full-scale ['fʊl'skeɪl] *adjective* complete and very thorough; ***the MD ordered a full-scale review of credit terms***

> the administration launched a full-scale investigation into maintenance procedures
>
> *Fortune*

full-service ['fʊl'sɜːvɪs] *adjective* that provides a full service; **full-service banking** = banking offering a whole range of services (including mortgages, loans, pensions, etc.) (NOTE: also called **one-stop banking**); **full-service broker** = broker who manages portfolios for clients, and gives advice on shares and financial questions in general (as opposed to an execution-only broker or discount broker)

> it's not worth selling something with only a slight loss: brokerage commission, especially if you trade with a full-service broker, will eat up any benefit
>
> *Smart Money*

> call three or four brokers and ask how they would price a certain bond in the amount you have to invest. If they can't find your bonds, you know you've got a stock-broker not a full-service broker
>
> *Fortune*

fully ['fʊli] *adverb* completely; **the offer was fully subscribed** = all the shares on offer were applied for, so the underwriters to the issue were not forced to buy any; **the shares are fully valued** = the market price of the shares is high enough, possibly too high; **fully-diluted earnings per share** = earnings per share calculated over the whole number of shares after convertible shares have been converted to ordinary shares; **fully-paid shares** = shares where the full face value has been paid; **fully paid-up capital** = all money paid for the issued capital shares

> issued and fully paid capital is $100 million
>
> *Hongkong Standard*

fund [fʌnd] **1** *noun* **(a)** money set aside for a special purpose; **contingency fund** = money set aside in case it is needed urgently; **pension fund** = money which provides pensions for retired members of staff; **sinking fund** = fund built up out of amounts of money put aside regularly to meet a future need, such as the repayment of a loan; *see also* INTERNATIONAL MONETARY FUND **(b)** money invested in an investment trust as part of a unit trust or given to a financial adviser to invest on behalf of a client; **capital-protected fund** = fund which guarantees the investor's capital and at the same time gives some growth; **equity fund** *or* **equity investment fund** = fund which is invested in equities, not in government securities or other funds; **equity growth fund** = fund invested in equities, aiming to provide capital growth; **growth fund** = fund which aims at providing capital growth rather than income; **growth-and-income fund** = fund which aims to provide both capital growth and income; **hedge fund** *see* HEDGE; **income fund** = fund which aims at providing a high income rather than capital growth; **index fund** = fund invested in a range of securities which aims to track the performance of a certain index; **managed fund** *or* **fund of funds** = unit trust fund which is invested in specialist funds within the group and can be switched from one specialized investment area to another; **tracker fund** = fund which tracks (i.e. follows closely) one of the stock market indices, such as the Footsie; **fund management** = dealing with the investment of sums of money on behalf of clients; **fund manager** = person who manages a the investments made by a fund in such a way as to fulfill the fund's stated objectives **2** *verb* to provide money for a purpose; **to fund a company** = to provide money for a company to operate; ***the company does not have enough resources to fund its expansion programme***

> the S&L funded all borrowers' development costs, including accrued interest
>
> *Barrons*

> capital-protected funds have sucked in millions of pounds from cautious investors
>
> *Investors Chronicle*

> a halfway house between the risk of shares and the protection of a deposit, capital-protected funds should be used in the long term to maximise the benefits of the capital protection and avoid the severe losses that the market can induce
>
> *Investors Chronicle*

> international equity investment funds have become extremely popular
>
> *Fortune*

> index funds provide an elegant means of investing in your chosen share markets over the long term
>
> *Money Observer*

> hands up if you understand the charges on your investment fund
>
> *The Times*

> real-estate investment trusts get, and deserve, much of the blame for inflating property prices across the country over the past 18 months. But their private counterparts, the so-called opportunity funds, are just as active and just as willing to pull the trigger at ever-higher price levels
>
> *Barron's*

> if you still do intend to invest in the long term ... then it still makes more sense to put money in a cheaper investment vehicle with full exposure to equities like a tracker fund
>
> *Investors Chronicle*

> fund managers have never conceived of their role as 'managing' money, in the sense of choosing where in the world they should invest. They simply state in their fund prospectuses where they will invest
>
> *Money Observer*

fundamental [fʌndə'mentl] **1** *adjective* basic or most important; **fundamental issues** = matters relating to a company's profits or assets; **fundamental research** *or* **analysis** = examination of the basic factors which affect a market **2** *noun* **fundamentals** = the basic realities of a stock market or of a company (such as its assets, profitability, dividends, etc.)

> with long-term fundamentals reasonably sound, the question for brokers is when does cheap become cheap enough?
>
> *Far Eastern Economic Review*

funded ['fʌndɪd] *adjective* backed by long-term loans; ***long-term funded capital;*** *GB* **funded debt** = (i) short-term debt which has been converted into long-term by selling long-term securities such as debentures to raise the money; (ii) part of the British National Debt which pays interest, but where there is no date for repayment of the principal

funding ['fʌndɪŋ] *noun* **(a)** providing money for spending; ***the bank is providing the funding for the new product launch*** **(b)** changing a short-term debt into a long-term loan; ***the capital expenditure programme requires long-term funding***

funds [fʌnz] *plural noun* **(a)** money which is available for spending; ***the company has no funds to pay for the research programme***; **the company called for extra funds** = the company asked for more money; **to run out of funds** = to come to end of the money available; **public funds** = government money available for expenditure; ***the cost was paid for out of public funds***; **shareholders' funds** = the capital and reserves of a company; **conversion of funds** = using money which does not belong to you for a purpose for which it is not supposed to be used; **to convert funds to another purpose** = to use money for a wrong purpose; **to convert funds to your own use** = to use someone else's money for yourself; **sources and uses of funds statement** = audited statement of where a company's funds come from and how they have been used during the period covered by a profit-and-loss account **(b)** *GB* **the Funds** = government stocks and securities; *see also* FED FUNDS

> small innovative companies have been hampered for lack of funds
>
> *Sunday Times*

> the company was set up with funds totalling NorKr 145m
>
> *Lloyd's List*

fungible ['fʌndʒəbl] *adjective* (security) which can be exchanged for another of the same type

fungibility [fʌndʒə'bɪlɪti] *noun* being exchangeable for something similar

funny money ['fʌni 'mʌni] *noun* strange types of shares or bonds offered by companies or their brokers, which are not the usual forms of loan stock

future ['fju:tʃə] **1** *adjective* referring to time to come or to something which has not yet happened; **future delivery** = delivery at a later date **2** *noun* time which has not yet happened; ***try to be more careful in future***; ***in future all reports must be sent to Australia by air***

futures ['fju:tʃəz] *plural noun* trading in shares, currency or commodities for delivery at a later date (they refer to fixed amounts, and are always available for sale at various dates); ***coffee rose 5% on the commodity futures market yesterday***; **futures contract** = contract for the purchase of commodities for delivery at a date in the future; **financial futures contract** = contract for the purchase of gilt-edged securities for delivery at a date in the future; **futures exchange** = commodity market which only deals in futures; **financial futures market** = market in gilt-edged securities for delivery at a date in the future

> COMMENT: a futures contract is a contract to purchase; if an investor is bullish, he will buy a contract, but if he feels the market will go down, he will sell one

> a number of specialized brokers will open an account on the buyer's behalf and then buy heavily leveraged palm-oil futures. For speculative investors, the object is to liquidate the contract before it comes due: they have no interest in taking possession of a container full of palm oil
>
> *Far Easter Economic Review*

Gg

G5, G7, G10 ['dʒiː 'faɪv *or* 'dʒiː 'sevn *or* 'dʒiː 'ten] *see* GROUP

GAAP = GENERALLY ACCEPTED ACCOUNTING PRINCIPLES

GAB = GENERAL ARRANGMENTS TO BORROW

gain [geɪn] **1** *noun* **(a)** increase, becoming larger; **gain in profitability** = becoming more profitable **(b)** increase in profit, price or value; ***oil shares showed gains on the Stock Exchange***; ***property shares put on gains of 10%-15%***; **capital gains** = money made by selling a fixed asset; **capital gains tax** = tax paid on capital gains; **short-term gains** = increase in price made over a short period **2** *verb* **(a)** to get or to obtain; **to gain control of a business** = to buy more than 50% of the shares so that you can direct the business **(b)** to rise in value; ***the dollar gained six points on the foreign exchange markets***

galloping inflation ['gæləpɪŋ ɪn'fleɪʃən] *noun* very rapid inflation which is almost impossible to reduce

gamma shares *or* **gamma securities** *or* **gamma stocks** ['gæmə] *noun* shares of companies which are not frequently traded on the London Stock Exchange, but which are listed; *see also* ALPHA, BETA, DELTA

gap [gæp] *noun* empty space; **gap in the market** = opportunity to make a product which is needed but which no one has sold before; ***to look for*** *or* ***to find a gap in the market***; ***this computer has filled a real gap in the market***; **dollar gap** = situation where the supply of dollars is not enough to satisfy the demand for them from overseas buyers; **trade gap** = difference in value between a country's imports and exports; **gap financing** = arranging extra loans (such as a bridging loan) to cover a purchase not covered by an existing loan

---

these savings are still not great enough to overcome the price gap between American products and those of other nations

Duns Business Month

---

garage ['gærɑːʒ] **1** *noun* part of the trading floor on the New York Stock Exchange **2** *verb* to put assets into another company so as to reduce tax liability

garnish ['gɑːnɪʃ] *verb US* to withhold salary or property in case of debt, unpaid tax, etc.

---

the tax advocate has authority to overrule many IRS actions, such as taxpayer levies, repossession and wage garnishing through enforced Taxpayer Assistance Orders (TAOs)

Smart Money

---

garnishee [gɑːnɪ'ʃiː] *noun* person who owes money to a creditor and is ordered by a court to pay that money to a creditor of the creditor, and not to the creditor himself; **garnishee order** court order, making a garnishee pay money not to the debtor, but to a third party

garnishment ['gɑːnɪʃmənt] *noun US* = GARNISHEE ORDER

GATT [gæt] = GENERAL AGREEMENT ON TARIFFS AND TRADE

gazump [gə'zʌmp] *verb* **to gazump someone** = to offer more money to buy a property that someone else is trying to buy, and so buy the property in his place

gazumping [gə'zʌmpɪŋ] *noun* offering more money for a house than another buyer has done, so as to be sure of buying it

GDP ['dʒiː 'diː 'piː] = GROSS DOMESTIC PRODUCT

gear [gɪə] *verb* **(a)** to link to or to connect with; ***bank interest rates are geared to American interest rates***; **salary geared to the cost of living** = salary which rises as the cost of living increases **(b) a company which is highly geared** *or* **a highly-geared company** = company which has a high proportion of its funds from borrowings as opposed to its equity capital

gearing ['gɪərɪŋ] *noun* **(a) equity gearing** = ratio between a company's borrowings at interest and its ordinary share capital; **income gearing** = ratio of the interest a company pays on its borrowing shown as a percentage of its pretax profits (before the interest is paid) **(b)** borrowing money at fixed interest which is then used to produce more money than the interest paid

> COMMENT: high gearing (when a company is said to be 'highly geared') indicates that the level of borrowings is high when compared to its ordinary share capital; a lowly-geared company has borrowings which are relatively low. High gearing has the effect of increasing a company's profitability when the company's trading is expanding; if the trading pattern slows down, then the high interest charges associated with gearing will increase the rate of slowdown

GEB = GUARANTEED EQUITY BOND

G8 ['dʒi: 'eɪt] = GROUP OF EIGHT

general ['dʒenərəl] *adjective* **(a)** ordinary, not special; **general expenses** = all kinds of minor expenses, the money spent on the day-to-day costs of running a business; **general fund** = unit trust with investments in a variety of stocks; **general insurance** = insurance covering theft, loss, damage, etc. (not life insurance); **general ledger** = book which records a company's income and expenditure in general; **general lien** = lien against the personal possessions of a borrower (but not against his house or land); **general manager** = manager in charge of the administration of a company; **general obligation bond (GO bond)** = a municipal or state bond issued to finance public undertakings such as roads, etc., but which is repaid out of general funds main administrative office of a company; **general partner** = partner in a partnership whose responsibility for its debts is not limited; **general PEP** = PEP which has shares of several companies in it, as opposed to a single company PEP **(b)** dealing with everything or with everybody; **general audit** = examining all the books and accounts of a company; **general average** = sharing of the cost of lost goods by all parties to an insurance (where some goods have been lost in an attempt to save the rest of the cargo); **general meeting** = meeting of all the shareholders of a company; *see also* ANNUAL GENERAL MEETING, EXTRAORDINARY GENERAL MEETING; **general undertaking** = undertaking signed by the directors of a company applying for a Stock Exchange listing, promising to work within the regulations of the Stock Exchange

General Agreement on Tariffs and Trade (GATT) ['dʒenrəl ə'gri:mənt ɒn 'tærɪfs ən 'treɪd] *see* WORLD TRADE ORGANIZATION

General Arrangements to Borrow (GAB) ['dʒenrəl ə'reɪnʒmənts tə 'bɒrəʊ] agreement between members of the G10 group of countries, by which members make funds available to the IMF to cover loans which it makes

Generally Accepted Accounting Principles (GAAP) *US* rules applied to accounting practice in the USA (the British equivalent are the SSAPs)

generation-skipping transfer tax (GSTT) [dʒenə'reɪʃnskɪpɪŋ 'trænsfə 'tæks] *noun US* tax on property left to grandchildren or great-grandchildren with the intention of avoiding paying estate duties

> the 55% GSTT applies when you give property to your grandchildren or great-grandchildren instead of to your children so you can reduce the number of times it's subject to estate tax
>
> *Fortune*

gensaki ['gensæki] *noun* Japanese bond market, dealing in bonds issued with agreements to repurchase at less than twelve months' notice

Gesellschaft [gə'zelʃɑ:ft] *German for* company; **Gesellschaft mit beschränkter Haftung (GmbH)** = private limited company

get back ['get 'bæk] *verb* to receive something which you had before; ***he got his initial investment back in two months***

get out ['get 'aʊt] *verb* **(a)** to produce something (on time); ***the accounts department got out the draft accounts in time for the meeting*** **(b)** to sell an investment; ***he didn't like the annual report, so he got out before the company collapsed***

get out of ['get 'aʊt əv] *verb* to stop trading in (a product or an area); ***the company is getting out of computers***; ***we got out of the South American market***

get round ['get 'raʊnd] *verb* to avoid; ***we tried to get round the embargo by shipping from Canada***

G5 ['dʒi: 'faɪv] = GROUP OF FIVE

GIB = GUARANTEED INCOME BOND

gift [gɪft] *noun* thing given to someone; **gift coupon** *or* **gift token** *or* **gift voucher** = card, bought in a store, which is given as a present and which must be exchanged in that store for goods; ***we gave her a gift token for her birthday***; **gift causa mortis** = gift may by someone 'in contemplation of death' (i.e. he knows he is about to die, and wants to avoid paying death tax); **gift inter vivos** = present given to another living person; *US* **gift tax** = tax on gifts (only gifts between husband and wife are exempt); **free gift** = present given by a shop to a customer who buys a certain amount of goods

gilts [gɪlts] *plural noun* British government bonds, bearing a fixed interest, which are traded on the Stock Exchange and can also be bought at Post Offices

gilt-edged ['gɪlt'edʒd] *adjective* investment which is very safe; **gilt-edged stock** *or* **gilt-edged securities** *or* **gilts** = (i) British government bonds; (ii) *US* any safe corporate bond with a AAA rating

Ginnie Mae ['dʒɪni 'meɪ] *US (informal)* = GOVERNMENT NATIONAL MORTGAGE ASSOCIATION

giro ['dʒaɪrəʊ] *noun* **giro system** *or* **bank giro** = banking system in which money can be transferred from one account to another without writing a cheque (the money is first removed from the payer's account and then credited to the payee's account; as opposed to a cheque payment, which is credited to the payee's account first and then claimed from the payer's account); ***he paid the invoice by bank giro transfer***

glamour stock ['glæmə 'stɒk] *noun* stock which is very popular with investors because it has risen in value and provided higher than average earnings over a period of time

global ['gləʊbəl] *adjective* referring to the whole world; **global economy** = the economy of the whole world

> but economically and politically, the major force on the planet may instead be the global economy - a point the economic crisis in East Asia has driven home in recent months
>
> *Smart Money*

> he points out that fund managers nowadays tend to look at sectors such as oils, pharmaceuticals and banks in a global context
>
> *Money Observer*

GmbH *German* = *GESELLSCHAFT MIT BESCHRANKTER HAFTUNG*

gnomes of Zurich ['nəʊmz əv 'zʊərɪk] *noun (informal)* important Swiss international bankers

GNP ['dʒi: 'en 'pi:] = GROSS NATIONAL PRODUCT

GNMA = GOVERNMENT NATIONAL MORTGAGE ASSOCIATION

go-ahead ['gəʊəhed] **1** *noun* **to give something the go-ahead** = to approve something, to say that something can be done; ***his project got a government go-ahead***; ***the board refused to give the go-ahead to the expansion plan*** **2** *adjective* energetic, keen to do well; ***he is a very go-ahead type***; ***she works for a go-ahead clothing company***

go back on ['gəʊ 'bæk ɒn] *verb* not to do what has been promised; ***two months later they went back on the agreement***

GO bond = GENERAL OBLIGATION BOND

go-go fund ['gəʊgəʊ 'fʌnd] *noun* fund which aims to give very high returns because it is invested in speculative stocks

going ['gəʊɪŋ] *adjective* **(a)** active, busy; **to sell a business as a going concern** = to sell a business as an actively trading company; **it is a going concern** = the company is working (and making a profit); **accounts prepared on a going-concern basis** = on the assumption that the company will continue to trade; *US* **going concern value** = the value of a corporation as it continues trading (in effect, the goodwill) as opposed to its breakup value **(b) the going price** = the usual or current price, the price which is being charged now; ***what is the going price for 1975 Volkswagen Beetles?***; **the going rate** = the usual or current rate of payment; ***we pay the going rate for typists***; ***the going rate for offices is £10 per square metre***

go into ['gəʊ 'ɪntʊ] *verb* **(a) to go into business** = to start in business; ***he went into business as a car dealer***; ***she went into business in partnership with her son*** **(b)** to examine carefully; ***the bank wants to go into the details of the inter-company loans***

gold [gəʊld] *noun* **(a)** very valuable yellow metal; ***to buy gold***; ***to deal in gold***; ***gold coins***; **gold bullion** = bars of gold; **gold fixing** = system where the world price for gold is set twice a day in US dollars on the London Gold Exchange and in Paris and Zurich **(b) a country's gold reserves** = a country's store of gold kept by a central bank; **the gold standard** = linking of the value of a currency to the value of a quantity of gold; **the pound came off the gold standard** = the pound stopped being linked to the value of gold; **gold point** = amount by which a currency which is linked to gold can vary in price **(c)** **gold shares** *or* **golds** = shares in gold mines

> COMMENT: gold is the traditional hedge against investment uncertainties. People buy gold in the form of coins or bars, because they think it will maintain its value when other investments such as government bonds, foreign currency, property, etc., may not be so safe. Gold is relatively portable, and small quantities can be taken from country to country if an emergency occurs. This view, which was prevalent when the political situation was uncertain, has not been borne out in recent years, and gold has not maintained its value for some time

gold bug ['gəʊld 'bʌg] *(informal)* person who believes that gold is the best investment

> an odd coalition of labor, protectionists, gold bugs and environmentalists opposes more US funds for the IMF, but they don't serve their country's interests
>
> *Barron's*

gold card ['gəʊld 'kɑːd] *noun* credit card issued to important customers (i.e., those with a certain level of income), which gives certain privileges, such as a higher spending limit than ordinary credit cards

gold-collar worker ['gəʊld'kɒlə 'wɜːkə] *noun* employee who earns a very high salary and bonuses

> young gold-collar workers don't give a damn about saving for retirement. They want to make money, move fast, have fun, find themselves, and do what they please
>
> *Fortune*

> in this economy the people with leverage are knowledge workers of a certain (young) age, so-called gold-collar workers. Anyone who's educated, smart, creative, computer literate, equipped with portable skills - and demanding
>
> *Fortune*

gold/silver ratio ['gəʊld'sɪlvə 'reɪʃəʊ] *noun* figure calculated as the number of ounces of silver it takes to buy one ounce of gold

golden ['gəʊldən] *adjective* made of gold, like gold; **golden hallo** = cash inducement paid to someone to encourage him to change jobs and move to another company; **golden handcuffs** = contractual arrangement to make sure that a valued member of staff stays in his job, by which he is offered special financial advantages if he stays and heavy penalties if he leaves; **golden handshake** = large, usually tax-free, sum of money given to a director who resigns from a company before the end of his service contract; ***when the company was taken over, the sales director received a golden handshake of £25,000***; **golden parachute** = special contract for a director of a company, which gives him advantageous financial terms if he has to resign when the company is taken over; **golden share** = share in a privatized company which is retained by the government and carries special privileges (such as the right to veto foreign takeover bids)

goldmine ['gəʊldmaɪn] *noun* mine which produces gold; **that shop is a little goldmine** = that shop is a very profitable business

go long ['gəʊ 'lɒŋ] *verb* to buy securities as a long-term investment

good [gʊd] **1** *adjective* not bad; **a good buy** = excellent item which has been bought cheaply; **to buy something in good faith** = to buy something thinking it is of good quality or that it has not been stolen or that it is not an imitation; **good till cancelled (GTC)** = order given to a broker to buy or sell as instructed until the order is cancelled **2** *noun (economics)* an item which is made and is for sale

goods [gʊdz] *plural noun* **(a)** **goods and chattels** = moveable personal possessions **(b)** items which can be moved and are for sale; **goods in bond** = imported goods held by the customs until duty is paid; **capital goods** = machinery, buildings and raw materials which are used to make other goods; **consumer goods** *or* **consumable goods** = goods bought by the general public and not by businesses; **dry goods** = cloth and clothes; **finished goods** = manufactured goods which are ready to be sold; **household goods** = items which are used in the home; **luxury goods** = expensive items which are not basic necessities; **manufactured goods** = items which are made by machine **(c)** *(in Canada)* **Goods and Services Tax (GST)** = tax on the sale of goods or the provision of services (similar to VAT)

> profit margins in the industries most exposed to

foreign competition - machinery, transportation equipment and electrical goods

Sunday Times

---

the minister wants people buying goods ranging from washing machines to houses to demand facts on energy costs

Times

---

goodwill [gʊd'wɪl] *noun* good reputation of a business, which can be calculated as part of a company's asset value, though separate from its tangible asset value (the goodwill can include the trading reputation, the patents, the trade names used, the value of a 'good site', etc., and is very difficult to establish accurately); ***he paid £10,000 for the goodwill of the shop and £4,000 for the stock***

go out ['gəʊ 'aʊt] *verb* **to go out of business** = to stop trading; ***the firm went out of business last week***

go private ['gəʊ 'praɪvət] *verb (of a public company)* to become a private company again, by concentrating all its shares in the hands of one or a few shareholders and removing its stock exchange listing

go public ['gəʊ 'pʌblɪk] *verb (of a private company)* to offer its shares to the general public for the first time

go short ['gəʊ 'ʃɔːt] *verb* to sell shares now which you have contracted to purchase at a later date, on the assumption that the market will fall further

gourde [guːəd] *noun* currency used in Haiti

govern ['gʌvən] *verb* to rule a country; ***the country is governed by a group of military leaders***

governance ['gʌvənəns] *noun* the philosophy of ruling, whether a state or a company; **corporate governance** = theory of the way companies should be run

---

the chairman has committed the cardinal sin in corporate governance - he acted against the wishes and interests of the shareholders

Investors Chronicle

---

government ['gʌvnmənt] *noun* **(a)** organization which administers a country; **central government** = main organization dealing with the affairs of the whole country; **local government** = organization dealing with the affairs of a small area of the country; **provincial government** *or* **state government** = organization dealing with the affairs of a province or of a state **(b)** coming from the government, referring to the government; ***local government finance***; ***central government borrowing***; ***government intervention*** *or* ***intervention by the government***; ***a government ban on investment in the country***; ***government regulations state that import duty has to be paid on luxury items***; **government bonds** *or* **government securities** *or* **gilt-edged securities** = bonds or other paper issued by the government on a regular basis as a method of borrowing money for government expenditure; *see also* TAP STOCK; **government support** = financial help given by the government; ***the computer industry does not rely on government support***

governmental [gʌvən'mentl] *adjective* referring to a government

government-backed ['gʌvnmənt'bækt] *adjective* backed by the government

government-controlled ['gʌvnməntkən'trəʊld] *adjective* under the direct control of the government; ***advertisements cannot be placed in the government-controlled newspapers***

Government National Mortgage Association (GNMA) *noun* US federal organization which provides backing for mortgages (also known as 'Ginnie Mae')

government-regulated ['gʌvnmənt'regjʊleɪtɪd] *adjective* regulated by the government

government-sponsored ['gʌvnmənt'spɒnsəd] *adjective* encouraged by the government and backed by government money; ***he is working in a government-sponsored scheme to help small businesses***

governor ['gʌvnə] *noun* **(a)** person in charge of an important institution; **the Governor of the Bank of England** = person (nominated by the British government) who is in charge of the Bank of England (NOTE: the American equivalent is the Chairman of the Federal Reserve Board) **(b)** *US* one of the members of the Federal Reserve Board

GPM = GRADUATED PAYMENT MORTGAGE

grace [greɪs] *noun* favour shown by granting a delay; **days of grace** *or* **grace period** *or* **period of grace** = time given to a debtor to repay a loan, or to pay the amount purchased using a credit card; ***we decided to give this creditor a period of two weeks' grace***

gradual ['grædʒʊəl] *adjective* slow, step by step; ***1997 saw a gradual return to profits***; ***his CV describes his gradual rise to the position of company chairman***

gradually ['grædʒʊəli] *adverb* slowly, step by step; ***the company has gradually become more profitable***; ***she gradually learnt the details of the import-export business***

graduate ['grædʒʊət] *noun* person who has a degree from a university or polytechnic; **graduate entry** = entry of graduates into employment with a company; **graduate training scheme** = training scheme for graduates; **graduate trainee** = person in a graduate training scheme

graduated ['grædʒʊeɪtɪd] *adjective* rising in steps according to quantity; **graduated income tax** = tax which rises in steps (each level of income is taxed at a higher percentage); US **graduated payment mortgage (GPM)** = mortgage where the monthly payments gradually rise over the lifetime of the mortgage (also called a 'jeep' mortgage); **graduated pension scheme** = pension scheme which is calculated on the salary of each person in the scheme; **graduated taxation** = tax system where the percentage of tax paid rises as the income rises

grand [grænd] **1** *adjective* important; **grand plan** = major plan; ***he explained his grand plan for redeveloping the factory site***; **grand total** = final total made by adding several subtotals **2** *noun (informal)* one thousand pounds or dollars; ***they offered him fifty grand for the information***

grant [grɑ:nt] **1** *noun* money given by the government to help pay for something; ***the laboratory has a government grant to cover the cost of the development programme***; ***the government has allocated grants towards the costs of the scheme***; **grant-aided scheme** = scheme which is funded by a government grant **2** *verb* to agree to give someone something; ***to grant someone a loan*** *or* ***a subsidy***; ***the local authority granted the company an interest-free loan to start up the new factory***

---

the budget grants a tax exemption for $500,000 in capital gains

Toronto Star

---

grantor [grɑ:ntə] *noun* person who grants a property to another

graph [grɑ:f] *noun* diagram which shows statistics as a drawing; ***to set out the results in a graph***; ***to draw a graph showing the rising profitability***; ***the sales graph shows a steady rise***; **graph paper** = special paper with many little squares, used for drawing graphs

gratia ['greɪʃə] *see* EX GRATIA

gratis ['grætɪs] *adverb* free, not costing anything; ***we got into the exhibition gratis***

gratuity [grə'tju:əti] *noun* money given to someone who has helped you; ***the staff are instructed not to accept gratuities*** (NOTE: also called **tip**)

graveyard ['greɪvjɑ:d] *noun* market where prices are low and no one is buying because investors prefer to remain liquid

greenback ['gri:nbæk] *noun* US *(informal)* dollar bill

---

just about a year ago, when the greenback was high, bears were an endangered species. Since then, the currency has fallen by 32% against the Deutschmark and by 30% against the Swiss franc

Financial Weekly

Green Book ['gri:n 'bʊk] *noun* US economic forecast prepared by the staff of the Federal Reserve Board

green card ['gri:n 'kɑ:d] *noun* **(a)** special British insurance certificate to prove that a car is insured for travel abroad???check **(b)** work permit for a person going to live in the USA

green currency ['gri:n 'kʌrənsi:] *noun* currency used in the EU for calculating agricultural payments; each country has an exchange rate fixed by the Commission, so there are 'green pounds', 'green francs', 'green marks', etc.

green day ['gri:n 'deɪ] *noun* US profitable day (NOTE: the opposite is **red day**)

greenmail ['gri:nmeɪl] *noun* making a profit by buying a large number of shares in a company, threatening to take the company over, and then selling the shares back to the company at a higher price

---

proposes that there should be a limit on greenmail, perhaps permitting payment of a 20% premium on a maximum of 8% of the stock

Duns Business Month

Green Paper ['gri:n 'peɪpə] *noun* report from the British government on proposals for a new law to be discussed in Parliament

green pound ['gri:n 'paʊnd] *noun* value of the British pound as used in calculating agricultural prices and subsidies in the EU

Gresham's Law ['greʃəmz lɔ:] law that 'bad money will drive out good': where two forms of money with the same denomination exist in the same market, the form with the higher metal value will be driven out of circulation when people hoard it and use the lower-rated form to spend (as when paper money and coins of the same denomination exist in the same market)

grey market ['greɪ 'mɑ:kɪt] *noun* unofficial market run by dealers, where new issues of shares are bought and sold before they officially become available for trading on the Stock Exchange (even before the share allocations are known)

gross [grəʊs] **1** *noun* twelve dozen (144); ***he ordered four gross of pens*** **2** *adjective* **(a)** total, with no deductions; **gross borrowings** = total of all monies borrowed by a company (such as overdrafts, long-term loans, etc.) but without deducting cash in bank accounts and on deposit; **gross dividend per share** = dividend per share paid before tax is deducted; **gross earnings** = total earnings before tax and other deductions; **gross income** *or* **gross salary** = salary before tax is deducted; **gross income yield** = the yield of an investment before tax is deducted; **gross margin** = (i) percentage difference between the unit manufacturing cost and the received price; (ii) difference between the total interest paid by a borrower and the cost of the loan to the lender; **gross profit** = profit calculated as sales income less the cost of sales; **gross receipts** = total amount of money received before expenses are deducted; **gross sales** = total sales before discounts; **gross turnover** = total turnover including discounts, VAT charged, etc.; **gross yield** = profit from investments before the deduction of tax **(b)** **gross domestic product (GDP)** = annual value of goods sold and services paid for inside a country; **gross national product (GNP)** = annual value of goods and services in a country including income from other countries **(c)** **gross tonnage** = total amount of space in a ship; **gross weight** = weight of both the container and its contents **3** *adverb* with no deductions; ***building society accounts can pay interest gross to non-taxpayers***; ***interest on these offshore funds is paid gross*** **4** *verb* **(a)** to make a gross profit; ***the group grossed £25m in 1997*** **(b)** **to gross up** = to calculate the percentage rate of a net investment as it would be before tax is deducted

> news that gross national product increased only 1.3% in the first quarter of the year sent the dollar down on foreign exchange markets
>
> *Fortune*

> gross wool receipts for the selling season to end June appear likely to top $2 billion
>
> *Australian Financial Review*

group [gru:p] **1** *noun* **(a)** several things or people together; ***a group of the staff has sent a memo to the chairman complaining about noise in the office*** **(b)** several companies linked together in the same organization; ***the group chairman*** *or* ***the chairman of the group***; ***group turnover*** *or* ***turnover for the group***; **group balance sheet** = consolidated balance sheet, the balance sheets of subsidiary companies grouped together into the balance sheet of the parent company; **group results** = results of a group of companies taken together **2** *verb* **to group together** = to put several items together; ***sales from six different agencies are grouped together under the heading 'European sales'***

Group of Five (G5) ['gru:p əv 'faɪv] central group of major industrial nations (France, Germany, Japan, UK and the USA), now expanded to form the G7

Group of Seven (G7) ['gru:p əv 'sevn] central group of major industrial nations (Canada, France, Germany, Italy, Japan, UK and the USA) who meet regularly to discussed problems of international trade and finance

Group of Eight (G8) ['gru:p əv 'eɪt] the G7 expanded to include Russia

Group of Ten (G10) ['gru:p əv 'ten] the major world economic powers working within the framework of the IMF: Belgium, Canada, France, Germany, Italy, Japan, Netherlands, Sweden, United Kingdom and the United States. There are in fact now eleven members, since Switzerland has joined the original ten. It is also called the 'Paris Club', since its first meeting was in Paris)

grow [grəʊ] *verb* to become larger; ***the company has grown from a small repair shop to a multinational electronics business***; ***turnover is growing at a rate of 15% per annum***; ***the computer industry grew fast in the 1980s*** (NOTE: **growing - grew - has grown**)

growth [grəʊθ] *noun* increase in size; **the company is aiming for growth** = is aiming to expand rapidly; **economic growth** = rate at which a country's national income grows; **external growth** = growth by buying other companies, rather than by expanding existing sales or products; **internal growth** = expansion of a company which is based on profits from its existing trading; **a growth area** *or* **a growth market** = an area where sales are increasing rapidly; **growth company** = company whose share price is expected to rise in value; **growth fund** = fund which aims at providing capital growth rather than income; **a growth industry** = industry which is expanding rapidly; **growth prospects** = potential for growth in a share; **growth rate** = speed at which something grows; **growth share** *or* **growth stock** = share which people think is likely to rise in value

> a general price freeze succeeded in slowing the growth in consumer prices
>
> *Financial Times*

> the thrift had grown from $4.7 million in assets in 1980 to $1.5 billion
>
> *Barrons*

> growth in demand is still coming from the private rather than the public sector
>
> *Lloyd's List*

> population growth in the south-west is again reflected by the level of rental values
>
> *Lloyd's List*

G7, G10 ['dʒi: 'sevən *or* 'dʒi: 'ten] = GROUP OF SEVEN, GROUP OF TEN

GST ['dʒi: 'es 'ti:] = GOODS AND SERVICES TAX (the Canadian equivalent of VAT)

> because the GST is applied only to fees for brokerage and appraisal services, the new tax does not appreciably increase the price of a resale home
>
> *Toronto Globe & Mail*

GSTT = GENERATION-SKIPPING TRANSFER TAX

GTC = GOOD TILL CANCELLED

guarani [gwɑ:ræ'ni:] currency used in Paraguay

guarantee [gærən'ti:] **1** *noun* **(a)** legal document which promises that a machine will work properly or that an item is of good quality; ***certificate of guarantee*** *or* ***guarantee certificate***; ***the guarantee lasts for two years***; ***it is sold with a twelve-month guarantee***; **the car is still under guarantee** = is still covered by the maker's guarantee **(b)** promise that someone will pay another person's debts if the latter is unable to pay them (NOTE: spelled **guaranty** in American English); **to go guarantee for someone** = to act as security for someone's debts **(c)** thing given as a security; ***to leave share certificates as a guarantee*** **2** *verb* to give a promise that something will happen; **to guarantee a debt** = to promise that you will pay a debt made by someone else; **to guarantee an associate company** = to promise that an associate company will pay its debts; **to guarantee a bill of exchange** = to promise that the bill will be paid; **the product is guaranteed for twelve months** = the manufacturer says that the product will work well for twelve months, and will mend it free of charge if it breaks down; **guaranteed wage** = wage which a company promises will not fall below a certain figure

Guaranteed Equity Bond (Geb) [gærən'ti:d 'ekwɪti 'bɒnd] *noun* bond which provides a return linked to one or more stock market indices (such as the FTSE 100 index) and guarantees a minimum return of the original capital invested

Guaranteed Income Bond (GIB) [gærən'ti:d 'ɪŋkʌm 'bɒnd] *noun* bond which guarantees a certain rate of interest over a certain period of time

> for basic-rate and higher-rate taxpayers, guaranteed income bonds (GIBs) offer some of the best risk-free returns around
>
> *Money Observer*

guarantor [gærən'tɔ:] *noun* person who promises to pay someone's debts; ***he stood guarantor for his brother***

guaranty ['gærənti] *US* = GUARANTEE (b)

guardian ['gɑ:diən] *noun* person appointed by law to act on behalf of someone (such as a child) who cannot act on his own behalf

guess [ges] **1** *noun* calculation made without any real information; ***the forecast of sales is only a guess***; **he made a guess at the pretax profits** = he tried to calculate roughly what the pretax profits would be; **it is anyone's guess** = no one really knows what is the right answer; **an informed guess** = a guess which is based on some information **2** *verb* **to guess (at) something** = to try to calculate something without any information; ***they could only guess at the total loss***; ***the***

sales director tried to guess the turnover of the Far East division

guesstimate ['gestɪmət] *noun (informal)* rough calculation

guilder ['gɪldə] currency used with the euro in the Netherlands, and also in Surinam; also called the florin (NOTE: usually written **fl** before or after figures: **fl25, 25fl**)

> the shares, which eased 1.10 guilders to fl49.80 earlier in the session, were suspended during the final hour of trading
>
> *Wall Street Journal*

Hh

haggle ['hægl] *verb* to discuss prices and terms and try to reduce them; ***to haggle about*** *or* ***over the details of a contract***; ***after two days' haggling the contract was signed***

haircut ['heəʌt] *noun US* **(a)** difference between the market value of a security and the amount lent to the owner using the security as collateral **(b)** estimate of possible loss in investments

half [hɑ:f] **1** *noun* one of two parts into which something is divided; ***the first half of the agreement is acceptable***; **the first half** *or* **the second half of the year** = the periods from January 1st to June 30th or from June 30th to December 31st; **we share the profits half and half** = we share the profits equally (NOTE: plural is **halves**) **2** *adjective* divided into two parts; **half a per cent** *or* **a half per cent** = 0.5%; **his commission on the deal is twelve and a half per cent** = 12.5%; **half a dozen** *or* **a half-dozen** = six; **to sell goods off at half price** = at 50% of the price for which they were sold before; **a half-price sale** = sale of all goods at half the price; **half-commission man** = dealer who introduces new clients to a stockbroker, and takes half the broker's commission as his fee

half-dollar ['hɑ:f'dɒlə] *noun US* fifty cents

half-life ['hɑ:f'laɪf] *noun* number of years needed to repay half the capital borrowed on mortgage

half-year ['hɑ:f'jɪə] *noun* six months of an accounting period; **first half-year** *or* **second half-year** = first six months or second six months of a company's accounting year; **to announce the results for the half-year to June 30th** *or* **the first half-year's results** = results for the period January 1st to June 30th; ***we look forward to improvements in the second half-year***

half-yearly ['hɑ:f'jɪəli] **1** *adjective* happening every six months, referring to a period of six months; ***half-yearly accounts***; ***half-yearly payment***; ***half-yearly statement***; ***a half-yearly meeting*** **2** *adverb* every six months; ***we pay the account half-yearly***

> economists believe the economy is picking up this quarter and will do better in the second half of the year
>
> *Sunday Times*

hallo [hə'ləʊ] *interjection* **golden hallo** = cash inducement paid to someone to encourage him to change jobs and move to another company

Hambrecht & Quist Technology Index American index based on the prices of 275 technology stocks

hammer ['hæmə] **1** *noun* **auctioneer's hammer** = wooden hammer used by an auctioneer to hit his desk, showing that an item has been sold; **to go under the hammer** = to be sold by auction; **all the stock went under the hammer** = all the stock was sold by auction **2** *verb* to hit hard; **to hammer the competition** = to attack and defeat the competition; **to hammer prices** = to reduce prices sharply

hammered ['hæməd] *adjective (on the London Stock Exchange)* **they were hammered** = the firm was removed from the Stock Exchange because it had failed

hammering ['hæmərɪŋ] *noun* **(a)** beating; **the company took a hammering in Europe** = the company had large losses in Europe or lost parts of its European markets; **we gave them a hammering** = we beat them commercially **(b)** *(on the London Stock Exchange)* announcement of the removal of a member firm because it has failed **(c)** *US* massive selling of stock on a stock market

> one of Britain's largest independent stockbrokers was hammered by the Stock Exchange yesterday, putting it out of business for good. The hammering leaves all clients of the firm in the dark about the value of their investments and the future of uncompleted financing deals
>
> *Guardian*

hand [hænd] *noun* **(a) to shake hands** = to hold someone's hand when meeting to show you are pleased to meet him or to show that an agreement has been reached; ***the two negotiating teams shook hands and sat down at the conference table***; **to shake hands on a deal** = to shake hands to show that a deal has been agreed **(b) by hand** = using the hands, not a machine; **to send a letter by hand** = to ask someone to carry and deliver a letter personally, not sending it through the post **(c) in hand** = kept in reserve; **balance in hand** *or* **cash in hand** = cash held to pay small debts and running costs; ***we have £10,000 in hand*** (NOTE: American English is **on hand**); **work in hand** = work which is in progress but not finished **(d) goods left on hand** = unsold goods left with the retailer or manufacturer; ***they were left with half the stock on their hands*** **(e) to hand** = here or present; **I have the invoice to hand** = I have the invoice in front of me **(f) show of hands** = vote where people show how they vote by raising their hands; ***the motion was carried on a show of hands*** **(g) to change hands** = to be sold to a new owner; ***the shop changed hands for £100,000*** **(h) note of hand** = document where someone promises to pay money at a stated time without conditions; **in witness whereof, I set my hand** = I sign as a witness

handcuffs ['hændkʌfs] *noun* **golden handcuffs** = contractual arrangement to make sure that a valued member of staff stays in his job, by which he is offered special financial advantages if he stays and heavy penalties if he leaves

hand in ['hænd 'ɪn] *verb* to deliver (a letter) by hand; **he handed in his notice** *or* **he handed in his resignation** = he resigned

handle ['hændl] *noun US (informal)* whole number of a share price quoted (it may be omitted in the quotation, leaving only the fraction)

handout ['hændaʊt] *noun* money paid to help someone in difficulties; ***the company only exists on handouts from the government***

handshake ['hænʃeɪk] *noun* **golden handshake** = large, usually tax-free, sum of money given to a director who resigns from a company before the end of his service contract; ***when the company was taken over, the sales director received a golden handshake of £25,000***

Hang Seng Index ['hæŋ 'seŋ 'ɪndeks] *noun* index of main share prices on the Hong Kong stock market

hard [hɑːd] *adjective* **(a)** strong, not weak; **to take a hard line in trade union negotiations** = to refuse to accept any proposal from the other side; **hard market** = market which is strong and not likely to fall **(b)** solid; **hard cash** = money in notes and coins which is ready at hand; ***he paid out £100 in hard cash for the chair***; **hard copy** = printout of a text which is on a computer, printed copy of a document which is on microfilm; ***he made the presentation with diagrams and ten pages of hard copy***; **hard disk** = computer disk which has a sealed case and can store large quantities of information **(c) hard currency** = currency of a country which has a strong economy and which can be changed into other currencies easily; ***exports which can earn hard currency for the poorest countries in Africa***; ***these goods must be paid for in hard currency***; ***a hard currency deal*** **(d) hard bargain** = bargain with difficult terms; **to drive a hard bargain** = to be a difficult negotiator; **to strike a hard bargain** = to agree a deal where the terms are favourable to you; **after weeks of hard bargaining** = after weeks of difficult discussions

> hard disks help computers function more speedily and allow them to store more information
>
> *Australian Financial Review*

> few of the paper millionaires sold out and transformed themselves into hard cash millionaires
>
> *Investors Chronicle*

harden ['hɑːdn] *verb* **prices are hardening** = are settling at a higher price

hardening ['hɑːdnɪŋ] *noun (of a market)* slowly moving upwards; *(of prices)* becoming settled at a higher level

hardness ['hɑːdnəs] *noun* **hardness of the market** = being strong or not being likely to fall

harmonization [hɑːmənaɪ'zeɪʃn] *noun* standardization, making things the same in several countries

> most EU countries have between 10 and 13 (public holidays) so we might gain by any attempt at 'harmonisation' - though business would have less reason to welcome more holidays than employees
>
> *Evening Standard*

harmonize ['hɑːmənaɪz] *verb* to make things such as tax rates or VAT rates the same in several countries

harmonized ['hɑːmənaɪzd] which has been made standard in several countries;

harmonized European index = method of calculating inflation which is standard throughout the EU

> at some stage, the Chancellor may want both to adopt the harmonized European index as our official measure of inflation, and to lower the target set for the Bank
>
> *The Times*

> the UK's inflation measure, the RPI, is sharply at odds with the harmonized European index
>
> *The Times*

hatchet man ['hætʃɪt 'mæn] *noun* recently appointed manager, whose job is to make staff redundant and reduce expenditure

haven ['heɪvn] *noun* safe place; **tax haven** = country where taxes are low which encourages companies to set up their main offices there

head [hed] **1** *noun* **(a)** most important person; **head of department** *or* **department head** = person in charge of a department **(b)** most important or main; ***head clerk***; ***head salesman***; **head buyer** = most important buyer in a department store; **head office** = main office, where the board of directors works and meets; *US* **head teller** = main teller in a bank (the UK equivalent is 'chief cashier') **(c) per head** = for each person; ***representatives cost on average £25,000 per head per annum*** **(d) heads of agreement** = draft agreement with not all the details complete **(e) head and shoulders** = term used by chartists showing a share price which rises to a peak, then falls slightly, then rises to a much higher peak, then falls sharply and rises to a lower peak before falling again, looking similar to a person's head and shoulders when shown on a graph **2** *verb* to be first; ***the two largest oil companies head the list of stock market results***

head for ['hed 'fɔː] *verb* to go towards; **the company is heading for disaster** = the company is going to collapse

headhunt ['hedhʌnt] *verb* to look for managers and offer them jobs in other companies; **he was headhunted** = he was approached by a headhunter and offered a new job

headhunter ['hedhʌntə] *noun* person or company that looks for top managers and offers them jobs in other companies

heading ['hedɪŋ] *noun* words at the top of a piece of text; ***items are listed under several headings; look at the figure under the heading 'Costs 85-86'***

headlease ['hedliːs] *noun* lease from a freehold owner to a lessee

headline inflation ['hedlaɪn ɪn'fleɪʃn] *noun* British inflation figure which includes items such as mortgage interest and local taxes, which are not included in the inflation figures for other countries

> the UK economy is at the uncomfortable stage in the cycle where two years of tight money are having the desired effect on demand: output is falling and unemployment is rising, but headline inflation and earnings are showing no sign of decelerating
>
> *Sunday Times*

headquarters (HQ) [hed'kwɔːtəz] *plural noun* main office, where the board of directors meets and works; ***the company's headquarters is in New York***; **divisional headquarters** = main office of a division of a company; **to reduce headquarters staff** = to have fewer people working in the main office

health [helθ] *noun* **(a)** being fit and well, not ill; *GB* **Health and Safety at Work Act** = Act of Parliament which rules how the health of workers should be protected by the companies they work for; **health insurance** = insurance which pays the cost of treatment for illness, especially when travelling abroad; **a private health scheme** = insurance which will pay for the cost of treatment in a private hospital, not a state one **(b) to give a company a clean bill of health** = to report that a company is trading profitably; **health warning** = notice printed on advertisements for investments, stating that the value of investments can fall as well as rise (this is a legal requirement in the UK)

> the main US banks have been forced to pull back from international lending as nervousness continues about their financial health
>
> *Financial Times*

healthy ['helθi] *adjective* **a healthy balance sheet** = balance sheet which shows a good profit; **the company made some very healthy profits** *or* **a very healthy profit** = the company made a large profit

heavily ['hevɪli] *adverb* **he is heavily in debt** = he has many debts; **they are heavily into property** = they have large investments in property; **the company has had to borrow heavily to repay its debts** = the company has had to borrow large sums of money; **the issue was heavily stagged** = large numbers of stags applied for the issue of new shares

> the steel company had spent heavily on new equipment
>
> *Fortune*

heavy ['hevi] *adjective* **(a)** large, in large quantities; ***a programme of heavy investment overseas***; ***he had heavy losses on the Stock Exchange***; ***the company is a heavy user of steel*** *or* ***a heavy consumer of electricity***; ***the government imposed a heavy tax on luxury goods***; **heavy costs** *or* **heavy expenditure** = spending large sums of money; **heavy market** = stock market where prices are falling; **heavy share price** = price on the London Stock Exchange which is over £10.00 per share, and so discourages the small investor (if the company wants to encourage more people to buy its shares, it may take steps to reduce the share price by splitting or issuing bonus shares) **(b)** having too many investments in the same type of share; ***his portfolio is heavy in banks*** (NOTE: the opposite is **light**) **(c) heavy industry** = industry which makes large products (such as steel bars, ships or railway lines); **heavy machinery** = large machines

> heavy selling sent many blue chips tumbling in Tokyo yesterday
>
> *Financial Times*

hectic ['hektɪk] *adjective* wild, very active; ***a hectic day on the Stock Exchange***; ***after last week's hectic trading, this week has been very calm***

hedge [hedʒ] **1** *noun* protection against a possible loss (by taking an action which is the opposite of an action taken earlier); **a hedge against inflation** = investment which should increase in value more than the increase in the rate of inflation; ***he bought gold as a hedge against exchange losses*** **2** *verb* to protect oneself (against the risk of a loss); **to hedge your bets** = to make investments in several areas so as to be protected against loss in one of them; **to hedge against inflation** = to buy investments which will rise in value faster than the increase in the rate of inflation; ***he should have hedged his future sales against price declines***

> the company has hedged its production until the year 2000 at $400, and effectively its entire reserves at $350
>
> *Fortune*

> during the 1970s commercial property was regarded by investors as an alternative to equities, with many of the same inflation-hedge qualities
>
> *Investors Chronicle*

hedge fund ['hedʒ 'fʌnd] *noun* partnership open to a small number of rich investors, which invests in equities, currency futures and derivatives and may produce high returns but carries a very high risk; **macro hedge fund** = hedge fund which invests in whole regions

> COMMENT: originally, hedge funds were funds planned to protect equity investments against possible falls on the stock market. Nowadays the term is applied to funds which take speculative positions in financial futures or equities, and are usually highly-geared: in other words, they do nothing to 'hedge' their holdings. They follow various investment strategies: some invest in 'distressed stocks' (companies which are almost bankrupt) in the hope that they might recover; some only invest in certain sectors or regions, such as oil exploration or emerging markets

> many hedge funds are actually funds of funds, using a wide portfolio of hedge fund managers to produce a balanced exposure for relatively small investors. They are usually referred to as multi-manager funds
>
> *Money Observer*

> hedge funds generally have in common an ability to sell short (that is, sell stocks you do not own), and to increase growth prospects - and risk - by borrowing to enhance the fund's assets
>
> *Money Observer*

> macro hedge funds aim to profit from major regional or global economic changes and their effects on markets. They make extensive use of leverage and derivatives
>
> *Money Observer*

the stock is a hedge fund - limited by the Securities and Exchange Commission to only wealthy individuals and qualified institutions

Smart Money

hedging ['hedʒɪŋ] *noun* protecting oneself against possible loss by buying investments at a fixed price for delivery later

Helsinki Stock Exchange (HEX) main stock exchange in Finland

hemline theory ['hemlaɪn 'θiːri] *noun* the theory that movements of the stock market reflect the current fashionable length of women's skirts (the shorter the skirt, the more bullish the market)

hereafter [hɪər'ɑːftə] *adverb* from this time on

hereby [hɪə'baɪ] *adverb* in this way, by this letter; ***we hereby revoke the agreement of January 1st 1982***

herewith [hɪə'wɪð] *adverb* together with this letter; ***please find the cheque enclosed herewith***

hereditament [herɪ'dɪtəmənt] *noun* property, including land and buildings

HEX = HELSINKI STOCK EXCHANGE; **Hex Index** = index of share prices on the Helsinki stock exchange

hidden ['hɪdn] *adjective* which cannot be seen; **hidden asset** = asset which is valued much less in the company's accounts than its true market value; **hidden reserves** = illegal reserves which are not declared in the company's balance sheet

high [haɪ] **1** *adjective* **(a)** large, not low; ***high overhead costs increase the unit price***; ***high prices put customers off***; ***they are budgeting for a high level of expenditure***; ***investments which bring in a high rate of return***; ***high interest rates are killing small businesses***; **high finance** = lending, investing and borrowing of very large sums of money organized by financiers; **high flier** = (i) person who is very successful or who is likely to get a very important job; (ii) share whose market price is rising rapidly; **high gearing** = situation where a company has a high level of borrowing compared to its share price; **high P/E ratio** = a high figure for the ratio between the market price of a share and the earnings per share (this suggests that investors expect earnings to grow); **high sales** = large amount of revenue produced by sales; **high taxation** = taxation which imposes large taxes on incomes or profits; **highest tax bracket** = the group which pays the most tax; **high volume (of sales)** = large number of items sold; **high yield** = dividend yield which is higher than is normal for the type of company **(b) highest bidder** = person who offers the most money at an auction; ***the property was sold to the highest bidder***; **a decision taken at the highest level** = decision taken by the most important person or group **2** *adverb* **prices are running high** = prices are above their usual level **3** *noun* point where prices or sales are very large; ***share prices have dropped by 10% since the high of January 2nd***; **highs and lows on the Stock Exchange** = list of shares which have reached a new high or low price in the previous day's trading; **sales volume has reached an all-time high** = has reached the highest point it has ever been at

the strong dollar which hit a seven-year high against the yen last week

Wall Street Journal

American interest rates remain exceptionally high in relation to likely inflation rates

Sunday Times

faster economic growth would tend to push US interest rates, and therefore the dollar, higher

Australian Financial Review

high-grade bond ['haɪgreɪd 'bɒnd] *noun* bond which has the highest rating (i.e., AAA)

high-income ['haɪ'ɪnkʌm] *adjective* which gives a high-percentage income; ***high-income shares***; ***a high-income portfolio***; **high-income bond (Hib)** = bond which aims to produce a high income

a Hib is generally linked to one or more stock market indices and provides a return which is specified at the outset. This return is guaranteed on the proviso that the indices to which it is linked either remain the same or increase during the bond's term. But if the indices fall only your initial capital will be returned

The Times

highly ['haɪli] *adverb* very; **highly-geared company** = company which has a high proportion of its funds from borrowings; **highly-paid** = earning a large salary; **highly-placed** = occupying an important post; ***the delegation met a highly-placed***

official in the Trade Ministry; **highly-priced** = with a large price; **she is highly thought of by the managing director** = the managing director thinks she is very competent

high-risk ['haɪ'rɪsk] *adjective* which involves more risk than normal; **high-risk investment** = investment which carries a higher risk than other investments

> as is always the case with higher-risk investments, we made some recommendations that lost ground
>
> *Smart Money*

high security area ['haɪ sɪ'kjʊərɪti 'eərɪə] *noun* special part of a bank with strong doors where cash can be kept safely

High Street ['haɪ 'stri:t] *noun* main shopping street in a British town; ***the High Street shops***; ***a High Street bookshop***; **the High Street banks** = main British banks which accept deposits from individual customers

high-tech ['haɪtek] *noun* **high-tech companies** = companies in advanced technological fields, such as computers, telecommunications, scientific research, etc.; **high-tech share** *or* **stock** = share in a technology sector, such as software or biotechnology

high-yield ['haɪ'ji:ld] *adjective* which gives a very high yield; **high-yield bonds** = JUNK BONDS

> in a leveraged buyout the acquirer raises money by selling high-yielding debentures to private investors
>
> *Fortune*

hike [haɪk] **1** *noun US* increase; **pay hike** = increase in salary **2** *verb US* to increase; ***the union hiked its demand to $3 an hour***

hire ['haɪə] **1** *noun* **(a)** paying money to rent a car, boat or piece of equipment for a time; ***car hire***; ***truck hire***; **car hire firm** *or* **equipment hire firm** = company which owns cars or equipment and lends them to customers for a payment; **hire car** = car which has been rented **(b)** *US* **for hire contract** = freelance contract; **to work for hire** = to work freelance **2** *verb* **(a) to hire staff** = to engage new staff to work for you; **to hire and fire** = to employ new staff and dismiss existing staff frequently; ***we have hired the best lawyers to represent us***; ***they hired a small company to paint the offices*** **(b) to hire a car** *or* **a crane** = to pay money to use a car or a crane for a time; ***he hired a truck to move his furniture*** **(c) to hire out cars** *or* **equipment** = to lend cars or equipment to customers who pay for their use

> COMMENT: an agreement to hire a piece of equipment, etc., involves two parties: the hirer and the owner. The equipment remains the property of the owner while the hirer is using it. Under a hire-purchase agreement, the equipment remains the property of the owner until the hirer has complied with the terms of the agreement (i.e., until he has paid all monies due)

hire purchase (HP) ['haɪə 'pɜ:tʃəs] *noun* system of buying something by paying a sum regularly each month; ***to buy a refrigerator on hire purchase***; **to sign a hire-purchase agreement** = to sign a contract to pay for something by instalments; **hire-purchase company** = company which provides money for hire purchase (NOTE: the American equivalent is **installment credit;** to buy something on hire purchase is **to buy something on an installment plan**)

hiring ['haɪərɪŋ] *noun* employing; ***hiring of new personnel has been stopped***

historic *or* **historical** [hɪs'tɒrɪk *or* hɪs'tɒrɪkəl] *adjective* which goes back over a period of time; **historic(al) cost** = actual cost of purchasing something which was bought some time ago; **historic cost depreciation** = depreciation based on the original cost of the asset; **historical figures** = figures which were current in the past; **historical trading range** = range of prices at which a share has been sold on the stock exchange over a period of time

> COMMENT: by tradition, a company's accounts are usually prepared on the historic cost principle - that assets are costed at their purchase price; with inflation, such assets are undervalued, and current-cost accounting or replacement-cost accounting may be preferred

> the Federal Reserve Board has eased interest rates in the past year, but they are still at historically high levels
>
> *Sunday Times*

> the bank stressed that short and long-term rates were at historically low levels
>
> *Financial Times*

hit [hɪt] *verb* **(a)** to have a (unpleasant) effect on; to affect; ***a falling yen could hit US and European markets as they were hit last year***

(b) to reach; ***the strong dollar which hit a seven-year high against the yen last week***

hive off ['haɪv 'ɒf] *verb* to split off part of a large company to form a smaller subsidiary, giving shares in this to its existing shareholders

hoard [hɔːd] *verb* to buy and store food in case of need; to keep cash instead of investing it

hoarder ['hɔːdə] *noun* person who buys and stores food in case of need; person who holds gold or cash without investing it

hoarding ['hɔːdɪŋ] *noun* **hoarding of supplies** = buying large quantities of money or food to keep in case of need

> as a result of hoarding, rice has become scarce with prices shooting up
>
> *Business Times (Lagos)*

hold [həʊld] **1** *noun* action of keeping something; **these shares are a hold** = these shares should be kept and not sold **2** *verb* **(a)** to own or to keep; ***he holds 10% of the company's shares*** **(b)** not to sell; **you should hold these shares** *or* **these shares are a hold - they look likely to rise** = you should keep these shares and not sell them; ***the redemption yield is the yield produced by bonds if they are held until redemption date*** **(c)** to make something happen; ***to hold a meeting*** *or* ***a discussion***; ***board meetings are held in the boardroom***; ***the AGM will be held on March 24th***; ***the receiver will hold an auction of the company's assets***; ***the accountants held a review of the company's accounting practices*** (NOTE: **holding - held**)

> as of last night, the bank's shareholders no longer hold any rights to the bank's shares
>
> *South China Morning Post*

hold back ['həʊld 'bæk] *verb* to wait, not to go forward; **investors are holding back until after the Budget** = investors are waiting until they hear the details of the Budget before they decide whether to buy or sell; **he held back from signing the lease until he had checked the details** = he delayed signing the lease until he had checked the details; **payment will be held back until the contract has been signed** = payment will not be made until the contract has been signed

holdback ['həʊldbæk] *noun* *US* part of a loan to a property developer which is not paid until the development is almost finished

hold down ['həʊld 'daʊn] *verb* **(a)** to keep at a low level; ***we are cutting margins to hold our prices down*** **(b) to hold down a job** = to manage to do a difficult job

> real wages have been held down; they have risen at an annual rate of only 1% in the last two years
>
> *Sunday Times*

holder ['həʊldə] *noun* **(a)** person who owns or keeps something; ***holders of government bonds*** *or* ***bondholders***; ***holder of stock*** *or* ***of shares in a company***; ***holder of an insurance policy*** *or* ***policy holder***; **credit card holder** = person who has a credit card; **debenture holder** = person who holds a debenture for money lent; **holder of record** = person who is registered as the owner of shares in a company; **holder in due course** = person who holds a negotiable instrument, such as a bill of exchange, and holds it in good faith, without knowing of any other claim against it **(b)** thing which keeps something or which protects something; **card holder** *or* **message holder** = frame which protects a card or a message; **credit card holder** = plastic wallet for keeping credit cards

holding ['həʊldɪŋ] *noun* **(a)** group of shares owned; ***he has sold all his holdings in the Far East***; ***the company has holdings in German manufacturing companies***; **key holding** = important block of shares owned by a single investor, which is large enough to influence the decisions of the board of directors; ***his key holding of 7% of the shares could influence the result of the takeover bid*** **(b) cross holdings** = situation where two companies own shares in each other in order to stop each from being taken over; ***the two companies have protected themselves from takeover by a system of cross holdings***

holding company ['həʊldɪŋ 'kʌmpni] *noun* (i) company which owns more than 50% of the shares in another company; (ii) company which exists only to own shares in subsidiary companies

hold on ['həʊld 'ɒn] *verb* to wait, not to change; **the company's shareholders should hold on and wait for a better offer** = they should keep their shares and not sell them

hold out for ['həʊld 'aʊt fɔː] *verb* to wait and ask for; **you should hold out for a 10% pay rise** = do not agree to a pay rise of less than 10%

> he will expect a buyer to pay a premium to the current price of 180p, and is likely to hold out for around 200p a share
>
> *Sunday Times*

hold to ['həʊld 'tu:] *verb* not to allow something to change; **we will try to hold him to the contract** = we will try to stop him going against the contract; **the government hopes to hold wage increases to 5%** = the government hopes that wage increases will not be more than 5%

hold up ['həʊld 'ʌp] *verb* **(a)** to stay at a high level; ***share prices have held up well***; ***sales held up during the tourist season*** **(b)** to delay; ***the shipment has been held up at the customs***; ***payment will be held up until the contract has been signed***; ***the strike will hold up dispatch for some weeks***

hologram ['hɒləgræm] *noun* three-dimensional picture which is used on credit cards as a means of preventing forgery

home ['həʊm] *noun* place where you live; **home banking** = system of banking using a computer terminal in your home to carry out various financial transactions (such as paying invoices); US **home equity credit** = loan made to a homeowner against the security of the equity in his property (i.e., the value of the property now less the amount outstanding on any mortgage); **home improvement loan** = loan made to a homeowner to pay for improvements to his home; **home office** = office organized inside your own home

> the old rules required that your home office be your primary place of business in order to qualify for deductions
>
> *Fortune*

> the new tax law clarifies who can deduct operating and depreciation expenses associated with home offices
>
> *Fortune*

honorarium [ɒnə'reərɪəm] *noun* money paid to a professional person, such as an accountant or a lawyer, when he does not ask for a fee (NOTE: plural is **honoraria**)

honorary ['ɒnərəri] *adjective* person who is not paid a salary; ***honorary secretary***; ***honorary president***

honour *US* **honor** ['ɒnə] *verb* to pay something because it is owed and is correct; ***to honour a bill***; ***the bank refused to honour his cheque***; **to honour a signature** = to pay something because the signature is correct

horse trading ['hɔ:s 'treɪdɪŋ] *noun* hard bargaining which ends with someone giving something in return for a concession from the other side

hostile ['hɒstaɪl] *adjective* not friendly; **hostile takeover bid** = takeover where the board of the company do not recommend it to the shareholders and try to fight it; **hostile bidder** *or* **hostile suitor** = person or company making a hostile bid

> its largest shareholders are the founding family, whose stake today has dwindled to about 6%, hardly enough to block a hostile bid
>
> *Fortune*

hot card ['hɒt 'kɑ:d] *noun* stolen credit card

hot money ['hɒt 'mʌni] *noun* money which is moved from country to country or from investment to investment to get the best interest rates

hot stock ['hɒt 'stɒk] *noun* stock (usually in a new issue) which rises rapidly on the Stock Exchange because of great demand

hour ['aʊə] *noun* **(a)** period of time lasting sixty minutes; **to work a thirty-five hour week** = to work seven hours a day each weekday; **we work an eight-hour day** = we work for eight hours a day, e.g. from 8.30 to 5.30 with one hour for lunch **(b)** sixty minutes of work; ***he earns £4 an hour***; ***we pay £6 an hour***; **to pay by the hour** = to pay people a fixed amount of money for each hour worked **(c) banking hours** = time when a bank is open for its customers; ***you cannot get money out of a bank outside banking hours***; **office hours** = time when an office is open; ***do not telephone during office hours***; **outside hours** *or* **out of hours** = when the office is not open; ***he worked on the accounts out of hours***; **the shares rose in after-hours trading** = in trading after the Stock Exchange had closed

house [haʊs] *noun* **(a)** building in which someone lives; **house property** = private houses, not shops, offices or factories; **house agent** = estate agent who deals in buying or selling houses **(b)** company; ***a French business house***; ***the largest London finance house***; ***he works for a broking house*** *or* ***a publishing house***; **clearing house** = central office where clearing banks exchange cheques; **discount house** = financial company which specializes in discounting bills; **export house** = company which specializes in the export of goods manufactured by other companies; **house journal** *or* **house magazine** *or* US **house organ** = magazine produced for the workers or shareholders in a company to give them news about the company; **house telephone** =

internal telephone for calling from one office to another

housecleaning ['haʊskli:nɪŋ] *noun* general reorganizing of a business; ***she has mainly been performing housecleaning measures***

house starts *or* **housing starts** ['haʊs 'stɑ:ts or 'haʊzɪŋ 'stɑ:ts] *plural noun* number of new private houses or flats of which the construction has begun during a year

housing authority bond ['haʊzɪŋ ɔ:'θɒrɪti 'bɒnd] *noun* bond issued by a US municipal housing authority to raise money to build dwellings

HP ['eɪtʃ 'pi:] = HIRE PURCHASE

hryvna ['χrɪvnə] *noun* currency used in the Ukraine

hurdle rate ['hɔ:dl 'reɪt] *noun* **(a)** rate of growth in a portfolio required to repay the final fixed redemption price of zero dividend preference shares; *see also* RATE, ZERO **(b)** minimum rate of return needed by a bank to fund a loan, the rate below which a loan is not profitable for the bank

> zeros with big negative hurdle rates promise lower returns than those with small negative hurdle rates
>
> *Sunday Times*

> at present nearly all zeros have negative hurdle rates, which means that trust assets could actually fall before the zeros are in danger
>
> *Sunday Times*

> these zeros have a life of 6.1 years, a gross redemption yield of 7.27% and a negative hurdle rate of 5%
>
> *Sunday Times*

hyper- ['haɪpə] *prefix meaning* very large

hyperinflation [haɪpərɪn'fleɪʃn] *noun* inflation which is at such a high percentage rate that it is almost impossible to reduce

hypothecation [haɪpɒθɪ'keɪʃn] *noun* **(a)** using property such as securities as collateral for a loan, but not transferring legal ownership to the lender (as opposed to a mortgage, where the lender holds the title to the property) **(b)** action of earmarking money derived from certain sources for certain related expenditure, as when investing taxes from private cars or petrol sales solely on public transport

Ii

IBO = INSTITUTIONAL BUYOUT

IBRD = INTERNATIONAL BANK FOR RECONSTRUCTION AND DEVELOPMENT (the World Bank)

ICAEW = INSTITUTE OF CHARTERED ACCOUNTANTS IN ENGLAND AND WALES

ICAI = INSTITUTE OF CHARTERED ACCOUNTANTS IN IRELAND

ICAS = INSTITUTE OF CHARTERED ACCOUNTANTS IN SCOTLAND

ICCH = INTERNATIONAL COMMODITIES CLEARING HOUSE

idle ['aɪdl] *adjective* **(a)** not working; ***2,000 employees were made idle by the recession*** **(b) idle machinery** *or* **machines lying idle** = machinery not being used **(c) idle capital** = capital not being used productively; **money lying idle** *or* **idle money** = money which is not being used to produce interest, which is not invested in business (also called 'barren money')

IFA = INDEPENDENT FINANCIAL ADVISER

> paying premiums throughout your life ofr a lump sum on death made good sense, especially to commission-hungry IFAs
>
> *Investors Chronicle*

IFC = INTERNATIONAL FINANCE CORPORATION a subsidiary of the World Bank which makes loans to private companies

> the IFC has agreed in principle to subscribe to a loan convertible into ordinary shares of 259 million krooni
>
> *The Banker*

IHT = INHERITANCE TAX

illegal [ɪ'li:gəl] *adjective* not legal, against the law

illegality [ɪlɪ'gæləti] *noun* being illegal

illegally [ɪ'li:gəli] *adverb* against the law; ***he was accused of illegally importing arms into the country***

illicit [ɪ'lɪsɪt] *adjective* not legal or not permitted; ***illicit sale of alcohol***; ***trade in illicit alcohol***

illiquid [ɪ'lɪkwɪd] *adjective* (i) (asset) which is not easy to change into cash; (ii) (company) which has no cash

ILO ['aɪ 'el 'əʊ] = INTERNATIONAL LABOUR ORGANIZATION

IMF ['aɪ 'em 'ef] = INTERNATIONAL MONETARY FUND

IMM = INTERNATIONAL MONETARY MARKET (part of the Chicago Mercantile Exchange)

immovable [ɪ'mu:vəbl] *adjective* which cannot be moved; **immovable property** = houses and other buildings on land

immunization [ɪmjunaɪ'zeɪʃn] *noun US* protecting the income from a portfolio of investments against any risk in a volatile stock market

impact ['ɪmpækt] *noun* shock, strong effect

> the strong dollar's deflationary impact on European economies as governments push up interest rates to support their sinking currencies
>
> *Duns Business Month*

impaired [ɪm'peəd] *adjective US* not certain, not perfect; **impaired credit** = situation where a person becomes less creditworthy than before; **impaired loans** = doubtful loans

implement ['ɪmplɪmənt] *verb* to put into action; ***to implement an agreement***

implementation [ɪmplɪmen'teɪʃən] *noun* putting into action; ***the implementation of new rules***

import 1 ['ɪmpɔ:t] *noun* **(a) imports** = goods brought into a country from abroad for sale; ***imports from Poland have risen to $1m a year***; **invisible imports** = services (such as banking, tourism) which are paid for in foreign currency; **visible imports** = real goods which are imported **(b) import ban** = forbidding imports; ***the government has***

imposed an import ban on arms; **import duty** = tax on goods imported into a country; **import levy** = tax on imports, especially in the EU a tax on imports of farm produce from outside the EU; **import licence** *or* **import permit** = government licence or permit which allows goods to be imported; **import quota** = fixed quantity of a particular type of goods which the government allows to be imported; ***the government has imposed an import quota on cars***; **import restrictions** = action taken by a government to reduce the level of imports (by imposing quotas, duties, etc.); **import surcharge** = extra duty charged on imported goods, to try to prevent them from being imported and to encourage local manufacture **2** [ɪm'pɔ:t] *verb* to bring goods from abroad into a country for sale; ***the company imports television sets from Japan***; ***this car was imported from France***; ***the union organized a boycott of imported cars***

European manufacturers rely heavily on imported raw materials which are mostly priced in dollars

Duns Business Month

---

importation [ɪmpɔ:'teɪʃən] *noun* act of importing; ***the importation of arms is forbidden***

importer [ɪm'pɔ:tə] *noun* person or company that imports goods; ***a cigar importer***; ***the company is a big importer of foreign cars***

import-export ['ɪmpɔ:t'ekspɔ:t] *adjective* dealing with both bringing foreign goods into a country and sending locally made goods abroad; ***import-export trade***; ***he works in import-export***

importing [ɪm'pɔ:tɪŋ] **1** *adjective* which imports; ***oil-importing countries***; ***an importing company*** **2** *noun* act of bringing foreign goods into a country for sale; ***the importing of arms into the country is illegal***

impose [ɪm'pəʊz] *verb* to put a tax or a duty on goods; ***to impose a tax on bicycles***; ***they tried to impose a ban on smoking***; ***the government imposed a special duty on oil***; ***the customs have imposed a 10% tax increase on luxury items***; ***the unions have asked the government to impose trade barriers on foreign cars***

imposition [ɪmpə'zɪʃən] *noun* putting a tax on goods or services

impound [ɪm'paʊnd] *verb* to take something away and keep it until a tax is paid; ***the customs impounded the whole cargo***

impounding [ɪm'paʊndɪŋ] *noun* act of taking something and keeping it until a tax is paid

imprest system ['ɪmprest 'sɪstəm] *noun* system of controlling petty cash, where cash is paid out against a written receipt and the receipt is used to get more cash to bring the float to the original level

imprinter [ɪm'prɪntə] *noun* hand-operated machine for printing the details of a customer's credit card on a sales voucher

improve [ɪm'pru:v] *verb* to make something better; to become better; ***they hope to improve the company's cash flow position***; ***we hope the cash flow position will improve or we will have difficulty in paying our bills***; **export trade has improved sharply during the first quarter** = export trade has increased; **improved offer** = offer which is larger or has better terms than the previous offer

---

we also invest in companies whose growth and profitability could be improved by a management buyout

Times

---

improvement [ɪm'pru:vmənt] *noun* **(a)** getting better; ***there is no improvement in the cash flow situation***; ***sales are showing a sharp improvement over last year*** **(b)** thing which is better; **improvement on an offer** = making a better offer

---

the management says the rate of loss-making has come down and it expects further improvement in the next few years

Financial Times

---

improve on [ɪm'pru:v 'ɒn] *verb* to do better than; **he refused to improve on his previous offer** = he refused to make a better offer

impulse ['ɪmpʌls] *noun* sudden decision; **impulse buying** = buying things which you have just seen, not because you had planned to buy them; ***the store puts racks of chocolates by the checkout to attract the impulse buyer***; **impulse purchase** = thing bought as soon as it is seen; **to do something on impulse** = to do something because you have just thought of it, not because it was planned

impute *verb* to pass the responsibility for something to someone else; **imputed value** = value which is given to figures, for which an accurate value cannot be calculated

imputation system *noun* system of taxation of dividends, where the company pays advance corporation tax on the dividends it pays to its shareholders, and the shareholders pay no tax on the dividends received, assuming that they pay tax at the standard rate (the ACT is shown as a tax credit which is imputed to the shareholder; the imputation system is used in the UK, Ireland, Australia, and other countries)

IMRO ['ɪmrəʊ] = INVESTMENT MANAGEMENT REGULATORY ORGANIZATION

> IMRO said that the bank had overcharged for registration fees and had failed to pay interest to customers on time
>
> *The Times*

inactive [ɪn'æktɪv] *adjective* not active or not busy; **inactive account** = bank account which is not used (i.e., no deposits or withdrawals are made) over a period of time (NOTE: the same as a **dormant account**); **inactive market** = stock market with few buyers or sellers

Inc [ɪŋk or ɪŋ'kɔ:pərcɪtɪd] *US* = INCORPORATED

incentive [ɪn'sentɪv] *noun* thing which encourages people to work better; **staff incentives** = pay and better conditions offered to workers to make them work better; **performance incentive** = extra payment to reward an employee's performance at work; **incentive bonus** *or* **incentive payment** = extra pay offered to a worker to make him work better; **incentive scheme** = plan to encourage better work by paying higher commission or bonuses; ***incentive schemes are boosting production***

> some further profit-taking was seen yesterday as investors continued to lack fresh incentives to renew buying activity
>
> *Financial Times*

> a well-designed plan can help companies retain talented employees and offer enticing performance incentives - all at an affordable cost
>
> *Fortune*

inchoate [ɪn'kəʊət] *adjective* (instrument) which is incomplete (i.e., where some of the details need to be filled in)

incidental [ɪnsɪ'dentl] **1** *adjective* which is not important, but connected with something else; **incidental expenses** = small amounts of money spent at various times in addition to larger amounts **2** *noun* **incidentals** = incidental expenses

include [ɪŋ'klu:d] *verb* to count something along with other things; ***the charge includes VAT***; ***the total comes to £1,000 including freight***; ***the total is £140 not including insurance and freight***; ***the account covers services up to and including the month of June***

inclusive [ɪŋ'klu:sɪv] *adjective* which counts something in with other things; ***inclusive of tax***; ***not inclusive of VAT***; **inclusive sum** *or* **inclusive charge** = charge which includes all costs

income ['ɪŋkʌm] *noun* **(a)** money which a person receives as salary or interest or dividends; **annual income** = money received during a calendar year; **disposable income** = income left after tax and national insurance have been deducted; **earned income** = money received as a salary or wages; **fixed income** = income which does not change from year to year; **gross income** = income before tax has been deducted; **gross income yield** = the yield of an investment before tax is deducted; **net income** = income left after tax has been deducted; **personal income** = income received by an individual person before tax is paid; **private income** = income from dividends, interest or rent which is not part of a salary; **retained income** = profits which are not paid out to shareholders as dividends; **unearned income** = money received from interest or dividends, not from salary, wages or profits of your business **(b) lower** *or* **upper income bracket** = groups of people who earn low or high salaries considered for tax purposes; **he comes into the higher income bracket** = he is in a group of people earning high incomes and therefore paying more tax; *see also* GUARANTEED INCOME BOND; **income fund** = fund which aims at providing a high income rather than capital growth; **income gearing** = ratio of the interest a company pays on its borrowings shown as a percentage of its pretax profits (before the interest is paid); **income shares** = shares in an investment trust which receive income from the investments, but do not benefit from the rise in capital value of the investments (the other form of shares in a split-level investment trust are capital shares, which increase in value as the value of the investments rises, but do not receive any income); **income units** = units in a unit trust, where the investor receives dividends in the form of income (as opposed to accumulation units where the dividend is left to accumulate as new units); **income yield** = actual percentage yield of government stocks, the fixed interest being shown as a percentage of the market price **(c) the government's incomes policy** = the government's ideas on how incomes should be controlled **(d) income tax** = (i) tax on a person's income (both earned and unearned); (ii) *also US* tax on the profits of a corporation; **income tax form** = form to be completed which declares all income to the tax office; **declaration of income** *or* **income tax return** = statement declaring income to the tax office; *see also* PAYE **(e)** money which an organization receives as gifts or from investments; ***the hospital has a large income from gifts*** **(f)** *US* **income statement** = accounts for a company which show expenditure and sales balanced to give a final profit or loss (NOTE: the British equivalent is the **profit and loss account)**

> there is no risk-free way of taking regular income from your money much higher than the rate of inflation
>
> *Guardian*

inconvertible [ɪnkən'vɜːtəbl] *adjective* (currency) which cannot be easily converted into other currencies

incorporate [ɪŋ'kɔːpəreɪt] *verb* **(a)** to bring something in to form part of a main group; ***income from the 1997 acquisition is incorporated into the accounts*** **(b)** to form a registered company; ***a company incorporated in 1985***; ***an incorporated company***; ***J. Doe Incorporated*** (NOTE: in the USA, **incorporated** is used as part of the name of the corporation, usually shortened to **Inc.)**

> COMMENT: a company is incorporated by drawing up a memorandum of association, which is lodged with Companies House. In the UK, a company is either a private limited company (they print Ltd after their name) or a public limited company (they print Plc after their name). A company must be a Plc to obtain a Stock Exchange listing. In the USA, there is no distinction between private and public companies, and all are called 'corporations'; they put Inc. after their name

incorporation [ɪŋkɔːpə'reɪʃən] *noun* act of incorporating a company; *see also* CERTIFICATE

increase 1 ['ɪŋkriːs] *noun* **(a)** growth, becoming larger; ***increase in tax*** *or* ***tax increase***; ***increase in price*** *or* ***price increase***; ***profits showed a 10% increase*** *or* ***an increase of 10% on last year***; **increase in the cost of living** = rise in the annual cost of living **(b)** higher salary; ***increase in pay*** *or* ***pay increase***; ***increase in salary*** *or* ***salary increase***; ***the government hopes to hold salary increases to 3%***; **he had two increases last year** = his salary went up twice; **cost-of-living increase** = increase in salary to allow it to keep up with higher cost of living; **merit increase** = increase in pay given to a worker whose work is good **2** [ɪn'kriːs] *verb* **(a)** to grow bigger or higher; ***profits have increased faster than the increase in the rate of inflation***; ***exports to Africa have increased by more than 25%***; ***the price of oil has increased twice in the past week***; **to increase in price** = to cost more; **to increase in size** *or* **in value** = to become larger or more valuable **(b) the company increased his salary to £20,000** = the company gave him a rise in salary to £20,000

> competition is steadily increasing and could affect profit margins as the company tries to retain its market share
>
> *Citizen (Ottawa)*

> turnover has potential to be increased to over 1 million dollars with energetic management and very little capital
>
> *Australian Financial Review*

increment ['ɪŋkrɪmənt] *noun* regular automatic increase in salary; **salary which rises in annual increments of £500** = each year the salary is increased by £500

incremental [ɪŋkrɪ'mentl] *adjective* which rises automatically in stages; **incremental cost** = cost of making a single extra unit above the number already planned; **incremental increase** = increase in salary according to an agreed annual increment; **incremental scale** = salary scale with regular annual salary increases

incubator [ɪŋkjuː'beɪtə] *noun* *US* **small business incubator** = centre which provides support for new businesses before they become really viable

> sometimes these organizations help support so-called small-business incubators at local universities. These institutions often provide such amenities as inexpensive office space, receptionists, and copy machines
>
> *Fortune*

incur [ɪŋ'kɜː] *verb* to make yourself liable to; **to incur the risk of a penalty** = to make it possible that you risk paying a penalty; **to**

incur debts *or* **costs** = to do something which means that you owe money or that you will have to pay costs; **the company has incurred heavy costs to implement the expansion programme** = the company has had to pay large sums of money (NOTE: **incurring - incurred**)

> the company blames fiercely competitive market conditions in Europe for a £14m operating loss last year, incurred despite a record turnover
>
> *Financial Times*

indebted [ɪn'detɪd] *adjective* owing money to someone; ***to be indebted to a property company***

indebtedness [ɪn'detɪdnəs] *noun* **state of indebtedness** = being in debt, owing money

indemnification [ɪndemnɪfɪ'keɪʃən] *noun* payment for damage

indemnify [ɪn'demnɪfaɪ] *verb* to pay for damage; ***to indemnify someone for a loss***

indemnity [ɪn'demnəti] *noun* guarantee of payment after a loss; compensation paid after a loss; ***he had to pay an indemnity of £100***; **letter of indemnity** = letter promising payment as compensation for a loss

indent 1 ['ɪndent] *noun* order placed by an importer for goods from overseas; ***he put in an indent for a new stock of soap*** **2** [ɪn'dent] *verb* **to indent for something** = to put in an order for something; ***the department has indented for a new computer***

indenture [ɪn'dentʃə] *noun* US formal agreement showing the terms of a bond issue

independent [ɪndɪ'pendənt] *adjective* free, not controlled by anyone; **independent company** = company which is not controlled by another company; **independent financial adviser (IFA)** = person who gives impartial advice on financial matters, who is not connected with any financial institution; **independent trader** *or* **independent shop** = shop which is owned by an individual proprietor, not by a chain; **the independents** = shops or companies which are owned by private individuals

index ['ɪndeks] **1** *noun* **(a)** list of items classified into groups or put in alphabetical order; **index card** = small card used for filing; **card index** = series of cards with information written on them, kept in a special order so that the information can be found easily; **index letter** *or* **number** = letter or number of an item in an index **(b)** regular statistical report which gives rises and falls in prices, etc., shown as a percentage of the previous figure; **growth index** = index showing how something has grown; **index number** = number which shows the percentage rise of something over a period of time; **cost-of-living index** = way of measuring the cost of living, shown as a percentage increase on the figure for the previous year; **Retail Price Index (RPI)** *or* US **Consumer Price Index (CPI)** = index showing how prices of consumer goods have risen over a period of time, used as a way of measuring inflation and the cost of living; **wholesale price index** = index showing rises and falls of prices of manufactured goods as they leave the factory **(c)** figure based on the current market price of certain shares on a stock exchange; *see* ALL-ORDINARIES, DOW JONES, FINANCIAL TIMES, FAZ, HANG SENG, NIKKEI, etc.; **index fund** = investment fund consisting of shares in all the companies which are used to calculate a Stock Exchange index (NOTE: plural is **indexes** or **indices** ['ɪndɪsiːz]) **2** *verb* to link a payment to an index; **indexed portfolio** = portfolio of shares in all the companies which form the basis of a stock exchange index

indexation [ɪndek'seɪʃn] *noun* linking of a payment or value to an index; **indexation of pensions** *or* **of wage increases** = linking of pensions or wage increases to the percentage rise in the cost of living

index-linked ['ɪndeks'lɪŋkt] *adjective* which rises automatically by the percentage increase in the cost of living; ***index-linked pensions***; ***his pension is index-linked***; ***index-linked government bonds***

> the index of industrial production sank 0.2 per cent for the latest month after rising 0.3 per cent in March
>
> *Financial Times*

> an analysis of the consumer price index for the first half of 1985 shows that the rate of inflation went down by 12.9 per cent
>
> *Business Times (Lagos)*

index tracker ['ɪndeks 'trækə] *noun* investor or fund manager who tracks an index

> what index-trackers do not offer is a means of determining the most vital choice - which mix of markets to invest in. Time spent on this mix does far more for your portfolio's performance than any work

choosing fund managers or individual shares

Money Observer

index-tracking ['ɪndeks 'trækɪŋ] *adjective* which tracks an index

on the fairly safe assumption that there is little to be gained in attempting to find the share or trust that outperforms everything else, there is every reason to buy an index-tracking fund

Money Observer

indicate ['ɪndɪkeɪt] *verb* to show; ***the latest figures indicate a fall in the inflation rate; our sales for 1998 indicate a move from the home market to exports***

indicator ['ɪndɪkeɪtə] *noun* thing which indicates; **coincident indicator** = indicator which coincides with economic activity (as opposed to leading indicators and lagging indicators); **government economic indicators** = statistics which show how the country's economy is going to perform in the short or long term; **lagging indicator** = indicator (such as the gross national product) which shows a change in economic trends later than other indicators; **leading indicator** = indicator (such as manufacturing order books) which shows a change in economic trends earlier than other indicators

it reduces this month's growth in the key M3 indicator from about 19% to 12%

Sunday Times

we may expect the US leading economic indicators for April to show faster economic growth

Australian Financial Review

other indicators, such as high real interest rates, suggest that monetary conditions are extremely tight

Economist

indirect [ɪndaɪ'rekt] *adjective* not direct; **indirect expenses** *or* **costs** = costs which are not directly attached to the making of a product (such as cleaning, rent, administration); **indirect labour costs** = costs of paying workers who are not directly involved in making a product (such as secretaries, cleaners); **indirect taxation** = taxes (such as sales tax) which are not paid direct to the government; ***the government raises more money by indirect taxation than by direct***

individual [ɪndɪ'vɪdjʊəl] **1** *noun* one single person; ***savings plan made to suit the requirements of the private individual*** **2** *adjective* single, belonging to one person; ***a pension plan designed to meet each person's individual requirements***

Individual Retirement Account (IRA) *US* private pension scheme, into which persons on lower incomes can make contributions (for people not covered by a company pension scheme); withdrawals can start when a person is 591/2 *see also* KEOGH, 410(k)

Individual Savings Account (ISA) British scheme by which individuals can invest for their retirement by putting a limited amount of money each year in a tax-free account (ISAs replace PEPs and TESSAs); *see also* LISA

inducement [ɪn'dju:smənt] *noun* thing which helps to persuade someone to do something; ***they offered him a company car as an inducement to stay***

industrial [ɪn'dʌstrɪəl] **1** *adjective* referring to manufacturing work; **industrial accident** = accident which takes place at work; **to take industrial action** = to go on strike or go-slow; **industrial bank** = finance house which lends to business customers; **industrial capacity** = amount of work which can be done in a factory or several factories; **industrial centre** = large town with many industries; *GB* **industrial court** *or* **industrial tribunal** = court which can decide in industrial disputes if both parties agree to ask it to judge between them; **industrial debenture** *or* **industrial loan** = debenture or loan raised by an industrial company; **industrial disputes** = arguments between management and workers; **industrial espionage** = trying to find out the secrets of a competitor's work or products, usually by illegal means; **industrial expansion** = growth of industries in a country or a region; **industrial injuries** = injuries which happen to workers at work; **industrial processes** = processes involved in manufacturing products in factories; **industrial relations** = relations between management and workers; **good industrial relations** = situation where management and workers understand each others' problems and work together for the good of the company; **industrial training** = training of new workers to work in an industry; **land zoned for light industrial use** = land where planning permission has been given to build small factories for light industry **2** *noun* **industrials** = shares in manufacturing companies

> indications of renewed weakness in the US economy were contained in figures on industrial production for April
>
> *Financial Times*

industrialization [ɪndʌstrɪəlaɪ'zeɪʃən] *noun* changing of an economy from being based on agriculture to industry

industrialize [ɪn'dʌstrɪəlaɪz] *verb* to set up industries in a country which had none before; **industrialized societies** = countries which have many industries

> central bank and finance ministry officials of the industrialized countries will continue work on the report
>
> *Wall Street Journal*

industry ['ɪndəstri] *noun* **(a)** all factories, companies or processes involved in the manufacturing of products; ***all sectors of industry have shown rises in output***; **basic industry** = most important industry of a country (such as coal, steel, agriculture); **a boom industry** *or* **a growth industry** = industry which is expanding rapidly; **heavy industry** = industry which deals in heavy raw materials (such as coal) or makes large products (such as ships or engines); **light industry** = industry making small products (such as clothes, books, calculators); **primary industry** = industry dealing with basic raw materials (such as coal, wood, farm produce); **secondary industry** = industry which uses basic raw materials to produce manufactured goods; **service industry** *or* **tertiary industry** = industry which does not produce raw materials or manufacture products but offers a service (such as banking, retailing, accountancy) **(b)** group of companies making the same type of product or in the same type of business; ***the aircraft industry***; ***the advertising industry***; ***the insurance industry***; ***the food processing industry***; ***the mining industry***; ***the petroleum industry***

> with the present overcapacity in the airline industry, discounting of tickets is widespread
>
> *Business Traveller*

ineligible [ɪn'elɪdʒɪbl] *adjective* not eligible; **ineligible bills** = bills of exchange which cannot be discounted by a central bank

inflate [ɪn'fleɪt] *verb* **(a) to inflate prices** = to increase prices without any reason; ***tourists don't want to pay inflated London prices*** **(b) to inflate the economy** = to make the economy more active by increasing the money supply

inflated [ɪn'fleɪtɪd] *adjective* **(a) inflated prices** = prices which are increased without any reason **(b) inflated currency** = currency which is too high in relation to other currencies

inflation [ɪn'fleɪʃən] *noun* situation where prices rise to keep up with increased production costs, with the result that the purchasing power of money falls; **we have 15% inflation** *or* **inflation is running at 15%** = prices are 15% higher than at the same time last year; ***to take measures to reduce inflation***; ***high interest rates tend to decrease inflation***; **rate of inflation** *or* **inflation rate** = percentage increase in prices over a twelve-month period; **inflation-proof** = (pension, etc.) which is index-linked, so that its value is preserved in times of inflation; **galloping inflation** *or* **runaway inflation** = very rapid inflation which it is almost impossible to reduce; **spiralling inflation** = inflation where price rises make workers ask for higher wages which then increase prices again; **a hedge against inflation** = investment which should increase in value more than the increase in the rate of inflation; **inflation accounting** = accounting system, where inflation is taken into account when calculating the value of assets; *see also* CURRENT COST ACCOUNTING, REPLACEMENT COST ACCOUNTING

COMMENT: the inflation rate in the UK is calculated on a series of figures, including prices of consumer items; petrol, gas and electricity; interest rates, etc. This gives the 'underlying' inflation rate which can be compared to that of other countries. The calculation can also include mortgage interest and local taxes which give the 'headline' inflation figure; this is higher than in other countries because of these extra items

> the decision by the government to tighten monetary policy will push the annual inflation rate above the year's previous high
>
> *Financial Times*

> when you invest to get a return, you want a 'real' return - above the inflation rate
>
> *Investors Chronicle*

inflationary [ɪn'fleɪʃnəri] *adjective* which tends to increase inflation; ***inflationary trends in the economy***; **the economy is in an inflationary spiral** = in a situation where price rises encourage higher wage demands which in turn make prices rise; **anti-inflationary measures** = measures to reduce inflation

inflow ['ɪnfləʊ] *noun* flowing in; **inflow of capital into the country** = capital which is coming into a country in order to be invested (NOTE: the opposite is **outflow**)

> they need to stop investors from withdrawing more money at a time when many other fund firms are continuing to receive fat inflows
>
> *Wall Street Journal*

> the dollar is strong because of capital inflows rather than weak because of the trade deficit
>
> *Duns Business Month*

influx ['ɪnflʌks] *noun* rushing in; ***an influx of foreign currency into the country***; ***an influx of cheap labour into the cities*** (NOTE: plural is **influxes**)

> the retail sector will also benefit from the expected influx of tourists
>
> *Australian Financial Review*

ingot ['ɪŋgət] *noun* bar of gold or silver

inherit [ɪn'herɪt] *verb* to get something from a person who has died; ***when her father died she inherited the shop***; ***he inherited £10,000 from his grandfather***

inheritance [ɪn'herɪtəns] *noun* property which is received from a dead person; **inheritance tax (IHT)** = tax on wealth or property above a certain amount, inherited after the death of someone (NOTE: the American equivalent is **death duty**)

initial [ɪ'nɪʃəl] **1** *adjective* first or starting; **initial capital** = capital which is used to start a business; ***he started the business with an initial expenditure*** *or* ***initial investment of £500;*** *US* **initial public offering (IPO)** = offering new shares in a corporation for sale to the public as a way of launching the corporation on the Stock Exchange (NOTE: the British equivalent for this is an **offer for sale**); **initial sales** = first sales of a new product; ***the initial response to the TV advertising has been very good***; **initial yield** = expected yield on a new unit trust **2** noun **initials** = first letters of the words in a name; ***what do the initials IMF stand for? the chairman wrote his initials by each alteration in the contract he was signing*** **3** *verb* to write your initials on a document to show you have read it and approved; ***to initial an amendment to a contract***; ***please initial the agreement at the place marked with an X***

> the founding group has subscribed NKr 14.5m of the initial NKr 30m share capital
>
> *Financial Times*

> career prospects are excellent for someone with potential, and initial salary is negotiable around $45,000 per annum
>
> *Australian Financial Review*

> shares of newly public companies posted their worst performance of the year last month as a spate of initial public offerings disappointed followers
>
> *Wall Street Journal*

initiate [ɪ'nɪʃɪeɪt] *verb* to start; ***to initiate discussions***

initiative [ɪ'nɪʃɪətɪv] *noun* decision to start something; **to take the initiative** = to decide to do something; **to follow up an initiative** = to take action once someone else has decided to do something

inject [ɪn'dʒekt] *verb* **to inject capital into a business** = to put money into a business

injection [ɪn'dʒekʃən] *noun* **a capital injection of £100,000** *or* **an injection of £100,000 capital** = putting £100,000 into an existing business

injunction [ɪn'dʒʌŋkʃən] *noun* court order telling someone not to do something; ***he got an injunction preventing the company from selling his car***; ***the company applied for an injunction to stop their rivals from marketing a similar product***

inland ['ɪnlənd] *adjective* **(a)** inside a country; **inland postage** = postage for a letter to another part of the country; **inland freight charges** = charges for carrying goods from one part of the country to another **(b)** *GB*; **the Inland Revenue** = British government department dealing with taxes (income tax, corporation tax, capital gains tax, inheritance tax, etc.) but not duties, such as Value Added Tax, which is collected by the Customs and Excise (NOTE: the American equivalent is the **Internal Revenue Service or IRS**)

in play [ˈɪn ˈpleɪ] phrase *(of a company)* being obviously up for sale or a possible takeover target

input [ˈɪnpʊt] **1** *noun* **(a) input of information** *or* **computer input** = data fed into a computer; **input lead** = lead for connecting the electric current to the machine **(b) inputs** = purchases by a company on which VAT has been paid; **input tax** = VAT paid on goods or services which a company buys **2** verb **to input information** = to put data into a computer

inquorate [ɪnˈkwɔːrət] *see note at* QUORUM

inside [ɪnˈsaɪd] **1** *adjective & adverb* in, especially in a company's office or building; ***we do all our design work inside***; **inside information** = information which is passed from people working in a company to people outside (and which can be valuable to investors in the company); **inside worker** = worker who works in the office or factory (not someone who works in the open air, not a salesman); *US* **inside director** = director who works full-time in a corporation (as opposed to an outside director) **2** *preposition* in; ***there was nothing inside the container***; ***we have a contact inside our rival's production department who gives us very useful information***

insider [ɪnˈsaɪdə] *noun* person who works in an organization and therefore knows its secrets; **insider buying** *or* **insider dealing** *or* **insider trading** = illegal buying or selling of shares by staff of a company or other persons who have secret information about the company's plans; **insider information;** *see* INSIDE INFORMATION

> COMMENT: in the USA, an insider is an officer or director of a company, or owner of 10% or more of a class of that company's shares. An insider must report any trade to the SEC by the 10th of the month following the transaction

> to really figure out the quality of insider buying, investors need to check the proxy statement
>
> *Smart Money*

> the main threat that will face companies from the new currency is found by dishonest insiders
>
> *Financial Times*

insolvent [ɪnˈsɒlvənt] *adjective* not able to pay debts; **he was declared insolvent** = he was officially stated to be insolvent

insolvency [ɪnˈsɒlvənsi] *noun* not being able to pay debts; **he was in a state of insolvency** = he could not pay his debts

> COMMENT: a company is insolvent when its liabilities are higher than its assets; if this happens it must cease trading

inspect [ɪnˈspekt] *verb* to examine in detail; ***to inspect a machine*** *or* ***an installation***; ***to inspect the accounts***; **to inspect products for defects** = to look at products in detail to see if they have any defects

inspection [ɪnˈspekʃən] *noun* close examination of something; ***to make an inspection*** *or* ***to carry out an inspection of a machine*** *or* ***an installation***; ***an inspection of a product for defects***; **to carry out a tour of inspection** = to visit various places, offices or factories to inspect them; **to issue an inspection order** = to order an official inspection; **VAT inspection** = visit by officials of the Customs and Excise Department to see if a company is correctly reporting its VAT; **inspection stamp** = stamp placed on something to show it has been inspected

inspector [ɪnˈspektə] *noun* official who inspects; **inspector of factories** *or* **factory inspector** = government official who inspects factories to see if they are safely run; **inspector of taxes** *or* **tax inspector** = official of the Inland Revenue who examines tax returns and decides how much tax people should pay; **inspector of weights and measures** = government official who inspects weighing machines and goods sold in shops to see if the quantities and weights are correct

inspectorate [ɪnˈspektərət] *noun* all inspectors; **the factory inspectorate** = all inspectors of factories

instability [ɪnstəˈbɪləti] *noun* being unstable, moving up and down; **period of instability in the money markets** = period when currencies fluctuate rapidly

instalment *or* *US* **installment** [ɪnˈstɔːlmənt] *noun* part of a payment which is paid regularly until the total amount is paid; ***the first instalment is payable on signature of the agreement***; **the final instalment is now due** = the last of a series of payments should be paid now; **to pay £25 down and monthly instalments of £20** = to pay a first payment of £25 and the rest in payments of £20 each month; **to miss an instalment** = not to pay an instalment at the right time

installment plan *or* **installment credit** *or* **installment sales** *or* **installment buying** [ɪn'stɔ:lmənt 'plæn or 'kredɪt or seɪlz or 'baɪɪŋ] *noun US* system of buying something by paying a sum regularly each month; ***to buy a car on an installment plan*** (NOTE: the British English equivalent is **hire purchase**)

instant ['ɪnstənt] *adjective* which happens immediately; **instant (access) account** = account which pays interest, but from which you can withdraw money when you need it

Institute of Chartered Accountants in England and Wales (ICAEW) professional body whose members are accountants in England and Wales

Institute of Chartered Accountants in Ireland (ICAI) professional body whose members are accountants in Ireland

Institute of Chartered Accountants in Scotland (ICAS) professional body whose members are accountants in Scotland

institution [ɪnstɪ'tju:ʃən] *noun* organization or society set up for a particular purpose; **financial institution** = bank, investment trust or insurance company whose work involves lending or investing large sums of money

institutional [ɪnstɪ'tju:ʃənl] *adjective* referring to a financial institution; **institutional buying** *or* **selling** = buying or selling shares by financial institutions; **institutional buyout (IBO)** = takeover of a company by a financial institution, which backs a group of managers who will run it; **institutional investors** = financial institutions which invest money in securities

> during the 1970s commercial property was regarded by big institutional investors as an alternative to equities
>
> *Investors Chronicle*

instruction [ɪn'strʌkʃən] *noun* order which tells someone what should be done; ***he gave instructions to his stockbroker to sell the shares immediately***; **to await instructions** = to wait for someone to tell you what to do; **to issue instructions** = to tell everyone what to do; **failing instructions to the contrary** = unless someone tells you to do the opposite

instrument ['ɪnstrəmənt] *noun* **(a)** tool, piece of equipment; ***the technician brought instruments to measure the output of electricity*** **(b)** legal document; especially, a document referring to a financial transaction; **financial instrument** = document showing that money has been lent or borrowed or passed from one account to another (such as a bill of exchange, certificate of deposit, IOU, etc.); **negotiable instrument** = document (such as a bill of exchange or a cheque) which can be exchanged for cash

insufficient funds [ɪnsə'fɪʃənt 'fʌndz] *noun US* not enough money in a checking account to pay a check that has been presented (NOTE: also called **not sufficient funds or NSF**)

insurable [ɪn'ʃʊərəbl] *adjective* which can be insured; **insurable interest** = the value of the thing insured which is attributed to the person who is taking out the insurance

insurance [ɪn'ʃʊərəns] *noun* **(a)** agreement that in return for regular small payments, a company will pay compensation for loss, damage, injury or death; **to take out an insurance against fire** = to pay a premium, so that if a fire happens, compensation will be paid; **to take out an insurance on the house** = to pay a premium, so that if the house is damaged compensation will be paid; **the damage is covered by the insurance** = the insurance company will pay for the damage; **to pay the insurance on a car** = to pay premiums to insure a car **(b)** **accident insurance** = insurance which will pay if an accident takes place; **car insurance** *or* **motor insurance** = insuring a car, the driver and passengers in case of accident; **comprehensive insurance** = insurance which covers against all risks which are likely to happen; **endowment insurance** = insurance where a sum of money is paid to the insured person on a certain date or to his heir if he dies before that date; **fire insurance** = insurance against damage by fire; **general insurance** = insurance covering theft, loss, damage, etc. (but not life insurance); **house insurance** = insuring a house and its contents against damage; **life insurance** = insurance which pays a sum of money when someone dies; **medical insurance** = insurance which pays the cost of medical treatment, especially when travelling abroad; **term insurance** = life insurance which covers a person's life for a fixed period of time; **third-party insurance** = insurance which pays compensation if someone who is not the insured person incurs loss or injury; **whole-life insurance** = insurance where the insured person pays premiums for all his life and the insurance company pays a sum when he dies **(c)** **insurance agent** *or* **insurance broker** = person who arranges insurance for clients; **insurance claim** = asking an insurance company to pay compensation for damage; **insurance company** = company whose business is to receive payments and pay compensation for loss or damage; **insurance contract** = agreement by an insurance company to insure; **insurance cover** = protection guaranteed by an insurance policy; **insurance policy** = document which shows the conditions of an insurance; **insurance premium** = payment made by the insured person to the insurer **(d)** *GB* **National Insurance** = state insurance, organized by the government, which pays for medical care, hospitals, unemployment benefits, etc.; **National Insurance contributions (NIC)** = money paid by a worker and the company each month to the National Insurance

insure [ɪn'ʃʊə] *verb* to have a contract with a company where, if regular small payments are made, the company will pay compensation for loss, damage, injury or death; ***to insure a house against fire***; ***to insure someone's life***; ***he was insured for £100,000***; ***to insure baggage against loss***; ***to insure against bad weather***; ***to insure against loss of earnings***; **the insured** = the party who will benefit from an insurance; **the life insured** = the person whose life is covered by a life assurance; **the sum insured** = the largest amount of money that an insurer will pay under an insurance

insurer [ɪn'ʃʊərə] *noun* company which insures; **Association of British Insurers (ABI)** = organization reprenting British companies which are authorized to transact insurance business (NOTE: that for life insurance, British English prefers to use the terms **assurance, assure, assurer**)

intangible [ɪn'tændʒəbl] *adjective* which cannot be touched; **intangible assets** *or* **intangibles** = assets which have a value, but which cannot be seen (such as goodwill, a patent or a trademark)

integrate ['ɪntɪgreɪt] *verb* to link things together to form one whole group

integration [ɪntɪ'greɪʃən] *noun* bringing several businesses together under a central control; **horizontal integration** = joining similar companies or taking over a company in the same line of business as yourself; **vertical integration** = joining business together which deal with different stages in the production or sale of a product

intensive [ɪn'tensɪv] adjective **capital-intensive industry** = industry which needs a large amount of capital investment in plant to make it work; **labour-intensive industry** = industry which needs large numbers of workers, where labour costs are high in relation to turnover

intent [ɪn'tent] *noun* what is planned; **letter of intent** = letter which states what a company intends to do if something happens

inter- ['ɪntə] *prefix* between; **inter-company dealings** = dealings between two companies in the same group; **inter-company comparisons** = comparing the results of one company with those of another in the same product area; **inter-dealer brokers** = brokers who act as intermediaries between dealers in government securities

inter-bank *adjective* between banks; **inter-bank deposits** = money which banks deposit with other banks; **inter-bank loan** = loan from one bank to another; **inter-bank market** = market where banks lend to or borrow from each other; **inter-bank rates** = rates of interest charged on inter-bank loans

interest ['ɪntrəst] **1** *noun* **(a)** payment made by a borrower for the use of money, calculated as a percentage of the capital borrowed; **simple interest** = interest calculated on the capital only, and not added to it; **compound interest** = interest which is added to the capital and then earns interest itself; **accrual of interest** = automatic addition of interest to capital; **accrued interest** = interest which is accumulating and is due for payment at a later date; **back interest** = interest which has not yet been paid; *US* **exact interest** = annual interest calculated on the basis of 365 days (as opposed to ordinary interest, calculated on 360 days); **fixed interest** = interest which is paid at a set rate; **high** *or* **low interest** = interest at a high or low percentage; *US* **ordinary interest** = annual interest calculated on the basis of 360 days (as opposed to exact interest, calculated on 365 days); **interest charges** = cost of paying interest; **interest cover** = being able to pay interest payments on a loan; **interest rate** *or* **rate of interest** = percentage charge for borrowing money; **interest rate margin** = difference between the interest a bank pays on deposits and the interest it charges on loans; **interest rate swap** = *see* SWAP; **interest-free credit** *or* **loan** = credit or loan where no interest is paid by the borrower; ***the company gives its staff interest-free loans*** **(b)** money paid as income on investments or loans; ***the bank pays 10% interest on deposits***; ***to receive interest at 5%***; ***the loan pays 5% interest***; ***deposit which yields*** *or* ***gives*** *or* ***produces*** *or* ***bears 5% interest***; ***account which earns interest at 10%*** *or* ***which earns 10% interest***; **interest-bearing deposits** = deposits which produce interest; **fixed-interest investments** = investments producing an interest which does not change; **fixed-interest securities** = securities (such as government bonds) which produce an interest which does not change **(c)** part of the ownership of something, such as money invested in a company giving a financial share in it; **beneficial interest** = situation where someone is allowed to occupy or receive rent from a house without owning it; **he has a controlling interest in the company** = he owns more than 50% of the shares and so can direct how the company is run; **life interest** = situation where someone benefits from a property as long as he is alive; **majority interest** *or* **minority interest** = situation where someone owns a majority or a minority of shares in a company; ***he has a majority interest in a supermarket chain***; **to acquire a substantial interest in the company** = to buy a large number of shares in a company; **to declare an interest** = to state in public that you own shares in a company **2** *verb* to attract someone's attention; ***he tried to interest several companies in his new invention***; **interested in** = paying attention to; ***the managing director is interested only in increasing profitability***

> since last summer American interest rates have dropped by between three and four percentage points
>
> *Sunday Times*

> a lot of money is said to be tied up in sterling because of the interest-rate differential between US and British rates
>
> *Australian Financial Review*

interested party ['ɪntrestɪd 'pɑːti] *noun* person or company with a financial interest in a company

interesting ['ɪntrəstɪŋ] *adjective* which attracts attention; ***they made us a very interesting offer for the factory***

interim ['ɪntərɪm] **1** adjective **interim dividend** = dividend paid at the end of a half-year; **interim payment** = payment of part of a dividend; **interim report** *or* **interim statement** = report given at the end of a half-year; **in the interim** = meanwhile, for the time being **2** *noun* statement of interim profits or dividends

> the company plans to keep its annual dividend unchanged at Y7.5 per share, which includes a Y3.75 interim payout
>
> *Financial Times*

intermediary [ɪntə'miːdjəri] *noun* person who is the link between two parties; **financial intermediary** = (i) institution which takes deposits or loans from individuals and lends money to clients; (ii) person or company which arranges insurance for a client, but is not itself an insurance company (banks, building societies, hire purchase companies, are all types of financial intermediaries)

intermediation [ɪntəmiːdi'eɪʃn] *noun* arrangement of finance or insurance by an intermediary

internal [ɪn'tɜːnl] *adjective* **(a)** inside a company; **we decided to make an internal appointment** = we decided to appoint an existing member of staff to the post, and not bring someone in from outside the company; **internal audit** = audit carried out by a department within the company; **internal audit department** *or* **internal auditor** = department or member of staff who audits the accounts of the company he works for; **internal control** = system set up by the management of a company to monitor and control the company's activities; **internal growth** = expansion of a company which is based on profits from its existing trading (as opposed to external growth, which comes from the acquisition of other companies); **internal rate of return (IRR)** = average annual yield of an investment, where the interest earned over a period of time is the same as the original cost of the investment; **internal telephone** = telephone which is linked to other phones in an office **(b)** inside a country or a region; **an internal flight** = flight to a town inside the same country; **the internal market** *or* **single European market** = the EU considered as one single market, with no tariff barriers between its member states; *US* **Internal Revenue Service (IRS)** = government department which deals with taxes (NOTE: the British equivalent is the **Inland Revenue**); **internal trade** = trade between various parts of a country

international [ɪntə'næʃənl] *adjective* working between countries; **international law** = laws governing relations between countries; **international money markets** = market, such as the Euromarket, the international market for lending or borrowing in eurocurrencies; **international trade** = trade between different countries

International Bank for Reconstruction and Development (IBRD) the official name of the World Bank

International Commodities Clearing House (ICCH) clearing house which deals in settlements of futures contracts in commodities and financial futures

International Finance Corporation (IFC) a subsidiary of the World Bank which makes loans to private companies

International Labour Organization (ILO) [ɪntə'næʃənl 'leɪbə ɔːgənaɪ'zeɪʃn] section of the United Nations, an organization which tries to improve working conditions and workers' pay in member countries

International Monetary Fund (IMF) [ɪntə'næʃənl 'mʌnɪtri 'fʌnd] (part of the United Nations) a type of bank which helps member states in financial difficulties, gives financial advice to members and encourages world trade

International Monetary Market (IMM) [ɪntə'næʃənl 'mʌnɪtri 'mɑːkɪt] part of the Chicago Mercantile Exchange dealing in financial futures

International Petroleum Exchange (IPE) London commodity exchange dealing in crude oil and natural gas futures (it is an investment exchange, recognized by the FSA)

internet ['ɪntənet] *noun* international electronic network that provides file and data transfer, together with electronic mail functions for millions of users round the world; anyone can use the internet; **internet bank** = system of having credit in an account on the internet, and using it to pay for purchases made on the internet; *see also* AUTHENTICATE, E-BUSINESS, MICROPAYMENTS, ELECTRONIC PURSE, VIRTUAL TOKENS

Interstate Commerce Commission (ICC) ['ɪntəsteɪt 'kɒmɜːs kə'mɪʃn] *noun US* federal agency which regulates business activity involving two or more of the states in the USA

intervene [ɪntə'viːn] *verb* to try to make a change in a system; **to intervene in a dispute** = to try to settle a dispute

intervention [ɪntə'venʃən] *noun* acting to make a change in a system; ***the government's intervention in the foreign exchange markets***; ***the central bank's intervention in the banking crisis***; ***the government's intervention in the labour dispute***; **official intervention** = attempt by a government to influence the exchange rate, by buying or selling foreign currency; **intervention mechanism** = methods used by central banks in maintaining exchange rate parities (such as buying or selling of foreign currency); **intervention price** = price at which the EU will buy farm produce which farmers cannot sell, in order to store it; *see note at* TARGET PRICE

inter vivos ['ɪntə 'vaɪvəs] *phrase* **gift inter vivos** = gift given to another living person; *US* **inter vivos trust** = trust set up by one person for another living person

intestate [ɪn'testət] adjective **to die intestate** = to die without having made a will

intraday ['ɪntrədeɪ] *adjective* within the day; ***the stock hit a new record of 86 intraday on Friday***; **intraday liquidity** = availability of cash in the banking system

> the 52-week high/low range columns show the highest and lowest intraday stock price
>
> *Barron's*

> the FTSE 100 index, having topped its old 6,179 peak in intraday trading, was hit by Wall Street weakness before Friday's rally in America sent it back to 5,941
>
> *Sunday Times*

> the document spells out the rules governing access to the system by NCBs and the tricky issue of access to indraday liquidity
>
> *The Banker*

intrinsic value *noun* value which exists as part of something, such as the value of an option (for a call option, it is the difference between the current price and the higher striking price)

introduce [ɪntrə'djuːs] *verb* to make someone get to know a new person or thing; **to introduce a client** = to bring in a new client and make him known to someone; **to introduce a new product on the market** = to produce a new product and launch it on the market

introduction [ɪntrə'dʌkʃən] *noun* **(a)** letter making someone get to know another person; ***I'll give you an introduction to the MD - he is an old friend of mine*** **(b)** bringing an established company to the Stock Exchange (i.e., getting permission for the shares to be traded on the Stock Exchange, used when a company is formed by a demerger from an existing larger company, and no new shares are being offered for sale); *compare* OFFER FOR SALE, PLACING

> as the group's shares are already widely held, the listing will be via an introduction
>
> *Sunday Times*

invalid [ɪn'vælɪd] *adjective* not valid or not legal; ***permit that is invalid***; ***claim which has been declared invalid***

invalidate [ɪn'vælɪdeɪt] *verb* to make something invalid; ***because the company has been taken over, the contract has been invalidated***

invalidation [ɪnvælɪ'deɪʃən] *noun* making invalid

invalidity [ɪnvə'lɪdəti] *noun* being invalid; ***the invalidity of the contract***

inventory ['ɪnvəntri] **1** *noun* **(a)** *especially US* stock or goods in a warehouse or shop; ***to carry a high inventory***; ***to aim to reduce inventory***; **inventory control** = system of checking that there is not too much stock in a warehouse, but just enough to meet requirements; **inventory financing** = using money from working capital to purchase stock for resale; **inventory turnover** = total value of stock sold during a year, divided by the value of the goods remaining in stock **(b)** list of the contents of a house for sale, of an office for rent, etc.; ***to draw up an inventory of fixtures***; **to agree the inventory** = to agree that the inventory is correct **2** *verb* to make a list of stock or contents (NOTE: the word 'inventory' is used in American English where British English uses the word 'stock'. So, the American 'inventory control' is 'stock control' in British English)

> a warehouse needs to tie up less capital in inventory and with its huge volume spreads out costs over bigger sales
>
> *Duns Business Month*

invest [ɪn'vest] *verb* **(a)** to put money into shares, bonds, a building society, hoping that it will produce interest and increase in value; ***he invested all his money in an engineering business***; ***she was advised to invest in real estate*** *or* ***in government bonds***; **to invest abroad** = to put money into shares or bonds in overseas countries **(b)** to spend money on something which you believe will be useful; ***to invest money in new machinery***; ***to invest capital in a new factory***

> we have substantial venture capital to invest in good projects
>
> *Times*

investment [ɪn'vesmənt] *noun* **(a)** placing of money so that it will increase in value and produce an income (either in an asset, such as a building, or by purchasing shares, placing money on deposit, etc.); ***they called for more government investment in new industries***; ***investment in real estate***; ***to make investments in oil companies***; **return on investment (ROI)** = interest or dividends shown as a percentage of the money invested **(b)** shares, bonds, deposits bought with invested money; **long-term investment** *or* **short-term investment** = shares, etc., which are likely to increase in value over a long or short period; **safe investment** = shares, etc., which are not likely to fall in value; **blue-chip investments** = risk-free shares of good companies; **he is trying to protect his investments** = he is trying to make sure that the money he has invested is not lost **(c)** **investment adviser** = person who advises people on what investments to make; **investment analyst** = person working for a stockbroking firm, who analyses the performance of companies in certain sectors of the market, or the performance of a market sector as a whole, or economic trends in general; *US* **investment bank** *or* **banker** = bank which deals with the underwriting of new issues, and advises corporations on their financial affairs (the British equivalent is an 'issuing house'); **investment company** *or* **investment trust** = company whose shares can be bought on the Stock Exchange, and whose business is to make money by buying and selling stocks and shares; **investment environment** = general economic situation in which an investment is made; **investment grant** = government grant to a company to help it to invest in new machinery; **investment income** = income (such as interest and dividends) from investments; **Investment Management Regulatory Organization (IMRO)** = self-regulatory organization which regulates managers of investment funds, such as pension funds, now part of the FSA; **Enterprise Investment Scheme (EIS)** = a scheme which provides income and CGT relief for people prepared to risk investing in a single unquoted or AIM-listed trading company

> Investors can become directors of the EIS companies in which they invest. The maximum investment is £150,000 pa
>
> *The Times*

> investment trusts, like unit trusts, consist of portfolios

of shares and therefore provide a spread of investments

Investors Chronicle

investment companies took the view that prices had reached rock bottom and could only go up

Lloyd's List

investor [ɪn'vestə] *noun* person who invests money; **the small investor** *or* **the private investor** = person with a small sum of money to invest; **the institutional investor** = organization (like a pension fund or insurance company) with large sums of money to invest; **investor protection** = legislation to protect small investors from unscrupulous investment brokers and advisers; **Investors in Industry (3i)** = finance group partly owned by the big British High Street banks, providing finance especially to smaller companies

investigate [ɪn'vestɪgeɪt] *verb* to examine something which may be wrong

investigation [ɪnvestɪ'geɪʃən] *noun* examination to find out what is wrong; ***to conduct an investigation into irregularities in share dealings***

invisible [ɪn'vɪzəbl] **1** adjective **invisible assets** = assets which have a value but which cannot be seen (such as goodwill or patents); **invisible earnings** = foreign currency earned by a country by providing services, receiving interests or dividends, but not selling goods; **invisible imports** *or* **exports** *or* **invisible trade** = services which are paid for in foreign currency or earn foreign currency without actually selling a product (such as banking or tourism) **2** *plural noun* **invisibles** = invisible imports and exports

invite [ɪn'vaɪt] *verb* to ask someone to do something, to ask for something; ***to invite someone to an interview***; ***to invite someone to join the board***; ***to invite shareholders to subscribe a new issue***; ***to invite tenders for a contract***

invitation [ɪnvɪ'teɪʃən] *noun* asking someone to do something; ***to issue an invitation to someone to join the board***; ***invitation to tender for a contract***; ***invitation to subscribe a new issue***

invoice ['ɪnvɔɪs] **1** *noun* **(a)** note asking for payment for goods or services supplied; ***your invoice dated November 10th***; ***they sent in their invoice six weeks late***; ***to make out an invoice for £250***; ***to settle*** *or* ***to pay an invoice***; **the total is payable within thirty days of invoice** = the total sum has to be paid within thirty days of the date on the invoice; **VAT invoice** = invoice which includes VAT **(b) invoice clerk** = office worker who deals with invoices; **invoice discounting** = method of obtaining early payment of invoices by selling them at a discount to a company which will receive payment of the invoices when they are paid (the debtor is not informed of this arrangement, as opposed to factoring, where the debtor is informed); **invoice price** = price as given on an invoice (including discount and VAT); **total invoice value** = total amount on an invoice, including transport, VAT, etc. **2** *verb* to send an invoice to someone; ***to invoice a customer***; **we invoiced you on November 10th** = we sent you the invoice on November 10th

invoicing ['ɪnvɔɪsɪŋ] *noun* sending of an invoice; ***our invoicing is done by the computer***; **invoicing department** = department in a company which deals with preparing and sending invoices; **invoicing in triplicate** = preparing three copies of invoices; **VAT invoicing** = sending of an invoice including VAT

involuntary *adjective* not willingly; *US* **involuntary bankruptcy** = application by creditors to have a person or corporation made bankrupt (the British equivalent is 'compulsory winding up')

inward ['ɪnwəd] *adjective* towards the home country; **inward bill** = bill of lading for goods arriving in a country; **inward investment** = investment from outside a country, as when a foreign company decides to set up a new factory there; **inward mission** = visit to your home country by a group of foreign businessmen

IOU ['aɪəʊ'ju:] *noun* = *I OWE YOU* signed document promising that you will pay back money borrowed; ***to pay a pile of IOUs***

IPE = INTERNATIONAL PETROLEUM EXCHANGE

IPO = INITIAL PUBLIC OFFERING

analysts think the parent will keep 35-45 per cent of the company, but will float the rest in a single IPO worth at least $2.5bn

Financial Times

IRA ['aɪ 'ɑ: 'eɪ] *US* = INDIVIDUAL RETIREMENT ACCOUNT; **Education IRA** = account in which people can contribute up to $500 annually for the education of a child or a grandchild under the age of 18. These contributions are not tax-deductible but can grow tax-free. There is no tax on withdrawals as long as the child uses them (by the time he or she is 30) to pay for higher education; *see also* SPOUSAL

> eligibility to fund an Education IRA phases out for singles with AGIs of $95,000 to $110,000 and for married couples filing jointly with AGIs of $150,000 to $160,000
>
> *Fortune*

IRR = INTERNAL RATE OF RETURN

irrecoverable [ɪrɪ'kʌvərəbl] *adjective* which cannot be recovered; **irrecoverable debt** = debt which will never be paid

irredeemable [ɪrɪ'di:məbl] *adjective* which cannot be redeemed; **irredeemable bond** = government bond which has no date of maturity and which therefore provides interest but can never be redeemed at full value (in the UK, the War Loan is irredeemable)

irregular [ɪ'regjʊlə] *adjective* not correct or not done in the correct way; ***irregular documentation***; ***this procedure is highly irregular***

irregularities [ɪregjʊ'lærətiz] *noun* things which are not done in the correct way and which are possibly illegal; ***to investigate irregularities in the share dealings*** *or* ***trading irregularities***

irrevocable [ɪ'revəkəbl] *adjective* which cannot be changed; **irrevocable acceptance** = acceptance which cannot be withdrawn; **irrevocable letter of credit** = letter of credit which cannot be cancelled or changed, except if agreed between the two parties involved

IRS ['aɪ 'ɑ: 'es] *US* = INTERNAL REVENUE SERVICE

ISA ['aɪsə] = INDIVIDUAL SAVINGS ACCOUNT; *see also* LISA

issuance ['ɪʃu:əns] *noun* action of issuing new shares or new bonds

> the bank's board also approved the issuance of up to $2 billion in bonds
>
> *Wall Street Journal*

> new issuance in most currency sectors has already closed for the year. Dealers are expecting at least two more Euroyen issues this week by Japanese companies. There could also be some new dollar issuance, but the deals are likely to be targeted
>
> *Wall Street Journal*

issue ['ɪʃu:] **1** *noun* selling or giving of new shares; **bonus issue** *or* **scrip issue** = new shares given free to shareholders; **issue of debentures** *or* **debenture issue** = borrowing money by giving lenders debentures; **issue of new shares** *or* **share issue** = selling new shares in a company to the public; **rights issue** = giving shareholders the right to buy more shares at a lower price; **new issues department** = section of a bank which deals with issues of new shares in companies; **issue price** = price of shares when they are offered for sale for the first time **2** *verb* to put out or to give out (for the first time); ***to issue a letter of credit***; ***to issue shares in a new company***; ***to issue a writ against someone***; ***the government issued a report on London's traffic***

issued ['ɪʃu:d] adjective **issued capital** = amount of capital which is formed of money paid for shares issued to shareholders; **issued price** = price of shares in a new company when they are offered for sale for the first time

issuer ['ɪʃu:ə] *noun* company which issues shares for sale; **credit card issuer** = bank or other financial institution that issues credit cards

> ask your credit-card issuer to lower the annual interest rate on your credit card
>
> *Smart Money*

issuing ['ɪʃu:ɪŋ] *adjective* which organizes an issue of shares; **issuing bank** *or* **issuing house** = bank which organizes the selling of shares in new companies (the US equivalent is an investment bank)

> the rights issue should overcome the cash flow problems
>
> *Investors Chronicle*

> the company said that its recent issue of 10.5 per cent convertible preference shares at A$8.50 a share has been oversubscribed
>
> *Financial Times*

issued and fully paid capital is $100 million

Hongkong Standard

IT ['aɪ 'ti:] = INFORMATION TECHNOLOGY

item ['aɪtəm] *noun* **(a)** thing for sale; **cash items** = goods sold for cash; **we are holding orders for out of stock items** = for goods which are not in stock; ***please find enclosed an order for the following items from your catalogue*** **(b)** piece of information; ***items on a balance sheet***; **item of expenditure** = goods or services which have been paid for and appear in the accounts; *see also* EXCEPTIONAL, EXTRAORDINARY **(c)** point on a list; **we will now take item four on the agenda** = we will now discuss the fourth point on the agenda

itemize ['aɪtəmaɪz] *verb* to make a detailed list of things; ***itemizing the sales figures will take about two days***; **itemized account** = detailed record of money paid or owed; **itemized statement** = bank statement where each transaction is recorded in detail; **itemized invoice** = invoice which lists each item separately

Jj

J curve [ˈdʒeɪ ˈkɜːv] *noun* line on a graph shaped like a letter 'J', with an initial short fall, followed by a longer rise (used to describe the effect of a falling exchange rate on a country's balance of trade)

jeep mortgage [ˈdʒiːp ˈmɔːgɪdʒ] *US (informal)* = GRADUATED PAYMENT MORTGAGE

job [dʒɒb] *noun* **(a)** order being worked on; **job lot** = small parcel of shares traded on a Stock Exchange **(b)** regular paid work; **office job** *or* **white-collar job** = job in an office; **to give up your job** = to resign from your work; **to look for a job** = to try to find work; **to retire from your job** = to leave work and take a pension; **to be out of a job** = to have no work **(c) job analysis** = detailed examination and report on the duties of a job; **job application** *or* **application for a job** = asking for a job in writing; **job centre** = government office which lists jobs which are vacant; **job classification** = describing jobs listed under various classes; **job creation scheme** = government-backed plan to make work for the unemployed; **job description** = official document from the management which says what a job involves; **job evaluation** = examining different jobs within an organization to see what skills and qualifications are needed to carry them out; **job satisfaction** = a worker's feeling that he is happy in his place of work and pleased with the work he does; **job security** = a worker's feeling that he has a right to keep his job, or that he will never be made redundant; **job specification** = very detailed description of what is involved in a job; **job title** = name given to a person in a certain job; **on-the-job training** = training given to workers at their place of work; **off-the-job training** = training given to workers away from their place of work (i.e. at a college)

> he insisted that the tax advantages be directed toward small businesses will help create jobs
>
> *Toronto Star*

jobber [ˈdʒɒbə] *noun* **(a)** *(formerly)* **(stock) jobber** = person who bought and sold shares from other traders on the Stock Exchange; **jobber's turn** = commission earned by a jobber when buying or selling shares **(b)** *US* wholesaler

> warehouse clubs buy directly from manufacturers, eliminating jobbers and wholesale middlemen
>
> *Duns Business Month*

jobbing [ˈdʒɒbɪŋ] noun **(stock) jobbing** = buying and selling shares from other traders on the Stock Exchange

jobless [ˈdʒɒbləs] noun **the jobless** = people with no jobs, the unemployed

> the contradiction between the jobless figures and latest economic review
>
> *Sunday Times*

joint [dʒɒɪnt] *adjective* **(a)** combined, with two or more organizations linked together; **joint commission of inquiry** *or* **joint committee** = commission or committee with representatives of various organizations on it; **joint management** = management done by two or more people; **joint venture** = situtation where two or more companies join together for one specific large business project **(b)** one of two or more people who work together or who are linked; ***joint beneficiary***; ***joint managing director***; ***joint owner***; ***joint signatory***; **joint account** = bank account for two people; **joint-life annuity** = annuity which continues to pay an amount to a spouse after the main beneficiary dies; *compare* SINGLE-LIFE ANNUITY; **joint ownership** = owning of a property by several owners; **joint-stock bank** = bank which is a public company quoted on the Stock Exchange; **joint-stock company** = formerly, a public company whose shares were owned by very many people (now called a Public Limited Company or Plc)

jointly [ˈdʒɒɪntli] *adverb* together with one or more other people; ***to own a property jointly***; ***to manage a company jointly***; ***they are jointly liable for damages***; *(of husband*

and wife) **to file jointly** = to make a joint tax declaration; **jointly and severally liable** = liable both as a group and as individuals

journal ['dʒɔːnl] *noun* book with the account of sales and purchases made each day

judge [dʒʌdʒ] *noun* person who decides in a legal case; ***the judge sent him to prison for embezzlement***

judgement *or* **judgment** ['dʒʌdʒmənt] *noun* legal decision or official decision; **to pronounce judgement** *or* **to give your judgement on something** = to give an official or legal decision about something; **judgment debtor** = debtor who has been ordered by a court to pay a debt; **judgment lien** = court order putting a lien on the property of a judgment debtor (NOTE: the spelling **judgment** is used by lawyers)

judicial [dʒu'dɪʃəl] *adjective* referring to the law; **judicial review** = (i) examination of a case a second time by a higher court because a lower court has acted wrongly; (ii) examination of administrative decisions by a court; **judicial processes** = the ways in which the law works

jump [dʒʌmp] **1** *noun* sudden rise; ***jump in prices***; ***jump in unemployment figures*** **2** *verb* to go up suddenly; ***oil prices have jumped since the war started***; ***share values jumped on the Stock Exchange***

jumpy ['dʒʌmpi] *adjective* nervous or excited; **the market is jumpy** = the stock market is nervous and share prices are likely to fluctuate

junior ['dʒuːnjə] *adjective* less important than something else; **junior capital** = capital in the form of shareholders' equity, which is repaid only after secured loans (called 'senior capital') have been paid if the firm goes into liquidation; **junior mortgage** = second mortgage; **junior security** = security which is repaid after other securities

junk [dʒʌŋk] *noun* rubbish; useless items; **junk bonds** = high-interest bonds raised as debentures on the security of a company which is the subject of a takeover bid (the security has a very low credit rating, and the bonds have a very low rating also); **junk mail** = advertising material sent through the post

> the big US textile company is running deep in the red, its junk bonds are trading as low as 33 cents on the dollar
>
> *Wall Street Journal*

jurisdiction [dʒʊərɪs'dɪkʃn] noun **within the jurisdiction of the court** = in the legal power of a court

Kk

K [keɪ] *abbreviation* one thousand; **'salary: £15K+'** = salary more than £15,000 per annum

keen [kiːn] *adjective* **(a)** eager or active; **keen competition** = strong competition; ***we are facing some keen competition from European manufacturers***; **keen demand** = wide demand; ***there is a keen demand for home computers*** **(b) keen prices** = prices which are kept low so as to be competitive; ***our prices are the keenest on the market***

keep [kiːp] *verb* **(a)** to do what is necessary; **to keep an appointment** = to be there when you said you would be; **to keep the books of a company** *or* **to keep a company's books** = to note the accounts of a company accurately **(b)** to hold items for sale or for information; **to keep someone's name on file** = to have someone's name on a list for reference **(c)** to hold things at a certain level; ***we must keep our mailing list up to date***; ***to keep spending to a minimum***; ***high interest rates have kept the pound at a high level***; ***the government is encouraging firms to keep prices low*** (NOTE: **keeping - kept**)

keep back ['kiːp 'bæk] *verb* to hold on to something which you could give to someone; ***to keep back information*** *or* ***to keep something back from someone***; ***to keep £10 back from someone's salary***

keeping ['kiːpɪŋ] noun **safe keeping** = being looked after carefully; ***we put the documents into the bank for safe keeping***

keep up ['kiːp 'ʌp] *verb* to hold at a certain high level; ***we must keep up the turnover in spite of the recession***; ***she kept up a keyboarding rate of sixty words per minute for several hours***

Keogh plan ['kiːəʊ 'plæn] *noun US* private pension system allowing self-employed businessmen and professionals to set up pension and retirement plans for themselves; people can invest up to a certain annual limit, and can hold a Keogh plan at the same time as they contribute to a corporation pension or to an IRA; funds can begin to be withdrawn from a plan at the age of 591/2 *compare* 401 (k) PLAN

kerb market *or* **kerb trading** ['kɜːb 'mɑːkɪt or 'treɪdɪŋ] *noun* unofficial after-hours market in shares, bonds or commodities

key [kiː] *noun* **(a)** piece of metal used to open a lock; **key money** = premium paid when taking over the keys of a flat or office which you are renting **(b)** part of a computer or typewriter which you press with your fingers; ***there are sixty-four keys on the keyboard***; **control key** = key on a computer which works part of a program; **function key** = key on a computer which has a specific task or sequence of instructions; ***tags can be allocated to function keys***; **shift key** = key which makes a typewriter or computer move to capital letters **(c)** important; ***key factor***; ***key industry***; ***key personnel***; ***key post***; ***key staff***; **key rate** = an interest rate which gives the basic rate on which other rates are calculated (the former bank base rate in the UK, or the Federal Reserve's discount rate in the USA)

keyboard ['kiːbɔːd] **1** *noun* part of a typewriter or computer with keys which are pressed to make a letter or figure; **qwerty keyboard** = English language keyboard, where the first letters are Q-W-E-R-T-Y; ***the computer has a normal qwerty keyboard*** **2** *verb* to press the keys on a keyboard to type something; ***he is keyboarding our address list***

keyboarder ['kiːbɔːdə] *noun* person who types information into a computer

keyboarding ['kiːbɔːdɪŋ] *noun* act of typing on a keyboard; ***keyboarding costs have risen sharply***

keypad ['kiːpæd] *noun* small keyboard; **numeric keypad** = part of a computer keyboard which is a programmable set of numbered keys

kickback ['kɪkbæk] *noun* illegal commission paid to someone (especially a government official) who helps in a business deal

kicker ['kɪkə] *noun* special inducement to buy a bond (such as making it convertible to shares at a preferential rate) *US* **equity kicker** = incentive given to people to lend a company money, in the form of a warrant to share in future earnings (the British equivalent is an 'equity sweetener')

kill [kɪl] verb *(informal)* **to kill an order** = to stop an order taking place after it has been instructed; ***'Kill that order' he shouted, but it was too late***

killing ['kɪlɪŋ] noun *(informal)* huge profit; ***he made a killing on the stock market***

kina ['ki:nə] *noun* currency used in Papua New Guinea

kind [kaɪnd] noun **payment in kind** = payment made by giving goods or food, but not money

kip [kɪp] *noun* currency used in Laos

kite [kaɪt] **1** *noun* **(a) to fly a kite** = to put forward a proposal to try to interest people; **kite flier** = person who tries to impress by putting forward a proposal; **kite-flying** = trying to impress by putting forward grand plans **(b)** *GB* **kite mark** = mark on goods to show they meet official standards **(c)** *(informal)* = ACCOMMODATION BILL **2** *verb* **(a)** *US* (i) to write cheques on one account and deposit them in another, withdrawing money from the second account before the cheques are cleared; (ii) to write cheques on one account and deposit them in a second account on the last day of the accounting period, thus showing the amount twice in the company's books, since the sum will not yet have been debited from the first account; (iii) to write a cheque for an amount which is higher than the total amount of money in the account, then deposit enough to cover the cheque **(b)** *GB* to use stolen credit cards or cheque books

kitty ['kɪti] *noun* money which has been collected by a group of people to be used later (such as for an office party); ***we all put £5 into the kitty***

knock down ['nɒk 'daʊn] verb **to knock something down to a bidder** = to sell something at an auction; ***the stock was knocked down to him for £10,000***

knockdown ['nɒkdaʊn] noun **knockdown prices** = very low prices; ***he sold me the car at a knockdown price***

knock off ['nɒk 'ɒf] *verb* to reduce a price by an amount; ***he knocked £10 off the price for cash***

knock-on effect ['nɒk 'ɒn ɪ'fekt] *noun* effect which an action will have on other situations; ***the strike by customs officers has had a knock-on effect on car production by slowing down exports of cars***

koruna [kə'rʊnə] *noun* currency used in the Czech Republic and Slovakia

krona ['krəʊnə] *noun* currency used in Sweden and Iceland

krone ['krəʊnə] *noun* currency used in Denmark and Norway

kroon [krəʊn] *noun* currency used in Estonia (NOTE: plural is **krooni**)

krugerrand ['kru:gərænd] *noun* gold coin weighing one ounce, minted in South Africa

kuna ['ku:nə] *noun* currency used in Croatia

kwacha ['kwætʃə] *noun* currency used in Malawi and Zambia

kwanza ['kwænzə] *noun* currency used in Angola

kyat ['kaɪət] *noun* currency used in Myanmar (formerly Burma)

Ll

L *US* measurement of money supply, calculated as M3 (broad money supply), plus Treasury bills, bonds and commercial paper

labour *US* **labor** ['leɪbə] *noun* **(a)** heavy work; **to charge for materials and labour** = to charge for both the materials used in a job and also the hours of work involved; **labour costs** *or* **labour charges** = cost of the workers employed to make a product (not including materials or overheads); **indirect labour costs** = cost of wages of workers who are not directly involved in making the product (such as secretaries, cleaners); **labour is charged at £5 an hour** = each hour of work costs £5 **(b)** workers, the workforce; **casual labour** = workers who are hired for a short period; **cheap labour** = workers who do not earn much money; **local labour** = workers recruited near a factory, not brought in from somewhere else; **organized labour** = workers who are members of trade unions; **skilled labour** = workers who have special knowledge or qualifications; **labour force** = all workers (either in a country or a company); ***the management has made an increased offer to the labour force***; ***we are setting up a factory in the Far East because of the cheap labour available***; **labour market** = number of workers who are available for work; **25,000 young people have left school and have come on to the labour market** = 25,000 people have left school and become available for work; **labour shortage** *or* **shortage of labour** = situation where there are not enough workers to fill jobs; **labour-intensive industry** = industry which needs large numbers of workers or where labour costs are high in relation to turnover **(c)** **labour disputes** = arguments between management and workers; **labour laws** *or* **labour legislation** = laws relating to the employment of workers; **labour relations** = relations between management and workers; *US* **labor union** = organization which represents workers who are its members in discussions about wages and conditions of work with management **(d)** **International Labour Organization (ILO)** = section of the United Nations which tries to improve working conditions and workers' pay in member countries

> the possibility that British goods will price themselves back into world markets is doubtful as long as sterling labour costs continue to rise faster than in competitor countries
>
> *Sunday Times*

> 70 per cent of Australia's labour force is employed in service activity
>
> *Australian Financial Review*

lack [læk] **1** *noun* not having enough; **lack of data** *or* **lack of information** = not having enough information; ***the decision has been put back for lack of up-to-date information***; **lack of funds** = not enough money; ***the project was cancelled because of lack of funds*** **2** *verb* not to have enough of something; ***the company lacks capital***

ladder ['lædə] *noun* *US* investment portfolio consisting of bonds with a series of maturity dates from very short-dated to long-dated; *compare* BAR-BELL

lading ['leɪdɪŋ] *noun* loading, putting goods on a ship; **bill of lading** = list of goods being shipped, which the transporter gives to the person sending the goods to show that they have been loaded

Laffer curve ['læfə 'kɜːv] *noun* chart showing that cuts in tax rates increase output in the economy

lag [læg] *verb* to be behind; to be slower than something; **lagging indicator** = indicator (such as the gross national product) which shows a change in economic trends later than other indicators (NOTE: the opposite is a **leading indicator**)

laissez-faire economy ['leseɪ'feə ɪ'kɒnəmi] *noun* economy where the government does not interfere because it believes it is right to let the economy run itself

lakh [læk] noun *(in India)* one hundred thousand (NOTE: ten lakh equal one crore)

lame duck ['leɪm 'dʌk] *noun* company which is in financial difficulties; ***the government has refused to help lame duck companies***

land [lænd] **1** *noun* **(a)** area of earth; **land agent** = person who runs a farm or a large area of land for someone; *GB* **land register** = register of land, showing who owns it and what buildings are on it; **land registration** = system of registering land and its owners; **land registry** = government office where land is registered; **land taxes** = taxes on the area of land owned **(b) Land** = one of the administrative states in Germany (NOTE: plural is **Länder**) **2** *verb* to put goods or passengers on to land after a voyage by sea or by air; **landed costs** = costs of goods which have been delivered to a port, unloaded and passed through customs

> two of the main pillars of Japan's ruling establishment - the big business community and the Finance Ministry - have clashed over a government plan to levy a new national tax on land on top of existing local land taxes
>
> *Far Eastern Economic Review*

Landeszentralbank [lændəztsen'trɑ:lbæŋk] *noun* the central bank in one of the German states, or Länder

landing ['lændɪŋ] *noun* **(a)** arrival of a plane on land; arrival of a passenger on land; **landing charges** = payment for putting goods on land and the customs duties; **landing order** = permit which allows goods to be unloaded into a bonded warehouse without paying customs duty **(b) hard landing** = change in economic strategy to counteract inflation which has serious results for the population (high unemployment, rising interest rates, etc.); **soft landing** = change in economic strategy to counteract inflation, which has only minor effects on the bulk of the population

landlord ['lænlɔ:d] *noun* person or company that owns a property which is let; **ground landlord** = person or company that owns the freehold of a property which is then let and sublet

lapse [læps] **1** noun **a lapse of time** = a period of time which has passed **2** *verb* to stop being valid, to stop being active; ***the guarantee has lapsed; the takeover bid was allowed to lapse when only 13% of the shareholders accepted the offer***; **to let an offer lapse** = to allow time to pass so that an offer is no longer valid; **lapsed option** = option which has not been taken up, and now has expired

large-sized ['lɑ:dʒ'saɪzd] *adjective* which is big, of a very large size; *(for UK tax purposes)* **large-sized company** = company which has a turnover of more than £5.75m or employs more than 250 staff; *compare* MEDIUM-SIZED, SMALL COMPANY

last [lɑ:st] *adjective & adverb* coming at the end of a series; **last quarter** = period of three months to the end of the financial year; **last trading day** = the last day when Stock Exchange trading takes place in an account, or the last day when futures trading takes place relating to a certain delivery month

last in first out (LIFO) ['lɑ:st 'ɪn 'fɜ:st 'aʊt] *noun* **(a)** redundancy policy, where the people who have been most recently appointed are the first to be made redundant **(b)** accounting method where stock is valued at the price of the latest purchases

lat ['læt] *noun* currency used in Latvia

launch [lɔ:ntʃ] **1** *noun* putting a company on the Stock Exchange for the first time **2** *verb* to put a company on the Stock Exchange for the first time

launder ['lɔ:ndə] *verb* to pass illegal profits, money from crime or drugs, or money which has not been taxed, etc., into the normal banking system in such a way that it is not possible to find out where it came from; ***to launder money through an offshore bank***

laundering ['lɔ:ndrɪŋ] noun **money laundering** = passing illegal money into the normal banking system

> although there have been few non-drug money laundering related prosecutions and convictions in the UK, there have been a number of recent cases where money laundering charges have been brought against parties who have received and dealt with the proceeds of the sale of counterfeit goods
>
> *Financial World*

law [lɔ:] *noun* **(a) laws** = rules by which a country is governed and the activities of people and organizations controlled; **labour laws** = laws concerning the employment of workers **(b) law** = all the laws of a country taken together; **civil law** = laws relating to arguments between individuals and the rights of individuals; **commercial law** = laws regarding business; **company law** = laws which refer to the way companies work; **contract law** *or* **the law of contract** = laws relating to private agreements; **criminal law** = laws relating to crime; **international law** = laws referring to the way countries deal with each other; **maritime law** *or* **the law of the sea** = laws referring to ships, ports, etc.; **inside the law** *or* **within the law** = obeying the laws of a country; **against** *or* **outside the law** = not according to the laws of a country; **to break the law** = to do something which is not allowed by law; ***he is breaking the law by selling goods on Sunday***; ***you will be breaking the law if you try to take that computer out of the country without an export licence*** **(c)** general rule; **law of supply and demand** = general rule that the amount of a product which is available is related to the needs of the possible customers; **law of diminishing returns** = general rule that as more factors of production (land, labour and capital) are added to the existing factors, so the amount they produce is proportionately smaller

lawful ['lɔ:fʊl] *adjective* acting within the law; **lawful practice** = action which is permitted by the law; **lawful trade** = trade which is allowed by law

lawsuit ['lɔ:su:t] *noun* case brought before a court; **to bring a lawsuit against someone** = to tell someone to appear in court to settle an argument; **to defend a lawsuit** = to appear in court to state your case

lawyer ['lɔ:jə] *noun* person who has studied law and can act for people on legal business; **commercial lawyer** *or* **company lawyer** = person who specializes in company law or who advises companies on legal problems; **international lawyer** = person who specializes in international law; **maritime lawyer** = person who specializes in laws concerning ships

lay off ['leɪ 'ɒf] *verb* **(a)** to stop employing staff, because there is no work **(b) to lay off risks** = to protect oneself against risk in one investment by making other investments

lay out ['leɪ 'aʊt] *verb* to spend money; ***we had to lay out half our cash budget on equipping the new factory***

LBO = LEVERAGED BUYOUT

L/C = LETTER OF CREDIT

LCE = LONDON COMMODITY EXCHANGE

LDC = LESS DEVELOPED COUNTRY

LDT = LICENSED DEPOSIT TAKER

lead [li:d] *noun* most important, in the front; **lead bank** = the main bank in a loan syndicate; **lead manager** = person who organizes a syndicate of underwriters for a new issue of securities; **lead underwriter** = underwriting firm which organizes the underwriting of a share issue (NOTE: the American equivalent is a **managing underwriter**)

leader ['li:də] *noun* **(a)** product which sells best; **a market leader** = (i) product which sells most in a market; (ii) company which has the largest share of a market; **loss-leader** = article which is sold very cheaply to attract customers **(b)** important share, share which is often bought or sold on the Stock Exchange

> market leaders may benefit from scale economies or other cost advantages; they may enjoy a reputation for quality simply by being at the top, or they may actually produce a superior product that gives them both a large market share and high profits
>
> *Accountancy*

leading ['li:dɪŋ] *adjective* most important; which comes first; ***leading industrialists feel the end of the recession is near***; ***leading shares rose on the Stock Exchange***; ***leading shareholders in the company forced a change in management policy***; ***they are the leading company in the field***; **leading indicator** = indicator (such as manufacturing order books) which shows a change in economic trends earlier than other indicators (NOTE: the opposite is a **lagging indicator**)

lead time ['li:d 'taɪm] *noun* time between deciding to place an order and receiving the product; ***the lead time on this item is more than six weeks***

lease [li:s] **1** *noun* **(a)** written contract for letting or renting a building or a piece of land or a piece of equipment for a period against payment of a fee; **long lease** = lease which runs for fifty years or more; ***to take an office building on a long lease***; **short lease** = lease which runs for up to two or three years; ***we have a short lease on our current premises***; ***to rent office space on a twenty-year lease***; **full repairing lease** = lease where the tenant has to pay for all repairs to the property; **headlease** = lease from the freehold owner to a tenant; **sublease** *or* **underlease** = lease from a tenant to another tenant; **the lease expires** *or* **runs out in 2005** = the lease comes to an end in 2005; **on expiration of the lease** = when the lease comes to an end; *see also* CONSUMER LEASE **(b) to hold an oil**

lease in the Gulf of Mexico = to have a lease on a section of the Gulf to explore for oil **2** *verb* **(a)** to let or rent offices or land or machinery for a period; ***to lease offices to small firms***; ***to lease equipment*** **(b)** to use an office or land or machinery for a time and pay a fee; ***to lease an office from an insurance company***; ***all our company cars are leased***

lease back ['li:s 'bæk] *verb* to sell a property or machinery to a company and then take it back on a lease; ***they sold the office building to raise cash, and then leased it back for twenty-five years***

lease-back ['li:sbæk] *noun* arrangement where property is sold and then taken back on a lease; ***they sold the office building and then took it back under a lease-back arrangement***

leasehold ['li:shəʊld] *noun & adjective* holding property on a lease from a freeholder (the ground landlord); ***they work from leasehold premises in the centre of town***; ***the company has some valuable leaseholds***; ***to buy a property leasehold***

leaseholder ['li:shəʊldə] *noun* person who holds a property on a lease

leasing ['li:sɪŋ] *noun* which leases; working under a lease; ***the company has branched out into car leasing***; ***an equipment-leasing company***; ***to run a copier under a leasing arrangement***; *see also* LESSEE

ledger ['ledʒə] *noun* book in which accounts are written; **bought ledger** *or* **purchase ledger** = book in which expenditure is noted; **bought ledger clerk** *or* **sales ledger clerk** = office worker who deals with the bought ledger or the sales ledger; **nominal ledger** *or* **general ledger** = book which records a company's income and expenditure in general; **payroll ledger** = list of staff and their salaries; **sales ledger** = book in which sales are noted

left [left] *adjective* **(a)** not right; ***the numbers run down the left side of the page***; ***put the debits in the left column*** **(b)** not with others; ***10m new shares were left with the underwriters when the offer was undersubscribed***; *see also* LEAVE

left-hand ['lefthænd] *adjective* belonging to the left side; ***the debits are in the left-hand column in the accounts***; ***he keeps the personnel files in the left-hand drawer of his desk***

legacy ['legəsi] *noun* property given by someone to someone else at his death

legal ['li:gəl] *adjective* **(a)** according to the law, allowed by the law; ***the company's action was completely legal***; **legal currency** = money which is legally used in a country; *US* **legal list** = list of blue-chip securities in which banks and financial institutions are allowed to invest by the state in which they are based; **legal tender** = coins or notes which can be legally used to pay a debt (small denominations cannot be used to pay large debts) **(b)** referring to the law; **to take legal action** = to sue someone, to take someone to court; **to take legal advice** = to ask a lawyer to advise about a legal problem; **legal adviser** = person who advises clients about the law; *GB* **legal aid** = government scheme where someone who has little money can have his legal expenses paid for him; **legal claim** = statement that someone owns something legally; ***he has no legal claim to the property***; **legal costs** *or* **legal charges** *or* **legal expenses** = money spent on fees to lawyers; **legal department** *or* **legal section** = section of a company dealing with legal matters; **legal expert** = person who knows a lot about the law; **legal holiday** = day when banks and other businesses are closed; **legal personality** = existence as a body and so ability to be affected by the law

legalization [li:gəlaɪ'zeɪʃən] *noun* making something legal

legalize ['li:gəlaɪz] *verb* to make something legal

legatee [legə'ti:] *noun* person who receives property from someone who has died

legislation [ledʒɪs'leɪʃən] *noun* laws; **labour legislation** = laws concerning the employment of workers

lek [lek] *noun* currency used in Albania

lempira [lem'pi:rə] *noun* currency used in Honduras

lend [lend] *verb* to allow someone to use something for a period; ***to lend something to someone*** *or* ***to lend someone something***; ***he lent the company money*** *or* ***he lent money to the company***; ***to lend money against security***; ***the bank lent him £50,000 to start his business*** (NOTE: **lending - lent**)

lender ['lendə] *noun* person who lends money; **lender of the last resort** = central bank which lends money to commercial banks when they are short of funds (in the UK, this is the Bank of England, and in the USA it is the Federal Reserve Banks); **mortgage lender** = company or institution which lends money on mortgages (these are banks and building societies); **Council of Mortgage Lenders** = organization which represents companies which provide mortgage lending to the residential market

lending ['lendɪŋ] *noun* act of letting someone use money for a time; **lending limit** = limit on the amount of money a bank can lend; **lending margin** = agreed spread (based on the LIBOR) for lending

> Japanese banks, responsible for half of all new international lending in the second half of the 1980s, have greatly reduced new lending
>
> *Financial Times*

leone [lɪ'əʊni] *noun* currency used in Sierra Leone

less [les] **1** *adjective* smaller than; of a smaller size or value than; ***we do not grant credit for sums of less than £100; he sold it for less than he had paid for it*** **2** *preposition* minus, with a sum removed; ***purchase price less 15% discount; interest less service charges*** **3** *adverb* not as much; **less developed countries (LDCs)** = countries in the Third World which are not economically advanced and borrowed heavily from commercial banks in the 1970s and 1980s to finance their industrial development, and so created an international debt crisis

lessee [le'siː] *noun* person who has a lease; person who pays money for a property he leases

lessor [le'sɔː] *noun* owner of a property who grants a lease on it

let [let] **1** *verb* to lend a house or an office or a farm to someone for a payment; **to let an office** = to allow someone to use an office for a time in return for payment of rent; **offices to let** = offices which are available to be leased by companies (NOTE: **letting - let**) **2** *noun* period of the lease of a property; ***they took the office on a short let***

let-out clause ['letaʊt 'klɔːz] *noun* clause which allows someone to avoid doing something in a contract; ***he added a let-out clause to the effect that the payments would be revised if the exchange rate fell by more than 5%***

letter ['letə] *noun* **(a)** piece of writing sent from one person or company to another to give information; **circular letter** = letter sent to many people; **covering letter** = letter sent with documents to say why they are being sent; **standard letter** = letter which is sent without change to various correspondents **(b)** **letter of acknowledgement** = letter which says that something has been received; **letters of administration** = letter given by a court to allow someone to deal with the estate of a person who has died; **letter of advice** = letter from one bank to another, advising that a transaction has taken place; **letter of allotment** *or* **allotment letter** = letter which tells someone how many shares in a new company he has been allotted; **letter of application** = letter in which someone applies for a job; **letter of appointment** = letter in which someone is appointed to a job; **letter of comfort** = (i) letter supporting someone who is trying to get a loan; (ii) letter from a company promising to lend money to a subsidiary; *see also* COMFORT; **letter of indemnity** = letter promising payment of compensation for a loss; **letter of intent** = (i) letter which states what a company intends to do if something happens; (ii) *US* letter from a private purchaser of shares, stating that the shares have been bought as an investment, and not for resale; **letters patent** = official document which gives someone the exclusive right to make and sell something which he has invented **(c)** **registered letter** = letter which is noted by the post office before it is sent, so that compensation can be claimed if it is lost **(d)** **to acknowledge receipt by letter** = to write a letter to say that something has been received

letter security *or* **letter stock** ['letə sɪ'kjʊərɪti] *noun US* share which has not been registered with the SEC and therefore can be sold privately, together with a letter of intent, or traded in the normal way if the owner files with the SEC using a Form 144

letter of credit (L/C) ['letə əv 'kredɪt] *noun* letter from a bank authorizing payment of a certain sum to a person or company (usually in another country); **irrevocable letter of credit** = letter of credit which cannot be cancelled or changed

letting ['letɪŋ] noun **letting agency** = agency which deals in property to let; **furnished lettings** = furnished property to let

leu [luː] *noun* currency used in Romania and Moldova

lev [lev] *noun* currency used in Bulgaria

level ['levl] **1** *noun* position; ***low levels of productivity*** *or* ***low productivity levels; to raise the level of employee benefits; to lower the level of borrowings***; **high level of investment** = large amount of money invested; **manning levels** *or* **staffing levels** = number of people required in each department of a company to do the work efficiently **2** *verb* **to level off** *or* **to level out** = to stop rising or falling; ***profits have levelled off over the last***

few years; ***prices are levelling out*** (NOTE: **levelling - levelled** but American spelling **leveling - leveled**)

> figures from the Fed on industrial production for April show a decline to levels last seen in June 1984
>
> *Sunday Times*

> applications for mortgages are running at a high level
>
> *Times*

> employers having got their staff back up to a reasonable level are waiting until the scope for overtime working is exhausted before hiring
>
> *Sydney Morning Herald*

leverage ['li:vərɪdʒ] *noun* **(a)** relation between a company's capital borrowed at a fixed interest and the value of its ordinary shares (also called 'gearing') **(b)** borrowing money at fixed interest which is then used to produce more money than the interest paid

> COMMENT: high leverage (or high gearing) has the effect of increasing a company's profitability when trading is expanding; if the company's trading slows down, the effect of high fixed-interest charges is to increase the rate of slowdown

leveraged ['li:vərɪdʒd] *adjective* using borrowings for finance; **leveraged buyout (LBO)** *or* **leveraged takeover** = buying all the shares in a company by borrowing money against the security of the assets of the company to be bought; **leveraged stock** = stock bought with borrowed money

> the offer came after management had offered to take the company private through a leveraged buyout for $825 million
>
> *Fortune*

levy ['levi] **1** *noun* money which is demanded and collected by the government; **capital levy** = tax on the value of a person's property and possessions; **import levy** = tax on imports, especially in the EU a tax on imports of farm produce from outside the EU; **levies on luxury items** = taxes on luxury items; **training levy** = tax to be paid by companies to fund the government's training schemes; *see also* DILUTION LEVY **2** *verb* to demand payment of a tax or some extra payment and to collect it; ***the government has decided to levy a tax on imported cars***; ***to levy a duty on the import of luxury items***; **to levy members for a new club house** = to ask members of the club to pay for the new building

> royalties have been levied at a rate of 12.5% of full production
>
> *Lloyd's List*

liability [laɪə'bɪləti] *noun* **(a)** being legally responsible for damage or loss, etc.; **to accept liability for something** = to agree that you are responsible for something; **to refuse liability for something** = to refuse to agree that you are responsible for something; **contractual liability** = legal responsibility for something as stated in a contract; **employers' liability insurance** = insurance to cover accidents which may happen at work, and for which the company may be responsible; **limited liability** = situation where someone's liability for debt is limited by law; **limited liability company** = company where a shareholder is responsible for repaying the company's debts only to the face value of the shares he owns **(b)** responsibility for a payment (such as the repayment of a loan); **liabilities** = debts of a business, including dividends owed to shareholders; ***the balance sheet shows the company's assets and liabilities***; **current liabilities** = debts which a company has to pay within the next accounting period (in a company's annual accounts, these would be debts which must be paid within the year and are usually payments for goods or services received); **long-term liabilities** = debts which are not due to be paid for some time; **he was not able to meet his liabilities** = he could not pay his debts; **to discharge your liabilities in full** = to pay everything which you owe

liable ['laɪəbl] *adjective* **(a) liable for** = legally responsible for; ***the customer is liable for breakages***; ***the chairman was personally liable for the company's debts*** **(b) liable to** = which is officially due to be paid; ***goods which are liable to stamp duty***

LIBID = LONDON INTERBANK BID RATE

LIBOR = LONDON INTERBANK OFFERED RATE

licence *US* **license** ['laɪsəns] *noun* official document which allows someone to do something; **import licence** *or* **export licence** = documents which allow goods to be exported or imported; **goods manufactured under licence** = goods made with the permission of the owner of the copyright or patent; **drinks licence** *or* **alcohol licence** *US* **liquor license** = permit to sell alcohol in a restaurant, etc.; ***he refused to renew the liquor license for his son's restaurant***

license ['laɪsəns] **1** *noun US* = LICENCE **2** *verb* to give someone official permission to do something; ***to license a company to manufacture spare parts***; ***she is licensed to run an employment agency***; **licensed dealer** = person who has been licensed by the DTI to buy and sell securities for individual clients; **licensed deposit-taker (LDT)** *or* **licensed institution** = deposit-taking institution, such as a building society, bank or friendly society, which is licensed to receive money on deposit from private individuals and to pay interest on it

licensee [laɪsən'si:] *noun* person who has a licence, especially to manufacture something

licensing ['laɪsənsɪŋ] *noun* which refers to licences; ***a licensing agreement***

lien [li:n] *noun* legal right to hold someone's goods and keep them until a debt has been paid; **general lien** = lien against the personal possessions of a borrower (but not against his house or land); *see also* BANKER'S LIEN

lieu [lju:] noun **in lieu of** = instead of; **she was given two months' salary in lieu of notice** = she was given two months' salary and asked to leave immediately

life [laɪf] *noun* **(a)** time when a person is alive; **life annuity** *or* **annuity for life** = annual payments made to someone as long as he is alive; **life expectancy** = number of years a person is likely to live; **life interest** *US* **life estate** = interest in a property which stops when a person dies; **whole-life insurance** = insurance where the insured person pays a fixed premium each year and the insurance company pays a sum when he dies; **the life assured** *or* **the life insured** = the person whose life has been covered by the life assurance **(b)** period of time something exists; ***the life of a loan***; ***during the life of the agreement***; **life of a contract** = remaining period of a futures contract before it expires; **shelf life of a product** = length of time during which a product can stay in the shop and still be good to use; *see also* HALF-LIFE

life assurance *or* **life insurance** ['laɪf ə'ʃʊərəns or ɪn'ʃʊərəns] *noun* insurance which pays a sum of money when someone dies, or at a certain date if he is still alive; **life assurance company** = company providing life assurance, but usually also providing other services such as investment advice

lifeboat ['laɪfbəʊt] *noun* boat used to rescue passengers from sinking ships; **lifeboat operation** = rescue of a company (especially of a bank) which is in difficulties

lifestyle ['laɪfstaɪl] *noun* way of living of a particular person or social group; *see also* AUDIT

Lifetime Individual Savings Account (LISA) British scheme by which individuals can invest for their retirement by putting a limited amount of money each year in a tax-free unit trust account; *see also* ISA

LIFFE = LONDON INTERNATIONAL FINANCIAL FUTURES AND OPTIONS EXCHANGE

LIFO = LAST IN FIRST OUT

light [laɪt] *adjective* **(a)** not heavy; **shares fell back in light trading** = shares lost value on a day when there was little business done on the Stock Exchange **(b)** not have enough of a certain type of share in a portfolio; ***his portfolio is light in banks*** (NOTE: the opposite is **heavy**)

lighten ['laɪtn] *verb* to sell shareholdings if a portfolio is too 'heavy' in a certain type of share

like-for-like ['laɪkfə'laɪk] *adverb* **on a like-for-like basis** = when comparing the same stores over different periods; **like-for-like store sales** = sales for the same stores over an earlier period

> the booksellers said like-for-like sales in the six weeks to January 2 were 6.3 per cent higher
>
> *The Times*

lilangeni [lɪlən'geni] *noun* currency used in Swaziland

limit ['lɪmɪt] **1** *noun* point at which something ends, point where you can go no further; **to set limits to imports** *or* **to impose import limits** = to allow only a certain amount of imports; **credit limit** = largest amount of money which a customer can borrow; **he has exceeded his credit limit** = he has borrowed more money than he is allowed; **lending limit** = restriction on the amount of money a bank can lend; **time limit** = maximum time which can be taken to do something; ***to set a time limit for acceptance of the offer***; *US* **limit order** = order to a broker to sell if a security falls to a certain price (NOTE: the British equivalent is **stop-loss order**); **limit 'up'** *or* **limit 'down'** = upper or lower limits to share price movements which are regulated by some stock exchanges **2** *verb* to stop something from going beyond a certain point; **the banks have limited their**

credit = the banks have allowed their customers only a certain amount of credit

limitation [lɪmɪˈteɪʃən] *noun* **(a)** act of allowing only a certain quantity of something; **limitation of liability** = making someone liable for only a part of the damage or loss; **time limitation** = amount of time available; ***the contract imposes limitations on the number of cars which can be imported*** **(b)** **statute of limitations** = law which allows only a certain amount of time (a few years) for someone to claim damages or property

limited [ˈlɪmɪtɪd] *adjective* restricted, not open; **limited market** = market which can take only a certain quantity of goods; **limited liability company** = company where each shareholder is responsible for the company's debts only to the face value of his shares (in the USA, profits are distributed to the shareholders as if it were a partnership); *see also* PARTNERSHIP; **private limited company** = company with a small number of shareholders, whose shares are not traded on the Stock Exchange (NOTE: shortened to **Ltd**); **Public Limited Company** = company whose shares can be bought on the Stock Exchange (NOTE: written as **plc** *or* **PLC**)

limiting [ˈlɪmɪtɪŋ] *adjective* which limits; ***a limiting clause in a contract***; ***the short holiday season is a limiting factor on the hotel trade***

line [laɪn] *noun* **(a)** long mark; ***he drew a thick line across the bottom of the column to show which figure was the total*** **(b)** row of letters or figures on a page; **bottom line** = last line in accounts, showing the net profit; ***the boss is interested only in the bottom line***; **line of credit** *US* **bank line** = (i) amount of money made available to a customer by a bank as an overdraft; (ii) *US* borrowing limit on a credit card; **to open a line of credit** *or* **a credit line** = to make credit available to someone **(c)** block of shares (traded on a Stock Exchange) **(d)** **line chart** *or* **line graph** = chart or graph using lines to indicate values

> the best thing would be to have a few more plants close down and bring supply more in line with current demand
>
> *Fortune*

link [lɪŋk] *verb* to join or to attach to something else; ***to link pensions to inflation***; ***his salary is linked to the cost of living***; ***to link bonus payments to productivity***; *see also* INDEX-LINKED

liquid [ˈlɪkwɪd] *adjective* easily converted to cash; containing a large amount of cash; **liquid assets** = cash, or bills which can easily be changed into cash; **to go liquid** = to convert as many assets as possible into cash; **liquid market** = market in a security where there are enough shares available to allow sales to take place without distorting the price (the opposite is a 'thin' market)

liquidate [ˈlɪkwɪdeɪt] verb **to liquidate a company** = to close a company and sell its assets; **to liquidate a debt** = to pay a debt in full; **to liquidate stock** = to sell stock to raise cash

liquidation [lɪkwɪˈdeɪʃən] *noun* **(a)** sale of assets for cash; closing of a company and selling of its assets; **the company went into liquidation** = the company was closed and its assets sold; **compulsory liquidation** = liquidation which is ordered by a court; **voluntary liquidation** = situation where a company itself decides it must close; **on a liquidation basis** = pricing of unit trusts at a very low bid price to encourage buyers (NOTE: also called **on a bid basis**) **(b)** **liquidation of a debt** = payment of a debt

liquidator [ˈlɪkwɪdeɪtə] *noun* person named to supervise the closing of a company which is in liquidation (he sells off the assets and pays the creditors; anything left over will be shared among the shareholders)

liquidity [lɪˈkwɪdəti] *noun* having cash, or assets which can be changed into cash; **liquidity crisis** = not having enough liquid assets; **liquidity ratio** = (i) liquid assets shown as a percentage of liabilities; (ii) proportion of bank deposits which a bank keeps in cash

lira [ˈlɪərə] *noun* currency used with the euro in Italy, and also in Turkey; ***the book cost 2,700 lira*** *or* ***L2,700*** (NOTE: plural is **lire; lira** is usually written **L** before figures: **L2,700**)

LISA [ˈliːsə] = LIFETIME INDIVIDUAL SAVINGS ACCOUNT; *compare* ISA

lis pendens [ˈliːs ˈpendenz] *Latin phrase meaning* pending suit

list [lɪst] **1** *noun* **(a)** several items written one after the other; ***list of products*** *or* ***product list***; ***to add an item to a list***; ***to cross an item off a list***; **address list** *or* **mailing list** = list of names and addresses of people and companies; **black list** = list of goods, companies or countries which are banned for trade **(b)** catalogue; **list price** = price as given in a catalogue; **price list** = sheet giving prices of goods for sale **2** *verb* **listed company** = company whose shares can be bought or sold on the Stock Exchange; **listed securities** = shares which can be bought or sold on the

Stock Exchange, shares which appear on the official Stock Exchange list

listing ['lɪstɪŋ] *noun* **(a) Stock Exchange listing** = being on the official list of shares which can be bought or sold on the Stock Exchange; ***the company is planning to obtain a Stock Exchange listing***; **Listing Agreement** = document which a company signs when being listed on the Stock Exchange, in which the company promises to abide by stock exchange regulations; **listing details** *or* **listing particulars** = (i) details of a company which are published when the company applies for a stock exchange listing (the US equivalent is the 'registration statement'); (ii) details of the institutions which are backing an issue; *US* **listing requirements** = conditions which must be met by a corporation before its stock can be listed on the New York Stock Exchange **(b) computer listing** = printout of a list of items taken from the data stored in a computer

> last month the group announced the £103.3m convertible bond issue to repay some of its debt, but it has been slow to publish listing particulars for the bond issue, and the delay has caused investors to be nervous
>
> *Financial Times*

> we could get a NASDAQ quote as a service to institutions in the US, but when it comes to dealing they usually just pick up the phone and deal through London. There was a trend for British companies to get the Big Board listing, but I don't go for that
>
> *Money Observer*

litas ['li:tæs] *noun* currency used in Lithuania

litigation [lɪtɪ'geɪʃən] *noun* the bringing of a lawsuit against someone

Little Board = AMERICAN STOCK EXCHANGE

lively ['laɪvli] adjective **lively market** = active stock market, with many shares being bought or sold

living ['lɪvɪŋ] *noun see* COST OF LIVING

Lloyd's (of London) ['lɔɪdz əv 'lʌndʌn] *noun* London international insurance market; **Lloyd's broker** = agent who represents a client who wants insurance and who arranges this insurance for him through a Lloyd's underwriting syndicate; **Lloyd's Register** = classified list showing details of all the ships in the world, with a rating of their seaworthiness; **ship which is A1 at Lloyd's** = ship in very good condition

> COMMENT: Lloyd's is an old-established insurance market; the underwriters who form Lloyd's are divided into syndicates, each made up of active underwriters who arrange the business and non-working underwriters (called 'names') who stand surety for any insurance claims which may arise. See also NAMES

LME = LONDON METAL EXCHANGE

load [ləud] **1** *verb* to put charges into a certain period or into certain payments; **back-end loaded** = (insurance or investment scheme) where commission is only charged when the investor withdraws his money from the scheme; **front-end loaded** = (insurance or investment scheme) where most of the management charges are incurred in the first year of the investment or insurance, and are not spread out over the whole period **2** *noun* part of the initial payment for something that covers the management charge or commission; **back-end load** = management charge or commission which is levied when the investor sells out of the fund; **load fund** = fund sold through a broker, with a high initial management charge or commission; **no-load fund** = fund sold directly by the fund company, with low management charges and no commission to a broker

> we started by eliminating load funds - with a muni fund, a load can eat up most of your first year's return
>
> *Smart Money*

> you can invest in two no-load funds with a solid performance record
>
> *Smart Money*

loan [ləun] **1** *noun* money which has been lent; **loan capital** = part of a company's capital which is a loan from an outside source which has to be repaid at a later date; **loan committee** = committee which examines applications for special loans, such as higher loans than normally allowed by a bank; **loan stock** = stock issued by a company at a fixed rate of interest, as a means of raising a loan; **convertible loan stock** = loan which can be exchanged for shares at a later date; **bank loan** = money lent by a bank; **bridging loan** = short-term loan to help someone buy a new house when he has not yet sold his old one; **government loan** = money lent by the government; **home loan** = loan by a bank or building society to help someone buy a house; **short-term loan** *or* **long-term loan** = loans which have to be repaid within a few weeks or some years; **soft loan** = loan (from a company to an employee or from one government to another) at a very low rate of interest or with no interest payable at all; **stock-purchasing loans** = loans from a company to members of staff to allow them to buy shares in the company; ***lots of big companies offer stock-purchasing loans***; **unsecured loan** = loan made with no security; *US* **loan participation** = grouping together by several banks to share a very large loan to one single customer; *see also* SHARK **2** *verb* to lend

> over the last few weeks, companies raising new loans from international banks have been forced to pay more, and an unusually high number of attempts to syndicate loans among banks has failed
>
> *Financial Times*

local ['ləʊkəl] **1** *adjective* referring to a particular area, especially one near where a factory or an office is based; **local authority** = elected section of government which runs a small area of the country; **local authority bond** = loan raised by a local authority in the form of a fixed- interest bond, repayable at a certain date (they are similar to Treasury bonds; the US equivalent is the municipal bond); **local authority deposits** = money deposited with a local authority to earn interest for the depositor; **local government** = elected administrative bodies which run areas of the country **2** *noun* **(a)** independent dealer in futures or options; independent trader on the LIFFE **(b)** *US* branch of a trade union

> each cheque can be made out for the local equivalent of £100 rounded up to a convenient figure
>
> *Sunday Times*

> the business agent for Local 414 of the Store Union said his committee will recommend that the membership ratify the agreement
>
> *Toronto Star*

> EU regulations insist that customers can buy cars anywhere in the EU at the local pre-tax price
>
> *Financial Times*

> local governments justify low assessment levels by arguing that land tax revenues should be proportionate to the costs of locally administered services and should not be linked to artificially inflated land prices
>
> *Far Eastern Economic Review*

lockbox ['lɒkbɒks] *noun US* **(a)** box at a post office which can be rented and can be opened only the person or company renting it **(b)** system where cheques sent to a Post Office box are picked up and deposited in a bank account

lock in(to) ['lɒk 'ɪntʊ] *verb* to be fixed to a certain interest rate or exchange rate; ***by buying francs forward the company is in effect locking itself into a pound-franc exchange rate of 10.06***; **to lock in profits** = to take profits, to sell investments at a profit to ensure that the profit is realized; ***the shares had become overpriced - it was time to lock in the profits***

> the next year or so might well see a significant fall in interest rates. This would be fine for borrowers, but no so good for those relying on income from savings. Fortunately, there are plenty of ways in which investors can lock into the present high level of interest rates for periods of up to five years or more
>
> *Money Observer*

locking up ['lɒkɪŋ 'ʌp] *noun* **the locking up of money in stock** = investing money in stock so that it cannot be used for other, possibly more profitable, investments

lock up ['lɒk 'ʌp] *verb* **to lock up capital** = to have capital invested in such a way that it cannot be used for other investments

lodge [lɒdʒ] *verb* **to lodge money with someone** = to deposit money with someone; **to lodge securities as collateral** = to put securities into a bank to be used as collateral for a loan

lodgement ['lɒdʒmənt] *noun* depositing money, cheques, etc., in an account

Lombard Rate ['lɒmbɑd 'reɪt] rate at which the German Bundesbank lends to commercial banks

> in Frankfurt, call money was steady at 8.15 per cent as dealers regarded any change in

official rates as unlikely at today's Bundesbank council meeting. The Lombard rate was increased to 8.50 from 8.00 per cent at the beginning of this month

Financial Times

London Bullion Market ['lʌndən 'bʊljən 'mɑːkɪt] international market dealing in gold and silver bullion and gold coins

London Commodity Exchange (LCE) [lʌndən kə'mɒdɪti ɪks'tʃeɪndʒ] London exchange dealing in commodities such as cotton, coffee, cocoa, etc., but not in metals

London Interbank Bid Rate (LIBID) ['lʌndən 'ɪntəbæŋk 'bɪd 'reɪt] rate at which banks are prepared to borrow from each other

London Interbank Offered Rate (LIBOR) ['lʌndən 'ɪntəbæŋk 'ɒfəd 'reɪt] rate at which banks offer to lend eurodollars to other banks

London International Financial Futures and Options Exchange (LIFFE) ['lʌndən ɪntə'næʃnəl faɪ'nænʃəl 'fjuːtʃəz ənd 'ɒpʃnz ɪks'tʃeɪndʒ] market where futures contracts are traded in financial instruments such as gilts, equity options, euroyen, US Treasury bonds, etc. and also commodities such as cocoa, coffee, wheat, potatoes, barley and sugar (it is an investment exchange, recognized by the FSA)

London Metal Exchange (LME) ['lʌndən 'metl ɪk'stʃeɪndʒ] commodity exchange dealing in aluminium, copper, lead, nickel, tin and zinc (it is an investment exchange, recognized by the FSA)

London Securities & Derivatives Exchange (OMLX) ['lʌndən sɪ'kjʊərɪtiz ɪk'stʃeɪndʒ] the London exchange where securities and derivatives are traded (it is an investment exchange, recognized by the FSA)

London Stock Exchange (LSE) ['lʌndən 'stɒk ɪk'stʃeɪndʒ] main British stock exchange where securities are bought and sold (it is an investment exchange, recognized by the FSA)

London Traded Options Market (LTOM) ['lʌndən 'treɪdɪd 'ɒpʃnz 'mɑːkɪt] market where options are traded

long [lɒŋ] **1** *adjective* **(a)** for a large period of time; **long bond** *US* **long coupon bond** = bond which will mature in more than ten years' time; **long credit** = credit terms which allow the borrower a long time to pay; **long lease** = lease of more than fifty years; **in the long term** = over a long period of time; **to take the long view** = to plan for a long period before current investment becomes profitable **(b) to be long of a stock** *or* **to go long** = to buy a share as a long-term investment on the assumption that the price will rise **2** noun **longs** = government stocks which will mature in over fifteen years' time

long-dated [lɒŋ'deɪtɪd] adjective **long-dated bills** = bills which are payable in more than three months' time; **long-dated stocks** = LONGS

long-range ['lɒŋ'reɪndʒ] *adjective* for a long period of time in the future; **long-range economic forecast** = forecast which covers a period of several years

long-tail business ['lɒŋ'teɪl 'bɪznəs] *noun* insurance business where a claim only arises some years after the insurance contract was taken out

long-term ['lɒŋtɜːm] adjective **on a long-term basis** = for a long period of time; **long-term borrowings** = borrowings which do not have to be repaid for some years; **long-term debts** = debts which will be repaid many years later; **long-term forecast** = forecast for a period of over three years; **long-term loan** = loan to be repaid many years later; **long-term objectives** = aims which will take years to achieve; **long-term security** = security which will mature in more than fifteen years' time

land held under long-term leases is not amortized

Hongkong Standard

the company began to experience a demand for longer-term mortgages when the flow of money used to finance these loans diminished

Globe and Mail (Toronto)

loophole ['luːphəʊl] noun **to find a loophole in the law** = to find a means of legally avoiding the law; **to find a tax loophole** = to find a means of legally not paying tax

because capital gains are not taxed but money taken out in profits is taxed, owners of businesses will be using accountants and tax experts to find loopholes in the law

Toronto Star

loose change ['luːs 'tʃeɪnʒ] *noun* money in coins

lose [lu:z] *verb* **(a)** not to have something any more; **to lose an order** = not to get an order which you were hoping to get; ***during the strike, the company lost six orders to American competitors***; **to lose control of a company** = to find that you have less than 50% of the shares and so are no longer able to direct the company **(b)** to have less money; ***he lost £25,000 in his father's computer company***; **the pound has lost value** = the pound is worth less **(c)** to drop to a lower price; ***the dollar lost two cents against the yen***; ***gold shares lost 5% on the market yesterday*** (NOTE: **losing - lost**)

loss [lɒs] *noun* **(a) loss of customers** = not keeping customers because of bad service, high prices, etc.; **loss of an order** = not getting an order which was expected; **the company suffered a loss of market penetration** = the company found it had a smaller share of the market; **compensation for loss of earnings** = payment to someone who has stopped earning money or who is not able to earn money; **compensation for loss of office** = payment to a director who is asked to leave a company before his contract ends **(b)** having less money than before, not making a profit; **the company suffered a loss** = the company did not make a profit; **to report a loss** = not to show a profit in the accounts at the end of the year; ***the company reported a loss of £1m on the first year's trading***; **capital loss** = loss made by selling assets; **the car was written off as a dead loss** *or* **a total loss** = the car was so badly damaged that the insurers said it had no value; **paper loss** = loss made when an asset has fallen in value but has not been sold; **trading loss** = situation where the company's receipts are less than its expenditure; **loss relief** = amount of tax not to be paid on one year's profit to offset a loss in the previous year; **at a loss** = making a loss, not making any profit; ***the company is trading at a loss***; ***he sold the shop at a loss***; **to cut your losses** = to stop doing something which was losing money **(c)** being worth less or having a lower value; ***shares showed losses of up to 5% on the Stock Exchange***

> against losses of FFr 7.7m in 1983, the company made a net profit of FFr 300,000 last year
>
> *Financial Times*

loss-leader ['lɒs'li:də] *noun* article which is sold at a loss to attract customers; ***we use these cheap films as a loss-leader***

lot [lɒt] *noun* **(a)** group of items sold together at an auction; ***to bid for lot 23***; ***at the end of the auction half the lots were unsold*** **(b)** group of shares which are sold; standard quantity sold on a commodity exchange; ***to sell a lot of shares***; ***to sell shares in small lots*** **(c)** *US* piece of land, especially one to be used for redevelopment

lottery ['lɒtəri] *noun* game where numbered tickets are sold and prizes given for some of the numbers; **the National Lottery** = British lottery, which takes place twice a week, where you have to try to forecast a series of six numbers

low [ləʊ] **1** *adjective* small, not high; ***low overhead costs keep the unit cost low***; ***we try to keep our wages bill low***; ***the company offered him a mortgage at a low rate of interest***; ***the pound is at a very low rate of exchange against the dollar***; ***our aim is to buy at the lowest price possible***; ***shares are at their lowest for two years***; **low coupon stocks** = government bonds which pay a low rate of interest; **low gearing** = not having much borrowing in proportion to your capital; **low yield** = yield on the share price which is low for the sector, suggesting that investors anticipate that the company will grow fast, and have pushed up the share price in expectation of growth; **the tender will go to the lowest bidder** = the contract will be awarded to the person who offers the best terms **2** *noun* point where prices or sales are very small; ***sales have reached a new low***; **highs and lows on the Stock Exchange** = list of shares which have reached a new high or low price in the previous day's trading; **shares have hit an all-time low** = shares have reached their lowest price ever

> after opening at 79.1 the index touched a peak of 79.2 and then drifted to a low of 78.8
>
> *Financial Times*

> the pound which had been as low as $1.02 earlier this year, rose to $1.30
>
> *Fortune*

> the trade-weighted dollar chart shows there has been a massive devaluation of the dollar since the mid-'80s and the currency is at its all-time low
>
> *Financial Weekly*

lower ['ləʊə] **1** *adjective* smaller, less high; ***a lower rate of interest***; ***sales were lower in December than in November*** **2** *verb* to make smaller or less expensive; ***to lower prices to secure a larger market share***; ***to lower the interest rate***

> Canadian and European negotiators agreed to a deal under which Canada could keep its quotas but lower its import duties
>
> *Globe and Mail (Toronto)*

lowering ['ləʊərɪŋ] *noun* making smaller or less expensive; ***lowering of prices***; ***we hope to achieve low prices with no lowering of quality***

low-profile ['ləʊ'prəʊfaɪl] adjective **low-profile company** = company which does not publicize itself much

> researchers discovered that when quarterly earnings exceed expectations, particularly with low-profile companies, the market generally underreacts
>
> *Smart Money*

loyalty ['lɔɪəlti] *noun* being faithful; **brand loyalty** *or* **loyalty to the brand** = inclination of a customer to keep buying the same brand of product

loyalty bonus ['lɔɪəltɪ 'bəʊnəs] *noun* special privileges given to shareholders who keep their shares for a certain period of time (used especially to attract investors to privatization issues)

LSE = LONDON STOCK EXCHANGE

Ltd ['lɪmɪtɪd] = LIMITED

LTOM = LONDON TRADED OPTIONS MARKET

lull [lʌl] *noun* quiet period; ***after last week's hectic trading this week's lull was welcome***

lump sum ['lʌmp 'sʌm] *noun* money paid in one single amount, not in several small sums; ***when he retired he was given a lump-sum bonus***; ***she sold her house and invested the money as a lump sum***

luxury items *or* **luxury goods** ['lʌkʃəri 'aɪtəmz] *noun* items which are not necessities (jewels, fur coats, etc.); **luxury tax** = extra tax levied on luxury goods

Mm

m = METRE, MILE, MILLION

M0 ['em 'nɔːt] narrowest British measure of money supply, including coins and notes in circulation plus the deposits of commercial banks with the Bank of England

M1 ['em 'wʌn] measure of money supply, including all coins and notes plus personal money in current accounts

M2 ['em 'tuː] measure of money supply, including coins and notes and personal money in current and deposit accounts

M3 ['em 'θriː] broadest measure of money supply, including coins and notes, personal money in current and deposit accounts, government deposits and deposits in currencies other than sterling; **£M3** = British measure of sterling money supply, including coins and notes, personal money in current and deposit accounts and government deposits; *see also* L, MONEY SUPPLY

> Bank of England calculations of notes in circulation suggest that the main component of the narrow measure of money supply, M0, is likely to have risen by 0.4 per cent after seasonal adjustments
>
> *Times*

M&A = MERGERS AND ACQUISITIONS

M&E fee = MORTALITY AND EXPENSE RISK CHARGE

machine [məˈʃiːn] *noun* **(a)** device which works with power from a motor; **adding machine** = machine which adds numbers; **copying machine** *or* **duplicating machine** = machine which makes copies of documents **(b) machine code** *or* **machine language** = instructions and information shown as a series of figures (0 and 1) which can be read by a computer; **machine-readable codes** = sets of signs or letters (such as bar codes, post codes) which a computer can read

macro- ['mækrəʊ] *prefix* very large, covering a wide area; **macroeconomics** = study of the economics of a whole area, whole industry, whole group of the population or whole country, in order to help in economic planning; *compare* MICROECONOMICS; **macro funds** = large hedge funds which bet on whole economies

magazine [mægəˈziːn] *noun* paper, usually with pictures, which comes out regularly, every month or every week; **business magazine** = magazine dealing with business affairs; **computer magazine** = magazine with articles on computers and programs; **house magazine** = magazine produced for the workers in a company to give them news of the company's affairs; **investment magazine** = magazine dealing with shares, unit trusts and other possible investments; **magazine insert** = advertising sheet put into a magazine when it is mailed or sold

magnetic [mægˈnetɪk] adjective **magnetic character reading (MCR)** *or* **magnetic ink character recognition (MICR)** = system that recognises characters by sensing magnetic ink (used on cheques); **magnetic ink** = special ink with magnetic particles in it, used for printing cheques; **magnetic strip** *US* **magnetic stripe** = black strip on credit cards and cashpoint cards, on which personal information about the account is recorded; **magnetic tape** *or* **mag tape** = plastic tape for recording information on a large computer

mail [meɪl] **1** *noun* **(a)** system of sending letters and parcels from one place to another; ***to put a letter in the mail***; ***the cheque was lost in the mail***; ***the invoice was put in the mail yesterday***; ***mail to some of the islands in the Pacific can take six weeks***; **by mail** = using the postal services, not sending something by hand or by messenger; **we sent the draft by first-class mail** = by the most expensive mail service, designed to be faster; **electronic mail (e-mail)** = system of sending messages from one computer to another, using the telephone lines **(b)** letters sent or received; ***has the mail arrived yet? to open the mail***; ***your cheque arrived in yesterday's mail***; ***my secretary opens my mail as soon as it arrives***; ***the receipt was in this morning's mail***; **incoming mail** = mail which arrives; **outgoing mail** = mail which is sent out; *see also* DIRECT

MAIL **2** *verb* to send something by post; ***to mail a letter; we mailed our order last Wednesday***

mail box ['meɪl 'bɒks] *noun* (i) place where mail is left; (ii) number where email messages are received

mailing ['meɪlɪŋ] *noun* sending something in the post; ***the mailing of publicity material***; **direct mailing** = sending of publicity material by post to possible buyers; **mailing list** = list of names and addresses of people who might be interested in a product; list of names and addresses of members of a society; ***his name is on our mailing list; to build up a mailing list***; **to buy a mailing list** = to pay a society, etc., money to buy the list of members so that you can use it to mail publicity material; **mailing piece** = leaflet suitable for sending by direct mail; **mailing shot** = leaflets sent by mail to possible customers

mail-order ['meɪl'ɔ:də] *noun* system of buying and selling from a catalogue, placing orders and sending goods by mail; **mail-order business** *or* **mail-order firm** *or* **mail-order house** = company which sells a product by mail; **mail-order catalogue** = catalogue from which a customer can order items to be sent by mail

main [meɪn] *adjective* most important; ***main office; main building; one of our main customers***; **the main market** = the London Stock Exchange (as opposed to the AIM market); *US* **Main Street** = most important street in a town, where the shops and banks are

mainstream corporation tax (MCT) ['meɪnstri:m kɒ:pə'reɪʃn 'tæks] *noun* total tax paid by a company on its profits (less any advance corporation tax, which a company has already paid when distributing profits to its shareholders in the form of dividends)

maintain [meɪn'teɪn] *verb* **(a)** to keep something going or working; ***to maintain good relations with your customers; to maintain contact with an overseas market*** **(b)** to keep something working at the same level; ***the company has maintained the same volume of business in spite of the recession; to maintain an interest rate at 5%***; **to maintain a dividend** = to pay the same dividend as the previous year

maintenance ['meɪntənəns] *noun* **(a)** keeping things going or working; ***maintenance of contacts; maintenance of supplies*** **(b)** keeping a machine in good working order; ***we offer a full maintenance service***; **maintenance contract** = contract by which a company keeps a piece of equipment in good working order **(c) maintenance fee** = fee charged for keeping an account or a contract going; ***many mutual fund companies and brokerage houses charge annual maintenance fees***

> the federal administration launched a full-scale investigation into the airline's maintenance procedures
>
> *Fortune*

majeure [mæ'ʒə:] *see* FORCE MAJEURE

major ['meɪdʒə] *adjective* important; **major shareholder** = shareholder with a large number of shares

majority [mə'dʒɒrəti] *noun* larger group than all others; **majority of the shareholders** = more than 50% of the shareholders; **the board accepted the proposal by a majority of three to two** = three members of the board voted to accept and two voted against; **majority vote** *or* **majority decision** = decision made after a vote according to the wishes of the largest group; **majority shareholding** *or* **majority interest** = group of more than half of all the shares in a company; **a majority shareholder** = person who owns more than half the shares in a company

> if the share price sinks much further the company is going to look tempting to any major takeover merchant
>
> *Australian Financial Review*

> monetary officials have reasoned that coordinated greenback sales would be able to drive the dollar down against other major currencies
>
> *Duns Business Month*

> a client base which includes many major commercial organizations and nationalized industries
>
> *Times*

make [meɪk] *verb* **(a)** to sign or to agree; ***to make a deal*** *or* ***to make an agreement***; **to make a bid for something** = to offer to buy something; *(of a marketmaker)* **to make a book** = to have a list of shares which he is prepared to buy or sell on behalf of clients; **to make a market in securities** = to offer to buy or sell securities on a selected list at any time; **to make a payment** = to pay; **to make a deposit** = to pay money as a deposit **(b)** to earn; to increase in value; ***he makes £50,000 a year*** *or* ***£25 an hour***; ***the shares made $2.92 in today's trading*** **(c) to make a profit** *or* **to make a loss** = to have more money or less money after a deal; **to make a killing** = to make a very large profit (NOTE: **making - made**)

make out ['meɪk 'aʊt] *verb* to write; ***to make out an invoice***; ***the bill is made out to Smith & Co.***; **to make out a cheque to someone** = to write someone's name on a cheque

make over ['meɪk 'əʊvə] *verb* to transfer property legally; ***to make over the house to your children***

maker ['meɪkə] *noun* **(a)** person who signs a promissory note in which he promises to pay money **(b) decision maker** = person who decides or who takes decisions; *see also* MARKETMAKER

make up ['meɪk 'ʌp] *verb* **(a)** to compensate for something; **to make up a loss** *or* **to make up the difference** = to pay extra so that the loss or difference is covered **(b) to make up accounts** = to complete the accounts

make up for ['meɪk 'ʌp 'fɔː] *verb* to compensate for something; ***to make up for a short payment*** *or* ***for a late payment***

maladministration ['mælədmɪnɪs'treɪʃən] *noun* incompetent administration

malfeasance [mæl'fiːzəns] *noun* unlawful act

manage ['mænɪdʒ] *verb* **(a)** to direct or to be in charge of; ***to manage a department***; ***to manage a branch office*** **(b)** *(of a central bank)* **to manage a currency** = to intervene in the markets to influence a currency's exchange rates; **managed float** = floating of a currency where the exchange rate is controlled by the central bank (NOTE: also called a **dirty float;** compare with **clean float**) **(c) to manage property** = to look after rented property for the owner; **managed fund** *or* **managed unit trust** = unit trust fund which is invested in specialist funds within the group and can be switched from one specialized investment area to another

> the research director will manage and direct a team of graduate business analysts reporting on consumer behaviour throughout the UK
>
> *Times*

manageable ['mænɪdʒəbl] *adjective* which can be dealt with easily; ***the interest payments, though high, are still manageable***; ***the company's financial problems are too large to be manageable***

management ['mænɪdʒmənt] *noun* **(a)** directing or running a business; ***to study management***; ***good management*** *or* ***efficient management***; ***bad management*** *or* ***inefficient management***; ***a management graduate*** *or* ***a graduate in management***; **line management** = organization of a business where each manager is responsible for doing what his superior tells him to do; **product management** = directing the making and selling of a product as an independent item; **management accountant** = accountant who prepares specialized information for managers so that they can make decisions; **management accounts** = financial information (on sales, costs, credit, profitability) prepared for a manager so that he can make decisions; **management consultant** = person who gives advice on how to manage a business; **management course** = training course for managers; **management by objectives** = way of managing a business by planning work for the managers and testing to see if it is completed correctly and on time; **management team** = a group of managers working together; **management techniques** = ways of managing a business; **management training** = training managers by making them study problems and work out ways of solving them; **management trainee** = young person being trained to be a manager **(b)** running a fund or investment portfolio for a client; **fund management** *or* **money management** = dealing with the investment of large sums of money on behalf of groups of clients; **portfolio management** = buying and selling shares by a person or by a specialist on behalf of a client **(c)** group of managers or directors; ***the management has decided to give an overall pay increase***; **top management** = the main directors of a company; **middle management** = the department managers of a company who carry out the policy set by the directors and organize the work of a group of workers; **management buyin** = purchase of a company by a group of outside directors; **management buyout (MBO)** = takeover of a company by a group of employees (usually senior managers and directors)

> this is the only retail fund offered by the top-performing institutional money-management firm
>
> *Smart Money*

> the management says that the rate of loss-making has come

down and it expects further improvement in the next few years

Financial Times

---

manager [ˈmænɪdʒə] *noun* **(a)** head of a department in a company; ***a department manager***; ***personnel manager***; **accounts manager** = head of the accounts department; **area manager** = manager who is responsible for the company's work (usually sales) in an area; **fund manager** = person who manages a the investments made by a fund in such a way as to fulfill the fund's stated objectives; **general manager** = manager in charge of the administration in a large company; *see also* MULTI-MANAGER FUND **(b)** person in charge of a branch; ***Mr Smith is the manager of our local Lloyds Bank***; ***the manager of our Zurich office is in London for a series of meetings***; **bank manager** = person in charge of a branch of a bank; **branch manager** = person in charge of a branch of a company

fund managers have never conceived of their role as 'managing' money, in the sense of choosing where in the world they should invest. They simply state in their fund prospectuses where they will invest

Money Observer

---

managerial [mæɪˈdʒiːəriəl] *adjective* referring to managers

the No. 1 managerial productivity problem in America is managers who are out of touch with their people and out of touch with their customers

Fortune

---

managership [ˈmænɪdʒəʃɪp] *noun* job of being a manager; ***after six years, he was offered the managership of a branch in Scotland***

managing [ˈmænɪdʒɪŋ] adjective **managing agent** = person who runs the day-to-day activities of a Lloyd's syndicate; **managing director** = director who is in charge of a whole company; **chairman and managing director** = managing director who is also chairman of the board of directors; *US* **managing underwriter** = underwriting firm which organizes the underwriting of a share issue (NOTE: the British equivalent is a **lead underwriter**)

manat [ˈmænæt] *noun* currency used in Turkmenistan

mandate [ˈmændeɪt] *noun* order which allows something to take place; **bank mandate** = written order to a bank, asking them to open an account and allowing someone to sign cheques on behalf of the account holder, giving specimen signatures, etc. (NOTE: the American equivalent is a **corporate resolution**)

mandatory [ˈmændətri] adjective **mandatory bid** = offer to purchase the shares of a company which has to be made when a shareholder acquires 30% of that company's shares; **mandatory meeting** = meeting which all members have to attend

manipulate [məˈnɪpjʊleɪt] *verb* **to manipulate accounts** = to make false accounts so that the company seems profitable; **to manipulate the market** = to work to influence share prices in your favour

manipulation [mənɪpjʊˈleɪʃən] noun **stock market manipulation** = trying to influence the price of shares by buying or selling in order to give the impression that the shares are widely traded

manipulator [məˈnɪpjʊleɪtə] noun **stock market manipulator** = person who tries to influence the price of shares in his own favour

marché [ˈmɑːʃeɪ] *French* market; *see also* MATIF

margin [ˈmɑːdʒɪn] *noun* **(a)** difference between the money received when selling a product and the money paid for it; **gross margin** = percentage difference between the unit manufacturing cost and the received price; **net margin** = percentage difference between received price and all costs, including overheads; **we are cutting our margins very fine** = we are reducing our margins to the smallest possible to be competitive; **our margins have been squeezed** = profits have been reduced because our margins have to be smaller to stay competitive **(b)** deposit paid when purchasing a futures contract; **margin call** = request for a purchaser of a futures contract or an option to pay more margin, since the fall in the price of the securities or commodity has removed the value of the original margin deposited **(c)** difference between interest paid to depositors and interest charged to borrowers (by a bank, building society, etc.) **(d)** extra space or time allowed; **margin of error** = number of mistakes which are accepted in a document or in a calculation; **safety margin** = time or space allowed for something to be safe; **margin of safety** = sales which are above the breakeven point

> profit margins in the industries most exposed to foreign competition - machinery, transportation equipment and electrical goods - are significantly worse than usual
>
> *Australian Financial Review*

marginal ['mɑːdʒɪnl] *adjective* **(a) marginal cost** = cost of making a single extra unit above the number already planned; **marginal pricing** = making the selling price the same as the marginal cost; **marginal rate of tax** *or* **marginal tax rate** = percentage of tax which a taxpayer pays at the top rate (which he therefore pays on every further pound or dollar he earns); **marginal revenue** = income from selling a single extra unit above the number already sold **(b)** not very profitable, hardly worth the money paid; ***marginal return on investment***; **marginal land** = land which is almost not worth farming; **marginal purchase** = thing which a buyer feels is only just worth buying

> pensioner groups claim that pensioners have the highest marginal rates of tax. Income earned by pensioners above $30 a week is taxed at 62.5 per cent, more than the highest marginal rate
>
> *Australian Financial Review*

marital ['mærɪtəl] *adjective* referring to a marriage; *US* **marital deductions** = that part of an estate which is not subject to estate tax because it goes to the dead person's spouse; **marital status** = the official state of a person, whether married, divorced or single

mark [mɑːk] *noun* **(a)** sign put on an item to show something; **assay mark** = hallmark, mark put on gold or silver items to show that the metal is of the correct quality; *GB* **kite mark** = mark on goods to show that they meet official standards **(b)** money used with the euro in Germany; ***the price is twenty-five marks***; ***the mark rose against the dollar*** (NOTE: usually written **DM** after a figure: **25DM.** Also called **Deutschmark, D-Mark**)

mark down ['mɑːk 'daʊn] *verb* to make lower; **to mark down a price** = to lower the price of something; ***this range has been marked down to $24.99***; ***we have marked all prices down by 30% for the sale***

mark-down ['mɑːkdaʊn] *noun* **(a)** reduction of the price of something to less than its usual price **(b)** percentage amount by which a price has been lowered; ***we have used a 30% mark-down to fix the sale price***

market ['mɑːkɪt] *noun* **(a)** place where a product might be sold; group of people who might buy a product; **home** *or* **domestic market** = market in the country where the selling company is based; ***sales in the home market rose by 22%*** **(b)** place where money or commodities are traded; **capital market** = place where companies can look for investment capital; **commodity market** = place where commodities are bought or sold; **the foreign exchange markets** = places where currencies are bought or sold; **forward markets** = places where foreign currency or commodities can be bought or sold for delivery at a later date; **money market** *or* **finance market** *or* **financial market** = place where large sums of money are lent or borrowed; **global financial markets** = world-wide finance markets; ***the global financial markets precipitated the Mexican crisis of 1994-95*** **(c) the Common Market** = the European Economic Community **(d) (stock) market** = place where shares are bought and sold; ***the market in oil shares was very active*** *or* ***there was a brisk market in oil shares***; **to sell at the market** = instruction to stockbroker to sell shares at the best price possible; **to buy shares in the open market** = to buy shares on the Stock Exchange, not privately; **market capitalization** = (i) value of a company calculated by multiplying the price of its shares on the Stock Exchange by the number of shares issued; (ii) value of all the shares listed on a stock market; **market forecast** = forecast of prices on the stock market; **market neutral funds** = hedge funds not related to general market movements, but which try to find opportunities to arbitrage temporary slight changes in the relative values of particular financial assets (NOTE: also called **relative value funds**); **market operator** = person who trades on a stock market or financial market; **market order** = order to a broker to buy or sell at the current price; **market price** = price at which a product can be sold; price at which a share stands a stock market; **market professionals** = people who work in a stock market, as brokers, analysts, etc.; **market purchases** = purchases of shares in a company on the normal stock market (by a company planning a takeover bid); **market sentiment** = general feeling among investors or financial analysts on a stock market (either optimistic or pessimistic) which can be influenced by external factors, and which will affect the prices of the shares themselves; *(of a company)* **to come to the market** = to apply for a Stock Exchange listing, by offering some of the existing shares for sale, or by floating it as a new company; **to bring a company to the market** = to arrange the flotation of a company's shares on the market; *(of a marketmaker)* **to make a market in securities** = to offer to buy or sell securities on a selected list at any time **(e) market analysis** = detailed examination and report on a market; **market cycle** = period during which a market expands, then slows down and then expands again; **market economist** = person who specializes in the study of financial structures and the return on investments in the stock market; **market forces** = influences on the sales which bring about a change in prices; **market leader** = company with the largest market share; ***we are the market leader in home computers***; **market opportunities** = possibility of finding new sales in a market; **market penetration** *or* **market share** = percentage of a total market which the sales of a company cover; ***we hope our new product range will increase our market share***; **market rate** = normal price in the market; ***we pay the market rate for secretaries*** *or* ***we pay secretaries the market rate***; **market research** = examining the possible sales of a product before it is put on the market; **market trends** = gradual changes taking place in a market; **market value** = value of a share, or a product or a company if sold today; *see also* ADJUSTER **(f)** possible sales of a certain type of product, demand for a certain type of product; **a growth market** = market where sales are likely to rise rapidly; **the labour market** = number of workers available for work; **25,000 graduates have come on to the labour market** = they have become available for work because they have left college **(g) the black market** = buying and selling goods in a way which is not allowed by law; ***there is a flourishing black market in spare parts for cars***; **to pay black market prices** = to pay high prices to get items which are not easily available **(h) a buyer's market** = market where goods are sold cheaply because there is little demand; **a seller's market** = market where the seller can ask high prices because there is a large demand for the product **(i) closed market** = market where a supplier deals with only one agent or distributor and does not supply any others direct; **free market economy** = system where the government does not interfere in business activity in any way; **open market** = market where anyone can buy and sell **(j) up market** *or* **down market** = more expensive or less expensive; **to go up market** *or* **to go down market** = to make products which appeal to a wealthy section of the market or to a wider, less wealthy, section of the market; **a down market** = a market which is falling or at its lowest level; **an up market** = a market which is rising or at its highest level **(k) to be in the market for secondhand cars** = to look for secondhand cars to buy; **to come on to the market** = to start to be sold; **to put something on the market** = to start to offer something for sale; ***they put their house on the market***; ***I hear the company has been put on the market***; **the company has priced itself out of the market** = the company has raised its prices so high that its products do not sell

---

the market cycle in which the big multinational companies excelled is coming to an end

Smart Money

---

global financial markets have trained their fire on the capitals of East Asia. One by one, from Bangkok to Seoul, they have crushed previously stable currencies

Smart Money

---

a few years earlier British Prime Minister John Major had declared that the UK would never delink its pound from European currencies. After global financial markets pulverized the British pound, the prime minister reversed himself 180 degrees

Smart Money

---

after the prime rate cut yesterday, there was a further fall in short-term market rates

Financial Times

---

market analysts described the falls in the second half of last week as a technical correction to a market which had been pushed by demand to over the 900 index level

Australian Financial Review

---

most discounted fares are sold by bucket shops but in today's competitive market any agent can supply them

Business Traveller

market leaders may benefit from scale economies or other cost advantages; they may enjoy a reputation for quality simply by being at the top, or they may actually produce a superior product that gives them both a large market share and high profits

Accountancy

how your emerging growth fund performs in a down market is just as important as in an up market

Smart Money

yet at this time of year, above all, market operators should know that their task is not to reflect the past, but to anticipate the future

The Times

marketability [mɑːkɪtəˈbɪlɪti] *noun* being able to be sold easily; ***the marketability of privatization shares***

marketable [ˈmɑːkɪtəbl] *adjective* which can be sold easily; **marketable securities** = stocks, shares, CDs, etc., which can be bought or sold on a stock market

they reported an astonishing $20.8 billion in cash and marketable securities at the end of last year

Fortune

marketing [ˈmɑːkɪtɪŋ] *noun* techniques used in selling a product (such as packaging, advertising, etc.); **marketing agreement** = contract by which one company will market another company's products; **marketing department** = department in a company which specializes in using marketing techniques to sell a product; **marketing manager** = person in charge of a marketing department; **marketing policy** *or* **marketing plans** = ideas of how the company's products are going to be marketed; ***to plan the marketing of a new product***

reporting to the marketing director, the successful applicant will be responsible for the development of a training programme for the new sales force

Times

marketmaker [ˈmɑːkɪtmeɪkə] *noun* person who buys or sells shares on the stock market and offers to do so in a certain list of securities (a marketmaker operates a book, listing the securities he is willing to buy or sell, and makes his money by charging a commission on each transaction)

marka *or* **markka** [ˈmɑːkə] *noun* currency used with the euro in Finland (NOTE: also called the **Finnmark**, written MK)

mark up [ˈmɑːk ˈʌp] *verb* to increase; **to mark prices up** = to increase prices; ***these prices have been marked up by 10%***

mark-up [ˈmɑːkʌp] *noun* **(a)** increase in price; ***we put into effect a 10% mark-up of all prices in June*** **(b)** amount added to the cost price to give the selling price; **we work to a 3.5 times mark-up** *or* **to a 350% mark-up** = we take the unit cost and multiply by 3.5 to give the selling price

MasterCard [ˈmæɑːstəˈkɑːd] *noun* international credit organization, backed by a group of banks (NOTE: another similar organization is **Visa International**)

matched bargains [ˈmætʃt ˈbɑːgɪnz] *noun* sales and purchases of shares which are conducted at the same time, where the buyers and sellers come together to agree on the price (as opposed to the 'quotation' system, where the marketmakers make the selling prices for shares); **to trade on a matched bargain basis** = to arrange to sell shares for a client and buy them for another client, without having to take a position in the shares

MATIF = MARCHE A TERME DES INSTRUMENTS FINANCIERS the French financial futures market

mature [məˈtjʊə] **1** adjective **mature economy** = fully developed economy **2** verb **bills which mature in three weeks' time** = bills which will be due for payment in three weeks

maturity [məˈtjʊərəti] noun **date of maturity** *or* **maturity date** = date when a government stock, an assurance policy or a debenture will become due for payment; **amount payable on maturity** = amount received by the insured person when the policy becomes mature; **maturity yield** *or* *US* **yield to maturity** = calculation of the yield on a fixed-interest investment, assuming it is bought at a certain price and held to maturity

May Day [ˈmeɪ ˈdeɪ] *noun* the change in practices on American Stock Exchanges which took place on 1st May 1975, with the removal of the system of fixed commissions; this allowed cheaper stock trading by brokers who did not offer any investment advice, and ultimately led to computerized financial dealing in general (NOTE: the British equivalent was **Big Bang**)

maximization [mæksɪmaɪˈzeɪʃən] *noun* making as large as possible; ***profit maximization*** *or* ***maximization of profit***

maximize [ˈmæksɪmaɪz] *verb* to make as large as possible; ***to maximize profits***

maximum [ˈmæksɪməm] **1** *noun* largest possible number or price or quantity; **up to a maximum of £10** = no more than £10; **to increase exports to the maximum** = as much as possible; ***it is the maximum the insurance company will pay*** (NOTE: plural is **maxima**) **2** *adjective* largest possible; ***maximum income tax rate*** *or* ***maximum rate of tax***; ***maximum load***; ***maximum production levels***; ***maximum price***; **to increase production to the maximum level** = as much as possible

MBO = MANAGEMENT BUYOUT

mean [miːn] **1** *adjective* average; ***mean annual increase***; **mean price** = average price of a share in a day's trading **2** *noun* average, figure calculated by adding several figures together and dividing by the number of figures added; ***unit sales are over the mean for the first quarter*** *or* ***above the first quarter mean***

means [miːnz] *plural noun* **(a)** way of doing something; ***air freight is the fastest means of getting stock to South America***; ***do we have any means of copying all these documents quickly?*** **(b)** money or resources; ***the company has the means to launch the new product***; ***such a level of investment is beyond the means of a small private company***; **means test** = inquiry into how much money someone earns to see if he is eligible for state benefits; **he has private means** = he has income from dividends or interest or rent which is not part of his salary

measure [ˈmeʒə] **1** *noun* **(a)** way of calculating size or quantity; **as a measure of the company's performance** = as a way of judging if the company's results are good or bad **(b)** type of action; **to take measures to prevent something happening** = to act to stop something happening; **to take crisis** *or* **emergency measures** = to act rapidly to stop a crisis developing; **an economy measure** = an action to save money; **fiscal measures** = tax changes made by the government to improve the working of the economy; **as a precautionary measure** = to prevent something taking place **2** verb **to measure a company's performance** = to judge how well a company is doing

measurement [ˈmeʒəmənt] *noun* way of judging something; ***growth measurement***; ***performance measurement*** *or* ***measurement of performance***; **measurement of profitability** = way of calculating how profitable something is

mechanic's lien [mɪˈkænɪks ˈliːn] *noun US* lien on buildings or other property which can be enforced by workmen until they have been paid

median [ˈmiːdiən] *noun* point in the middle of a list of numbers or values

medium [ˈmiːdiəm] **1** *adjective* middle or average; ***the company is of medium size*** **2** noun **mediums** *or* **medium-dated stocks** = government stocks which mature in seven to fifteen years' time (NOTE: plural for (a) is **media**)

medium-sized company [ˈmiːdiəm ˈsaɪzd ˈkʌmpni] noun *(for UK tax purposes)* company which has a turnover of less than £5.75m and does not employ more than 250 staff (companies of this size can file modified accounts with the Registrar of Companies)

medium-term [ˈmiːdiəm ˈtɜːm] *adjective* referring to a point between short term and long term; **medium-term bond** = bond which matures within five to fifteen years; **medium-term forecast** = forecast for two or three years; **medium-term loan** = bank loan for three to five years

meet [miːt] *verb* **(a)** to be satisfactory for; **we will try to meet your price** = we will try to offer a price which is acceptable to you; **they failed to meet the deadline** = they were not able to complete in time **(b)** to pay for; ***to meet someone's expenses***; ***the company will meet your expenses***; ***he was unable to meet his mortgage repayments*** (NOTE: **meeting - met**)

---

if corporate forecasts are met, sales will exceed $50 million next year

Citizen (Ottawa)

---

meeting [ˈmiːtɪŋ] *noun* **(a)** coming together of a group of people; **board meeting** = meeting of the directors of a company; **general meeting** *or* **meeting of shareholders** *or* **shareholders' meeting** = meeting of all the shareholders of a company, meeting of all the members of a society; *see also* ANNUAL GENERAL MEETING, EXTRAORDINARY GENERAL MEETING **(b) to hold a meeting** = to organize a meeting of a group of people; ***the meeting will be held in the committee room***; **to open a meeting** = to start a meeting; **to conduct a meeting** = to be in the chair for a meeting; **to close a meeting** = to end a meeting; **to address a meeting** = to speak to a meeting; **to put a resolution to a meeting** = to ask a meeting to vote on a proposal

> in proportion to your holding you have a stake in every aspect of the company, including a vote in the general meetings
>
> *Investors Chronicle*

mega-cap ['megəkæp] *noun* share with the very highest capitalization and growth; *see also* CAP, MICROCAP, MIDCAP, SMALL-CAP

> Wall Street's performance in the last three years or so has been dominated by the so-called mega-caps
>
> *Investors Chronicle*

member ['membə] *noun* **(a)** person who belongs to a group or a society, such as a member of a stock exchange; **ordinary member** = person who pays a subscription to belong to a group; **member's agent** = person who works on behalf of the names in a Lloyd's syndicate **(b)** shareholder in a company **(c)** organization which belongs to a society; ***the member countries of the EU***; ***the members of the United Nations***; ***the member companies of a trade association***; *US* **member bank** = bank which is part of the Federal Reserve system; **member firm** = stockbroking firm which is a member of a stock exchange; **Member States** = states which are members of an organization such as the EU or the UN

> Member States have been left with the option to restrict this four week holiday to three weeks until November 1999
>
> *Evening Standard*

> it will be the first opportunity for party members and trade union members to express their views on the tax package
>
> *Australian Financial Review*

> in 1984 exports to Canada from the member-states of the European Community jumped 38 per cent
>
> *Globe and Mail (Toronto)*

membership ['membəʃɪp] *noun* all the members of an organization

> the bargaining committee will recommend that its membership ratify the agreement at a meeting called for June
>
> *Toronto Star*

memorandum (and articles) of association [memə'rændəm] *noun* legal document setting up a limited company and giving details of its name, aims, directors, and registered office

mercantile ['mə:kəntaɪl] *adjective* commercial; *US* **mercantile agency** = agency which supplies credit ratings (NOTE: British English is a **credit agency**); **mercantile agent** = (i) *GB* agent who trades on behalf of another person or company; (ii) *US* person who supplies credit ratings on corporations or individuals; **mercantile country** = country which earns income from trade; **mercantile law** = laws relating to business; **mercantile marine** = all the commercial ships of a country

merchant ['mə:tʃənt] *noun* company, retail outlet, etc., which accepts a certain type of credit card for purchases; **merchant number** = number of the merchant, printed at the top of the report slip when depositing credit card payments

merchant bank ['mə:tʃənt 'bæŋk] *noun* **(a)** bank which arranges loans to companies and deals in international finance, buys and sells shares, launches new companies on the Stock Exchange but does not provide normal banking services to the general public; **merchant banker** = person who has a high position in a merchant bank **(b)** *US* bank which operates a credit card system (accepting payment on credit cards from retailers or 'merchants')

merchant navy *or* **merchant marine** ['mə:tʃənt 'neɪvi or mə'ri:n] *noun* all the commercial ships of a country

merge [mə:dʒ] *verb* to join together; ***the two companies have merged***; ***the firm merged with its main competitor***

merger ['mə:dʒə] *noun* joining together of two or more companies (usually as the result of an agreed takeover bid); ***as a result of the merger, the company is the largest in the field***; **merger accounting** = way of presenting the accounts of a newly acquired company within the group accounts, so as to show it in the best possible light

metal ['metl] *noun* material (either an element or a compound) which can carry heat and electricity; **base metals** = ordinary metals used in industry, such as aluminium and lead;

precious metals = very valuable metals, such as gold and platinum

> COMMENT: only some metals are traded as commodities: these are the base metals aluminium, copper, lead, nickel, tin, zinc (which are traded on the London Metal Exchange) and the precious metals gold, silver, platinum and palladium which are traded on the London Bullion Market, COMEX, and other exchanges

method ['meθəd] *noun* way of doing something; ***a new method of making something*** *or* ***of doing something; what is the best method of payment? his organizing methods are out of date; their manufacturing methods*** *or* ***production methods are among the most modern in the country***; **time and method study** = examining the way in which something is done to see if a cheaper or quicker way can be found

metical ['metɪkæl] *noun* currency used in Mozambique

mezzanine class stock ['metsəni:n 'klɑ:s 'stɒk] *noun* type of common stock rated at a level below the top double-A or triple-A ratings

> although the triple-A and double-A classes do well, the mezzanine classes of the current crop - those rated single-A and triple-B - are showing signs of weakness
>
> *Barron's*

mezzanine finance ['metsəni:n faɪ'næns] *noun* provision of finance for a company after the start-up finance has been provided

> COMMENT: mezzanine finance is less risky than start-up finance, since the company has usually already started trading; this type of finance is aimed at consolidating the company's trading position before it is floated on a stock exchange

MFN = MOST FAVOURED NATION

Mibtel index of share prices on the Milan stock exchange in Italy

micro- ['maɪkrəʊ] *prefix* very small; **microeconomics** = study of the economics of groups of people or single companies; *compare* MACROECONOMICS

microcap ['maɪkrəʊkæp] *noun & adjective* **microcap stocks** = shares of companies with very small capitalization; *see also* CAP, MEGA-CAP, MIDCAP, SMALL-CAP

microfiche ['maɪkrəfi:ʃ] *noun* index sheet, made of several microfilm photographs; ***we hold our records on microfiche***

microfilm ['maɪkrəfɪlm] **1** *noun* roll of film on which a document is photographed in very small scale; ***we hold our records on microfilm*** **2** *verb* to make a very small scale photograph; ***send the 1990 correspondence to be microfilmed*** *or* ***for microfilming***

micropayments ['maɪkrəʊpeɪmənts] *noun* technology developed to allow visitors to spend very small amounts of money (normally for information) on an internet site

> COMMENT: when purchasing goods or spending more than ú5 on an internet site it is commercially viable for the retailer to accept payment by credit card or any other form of e-money. When charging very small amounts (normally a few pence or cents) for information it is not worth while paying using a standard credit card. Micropayments allow the retailer to debit the visitor's e-purse or bank account directly.

mid- [mɪd] *prefix* middle; **from mid-1998** = from the middle of 1998; ***the factory is closed until mid-July***

mid-cap *or* **midcap** ['mɪdkæp] *noun & adjective* **midcap stocks** = shares of companies with medium-sized capitalization (on the London Stock Exchange between £300m and £2.5bn capitalization); ***a portfolio manager specializing in midcap stocks***; *see also* CAP, MEGA-CAP, MICRO-CAP, SMALL-CAP

middle ['mɪdl] *adjective* in the centre or between two points; **middle management** = department managers in a company, who carry out the policy set by the directors and organize the work of a group of workers; **middle price** = price between the buying and selling price (usually shown in indices); **middle rate** = exchange rate between the buy and sell rates for a foreign currency

middle-income ['mɪdl'ɪŋkʌm] adjective **people in the middle-income bracket** = people with average incomes, not very high or very low

middleman ['mɪdlmæn] *noun* businessman who buys from the manufacturer and sells to the public; person who negotiates with large companies on behalf of personal clients; ***he arranged his car insurance direct with the insurance company, without going through a middleman***

mid-month ['mɪd'mʌnθ] *adjective* taking place in the middle of the month; ***mid-month accounts***

mid-sized *or* **midsize** ['mɪdsaɪzd] *adjective US* **mid-sized company** = company which is larger than a small company but smaller than a large company (NOTE: in British English **medium-sized**)

mid-week ['mɪd'wi:k] *adjective* which happens in the middle of a week; ***the mid-week lull in sales***

mill [mɪl] *noun US* one-fifth of a cent

million ['mɪljən] number 1,000,000; ***the company lost £10 million in the African market***; ***our turnover has risen to $13.4 million*** (NOTE: can be written **m** after figures: **$5m:** say 'five million dollars')

millionaire [mɪljə'neə] *noun* person who has more than one million pounds; **dollar millionaire** = person who has more than one million dollars; **paper millionaire** = person who owns shares which, if sold, would be worth one million pounds or dollars

min = MINUTE, MINIMUM

mini- ['mɪni] *prefix* very small

minibudget ['mɪnibʌdʒɪt] *noun* interim statement about financial plans from a finance minister

minimum ['mɪnɪməm] **1** *noun* smallest possible quantity or price or number; ***to keep expenses to a minimum***; ***to reduce the risk of a loss to a minimum***; **Minimum Lending Rate (MLR)** = formerly, the rate at which the Bank of England used to lend to other banks (now called the 'base rate') (NOTE: plural is **minima** or **minimums**) **2** *adjective* smallest possible; **minimum balance** = smallest amount of money which must be kept in an account to qualify for the services provided; ***to pay no charges a minimum balance of £5000 is required***; **minimum dividend** = smallest dividend which is legal and accepted by the shareholders; **minimum payment** = smallest payment necessary; **minimum quantity** = smallest quantity which is acceptable; **minimum reserves** = smallest amount of reserves which a commercial bank must hold with a central bank; **minimum wage** = lowest hourly wage which a company can legally pay its workers

mining ['maɪnɪŋ] *see also* DATA

minister ['mɪnɪstə] *noun* member of a government who is in charge of a ministry; ***a government minister***; ***the Minister of Trade*** *or* ***the Trade Minister***; ***the Minister of Foreign Affairs*** *or* ***the Foreign Minister***; *see also* SECRETARY

> COMMENT: in the USA, heads of government departments are called **secretary: the Secretary for Commerce;** in the UK, heads of government departments are called **Secretary of State: the Secretary of State for Defence**

ministry ['mɪnɪstri] *noun* department in the government; ***he works in the Ministry of Finance*** *or* ***the Finance Ministry***; ***he is in charge of the Ministry of Information*** *or* ***of the Information Ministry***; ***a ministry official*** *or* ***an official from the ministry*** (NOTE: in both the UK and the USA, important ministries are called **departments: the Department of Trade and Industry; the Commerce Department**)

minor ['maɪnə] **1** *adjective* less important; ***minor expenditure***; ***minor shareholders*** **2** *noun* person less than eighteen years old

minority [maɪ'nɒrəti] *noun* number or quantity which is less than half of the total; ***a minority of board members opposed the chairman***; **minority shareholding** *or* **minority interest** = group of shares which are less than one half of the shares in a company; **minority shareholder** = person who owns a group of shares but less than half of the shares in a company; **in the minority** = being fewer than half; ***shareholders opposing the scheme were in the minority***

mint [mɪnt] **1** *noun* factory where coins are made **2** *verb* to make coins

minus ['maɪnəs] **1** *adverb* less, without; ***net salary is gross salary minus tax and National Insurance deductions***; ***gross profit is sales minus production costs*** **2** adjective **the accounts show a minus figure** = show that more has been spent than has been received; **minus factor** = unfavourable factor; ***to have lost sales in the best quarter of the year is a minus factor for the sales team*** **3** *noun* printed sign (-) showing a loss or decrease; ***at the end of the day the index showed a series of minuses, with very few pluses***

MIRAS ['maɪrəs] = MORTGAGE INTEREST RELIEF AT SOURCE

mirror ['mirə] noun **mirror fund** = investment trust where the manager also runs a unit trust with the same objectives

misappropriate [mɪsə'prəuprɪeɪt] *verb* to use illegally money which is not yours, but with which you have been trusted

misappropriation [mɪsəprəuprɪ'eɪʃən] *noun* illegal use of money by someone who is not the owner but who has been trusted to look after it

miscalculate [mɪsˈkælkjuleɪt] *verb* to calculate wrongly; ***the salesman miscalculated the discount, so we hardly broke even on the deal***

miscalculation [mɪskælkjuˈleɪʃən] *noun* mistake in calculating

miscount 1 [ˈmɪskaʊnt] *noun* mistake in counting **2** [mɪsˈkaʊnt] *verb* to count wrongly; ***the shopkeeper miscounted, so we got twenty-five boxes instead of two dozen***

misfeasance [mɪsˈfi:zəns] *noun* doing something in an improper way

mismanage [mɪsˈmænɪdʒ] *verb* to manage badly

mismanagement [mɪsˈmænɪdʒmənt] *noun* bad management; ***the company failed because of the chairman's mismanagement***

misrepresent [mɪsrepriˈzent] *verb* to report facts wrongly

misrepresentation [mɪsreprɪzenˈteɪʃən] *noun* wrongly reporting facts; **fraudulent misrepresentation** = giving someone wrong information in order to cheat him

mistake [mɪˈsteɪk] *noun* wrong action or wrong decision; **to make a mistake** = to do something wrong; ***the shop made a mistake and sent the wrong items***; ***there was a mistake in the address***; ***she made a mistake in addressing the letter***; **by mistake** = in error, wrongly; ***they sent the wrong items by mistake***; ***she put my letter into an envelope for the chairman by mistake***

Mittelstand [ˈmɪtəlʃtænt] *German* sector of medium-sized companies

misuse [mɪsˈju:s] *noun* wrong use; ***misuse of funds*** *or* ***of assets***

mixed [mɪkst] *adjective* **(a)** of different sorts or of different types together; **mixed economy** = system which contains both nationalized industries and private enterprise **(b)** neither good nor bad

> prices closed on a mixed note after a moderately active trading session
>
> *Financial Times*

MMC = MONOPOLIES AND MERGERS COMMISSION

mobilize [ˈməʊbɪlaɪz] *verb* to bring together, especially to fight an enemy; **to mobilize capital** = to collect capital to support something; **to mobilize resources to defend a takeover bid** = to get the support of shareholders, etc., to stop a company being taken over

mode [məʊd] *noun* way of doing something; **mode of payment** = way in which payment is made (such as cash or cheque)

model [ˈmɒdl] noun **computer model** = system for calculating investment opportunities, used by fund managers to see the right moment to buy or sell; **economic model** = computerized plan of a country's economic system, used for forecasting economic trends; **pricing model** = computerized system for calculating a price, based on costs, anticipated margins, etc.; **model risk** = possibility that a computer model used when investing may have a flaw which makes it function badly in extreme market conditions

> model-based techniques are not only used by market practitioners in trading decisions, but are also tools used by the Bank for International Settlements, the Federal Reserve and the EU
>
> *Financial World*

> on the basis of historical pricing relationships, computer models calculate the exact point at which to enter a buy/sell order and the appropriate size of transaction
>
> *Financial World*

modem [ˈməʊdem] *noun* device which links a computer to the telephone line, allowing data to be sent from one computer to another

modest [ˈmɒdɪst] *adjective* small; ***oil shares showed modest gains over the week's trading***

modified accounts [ˈmɒdɪfaɪd əˈkaʊnts] *noun* less detailed annual accounts which can be deposited with the Registrar of Companies by small or medium-sized companies

momentum [məˈmentəm] *noun* movement upwards of share prices, suggesting that prices will continue to rise; **momentum investor** = investor who buys shares which seem to be moving upwards

> I am not a momentum investor. I look for quality and value, companies that have not shown rapid outperformance, or which have not moved at all, or which offer value relative to their peer group
>
> *Money Observer*

momentum is rapidly becoming established as a big stock market theme

Financial Times

monetarism ['mʌnɪtərɪzm] *noun* theory that the amount of money in the economy affects the level of prices, so that inflation can be controlled by regulating money supply

monetarist ['mʌnɪtərɪst] **1** *noun* person who believes in monetarism and acts accordingly **2** *adjective* according to monetarism; ***monetarist theories***

monetary ['mʌnɪtəri] *adjective* referring to money or currency; **monetary control** = control of money supply; **monetary standard** = fixing of a fixed exchange rate for a currency; **monetary targets** = figures such as the money supply, PSBR, etc., which are given as targets by the government when setting out its budget for the forthcoming year; **the international monetary system** = methods of controlling and exchanging currencies between countries; **monetary unit** = standard currency in a country (the pound, the dollar, the franc, etc.) or within a group of countries (the CFA franc, the euro, etc.); *see also* EUROPEAN MONETARY UNION, INTERNATIONAL MONETARY FUND

a draft report on changes in the international monetary system

Wall Street Journal

monetary policy ['mʌnɪtəri 'pɒlɪsi] noun **the government's monetary policy** = the government's policy relating to finance (money supply, bank interest rates, government expenditure and borrowing)

the decision by the government to tighten monetary policy will push the annual inflation rate above the year's previous high

Financial Times

it is not surprising that the Fed started to ease monetary policy some months ago

Sunday Times

Monetary Policy Committee (MPC) ['mʌnɪtəri 'pɒlɪsi kə'mɪti] committee of the Bank of England, chaired by the governor of the Bank, which has responsibility for setting interest rates independently of the British government; the aim is to set rates with a view to keeping inflation at a certain level, and avoiding deflation

Its Monetary Policy Committee (MPC) gets an opportunity to reveal whether it is still affected by the Christmas spirit when it meets this Wednesday

The Times

The Fed next meets to consider interest rates on February 3 and 4, just one day ahead of the February MPC meeting

The Times

money ['mʌni] *noun* **(a)** coins and notes used for buying and selling; **to earn money** = to have a salary; **to earn good money** = to have a large salary; **to lose money** = to make a loss, not to make a profit; **the company has been losing money for months** = the company has been working at a loss; **to get your money back** = to make enough profit to cover your original investment; **to make money** = to make a profit; **to put money into the bank** = to deposit money into a bank account; **to put money into a business** = to invest money in a business; ***he put all his redundancy money into a shop***; **to put money down** = to pay cash, especially as a deposit; ***he put £25 down and paid the rest in instalments***; **money at call** *or* **call money** = money loaned for which repayment can be demanded without notice (used by commercial banks, placing money on very short- term deposit with discount houses); **cheap money** = money which can be borrowed at a low rate of interest; **danger money** = extra salary paid to workers in dangerous jobs; **dear money** = money which has to be borrowed at a high rate of interest; **easy money** = money which can be earned with no difficulty; ***selling insurance is easy money***; **hot money** = money which is moved from country to country to get the best returns; **paper money** = money in notes, not coins; **ready money** = cash, money which is immediately available; **money lying idle** = money not being used to produce interest; **they are worth a lot of money** = they are valuable; *see also* LAUNDERING **(b) money broker** = dealer operating in the interbank and foreign exchange markets; **money management** = dealing with the investment of large sums of money on behalf of groups of clients; **money markets** = markets for buying and selling short-term loans or financial instruments such as Treasury bills and CDs, which can be easily converted to cash; ***the international money markets are nervous***; *see also* BASIS; **money market fund** = investment fund, which only invests in CDs, Treasury bills, etc.; **money market instruments** = short-term investments, such as CDs, which can be easily turned to cash and are traded on the money markets; **money rates** = rates of interest for borrowers or lenders **(c)** *(traded options)* **at the money** = option to sell at the same price as the share currently is trading at; **in the money** = option to buy at a lower price or to sell at a higher price than the share is currently at; **out of the money** = option to buy at a higher price or to sell at a lower price than a share is currently trading at

moneylender ['mʌni'lendə] *noun* person who lends money at interest

money-making ['mʌni'meɪkɪŋ] *adjective* which makes money; ***a money-making plan***

money order ['mʌni 'ɔ:də] *noun* document which can be bought for sending money through the post; **foreign money order** *or* **international money order** *or* **overseas money order** = money order in a foreign currency which is payable to someone living in a foreign country

money-spinner ['mʌni'spɪnə] *noun* item which sells very well or which is very profitable

money supply ['mʌni sʌ'plaɪ] *noun* amount of money which exists in circulation in a country

> COMMENT: money supply is believed by some to be at the centre of control of a country's economy. If money supply is tight (i.e., the government restricts the issue of new notes, reduces the possibility of lending, etc.) the amount of money available in the economy is reduced and thus may reduce spending. Money supply is calculated in various ways: **M0** (or narrow money supply), including coins and notes in circulation plus the deposits of commercial banks with the Bank of England; **M1,** including all coins and notes plus personal money in current accounts; **M2,** including coins and notes and personal money in current and deposit accounts; **M3,** or the broader money supply, including coins and notes, personal money in current and deposit accounts, government deposits and deposits in currencies other than sterling (called **£M3** in Britain). In the USA, money supply also includes **L,** which is calculated as M3, plus Treasury bills, bonds and commercial paper

monies ['mʌniz] *noun* sums of money; ***monies owing to the company***; ***to collect monies due***

monitor ['mɒnɪtə] **1** *noun* screen (like a TV screen) on a computer **2** *verb* to check or to examine how something is working; ***he is monitoring the progress of sales***; ***how do you monitor the performance of a unit trust?***

monopoly [mə'nɒpəli] *noun* situation where one person or company controls all the market in the supply of a product; **public monopoly** *or* **state monopoly** = situation where the state is the only supplier of a product or service (such as the Post Office, the coal industry,etc.); **Monopolies and Mergers Commission (MMC)** = government organization which examines takeover bids at the request of the Office of Fair Trading, to see if a successful bid would result in a monopoly and so harm the consumer by reducing competition

month [mʌnθ] *noun* one of twelve periods which make a year; ***the company pays him £100 a month***; ***he earns £2,000 a month***; ***bills due at the end of the current month***; **calendar month** = whole month as on a calendar; **paid by the month** = paid once each month; **to give a customer two months' credit** = to allow a customer to pay not immediately, but after two months

month end ['mʌnθ 'end] *noun* the end of a calendar month, when accounts are usually drawn up; ***month-end accounts***

monthly ['mʌnθli] **1** *adjective* happening every month, which is received every month; ***monthly payments***; ***he is paying for his car by monthly instalments***; ***my monthly salary cheque is late***; **monthly statement** = statement sent to a customer at the end of each month, itemizing transactions which have taken place in his account; **monthly ticket** = ticket for travel which is good for one month **2** *adverb* every month; ***to pay monthly***; ***the account is credited monthly***

Moody's Investors Service ['mu:diz] American rating organization, which gives a rating showing the reliability of a debtor organization (its ratings run from AAA to C); it also issues ratings on municipal bonds, running from MIG1 (the highest rating) to MIG4

moonlight ['mu:nlaɪt] verb *(informal)* to do a second job for cash (often in the evening) as well as a regular job

moonlighter ['mu:nlaɪtə] *noun* person who moonlights

moonlighting ['mu:nlaɪtɪŋ] *noun* doing a second job; ***he makes thousands a year from moonlighting***

moratorium [mɒrə'tɔ:riəm] *noun* temporary stop to repayments of interest or capital of money owed; ***the banks called for a***

moratorium on payments (NOTE: plural is **moratoria**)

Morningstar [ˈmɔːnɪŋstɑː] *US* agency which gives ratings to mutual funds

> the fund has earned Morningstar's highest rating - five star - for its overall risk-adjusted performance
>
> *Smart Money*

> the fund was awarded a four-star rating for its overall risk-adjusted performance by Morningstar
>
> *Smart Money*

mortality [mɔːˈtæləti] noun **mortality rate** = number of deaths shown as a percentage of the total population; *US* **mortality and expense risk charge (M&E fee)** = an extra charge to pay on some annuities to guarantee that if the policyholder dies his heirs will receive a benefit, and also that the insurance company will be compensated for an annuitant who lives longer than he or she should according to the mortality tables

mortgage [ˈmɔːgɪdʒ] **1** *noun* **(a)** (i) legal agreement where someone lends money to another person so that he can buy a property, the property being the security; (ii) money lent in this way; ***to take out a mortgage on the a house***; ***to buy a house with a £20,000 mortgage***; **mortgage arrears** = being late in paying mortgage payments; **mortgage payments** = money paid each month as interest on a mortgage, plus repayment of a small part of the capital borrowed; **mortgage relief** = reduction in tax on interest paid on a mortgage; **to foreclose on a mortgaged property** = to sell a property because the owner cannot repay money which he has borrowed, using the property as security; **to pay off a mortgage** = to pay back the principal and all the interest on a loan to buy a property **(b) mortgage bank** = bank which lends money to purchasers of properties, on the security of the property; **mortgage bond** = certificate showing that a mortgage exists and that property is security for it; **mortgage broker** = person who arranges mortgages, by putting a borrower in touch with a possible lender; **mortgage debenture** = debenture where the loan is secured against the company's property; **mortgage famine** = situation where there is not enough money available to offer mortgages to house buyers; **mortgage lender** = financial institution such as a bank or building society that lends money to people buying property; **mortgage queue** = list of people waiting for mortgages; *US* **mortgage REIT** = trust which provides mortgages to property developers; **first mortgage** = main mortgage on a property; **second mortgage** = further mortgage on a property which is already mortgaged; *see also* ENDOWMENT MORTGAGE, REPAYMENT MORTGAGE **2** *verb* to accept a loan with a property as security; ***the house is mortgaged***; ***he mortgaged his house to set up in business***

mortgage-backed [ˈmɔːgɪdʒˈbækt] adjective **mortgage-backed securities** = shares which are backed by the security of a mortgage; *see also* COMMERCIAL

mortgagee [mɔːgəˈdʒiː] *noun* person or company which lends money for someone to buy a property

mortgage interest relief at source (MIRAS) [ˈmɔːgɪdʒ ˈɪntrəst rɪˈliːf ət ˈsɔːs] scheme by which the borrower may repay interest on a mortgage less the standard rate tax which he would otherwise have to pay on it (i.e., he does not pay the full interest and then reclaim the tax)

> COMMENT: Mortgage Interest Relief at Source (MIRAS) is given in the UK to individuals paying interest on a mortgage; the relief is calculated at the basic rate of income tax multiplied by the interest due on the first part of the loan and is deducted from the individual's monthly payments; the amount of the loan eligible for MIRAS is being gradually reduced and will eventually be phased out altogether

mortgager *or* **mortgagor** [ˈmɔːgɪdʒə] *noun* person who borrows money to buy a property

> mortgage money is becoming tighter. Applications for mortgages are running at a high level and some building societies are introducing quotas
>
> *Times*

> for the first time since mortgage rates began falling a financial institution has raised charges on homeowner loans
>
> *Globe and Mail (Toronto)*

most favoured nation (MFN) [ˈməʊst ˈfeɪvəd ˈneɪʃən] *noun* country which has the best trade terms; **most-favoured-nation clause** = agreement between two countries that each will offer the best possible terms in commercial contracts; ***the USA has agreed to offer the country MFN status***

mounting ['maʊntɪŋ] *adjective* increasing; ***he resigned in the face of mounting pressure from the shareholders***; ***the company is faced with mounting debts***

mount up ['maʊnt 'ʌp] *verb* to increase rapidly; ***costs are mounting up***

move [mu:v] *verb* to propose formally that a motion be accepted by a meeting; ***he moved that the accounts be agreed***; ***I move that the meeting should adjourn for ten minutes***

movement ['mu:vmənt] *noun* changing position, going up or down; ***movements in the money markets***; ***cyclical movements of trade***; **movements of capital** = changes of investments from one country to another; **price movement** = change in prices of shares or commodities

mover ['mu:və] *noun* person who proposes a motion

moving average ['mu:vɪŋ 'ævrɪdʒ] *noun* average of share prices on a stock market, where the calculation is made over a period which moves forward regularly

> COMMENT: the commonest are 100-day or 200-day averages, or 10- or 40-week moving averages; the average is calculated as the average figure for the whole period, and moves forward one day or week at a time; these averages are often used by chartists

MPC = MONETARY POLICY COMMITTEE

multi- ['mʌlti] *prefix* referring to many things

> factory automation is a multi-billion-dollar business
>
> *Duns Business Month*

multicurrency ['mʌlti'kʌrənsi] *adjective* in several currencies; **multicurrency loan** = loan in several currencies

multilateral ['mʌlti'lætərəl] *adjective* between several parties; ***a multilateral agreement***; **multilateral netting** = method of putting together sums from various sources into one currency (used by groups of banks trading in several currencies at the same time); **multilateral trade** = trade between several countries

multi-manager fund ['mʌlti'mænɪdʒə 'fʌnd] *noun* hedge fund which uses a wide portfolio of fund managers to produce a balanced exposure for relatively small investors; *see also* HEDGE FUND, MANAGER

multimillion ['mʌlti'mɪljən] *adjective* referring to several million pounds or dollars; ***they signed a multimillion pound deal***

multimillionaire ['mʌltimɪljə'neə] *noun* person who owns several million pounds or dollars

multinational ['mʌlti'næʃənl] *noun* company which has branches or subsidiary companies in several countries; ***the company has been bought by one of the big multinationals*** (NOTE: also called a **multinational company**)

multiple ['mʌltɪpl] **1** *adjective* many; **multiple applications** = several applications for a new issue of shares, made by the same person, but under different names (in some share issues, people making multiple applications may be prosecuted); **multiple store** = one store in a chain of stores; **multiple ownership** = situation where something is owned by several parties jointly **2** *noun* **(a)** **share on a multiple of 5** = share with a P/E ratio of 5 (i.e., 5 is the result when dividing the current market price by the dividend) **(b)** company with stores in several different towns; ***it isn't cheap at more than 21 times projected 1998 operating profits, one of the highest multiples ever***; ***since 1985, the average multiple on the Goldman Sachs index of large-cap growth stocks has been 1.29 times that of the S&P 500***; *see also* PRICE/EARNINGS MULTIPLE

> the company's got a low multiple and the stock is trading for half of where it should be
>
> *Fortune*

multiply ['mʌltɪplaɪ] *verb* **(a)** to calculate the sum of various numbers repeated a certain number of times; ***to multiply twelve by three***; ***square measurements are calculated by multiplying length by width*** **(b)** to grow or to increase; ***profits multiplied in the boom years***

multiplication [mʌltɪplɪ'keɪʃən] *noun* act of multiplying; **multiplication sign** = sign (x) used to show that a number is being multiplied by another

multiplier ['mʌltɪplaɪə] *noun* number which multiplies another; factor which tends to multiply something (as the effect of new expenditure on total income and reserves)

muni ['mjʊni] noun *(informal)* = MUNICIPAL BOND

municipal bond [mjʊ'nɪsɪpəl 'bɒnd] *noun* *US* bond issued by a town or local area (the

British equivalent is a 'local authority bond') (NOTE: usually called **munis**); **municipal bond fund** *or* **muni fund** = fund invested in municipal bonds

> because muni funds produce relatively low yields, costs are extremely important
>
> *Smart Money*

> the yield on long-term munis, now just under 5 percent, is about 87 percent that of Treasurys
>
> *Smart Money*

> the good news is that municipal bonds are, indeed, a pretty good investment these days
>
> *Smart Money*

Murphy's law ['mɜːfɪz 'lɔː] *noun* law, based on wide experience, which says that in commercial life if something can go wrong it will go wrong, or that when you are thinking that things are going right, they will inevitably start to go wrong

mutual ['mjuːtʃʊəl] *adjective* belonging to two or more people; **mutual company** = insurance company which belongs to its policy holders or savings bank which belongs to its depositors (who may receive dividends from it); *US* **mutual funds** = organizations which take money from small investors and invest it in stocks and shares for them, the investment being in the form of units in the fund (similar to the British 'unit trusts'); **stock mutual funds** = mutual funds where the money is invested in corporate stocks as opposed to bonds or government securities, etc.

> purchases of stock mutual funds have stabilized after strong growth in 1996
>
> *Barron's*

MVA = MARKET VALUE ADDED; MARKET VALUE ADJUSTER

Nn

nail [neɪl] noun **to pay on the nail** = to pay promptly, to pay rapidly

naira ['naɪrə] *noun* currency used in Nigeria (NOTE: no plural; naira is usually written **N** before figures: **N2,000** say 'two thousand naira')

naked ['neɪkɪd] *adjective* without any hedge or without any reserves to protect a position

name [neɪm] *noun* **(a)** word used to call a thing or a person; **brand name** = name of a particular make of product; **corporate name** = name of a large corporation; **under the name of** = using a particular name; **trading under the name of 'Best Foods'** = using the name 'Best Foods' as a commercial name, but not the name of the company **(b)** person who provides security for insurance arranged by a Lloyd's of London syndicate

> COMMENT: Lloyd's is an old-established insurance market; the underwriters who form Lloyd's are divided into syndicates, each made up of active underwriters who arrange the business and non-working underwriters (called 'names') who stand surety for any insurance claims which may arise. Because of large losses by some syndicates in the early 1990s, some names were made bankrupt

named ['neɪmd] adjective **person named in the policy** = person whose name is given on an insurance policy as the person insured

narrow market ['nærəʊ 'mɑːkɪt] *noun* market in a share where few shares are available for sale, and where the price can vary sharply according to the demand

NASDAQ ['næzdæk] = NATIONAL ASSOCIATION OF SECURITIES DEALERS AUTOMATED QUOTATIONS the NASDAQ system provides quotations via computer for the US over-the-counter market, and also for some large corporations listed on the NYSE (NOTE: the British equivalent is **SEAQ**)

nation ['neɪʃən] *noun* country and the people living in it; **the United Nations** = organization linking almost all countries in the world; *see also* MOST FAVOURED NATION

national ['næʃənl] *adjective* referring to a particular country; **National Association of Securities Dealers Automated Quotation system;** *see* NASDAQ; *US* **national bank** = bank which is chartered by the federal government and is part of the Federal Reserve system (as opposed to a 'state bank'); **national central bank (NCB)** = one of central banks of the countries which form the eurozone, under the overall European Central Bank; **national currency** = official currency of a country, which is legal tender in that country; **the National Debt** = money borrowed by a government; **national income** = value of income from the sales of goods and services in a country; *GB* **National Insurance** = state insurance which pays for medical care, hospitals, unemployment benefits, etc.; **National Insurance contributions (NIC)** = money paid into the National Insurance scheme by the employer and the worker; **gross national product (GNP)** = annual value of goods and services in a country including income from other countries; *GB* **National Savings (NS)** = savings scheme for small investors run by the Post Office (including a savings bank, savings certificates and premium bonds); **National Savings Certificates** *or* **NS certificates** = certificates showing that someone has invested in National Savings (the NS issues certificates with stated interest rates and stated maturity dates, usually five or ten years)

nationality [næʃə'næləti] noun **he is of British nationality** = he is a British citizen; **nationality declaration** = declaration on some share application forms that the applicant is of a certain nationality (some shares cannot be held by persons who are not British)

nationalize ['næʃənəlaɪz] *verb* to put a privately-owned industry under state ownership and control; ***the government are planning to nationalize the banking system***; *the opposite is* PRIVATIZATION, PRIVATIZE

nationalized ['næʃənəlaɪzd] adjective **nationalized industry** = industry which was privately owned, but is now owned by the state

nationalization [næʃənəlaɪ'zeɪʃən] *noun* taking over of private industry by the state

NAV = NET ASSET VALUE

NB ['en'bi:] = NOTE

NCB = NATIONAL CENTRAL BANK

near-liquid asset *or* **near money** ['nɪə'lɪkwɪd 'æsɪt or 'nɪə 'mʌni] *noun* asset which can easily be converted to cash

negative ['negətɪv] *adjective* **the answer was in the negative** = the answer was 'no'; **negative carry** = deal where the cost of finance is more than the return on the capital used; **negative cash flow** = situation where a company is spending more money than it receives; **negative equity** = situation where a house bought with a mortgage becomes less valuable than the money borrowed to buy it (because of falling house prices); **negative yield curve** = situation where the yield on a long-term investment is less than that on a short-term investment (NOTE: the opposite is **positive**)

neglected [nɪ'glektɪd] *adjective* not well looked after; ***bank shares have been a neglected sector of the market this week***; **neglected business** = company which has not been actively run by its owners and could therefore do better; **neglected shares** = shares which are not bought or sold often

negligence ['neglɪdʒəns] noun **gross negligence** = act showing very serious neglect of duty towards other people

---

`if your card is misused before you tell us of its loss or theft, your liability will be limited to a maximum of £50, unless you have acted fraudulently or with gross negligence`

Banking Code

---

negligible ['neglɪdʒəbl] adjective **shares of negligible value** = shares which are considered by the income tax to have no value, because the company has ceased to exist (companies in receivership are not of negligible value, though they may end up in that category)

negotiable [nɪ'gəʊʃəbl] *adjective* **(a)** which can be negotiated **(b)** (document) which can easily be transferred to another person; **not negotiable** = which cannot be exchanged for cash; **'not negotiable'** = words written on a cheque to show that it can be paid only to a certain person; **negotiable certificate of deposit** *or* **negotiable CD** = receipt issued by a bank for a large sum deposited with the bank, which acts as an interest-bearing deposit; **negotiable cheque** = cheque made payable to bearer (i.e. to anyone who holds it); **negotiable instrument** = document (such as a bill of exchange, or cheque) which can be exchanged for cash; *US* **negotiable order of withdrawal** = cheque written on a NOW account; *see also* NOW ACCOUNT; **negotiable paper** = document which can be transferred from one owner to another for money

---

`initial salary is negotiable around $45,000 per annum`

Australian Financial Review

---

negotiate [nɪ'gəʊʃɪeɪt] verb **to negotiate with someone** = to discuss a problem formally with someone, so as to reach an agreement; ***the management refused to negotiate with the union***; **to negotiate terms and conditions** *or* **to negotiate a contract** = to discuss and agree terms of a contract; **he negotiated a £250,000 loan with the bank** = he came to an agreement with the bank for a loan of £250,000; **negotiated commission** = broker's commission which is not fixed, but which is negotiated between the client and the broker

---

`many of the large travel agency chains are able to negotiate even greater discounts`

Duns Business Month

---

negotiation [nɪgəʊʃɪ'eɪʃən] *noun* discussion of terms and conditions to reach an agreement; **contract under negotiation** = contract which is being discussed; **a matter for negotiation** = something which must be discussed before a decision is reached; **to enter into negotiations** *or* **to start negotiations** = to start discussing a problem; **to resume negotiations** = to start discussing a problem again, after talks have stopped for a time; **to break off negotiations** = to refuse to go on discussing a problem; **to conduct negotiations** = to negotiate; **negotiations broke down after six hours** = discussions stopped because no agreement was possible; **pay negotiations** *or* **wage negotiations** = discussions between management and workers about pay

---

`after three days of tough negotiations, the company reached agreement with its 1,200 unionized workers`

Toronto Star

---

negotiator [nɪ'gəʊʃɪeɪtə] *noun* **(a)** person who discusses with the aim of reaching an agreement; **an experienced union negotiator** = member of a union who has a lot of experience of discussing terms of employment with management **(b)** *GB* person who works in an estate agency

nest egg ['nest 'eg] *noun* money which someone has saved over a period of time (usually kept in an interest-bearing account, and intended for use after retirement)

net [net] **1** *adjective* **(a)** price, weight or pay, etc., after all deductions have been made; **net asset value (NAV)** *or* **net worth** = total value of a company after deducting the money owed by the company (it is the value of shareholders' capital plus any money retained from profits); **net asset value per share** = value of a company calculated by dividing the shareholders' funds by the number of shares issued; **net borrowings** = a company's borrowings, less any cash the company is holding in its bank accounts; **net cash flow** = difference between more money coming in and less money going out of a firm; **net change on the day** = difference between the opening price of a share at the beginning of a day's trading and the closing price at the end; **net current assets** *or* **net working capital** = current assets of a company (cash and stocks) less any liabilities, which a company needs to be able to continue trading; **net dividend per share** = dividend per share after deduction of personal income tax; **net earnings** *or* **net income** = total earnings of a business after tax and other deductions; **net income** *or* **net salary** = person's income which is left after taking away tax and other deductions; **net interest margin** = the difference between what a bank receives in interest on loans and what it pays out in interest on deposits; **net loss** = actual loss, after deducting overheads; **net margin** = net profit shown as a percentage of sales; **net price** = (i) price of goods or services which cannot be reduced by a discount; (ii) price paid for a share, where no commission is payable to the broker; **net profit** = result where income from sales is more than all expenditure; **net profit before tax** = profit of a company after expenses have been deducted but before tax has been paid; **net receipts** = receipts after deducting commission, tax or discounts, etc.; **net return** = return on an investment after tax has been paid; **net sales** = sales less damaged or returned items, discounts to retailers, etc.; **net weight** = weight of goods after deducting the weight of packaging material and container (NOTE: the spelling **nett** is sometimes used on containers); **net working capital** = NET CURRENT ASSETS; **net worth** = NET ASSET VALUE; **net yield** = profit from investments after deduction of tax **(b) terms strictly net** = payment has to be the full price, with no discount allowed **2** *verb* **(a)** to make a true profit; ***to net a profit of £10,000*** **(b) to net out** = to balance debits and credits to give a net result; **bilateral netting** = settling of contracts between two banks to give a new position; **multilateral netting** = method of putting together sums from various sources into one currency (used by groups of banks trading in several currencies at the same time)

> Out of its earnings a company will pay a dividend. When shareholders receive this it will be net, that is, it will have had tax deducted at 25 per cent
>
> *Investors Chronicle*

> in each of the years 1986 to 1989, Japan pumped a net sum of the order of $100bn into foreign securities markets, notably into US government bonds. In 1988, Germany was also a significant supplier of net capital to the tune of $45bn
>
> *Financial Times Review*

new [nju:] *adjective* recent, not old; **under new management** = with a new owner; **new issue** = issue of new shares to raise finance for a company; **new issue market** = market where companies can raise finance by issuing new shares, or by a flotation; **new issue sale** = sale of a new issue of shares; **new issues department** = section of a bank which deals with issues of new shares; **new money** = finance provided by a new issue of shares or by the transfer of money from one account to another; **new time** = the next account on a Stock Exchange (where sales in the last few days of the previous account are credited to the following account)

New York Cotton Exchange (NYCE) ['nju: 'jɔ:k 'kɒtən ɪks'tʃeɪnʒ] commodity exchange, based in New York, dealing in cotton and other commodities, and also in financial futures through the NYFE

New York Futures Exchange (NYFE) ['nju: 'jɔ:k 'fju:tʃəz ɪks'tʃeɪnʒ] financial futures and options exchange, based in New York, part of the NYCE

New York Stock Exchange (NYSE) ['nju: 'jɔ:k 'stɒk ɪks'tʃeɪnʒ] the main US stock exchange, situated on Wall Street in New York (NOTE: also called **Big Board**)

ngultrum ['ŋgʌltrəm] *noun* currency used in Bhutan

NIC = NATIONAL INSURANCE CONTRIBUTIONS

niche [ni:ʃ] *noun* special place in a market, occupied by one company; **niche company** = company specializing in a particular type of produce or service, which occupies a market niche

nickel ['nɪkl] *noun* **(a)** valuable metal traded on commodity exchanges, such as the London Metal Exchange **(b)** *US* five cent coin

NIF = NOTE ISSUANCE FACILITY

night [naɪt] noun **night safe** *US* **night collection box** = safe in the outside wall of a bank where money and documents can be deposited at night using a special door

Nikkei Average ['nɪkeɪ 'ævrɪdʒ] index of prices on the Tokyo Stock Exchange, based on about 200 leading shares

nil [nɪl] *noun* zero or nothing; ***to make a nil return***; ***the advertising budget has been cut to nil***; **nil paid shares** = new shares which have not yet been paid for

No. = NUMBER

no-claims bonus ['nəʊ'kleɪmz 'bəʊnəs] *noun* reduction of premiums on an insurance policy because no claims have been made

nominal ['nɒmɪnl] *adjective* **(a)** very small (payment); ***we make a nominal charge for our services***; ***they are paying a nominal rent*** **(b)** **nominal capital** = the total of the face value of all the shares which a company is authorized to issue; **nominal interest rate** = interest rate expressed as a percentage of the face value of a bond, not on its market value; **nominal ledger** = general accounts book showing income and expenditure; **nominal value** *or* **face value** *or* **par value** = value written on a share, a coin or a banknote

nominate ['nɒmɪneɪt] *verb* to suggest someone, to name someone for a job; **to nominate someone to a post** = to appoint someone to a post without an election; **to nominate someone as proxy** = to name someone as your proxy

nomination [nɒmɪ'neɪʃən] *noun* act of nominating

nominee [nɒmɪ'ni:] *noun* person who is nominated, especially someone who is appointed to deal with financial matters on your behalf; **nominee account** = account held on behalf of someone

> COMMENT: most shares are now held in nominee accounts, especially where computerized share dealing takes place. The disadvantage for the shareholder is that he or she does not see the company reports, and will not be eligible for any shareholder perks. Shares can also be purchased and held in nominee accounts so that the identity of the owner of the shares cannot be discovered

non- [nɒn] *prefix* not

> the reforms which took effect on 1 April 1998, greatly increased the ability of Japanese citizens to hold non-yen financial assets, such as dollar deposits in foreign banks
>
> *The Banker*

non-acceptance ['nɒnək'septəns] *noun* situation where the person who is to pay a bill of exchange does not accept it

non-bank ['nɒn'bæŋk] *noun* financial institution which is not a commercial bank according to the official definition (so an institution which only makes loans, and does not take deposits does not fall within the official definition of a bank and is not subject to the same regulations)

> all types of debt in the US have risen in recent years, but the sharpest climb by far has been in debt owed to non-bank institutions
>
> *Wall Street Journal*

noncash items [nɒn'kæʃ 'aɪtəmz] *noun* cheques, drafts, etc., which are not in the form of cash

noncompete agreement ['nɒnkʌm'pi:t ə'gri:mənt] *noun* *US* type of contract of employment by which an employee guarantees that he will not work for a competing firm after leaving his job

> to prevent managers from losing clients, some employers are taking their ex-employees to court, accusing them of violating noncompete agreements
>
> *Barron's*

non-contributory ['nɒnkən'trɪbjʊtəri] adjective **non-contributory pension scheme** = pension scheme where the employee does not make any contributions and the company pays everything; ***the company pension scheme is non-contributory***

nondeductible ['nɒndɪ'dʌktɪbl] *adjective* which cannot be deducted from income tax

> you'll pay taxes on the earnings you eventually withdraw from a nondeductible, traditional IRA
>
> *Fortune*

non-delivery ['nɒndɪ'lɪvəri] *noun* situation where something is not delivered

non-durables ['nɒn'djʊərəblz] *plural noun* goods which are used up soon after they have been bought (such as food, newspapers)

non-exec ['nɒnɪg'zek] noun *(informal)* NON-EXECUTIVE DIRECTOR

non-executive director ['nɒnɪg'zekjʊtɪv dɪ'rektə] *noun* director who attends board meetings and gives advice, but does not work full-time for the company, and is paid a fee for his or her advice (NOTE: also called an **outside director**)

> COMMENT: non-executive directors keep an eye on the way the company is run, and in particular make sure that the executive directors are doing their work properly. They may also intervene in disputes between directors, or between shareholders and directors

non-feasance ['nɒn'fi:zəns] *noun* not doing something which should be done by law

non-interest ['nɒn'ɪntrəst] *noun* a bank's income from fees and charges, as opposed to income from interest

nonmember bank [nɒn'membə 'bæŋk] *noun US* bank which is not a member of the Federal Reserve System

non-negotiable instrument ['nɒnnɪgəʊʃəbl 'ɪnstrəmənt] *noun* document (such as a crossed cheque) which cannot be exchanged for cash

non-payment ['nɒn'peɪmənt] noun **non-payment of a debt** = not paying a debt due

non-performing loan ['nɒnpə'fɔ:mɪŋ 'ləʊn] *noun US* loan where the borrower is not likely to pay any interest nor to repay the principal (as in the case of loans to Third World countries by western banks)

non profit-making organization *US* **non-profit corporation** ['nɒn'prɒfit'meɪkɪŋ ɔ:gənaɪ'zeɪʃən or 'nɒn'prɒfit kɔ:pə'reɪʃən] *noun* organization (such as a charity) which is not allowed by law to make a profit; ***non-profit-making organizations are exempted from tax***

non-recurring items ['nɒnrɪ'kə:rɪŋ 'aɪtəmz] *noun* special items in a set of accounts which appear only once

non-refundable ['nɒnrɪ'fʌndəbl] *adjective* which will not be refunded; ***non-refundable deposit***

nonregulated ['nɒn'regjuleɪtɪd] *adjective* which is not subject to government regulations; ***the banking industry was totally nonregulated in the nineteenth century***; ***a nonregulated subsidiary that builds and manages energy projects for industrial customers***

non-resident ['nɒn'rezɪdənt] *noun* person who is not considered a resident of a country for tax purposes; ***he has a non-resident bank account***

non-statutory ['nɒn'stætju:təri] *adjective* not covered by legislation

non-taxable ['nɒn'tæksəbl] *adjective* which is not subject to tax; ***non-taxable income***

non-voting shares ['nɒn'vəʊtɪŋ 'ʃeəz] *noun* shares which do not allow the shareholder to vote at meetings

nostro account ['nɒstrəʊ ə'kaʊnt] *noun* account which a bank has with a correspondent bank in another country; *see also* VOSTRO ACCOUNT

notary public ['nəʊtəri 'pʌblɪk] *noun* lawyer who has the authority to witness documents and spoken statements, making them official (NOTE: plural is **notaries public**)

note [nəʊt] *noun* **(a)** short document or short piece of information; **advice note** = written notice to a customer giving details of goods ordered and shipped but not yet delivered; **contract note** = note showing that shares have been bought or sold but not yet paid for; **cover note** = letter from an insurance company giving details of an insurance policy and confirming that the policy exists; **covering note** = letter sent with documents to explain why you are sending them; **credit note** = note showing that money is owed to a customer; **debit note** = note showing that a customer owes money; ***we undercharged Mr Smith and had to send him a debit note for the extra amount***; **delivery note** = list of goods being delivered, given to the customer with the goods; **dispatch note** = note saying that goods have been sent; **note of hand** *or* **promissory note** = document stating that someone promises to pay an amount of money on a certain date **(b)** paper showing that money has been borrowed; **note issuance facility (NIF)** = credit facility where a company obtains a loan underwritten by banks and can issue a series of short-term eurocurrency notes to replace others which have expired; **promissory note** = document stating that someone promises to pay an amount of money on a certain date **(c) bank note** *or* **currency note** = piece of printed paper money; ***a £5 note***; ***he pulled out a pile of used notes*** **(d)** short piece of writing; **notes to the accounts** = notes attached to a company's accounts by the auditors to explain items in the accounts or to explain the principles of accounting used

notice ['nəʊtɪs] *noun* **(a)** piece of written information; ***the company secretary pinned up a notice about the pension scheme***; **copyright notice** = note in a book showing who owns the copyright and the date of ownership **(b)** official warning that a contract is going to end or that terms are going to be changed; **until further notice** = until different instructions are given; ***you must pay £200 on the 30th of each month until further notice*** **(c)** time allowed before something takes place; **at short notice** = with very little warning; ***the bank manager will not see anyone at short notice***; **you must give seven days' notice of withdrawal** = you must ask to take money out of the account seven days before you want it

notional ['nəʊʃənl] *adjective* probable but not known exactly, not quantifiable; **notional income** = invisible benefit which is not money or goods and services; **notional rent** = sum put into accounts as rent where the company owns the building it is occupying and so does not pay an actual rent

not sufficient funds (NSF) [nɒt sə'fɪʃnt 'fʌndz] *noun US* not enough money in a checking account to pay a check that has been presented (NOTE: also called **insufficient funds**)

nought [nɔːt] number 0; ***a million pounds can be written as '£1m' or as one and six noughts*** (NOTE: **nought** is commoner in British English; in American English, **zero** is more usual)

novation [nə'veɪʃn] *noun* agreement to change a contract by substituting a third party for one of the two original parties

NOW account ['naʊ ə'kaʊnt] *noun US* = NEGOTIABLE ORDER OF WITHDRAWAL interest-bearing account with a bank or savings and loan association, on which cheques (called 'negotiable orders of withdrawal') can be drawn

NSF = NOT SUFFICIENT FUNDS

number ['nʌmbə] **1** *noun* **(a)** quantity of things or people; ***the number of persons on the payroll has increased over the last year***; ***the number of days lost through strikes has fallen***; ***the number of shares sold*** **(b)** written figure; ***batch number***; ***cheque number***; ***invoice number***; ***order number***; ***page number***; **account number** = special number given to an account, either a bank account (it appears on cheques) or a customer account; **box number** = reference number used when asking for mail to be sent to a post office or when asking for replies to an advertisement to be sent to the newspaper's offices; ***please reply to Box No. 209***; **index number** = (i) number of something in an index; (ii) number showing the percentage rise of something over a period (NOTE: often written **No.** with figures) **(c)** amount in figures; **earnings number** = profits expressed as a percentage; **growth number** = growth expressed as a percentage **2** *verb* to put a figure on a document; ***to number an order***; ***I refer to your invoice numbered 1234***; **numbered account** = bank account (usually in Switzerland) which is referred to only by a number, the name of the person holding it being kept secret

> the difficulty of hitting an earnings number just right, particularly in high technology shares
>
> *Fortune*

> he consistently pulls in some of the best earnings and growth numbers in the industry
>
> *Fortune*

> though most companies are meeting their 1997 numbers, the market is beginning to sense an uneasiness about the year ahead
>
> *Smart Money*

number cruncher ['nʌmbə 'krʌntʃə] noun *(informal)* person who makes calculations involving large figures

> the number crunchers get to work here to calculate a 'hurdle rate', which shows the average annual rate by which the trust underlying assets must grow, in order for the zeros to be repaid
>
> *Sunday Times*

numeric *or* **numerical** [njʊ'merɪk *or* njʊ'merɪkl] *adjective* referring to numbers; **in numerical order** = in the order of figures (such as 1 before 2, 33 before 34); ***file these***

invoices in numerical order; **numeric data** = data in the form of figures; **numeric keypad** = part of a computer keyboard which is a programmable set of numbered keys

NV = NAAMLOZE VENOOTSCHAP Dutch private limited company

NYCE = NEW YORK COTTON EXCHANGE

NYFE = NEW YORK FUTURES EXCHANGE

NYSE = NEW YORK STOCK EXCHANGE

Oo

O & M = ORGANIZATION AND METHODS

objective [əb'dʒektɪv] **1** *noun* something which you try to do; ***the company has achieved its objectives***; ***we set the sales force certain objectives***; **long-term objective** *or* **short-term objective** = aim which you hope to achieve within a few years or a few months; **management by objectives** = way of managing a business by planning work for the managers to do and testing if it is completed correctly and on time **2** *adjective* considered from a general point of view not from that of the person involved; ***to carry out an objective survey of the market***

obligate ['ɒblɪgeɪt] verb **to be obligated to do something** = to have a legal duty to do something

obligation [ɒblɪ'geɪʃən] *noun* **(a)** duty to do something; **to be under an obligation to do something** = to feel it is your duty to do something; ***there is no obligation to buy***; ***to be under no obligation to do something***; **he is under no contractual obligation to buy** = he has signed no contract which forces him to buy; **to fulfil your contractual obligations** = to do what is stated in a contract which you have signed; **two weeks' free trial without obligation** = the customer can try the item at home for two weeks without having to buy it at the end of the test **(b)** duty to pay a debt; **to meet your obligations** = to pay your debts **(c)** *(French)* bond

o.b.o. ['əʊ 'bi: 'əʊ] = OR BEST OFFER

occupational [ɒkju'peɪʃənl] *adjective* referring to a job; **occupational accident** = accident which takes place at work; **occupational pension scheme** = pension scheme where the worker gets a pension from the company he has worked for

occupier ['ɒkjupaɪə] *noun* person who lives in a property; **beneficial occupier** = person who occupies a property but does not own it fully; **owner-occupier** = person who owns the property in which he lives

odd [ɒd] *adjective* **(a)** **odd numbers** = numbers (like 17 or 33) which cannot be divided by two; ***odd-numbered buildings*** *or* ***buildings with odd numbers are on the south side of the street*** **(b)** **a hundred odd** = approximately one hundred; **keep the odd change** = keep the small change which is left over **(c)** **odd lot** = group of miscellaneous items, such as a small block of shares

OECD ['əʊ 'i: 'si: 'di:] = ORGANIZATION FOR ECONOMIC CO-OPERATION AND DEVELOPMENT

Oeics ['əʊɪks] = OPEN-ENDED INVESTMENT COMPANIES

OFEX ['ɒfeks] *noun* private trading facilities for buying and selling shares in companies which are not quoted on the London Stock Exchange (the market is not subject to Stock Exchange regulations)

off [ɒf] **1** *adverb* **(a)** taken away from a price; ***we give 5% off for quick settlement*** **(b)** lower than (a previous price); ***the shares closed 2% off*** **2** *preposition* **(a)** away from a price; ***to take £25 off the price***; ***these carpets are sold at £25 off the marked price***; ***we give 10% off our normal prices*** **(b)** not included; **items off balance sheet** *or* **off balance sheet items** = financial items which do not appear in a company's balance sheet as assets (such as leased equipment); **off balance sheet financing** = financing by leasing equipment instead of buying it, so that it does not appear in the balance sheet as an asset

> its stock closed Monday at $21.875 a share in NYSE composite trading, off 56% from its high last July
>
> *Wall Street Journal*

> the active December long gilt contract on the LIFFE slipped to close at 83-12 from the opening 83-24. In the cash market, one long benchmark - the 113/4issue of 2003-07 - closed 1011/2to yield 11.5 per cent, off more than 5/8 on the day
>
> *Financial Times*

offer ['ɒfə] **1** *noun* **(a)** statement that you are willing to pay a certain amount of money to buy something; ***to make an offer for a***

company; ***he made an offer of £10 a share***; ***we made a written offer for the house***; ***£1,000 is the best offer I can make***; ***to accept an offer of £1,000 for the car***; **the house is under offer** = someone has made an offer to buy the house and the offer has been accepted provisionally; **we are open to offers** = we are ready to discuss the price which we are asking; **cash offer** = being ready to pay in cash; **offer price** = price at which investors buy new shares or units in a unit trust (the opposite, i.e., the selling price, is called the 'bid price'; the difference between the two is the 'spread') **(b)** statement that you are willing to sell something for a certain amount of money; **offer for sale** = situation where a company advertises new shares for sale to the public as a way of launching the company on the Stock Exchange (the other ways of launching a company are a 'tender' or a 'placing'); **offer for subscription** = similar to an offer for sale, except there is a minimum level of subscription for the shares, and if this is not reached the offer is withdrawn (NOTE: the American equivalent for this is **public offering**) **(c)** statement that a company is prepared to buy another company's shares and take the company over; **offer document** = formal document where a company offers to buy shares at a certain price as part of a takeover bid; **offer period** = time during which a takeover bid for a company is open **(d) he received six offers of jobs** *or* **six job offers** = six companies told him he could have a job with them **(e) bargain offer** = sale of a particular type of goods at a cheap price; ***this week's bargain offer - 30% off all carpet prices***; **introductory offer** = special price offered on a new product to attract customers; **special offer** = goods put on sale at a specially low price; ***we have a range of men's shirts on special offer*** **(f)** *(in advertisements)* **or near offer** *US* **or best offer** *or* **or nearest offer** = or an offer of a price which is slightly less than the price asked; ***the car is for sale at £2,000 or near offer*** (NOTE: often shortened to **o.n.o., o.b.o.**) **2** *verb* **(a)** to say that you are willing to pay a certain amount of money for something; ***to offer someone £100,000 for his house***; ***he offered £10 a share***; **offered market** = market where there are more sellers than buyers; **offered price** = price at which shares are offered for sale by a marketmaker on the Stock Exchange (the opposite, i.e., the price at which an investor sells shares, is the 'bid price'; the difference between the two is the 'spread') **(b)** to say that you are willing to sell something; ***we offered the house for sale*** **(c)** to say that you are willing to do something; **to offer someone a job** = to tell someone that he can have a job in your company; ***he was offered a directorship with Smith Ltd***; **offered rate** = rate of interest at which banks are prepared to lend each other money

offering ['ɒfrɪŋ] *noun* action of stating that you are prepared to sell something at a certain price; **offering circular** = document which gives information about a company whose shares are being sold to the public for the first time; *US* **initial public offering (IPO)** = offering new shares in a corporation for sale to the public as a way of launching the corporation on the Stock Exchange (NOTE: the British equivalent for this is an **offer for sale**)

> shares of newly public companies posted their worst performance of the year last month as a spate of initial public offerings disappointed followers
>
> *Wall Street Journal*

> if the partnership supports a sale, a public offering of shares would be set for as early as the fourth quarter
>
> *Wall Street Journal*

office ['ɒfɪs] *noun* **(a)** set of rooms where a company works or where business is done; **branch office** = less important office, usually in a different town or country from the main office; **head office** *or* **main office** = office building where the board of directors works and meets; *GB* **registered office** = office address of a company which is officially registered with the Companies' Registrar **(b) office block** *or* **a block of offices** = building which contains only offices; **office hours** = time when an office is open; ***open during normal office hours***; ***do not telephone during office hours***; ***the manager can be reached at home out of office hours***; **office space** *or* **office accommodation** = space available for offices or occupied by offices; **office staff** = people who work in offices; **for office use only** = something which must only be used in an office **(c)** room where someone works and does business; **back office** = (i) the part of a broking firm where the paperwork involved in buying and selling shares is processed; (ii) *US* part of a bank where cheques are processed, statements of account drawn up, etc.) (iii) *US* general administration department of a company (NOTE: also called **operations department**) **(d) employment office** = office which finds jobs for people; **general office** = main administrative office in a company;

information office = office which gives information to tourists or visitors; **inquiry office** = office where someone can answer questions from members of the public **(e)** *GB* government department; **the Foreign Office** = ministry dealing with foreign affairs; **the Home Office** = ministry dealing with the internal affairs of the country; *see also* SERIOUS FRAUD OFFICE **(f)** post or position; **compensation for loss of office** = payment to a director who is asked to leave a company before his contract ends

Office of Fair Trading (OFT) ['ɒfis əv 'feə 'treɪdɪŋ] government department which protects consumers against unfair or illegal business; it also decides if a takeover bid is in the interests of the ordinary customers of the two companies concerned, and may refer such a bid to the Monopolies and Mergers Commission for investigation

Office of Management and Budget (OMB) ['ɒfis əv 'mænɪdʒmənt ənd 'bʌdʒɪt] *US* government department which prepares the budget for the president

officer ['ɒfisə] *noun* person who has an official position; **the company officers** *or* **the officers of a company** = the main executives or directors of a company; **customs officer** = person working for the Customs and Excise Department; **information officer** = person who gives information about a company or about a government department to the public; **personnel officer** = person who deals with the staff, especially interviewing new workers; **training officer** = person who deals with the training of staff in a company

official [ə'fɪʃəl] *adjective* **(a)** from a government department or organization; **speaking in an official capacity** = speaking officially; **to go through official channels** = to deal with officials, especially when making a request; **the official exchange rate** = exchange rate which is imposed by the government; ***the official exchange rate is ten to the dollar, but you can get twice that on the black market***; **official intervention** = attempt by a government to influence the exchange rate, by buying or selling foreign currency; **Official List** = daily publication by the London Stock Exchange of the highest and lowest prices recorded for each share during the trading session; **official market** = the market in shares on the London Stock Exchange (as opposed to the grey market); **the official receiver** = official who is appointed by the courts to run a company which is in financial difficulties, to pay off its debts as far as possible, and to close it down **2** *noun* person working in a government department; **customs official** = person working in the Customs and Excise Department; **high official** = important person in a government department; **minor official** = person in a low position in a government department; **top official** = very important person in a government department

officialese [əfɪʃə'li:z] *noun* language used in government documents which can be difficult to understand

officio [ə'fɪʃiəʊ] *see* EX OFFICIO

offload [ɒf'ləʊd] *verb* to pass something which is not wanted to someone else; **to offload excess stock** = to try to sell excess stock; **to offload costs onto a subsidiary company** = to try to get a subsidiary company to pay some charges so as to reduce tax (NOTE: you offload something **from** a thing or person **onto** another thing or person)

> unless your investment outlook is apocalyptic, do not offload your equity holdings and pile into gilts - you have already missed the boat
>
> *Money Observer*

offre publique d'achat (OPA) ['ɒfr pub'li:k 'dæʃæ] *French* takeover bid

offset [ɒf'set] *verb* to balance one thing against another so that they cancel each other out; ***to offset losses against tax***; ***foreign exchange losses more than offset profits in the domestic market*** (NOTE: **offsetting - offset**)

offshore [ɒf'ʃɔ:] *adjective & adverb* **(a)** on an island or in the sea near to land; ***offshore oil field***; ***offshore oil platform*** **(b)** based outside a country (especially in a tax haven); **offshore account** = account in a tax haven; **offshore banking** = banking in a tax haven; **offshore fund** = fund which is based outside the UK, and usually in a country which has less strict taxation than in the UK, such as the Bahamas, etc.; **offshore investments** = investments which are sold and run by companies licensed in an offshore tax haven, such as Jersey, Guernsey, and the Isle of Man

> the countries most frequently used for traditional tax haven operations now prefer to be known as 'offshore financial centres'
>
> *Accountancy*

off-the-job training ['ɒfðədʒɒb 'treɪnɪŋ] *noun* training given to workers away from their place of work (such as at a college or school)

off-the-shelf company ['ɒfðə'ʃelf 'kʌmpni] *noun* company which has already been registered by an accountant or lawyer, and which is ready for sale to someone who wants to set up a new company quickly

OFT = OFFICE OF FAIR TRADING

oil shares ['ɔɪl 'ʃeəz] *noun* shares in companies engaged in extracting or selling oil and petrol; **oil-exporting countries** = countries which produce oil and sell it to others; **oil-importing countries** = countries which import oil; **oil-producing countries** = countries which produce oil

Old Lady of Threadneedle Street ['əʊld 'leɪdi əv θred'ni:dl 'stri:t] noun *(informal)* the Bank of England

OMB = OFFICE OF MANAGEMENT AND BUDGET

ombudsman ['ɒmbʊdzmən] *noun* an official who investigates complaints by the public against government departments or other large organizations

> COMMENT: there are several ombudsmen: the main one is the Parliamentary Commissioner, who is a civil servant who investigates complaints against government departments. The Banking Ombudsman and the Building Societies Ombudsman are independent officials who investigates complaints by the public against banks or building societies

omission [ə'mɪʃən] *noun* thing which has been omitted; **errors and omissions excepted** = words written on an invoice to show that the company has no responsibility for mistakes in the invoice

omit [ə'mɪt] *verb* not to do something which should be done; *US* **to omit a dividend** = to pay no dividend in a certain year (NOTE: the British equivalent is **to pass a dividend**)

OMLX = LONDON SECURITIES & DERIVATIVES EXCHANGE

oncosts ['ɒnkɒsts] *plural noun* fixed costs, money paid in producing a product which does not increase with the quantity of the product made

one-man ['wɒn'mæn] adjective **one-man business** *or* **firm** *or* **company** *or* **operation** = business run by one person alone with no staff or partners (NOTE: also informally called a **one-man band**)

one-off ['wɒnɒf] *adjective* done or made only once; ***one-off item***; ***one-off deal***

one-sided ['wɒn'saɪdɪd] *adjective* which favours one side and not the other in a negotiation; ***one-sided agreement***

one-stop banking ['wɒn'stɒp 'bæŋkɪŋ] *noun* banking organization offering a whole range of services (including mortgages, loans, pensions, etc.) (NOTE: also called **full-service banking**)

one-stop shopping ['wɒn'stɒp 'ʃɒpɪŋ] *noun* taking a range of financial services from a single organization (a bank may offer loans, mortgages, pensions, insurance as well as the normal personal banking services) (NOTE: also called a **financial supermarket**)

one-way ['wɒnweɪ] adjective **one-way ticket** = ticket for a journey from one place to another; **one-way trade** = situation where one country sells to another, but does not buy anything in return

one-year money ['wɒnjə: 'mʌni] *noun* money placed for one year

onerous ['ɒnərəs] *adjective* needing a lot of effort or money; **the repayment terms are particularly onerous** = the loan is particularly difficult to pay back

on line *or* **online** [ɒn'laɪn] *adverb* linked directly to a mainframe computer; ***the sales office is on line to the warehouse***; ***we get our data on line from the stock control department***; ***you can get real-time stock quotes on-line***; ***on-line stock trading via the Internet***

o.n.o. ['əʊ 'en 'əʊ] = OR NEAR OFFER

on-the-job training ['ɒnðədʒɒb 'treɪnɪŋ] *noun* training given to workers at their place of work

OPA ['əʊ 'peɪ 'æ] *French* = *OFFRE PUBLIQUE D'ACHAT*

OPEC ['əʊpek] = ORGANIZATION OF PETROLEUM EXPORTING COUNTRIES

open ['əʊpən] **1** *adjective* **(a)** at work, not closed; ***not many banks are open on Saturdays***; ***our offices are open from 9 to 6***; ***they are open for business every day of the week*** **(b)** ready to accept something; **the job is open to all applicants** = anyone can apply for the job; **open to offers** = ready to accept a reasonable offer; **the company is open to offers for the empty factory** = the company is ready to discuss an offer which is lower than the suggested price **(c) open account** = unsecured credit, amount owed with no security; **open cheque** = cheque which is not crossed and can be cashed anywhere; **open credit** = bank credit given to good customers without security up to a certain maximum sum; **open market** = market where anyone can buy or sell; **to buy shares on the open market** = to buy shares on the Stock Exchange, not privately; **open market operation** = sale or purchase of government stock by ordinary investors, used by the government as a means of influencing money supply; **open ticket** = ticket which can be used on any date; *see also* OPEN OUTCRY SYSTEM **2** *verb* **(a)** to start a new business working; ***she has opened a shop in the High Street; we have opened an office in London*** **(b)** to start work or to be at work; ***the office opens at 9 a.m.; we open for business on Sundays*** **(c)** to begin; **to open negotiations** = to begin negotiating; ***he opened the discussions with a description of the product; the chairman opened the meeting at 10.30*** **(d)** to start or to allow something to start; ***to open a bank account; to open a line of credit; to open a loan*** **(e) the shares opened lower** = share prices were lower at the beginning of the day's trading

open-ended *US* **open-end** ['əupən'endɪd *or* 'əupən'end] **1** *adjective* with no fixed limit or with some items not specified; **open-ended credit** = REVOLVING CREDIT; **open-ended fund** = fund (such as a unit trust) where investors buy units, the money paid being invested in a range of securities (as opposed to a closed fund, such as an investment trust, where the investor buys shares in the trust company, and receives dividends) **2** *verb US* **to open-end** = to make a fund open-ended

---

it was trading at a steep discount, with an eye toward open-ending the fund

Barron's

Open-ended investment company (Oeic) ['əupən'endɪd ɪn'vestmənt 'kʌmpni] *noun* new form of unit trust, in which the investor purchases shares at a single price, as opposed to the offer/bid pricing system used by ordinary unit trusts

---

Oeics are 'open-ended' accepting any amount of investors' money on an on-going basis, but structured as a company with shares. Most importantly, the shares have a single price for both buying and selling

The Times

---

opening ['əupənɪŋ] **1** *noun* **(a)** act of starting a new business; ***the opening of a new branch; the opening of a new market*** *or* ***of a new distribution network*** **(b) opening hours** = hours when a shop or business is open **2** *adjective* at the beginning, first; **opening balance** = balance at the beginning of an accounting period; **opening bid** = first bid at an auction; **opening entry** = first entry in an account; **opening price** = price at the start of the day's trading; **opening stock** = stock at the beginning of the accounting period

---

after opening at 79.1 the index touched a peak of 79.2 and then drifted to a low of 78.8

Financial Times

---

operate ['ɒpəreɪt] *verb* to do business; ***the company mainly operates in the Far East***

---

the company gets valuable restaurant locations which will be converted to the family-style restaurant chain that it operates and franchises throughout most parts of the US

Fortune

---

operating ['ɒpəreɪtɪŋ] *noun* general running of a business or of a machine; **operating budget** = forecast of income and expenditure over a period of time; **operating costs** *or* **operating expenses** = costs of the day-to-day organization of a company; **operating manual** = book which shows how to work a machine; **operating earnings** *or* **operating profit** *or* **operating income** = profit made by a company in its usual business (usually calculated after tax has been paid); **operating loss** = loss made by a company in its usual business (usually calculated after tax has been paid); **operating system** = the main program which operates a computer

---

we mined just under four million ounces of gold last year - the most by any North American company ever. Operating earnings climbed 70%

Fortune

---

in the next quarter the company will save over $50 million in operating income from deals

Smart Money

---

the company blamed over-capacity and competitive market conditions in Europe for a £14m operating loss last year

Financial Times

---

operation [ɒpə'reɪʃən] *noun* **(a)** business organization and work; ***the company's***

operations in West Africa; *he heads up the operations in Northern Europe;* US **operations department** = general administration department of a company (NOTE: also called **back office**); **operations review** = examining the way in which a company or department works to see how it can be made more efficient and profitable; **a franchising operation** = selling licences to trade as a franchise **(b) Stock Exchange operation** = buying or selling of shares on the Stock Exchange

> a leading manufacturer of business, industrial and commercial products requires a branch manager to head up its mid-western Canada operations based in Winnipeg
>
> *Globe and Mail (Toronto)*

operational [ɒpə'reɪʃənl] *adjective* referring to how something works; **operational budget** = forecast of expenditure on running a business; **operational costs** = costs of running a business; **operational gearing** = situation where a company has high fixed costs which are funded by borrowings; **operational planning** = planning how a business is to be run; **operational research** = study of a company's way of working to see if it can be made more efficient and profitable

operator ['ɒpəreɪtə] *noun* person who runs a business; *(on the Stock Exchange)* person who buys and sells shares hoping to make a quick profit

> a number of block bookings by American tour operators have been cancelled
>
> *Economist*

OPM ['əʊ 'pi: 'em] = OTHER PEOPLE'S MONEY money which a business 'borrows' from its creditors, such as by not paying invoices on schedule, and so avoids using its own funds

opportunity [ɒpə'tju:nəti] *noun* situation where you can do something successfully; **investment opportunities** *or* **sales opportunities** = possibilities for making investments or sales which will be profitable; **a market opportunity** = possibility of going into a market for the first time; **opportunity cost** = value of another method of investment which could have been used, instead of the one adopted

oppose [ə'pəʊz] *verb* to try to stop something happening; to vote against something; *a minority of board members opposed the motion*; *we are all opposed to the takeover*

optimal ['ɒptɪməl] *adjective* best

optimism ['ɒptɪmɪzm] *noun* being sure that everything will work out well; *he has considerable optimism about sales possibilities in the Far East*; **market optimism** = feeling that the stock market will rise (NOTE: the opposite is **pessimism**)

optimistic [ɒptɪ'mɪstɪk] *adjective* feeling sure that everything will work out well; **he takes an optimistic view of the exchange rate** = he expects the exchange rate will go in his favour (NOTE: the opposite is **pessimistic**)

optimum ['ɒptɪməm] *adjective* best; *the market offers optimum conditions for sales*

option ['ɒpʃən] *noun* **(a) option to purchase** *or* **to sell** = giving someone the possibility to buy or sell something within a period of time; **first option** = allowing someone to be the first to have the possibility of deciding something; **to grant someone a six-month option on a product** = to allow someone six months to decide if he wants to be the agent or if he wants to manufacture the product, etc.; **to take up an option** *or* **to exercise an option** = to accept the option which has been offered and to put it into action; *he exercised his option or he took up his option to acquire sole marketing rights to the product*; **I want to leave my options open** = I want to be able to decide what to do when the time is right; **to take the soft option** = to decide to do something which involves the least risk, effort or problems **(b)** *(Stock Exchange)* giving someone the right to buy or sell a security, a financial instrument, a commodity, etc., at a certain price on a certain date; **call option** = option to buy shares at a certain price; **double option** = option to buy or sell at a certain price in the future (a combination of call and put options); **put option** = option to sell shares at a certain price; **share option** = right to buy or sell shares at a certain price at a time in the future; **stock option** = right to buy shares at a cheap price given by a company to its employees; **writer of an option** = person who sells an option; **option contract** = right to buy or sell shares at a fixed price; **option dealing** *or* **option trading** = buying and selling share options; **traded options** = options to buy or sell shares at a certain price at a certain date in the future, which themselves can be bought or sold (in London, this is done through the Traded Options Market or TOM); **option holder** = person who holds an option (i.e., who has bought an option)

optional ['ɒpʃənl] *adjective* which can be added if the customer wants; ***the insurance cover is optional***

order ['ɔ:də] *noun* **(a)** arrangement of records (filing cards, invoices, etc.); **alphabetical order** = arrangement by the letters of the alphabet (A, B, C, etc.); **chronological order** = arrangement by the order of the dates; ***the reports are filed in chronological order***; **numerical order** = arrangement by numbers; ***put these invoices in numerical order*** **(b)** document which allows money to be paid to someone; ***he sent us an order on the Chartered Bank***; **banker's order** *or* **standing order** = order written by a customer asking a bank to make a regular payment; ***he pays his subscription by banker's order***; **money order** = document which can be bought for sending money through the post **(c) pay to Mr Smith or order** = pay money to Mr Smith or as he orders; **pay to the order of Mr Smith** = pay money directly into Mr Smith's account; **order cheque** = cheque which is paid to a named person with the words 'or order' after the payee's name, showing that he can endorse it and pass it to someone else if he wishes **(d)** *(Stock Exchange)* instruction to a broker to buy or sell; **market order** = order to a broker to buy or sell at the current price; **stop-loss order** = instruction to a stockbroker to sell a share if the price falls to a certain level **(e)** official request for goods to be supplied; **to fill** *or* **to fulfil an order** = to supply items which have been ordered; **purchase order** = official paper which places an order for something; **order fulfilment** = supplying items which have been ordered; **terms: cash with order** = the goods will be supplied only if payment in cash is made at the same time as the order is placed; **items available to order only** = items which will be manufactured only if someone orders them; **on order** = ordered but not delivered; **unfulfilled orders** *or* **back orders** *or* **outstanding orders** = orders received in the past and not yet supplied; **order book** = record of orders; **the company has a full order book** = it has enough orders to work at full capacity; **a pad of order forms** = a pad of blank sheets for orders to be written on

order-driven system ['ɔ:də'drɪvn 'sɪstəm] price system on a stock exchange, where prices vary according to the level of orders (as opposed to a 'quote-driven' system)

in the view of some professionals, an order-driven market where investors' buy and sell orders are matched, might prove more appropriate for private individuals than the present marketmaking system which concentrates on high turnover shares

Accountancy

ordinary ['ɔ:dnri] *adjective* **(a)** normal, not special; **ordinary resolution** = resolution put before an AGM, usually referring to some general procedural matter, and which requires a simple majority of votes to be accepted; **ordinary shares** = normal shares in a company, which have no special bonuses or restrictions (NOTE: the American term is **common stock**); **ordinary shareholder** = person who owns ordinary shares in a company; **ordinary share capital** = capital of a company in the form of money paid for ordinary shares; **FT Ordinary Share Index** = index based on the market prices of thirty blue-chip companies (this index is the oldest of the FT indices, and is now considered too narrow to have much relevance) **(b)** *US* **ordinary interest** = annual interest calculated on the basis of 360 days (as opposed to 'exact interest' which is calculated on 365 days)

organic growth [ɔ:'gænɪk 'grəʊθ] *noun* internal growth, the expansion of a company which is based on profits from its existing trading (as opposed to external growth, which comes from the acquisition of other companies)

organization [ɔ:gənaɪ'zeɪʃən] *noun* **(a)** way of arranging something so that it works efficiently; ***the chairman handles the organization of the AGM***; ***the organization of the group is too centralized to be efficient***; ***the organization of the head office into departments***; **organization and methods (O&M)** = examining how an office works, and suggesting how it can be made more efficient; **organization chart** = list of people working in various departments, showing how a company or office is organized; **line organization** = organization of a business where each manager is responsible for doing what his superior tells him to do **(b)** group or institution which is arranged for efficient work; **a government organization** = official body, run by the government; **a travel organization** = body representing companies in the travel business; **an employers' organization** = group of employers with similar interests

working with a client base which includes many major commercial organizations and nationalized industries

Times

organizational [ɔ:gənaɪ'zeɪʃənl] *adjective* referring to the way in which something is organized; ***the paper gives a diagram of the company's organizational structure***

Organization for Economic Co-operation and Development (OECD) organization of 29 industrialized countries, aimed at encouraging international trade, wealth and employment in member countries, etc.

Organization of Petroleum Exporting Countries (OPEC) group of major countries who are producers and exporters of oil

organize ['ɔ:gənaɪz] *verb* to arrange something so that it works

we organize a rate with importers who have large orders and guarantee them space at a fixed rate so that they can plan their costs

Lloyd's List

originating fee [ə'rɪdʒɪneɪtɪŋ 'fi:] *noun US* front-end fee charged to cover the costs of dealing with an application for a loan

orphan stock ['ɔ:fən 'stɒk] *noun* neglected share, which is not often recommended by market analysts

the market could not get enough Britannic shares yesterday, fuelling an 11 per cent stock price rise. But aside from the boost provided by the orphan assets, where is the new profit going to come from?

The Times

OTC = OVER-THE-COUNTER

other people's money ['ʌðə 'pi:plz 'mʌni:] *see* OPM

ouguiya [u:'gi:jə] *noun* currency used in Mauretania

ounce [aʊns] *noun* measure of weight which equals 28 grams; **troy ounce** = measurement of weight for gold and other metals, such as silver and platinum (= 31.10 grammes) (NOTE: in writing, often shortened to **oz.** after figures: **25.2oz.**)

out [aʊt] *adverb* **(a)** on strike; ***the workers have been out on strike for four weeks***; ***as soon as the management made the offer, the staff came out***; ***the shop stewards called the workforce out*** **(b) to be out** = to be wrong in calculating something; ***the balance is £10 out***; **we are £20,000 out in our calculations** = we have £20,000 too much or too little; **out of the money** = option to buy at a higher price or to sell at a lower price than a share is currently trading at

outbid [aʊt'bɪd] *verb* to offer a better price than someone else; ***we offered £100,000 for the warehouse, but another company outbid us*** (NOTE: **outbidding - outbid**)

outcry ['əʊtkraɪ] noun **open outcry system** = system of buying and selling used in some exchanges, where the brokers shout prices, offers or orders to each other

trading on the small floor is by open outcry, but conditions have grown so crowded that resilient vocal cords and a flair for attracting attention are essential for getting through the day's business

Financial Times

outflow ['aʊtfləʊ] *noun* **(a) outflow of capital from a country** = capital which is sent out of a country for investment abroad **(b) outflows** = withdrawal of money invested in a fund (NOTE: the opposite is **inflow**)

Nigeria recorded foreign exchange outflow of N972.9 million for the month of June 1985

Business Times (Lagos)

a spokesman for the company declined to comment about the outflows, but performance has been a problem

Wall Street Journal

they've been grappling with the outflows of investor cash for some time, and management doesn't expect the bleeding to stop until at least next year

Wall Street Journal

outgoings [aʊt'gəʊɪŋz] *plural noun* money which is paid out

outlay ['aʊtleɪ] *noun* money spent, expenditure; **capital outlay** = money spent on fixed assets (such as property, machinery, furniture); **for a modest outlay** = for a small sum

outlook ['aʊtlʊk] *noun* view of what is going to happen in the future; ***the economic outlook is not good***; ***the stock market outlook is worrying***

> American demand has transformed the profit outlook for many European manufacturers
>
> *Duns Business Month*

out-of-date cheque ['aʊt əv 'deɪt 'tʃek] *noun* cheque which has not been cleared because its date is too old, normally more than six months

out-of-favour *US* **out-of-favor** ['əʊt əv 'feɪvə] *adjective and adverb* neglected, not liked

> they also look for less risky out-of-favor company on the verge of a comeback
>
> *Smart Money*

> the funds that did the best were those that held both growth companies with rising earnings and value, or out-of-favor stocks
>
> *Smart Money*

out of pocket ['aʊt əv 'pɒkɪt] *adjective & adverb* having paid out money personally; ***the deal has left me out of pocket***; **out-of-pocket expenses** = amount of money paid to an employee to pay him back for his own money which he has spent on company business

outperform [əʊtpə'fɔːm] *verb* to do better than other companies

> he demonstrated that small companies and those with a low price/book ratio outperform over time
>
> *Smart Money*

> these funds can often outperform when the market gets unsettling
>
> *Smart Money*

> on the fairly safe assumption that there is little to be gained in attempting to find the share or trust that outperforms everything else, there is every reason to buy an index-tracking fund
>
> *Money Observer*

outperformance [əʊtpə'fɔːməns] *noun* doing better than other companies

> our argument was that despite the extra volatility investors would shoulder, there was real opportunity for outperformance
>
> *Smart Money*

output ['aʊtpʊt] *noun* amount which a company or a person or a machine produces; ***output has increased by 10%***; ***25% of our output is exported***; **output per hour** = amount produced in one hour; **output bonus** = extra payment for increased production; **output tax** = VAT charged by a company on goods or services sold

> crude oil output plunged during the last month and is likely to remain near its present level for the near future
>
> *Wall Street Journal*

outright ['aʊtraɪt] *adverb & adjective* completely; **to purchase something outright** *or* **to make an outright purchase** = to buy something completely, including all rights in it

outsell [aʊt'sel] *verb* to sell more than someone; ***the company is easily outselling its competitors*** (NOTE: **outselling - outsold**)

outside ['aʊtsaɪd] *adjective & adverb* not in a company's office or building; **to send work to be done outside** = to send work to be done in other offices; **outside office hours** = when the office is not open; **outside dealer** = person who is not a member of the Stock Exchange but is allowed to trade; **outside director** = director who is not employed by the company, a non-executive director; **outside line** = line from an internal office telephone system to the main telephone exchange; **outside shareholders** = minority shareholders; **outside worker** = worker who does not work in a company's offices

outstanding [aʊt'stændɪŋ] *adjective* not yet paid or completed; **outstanding cheque** = cheque which has been written and therefore has been entered in the company's ledgers, but which has not been presented for payment and so has not been debited from the company's bank account; **outstanding debts** = debts which are waiting to be paid; **outstanding orders** = orders received but not yet supplied; **what is the amount outstanding?** = how much money is still owed?; **matters outstanding from the previous meeting** = questions which were not settled at the previous meeting

outturn ['aʊttɜːn] *noun* amount produced by a country or company

outvote [aʊt'vəʊt] *verb* to defeat in a vote; **the chairman was outvoted** = the majority voted against the chairman

overall [əʊvər'ɔːl] *adjective* covering or including everything; **although some divisions traded profitably, the company**

reported an overall fall in profits = the company reported a general fall in profits; **overall plan** = plan which covers everything

overbook [əʊvəˈbʊk] *verb* to book more people than there are seats or rooms available; ***the hotel or the flight was overbooked***

overbooking [əʊvəˈbʊkɪŋ] *noun* booking of more people than there are seats or rooms available

overborrowed [əʊvəˈbɒrəʊd] *adjective* (company) which has very high borrowings compared to its assets, and has difficulty in meeting its interest payments

overbought [əʊvəˈbɔːt] *adjective* having bought too much; **the market is overbought** = prices on the stock market are too high, because there have been too many buyers

> they said the market was overbought when the index was between 860 and 870 points
>
> *Australian Financial Review*

overcapacity [əʊvəkəˈpæsɪti] *noun* unused capacity for producing something

> with the present overcapacity situation in the airline industry the discounting of tickets is widespread
>
> *Business Traveller*

overcapitalized [əʊvəˈkæpɪtəlaɪzd] *adjective* with more capital in a company than it needs

overcharge 1 [ˈəʊvətʃɑːdʒ] *noun* charge which is higher than it should be; ***to pay back an overcharge*** **2** [əʊvəˈtʃɑːdʒ] *verb* to ask too much money; ***they overcharged us for meals***; ***we asked for a refund because we had been overcharged***

overdraft [ˈəʊvədrɑːft] *noun* **(a)** *GB* amount of money which a company or person can withdraw from a bank account with the bank's permission, and which is more than there is in the account (NOTE: in American English this is **overdraft protection**); ***the bank has allowed me an overdraft of £5,000***; **overdraft facilities** = arrangement with a bank to have an overdraft; **we have exceeded our overdraft facilities** = we have taken out more than the overdraft allowed by the bank; **overdraft limit** = total which is agreed between the bank and a customer as the maximum amount the customer's account may be overdrawn; **to exceed your overdraft limit** = to write cheques on your account which take your overdraft past its agreed limit **(b)** *US* amount of a cheque which is more than the money in the account on which it is drawn

overdraw [əʊvəˈdrɔː] *verb* to take out more money from a bank account than there is in it; **your account is overdrawn** *or* **you are overdrawn** = you have paid out more money from your account than you have in it (NOTE: **overdrawing - overdrew - overdrawn**)

overdue [əʊvəˈdjuː] *adjective* which has not been paid on time; **interest payments are three weeks overdue** = interest payments which should have been made three weeks ago; *compare* OUTSTANDING

overestimate [əʊvərˈestɪmeɪt] *verb* to think something is larger or worse than it really is; ***he overestimated the amount of time needed to fit out the factory***

overexposure [əʊvəɪkˈspəʊʒə] *noun* being too exposed to risky loans

overextend [əʊvərɪkˈstend] verb **the company overextended itself** = the company borrowed more money than its assets would allow

overfunding [əʊvəˈfʌndɪŋ] *noun* situation where the government borrows more money than it needs for expenditure, by selling too much government stock

overgeared [əʊvəˈgiːəd] *adjective* (company) which has high borrowings in comparison to its assets

overhang [əʊvəˈhæŋ] **1** verb *(of a large number of shares)* **to overhang the market** = to be available for sale, and so depress the share price **2** *noun* large quantity of shares or of a commodity or of unsold stock available for sale, which has the effect of depressing the market price

> according to a gold trader, the central bank overhang accounted for much of gold's recent dismal performance (along with the short sales by hedge funds)
>
> *Fortune*

> unexpectedly weak retail sales warned that retailers could be facing significant stock overhangs after a dismal Christmas
>
> *The Times*

overhead [ˈəʊvəhed] **1** adjective **overhead costs** *or* **expenses** = money spent on the day-to-day cost of a business; **overhead budget** = plan of probable overhead costs **2** noun **overheads** *US* **overhead** = costs of the day-to-day running of a business or of part of a business (i.e., any cost, other than the cost of the goods offered for sale); ***the sales revenue covers the manufacturing costs but not the overheads***

> it ties up less capital in inventory and with its huge volume spreads out costs over bigger sales; add in low overhead (i.e. minimum staff, no deliveries, no credit cards) and a warehouse club can offer bargain prices
>
> *Duns Business Month*

overheating [əʊvəˈhiːtɪŋ] *noun* rise in industrial activity in an economy, leading to a rise in inflation (the economy is then said to be 'overheated')

overnight [əʊvəˈnaɪt] *adverb* from the evening of one day to the morning of the next; **overnight money** = money deposited for less than 24 hours; **overnight repo** = repurchase agreement, where banks sell securities for cash and repurchase them the next day at a higher price (used by central banks as a means of regulating the money markets)

overpay [əʊvəˈpeɪ] *verb* **(a)** to pay too much; ***we overpaid the invoice by $245*** **(b)** to pay an extra amount to reduce the total capital borrowed on a mortgage; *see also* ANNUAL REST SYSTEM

overpaid [əʊvəˈpeɪd] *adjective* paid too much; ***our staff are overpaid and underworked***

overpayment [əʊvəˈpeɪmənt] *noun* **(a)** paying too much **(b)** payment of a lump sum to reduce the capital borrowed on a mortgage

overrated [əʊvəˈreɪtɪd] *adjective* valued more highly than it should be; ***the effect of the dollar on European business cannot be overrated***; ***their 'first-class service' is very overrated***

overrider *or* **overriding commission** [ˈəʊvəraɪdə or ˈəʊvəraɪdɪŋ kəˈmɪʃən] *noun* special extra commission which is above all other commissions

overseas [əʊvəˈsiːz] **1** *adjective* across the sea or to foreign countries; **overseas bank** = (i) British bank which mainly trades overseas; (ii) foreign bank with branches in the UK; **overseas division** = section of a company dealing with trade with other countries; **overseas markets** = markets in foreign countries; **overseas funds** = investment funds based in other countries; **overseas trade** = trade with foreign countries **2** *noun* foreign countries; ***the profits from overseas are far higher than those of the home division***

oversell [əʊvəˈsel] *verb* to sell more than you can produce; **he is oversold** = he has agreed to sell more product than he can produce; **the market is oversold** = stock market prices are too low, because there have been too many sellers (NOTE: **overselling - oversold**)

overspend [əʊvəˈspend] *verb* to spend too much; **to overspend your budget** = to spend more money than is allowed in your budget (NOTE: **overspending - overspent**)

overspending [əʊvəˈspendɪŋ] *noun* spending more than is allowed; ***the board decided to limit the overspending by the production departments***

overstock [əʊvəˈstɒk] **1** *verb* to have more stock than is needed; **to be overstocked with spare parts** = to have too many spare parts in stock **2** *plural noun* US **overstocks** = more stock than is needed to supply orders; ***we will have to sell off the overstocks to make room in the warehouse***

> Cash paid for your stock: any quantity, any products, overstocked lines, factory seconds
>
> *Australian Financial Review*

oversubscribe [əʊvəsʌbˈskraɪb] verb **the share offer was oversubscribed six times** = people applied for six times as many new shares as were available

oversubscription [əʊvəsʌbˈskrɪpʃn] *noun* subscribing for more shares in a new issue than are being issued

over-the-counter (OTC) [əʊvəðəˈkaʊntə] *adjective* US **over-the-counter market** = market in shares which are not listed on the Stock Exchange; **over-the-counter sales** = legal selling of shares which are not listed in the official Stock Exchange list (usually carried out by telephone); ***this share is available on the over-the-counter market***

overtime [ˈəʊvətaɪm] **1** *noun* hours worked more than the normal working time; ***to work six hours' overtime***; ***the overtime rate is one and a half times normal pay***; **overtime ban** = order by a trade union which forbids overtime work by its members; **overtime pay** = pay for extra time worked **2** *adverb* **to work overtime** = to work longer hours than in the contract of employment

overtrading [əuvə'treɪdɪŋ] noun *(of a company)* trading too much, so that it runs short of cash

overvalue [əuvə'væljuː] *verb* to give a higher value than is right; **these shares are overvalued at £1.25** = the shares are worth less than the £1.25 for which they are selling; **the pound is overvalued against the dollar** = the exchange rate gives too many dollars to the pound, given the strength of the two countries' economies (NOTE: the opposite is **undervalued**)

owe [əu] *verb* to have to pay money; ***he owes the bank £250,000***; **he owes the company for the stock he purchased** = he has not paid for the stock

owing ['əuɪŋ] *adjective* which is owed; ***money owing to the directors***; ***how much is still owing to the company by its debtors?***

own [əun] *verb* to have or to possess; ***he owns 50% of the shares***; **a wholly-owned subsidiary** = a subsidiary which belongs completely to the parent company; **a state-owned industry** = an industry which is nationalized

owner ['əunə] *noun* person who owns something; ***the owners of a company are its shareholders***; **sole owner** = person who owns something by himself; **owners' equity** = value of the shares in a company owned by the owners of the company; **owner-occupier** = person who owns and lives in a house; **goods sent at owner's risk** = situation where the owner has to insure the goods while they are being transported

ownership ['əunəʃɪp] *noun* act of owning something; **common** *or* **collective ownership** = situation where a business is owned by the workers who work in it; **joint ownership** = situation where two people own the same property; **public ownership** *or* **state ownership** = situation where an industry is nationalized; **private ownership** = situation where a company is owned by private shareholders; **the ownership of the company has passed to the banks** = the banks have become owners of the company

oz = OUNCE

Pp

P&L = PROFIT AND LOSS

P* ['pi: 'stɑ:] *US* measure of M2 shown as a ratio of the velocity of money, used as an indication of inflation

p.a. = PER ANNUM

pa'anga [pæ'æŋgə] *noun* currency used in Tonga

Pacific Rim [pə'sɪfɪk 'rɪm] *noun* countries on the edge of the Pacific Ocean: Hong Kong, Japan, Korea, Malaysia, Singapore, Thailand, Taiwan, etc.

> Pacific Rim equities may appear cheap, but investors should remain wary of them
>
> *Investors Chronicle*

package ['pækɪdʒ] *noun* group of different items joined together in one deal; **pay package** *or* **salary package** *US* **compensation package** = salary and other benefits offered with a job; ***the job carries an attractive salary package***; **package deal** = agreement where several different items are agreed at the same time

> the remuneration package will include an attractive salary, profit sharing and a company car
>
> *Times*

Pac-man ['pækmæn] *noun* method of defence against a takeover bid, where the target company threatens to take over the company which is trying to take it over

> the Pac-man defence, where a target company turns the tables on an unwanted predator and makes a bid for the bidder, was last used in the UK ten years ago
>
> *Financial Times*

paid [peɪd] *adjective* with money given **(a) paid holidays** = holidays where the worker's wages are still paid even though he is not working **(b) paid assistant** = assistant who receives a salary **(c)** which has been settled; ***carriage paid***; ***tax paid***; **paid bills** = bills which have been settled; ***the invoice is marked 'paid'*** **(d) paid-in capital** = capital in a business which has been provided by its shareholders (usually in the form of payments for shares above their par value); **paid-up capital** = all money paid by shareholders for the issued capital shares; **paid-up shares** = shares which have been completely paid for by the shareholders; *see also* PARTLY PAID, PAY UP

PAN = PRIMARY ACCOUNT NUMBER

panel ['pænl] noun **panel of experts** = group of people who give advice on a problem; **consumer panel** = group of consumers who report on goods they have used so that the manufacturer can improve the goods, or use the consumers' reports in his advertising; **Panel on Takeovers and Mergers** *or* **Takeover Panel** = non-statutory body which examines takeovers and applies the City Code on Takeovers and Mergers

panic ['pænɪk] *noun* state of being frightened; **panic buying** = rush to buy something at any price because stocks may run out or because the price may rise; ***panic buying of sugar*** *or* ***of dollars***; **panic selling of sterling** = rush to sell sterling at any price because of possible devaluation

paper ['peɪpə] *noun* **(a) on paper** = in theory; ***on paper the system is ideal, but we have to see it working before we will sign the contract***; **paper loss** = loss made when an asset has fallen in value but has not been sold; **paper gain** *or* **paper profit** = profit made when an asset has increased in value but has not been sold (NOTE: also called **unrealized profit**); **paper millionaire** = person who owns shares or bonds which, if he sold them, would make him a millionaire **(b)** documents which can represent money (bills of exchange, promissory notes, etc.); **bankable paper** = document which a bank will accept as security for a loan; **negotiable paper** = document which can be transferred from one owner to another for money **(c)** shares in the form of share certificates; **paper offer** = takeover bid, where the purchasing company offers its shares in exchange for shares in the company being taken over (as opposed to a cash offer) **(d) paper money** *or* **paper currency** = banknotes

the profits were tax-free and the interest on the loans they incurred qualified for income tax relief; the paper gains were rarely changed into spending money

Investors Chronicle

paperchase ['peɪpətʃeɪs] *noun* takeover bid where the purchasing company issues large numbers of new shares to offer in exchange for the shares in the company being bought

paperwork ['peɪpəwɜ:k] *noun* office work, especially writing memos and filling in forms; ***exporting to Russia involves a large amount of paperwork***

par [pɑ:] *adjective & noun* equal, at the same price; **par value** = face value, the value printed on a share certificate; **shares at par** = shares whose market price is the same as their face value; **shares above par** *or* **below par** = shares with a market price higher or lower than their par value

parachute ['pærəʃu:t] *noun* **golden parachute** = special contract for a director of a company, which gives him advantageous financial terms if he has to resign when the company is taken over

parallel markets ['pærælel 'mɑ:kɪts] *noun* money markets, where institutions such as banks, or organizations such as local authorities, can lend or borrow money without having to go through the main money markets (securities traded on the parallel markets include certificates of deposit, local authority bonds, etc.)

parameter [pə'ræmɪtə] *noun* fixed limit; ***the budget parameters are fixed by the finance director***; ***spending by each department has to fall within certain parameters***

parcel ['pɑ:sl] noun **parcel of shares** = group of shares (such as 50 or 100) which are sold as a group; ***the shares are on offer in parcels of 2000***

parent company ['peərənt 'kʌmpni] *noun* company which owns more than 50% of the shares of another company; *compare* HOLDING COMPANY

Pareto's Law [pə'ri:təʊz 'lɔ:] *noun* the theory that a small percentage of a total can have a large effect on the rest (also called the 80/20 law, because 80/20 is the normal ratio between majority and minority figures: so 20% of accounts produce 80% of turnover; 80% of GDP enriches 20% of the population, etc.)

pari passu ['pæri 'pæsu:] *Latin phrase* meaning 'equally'; ***the new shares will rank pari passu with the existing ones***

Paris Club ['pærɪs 'klʌb] the Group of Ten, the major world economic powers working within the framework of the IMF (there are in fact eleven: Belgium, Canada, France, Germany, Italy, Japan, Netherlands, Sweden, Switzerland, United Kingdom and the United States. It is called the 'Paris Club' because its first meeting was in Paris)

the country has reached a debt rescheduling agreement with the Paris club of government creditors

The Banker

parity ['pærəti] *noun* (i) being at an equal price with something else; (ii) the base figures, against which other figures are compared; (iii) official exchange rate against another currency, such as the dollar; **the pound fell to parity with the dollar** = (i) the pound fell to a point where one pound equalled one dollar; (ii) the pound fell to a point where it was at its official exchange rate with the dollar

the draft report on changes in the international monetary system casts doubt about any return to fixed exchange-rate parities

Wall Street Journal

Parkinson's law ['pɑ:kɪnsnz 'lɔ:] *noun* law, based on wide experience, that in business as in government the amount of work increases to fill the time available for it

part [pɑ:t] *noun* **(a) in part** = not completely; ***to contribute in part to the costs*** *or* ***to pay the costs in part*** **(b) part-owner** = person who owns something jointly with one or more other persons; ***he is part-owner of the restaurant***; **part-ownership** = situation where two or more persons own the same property **(c) part exchange** = giving an old product as part of the payment for a new one; ***they refused to take my old car as part exchange for the new one***; **part-paid** = PARTLY PAID; **part payment** = paying of part of a whole payment; ***I gave him £250 as part payment for the car***; **part delivery** *or* **part order** *or* **part shipment** = delivering or shipping only some of the items in an order

partial ['pɑ:ʃəl] *adjective* not complete; **partial loss** = situation where only part of the insured property has been damaged or lost; **he got partial compensation for the damage to his house** = he was compensated for part of the damage

participate [pɑːˈtɪsɪpeɪt] *verb* to take part in; **participating preference shares** US **participating preferred stock** = preference shares which get an extra bonus dividend if company profits reach a certain level

participation [pɑːtɪsɪˈpeɪʃən] *noun* taking part; **participation fee** = fee paid to a bank for taking part in underwriting a loan

participator [pɑːˈtɪsɪpeɪtə] *noun* person who has an interest in a company (an ordinary or preference shareholder, a creditor, the owner of rights to shares, etc.)

particular average [pəˈtɪkjʊlə] *noun* situation where part of a shipment is lost or damaged and the insurance costs are borne by the owner of the lost goods (he receives no compensation from the other owners of the shipment)

partly [ˈpɑːtli] *adverb* not completely; **partly-paid capital** = capital which represents partly-paid shares; **partly-paid shares** = shares where the shareholders have not paid the full face value; **partly-secured creditors** = creditors whose debts are not fully covered by the value of the security

partner [ˈpɑːtnə] *noun* person who works in a business and has an equal share in it with others; ***he became a partner in a firm of solicitors***; **active partner** *or* **working partner** = partner who works in a partnership; **junior partner** *or* **senior partner** = person who has a small or large part of the shares in a partnership; **sleeping partner** US **silent partner** = partner who has a share in a business but does not work in it

partnership [ˈpɑːtnəʃɪp] *noun* **(a)** unregistered business where two or more people share the risks and profits equally; **to go into partnership with someone** = to join with someone to form a partnership; **to offer someone a partnership, to take someone into partnership with you** = to have a working business and bring someone in to share it with you; **to dissolve a partnership** = to bring a partnership to an end; **partnership agreement** *or* **articles of partnership** = document setting up a partnership, giving the details of the business and the amount each partner is contributing to it **(b) general partnership** = partnership where the liability of each partner is not limited; **limited partnership** = registered business where the liability of the partners is limited to the amount of capital they have each provided to the business and where the partners may not take part in the running of the business

party [ˈpɑːti] *noun* **(a)** company or person involved in a legal dispute or legal agreement; ***one of the parties to the suit has died***; ***the company is not a party to the agreement*** **(b) third party** = any third person, in addition to the two main people involved in a contract; **third party insurance** *or* **third party policy** = insurance to cover damage to any person who is not one of the people named in the insurance contract (that is, not the insured person nor the insurance company)

pass [pɑːs] *verb* **(a) to pass a dividend** = to pay no dividend in a certain year (NOTE: American English is also **to omit a dividend**) **(b)** to approve; ***the finance director has to pass an invoice before it is sent out***; ***the loan has been passed by the board***; **to pass a resolution** = to vote to agree to a resolution; ***the meeting passed a proposal that salaries should be frozen*** **(c)** to be successful; ***she has passed all her exams and now is a qualified accountant***

passbook [ˈpɑːsbʊk] *noun* book given to a customer by a bank or building society, which shows money which the customer deposits or withdraws from the account; **passbook account** = account which carries a passbook

> instead of customers having transactions recorded in their passbooks, they will present plastic cards and have the transactions printed out on a receipt
>
> *Australian Financial Review*

passive [ˈpæsɪv] *adjective* not taking any action; US **passive investor** = SLEEPING PARTNER; **passive stake** = shareholding where the shareholder takes no active part in running the company

> she's selling off passive stakes in businesses like medical publishing and satellite TV
>
> *Fortune*

pass off [ˈpɑːs ˈɒf] verb **to pass something off as something else** = to pretend that it is another thing in order to cheat a customer

password [ˈpɑːswɔːd] noun *(for telephone or home banking service)* special word which a user has to give when carrying out operations on an account by phone

pataca [pæˈtækə] *noun* currency used in Macao

patent ['peɪtənt or 'pætənt] **1** *noun* **(a)** official document showing that a person has the exclusive right to make and sell an invention; ***to take out a patent for a new type of light bulb***; ***to apply for a patent for a new invention***; **letters patent** = official term for a patent; **patent applied for** *or* **patent pending** = words on a product showing that the inventor has applied for a patent for it; **to forfeit a patent** = to lose a patent because payments have not been made; **to infringe a patent** = to make and sell a product which works in the same way as a patented product and not pay a royalty for it; **infringement of patent** *or* **patent infringement** = act of illegally making or selling a product which is patented **(b) patent agent** = person who advises on patents and applies for patents on behalf of clients; **to file a patent application** = to apply for a patent; **patent office** = government office which grants patents and supervises them; **patent rights** = rights which an inventor holds under a patent **2** *verb* **to patent an invention** = to register an invention with the patent office to prevent other people from copying it

patented ['peɪtəntɪd or 'pætəntɪd] *adjective* which is protected by a patent

pathfinder prospectus ['pɑːθfaɪndə prə'spektəs] *noun* preliminary prospectus about a company which is going to be launched on the Stock Exchange, sent to potential major investors before the issue date, giving details of the company's background, but not giving the price at which shares will be sold

pattern ['pætən] *noun* general way in which something usually happens; **pattern of trade** *or* **trading pattern** = general way in which trade is carried on; ***the company's trading pattern shows high export sales in the first quarter and high home sales in the third quarter***

pawn [pɔːn] **1** noun **to put something in pawn** = to leave a valuable object with someone in exchange for a loan which has to be repaid if you want to take back the object; **to take something out of pawn** = to repay the loan and so get back the object which has been pawned; **pawn ticket** = receipt given by the pawnbroker for the object left in pawn **2** verb **to pawn a watch** = to leave a watch with a pawnbroker who gives a loan against it

pawnbroker ['pɔːnbrəʊkə] *noun* person who lends money against the security of valuable objects

pawnshop ['pɔːnʃɒp] *noun* pawnbroker's shop

pay [peɪ] **1** *noun* **(a)** salary or wageor money given to someone for regular work; **back pay** = salary which has not been paid; **basic pay** = normal salary without extra payments; **take-home pay** = pay left after tax and insurance have been deducted; **holidays with pay** = holiday which a worker can take by contract and for which he is paid; **unemployment pay** = money given by the government to someone who is unemployed **(b) pay day** = day on which wages are paid to workers (usually Friday for workers paid once a week, and during the last week of the month for workers who are paid once a month); **pay negotiations** *or* **pay talks** = discussions between management and workers about pay increases; **pay packet** = envelope containing the pay slip and the cash pay; **pay rise** = increase in pay; **pay slip** = piece of paper showing the full amount of a worker's pay, and the money deducted as tax, pension and insurance contributions **(c) pay desk** = place in a store where you pay for goods bought; **pay phone** = telephone which works if you put coins into it **2** *verb* **(a)** to give money to buy an item or a service; ***to pay £1,000 for a car***; ***how much did you pay to have the office cleaned?***; **to pay in advance** = to give money before you receive the item bought or before the service has been completed; ***we had to pay in advance to have the new telephone system installed***; **to pay in instalments** = to give money for an item by giving small amounts regularly; ***we are paying for the computer by paying instalments of £50 a month***; **to pay cash** = to pay the complete sum in cash; **'pay cash'** = words written on a crossed cheque to show that it can be paid in cash if necessary; **to pay by cheque** = to pay by giving a cheque, not by using cash or credit card; **to pay by credit card** = to pay, using a credit card and not a cheque or cash **(b)** to give money; **to pay on demand** = to pay money when it is asked for, not after a period of credit; **please pay the sum of £10** = please give £10 in cash or by cheque; **to pay a dividend** = to give shareholders a part of the profits of a company; ***these shares pay a dividend of 1.5p***; **to pay interest** = to give money as interest on money borrowed or invested; ***building societies pay an interest of 10%***; GB **pay as you earn (PAYE)** US **pay-as-you-go** = tax system, where income tax is deducted from the salary before it is paid to the worker; GB **pay-as-you-go** = payment system where the purchaser pays in small instalments as he uses the service **(c)** to give a worker money for work done; **to be paid by the hour** = to get money for each hour worked; **to be paid at piece-work rates**

= to get money for each piece of work finished **(d)** to give money which is owed or which has to be paid; ***to pay a bill***; ***to pay an invoice***; ***to pay duty on imports***; ***to pay tax*** **(e)** **to pay a cheque into an account** = to deposit money in the form of a cheque (NOTE: **paying - paid**)

> the yield figure means that if you buy the shares at their current price you will be getting 5% before tax on your money if the company pays the same dividend as in its last financial year
>
> *Investors Chronicle*

> recession encourages communication not because it makes redundancies easier, but because it makes low or zero pay increases easier to accept
>
> *Economist*

payable ['peɪəbl] *adjective* which is due to be paid; **payable in advance** = which has to be paid before the goods are delivered; **payable on delivery** = which has to be paid when the goods are delivered; **payable on demand** = which must be paid when payment is asked for; **payable at sixty days** = which has to be paid by sixty days after the date of invoice; **cheque made payable to bearer** = cheque which will be paid to the person who has it, not to any particular name written on it; **shares payable on application** = shares which must be paid for when you apply to buy them; **accounts payable** = money owed by a company; **bills payable** = bills which a debtor will have to pay; **electricity charges are payable by the tenant** = the tenant (and not the landlord) must pay for the electricity

pay back ['peɪ 'bæk] *verb* to give money back to someone; ***to pay back a loan***; ***I lent him £50 and he promised to pay me back in a month***; ***he has never paid me back for the money he borrowed***

payback ['peɪbæk] *noun* paying back money which has been borrowed; **payback clause** = clause in a contract which states the terms for repaying a loan; **payback period** = (i) period of time over which a loan is to be repaid; (ii) time taken for the total interest on an investment to equal the amount of the initial investment

pay cheque *or* **paycheck** ['peɪtʃek] *noun* monthly cheque which pays a salary to an employee

pay down ['peɪ 'daʊn] verb **to pay money down** = to make a deposit; ***he paid £50 down and the rest in monthly instalments***

paydown ['peɪdaʊn] *noun US* repayment of part of a sum which has been borrowed

PAYE ['pi: 'eɪ 'waɪ 'i:] = PAY AS YOU EARN

payee [peɪ'i:] *noun* person who receives money from someone; person whose name is on a cheque

payer ['peɪə] *noun* **(a)** person who gives money to someone; **slow payer** = person or company that does not pay their debts on time; ***they are well known as slow payers*** **(b)** **payer bank** = bank which pays a cheque drawn on one of its accounts

paying ['peɪɪŋ] **1** *adjective* **(a)** which makes a profit; ***it is a paying business***; **it is not a paying proposition** = it is not a business which is going to make a profit **(b)** which pays; **paying agent** = bank which pays dividend or interest to a bondholder **2** *noun* giving money; ***the paying of a debt***; **paying-in book** = book of forms for paying money into a bank account or building society; **paying-in slip** = form which is filled in when money is being deposited in a bank account or building society

payment ['peɪmənt] *noun* **(a)** giving money; ***payment in cash*** *or* ***cash payment***; ***payment by cheque*** *or* ***cheque payment***; ***payment of interest*** *or* ***interest payment***; **payment on account** = paying part of the money owed; **full payment** *or* **payment in full** = paying all money owed; **payment on invoice** = paying money as soon as an invoice is received; **payment in kind** = paying by giving goods or food, but not money; **payment by results** = money given which increases with the amount of work done or goods produced; **payment date** = date when a payment should be or has been made; **payment order** = order to someone to make a payment **(b)** money paid; **back payment** = paying money which is owed; **deferred payments** = money paid later than the agreed date; ***the company agreed to defer payments for three months***; **down payment** = part of a total payment made in advance; **repayable in easy payments** = repayable with small sums regularly; **incentive payments** = extra pay offered to a worker to make him work better; *see also* BALANCE OF PAYMENTS

pay off ['peɪ 'ɒf] *verb* **(a)** to finish paying money which is owed; ***to pay off a mortgage***; ***to pay off a loan*** **(b)** to pay all the money owed to someone and terminate his employment; ***when the company was taken***

over the factory was closed and all the workers were paid off

payoff ['peɪɒf] *noun* money paid to finish paying something which is owed; **payoff period** = PAYBACK PERIOD

pay out ['peɪ 'aʊt] *verb* to give money; ***the company pays out thousands of pounds in legal fees***; ***we have paid out half our profits in dividends***

payout ['peɪaʊt] *noun* **(a)** money paid out; **dividend payout** = money paid as dividends to shareholders; ***although the stock's dividend payout ratio has been below average, the rate of increase has been above average*** **(b)** money paid to help someone in difficulties; ***the company only exists on payouts from the government***

> after a period of recession followed by a rapid boost in incomes, many tax payers embarked upon some tax planning to minimize their payouts
>
> *Australian Financial Review*

payroll ['peɪrəʊl] *noun* list of people employed and paid by a company; money paid by a company in salaries; ***the company has 250 on the payroll***; **payroll ledger** = list of staff and their salaries; **payroll tax** = tax on the people employed by a company

pay up ['peɪ 'ʌp] *verb* to give money which is owed; ***the company only paid up when we sent them a letter from our solicitor***; ***he finally paid up six months late***; **amount paid up** = amount paid for a new issue of shares, either the total payment or the first instalment, if the shares are offered with instalment payments; *see also* PAID UP

PC = PERSONAL COMPUTER

PCB = PETTY CASH BOOK

P/E ['pi:'i:] *abbreviation* = *PRICE/EARNINGS*; **P/E ratio (price/earnings ratio** *or* **PER)** = PRICE/EARNINGS RATIO

peak [pi:k] **1** *noun* highest point; ***the peaks and troughs of the stock market***; **time of peak demand** = time when something is being used most; **peak output** = highest output; **peak year** = best year, year when the largest quantity of products was produced or when sales were highest; ***the shares reached their peak in January***; ***the share index has fallen 10% since the peak in January*** **2** *verb* to reach the highest point; ***the balance of payments deficit peaked in January***; ***shares have peaked and are beginning to slip back***

peanuts ['pi:nʌts] *noun (informal)* small amount of money

pecuniary [pɪ'kju:niəri] *adjective* referring to money; **he gained no pecuniary advantage** = he made no profit

peddle ['pedl] *verb* to sell goods from door to door or in the street

peg [peg] **1** *noun* fixed rate; **adjustable peg** = currency which is pegged to another, but with the possibility of adjusting the exchange rate from time to time; **crawling peg** = method of fixing exchange rates, but allowing them to move up or down slowly **2** *verb* to hold something at a certain level or price; **to peg a currency** = to fix an exchange rate for a currency which previously was floating; **to peg prices** = to fix prices to stop them rising; **to peg wage increases to the cost-of-living index** = to limit increases in wages to the increases in the cost-of-living index (NOTE: **pegging - pegged**)

> adjustable peg exchange rates are extremely vulnerable to destabilizing expectations. Economic agents have to guess not just whether the authorities mean what they say, but whether other private participants believe them
>
> *Financial Times*

penalize ['pi:nəlaɪz] *verb* to punish or to fine; ***to penalize a supplier for late deliveries***; ***they were penalized for bad service***

penalty ['penlti] *noun* **(a)** punishment (such as a fine) which is imposed if something is not done; **penalty clause** = clause which lists the penalties which will be imposed if the contract is not obeyed; ***the contract contains a penalty clause which fines the company 1% for every week the completion date is late*** **(b)** money withheld from an investor if he or she withdraws money from an interest-bearing account early

penalty-free ['penəlti'fri:] *adjective* without incurring any penalty, without losing any interest on money invested; ***penalty-free withdrawal***

pence [pens] *see* PENNY

penny ['peni] *noun* **(a)** *GB* small coin, of which one hundred make a pound (NOTE: usually written **p** after a figure: **26p**; the plural is **pence**) **(b)** *US (informal)* small coin, one cent

penny shares *or* **penny stocks** ['peni 'ʃeəz *or* 'peni 'stɒks] *noun* very cheap shares, costing less than £1 or $1

COMMENT: these shares can be considered as a good speculation, since buying even large numbers of them does not involve a large amount of money, and the share price of some companies can rise dramatically; the price can of course fall, but in the case of penny shares, the loss is not likely to be as much as with shares with a higher market value

pension ['penʃən] **1** *noun* **(a)** money paid regularly to someone who no longer works, paid either by the state or by a private company; **retirement pension** *or* **old age pension** = state pension given to a man who is over 65 or and woman who is over 60; **government pension** *or* **state pension** = pension paid by the state; **occupational pension** = pension which is paid by the company by which a worker has been employed; **portable pension** = pension entitlement which can be moved from one company to another without loss (as a worker changes jobs); **pension contributions** = money paid by a company or worker into a pension fund; **pension funds** = investments managed by pension companies to produce pensions for investors **(b) pension plan** *or* **pension scheme** = plan worked out by an insurance company which arranges for a worker to pay part of his salary over many years and receive a regular payment when he retires; **company pension scheme** = pension which is organized by a company for its staff; ***he decided to join the company's pension scheme***; **contributory pension scheme** = scheme where the worker has to pay a proportion of his salary; **graduated pension scheme** = pension scheme where the benefit is calculated as a percentage of the salary of each person in the scheme; **non-contributory pension scheme** = scheme where the employer pays in all the money on behalf of the worker; **personal pension plan (PPP)** = pension plan which applies to one worker only, usually a self-employed person, not to a group; *see also* PORTABLE **(c) pension entitlement** = amount of pension which someone has the right to receive when he retires; **pension fund** = fund which receives contributions from employers and employees, being the money which provides pensions for retired members of staff **2** verb **to pension someone off** = to ask someone to retire and take a pension

permanent workers' pensions are funded on a pay-as-you-go basis, with enterprises contributing a portion of permanent employees' total wages to a pool. Contract workers' pension pools are separately funded: enterprises contribute 15% of contract workers' total wages, plus individual deductions of up to 3%

Far Eastern Economic Review

pensionable ['penʃənəbl] *adjective* able to receive a pension; **pensionable age** = age after which someone can take a pension

pensioner ['penʃənə] *noun* person who receives a pension; **old age pensioner** = person who receives the retirement pension

People's Bank of China ['pi:plz 'bæŋk əv 'tʃaɪnə] the Central Bank of China

PEP [pep] = PERSONAL EQUITY PLAN

peppercorn rent ['pepəkɔ:n 'rent] *noun* very small or nominal rent; ***to pay a peppercorn rent; to lease a property for*** *or* ***at a peppercorn rent***

PER = PRICE/EARNINGS RATIO

per [pɔ:] *preposition* **(a) as per** = according to; **as per invoice** = as stated in the invoice; **as per sample** = as shown in the sample; **as per previous order** = according to the details given in our previous order **(b)** at a rate of; **per hour** *or* **per day** *or* **per week** *or* **per year** = for each hour or day or week or year; ***the rate is £5 per hour; he makes about £250 per month***; **we pay £10 per hour** = we pay £10 for each hour worked; **the earnings per share** = dividend received by each share; **the average sales per representative** = the average sales achieved by one representative; **per head** = for each person

a 100,000 square-foot warehouse generates $600 in sales per square foot of space

Duns Business Month

per annum ['pər 'ænəm] *adverb* in a year; ***what is their turnover per annum?***

per capita ['pə 'kæpɪtə] *adjective & adverb* for each person; **average income per capita** *or* **per capita income** = average income of one person; **per capita expenditure** = total money spent divided by the number of people involved

per cent *or* **percent** ['pə 'sent] *adjective & adverb* out of each hundred *or* for each hundred; **10 per cent** = ten in every hundred; ***what is the increase per cent? fifty per cent of nothing is still nothing***

this would represent an 18 per cent growth rate - a slight

slackening of the 25 per cent turnover rise in the first half

Financial Times

buildings are depreciated at two per cent per annum on the estimated cost of construction

Hongkong Standard

percentage [pə'sentɪdʒ] *noun* amount shown as part of one hundred; **percentage discount** = discount calculated at an amount per hundred; **percentage increase** = increase calculated on the basis of a rate for one hundred; **percentage point** = one per cent

state-owned banks cut their prime rates a percentage point to 11%

Wall Street Journal

a good percentage of the excess stock was taken up during the last quarter

Australian Financial Review

the Federal Reserve Board, signalling its concern about the weakening American economy, cut the discount rate by one-half percentage point to 6.5%

Wall Street Journal

percentile [pə'sentaɪl] *noun* a percentage point, one of a series of ninety-nine figures below which a certain percentage of the total falls

perform [pə'fɔ:m] *verb* to do well or badly; **how did the shares perform?** = did the shares go up or down?; **the company** *or* **the shares performed badly** = the company's share price fell; *see also* UNDERPERFORM

performance [pə'fɔ:məns] *noun* **(a)** way in which someone does his work; **performance-linked bonus** = bonus calculated against the performance of a worker or group of workers; **performance of personnel against objectives** = how personnel have worked, measured against the objectives set; **performance review** = yearly interview between a manager and each worker to discuss how the worker has worked during the year; **job performance** = doing a job well or badly; *see also* INCENTIVE **(b)** way in which a share increases in value; **the poor performance of the shares on the stock market** = the fall in the share price on the stock market; ***last year saw a dip in the company's performance***; **as a measure of the company's performance** = as a way of judging if the company's results are good or bad; **earnings performance** = way in which shares earn dividends; **performance fund** = fund invested in shares to provide capital growth, but probably with less dividend income than usual; **performance share** = share which is likely to show capital growth, though perhaps not income; these are usually riskier shares than those which provide income

inflation-adjusted GNP edged up at a 1.3% annual rate, its worst performance since the economic expansion began

Fortune

if you consider that successful fund managers in the conventional sphere might make a mere £250,000 or so in a good year, compared to a performance-linked bonus running into the millions after a good run with a hedge fund

Money Observer

period ['pɪərɪəd] *noun* **(a)** length of time; ***for a period of time*** *or* ***for a period of months*** *or* ***for a six-year period***; ***turnover for a period of three months***; ***sales over the holiday period***; ***to deposit money for a fixed period*** **(b) accounting period** *or* **period of account** = period of time at the end of which the firm's accounts are made up

periodic *or* **periodical** [pɪərɪ'ɒdɪk or pɪərɪ'ɒdɪkəl] *adjective* from time to time; ***a periodic review of the company's performance***

perks [pɜ:ks] *plural noun* extra items given by a company to workers in addition to their salaries (such as company cars, private health insurance); **shareholder perks** = special offers which are available only to shareholders (such as discounts on travel or hotel accommodation) (NOTE: also called **fringe benefits**)

permanent ['pɜ:mənənt] adjective **permanent interest-bearing share (PIB)** = share issued by a building society to attract investment capital (the yield is quite high, since the capital investment is not guaranteed)

permit 1 ['pɜ:mɪt] *noun* official document which allows someone to do something; **export permit** *or* **import permit** = official document which allows goods to be exported or imported; **work permit** = official document which allows someone who is not a citizen to work in a country **2** [pə'mɪt] *verb* to allow someone to do something; ***this***

document permits you to export twenty-five computer systems

perpetual inventory [pə'petjuəl 'ɪnvəntri] *noun* stock recording and valuation system where each item of stock purchased is added to the total and each item sold is deducted, so that the stock figures are always correct and up-to-date

per pro ['pɜː 'prəʊ] = PER PROCURATIONEM with the authority of; ***the secretary signed per pro the manager***

perquisites ['pɜːkwɪzɪts] *plural noun* = *PERKS*

person ['pɜːsn] *noun* **(a)** someone (a man or woman); ***insurance policy which covers a named person***; **the persons named in the contract** = people whose names are given in the contract; **the document should be witnessed by a third person** = someone who is not named in the document should witness it **(b) in person** = someone himself or herself; **this important package is to be delivered to the chairman in person** = the package has to be given to the chairman himself (and not to his secretary, assistant, etc.)

personal ['pɜːsənl] *adjective* referring to one person; **personal allowances** = part of a person's income which is not taxed; **personal assets** = moveable assets which belong to a person; **personal banker** = bank employee who looks after a client, and is the one whom the client contacts when there are problems; **personal call** = telephone call where you ask the operator to connect you with a particular person; **personal computer (PC)** = small computer which can be used at home; *(of a bank)* **personal customer** = individual who has an account with a bank, as opposed to a business customer; **personal effects** *or* **personal property** = things which belong to someone; **personal income** = income received by an individual person before tax is paid; *(used for identification)* **selected personal information** = information, such as the post code of your home, or the maiden name of your mother, used for identification purposes; **personal loan** = loan to a person for household or other personal use, not for business use; **personal pension plan (PPP)** = pension plan which applies to one worker only, usually a self-employed person, not to a group; **personal sector** = part of the investment market which is owned by private investors (as opposed to the corporate or institutional sector); **apart from the family shares, he has a personal shareholding in the company** = apart from shares belonging to his family as a group, he has shares which he owns himself; **the car is for his personal use** = the car is for him to use himself

Personal Equity Plan (PEP) ['pɜːsnəl 'ekwɪti 'plæn] *noun* government-backed scheme to encourage share-ownership and investment in industry, where individual taxpayers can each invest a certain amount of money in shares each year, and not pay tax on either the income or the capital gains, provided that the shares are held for a certain period of time (replaced by ISAs in April 1999, but existing schemes will continue); **self-select Pep** = a general Pep, usually sold by stockbrokers, that allows the investor to choose which investments to hold in the Pep; **single-company Pep** = Pep which holds shares in one single company (up to £3,000 can be invested in the shares of just one company and protected from tax in this way)

> COMMENT: there are several types of equity Pep: the single company Pep, where only shares in one company are allowed, and the general Pep, where shares in several companies can be held or other types of investment

Personal Identification Number (PIN) ['pɜːsnəl aɪdentɪfɪ'keɪʃn 'nʌmbə] *noun* unique number allocated to the holder of a credit card, by which he can enter an automatic banking system, as, for example, to withdraw cash from an ATM or to pay through an EFTPOS terminal

Personal Investment Authority (PIA) ['pɜːsnəl ɪn'vestmənt ɔː'θɒrɪti] self-regulatory body which regulates financial advisers, insurance brokers, etc., who give financial advice or arrange financial services for clients, now part of the FSA

personalized ['pɜːsnəlaɪzd] *adjective* with the name or initials of a person printed on it; ***personalized cheques***; ***personalized briefcase***

peseta [pə'seɪtə] *noun* currency used with the euro in Spain (NOTE: usually written **ptas** after a figure: **2,000ptas**)

peso ['peɪsəʊ] *noun* currency used in Mexico and many other countries such as Argentina, Bolivia, Chile, Colombia, Cuba, Dominican Republic, Philippines, and Uruguay

pessimism ['pesɪmɪzm] *noun* expecting that everything will turn out badly; ***there is considerable pessimism about job opportunities***; **market pessimism** *or* **pessimism on the market** = feeling that the stock market prices will fall (NOTE: the opposite is **optimism**)

> falling interest rates are good news for UK equities but might provoke further pessimism in consumers
>
> *Investors Chronicle*

pessimistic [pesɪˈmɪstɪk] *adjective* feeling sure that things will work out badly; **he takes a pessimistic view of the exchange rate** = he expects the exchange rate to fall (NOTE: the opposite is **optimistic**)

peter out [ˈpi:tə ˈaʊt] *verb* to come to an end gradually

> economists believe the economy is picking up this quarter and will do better in the second half of the year, but most expect growth to peter out in 1986
>
> *Sunday Times*

Peter principle [ˈpi:tə ˈprɪnsəpl] *noun* law, based on wide experience, that people are promoted until they occupy positions for which they are incompetent

petrocurrency [ˈpetrəʊkʌrənsi] *noun* foreign currency which is earned by exporting oil

petrodollar [ˈpetrəʊdɒlə] *noun* dollar earned by a country from exporting oil, then invested outside that country

petroleum [pəˈtrəʊljəm] *noun* raw natural oil, found in the ground; **crude petroleum** = raw petroleum which has not been processed; **petroleum exporting countries** = countries which produce petroleum and sell it to others; **petroleum industry** = industry which uses petroleum to make other products (petrol, soap, etc.); **petroleum products** = products (such as petrol, soap, paint) which are made from crude petroleum; **petroleum revenues** = income from selling oil

petty [ˈpeti] *adjective* not important; **petty cash** = small amount of money kept in an office to pay small debts; **petty cash book (PCB)** = book in which petty cash payments are noted; **petty cash box** = locked metal box in an office where the petty cash is kept; **petty expenses** = small sums of money spent

P45 [ˈpi: ˈfɔ:tiˈfaɪv] *noun* form given to someone who is leaving a job, either through redundancy, dismissal or simply going to work somewhere else (NOTE: the equivalent in the USA is the **pink slip**)

PGP [ˈpi:ˈdʒi:ˈpi:] = PRETTY GOOD PRIVACY method of encrypting information so that only the intended recipient can read the message; often used to send credit card details via electronic mail

phase [feɪz] *noun* period, part of something which takes place; ***the first phase of the expansion programme***

phase in [ˈfeɪz ˈɪn] *verb* to bring something in gradually; ***the new invoicing system will be phased in over the next two months***

phase out [ˈfeɪz ˈaʊt] *verb* to remove something gradually; ***Smith Ltd will be phased out as a supplier of spare parts***

> the budget grants a tax exemption for $500,000 in capital gains, phased in over the next six years
>
> *Toronto Star*

phoenix company [ˈfi:nɪks ˈkʌmpəni] *noun* company formed by the directors of a company which has gone into receivership, which trades in the same way as the first company, and in most respects (except its name) seems to be exactly the same as the first company

physical [ˈfɪzɪkl] **1** *adjective* **(a) physical stock check** = counting actual items of stock (as opposed to checking ledger entries) **(b) physical market** = commodity market where purchasers actually buy the commodities (as opposed to the futures market, where they buy and sell the right to purchase commodities at a future date); **physical price** = current cash price for a commodity for immediate delivery **2** *noun* **physicals** = actual commodities which are sold on the current market (as opposed to futures)

PIA = PERSONAL INVESTMENT AUTHORITY

PIB = PERMANENT INTEREST BEARING SHARE

pick [pɪk] **1** *verb* to choose or select; **to pick stocks** = to select which shares to buy **2** *noun* thing chosen; ***the former research analyst never before talked to the press about his stock picks***

> my style of investing has gone from insanely stupid - namely, trying to pick stocks - to fairly sensible - namely, buying the index
>
> *Smart Money*

picker [ˈpɪkə] noun **stock picker** = person who invests by choosing which shares to buy

picking [ˈpɪkɪŋ] noun *see* STOCKPICKING

pick up ['pɪk 'ʌp] *verb* to get better or to improve; ***business** or **trade is picking up***

piece rate ['pi:s 'reɪt] *noun noun* rate of pay for a product produced or for a piece of work done and not paid for at an hourly rate; ***to earn piece rates***

piecework ['pi:swɜ:k] *noun* work for which workers are paid for the products produced or for the pieces of work done and not at an hourly rate

pie chart ['paɪ 'tʃɑ:t] *noun* diagram where information is shown as a circle cut up into sections of different sizes

piggybacking ['pɪgibækɪŋ] *noun US* selling existing shares in a company, as well as new shares being offered for sale for the first time

PIN ['pɪn 'nʌmbə] = PERSONAL IDENTIFICATION NUMBER

pink slip ['pɪŋk 'slɪp] *noun US* official letter given to someone who is leaving a job, either through redundancy or dismissal (NOTE: the equivalent in Britian is the **P45**)

Pink 'Un ['pɪŋk 'ʌn] *(informal)* = FINANCIAL TIMES (because it is printed on pink paper)

pit [pɪt] *noun US* part of a stock exchange or of a commodities exchange where dealers trade (NOTE: also called **the ring;** British English for this is **the trading floor**)

P&L ['pi: ənd 'el] = PROFIT AND LOSS (ACCOUNT)

place [pleɪs] *verb* **(a)** to put; ***to place $25,000 on deposit***; **to place money in an account** = to deposit money in an account; **to place a contract** = to decide that a certain company shall have the contract to do work; **to place something on file** = to file something **(b) to place a block of shares** = to find a buyer for a block of shares; **to place an issue** = to find buyers (usually a small number of investors) for all of a new issue of shares

placement ['pleɪsmənt] *noun* **(a)** finding work for someone **(b)** *US* finding buyers for an issue of new shares; **direct placement** = placing new shares directly with purchasers, without going through a broker (NOTE: the British equivalent is **placing**)

placing ['pleɪsɪŋ] *noun* finding a single buyer or a group of institutional buyers for a large number of shares in a new company or a company which is going public; **the placing of a line of shares** = finding a purchaser for a block of shares which was overhanging the market; **public placing** = offering a new issue of shares to certain investing institutions, though not to private investors in general; **vendor placing** = arranging for an issue of new shares to be bought by institutions, as a means of financing the purchase of another company

plaintiff ['pleɪntɪf] *noun* person who starts a legal action against someone

plain vanilla swap ['pleɪn və'nɪlə 'swɒp] *noun* interest rate swap, where a company with fixed interest borrowings may swap them for variable interest borrowings of another company; *see also* SWAP

plan [plæn] **1** *noun* **(a)** organized way of doing something; **contingency plan** = plan which will be put into action if something happens which no one expects to happen; **the government's economic plans** = the government's proposals for running the country's economy; **a Five-Year Plan** = proposals for running a country's economy over a five-year period **(b)** way of saving or investing money; ***investment plan***; ***pensions plan***; ***savings plan*** **2** *verb* to organize carefully how something should be done; **to plan for an increase in bank interest charges** = to change a way of doing things because you think there will be an increase in bank interest charges; **to plan investments** = to propose how investments should be made (NOTE: **planning - planned**)

> the benefits package is attractive and the compensation plan includes base, incentive and car allowance totalling $50,000+
>
> *Globe and Mail (Toronto)*

planned [plænd] adjective **planned economy** = system where the government plans all business activity

planner ['plænə] *noun* **(a)** person who plans; **the government's economic planners** = people who plan the future economy of the country for the government **(b) desk planner** *or* **wall planner** = book or chart which shows days, weeks and months so that the work of an office can be shown by diagrams

planning ['plænɪŋ] *noun* organizing how something should be done, especially how a company should be run to make increased profits; ***long-term planning** or **short-term planning***; **economic planning** = planning the future financial state of the country for the government; **corporate planning** = planning the future financial state of a group of companies; **manpower planning** = planning to get the right number of workers in each job; **tax planning** = planning how to avoid paying too much tax, by investing in tax-exempt savings schemes, offshore trusts, etc.

plastic money ['plæstɪk 'mʌni] *noun* credit cards and charge cards

platinum ['plætɪnəm] *noun* rare precious metal traded on bullion markets; **platinum card** = special credit card for people with very large incomes

play [pleɪ] *noun* **in play** = likely to be the object of a takeover; **company in play** = company which is being targeted by several takeover bids; *see also* ASSET PLAY

PLC *or* **plc** ['pi: 'el 'si:] = PUBLIC LIMITED COMPANY

pledge [pledʒ] **1** *noun* object given to a pawnbroker as security for money borrowed; **to redeem a pledge** = to pay back a loan and interest and so get back the security; **unredeemed pledge** = pledge which the borrower has not taken back because he has not repaid the loan **2** *verb* **to pledge share certificates** = to deposit share certificates with a lender as security for money borrowed (the title to the certificates is not transferred and the certificates are returned when the debt is repaid)

pledgee [ple'dʒi:] *noun* person who receives an item as a pledge against a loan

pledgor ['pledʒə] *noun* person who pledges his property as security for a loan

plenary meeting *or* **plenary session** ['pli:nəri 'mi:tɪŋ or 'pli:nəri 'seʃn] *noun* meeting at a conference when all the delegates meet together

plough back *US* **plow back** ['plaʊ 'bæk] *verb* **to plough back profits into the company** = to invest the profits in the business (and not pay them out as dividends to the shareholders) by using them to buy new equipment or create new products

plug [plʌg] *verb* to block or to stop; ***the company is trying to plug the drain on cash reserves*** (NOTE: **plugging - plugged**)

plummet *or* **plunge** ['plʌmɪt or plʌnʒ] *verb* to fall sharply; ***share prices plummeted*** *or* ***plunged on the news of the devaluation***

> in the first six months of this year secondhand values of tankers have plummeted by 40%
>
> *Lloyd's List*

> crude oil output plunged during the past month
>
> *Wall Street Journal*

plus [plʌs] **1** *preposition* **(a)** added to; ***his salary plus commission comes to more than £25,000; production costs plus overheads are higher than revenue*** **(b)** more than; **houses valued at £160,000 plus** = houses valued at over £160,000 **2** *adjective* favourable, or good and profitable; ***a plus factor for the company is that the market is much larger than they had originally thought***; **the plus side of the account** = the credit side of the account; **on the plus side** = this is a favourable point; ***on the plus side, we must take into account the new product line*** **3** *noun* **(a)** printed sign (+) showing an addition or increase; ***at the end of the day the index showed a series of pluses, with very few minuses*** **(b)** a good or favourable point; ***to have achieved £1m in new sales in less than six months is certainly a plus for the sales team***

pm = PREMIUM

pocket ['pɒkɪt] noun **pocket calculator** *or* **pocket diary** = calculator or diary which can be carried in the pocket; **to be £25 in pocket** = to have made a profit of £25; **to be £25 out of pocket** = to have lost £25; *see also* OUT OF POCKET

point [pɔɪnt] *noun* **(a)** place or position; **point of sale (POS)** = place where a product is sold (such as a shop); *see also* EFTPOS; **point of sale material** *or* **POS material** = display material (such as posters, dump bins) to advertise a product where it is being sold; **point of sale terminal** *or* **POS terminal** = electronic cash terminal at a pay desk which records transactions and stock movements automatically when an item is bought; **breakeven point** = position at which sales cover costs but do not show a profit; **customs entry point** = place at a border between two countries where goods are declared to customs **(b)** **(decimal) point** = dot which indicates the division between a whole unit and its smaller parts (such as 4.25); *see note at* DECIMAL) **(c)** a unit for calculations; **basis point** = one hundredth of a percentage point (0.01%), the basic unit used in measuring market movements; **percentage point** = 1 per cent; **half a percentage point** = 0.5 per cent; **the dollar gained two points** = the dollar increased in value against another currency by two hundredths of a cent; **government stocks rose by one point** = they rose by £1; **the exchange fell ten points** = the stock market index fell by ten units

> sterling M3, the most closely watched measure, rose by 13% in the year to August - seven percentage points faster than the rate of inflation
>
> *Economist*

> banks refrained from quoting forward US/Hongkong dollar exchange rates as premiums of 100 points replaced discounts of up to 50 points
>
> *South China Morning Post*

poison pill ['pɔɪzn 'pɪl] *noun* action taken by a company to make itself less attractive to a potential takeover bid

> COMMENT: in some cases, the officers of a company will vote themselves extremely high redundancy payments if a takeover is successful; or a company will borrow large amounts of money and give it away to the shareholders as dividends, so that the company has an unacceptably high level of borrowing

polarization [pəʊləraɪ'zeɪʃn] noun **market polarization** = situation where a market is concentrated round a few suppliers or traders

> the firm consequently concludes that today's market polarization is very unlikely to end the same way that it did in the 1970s
>
> *Investors Chronicle*

policy ['pɒlɪsi] *noun* **(a)** decisions on the general way of doing something; ***government policy on wages*** *or* ***government wages policy***; ***the government's prices policy*** *or* ***incomes policy***; ***the country's economic policy***; ***a company's trading policy***; **the government made a policy statement** *or* **made a statement of policy** = the government declared in public what its plans were; **budgetary policy** = policy of expected income and expenditure **(b) company policy** = the company's agreed plan of action or the company's way of doing things; ***what is the company policy on credit? it is against company policy to give more than thirty days' credit***; ***our policy is to submit all contracts to the legal department*** **(c) insurance policy** = document which shows the conditions of an insurance contract; **accident policy** = insurance contract against accidents; **all-risks policy** = insurance which covers risks of any kind, with no exclusions; **comprehensive** *or* **all-in policy** = insurance which covers all risks; **contingent policy** = insurance which pays out only if something happens (as if the person named in the policy dies before the person due to benefit); **endowment policy** = insurance where a sum of money is paid to the insured person on a certain date, or to his estate if he dies earlier; **policy holder** = person who is insured by an insurance company; **to take out a policy** = to sign the contract for an insurance and start paying the premiums; ***she took out a life insurance policy*** *or* ***a house insurance policy***; **the insurance company made out a policy** *or* **drew up a policy** = the company wrote the details of the contract on the policy

poll [pəʊl] *noun* vote using voting papers, used to determine the result of a vote at an AGM where a show of hands is inconclusive

pool [pu:l] **1** *noun* **(a)** unused supply; ***a pool of unemployed labour*** *or* ***of expertise*** **(b)** *US* group of mortgages and other collateral used to back a loan **2** verb **to pool interests** = to exchange shares between companies when a merger takes place; **to pool resources** = to put all resources together so as to be more powerful or profitable

poor [pɔ:] *adjective* **(a)** without much money; ***the company tries to help the poorest members of staff with soft loans***; ***it is one of the poorest countries in the world*** **(b)** not very good; ***poor quality***; ***poor service***; ***poor turnround time of orders*** *or* ***poor order turnround time***

poorly ['pɔ:li] *adverb* badly; ***the offices are poorly laid out***; ***the plan was poorly presented***; **poorly-paid staff** = staff with low wages

pork bellies ['pɔ:k 'beliz] *noun* meat from the underside of pig carcasses used to make bacon, traded as futures on some American exchanges

portability ['pɔ:təbɪlɪti] *noun* being able to be moved around

> the key feature of a personal pension plan for employees is portability
>
> *Money Observer*

portable ['pɔ:təbl] **1** *adjective* which can be carried; ***a portable computer*** *or* ***a portable typewriter***; **portable pension** = pension rights which a worker can take with him from one company to another as he changes jobs; **portable pension plan** = pension plan which allows a worker to carry his pension entitlements from one company to another as he changes jobs **2** *noun* **a portable** = a computer or typewriter which can be carried

portfolio [pɔːt'fəʊljəʊ] *noun* group of loans, mortgages, investments, etc., all belonging to the same individual or company; **loan portfolio** = all the loans which a financial institution has made and which are still outstanding; **mortgage portfolio** = all the mortgages made by a bank or building society which have not been paid off; **property portfolio** = all the investment property which belongs to one person or company; **a portfolio of shares** = all the shares owned by a single investor; **portfolio investments** = investments in shares and government stocks (as opposed to investments in property, etc.); **portfolio management** = buying and selling shares to make profits for a single investor; **portfolio theory** = basis for managing a portfolio of investments (a mix of safe stocks and more risky ones); **portfolio value** = value of someone's portfolio of investments

POS *or* **p.o.s.** ['piː 'əʊ 'es] = POINT OF SALE

position [pə'zɪʃən] *noun* **(a)** situation or state of affairs; **what is the cash position?** = what is the state of the company's current account?; **bargaining position** = statement of position by one group during negotiations **(b)** state of a person's current financial holding in a stock; *(of a marketmaker)* **to take a position in a share** = to buy shares on your own account, expecting to sell them later at a profit; **to take a bear position** = to act on the assumption that the market will fall; **bull position** = buying shares in the hope that they will rise; **to close a position** = to arrange your affairs so that one no longer has any liability to pay (as by selling all your securities or when a purchaser of a futures contract takes on a sales contract for the same amount to offset the risk); **to cover a position** = to have enough money to pay for a forward purchase; **long position** = situation where an investor sells long (i.e., sells forward shares which he owns); **short position** = situation where an investor sells short (i.e., sells forward shares which he does not own)

positive ['pɒzɪtɪv] adjective **positive carry** = deal where the cost of the finance is less than the return; **positive cash flow** = situation where more money is coming in than is being spent; **cash positive** = having cash in hand, as opposed to debts and overdrafts; **positive yield curve** = situation where the yield on a short-term investment is less than that on a long-term investment (NOTE: the opposite is **negative**)

---

as the group's shares are already widely held, the listing will be via an introduction. It will also be accompanied by a deeply-discounted £25m rights issue, leaving the company cash positive

Sunday Times

---

possess [pə'zes] *verb* to own; ***the company possesses property in the centre of the town***; ***he lost all he possessed in the collapse of his company***

possession [pə'zeʃən] *noun* **(a)** owning something; **the documents are in his possession** = he is holding the documents; **vacant possession** = being able to occupy a property immediately after buying it because it is empty; ***the property is to be sold with vacant possession*** **(b)** **possessions** = property, things owned; ***they lost all their possessions in the fire***

post [pəʊst] **1** *noun* system of sending letters and parcels from one place to another; ***to send an invoice by post***; ***the cheque is in the post***; ***the statement was lost in the post***; **to send a reply by return of post** = to reply to a letter immediately; **letter post** *or* **parcel post** = service for sending letters or parcels **2** *verb* **(a)** **to post an entry** = to transfer an entry to an account; **to post up a ledger** = to keep a ledger up to date **(b)** **to post an increase** = to let people know that an increase has taken place

---

Toronto stocks closed at an all-time high, posting their fifth day of advances in heavy trading

Financial Times

---

over the past 10 years, mutual funds shunned by investors in one year went on to post better performance than funds that won the popularity contest

Smart Money

---

that may help quant funds post stable returns in what looks to be a difficult 1998

Smart Money

---

it posted a record $4 billion in revenues during fiscal 1997

Fortune

---

the troubled retailer, which posted a shock profit warning last week, has lost its triple-A credit rating and been warned that the rating will be slashed

```
again if a clear recovery strategy does not emerge
```
Sunday Business

postal ['pəʊstəl] *adjective* referring to the post; **postal account** = bank account where all dealings are done by post, so reducing overhead costs and allowing a higher interest to be paid; **postal charges** *or* **postal rates** = money to be paid for sending letters or parcels by post; ***postal charges are going up by 10% in September***; **postal order** = document bought at a post office, as a method of paying small amounts of money by post

post-balance sheet event ['pəʊst'bæləns 'ʃi:t ɪ'vent] *noun* something which happens after the end of a company's financial year, when the draft accounts is drawn up, and before the time when the balance sheet is officially approved by the directors

postdate ['pəʊs'deɪt] *verb* to put a later date on a document; ***he sent us a postdated cheque***; ***his cheque was postdated to June***

posting ['pəʊstɪŋ] *noun* action of entering transactions in accounts

potential [pə'tenʃəl] **1** *adjective* possible; **potential customers** = people who could be customers; **potential market** = market which could be exploited **2** *noun* possibility of becoming something; **share with growth potential** *or* **with a potential for growth** = share which is likely to increase in value; **product with considerable sales potential** = product which is likely to have very large sales; **to analyse the market potential** = to examine the market to see how large it possibly is; **earning potential** = amount of money which someone should be able to earn, amount of dividend which a share is capable of earning

```
career prospects are excellent for someone with growth potential
```
Australian Financial Review

```
for sale: established general cleaning business; has potential to be increased to over 1 million dollar turnover
```
Australian Financial Review

pound [paʊnd] *noun* **(a)** measure of weight (= 0.45 kilos); ***to sell oranges by the pound***; ***a pound of oranges***; ***oranges cost 50p a pound*** (NOTE: usually written **lb** after a figure: **25lb**) **(b)** currency used in the UK, with the euro in Ireland (also called the punt), and in many other countries including Cyprus, Egypt, Lebanon, Malta and Syria **(c)** in particular, the currency of the UK; **pound sterling** = official term for the British currency; ***a pound coin***; ***a five pound note***; ***it costs six pounds***; ***the pound/dollar exchange rate*** (NOTE: usually written **£** before a figure: **£25**); **pound-cost averaging** = buying securities at different times, but always spending the same amount of money (NOTE: in the USA, this is called **dollar cost averaging**)

poundage ['paʊndɪdʒ] *noun* (i) rate charged per pound in weight; (ii) tax charged per pound in value

power ['paʊə] *noun* **(a)** strength or ability; **purchasing power** = quantity of goods which can be bought by a group of people or with a sum of money; ***the purchasing power of the school market***; ***the purchasing power of the pound has fallen over the last five years***; **the power of a consumer group** = ability of a group to influence the government or manufacturers; **bargaining power** = strength of one person or group when discussing prices or wages; **earning power** = amount of money someone should be able to earn; ***he is such a fine designer that his earning power is very large***; **borrowing power** = amount of money which a company can borrow **(b)** force or legal right; **executive power** = right to act as director or to put decisions into action; **power of appointment** = power of a trustee to dispose of interests in property to another person; **power of attorney** = legal document which gives someone the right to act on someone's behalf in legal matters; **the full power of the law** = the full force of the law when applied; ***we will apply the full power of the law to get possession of our property again***

p.p. ['pi:'pi:] *verb* = *PER PROCURATIONEM*; **to p.p. a letter** = to sign a letter on behalf of someone; ***the secretary p.p.'d the letter while the manager was at lunch***

PPP = PERSONAL PENSION PLAN

practice ['præktɪs] *noun* way of doing things; ***his practice was to arrive at work at 7.30 and start counting the cash***; **business practices** *or* **industrial practices** *or* **trade practices** = ways of managing or working in business, industry or trade; **restrictive practices** = ways of working which make people less free (such as stopping, by trade unions, of workers from doing certain jobs, or by stores not allowing customers a free choice of product); **best practice** = best way of working in a business or trade, as detailed in a code of practice; **sharp practice** = way of doing business which is not honest, but is not illegal; **code of practice** = rules drawn up by an association which the members must follow when doing business

preannouncement [priə'naʊnsmənt] *noun* announcement of something earlier than the date on which it should normally be announced

> this January proved even more tense than most because the previous month featured an unusual number of so-called preannouncements whereby several companies put Wall Street on notice even before the quarter ended that they would not meet their expected earnings number
>
> *Smart Money*

predator ['predətə] *noun* individual (or company) who spends most of his time looking for companies to purchase cheaply

predict [prɪ'dɪkt] *verb* to say that something will certainly happen

> lower interest rates are a bull factor for the stock market and analysts predict that the Dow Jones average will soon challenge the 1,300 barrier
>
> *Financial Times*

predictability [prɪdɪktə'bɪlɪti] *noun* ability to be predicted

> there is a high degree of predictability about the company, so its earnings and cash flow can be projected several years into the future
>
> *Smart Money*

pre-empt [pri'empt] *verb* to get an advantage by doing something quickly before anyone else; ***they staged a management buyout to pre-empt a takeover bid***

pre-emption right [pri'empʃn 'raɪt] *noun* right of an existing shareholder to be first to buy a new stock issue

pre-emptive [pri'emptɪv] *adjective* which has an advantage by acting early; **pre-emptive strike against a takeover bid** = rapid action taken to prevent a takeover bid; **a pre-emptive right** = (i) right of a government or of a local authority to buy a property before anyone else; (ii) right of an existing shareholder to be first to buy a new stock issue (so as to be able to maintain his percentage holding)

preference ['prefrəns] *noun* thing which is preferred; thing which has an advantage over something else; **preference shares** = shares (often with no voting rights) which receive their dividend before all other shares and which are repaid first (at face value) if the company is liquidated (NOTE: American English is **preferred stock**); **preference shareholders** = owners of preference shares; **cumulative preference share** = preference share where the dividend will be paid at a later date even if the company cannot pay a dividend in the current year

> COMMENT: preference shares, because they have less risk than ordinary shares, normally carry no voting rights

preferential [prefə'renʃəl] *adjective* showing that something is preferred more than another; **preferential creditor** = creditor who must be paid first if a company is in liquidation; **preferential duty** *or* **preferential tariff** = special low rate of tax; **preferential shares** = shares (part of a new issue) which are set aside for the employees of the company; **preferential terms** *or* **preferential treatment** = terms or way of dealing which is better than usual; ***subsidiary companies get preferential treatment when it comes to subcontracting work***

preferred [prɪ'fɜːd] adjective **preferred creditor** = creditor who must be paid first if a company is in liquidation; *US* **preferred stock** = shares which receive their dividend before all other shares, and which are repaid first (at face value) if the company is in liquidation (NOTE: British English is **preference shares**); *US* **cumulative preferred stock** = preference share where the dividend will be paid at a later date even if the corporation cannot pay a dividend in the current year

pre-financing ['priːfaɪ'nænsɪŋ] *noun* financing in advance

prelim ['priːlɪm] noun *(informal)* = PRELIMINARY ANNOUNCEMENT

preliminary [prɪ'lɪmɪnəri] *adjective* early, happening before anything else; **preliminary discussion** *or* **a preliminary meeting** = discussion or meeting which takes place before the main discussion or meeting starts; **preliminary announcement** = announcement of a company's full-year results, given out to the press before the detailed annual report is released; *US* **preliminary prospectus** = first prospectus for a new share issue, produced to see the market reaction to the proposed issue, but without giving a price for the new shares (also called a 'red herring'; similar to the British 'pathfinder prospectus')

> preliminary indications of the level of business investment and activity during the March quarter will be available this week
>
> *Australian Financial Review*

pre-market trading ['pri:'mɑ:kɪt 'treɪdɪŋ] *noun* trading before a Stock Exchange officially opens in the morning

premium ['pri:mjəm] *noun* **(a)** payment to encourage someone; **premium offer** = free gift offered to attract more customers **(b)** **insurance premium** = annual payment made by the insured person or company to an insurance company; ***you pay either an annual premium of £360 or twelve monthly premiums of £32***; **additional premium** = payment made to cover extra items in an existing insurance; **premium income** = income which an insurance company derives from premiums paid by insured persons **(c)** amount to be paid to a landlord or a tenant for the right to take over a lease; ***flat to let with a premium of £10,000***; ***annual rent: £8,500, premium: £25,000*** **(d)** rate above a previous rate; **exchange premium** = extra cost above the normal rate for buying foreign currency; ***the dollar is at a premium***; **shares sold at a premium** = (i) shares whose price is higher than their asset value or par value; (ii) new shares whose market price is higher than their issue price; ***most of the shares in our portfolio trade at premiums*** (NOTE: the opposite is **shares at a discount**)

> greenmail, the practice of buying back stock at a premium from an acquirer who threatens a takeover
>
> *Duns Business Month*

premium bonds ['pri:miəm 'bɒndz] British government bonds, part of the national savings scheme, which pay no interest, but give the owner the chance to win a monthly prize

prepaid [pri:'peɪd] *adjective* paid in advance; **carriage prepaid** = note showing that the transport costs have been paid in advance; **prepaid reply card** = stamped addressed card which is sent to someone so that he can reply without paying the postage

prepay [pri:'peɪ] *verb* to pay in advance (NOTE: **prepaying - prepaid**)

prepayment [pri:'peɪmənt] *noun* **(a)** payment in advance; **to ask for prepayment of a fee** = to ask for the fee to be paid before the work is done **(b)** *US* repayment of the principal of a loan before it is due; **prepayment penalty** = charge levied on someone who repays a loan (such as a mortgage) before it is due

present 1 ['preznt] *adjective* **(a)** happening now; ***the shares are too expensive at their present price***; ***what is the present address of the company?*** **(b)** being there when something happens; ***only six directors were present at the board meeting*** **2** [prɪ'zent] *verb* to bring or send and show a document; **to present a bill for acceptance** = to send a bill for payment by the person who has accepted it; **to present a bill for payment** = to send a bill to be paid

presentation [prezən'teɪʃən] *noun* showing a document; **cheque payable on presentation** = cheque which will be paid when it is presented; **free admission on presentation of this card** = you do not pay to go in if you show this card

presentment [prɪ'zentmənt] *noun US* = PRESENTATION

present value (PV) ['preznt 'vælju:] *noun* **(a)** the value something has now; ***in 1974 the pound was worth five times its present value*** **(b)** (i) sum of money which if invested now at a given rate of interest would produce a certain amount in the future; (ii) price which a share must reach in the future to be the equivalent of today's price, taking inflation into account

press [pres] *noun* newspapers and magazines; **the local press** = newspapers which are sold in a small area of the country; **the national press** = newspapers which sell in all parts of the country; **press conference** = meeting where reporters from newspapers are invited to hear news of a new product, of a court case or of a takeover bid, etc.; **press coverage** = reports about something in the press; ***we were very disappointed by the press coverage of the new car***; **press cutting** = piece cut out of a newspaper or magazine, which refers to an item which you find interesting; ***we have kept a file of press cuttings about the new car***; **press recommendation** = share which has been tipped as a buy in the financial column of a newspaper; **press release** = sheet giving news about something which is sent to newspapers and TV and radio stations so that they can use the information

pressing ['presɪŋ] *adjective* urgent; **pressing engagements** = meetings which have to be attended; **pressing bills** = bills which have to be paid

pressure ['preʃə] *noun* something which forces you to do something; **he was under considerable financial pressure** = he was forced to act because he owed money; **to put pressure on someone to do something** = to try to force someone to do something; **the pound has come under pressure on the foreign exchanges** = many people have been trying to sell pounds, and this has brought down its exchange rate; ***the group tried to put pressure on the government to act***; ***the banks put pressure on the company to reduce its borrowings***; **working under high pressure** = working with customers asking for supplies urgently, with a manager telling you to work faster; **pressure group** = group of people who try to influence the government or the local town council, etc.

> changes in interest rates put a different complexion on the currency market yesterday. The main factor was Thursday's increase in the Bundesbank's Lombard rate. This has resulted in downward pressure on some currencies or has forced central banks to move rates higher
>
> *Financial Times*

pre-tax *or* **pretax** ['pri:tæks] *adjective* before tax has been deducted or paid; **pretax profit** = profit before tax has been paid; ***the dividend paid is equivalent to one quarter of the pretax profit***

> the company's goals are a growth in sales of up to 40 per cent, a rise in pre-tax earnings of nearly 35 per cent and a rise in after-tax earnings of more than 25 per cent
>
> *Citizen (Ottawa)*

> EU regulations which came into effect in July insist that customers can buy cars anywhere in the EU at the local pre-tax price
>
> *Financial Times*

previous ['pri:vjəs] *adjective* which existed before; **previous balance** = balance in an account at the end of the accounting period before the current one

prey [preɪ] *noun* company which is being attacked by another (the 'predator') in a takeover bid

price [praɪs] **1** *noun* **(a)** money which has to be paid to buy something; **agreed price** = price which has been accepted by both the buyer and seller; **all-in price** = price which covers all items in a purchase (goods, insurance, delivery, etc.); **asking price** = price which the seller is hoping to be paid for the item when it is sold; **bargain price** = very cheap price; **catalogue price** *or* **list price** = price as marked in a catalogue or list; **competitive price** = low price aimed to compete with a rival product; **cost price** = selling price which is the same as the price which the seller paid for the item (either the manufacturing price or the wholesale price); **cut price** = very cheap price; **discount price** = full price less a discount; **factory price** *or* **price ex factory** = price not including transport from the maker's factory; **factory gate prices** = manufacturers' prices in general; **fair price** = good price for both buyer and seller; **firm price** = price which will not change; ***they are quoting a firm price of $1.23 a unit***; **going price** *or* **current price** *or* **usual price** = the price which is being charged now; **to sell goods off at half price** = to sell goods at half the price at which they were being sold before; **market price** = price at which a product can be sold; **net price** = price which cannot be reduced by a discount; **retail price** = price at which the retailer sells to the final customer; **Retail Price Index (RPI)** = index which shows how prices of consumer goods have increased or decreased over a period of time; **spot price** = price for immediate delivery of a commodity; ***the spot price of oil on the commodity markets***; **street price** *or* **shop price** = RETAIL PRICE; ***both machines go for $150 (street price), including a headset microphone***; **wholesale price** = price of a product which is sold by a wholesaler; **Wholesale Price Index** = index showing the rises and falls of wholesale prices of manufactured goods (usually moving about two months before a similar movement takes place on the Retail Price Index) **(b) price ceiling** = highest price which can be reached; **price change** = amount by which the price of a share moves during a day's trading; **price control** = legal measures to stop prices rising too fast; **price cutting** = sudden lowering of prices; **price war** *or* **price-cutting war** = competition between companies to get a larger market share by cutting prices; **price differential** = difference in price between products in a range; **price fixing** = illegal agreement between companies to charge the same price for competing products; **price label** *or* **price tag** = label which shows a price; ***the takeover bid put a $2m price tag on the company***; **price list** = sheet giving prices of goods for sale; **price movement** = change in prices of shares or commodities; **price range** = series of prices for similar products from different suppliers; **cars in the £8-9,000 price range** = cars of different makes, selling for between £8,000 and £9,000; **price-sensitive product** = product which will not sell if the price is increased **(c) to increase in price** = to become more expensive; ***petrol has increased in price*** *or* ***the price of petrol has increased***; **to increase prices** *or* **to raise prices** = to make items more expensive; **we will try to meet your price** = we will try to offer a price which is acceptable to you; **to cut prices** = to reduce prices suddenly; **to lower prices** *or* **to reduce prices** = to make items cheaper **(d)** *(on the Stock Exchange)* **asking price** = price which sellers are asking for shares; **closing price** = price at the end of a day's trading; **opening price** = price at the start of a day's trading **2** *verb* to give a price to a product; ***car priced at £5,000***; **competitively priced** = sold at a low price which competes with that of similar goods from other companies; **the company has priced itself out of the market** = the company has raised its prices so high that its products do not sell

> that British goods will price themselves back into world markets is doubtful as long as sterling labour costs continue to rise
>
> *Sunday Times*

> the average price per kilogram for this season has been 300c
>
> *Australian Financial Review*

> European manufacturers rely heavily on imported raw materials which are mostly priced in dollars
>
> *Duns Business Month*

> after years of relying on low wages for their competitive edge, Spanish companies are finding that rising costs and the strength of the peseta are pricing them out of the market
>
> *Wall Street Journal*

price/book ratio [ˈpraɪsbʊk ˈreɪʃɪəʊ] *noun* ratio of the price of a stock to its book value

> I wanted stocks with a P/E and price/book ratio below the average for the Standard & Poor's 500-stock index
>
> *Smart Money*

> he demonstrated that small companies and those with a low price/book ratio outperform over time
>
> *Smart Money*

price/earnings ratio (P/E ratio *or* **PER)** [ˈpraɪs ˈɜːnɪŋz ˈreɪʃəʊ] *noun* ratio between the current market price of a share and the earnings per share (the current dividend it produces) calculated by dividing the market price by the earnings per share; ***these shares sell at a P/E ratio of 7***; ***the price to earnings ratio is the quoted price of a share divided by its EPS***

> COMMENT: the P/E ratio is an indication of the way investors think a company will perform in the future, as a high market price suggests that investors expect earnings to grow and this gives a high P/E figure; a low P/E figure implies that investors think that earnings are not likely to rise

price/earnings multiple *or* **P/E multiple** *US* = PRICE/EARNINGS RATION

> the company's price/earnings multiple fell to 15 from 20 because of concerns over its Asian exposure
>
> *Smart Money*

> typical stock in Standard & Poor's 500 now carries a price/earnings multiple of 25
>
> *Fortune*

pricing [ˈpraɪsɪŋ] *noun* giving a price to a product; **pricing policy** = a company's policy in giving prices to its products; ***our pricing policy aims at producing a 35% gross margin***; **common pricing** = illegal fixing of prices by several businesses so that they all charge the same price; **competitive pricing** = putting a low price on a product so that it competes with similar products from other companies; **marginal pricing** = making the selling price the same as the cost of a single extra unit above the number already planned

primary [ˈpraɪməri] *adjective* **(a)** basic; **primary commodities** = raw materials or food; **primary industry** = industry dealing with basic raw materials (such as coal, wood, farm produce); **primary products** = products (such as wood, milk, fish) which are basic raw materials **(b)** first, most important; **primary**

account number (PAN)** = series of figures on a credit card, which are the number of the issuing bank and the personal number of the account; **primary dealer** = marketmaker dealing in government stocks; **primary market** = market where new securities or bonds are issued (if they are resold, it is on the secondary market); *compare* SECONDARY

> analysts are betting that US issuers will be a driving force in the primary market for these securities over the next few years
>
> *Wall Street Journal*

> farmers are convinced that primary industry no longer has the capacity to meet new capital taxes or charges on farm inputs
>
> *Australian Financial Review*

prime [praɪm] *adjective* **(a)** most important; **prime sites** = most valuable commercial sites (in main shopping streets, etc.) as opposed to secondary sites; **prime time** = most expensive advertising time for TV commercials; ***we are putting out a series of prime-time commercials*** **(b)** basic; **prime bills** = bills of exchange which do not involve any risk; **prime cost** = cost involved in producing a product, excluding overheads

prime rate *or* **prime** [ˈpraɪm ˈreɪt] *noun US* best rate of interest at which an American bank lends to its customers

> the base lending rate, or prime rate, is the rate at which banks lend to their top corporate borrowers
>
> *Wall Street Journal*

COMMENT: not the same as the British bank base rate, which is only a notional rate, as all bank loans in the UK are at a certain percentage point above the base rate

priming [ˈpraɪmɪŋ] noun *see* PUMP PRIMING

principal [ˈprɪnsəpl] **1** *noun* **(a)** person or company that is represented by an agent; ***the agent has come to London to see his principals*** **(b)** person acting for himself, such as a marketmaker buying securities on his own account **(c)** money lent or borrowed on which interest is paid; ***to repay principal and interest*** **2** *adjective* most important; ***the principal shareholders asked for a meeting***; ***the country's principal products are paper and wood***

> when you buy a muni, your broker is generally acting as a principal (selling bonds from inventory) rather than a broker (an agent who matches buyers and sellers)
>
> *Fortune*

> the company was set up with funds totalling NorKr 145m with the principal aim of making capital gains on the secondhand market
>
> *Lloyd's List*

principle [ˈprɪnsəpl] *noun* basic point, general rule; **in principle** = in agreement with a general rule; **agreement in principle** = agreement with the basic conditions of a proposal

prior [ˈpraɪə] *adjective* earlier; **prior agreement** = agreement which was reached earlier; **without prior knowledge** = without knowing before; **prior charge** = security (such as a preference share) which is repaid before other securities when a company goes into liquidation; **prior-charge capital** = capital in the form of preference shares

priority [praɪˈɒrəti] noun **to have priority** = to have the right to be first; **to have priority over or to take priority over something** = to be more important than something; ***reducing overheads takes priority over increasing turnover***; ***debenture holders have priority over ordinary shareholders***; **to give something top priority** = to make something the most important item

privacy [ˈpraɪvəsi] *noun* method of ensuring that a person's personal or credit card payment details cannot be intercepted and read when transferred over the internet; ***to be sure of privacy, I only enter my credit card details on a web site with SSL security***; *see also* AUTHENTICATION, PGP

private [ˈpraɪvət] *adjective* **(a)** belonging to a single person, not to a company nor to the state; **letter marked 'private and confidential'** = letter which must not be opened by anyone other than the person it is addressed to; **private client** *or* **private customer** = (i) client dealt with by a salesman as a person, not as a company; (ii) individual investor who is the client of a stockbroker; **private client stockbroker** = stockbroker who deals on behalf of private investors; **private income** = income from dividends, interest or rents which is not part of a salary; **private investor** = ordinary person with money to invest; **private placing** *US* **private**

placement = placing a new issue of shares with a group of selected financial institutions; **private property** = property which belongs to a private person, not to the public **(b) private (limited) company** = (i) company with a small number of shareholders whose shares are not traded on the Stock Exchange; (ii) subsidiary company whose shares are not listed on the Stock Exchange, while those of its parent company are; *(of a public company)* **to go private** = to become a private company again, by concentrating all its shares in the hands of one or a few shareholders and removing its stock exchange listing; *see also* PUBLIC-TO-PRIVATE, TAKE-PRIVATE **(c) private enterprise** = businesses which are owned by private shareholders, not by the state; ***the project is funded by private enterprise***; **the private sector** = all companies which are owned by private shareholders, not by the state

> in the private sector the total number of new house starts was 3 per cent higher than in the corresponding period last year, while public sector starts were 23 per cent lower
>
> *Financial Times*

> management had offered to take the company private through a leveraged buyout for $825 million
>
> *Fortune*

> private-client stockbrokers are suggesting investors should take a look at zero-dividend preference shares
>
> *Sunday Times*

privatization [praɪvətaɪ'zeɪʃən] *noun* selling a nationalized industry to private owners

privatize ['praɪvətaɪz] *verb* to sell a nationalized industry to private owners

pro [prəʊ] *preposition* for; **pro tem** = for the time being. temporarily; **per pro** = with the authority of; ***the secretary signed per pro the manager***

probate ['prəʊbeɪt] *noun* proving legally that a document, especially a will, is valid; **the executor was granted probate** = the executor was told officially that the will was valid; **probate court** = court which examines wills to see if they are valid

procedure [prə'siːdʒə] *noun* way in which something is done; ***to follow the proper procedure***; **this procedure is very irregular** = this is not the set way to do something; **accounting procedures** = set ways of doing the accounts of a company; **disciplinary procedure** = way of warning a worker that he is breaking the rules of a company; **complaints procedure** *or* **grievance procedure** = way of presenting complaints formally from a trade union to a management; **dismissal procedures** = correct way to dismiss someone, following the rules in the contract of employment

proceed [prə'siːd] *verb* to go on or to continue; ***the negotiations are proceeding slowly***; **to proceed against someone** = to start a legal action against someone; **to proceed with something** = to go on doing something; ***shall we proceed with the committee meeting?***

proceedings [prə'siːdɪŋz] *plural noun* **(a) conference proceedings** = written report of what has taken place at a conference **(b) legal proceedings** = legal action, lawsuit; ***to take proceedings against someone***; ***the court proceedings were adjourned***; **to institute proceedings against someone** = to start a legal action against someone

proceeds ['prəʊsiːdz] *plural noun* **the proceeds of a sale** = money received from a sale after deducting expenses; ***he sold his shop and invested the proceeds in a computer repair business***

process ['prəʊses] **1** *noun* **(a) industrial processes** = processes involved in manufacturing products in factories; **decision-making processes** = ways in which decisions are reached **(b) the due processes of the law** = the formal work of a legal action **2** *verb* **(a) to process figures** = to sort out information to make it easily understood; ***the sales figures are being processed by our accounts department***; ***data is being processed by our computer*** **(b)** to deal with something in the usual routine way; ***to process an insurance claim***; ***orders are processed in our warehouse***

processing ['prəʊsesɪŋ] *noun* **(a)** sorting of information; ***processing of information*** *or* ***of statistics***; **batch processing** = computer system, where information is collected into batches before being loaded into the computer; **data processing** *or* **information processing** = selecting and examining data in a computer to produce information in a special form; **word processing** *or* **text processing** = working with words, using a computer to produce, check and change texts, reports, letters, etc. **(b) the processing of a claim for insurance** = putting a claim for insurance through the usual office routine in the insurance company; **order processing** = dealing with orders

produce [prə'dju:s] *verb* **(a)** to bring out; ***he produced documents to prove his claim; the negotiators produced a new set of figures; the customs officer asked him to produce the relevant documents*** **(b)** to make or to manufacture; ***to produce cars** or **engines** or **books***; **to mass produce** = to make large quantities of a product **(c)** to give an interest; ***investments which produce about 10% per annum***

product ['prɒdʌkt] *noun* **(a)** thing which is made or manufactured; **basic product** = main product made from a raw material; **by-product** = secondary product made as a raw material is being processed; **end product** *or* **final product** *or* **finished product** = product made at the end of a production process **(b)** manufactured item for sale; **product advertising** = advertising a particular named product, not the company which makes it; **product analysis** = examining each separate product in a company's range to see why it sells, who buys it, etc.; **product design** = design of consumer products; **product development** = improving an existing product line to meet the needs of the market; **product engineer** = engineer in charge of the equipment for making a product; **product line** *or* **product range** = series of different products made by the same company which form a group (such as cars in different models, pens in different colours, etc.); **product management** = directing the making and selling of a product as an independent item; **product mix** = group of quite different products made by the same company **(c) gross domestic product (GDP)** = annual value of goods sold and services paid for inside a country; **gross national product (GNP)** = annual value of goods and services in a country, including income from other countries

production [prə'dʌkʃən] *noun* **(a)** showing something; **on production of** = when something is shown; ***the case will be released by the customs on production of the relevant documents; goods can be exchanged only on production of the sales slip*** **(b)** making or manufacturing of goods for sale; ***production will probably be held up by industrial action; we are hoping to speed up production by installing new machinery***; **batch production** = production in batches; **domestic production** = production of goods in the home market; **mass production** = manufacturing of large quantities of goods; **rate of production** *or* **production rate** = speed at which items are made; **production cost** = cost of making a product; **production department** = section of a company which deals with the making of the company's products; **production line** = system of making a product, where each item (such as a car) moves slowly through the factory with new sections added to it as it goes along; **production manager** = person in charge of the production department; **production unit** = separate small group of workers producing a certain product

productive [prə'dʌktɪv] *adjective* which produces; **productive capital** = capital which is invested to give interest; **productive discussions** = useful discussions which lead to an agreement or decision

productivity [prɒdʌk'tɪvɪti] *noun* (i) rate of output per worker or per machine in a factory; (ii) rate of return per unit (pound, dollar, etc.) of capital; ***bonus payments are linked to productivity; the company is aiming to increase productivity; productivity has fallen** or **risen since the company was taken over***; **productivity agreement** = agreement to pay a productivity bonus; **productivity bonus** = extra payments made to workers because of increased production; **productivity drive** = extra effort to increase productivity

> though there has been productivity growth, the absolute productivity gap between many British firms and their foreign rivals remains
>
> *Sunday Times*

profession [prə'feʃən] *noun* **(a)** work which needs special skills learnt over a period of time; ***the managing director is an accountant by profession*** **(b)** group of specialized workers; **the accounting profession** = all qualified accountants; **the banking profession** = all qualified bankers; **the legal profession** = all qualified lawyers

professional [prə'feʃənl] *adjective* **(a)** referring to one of the professions; ***the accountant sent in his bill for professional services; we had to ask our lawyer for professional advice on the contract***; **a professional man** = man who works in one of the professions (such as a lawyer, doctor, accountant); **professional qualifications** = documents showing that someone has successfully finished a course of study which allows him to work in one of the professions **(b)** doing work for money; **he is a professional troubleshooter** = he makes his living by helping companies to sort out their problems

> one of the key advantages of an accountancy qualification is its worldwide marketability. Other professions are not so lucky: lawyers, for example, are much more limited in where they can work
>
> *Accountancy*

profit ['prɒfit] *noun* **(a)** money gained from a sale which is more than the money spent; **clear profit** = profit after all expenses have been paid; ***we made $6,000 clear profit on the deal***; **excess profit** = profit which is higher than what is thought to be normal; **excess profits tax** = tax on excess profits; **gross profit** = profit calculated as sales income less the cost of the goods sold; **healthy profit** = quite a large profit; **net profit** = result where income from sales is larger than all expenditure; **net profit before tax** = profit of a company after expenses have been deducted but before tax has been paid; **operating profit** = result where sales from normal business activities are higher than the costs; **paper profit** = profit on an asset which has increased in price but has not been sold; ***he is showing a paper profit of £25,000 on his investment***; **trading profit** = result where the company' receipts are higher than its expenditure; **profit margin** = percentage difference between sales income and the cost of sales; **pretax profit margin** = the pretax profit shown as a percentage of turnover in a profit and loss account; **profits tax** *or* **tax on profits** = tax to be paid on profits; **profit before tax** *or* **pretax profit** = profit before any tax has been paid (NOTE: also called **profit on ordinary activities before tax**); **profit after tax** *or* **net profit** = profit after tax has been paid **(b) to take your profit** = to sell your shares at a higher price than was paid for them, and so realise the profit, rather than to keep them as an investment; *see also* PROFIT-TAKING; **to show a profit** = to make a profit and state it in the company accounts; ***we are showing a small profit for the first quarter***; **to make a profit** = to have more money as a result of a deal; **to move into profit** = to start to make a profit; ***the company is breaking even now, and expects to move into profit within the next two months***; **to sell at a profit** = to sell at a price which gives you a profit

> because capital gains are not taxed and money taken out in profits and dividends is taxed, owners of businesses will be using accountants and tax experts to find loopholes in the law
>
> *Toronto Star*

profitability [prɒfitə'bɪləti] *noun* **(a)** ability to make a profit **(b)** amount of profit made as a percentage of costs; **measurement of profitability** = way of calculating how profitable something is

profitable ['prɒfitəbl] *adjective* which makes a profit

profitably ['prɒfitəbli] *adverb* making a profit

profit and loss account (P&L account) ['prɒfit ən 'lɒs ə'kaʊnt] *noun* accounts for a company with expenditure and income over a period of time, almost always one calendar year, balanced to show a final profit or loss (the balance sheet shows the state of a company's finances at a certain date; the profit and loss account shows the movements which have taken place since the last balance sheet) (NOTE: the American equivalent is the **profit and loss statement** or **income statement**)

> the bank transferred $5 million to general reserve compared with $10 million in 1983 which made the consolidated profit and loss account look healthier
>
> *Hongkong Standard*

profit centre ['prɒfit 'sentə] *noun* person or department considered separately for the purposes of calculating a profit

profiteer [prɒfi'tɪə] *noun* person who makes too much profit, especially when goods are rationed or in short supply

profiteering [prɒfi'tɪərɪŋ] *noun* making too much profit

profit-making ['prɒfitmeɪkɪŋ] *adjective* which makes a profit; ***the whole project was expected to be profit-making by 1993***; *see also* NON PROFIT-MAKING

profit-sharing ['prɒfitʃeərɪŋ] *noun* arrangement where workers get a share of the profits of the company they work for; ***the company runs a profit-sharing scheme***

profit-taker ['prɒfitteɪkə] *noun* person who sells an investment in order to realise a profit

profit-taking ['prɒfitteɪkɪŋ] *noun* selling investments to realize the profit, rather than keeping them; ***share prices fell under continued profit-taking***

> some profit-taking was seen yesterday as investors

continued to lack fresh incentives to renew buying activity

Financial Times

---

pro forma ['prəʊ 'fɔːmə] **1** noun **pro forma (invoice)** = invoice sent to a buyer before the goods are sent, so that payment can be made or that business documents can be produced; ***they sent us a pro forma***; ***we only supply that account on pro forma*** **2** *verb* to send a pro forma invoice; ***can you pro forma this order?***

program ['prəʊgræm] **1** noun **computer program** = instructions to a computer telling it to do a particular piece of work; ***to buy a word-processing program***; ***the accounts department is running a new payroll program***; **program trading** = buying and selling shares according to instructions given by a computer program (the computer is programmed to buy or sell when certain prices are reached or when a certain volume of sales on the market is reached); **program trader** = person who buys or sells according to a computer program **2** *verb* to write a program for a computer; **to program a computer** = to install a program in a computer; ***the computer is programmed to print labels***; **programmed trading** = PROGRAM TRADING (NOTE: **programming - programmed)**

---

contrary to what is commonly believed, there appears to be little or no connection between stock-market volatility and program trading

Barron's

---

program trading is defined by the exchange as purchases or sales of 15 or more stocks with a combined value of at least $1 million. While it's often been considered to be synonymous with index arbitrage (buying or selling a basket of stocks against an index option or future), that form of trading is just one small part of it

Barron's

---

programme *US* **program** ['prəʊgræm] *noun* plan of things which will be done; ***development programme***; ***research programme***; ***training programme***; ***to draw up a programme of investment*** *or* ***an investment programme***

programmable [prəʊ'græməbl] *adjective* which can be programmed

programmer ['prəʊgræmə] noun **computer programmer** = person who writes computer programs

programming ['prəʊgræmɪŋ] noun **computer programming** = writing programs for computers; **programming engineer** = engineer in charge of programming a computer system; **programming language** = system of signs, letters and words used to instruct a computer

progress 1 ['prəʊgres] *noun* movement of work forward; ***to report on the progress of the work or of the negotiations***; **to make a progress report** = to report how work is going; **in progress** = which is being done but is not finished; **work in progress** = value of goods being manufactured which are not complete at the end of an accounting period; **progress payments** = payments made as each stage of a contract is completed; ***the fifth progress payment is due in March*** **2** [prə'gres] *verb* to move forward or to go ahead; ***the contract is progressing through various departments***

progressive [prə'gresɪv] *adjective* which moves forward in stages; **progressive taxation** = taxation system where tax levels increase as the income is higher (also called 'graduated taxation')

prohibitive [prə'hɪbɪtɪv] *adjective* with a price so high that you cannot afford to pay it; ***the cost of redeveloping the product would be prohibitive***

project ['prɒdʒekt] *noun* **(a)** plan; ***he has drawn up a project for developing new markets in Europe*** **(b)** particular job of work which follows a plan; ***we are just completing an engineering project in North Africa***; ***the company will start work on the project next month***; **project analysis** = examining all costs or problems of a project before work on it is started; **project engineer** = engineer in charge of a project; **project manager** = manager in charge of a project

projected [prə'dʒektɪd] *adjective* planned or expected; **projected sales** = forecast of sales; ***projected sales in Europe next year should be over £1m***

projection [prə'dʒekʃən] *noun* forecast of something which will happen in the future; ***projection of profits for the next three years***; ***the sales manager was asked to draw up sales projections for the next three years***

promise ['prɒmɪs] **1** *noun* saying that you will do something; **to keep a promise** = to do what you said you would do; ***he says he will pay next week, but he never keeps his***

promises; **to go back on a promise** = not to do what you said you would do; ***the management went back on its promise to increase salaries across the board***; **a promise to pay** = a promissory note **2** *verb* to say that you will do something; ***they promised to pay the last instalment next week***

promissory note [prə'mɪsəri 'nəʊt] *noun* document stating that someone promises to pay an amount of money on a certain date

promote [prə'məʊt] *verb* **(a)** to give someone a more important job; ***he was promoted from salesman to sales manager*** **(b)** to advertise; **to promote a new product** = to increase the sales of a new product by a sales campaign by TV commercials or free gifts or by giving discounts; ***they are promoting beef at 25% off this week*** **(c) to promote a new company** = to organize the setting up of a new company

promoter [prə'məʊtə] noun **company promoter** = person who organizes the setting up of a new company

promotion [prə'məʊʃən] *noun* **(a)** moving up to a more important job; ***promotion chances*** *or* ***promotion prospects***; ***he ruined his chances of promotion when he argued with the managing director***; **to earn promotion** = to work hard and efficiently and so be promoted **(b) promotion of a company** = setting up a new company **(c) promotion of a product** = selling a new product by publicity, by a sales campaign, TV commercials, free gifts, or by giving special discounts; ***promotion budget***; ***promotion team***; ***sales promotion***; ***special promotion***

promotional [prə'məʊʃənl] *adjective* used in an advertising campaign; **promotional budget** = forecast cost of promoting a new product

prompt [prɒmpt] *adjective* **(a)** rapid, done immediately; **prompt payer** = company which pays its bills rapidly; **prompt payment** = payment made rapidly; **prompt supplier** = supplier who delivers orders rapidly **(b) prompt date** = date for delivery, stated on a futures contract

> they keep shipping costs low and can take advantage of quantity discounts and other allowances for prompt payment
>
> *Duns Business Month*

proof [pru:f] *noun* thing which shows that something is true; **documentary proof** = proof in the form of a document

-proof [pru:f] *suffix* which prevents something harming; **inflation-proof pension** = pension which will rise to keep pace with inflation

property ['prɒpəti] *noun* **(a) personal property** = things which belong to a person; ***the storm caused considerable damage to personal property***; ***the management is not responsible for property left in the hotel rooms*** **(b)** land and buildings; ***damage to property*** *or* ***property damage***; ***the commercial property market is booming***; **property bond** = investment in a fund invested in properties or in property companies; **property company** = company which buys buildings to lease them; **property developer** = person who buys old buildings or empty land and builds new buildings for sale or rent; **the property market** = (i) the market in letting commercial properties; (ii) the market in developing commercial properties as investments; (iii) buying or selling residential properties by individual homeowners; **property shares** = shares in property companies; **property tax** = tax paid on building or land (such as the rates in the UK); **commercial property** = building used as offices or shops; **industrial property** = factories or other buildings used for industrial purposes; **private property** = property which belongs to a private person and not to the public; **residential property** = houses or flats owned or occupied by individual residents **(c)** a building; ***we have several properties for sale in the centre of the town***

proportion [prə'pɔ:ʃən] *noun* part (of a total); ***a proportion of the pre-tax profit is set aside for contingencies***; ***only a small proportion of our sales comes from retail shops***; **in proportion to** = showing how something is related to something else; ***profits went up in proportion to the fall in overhead costs***; ***sales in Europe are small in proportion to those in the USA***

proportional [prə'pɔ:ʃənl] *adjective* directly related; ***the increase in profit is proportional to reduction in overheads***

proportionately [prə'pɔ:ʃənətli] *adverb* in proportion

proprietary [prə'praɪətəri] *adjective* **(a)** product (such as a medicine) which is made and owned by a company; **proprietary drug** = drug which is made by a particular company and marketed under a brand name **(b)** *(in South Africa and Australia)* **proprietary company (pty)** = private limited company

pro rata ['prəʊ 'rɑ:tə] *adjective & adverb* at a rate which varies according to the size or importance of something; ***a pro rata payment***; ***to pay someone pro rata***; **dividends are paid pro rata** = dividends are paid according to the number of shares held

prospects ['prɒspekts] *noun* possibilities for the future; **his job prospects are good** = he is very likely to find a job; **prospects for the market** *or* **market prospects are worse than those of last year** = sales in the market are likely to be lower than they were last year; **growth prospects** = potential for growth in a share

prospective [prə'spektɪv] *adjective* which may happen in the future; **prospective dividend** = dividend which a company expects to pay at the end of the current year (NOTE: also called **forecast dividend**); **prospective P/E ratio** = P/E ratio expected in the future on the basis of forecast dividends

prospectus [prə'spektəs] *noun* (i) document which gives information to attract buyers or customers; (ii) document which gives information about a company whose shares are being sold to the public for the first time; **pathfinder prospectus** US **preliminary prospectus** = preliminary prospectus about a company which is going to be launched on the Stock Exchange, sent to potential major investors before the issue date, giving details of the company's background, but not giving the price at which shares will be sold (also called a 'red herring') (NOTE: plural is **prospectuses**)

> every new float must issue a prospectus detailing the financial state of the company and likely benefits for shareholders
>
> *The Times*

> when the prospectus emerges, existing shareholders and any prospective new investors can find out more by calling the free share information line; they will be sent a leaflet. Non- shareholders who register in this way will receive a prospectus when it is published; existing shareholders will be sent one automatically
>
> *Financial Times*

prosperous ['prɒspərəs] *adjective* rich; ***a prosperous shopkeeper***; ***a prosperous town***

prosperity [prɒ'sperəti] *noun* being rich; **in times of prosperity** = when people are rich

protect [prə'tekt] *verb* to defend something against harm; **to protect an industry by imposing tariff barriers** = to stop a local industry from being hit by foreign competition by taxing foreign products when they are imported

protection [prə'tekʃən] *noun* thing which protects; ***the legislation offers no protection to part-time workers***; **consumer protection** = protecting consumers against unfair or illegal traders

protectionism [prə'tekʃənɪzm] *noun* restriction of imports into a country to protect the country's own native industry

protective [prə'tektɪv] *adjective* which protects; **protective tariff** = tariff which tries to ban imports to stop them competing with local products

pro tem ['prəʊ 'tem] *adverb* temporarily, for a time

protest 1 ['prəʊtest] *noun* official document which states that a bill of exchange has not been paid **2** [prə'test] verb **to protest a bill** = to draw up a document to prove that a bill of exchange has not been paid

provide [prə'vaɪd] *verb* **(a) to provide for** = to allow for something which may happen in the future; ***the contract provides for an annual increase in charges***; ***£10,000 of expenses have been provided for in the budget*** **(b)** to put money aside in accounts to cover expenditure or losses in the future; ***£25,000 is provided against bad debts***

provident ['prɒvɪdənt] *adjective* which provides benefits in case of illness, old age, etc.; ***a provident fund***; ***a provident society***

provision [prə'vɪʒən] *noun* **(a) to make provision for** = to see that something is allowed for in the future; **there is no provision for** *or* **no provision has been made for car parking in the plans for the office block** = the plans do not include space for cars to park **(b) provisions** = money put aside in accounts for anticipated expenditure (if the expenditure is not certain, then the money set aside is called 'contingent liability'); ***the bank has made a £2m provision for bad debts*** *or* ***a $5bn provision against Third World loans*** **(c)** legal condition; **we have made provision to this effect** = we have put into the contract terms which will make this work

> mortgage banks are unlikely to see more than a fraction of the bad debt provisions of other lenders
>
> *Investors Chronicle*

provisional [prəˈvɪʒənl] *adjective* temporary, not final or permanent; ***provisional forecast of sales; provisional budget; they faxed their provisional acceptance of the contract***

provisionally [prəˈvɪʒnəli] *adverb* not finally; ***the contract has been accepted provisionally***

proxy [ˈprɒksi] *noun* **(a)** document which gives someone the power to act on behalf of someone else; ***to sign by proxy***; **proxy vote** = votes made by proxy; ***the proxv votes were all in favour of the board's recommendation*** **(b)** person who acts on behalf of someone else; ***to act as proxy for someone; shareholders who are unable to attend the AGM are asked to appoint proxies***; **proxy form** *or* **proxy card** = form which a shareholder receives with his invitation to attend an AGM, which he fills in if he wants to appoint a proxy to vote for him on a resolution; **proxy statement** = document filed with the SEC outlining executive pay packages, option grants and other perks, and also giving details of dealings by executives in shares of the company

prudent [ˈpruːdənt] *adjective* careful, not taking any risks; **prudent man rule** = rule that trustees who make financial decisions on behalf of other people should act carefully (as a normal prudent person would)

prudential [prəˈdenʃl] *adjective* which is careful, prudent; **prudential ratio** = ratio of capital to assets which a bank feels it is prudent to have, according to EC regulations

PSBR = PUBLIC SECTOR BORROWING REQUIREMENT

ptas [pəˈseɪtəz] = PESETAS

Pte; *(Singapore)* = PRIVATE LIMITED COMPANY

Pty = PROPRIETARY COMPANY; *(Australia)* **Pty Ltd** = private limited company

public [ˈpʌblɪk] *adjective* **(a)** referring to all the people in general; **public holiday** = day when all workers rest and enjoy themselves instead of working; **public utilities** = companies (such as electricity, gas, transport, etc.) which provide a service used by the whole community **(b)** referring to the government or the state; **public expenditure** = spending of money by the local or central government; **public finance** = the raising of money by governments (by taxes or borrowing) and the spending of it; **public funds** = government money available for expenditure; **public ownership** = situation where the government owns a business, i.e., where an industry is nationalized; **public spending** = spending by the government or by local authorities **(c) the company is going public** = the company is going to place some of its shares for sale on the stock market so that anyone can buy them; *US* **public offering** = offering new shares in a corporation for sale to the public as a way of launching the corporation on the Stock Exchange (NOTE: the British equivalent for this is an **offer for sale**); **public placing** = offering a new issue of shares to the public

> since the company went public in 1922, its stock is up tenfold
>
> *Fortune*

Public Limited Company (Plc) [ˈpʌblɪk ˈlɪmɪtɪd ˈkʌmpni] *noun* company whose shares are listed on the Stock Exchange

public sector [ˈpʌblɪk ˈsektə] *noun* nationalized industries and services; ***a report on wage rises in the public sector*** *or* ***on public sector wage settlements***; **Public Sector Borrowing Requirement (PSBR)** = amount of money which a government has to borrow to pay for its own spending (i.e., the difference between the government's expenditure and its income)

public-to-private deal [ˈpʌblɪk tθ ˈpraɪvət ˈdiːl] *noun* arrangement by which a quoted company leaves the Stock Exchange and becomes a privately owned investment; *see also* TAKE-PRIVATE

> public-to-private deals are just one feature of an evolving and increasingly mature corporate finance sector in the North West
>
> *Investors Chronicle*

pula [ˈpjuːlə] *noun* currency used in Botswana

pull off [ˈpʊl ˈɒf] verb *(informal)* to succeed in negotiating a deal

pull out [ˈpʊl ˈaʊt] *verb* to stop being part of a deal or agreement; ***our Australian partners pulled out of the contract***

pump [pʌmp] *verb* to put something in by force; ***the banks have been pumping money into the company to keep it afloat***

> in each of the years 1986 to 1989, Japan pumped a net sum of the order of $100bn into foreign securities, notably into US government bonds
>
> *Financial Times Review*

pump priming ['pʌmp 'praɪmɪŋ] *noun* government investment in new projects which it hopes will benefit the economy

punt [pʌnt] **1** *noun* **(a)** currency used in the Republic of Ireland **(b)** *(informal)* gamble; ***these shares are probably worth a punt*** **2** *verb* to gamble or to bet (on something)

punter ['pʌntə] *noun* person who gambles or who hopes to make money on the Stock Exchange

purchase ['pɜ:tʃəs] **1** *noun* thing which has been bought; **to make a purchase** = to buy something; *US* **purchase acquisition** = full consolidation, where the assets of a subsidiary company which has been purchased are included into the parent company's balance sheet, and the premium paid for the goodwill is written off against the year's earnings (the British equivalent is 'acquisition accounting'); **purchase book** = records of purchases; **purchase ledger** = book in which expenditure is noted; **purchase order** = official order made out by a purchasing department for goods which a company wants to buy; ***we cannot supply you without a purchase order number***; **purchase price** = price paid for something; **purchase tax** = tax paid on things which are bought; **bulk purchase** *or* **quantity purchase** = buying of large quantities of goods at low prices; **cash purchase** = purchase made in cash; **hire purchase** = system of buying something by paying a sum regularly each month; ***he is buying a refrigerator on hire purchase***; **hire purchase agreement** = contract to pay for something by instalments **2** *verb* to buy; **to purchase something for cash** = to pay cash for something

purchaser ['pɜ:tʃəsə] *noun* person or company that purchases; **the company is looking for a purchaser** = the company is trying to find someone who will buy it; ***the company has found a purchaser for its warehouse***

purchasing ['pɜ:tʃəsɪŋ] *noun* buying; **purchasing department** = section of a company which deals with buying of stock, raw materials, equipment, etc.; **purchasing manager** = head of a purchasing department; **purchasing officer** = person in a company or organization who is responsible for buying stock, raw materials, equipment, etc.; **purchasing power** = quantity of goods which can be bought by a group of people, with an amount of money; ***the decline in the purchasing power of the pound***; **central purchasing** = purchasing organized by the main office for all departments or branches

purse [pɜ:s] *noun* small, usually leather, bag for keeping money in; **electronic purse** *or* **e-purse** = concept developed to provide a way of holding a virtual token when shopping on the internet; ***you should treat your electronic purse like cash in a wallet***; *see also* VIRTUAL TOKEN

push [pʊʃ] verb **to push a share** = to try to persuade investors to buy a share (using forceful means)

put [pʊt] **1** noun **put option** = right to sell shares at a certain price at a certain date (NOTE: the opposite is a **call option**) **2** *verb* to place or to fix; **the accounts put the stock value at £10,000** = the accounts state that the value of the stock is £10,000; **to put a proposal to the vote** = to ask a meeting to vote for or against a proposal; **to put a proposal to the board** = to ask the board to consider a suggestion (NOTE: **putting - put**)

put down ['pʊt 'daʊn] *verb* **(a)** to make a deposit; ***to put down money on a house*** **(b)** to write an item in a ledger or account book; ***to put down a figure for expenses***

put in ['pʊt 'ɪn] verb **to put in a bid for something** = to offer (usually in writing) to buy something; **to put in an estimate for something** = to give someone a written calculation of the probable costs of carrying out a job; **to put in a claim for damage** = to ask an insurance company to pay for damage

put into ['pʊt 'ɪntʊ] verb **to put money into a business** = to invest money in a business

put on ['pʊt 'ɒn] verb **to put an item on the agenda** = to list an item for discussion at a meeting; **to put an embargo on trade** = to forbid trade; **property shares put on gains of 10%-15%** = shares in property companies increased in value by 10%-15%

put up ['pʊt 'ʌp] *verb* **(a) who put up the money for the shop?** = who provided the investment money for the shop to start?; **to put something up for sale** = to advertise that something is for sale; ***when he retired he decided to put his town flat up for sale*** **(b)** to increase, to make higher; ***the shop has put up all its prices by 5%***

PV = PRESENT VALUE

pyramid selling ['pɪrəmɪd 'selɪŋ] *noun* illegal way of selling goods to the public, where each selling agent pays for the right to sell and sells that right to other agents, so that in the end the commissions earned by the sales of goods will never pay back the agents for the payments they themselves have already made

pyramiding [ˈpɪrəmɪdɪŋ] *noun* **(a)** building up a major group by acquiring controlling interests in many different companies, each larger than the original company **(b)** illegally using new investors' deposits to pay the interest on the deposits made by existing investors

Qq

quadruplicate [kwɒ'druːplɪkət] noun **in quadruplicate** = with the original and three copies; ***the invoices are printed in quadruplicate***

qualification [kwɒlɪfɪ'keɪʃn] *noun* **(a)** proof that you have completed a specialized course of study; ***to have the right qualifications for the job***; **professional qualifications** = documents which show that someone has successfully finished a course of study which allows him to work in one of the professions **(b) period of qualification** = time which has to pass before someone qualifies for something **(c) auditors' qualification** = notes from the auditors of a company's accounts, stating that in their opinion items in the accounts are not a true reflection of the company's financial position; *see also* QUALIFIED AUDIT REPORT

qualified ['kwɒlɪfaɪd] *adjective* **(a)** having passed special examinations in a subject; ***she is a qualified accountant***; ***we have appointed a qualified designer to supervise the new factory project***; **highly qualified** = with very good results in examinations **(b)** with some reservations or conditions; ***qualified acceptance of a contract***; ***the plan received qualified approval from the board*** **(c) qualified accounts** = accounts which have been noted by the auditors because they contain something with which the auditors do not agree; **qualified auditors' report** *or* **qualified audit report** *US* **qualified opinion** = report from a company's auditors which points out items in accounts with which the auditors do not agree

> applicants will be professionally qualified and ideally have a degree in Commerce and post graduate management qualifications
>
> *Australian Financial Review*

qualify ['kwɒlɪfaɪ] *verb* **(a) to qualify for** = to be in the right position for, to be entitled to; ***the company does not qualify for a government grant***; ***she qualifies for unemployment pay*** **(b) to qualify as** = to follow a specialized course and pass examinations so that you can do a certain job; ***she has qualified as an accountant***; ***he will qualify as a solicitor next year*** **(c) the auditors have qualified the accounts** = the auditors have found something in the accounts of the company which they do not agree with, and have noted it

> federal examiners will also determine which of the privately insured savings and loans qualify for federal insurance
>
> *Wall Street Journal*

qualifying ['kwɒlɪfaɪɪŋ] *adjective* **(a) qualifying period** = time which has to pass before something qualifies for a grant or subsidy, etc.; ***there is a six-month qualifying period before you can get a grant from the local authority;*** *US* **qualifying ratio** = calculation of how much mortgage a borrower can afford, by comparing his monthly incoming against his monthly outgoings **(b) qualifying distribution** = payment of a dividend to a shareholder, on which advance corporation tax is paid; **qualifying shares** = number of shares which you need to earn to get a bonus issue, to be a director of the company, etc.

quality ['kwɒlɪti] noun **flight to quality** = tendency of investors to buy safe blue-chip securities when the economic outlook is uncertain

> the flight to quality has been underway for some time and gilt prices have risen sharply as result
>
> *Money Observer*

quant funds ['kwɒnt 'fʌndz] = QUANTITATIVE FUNDS

> since quant funds use computers to pick stocks that fit certain criteria and then ignore Wall Street's euphoria or disappointment about them, that can give a fund a leg up in a volatile market
>
> *Smart Money*

quantify ['kwɒntɪfaɪ] *verb* **to quantify the effect of something** = to show the effect of something in figures; ***it is impossible to quantify the effect of the new legislation on our turnover***

quantifiable ['kwɒntɪfaɪəbl] *adjective* which can be quantified; ***the effect of the change in the discount structure is not quantifiable***

quantitative ['kwɒntɪtətɪv] *adjective* referring to quantities or to quantity; **quantitative funds** *or* **quant funds** = funds which invest according to the instruction given by a computer model; ***with quantitative mutual funds, it's a machine that does the thinking***

> the EC demands that Japan abolish quantitative restrictions and cut import tariffs in three sectors: food, fish products and leather
>
> *Times*

quantity ['kwɒntəti] *noun* large amount; ***the company offers a discount for quantity purchase***; **quantity discount** = discount given to a customer who buys large quantities of goods

quantum meruit ['kwɒntʌm 'meruɪt] *Latin phrase* meaning 'as much as has been earned'

quarter ['kwɔːtə] *noun* **(a)** one of four equal parts; **a quarter of a litre** *or* **a quarter litre** = 250 millilitres; **a quarter of an hour** = 15 minutes; **three quarters** = 75%; ***three quarters of the staff are less than thirty years old***; ***he paid only a quarter of the list price*** **(b)** period of three months; **first quarter, second quarter, third quarter, fourth quarter** *or* **last quarter** = periods of three months from January to the end of March, from April to the end of June, from July to the end of September, from October to the end of the year; ***the instalments are payable at the end of each quarter***; ***the first quarter's rent is payable in advance*** **(c)** US *(informal)* 25 cent coin

> corporate profits for the first quarter showed a 4 per cent drop from last year's final three months
>
> *Financial Times*

> economists believe the economy is picking up this quarter and will do better still in the second half of the year
>
> *Sunday Times*

quarter day ['kwɑːtə 'deɪ] *noun* day at the end of a quarter, when rents and fees, etc., should be paid

> COMMENT: in England, the quarter days are 25th March (Lady Day), 24th June (Midsummer Day), 29th September (Michaelmas Day) and 25th December (Christmas Day)

quarterly ['kwɔːtəli] **1** *adjective & adverb* happening every three months, happening four times a year; ***there is a quarterly charge for electricity***; ***the bank sends us a quarterly statement***; ***we agreed to pay the rent quarterly*** *or* ***on a quarterly basis*** **2** *noun* US the results of a corporation, produced each quarter

> he and his competitors are judged on three broad criteria: the stock they recommend for purchase or sale, the accuracy of their estimates of quarterly and annual earnings and their ability to forecast into the future
>
> *Smart Money*

quartile ['kwɔːtaɪl] *noun* one of three figures below which 25%, 50% or 75% of a total falls

quasi- ['kweɪzaɪ] *prefix* almost, which seems like; ***a quasi-official body***

quasi-loan ['kweɪzaɪ'ləʊn] *noun* agreement between two parties where one agrees to pay the other's debts, provided that the second party agrees to reimburse the first at some later date

quasi-public corporation ['kweɪzaɪ'pʌblɪk kɔːpə'reɪʃn] *noun* US American institution which is privately owned, but which serves a public function (such as the Federal National Mortgage Association)

queue [kjuː] **1** *noun* **(a)** line of people waiting one behind the other; ***to form a queue*** *or* ***to join a queue***; ***queues formed at the doors of the bank when the news spread about its possible collapse***; **dole queue** = line of people waiting to collect their unemployment benefit **(b)** series of documents (such as orders, application forms) which are dealt with in order; **his order went to the end of the queue** = his order was dealt with last; **mortgage queue** = list of people waiting for mortgages **2** *verb* to form a line one after the other for something; ***when food was rationed, people had to queue for bread***; ***we queued for hours to get tickets***; ***a list of***

companies queueing to be launched on the Stock Exchange

quetzal ['kwetzəl] *noun* currency used in Guatemala

quick [kwɪk] *adjective* fast, not taking any time; ***the company made a quick recovery***; ***he is looking for a quick return on his investments***; ***we are hoping for a quick sale***; **quick assets** = cash, or bills which can easily be changed into cash; **to make a quick buck** = to make a profit very quickly; **quick ratio** = ratio of liquid assets (that is, current assets less stock) to current liabilities, giving an indication of a company's solvency (NOTE: also called **acid test ratio**)

quid pro quo ['kwɪd 'prəʊ 'kwəʊ] *noun* money paid or action carried out in return for something; ***he agreed to repay the loan early, and as a quid pro quo the bank released the collateral***

quiet ['kwaɪət] *adjective* calm, not excited; ***the market is very quiet***; ***currency exchanges were quieter after the government's statement on exchange rates***

quitclaim ['kwɪtkleɪm] *noun* release of someone from any claim that might exist against him or that he might have on something

quorum ['kwɔːrəm] *noun* number of people who have to be present at a meeting to make it valid; **to have a quorum** = to have enough people present for a meeting to go ahead; ***do we have a quorum?***

> COMMENT: if there is a quorum at a meeting, the meeting is said to be 'quorate'; if there aren't enough people present to make a quorum, the meeting is 'inquorate'

quota ['kwəʊtə] *noun* fixed amount of something which is allowed; **import quota** = fixed quantity of a particular type of goods which the government allows to be imported; ***the government has imposed a quota on the importation of cars***; ***the quota on imported cars has been lifted***; **quota system** = system where imports or supplies are regulated by fixing maximum amounts; **to arrange distribution through a quota system** = to arrange distribution by allowing each distributor only a certain number of items

> Canada agreed to a new duty-free quota of 600,000 tonnes a year
>
> *Globe and Mail (Toronto)*

quotation [kwəʊ'teɪʃn] *noun* **(a)** estimate of how much something will cost; ***they sent in their quotation for the job***; ***to ask for quotations for refitting the shop***; ***his quotation was much lower than all the others***; ***we accepted the lowest quotation*** **(b) quotation on the Stock Exchange** *or* **Stock Exchange quotation** = listing of the price of a share on the Stock Exchange; **the company is going for a quotation on the Stock Exchange** = the company has applied to the Stock Exchange to have its shares listed; ***we are seeking a stock market quotation***

quote ['kwəʊt] **1** *verb* **(a)** to repeat words used by someone else; to repeat a reference number; ***he quoted figures from the annual report***; ***in reply please quote this number***; ***when making a complaint please quote the batch number printed on the box***; ***he replied, quoting the number of the account*** **(b)** to estimate, to say what costs may be; ***to quote a price for supplying stationery***; ***their prices are always quoted in dollars***; ***he quoted me a price of £1,026***; ***can you quote for supplying 20,000 envelopes?*** **2** *noun* **(a)** *(informal)* estimate of how much something will cost; ***to give someone a quote for supplying computers***; ***we have asked for quotes for refitting the shop***; ***his quote was the lowest of three***; ***we accepted the lowest quote*** **(b) stock quote** = current price of a share on a stock exchange; **quote-driven system** = system of working a stock market, where marketmakers quote a price for a stock (as opposed to an order-driven system)

> the company offers an information-services package, including e-mail, stock quotes, weather and sports for $9.95 a month
>
> *Smart Money*

> banks operating on the foreign exchange market refrained from quoting forward US/Hongkong dollar exchange rates
>
> *South China Morning Post*

quoted ['kwəʊtɪd] adjective **quoted company** = company whose shares can be bought or sold on the Stock Exchange; **quoted shares** = shares which can be bought or sold on the Stock Exchange

> a Bermudan-registered company quoted on the Luxembourg stock exchange
>
> *Lloyd's List*

qty = QUANTITY

Rr

R&D ['ɑːr ən 'diː] = RESEARCH AND DEVELOPMENT; ***the R&D department***; ***the company spends millions on R&D***

racket ['rækɪt] *noun* illegal deal which makes a lot of money; ***he runs a cut-price ticket racket***

racketeer [rækə'tɪə] *noun* person who runs a racket

racketeering [rækə'tɪərɪŋ] *noun US* crime of carrying on an illegal business to make money

rack rent ['ræk 'rent] *noun* (i) very high rent; (ii) full yearly rent of a property let on a normal lease

raid [reɪd] *noun* sudden attack; **raid alarm** = automatic alarm in a bank which goes off when a robbery is taking place; *see also* BEAR RAID, DAWN RAID

raider ['reɪdə] *noun* person or company which buys a stake in another company before making a hostile takeover bid (also called a 'corporate raider')

> bear raiding involves trying to depress a target company's share price by heavy selling of its shares, spreading adverse rumours or a combination of the two. As an added refinement, the raiders may sell short. The aim is to push down the price so that the raiders can buy back the shares they sold at a lower price
>
> *Guardian*

raise [reɪz] **1** *noun US* increase in salary; ***he asked the boss for a raise***; ***she is pleased - she has had her raise*** (NOTE: British English is **rise**) **2** *verb* **(a) to raise a cheque** = to write out a cheque, either by hand or by machine; **to raise an invoice** = to write out an invoice **(b)** to increase or to make higher; ***the government has raised the tax levels***; ***air fares will be raised on June 1st***; ***the company raised its dividend by 10%***; ***when the company raised its prices, it lost half of its share of the market; US* raised check** = cheque where the amount has been increased by hand illegally **(c)** to obtain (money) or to organize (a loan); ***the company is trying to raise the capital to fund its expansion programme***; ***the government raises more money by indirect taxation than by direct***; ***where will he raise the money from to start up his business?***

> the company said yesterday that its recent share issue has been oversubscribed, raising A$225.5m
>
> *Financial Times*

> investment trusts can raise capital, but this has to be done as a company does, by a rights issue of equity
>
> *Investors Chronicle*

> over the past few weeks, companies raising new loans from international banks have been forced to pay more
>
> *Financial Times*

rake in ['reɪk 'ɪn] *verb* to gather together; **to rake in cash** *or* **to rake it in** = to make a lot of money

rake-off ['reɪkɒf] *noun* commission; ***the group gets a rake-off on all the company's sales***; ***he got a £100,000 rake-off for introducing the new business***

rally ['ræli] **1** *noun* rise in price when the trend has been downwards; ***shares staged a rally on the Stock Exchange***; ***after a brief rally shares fell back to a new low*** **2** *verb* to rise in price, when the trend has been downwards; ***shares rallied on the news of the latest government figures***

> when Japan rallied, it had no difficulty in surpassing its previous all-time high, and this really stretched the price-earnings ratios into the stratosphere
>
> *Money Observer*

> bad news for the US economy ultimately may have been the cause of a late rally in stock prices yesterday
>
> *Wall Street Journal*

ramp [ræmp] *noun* buying of shares in order to force up the price (as when a company buys its own shares illegally during a takeover bid)

rand [rænd] *noun* currency used in South Africa

random ['rændəm] *adjective* done without making any special choice; **random check** = check on items taken from a group without any special choice; **random error** = computer error which has no special reason; **random sample** = sample for testing taken without any choice; **random sampling** = choosing samples for testing without any special selection; **random walk** = movement which cannot be predicted (used to describe movements in share prices which cannot be forecast)

range [reɪndʒ] *noun* scale of items from a low point to a high one; **range of prices** *or* **trading range** = difference between the highest and lowest price for a share or bond over a period of time; **historical trading range** = range of prices at which a share has been sold on the stock exchange over a long period of time; *US* **range forward** = forward currency contract which includes an option to purchase currency futures and so has the effect of limiting potential exchange losses

rank [ræŋk] **1** *noun* position in a company or an organization; ***all managers are of equal rank***; **in rank order** = in order according to position of importance **2** *verb* **(a)** to classify in order; ***candidates are ranked in order of appearance*** **(b)** to be in a certain position; ***the non-voting shares rank equally with the voting shares***; ***deferred ordinary shares do not rank for dividend***

> in a separate development, the Geneva-based bank confirmed that it has accelerated the six Swiss bond issues. Acceleration means the bonds become payable immediately and allows bondholders to rank alongside the company's other creditors
>
> *Times*

rata ['rɑːtə] *see* PRO RATA

rate [reɪt] *noun* **(a)** money charged for time worked or work completed; **all-in rate** = price which covers all items in a purchase (such as delivery, tax and insurance, as well as the goods themselves); **fixed rate** = charge which cannot be changed; **flat rate** = charge which always stays the same; ***a flat-rate increase of 10%***; ***we pay a flat rate for electricity each quarter***; ***he is paid a flat rate of £2 per thousand***; **freight rates** = charges for transporting goods; **full rate** = full charge, with no reductions; **the going rate** = the usual or the current rate of payment; **letter rate** *or* **parcel rate** = postage (calculated by weight) for sending a letter or a parcel; **the market rate** = normal price in the market; ***we pay the going rate*** *or* ***the market rate for typists***; ***the going rate for offices is £20 per square foot***; **night rate** = cheap rate for telephone calls at night; **reduced rate** = specially cheap charge **(b) depreciation rate** = rate at which an asset is depreciated each year in the company accounts; **discount rate** = percentage taken by a bank when it buys bills; **insurance rates** = amount of premium which has to be paid per £1000 of insurance **(c)** amount of interest paid; **interest rate** *or* **rate of interest** = percentage charge for borrowing money; **rate of return** = amount of interest or dividend which comes from an investment, shown as a percentage of the money invested; **(bank) base rates** = basic rate of interest which a bank uses to calculate the actual rate of interest on loans to customers; *see also* HURDLE **(d)** value of one currency against another; ***what is today's rate*** *or* ***the current rate for the dollar?***; **cross rate** = exchange rate between two currencies expressed in a third currency; **exchange rate** *or* **rate of exchange** = rate at which one currency is exchanged for another; **to calculate costs on a fixed exchange rate** = to calculate costs on an exchange rate which does not change; **forward rate** = rate for purchase of foreign currency at a fixed price for delivery at a later date **(e)** amount or number or speed compared with something else; ***the rate of increase in redundancies***; ***the rate of absenteeism*** *or* ***the absenteeism rate always increases in fine weather***; **birth rate** = number of children born per 1,000 of the population; **call rate** = number of calls (per day or per week) which a salesman makes on customers; **error rate** = number of mistakes per thousand entries or per page; **rate of sales** = speed at which units are sold **(f)** *GB* **rates** = local taxes on all property; **uniform business rate (UBR)** = tax levied on business property which is the same percentage for the whole country

> state-owned banks cut their prime rate a percentage point to 11%
>
> *Wall Street Journal*

> the unions had argued that public sector pay rates had slipped behind rates applying in private sector employment
>
> *Australian Financial Review*

> royalties have been levied at a rate of 12.5% of full production
>
> *Lloyd's List*

rateable ['reɪtəbl] adjective **rateable value** = value of a commercial property as a basis for calculating local taxes

ratepayer ['reɪtpeɪə] noun **business ratepayer** = business which pays local taxes on a shop, office, factory, etc.

rating ['reɪtɪŋ] *noun* **(a)** putting in order of value or of merit; **credit rating** = amount which a credit agency feels a customer will be able to repay; **merit rating** = judging how well a worker does his work, so that he can be paid according to merit; **performance rating** = judging how well a share or a company has performed; **stockmarket rating** = price of a share on the stockmarket, which shows how investors and financial advisers generally consider the value of the company; **rating agency** = organization which gives a rating to companies or other organizations issuing bonds; *see also* RERATING **(b) ratings** = estimated number of people who watch TV programmes; ***the show is high in the ratings, which means it will attract good publicity*** **(c)** valuing of property; **rating officer** = official in a local authority who decides the rateable value of a commercial property

ratio ['reɪʃɪəʊ] *noun* proportion or quantity of something compared to something else; ***the ratio of successes to failures***; ***our product outsells theirs by a ratio of two to one***; **ratio analysis** = method of analyzing the performance of a company by showing the figures in its accounts as ratios and comparing them with those of other companies; **cost-income ratio** = ratio between the costs involved in running a business and the income the business produces; *see also* PRICE/EARNINGS RATIO

> the life insurer has suggested a merger is the answer, arguing that the increased volumes of sales would reduce cost-income ratios
>
> *The Times*

raw [rɔ:] *adjective* in the original state, not processed; **raw data** = data as it is put into a computer, without being analysed; **raw materials** = substances which have not been manufactured (such as wool, wood, sand)

> it makes sense for them to produce goods for sale back home in the US from plants in Britain where raw materials are relatively cheap
>
> *Duns Business Month*

R/D = REFER TO DRAWER

RDG = REGIONAL DEVELOPMENT GRANT

re- [ri:] *prefix* again

react [ri'ækt] verb **to react to** = to do or to say something in reply to what someone has done or said; ***shares reacted sharply to the fall in the exchange rate***

reaction [ri'ækʃən] *noun* (i) change or action in reply to something said or done; (ii) slight price movement (up or down); ***the reaction of the shares to the news of the takeover bid***

read [ri:d] *verb* to look at printed words and understand them; ***the terms and conditions are printed in very small letters so that they are difficult to read***; **can the computer read this information?** = can the computer take in this information and understand it or analyze it?

readable ['ri:dəbl] *adjective* which can be read; **machine-readable codes** = sets of signs or letters (such as bar codes, post codes) which can be read and understood by a computer; **the data has to be presented in computer-readable form** = in a form which a computer can read

reader/sorter ['ri:də'sɔ:tə] *noun* machine in a bank which reads cheques and sorts them automatically

readjust [ri:ə'dʒʌst] *verb* to adjust again; ***to readjust prices to take account of the rise in the costs of raw materials***; ***shares prices readjusted quickly to the news of the devaluation***

readjustment [ri:ə'dʒʌstmənt] *noun* act of readjusting; ***a readjustment in pricing***; ***after the devaluation there was a period of readjustment in the exchange rates***

ready ['redi] adjective **ready cash** = money which is immediately available for payment; **these items find a ready sale in the Middle East** = these items sell rapidly or easily in the Middle East

real [rɪəl] *adjective* **(a)** (price, etc.) shown in terms of money adjusted for inflation; **real income** *or* **real wages** = income which is available for spending after tax, etc., has been deducted and after inflation has been taken into account; **real interest rate** = interest rate after taking inflation into account; **real money** = cash used for settling debts (as opposed to cheques, drafts, etc.); **real rate of return** = actual rate of return, calculated after taking inflation into account; **real value** = value of an investment which is kept the same (by index- linking, for example); **in real terms** = actually or really; ***prices have gone up by 3% but with inflation running at 5% that is a fall in real terms*** **(b) real time** = time when a computer is working on the processing of data while the problem to which the data refers is actually taking place; **real-time system** = computer system where data is inputted directly into the computer which automatically processes it to produce information which can be used immediately; **real-time gross settlement (RTGS) system** = international system for making computerized transfers of money; *see also* TARGET **(c) real estate** = property (land or buildings); ***he made his money from real estate deals in the 1970s;*** *US* **real estate agent** = person who sells property for customers; *US* **real estate investment trust (REIT)** = public trust company which invests only in property; *see also* EQUITY REIT, MORTGAGE REIT

---

real wages have been held down dramatically: they have risen as an annual rate of only 1% in the last two years

Sunday Times

---

sterling M3 rose by 13.5% in the year to August - seven percentage points faster than the rate of inflation and the biggest increase in real terms since 1972-3

Economist

---

on top of the cost of real estate, the investment in inventory and equipment to open a typical warehouse comes to around $5 million

Duns Business Month

---

real [reɪ'æl] *noun* currency used in Brazil (NOTE: written as **R$** before the sum in transactions: **R$1500)**

realizable [rɪə'laɪzəbl] adjective **realizable assets** = assets which can be sold for money

realization [rɪəlaɪ'zeɪʃən] *noun* **(a)** making real; **the realization of a project** = putting as project into action **(b) realization of assets** = selling of assets for money

realize ['rɪəlaɪz] *verb* **(a)** to make something become real; **to realize a project** *or* **a plan** = to put a project or a plan into action **(b)** to sell for money; ***to realize property*** *or* ***assets***; ***the sale realized £100,000***; **realized profit** = actual profit made when something is sold (as opposed to paper profit)

realtor ['rɪəltə] *noun* *US* person who sells real estate for customers

realty ['rɪəlti] *noun* property or real estate

reasonable ['ri:zənəbl] *adjective* **(a)** sensible, not annoyed; **no reasonable offer refused** = we will accept any offer which is not extremely low **(b)** moderate, not expensive; ***the restaurant offers good food at reasonable prices***

reassess [ri:ə'ses] *verb* to assess again

reassessment [ri:ə'sesmənt] *noun* new assessment

reassure [ri:ə'ʃɔ:] *verb* **(a)** to make someone less worried; ***the markets were reassured by the government statement on import controls*** **(b)** to reinsure, to spread the risk of an insurance by asking another insurance company to cover part of it and receive part of the premium

reassurance [ri:ə'ʃʊərəns] *noun* (i) making someone less worried; (ii) reinsurance

rebate ['ri:beɪt] *noun* **(a)** reduction in the amount of money to be paid; ***to offer a 10% rebate on selected goods***; **brokerage rebates** = percentage of the commission paid to a broker which is returned to the customer as an incentive to do more business **(b)** money returned to someone because he has paid too much; ***he got a tax rebate at the end of the year***

---

prosecutors accused him of illegally funnelling brokerage rebates - some call them kickbacks - to his customers

Barron's

---

rebound [rɪ'baʊnd] *verb* to go back up again quickly; ***the market rebounded on the news of the government's decision***

recapitalization [ri:kæpɪtəlaɪ'zeɪʃn] *noun* change in the capital structure of a company (as when new shares are issued), especially when undertaken to avoid the company going into liquidation

recapitalize [ri:'kæpɪtəlaɪz] *verb* to change the capital structure of a company (as by issuing new shares), especially to avoid the company going into liquidation

> he estimates that banks and companies in Asia require $109 billion to recapitalize
>
> *Wall Street Journal*

> restructuring and recapitalizing the region's banks is the key to recovery for financial markets and economies in countries from Japan to Indonesia
>
> *Wall Street Journal*

recd = RECEIVED

receipt [rɪ'siːt] **1** *noun* **(a)** paper showing that money has been paid or that something has been received; ***customs receipt***; ***rent receipt***; ***receipt for items purchased***; ***please produce your receipt if you want to exchange items***; **receipt book** *or* **book of receipts** = book of blank receipts to be filled in when purchases are made **(b)** act of receiving something; **to acknowledge receipt of a letter** = to write to say that you have received a letter; ***we acknowledge receipt of your letter of the 15th***; ***goods will be supplied with thirty days of receipt of order***; ***invoices are payable within thirty days of receipt***; ***on receipt of the notification, the company lodged an appeal*** **(c) receipts** = money taken in sales; ***to itemize receipts and expenditure***; ***receipts are down against the same period of last year***; **receipts and payments basis** = method of preparing the accounts of a business, where receipts and payments are shown at the time when they are made (as opposed to showing debits or credits which are outstanding at the end of the accounting period; also called 'cash basis') **2** *verb* to stamp or to sign a document to show that it has been received; to stamp an invoice to show that it has been paid

> the public sector borrowing requirement is kept low by treating the receipts from selling public assets as a reduction in borrowing
>
> *Economist*

> gross wool receipts for the selling season to end June appear likely to top $2 billion
>
> *Australian Financial Review*

receivable [rɪ'siːvəbl] *adjective* which can be received; **accounts receivable** = money owed to a company; **bills receivable** = bills which a creditor will receive

receivables [rɪ'siːvəblz] *plural noun* money which is owed to a company

receive [rɪ'siːv] *verb* to get something which has been delivered; ***we received the payment ten days ago***; ***the workers have not received any salary for six months***; ***the goods were received in good condition***; **'received with thanks'** = words put on an invoice to show that a sum has been paid

receiver [rɪ'siːvə] *noun* **(a)** person who receives something; ***the receiver of the shipment*** **(b) official receiver** = official who is appointed by the courts to run a company which is in financial difficulties, to pay off its debts as far as possible, and to close it down; ***the court appointed a receiver for the company***; ***the company is in the hands of the receiver***

receivership [rɪ'siːvəʃɪp] noun **the company went into receivership** = the company was put into the hands of a receiver

receiving [rɪ'siːvɪŋ] *noun* **(a)** act of getting something which has been delivered; **receiving bank** = bank which receives money via electronic transfer; **receiving clerk** = official who works in a receiving office; **receiving department** = section of a company which deals with incoming goods or payments; **receiving office** = office where goods or payments are received **(b) receiving order** = order from a court appointing a receiver to a company

recession [rɪ'seʃən] *noun* fall in trade or in the economy of a country; ***the recession has reduced profits in many companies***; ***several firms have closed factories because of the recession***

> COMMENT: there a various ways of deciding if a recession is taking place: the usual one is when the GNP falls for two consecutive quarters

reciprocal [rɪ'sɪprəkəl] *adjective* applying from one country or person or company to another and vice versa; ***reciprocal agreement***; ***reciprocal contract***; **reciprocal holdings** = situation where two companies own shares in each other to prevent takeover bids; **reciprocal trade** = trade between two countries

reciprocate [rɪ'sɪprəkeɪt] *verb* to do the same thing to someone as he has just done to you; ***they offered us an exclusive agency for their cars and we reciprocated with an offer of the agency for our buses***

in 1934 Congress authorized President Roosevelt to seek lower tariffs with any country willing to reciprocate

Duns Business Month

reckon ['rekən] *verb* to calculate; ***to reckon the costs at £25,000***; ***we reckon the loss to be over £1m***; ***they reckon the insurance costs to be too high***

reclamation [reklə'meɪʃn] *noun* *US* action of recovering money owed by a bank or securities firm to a customer because of an error

recognize ['rekəgnaɪz] verb **to recognize a union** = to accept that a union can act on behalf of staff; **recognized agent** = agent who is approved by the company for which he acts; **recognized investment exchange (RIE)** = stock exchange, futures exchange or commodity exchange recognized by the FSA; **recognized professional body (RPB)** = professional body which is in charge of the regulation of the conduct of its members and is regognized by the FSA

recommended retail price (RRP) [rekə'mendɪd 'ri:teɪl 'praɪs] *noun* price which a manufacturer suggests a product should be sold at on the retail market, though often reduced by the retailer

reconcile ['rekənsaɪl] *verb* to make two accounts or statements agree; ***to reconcile one account with another***; ***to reconcile the accounts***

reconciliation *US* **reconcilement** [rekənsɪlɪ'eɪʃən or 'rekənsaɪlmənt] *noun* making two accounts or statements agree; **bank reconciliation** *US* **account reconcilement** = making sure that the bank statements agree with the company's ledgers; **reconciliation statement** = statement which explains how two accounts can be made to agree

record 1 ['rekɔ:d] *noun* **(a)** report of something which has happened; ***the chairman signed the minutes as a true record of the last meeting***; **record book** = book in which minutes of meetings are kept; **for the record** *or* **to keep the record straight** = to note something which has been done; ***for the record, I would like these sales figures to be noted in the minutes***; **on record** = correctly reported; ***the chairman is on record as saying that profits are set to rise***; **off the record** = unofficially, in private; ***he made some remarks off the record about the disastrous home sales figures*** **(b) records** = documents which give information; ***the names of customers are kept in the company's records***; ***we find from our records that our invoice number 1234 has not been paid***; **date of record** *or* **record date** = date when a shareholder must be registered to qualify for a dividend; **holder of record** = person who is registered as the owner of shares in a company at a certain date **(c)** description of what has happened in the past; **track record** = success or failure of a company or salesman in the past **(d)** which is better or worse than anything before; **record sales** *or* **record losses** *or* **record profits** = sales or losses or profits which are higher than ever before; ***1997 was a record year for the company***; ***sales for 1998 equalled the record of 1994***; ***our top salesman has set a new record for sales per call***; **we broke our record for June** = we sold more than we have ever sold before in June **2** [rɪ'kɔ:d] *verb* to note or to report; ***the company has recorded another year of increased profits***; ***your complaint has been recorded and will be investigated***; **recorded delivery** = mail service where the letters are signed for by the person receiving them

record-breaking ['rekɔ:d'breɪkɪŋ] *adjective* which is better than anything which has happened before; ***we are proud of our record-breaking profits this year***

recording [rɪ'kɔ:dɪŋ] *noun* making of a note; ***the recording of an order*** *or* ***of a complaint***; **recording of a lien** = note in the public records showing a lien on a property (such as a mortgage)

recoup [rɪ'ku:p] verb **to recoup your losses** = to get back money which you thought you had lost

it only took two years for investors to recoup their money after the stock-market crash of 1987

Sunday Times

recourse [rɪ'kɔ:s] *noun* right of a lender to compel a borrower to repay money borrowed; **to decide to have recourse to the courts to obtain money due** = to decide in the end to sue someone to obtain money owed

recover [rɪ'kʌvə] *verb* **(a)** to get back something which has been lost; ***he never recovered his money***; ***the initial investment was never recovered***; ***to recover damages from the driver of the car***; ***to start a court action to recover property*** **(b)** to get better, to rise; ***the market has not recovered from the rise in oil prices***; ***the stock market fell in the morning, but recovered during the afternoon***

recoverable [rɪ'kʌvərəbl] *adjective* which can be got back; **recoverable ACT** = advance corporation tax which can be set against corporation tax payable for the period; **recoverable amount** = value of an asset, either the price it would fetch if sold, or its value to the company when used (whichever is the larger figure)

recovery [rɪ'kʌvri] *noun* **(a)** getting back something which has been lost; ***we are aiming for the complete recovery of the money invested***; ***to start an action for recovery of property*** **(b)** movement upwards of shares or of the economy; ***the economy staged a recovery***; ***the recovery of the economy after a slump***; **recovery shares** = shares which are likely to go up in value because the company's performance is improving

rectify ['rektɪfaɪ] *verb* to correct something, to make something right; ***to rectify an entry***

recurrent [rɪ'kʌrənt] *adjective* which happens again and again; ***a recurrent item of expenditure***

recurring [rɪ'kɜːrɪŋ] *adjective* which happens again and again; **recurring payments** = payments, such as mortgage interest or payments on a hire purchase agreement, which are made each month

recycle ['riː'saɪkl] *verb* to use money in a different way (as by investing profits from industry in developing environmental resources)

> oil producers are probably in a better position to recycle the money than they were in the 1970s, but the money will be spent in different ways
>
> *Financial Times Review*

> the balance of payments deficit of the United States (and to a lesser degree, the UK) was being offset by the recycled surpluses of Japan and Germany
>
> *Financial Times Review*

recycling ['riː'saɪklɪŋ] *noun* deposits made by banks into a bank which is in difficulties, in order to keep it afloat

red [red] *noun* **in the red** = showing a debit or loss; ***my bank account is in the red***; ***the company went into the red in 1997***; ***the company is out of the red for the first time since 1994***

Red Book ['red 'bʊk] *noun* document published on Budget Day, with the text of the Chancellor of the Exchequer's financial statement and budget

red clause credit ['red 'klɔːz 'kredɪt] *noun* letter of credit authorizing the holder to receive an advance payment, usually so that he can continue trading

red day ['red 'deɪ] *noun US* day which is not profitable (NOTE: the opposite is **green day**)

redeem [rɪ'diːm] *verb* **(a)** to pay off a loan or a debt; ***to redeem a mortgage***; ***to redeem a debt*** **(b)** **to redeem a bond** = to sell a bond for cash

redeemable [rɪ'diːməbl] *adjective* which can be sold for cash; **redeemable government stock** = stock which can be redeemed for cash at some time in the future (in the UK, only the War Loan is irredeemable); **redeemable preference share** = preference share which must be bought back by the company at a certain date and for a certain price (the company will set aside money into a special fund for the purpose of redeeming these shares at due date); **redeemable security** = security which can be redeemed at its face value at a certain date in the future

redemption [rɪ'dempʃən] *noun* **(a)** repayment of a loan or of a debt; **redemption date** = date on which a loan, etc., is due to be repaid; **redemption before due date** = paying back a loan before the date when repayment is due; **redemption value** = value of a security when redeemed; **redemption yield** = yield on a security including interest and its redemption value **(b)** repayment of a mortgage; **equity of redemption** = right of a mortgagor to redeem the estate by paying off the principal and interest

> the amount that a zero promises on redemption compared to the purchase price is translated by the stockbrokers into an equivalent annual interest rate, bearing in mind the number of years the trust has to run. This figure is called the 'gross redemption yield'
>
> *Sunday Times*

> these zeros have 12.5 years to run, and here, the hurdle rate is -0.6%: much less margin of error therefore. In return for the higher risk, the gross redemption yield is higher, at 7.3%
>
> *Sunday Times*

red herring ['red 'herɪŋ] *noun* US a preliminary prospectus, the first prospectus for a new share issue, produced to see the market reaction to the proposed issue, but without giving a price for the new shares (similar to the British 'pathfinder prospectus'; called this because the first page has a notice printed in red which states that it is not a full offer)

rediscount ['ri:'dɪskaunt] *verb (of a central bank)* to discount a bill of exchange which has already been discounted by a commercial bank

redistribute [ri:dɪs'trɪbju:t] *verb* to move items or work or money to different areas or people; ***the government aims to redistribute wealth by taxing the rich and giving grants to the poor***

redistribution [ri:dɪstrɪ'bju:ʃən] noun **redistribution of risk** = spreading the risk of an investment or of an insurance among various insurers; **redistribution of wealth** = sharing wealth among the whole population

redlining ['red'laɪnɪŋ] *noun* illegal practice of discriminating against prospective borrowers because of the area of the town in which they live

red tape ['red 'teɪp] *noun* official paperwork which takes a long time to complete; ***the Australian joint venture has been held up by government red tape***

reduce [rɪ'dju:s] *verb* to make smaller or lower; ***to reduce expenditure***; ***to reduce a price***; ***to reduce taxes***; ***prices have been reduced by 15%***; ***the government's policy is to reduce inflation to 5%***; **to reduce staff** = to sack employees in order to have a smaller number of staff; **reducing balance method** = method of depreciating assets, where the asset is depreciated at a constant percentage of it cost each year

reduced [rɪ'dju:st] *adjective* lower; ***reduced prices have increased unit sales***

reduction [rɪ'dʌkʃən] *noun* lowering (of prices, etc.); ***price reductions***; ***tax reductions***; ***staff reductions***; ***reduction of expenditure***; ***reduction in demand***; ***the company was forced to make job reductions***

redundancy [rɪ'dʌndənsi] *noun* being no longer employed, because the job is no longer necessary; **redundancy payment** = payment made to a worker to compensate for losing his job; **redundancy rebate** = payment made to a company to compensate for redundancy payments made; *see also* VOLUNTARY REDUNDANCY

redundant [rɪ'dʌndənt] *adjective* **(a)** more than is needed, useless; ***redundant capital***; ***redundant clause in a contract***; ***the new legislation has made clause 6 redundant*** **(b)** **to make someone redundant** = to decide that a worker is not needed any more; **redundant staff** = staff who have lost their jobs because they are not needed any more

re-export 1 ['ri:'ekspɔ:t] *noun* exporting of goods which have been imported; ***re-export trade***; ***we import wool for re-export***; ***the value of re-exports has increased*** **2** [ri:eks'pɔ:t] *verb* to export something which has been imported

re-exportation [ri:ekspɔ:'teɪʃən] *noun* exporting goods which have been imported

ref [ref] = REFERENCE

refer [rɪ'fɜ:] verb **the bank referred the cheque to drawer** = the bank returned the cheque to person who wrote it because there was not enough money in the account to pay it; **'refer to drawer' (R/D)** = words written on a cheque which a bank refuses to pay and returns it to the person who wrote it (NOTE: **referring - referred**)

reference ['refrəns] *noun* **(a)** **terms of reference** = areas which a committee or an inspector can deal with; ***under the terms of reference of the committee, it cannot investigate complaints from the public***; ***the committee's terms of reference do not cover exports*** **(b)** mentioning or dealing with; ***with reference to your letter of May 25th*** **(c)** numbers or letters which make it possible to find a document which has been filed; ***our reference: PC/MS 1234***; ***thank you for your letter (reference 1234) please quote this reference in all correspondence***; ***when replying please quote reference 1234*** **(d)** written report on someone's character, ability, etc.; ***to write someone a reference*** *or* ***to give someone a reference***; ***to ask applicants to supply references***; **letter of reference** = letter in which an employer or former employer recommends someone for a job; **banker's reference** *or* **bank reference** = details of a company's bank, account number, etc., supplied so that a client can check if the company is a risk; **to ask a company for trade references** *or* **for bank references** *or* **banker's reference** = to ask for reports from traders or a bank on the company's financial status and reputation

refinance [ri:'faɪnæns] *verb* (i) to arrange to take over an existing loan; (ii) to extend a loan by exchanging it for a new one (normally done when the terms of the new loan are better); (iii) to add to an existing loan

> if you recently refinanced your home for a second time, you've probably got a tax break coming
>
> *Smart Money*

> as anyone who has ever refinanced a mortgage knows, trimming 1% off expense ratios on an account held over a 30-year period can result in substantial savings
>
> *Fortune*

refinancing [riːfaɪˈnænsɪŋ] noun **refinancing of a loan** = taking out a new loan to pay back a previous loan; **mortgage refinancing** = arranging to increase a mortgage on a property so as to pay for improvements to the property

> the refinancing consisted of a two-for-five rights issue, which took place in September this year, to offer 55.8m shares at 2p and raise about £925,000 net of expenses
>
> *Accountancy*

> the typical refinancing, worthy of note, involves a larger loan because the borrower has more equity in his home than he did when he got the initial mortgage
>
> *Barron's*

> home refinancing has become a modern form of mortgage debt
>
> *Barron's*

reflate [riːˈfleɪt] verb **to reflate the economy** = to stimulate the economy by increasing the money supply or by reducing taxes (often leading to increased inflation); ***the government's attempts to reflate the economy were not successful***

reflation [riːˈfleɪʃən] *noun* act of stimulating the economy by increasing the money supply or by reducing taxes

reflationary measures [riːˈfleɪʃnəri ˈmeʒəz] *noun* acts which are likely to stimulate the economy

refund 1 [ˈriːfʌnd] *noun* money paid back; ***to ask for a refund***; ***she got a refund after she had complained to the manager***; **full refund** *or* **refund in full** = refund of all the money paid; ***he got a full refund when he complained about the service*** **2** [rɪˈfʌnd] *verb* to pay back money; ***to refund the cost of postage***; ***all money will be refunded if the goods are not satisfactory***

refundable [rɪˈfʌndəbl] *adjective* which can be paid back; ***refundable deposit***; ***the entrance fee is refundable if you purchase £5 worth of goods***

refunding [rɪˈfʌndɪŋ] *noun* funding of a debt again by the government, by issuing new stock to replace stock which is about to mature

region [ˈriːdʒən] *noun* large area of a country

regional [ˈriːdʒənl] *adjective* referring to a region; **regional development grant (RDG)** = grant given to encourage a business to establish itself in a certain part of the country; **regional planning** = planning the industrial development of a region; *US* **regional bank** = bank which services one part of the country; **regional stock exchange** = stock exchange which is not in the main finance centre (i.e., not in New York or London)

register [ˈredʒɪstə] **1** *noun* **(a)** official list; ***to enter something in a register***; ***to keep a register up to date***; **companies' register** *or* **register of companies** = list of companies, showing their directors and registered addresses; **register of debentures** *or* **debenture register** = list of debenture holders of a company; **register of directors** = official list of the directors of a company which has to be sent to the registrar of companies; **register of interests in shares** = list kept by a company of those shareholders who own more than 3% of its shares; **land register** = list of pieces of land, showing who owns each and what buildings are on it; **Lloyd's register** = classified list showing details of all the ships in the world; **register of shareholders** *or* **share register** = list of shareholders in a company with their addresses **(b) cash register** = machine which shows and adds the prices of items bought in a shop, with a drawer for keeping the cash received **2** *verb* **(a)** to write something in an official list; ***to register a company***; ***to register a sale***; ***to register a property***; ***to register a trademark*** **(b)** to send (a letter) by registered post; ***I registered the letter, because it contained some money***

registered [ˈredʒɪstəd] *adjective* **(a)** which has been noted on an official list; ***registered share transaction***; ***registered trademark; US*** **registered check** = cheque written on a bank account on behalf of a client who does not have a bank account himself; **registered company** = company which has been officially set up and registered with the Registrar of Companies; **the company's registered office** = the head office of the company as noted in the register of companies; **registered security** = security (such as a share in a quoted company) which is registered with Companies House and whose holder is listed in the company's share register **(b) registered letter** *or* **registered parcel** = letter or parcel which is noted by the post office before it is sent, so that compensation can be claimed if it is lost; ***to send documents by registered mail*** *or* ***registered post***

registrar [redʒɪs'trɑː] *noun* person who keeps official records; **the company registrar** = person who keep the share register of a company; **the Registrar of Companies** = government official whose duty is to ensure that companies are properly registered, and that, when registered, they file accounts and other information correctly (he is in charge of the Companies Registration Office or Companies House)

registration [redʒɪs'treɪʃən] *noun* **(a)** act of having something noted on an official list; ***registration of a trademark*** *or* ***of share ownership***; **certificate of registration** *or* **registration certificate** = document showing that an item has been registered; **registration fee** = money paid to have something registered, money paid to attend a conference; **registration number** = official number (such as the number of a car); *US* **registration statement** = document which gives information about a company when registering and listing on a stock exchange (the British equivalent is the 'listing particulars') **(b) Companies Registration Office (CRO)** = office of the Registrar of Companies, official organization where the records of companies must be deposited, so that they can be inspected by the public (NOTE: usually called **Companies House**); **land registration** = system of registering land and its owners

regression analysis [rɪ'greʃn ə'næləsɪs] *noun* method of discovering the relationship between one variable and any number of other variables giving a coefficient by which forecasts can be made, the technique used by statisticians to forecast the way in which something will behave

regressive taxation [rɪ'gresɪv tæk'seɪʃn] *noun* taxation in which tax gets progressively less as income rises (the opposite of 'progressive taxation')

regular ['regjʊlə] *adjective* which happens or comes at the same time each day or each week or each month or each year; **regular income** = income which comes in every week or month; ***she works freelance so she does not have a regular income***

regulate ['regjʊleɪt] *verb* **(a)** to adjust something so that it works well or is correct **(b)** to change or maintain something by law; **prices are regulated by supply and demand** = prices are increased or lowered according to supply and demand; **regulated consumer credit agreement** = credit agreement according to the Consumer Credit Act; **government-regulated price** = price which is imposed by the government

regulation [regjʊ'leɪʃən] *noun* **(a)** act of making sure that something will work well; ***the regulation of trading practices***; **regulation agency** = organization which sees that members of an industry follow government regulations; *see also* DEREGULATION, SELF-REGULATION **(b) regulations** = laws, rules set out by government; ***the new government regulations on housing standards***; ***fire regulations*** *or* ***safety regulations***; ***regulations concerning imports and exports***

> EU regulations which came into effect in July insist that customers can buy cars anywhere in the EU at the local pre-tax price
>
> *Financial Times*

> a unit trust is established under the regulations of the Department of Trade, with a trustee, a management company and a stock of units
>
> *Investors Chronicle*

regulator ['regjʊleɪtə] *noun* person whose job it is to see that regulations are followed; **unitary regulator** = single regulator, where before there were several; ***the new unitary regulator is the Financial Services Authority***

> the regulators have sought to protect investors and other market participants from the impact of a firm collapsing
>
> *Banking Technology*

regulatory [regjʊ'leɪtəri] *adjective* which applies regulations; **regulatory powers** = powers to enforce government regulations; *see also* SELF-REGULATORY

reimburse [riːɪm'bɜːs] verb **to reimburse someone his expenses** = to pay someone back for money which he has spent; ***you will be reimbursed for your expenses*** *or* ***your expenses will be reimbursed***

reimbursement [riːɪm'bɜːsmənt] *noun* paying back money; ***reimbursement of expenses***

reinstatement [riːɪn'steɪtmənt] *noun* giving a borrower back his former credit status after he has paid off outstanding debts

reinsurance [riːɪn'ʃʊərəns] *noun* insurance where a second insurer (the reinsurer) agrees to cover part of the risk insured by the first insurer

reinsure [riːɪn'ʃʊə] *verb* to spread the risk of an insurance, by asking another insurance company to cover part of it and receive part of the premium

reinsurer [riːɪn'ʃʊərə] *noun* insurance company which accepts to insure part of the risk for another insurer

reintermediation /[riːɪntəmiːdi'eɪʃn] *noun* withdrawing funds from investments such as shares or bonds and transferring them into cash deposits in banks (NOTE: the opposite is **disintermediation**)

reinvest [riːɪn'vest] *verb* to invest again; ***he reinvested the money in government stocks***

reinvestment [riːɪn'vestmənt] *noun* investing again in the same securities; investing a company's earnings in its own business by using them to create new products for sale

> many large US corporations offer shareholders the option of reinvesting their cash dividend payments in additional company stock at a discount to the market price. But to some big securities firms these discount reinvestment programs are an opportunity to turn a quick profit
>
> *Wall Street Journal*

REIT *US* = REAL ESTATE INVESTMENT TRUST; *see also* EQUITY REIT, MORTGAGE REIT

reject 1 ['riːdʒekt] *noun* thing which has been thrown out because it is not of the usual standard; ***sale of rejects*** *or* ***of reject items***; ***to sell off reject stock*** **2** [rɪ'dʒekt] *verb* to refuse to accept, to say that something is not satisfactory; **the company rejected the takeover bid** = the directors recommended that the shareholders should not accept the bid

rejection [rɪ'dʒekʃən] *noun* refusal to accept, such as the refusal to give a customer credit; ***the board recommended rejection of the bid***

related [rɪ'leɪtɪd] *adjective* connected or linked; **related company** = company which is partly owned by another company; **earnings-related contributions** = contributions to social security which rise as the worker's earnings rise; **earnings-related pension** = pension which is linked to the size of the salary

relative value funds ['relətɪv 'væljuː 'fʌndz] *noun* hedge funds not related to general market movements, but which try to find opportunities to arbitrage temporary slight changes in the relative values of particular financial assets (NOTE: also called **market neutral funds**)

release [rɪ'liːs] **1** *noun* **(a)** setting free; ***release from a contract***; ***release of goods from customs***; **release note** *or* **bank release** = note from a bank to say that a bill of exchange has been paid **(b) day release** = arrangement where a company allows a worker to go to college to study for one day each week; ***the junior sales manager is attending a day release course*** **2** *verb* **(a)** to free; ***to release goods from customs***; ***the customs released the goods against payment of a fine***; ***to release someone from a debt*** **(b)** to make something public; ***the company released information about the new mine in Australia***; ***the government has refused to release figures for the number of unemployed women*** **(c) to release dues** = to send off orders which had been piling up while a product was out of stock

> pressure to ease monetary policy mounted yesterday with the release of a set of pessimistic economic statistics
>
> *Financial Times*

> the national accounts for the March quarter released by the Australian Bureau of Statistics showed a real increase in GDP
>
> *Australian Financial Review*

relevant ['reləvənt] *adjective* which has to do with what is being discussed; ***which is the relevant government department? can you give me the relevant papers?***

relief [rɪ'liːf] *noun* help; **tax relief** = allowing someone to pay less tax; **there is full tax relief on mortgage interest payments** = no tax is payable on income used to pay interest on a mortgage; **mortgage interest relief** = allowing someone to pay no tax on mortgage interest payments up to a certain level; *see also* MORTGAGE INTEREST RELIEF AT SOURCE; **relief shift** = shift which comes to take the place of another shift, usually the shift between the day shift and the night shift

reminder [rɪ'maɪndə] *noun* letter to remind a customer that he has not paid an invoice; ***to send someone a reminder***

remission [rɪ'mɪʃən] noun **remission of taxes** = refund of taxes which have been overpaid

remit [rɪ'mɪt] *verb* to send (money); ***to remit by cheque***; **remitting bank** = bank into which a person has deposited a cheque, and which has the duty to collect the money from the account of the writer of the cheque (NOTE: **remitting - remitted**)

remittance [rɪ'mɪtəns] *noun* money which is sent (to pay back a debt, to pay an invoice, etc.); ***please send remittances to the treasurer***; ***the family lives on a weekly remittance from their father in the USA***; **remittance advice** *or* **remittance slip** = advice note sent with payment, showing why it is being made (i.e., quoting the invoice number or a reference number)

remunerate [rɪ'mju:nəreɪt] *verb* to pay someone for doing something; ***to remunerate someone for their services***

remuneration [rɪmju:nə'reɪʃən] *noun* payment for services; ***she has a monthly remuneration of £400***

remunerative [rɪ'mju:nərətɪv] *adjective* (job) which pays well; ***he is in a very remunerative job***

render ['rendə] verb **to render an account** = to send in an account; ***payment for account rendered***; ***please find enclosed payment per account rendered***

renege [rɪ'neɪg] verb *(formal)* **to renege on a promise** = not to do something which you had promised to do; ***I was furious when he reneged on the deal***

> they would renege on a job they'd accepted if a better one came along
>
> *Fortune*

renegotiate [ri:nɪ'gʊʃieɪt] *verb* to negotiate again; ***the company was forced to renegotiate the terms of the loan***

renew [rɪ'nju:] *verb* to continue something for a further period of time; ***to renew a bill of exchange*** *or* ***to renew a lease***; **to renew a subscription** = to pay a subscription for another year; **to renew an insurance policy** = to pay the premium for another year's insurance

renewal [rɪ'nju:əl] *noun* act of renewing; ***renewal of a lease*** *or* ***of a subscription*** *or* ***of a bill***; ***the lease is up for renewal next month***; ***when is the renewal date of the bill?***; **renewal notice** = note sent by an insurance company asking the insured person to renew the insurance; **renewal premium** = premium to be paid to renew an insurance

renminbi ['renmɪnbi:] *noun* currency used in China (NOTE: also called the **yuan**)

rent [rent] **1** *noun* money paid to use an office or house or factory for a period of time; **high rent** *or* **low rent** = expensive or cheap rent; ***rents are high in the centre of the town***; ***we cannot afford to pay High Street rents***; ***to pay three months' rent in advance***; **back rent** = rent owed; **the flat is let at an economic rent** = at a rent which covers all costs to the landlord; **ground rent** = rent paid by the main tenant to the ground landlord; **nominal rent** = very small rent; **rent control** = government regulation of rents; **income from rents** *or* **rent income** = income from letting offices, houses, etc.; **rent review** = increase in rents which is carried out during the term of a lease (most leases allow for rents to be reviewed every three or five years) **2** *verb* **(a)** to pay money to hire an office, house, factory or piece of equipment for a period of time; ***to rent an office*** *or* ***a car***; ***he rents an office in the centre of town***; ***they were driving a rented car when they were stopped by the police*** **(b) to rent (out)** = to own a car or office, etc., and let it to someone for money; ***we rented part of the building to an American company***

rental ['rentl] *noun* money paid to use an office, house, factory, car or piece of equipment, etc., for a period of time; ***the telephone rental bill comes to over £500 a quarter***; **rental income** *or* **income from rentals** = income from letting offices, houses, etc.; **rental value** = full value of the rent for a property if it were charged at the current market rate (i.e., calculated between rent reviews); **car rental firm** = company which specializes in offering cars for rent; **fleet rental** = renting all a company's cars from the same company at a special price

> top quality office furniture: short or long-term rental 50% cheaper than any other rental company
>
> *Australian Financial Review*

> office rental growth has been faster in Britain in the first six months of this year
>
> *Lloyd's List*

rente [rɒnt] *French* government annuity

renunciation [rɪnʌnsi'eɪʃən] *noun* act of giving up ownership of shares; **letter of renunciation** = form sent with new shares, which allows the person who has been allotted the shares to refuse to accept them and so sell them to someone else

reorder [ri:'ɔ:də] **1** *noun* further order for something which has been ordered before; ***the product has only been on the market ten days and we are already getting reorders***; **reorder interval** = period of time before a new order for a stock item is placed; **reorder level** = minimum amount of stock of an item which must be reordered when stock falls to this amount **2** *verb* to place a new order for something; ***we must reorder these items because stock is getting low***

reorganization [riɔ:gənaɪ'zeɪʃən] *noun* action of organizing a company in a different way (as in the USA, when a bankrupt company applies to be treated under Chapter 11 while it is being reorganized)

repatriation [ri:pætri'eɪʃn] *noun* return of foreign investments to the home country of their owner

repay [rɪ'peɪ] *verb* to pay back; ***to repay money owed***; ***the company had to cut back on expenditure in order to repay its debts***; **he repaid me in full** = he paid me back all the money he owed me (NOTE: **repaying - repaid**)

repayable [rɪ'peɪəbl] *adjective* which can be paid back; ***loan which is repayable over ten years***

repayment [rɪ'peɪmənt] *noun* paying back; money which is paid back; ***the loan is due for repayment next year***; **he fell behind with his mortgage repayments** = he was late in paying back the instalments on his mortgage; **repayment mortgage** = mortgage where the borrower pays back both interest and capital over the period of the mortgage (as opposed to an endowment mortgage, where only the interest is repaid, and an insurance is taken out to repay the capital at the end of the term of the mortgage)

replacement [rɪ'pleɪsmənt] noun **replacement cost** *or* **cost of replacement** = cost of an item to replace an existing asset; **replacement cost accounting** = method of accounting, where assets are valued at the amount it would cost to replace them, rather than at the original cost; **replacement cost depreciation** = depreciation based on the actual cost of replacing the asset in the current year; **replacement price** = price at which the replacement for an asset would have to be bought; **replacement value** = value of something for insurance purposes if it were to be replaced; ***the computer is insured at its replacement value***

repo ['ri:pəʊ] *(informal)* = REPURCHASE AGREEMENT

report [rɪ'pɔ:t] **1** *noun* **(a)** statement describing what has happened, describing a state of affairs; ***to draft a report***; ***to make a report*** *or* ***to present a report*** *or* ***to send in a report***; ***the sales manager reads all the reports from the sales team***; ***the chairman has received a report from the insurance company***; **the company's annual report** *or* **the chairman's report** *or* **the directors' report** = document sent each year by the chairman of a company or the directors to the shareholders, explaining what the company has done during the year; **confidential report** = secret document which must not be shown to other people; **feasibility report** = document which says if something can be done; **financial report** = document which gives the financial position of a company *or* of a club, etc.; **the treasurer's report** = document from the honorary treasurer of a society to explain the financial state of the society to its members **(b)** official document from a government committee; ***the government has issued a report on the credit problems of exporters*** **2** *verb* **(a)** to make a statement describing something; ***he reported the damage to the insurance company***; ***we asked the bank to report on his financial status*** **(b)** to publish the results of a company for a period and declare the dividend; **reporting season** = period when many large companies declare their dividends; ***the banks reporting season starts in February*** (NOTE: in American English also called the **earnings season**) **(b) to report to someone** = to be responsible to or to be under someone; ***he reports direct to the managing director***; ***the salesmen report to the sales director***

---

a draft report on changes in the international monetary system

Wall Street Journal

---

responsibilities include the production of premium quality business reports

Times

> the research director will manage a team of business analysts monitoring and reporting on the latest development in retail distribution
>
> *Times*

> the successful candidate will report to the area director for profit responsibility for sales of leading brands
>
> *Times*

repossess [ri:pə'zes] *verb* to take back an item which someone is buying under a hire-purchase agreement or mortgage agreement, because the purchaser cannot continue the payments; ***when he fell behind with the mortgage repayments, the bank repossessed his flat***

repossession [ri:pə'zeʃn] *noun* act of repossessing; ***repossessions are increasing as people find it difficult to meet mortgage repayments***

represent [reprɪ'zent] *verb* **(a)** to work for a company, showing goods or services to possible buyers; ***he represents an American car firm in Europe***; ***our French distributor represents several other competing firms*** **(b)** to act for someone; ***he sent his solicitor and accountant to represent him at the meeting***; ***three managers represent the workforce in discussions with the directors***

re-present [ri:prɪ'zent] *verb* to present something again; ***he re-presented the cheque two weeks later to try to get payment from the bank***

representation [reprɪzen'teɪʃən] *noun* **(a)** act of selling goods for a company; ***we offered them exclusive representation in Europe***; ***they have no representation in the USA*** **(b)** having someone to act on your behalf; ***the minority shareholders want representation on the board***

representative [reprɪ'zentətɪv] **1** *adjective* which is an example of what all others are like; ***we displayed a representative selection of our product range***; ***the sample chosen was not representative of the whole batch*** **2** *noun* **(a) sales representative** = person who works for a company, showing goods or services for sale; ***we have six representatives in Europe***; ***they have vacancies for representatives to call on accounts in the north of the country*** **(b)** company which works for another company, selling their goods; ***we have appointed Smith & Co our exclusive representatives in Europe*** **(c)** person who acts on someone's behalf; ***she sits on the board as the representative of the bank***; ***he sent his solicitor and accountant to act as his representatives at the meeting***; ***the board refused to meet the representatives of the workforce***

reprice [ri:'praɪs] *verb* to change the price on an item (usually, to increase its price), or to change the interest rate on deposits or loans

repudiate [rɪ'pju:dɪeɪt] *verb* to state publicly that you refuse to repay a loan

repurchase ['ri:'pɜ:tʃəs] *verb* to buy something again, especially something which you have recently bought and then sold; **repurchase agreement** *or* **repo** = agreement, where a bank agrees to buy something and sell it back later (in effect, giving a cash loan to the seller; this is used especially to raise short-term finance, very short-term in the case of overnight repo)

require [rɪ'kwaɪə] *verb* **(a)** to ask for or to demand something; ***to require a full explanation of expenditure***; ***the law requires you to submit all income to the tax authorities*** **(b)** to need; ***the document requires careful study***; ***to write the program requires a computer specialist***

requirement [rɪ'kwaɪəmənt] *noun* what is needed; **public sector borrowing requirement (PSBR)** = amount of money which a government has to borrow to pay for its own spending

requirements [rɪ'kwaɪəmənts] *plural noun* things which are needed; **the requirements of a market** *or* **market requirements** = things which are needed by the market; **budgetary requirements** = spending or income needed to meet budget forecasts

requisition [rekwɪ'zɪʃən] **1** *noun* official order for something; ***what is the number of your latest requisition?***; **cheque requisition** = official note from a department to the company accounts staff asking for a cheque to be written **2** *verb* to put in an official order for something; to ask for supplies to be sent

rerate ['ri:reɪt] *verb* to change the rating of a share on the Stock Exchange (either upwards or downwards)

rerating [ri:'reɪtɪŋ] *noun* reconsidering the value of a share on the Stock Exchange, either upwards or downwards

resale [ri:'seɪl] *noun* selling goods which have been bought; ***to purchase something for resale***; ***the contract forbids resale of the goods to the USA***

resale price maintenance (RPM) ['ri:seɪl 'praɪs 'meɪntənəns] *noun* system where the price for an item is fixed by the manufacturer and the retailer is not allowed to sell it for a lower price

reschedule [ri:'ʃedju:l] *verb* to arrange new credit terms for the repayment of a loan; ***Third World countries which are unable to keep up the interest payments on their loans from western banks, have asked for their loans to be rescheduled***

> the country has reached a debt rescheduling agreement with the Paris club of government creditors
>
> *The Banker*

rescind [rɪ'sɪnd] *verb* to annul or to cancel; ***to rescind a contract*** *or* ***an agreement***

rescission [rɪ'sɪʒn] *noun* act of rescinding a contract

rescue ['reskju:] **1** *noun* saving someone or something from danger; **rescue operation** = arrangement by a group of people to save a company from collapse; ***the banks planned a rescue operation for the company*** **2** *verb* to save someone or something from danger; ***the company nearly collapsed, but was rescued by the banks***

> the US government's rescue of the savings and loan industry may come to a halt in a few weeks because Congress adjourned yesterday without approving needed funds. This is certain to increase the cost of the rescue, the largest ever in the US
>
> *Financial Times*

research [rɪ'sɜ:tʃ] **1** *noun* trying to find out facts or information; **consumer research** = research into why consumers buy goods and what goods they may want to buy; **market research** = examining the possible sales of a product and the possible customers for it before it is put on the market; **research and development (R & D)** = scientific investigation which leads to making new products or improving existing products; ***the company spends millions on research and development***; **research and development expenditure** = money spent on R & D; **research department** = section of a broker's office which does research into companies **2** *verb* to study, to try to find out information about something

researcher [rɪ'sɜ:tʃə] *noun* person who carries out research

resell [ri:'sel] *verb* to sell something which has just been bought

reseller [ri:'selə] *noun* person who sells something he has just bought

reserve [rɪ'zɜ:v] *noun* **(a) reserves** = money from profits not paid as dividend, but kept back by a company in case it is needed for a special purpose; **accumulated reserves** = reserves which a company has put aside over a period of years; **bank reserves** = cash and securities held by a bank to cover deposits; **capital reserves** *or* **reserve capital** *or* **reserve liability** = money from profits, which forms part of the capital of a company and can be used for distribution to shareholders only when a company is wound up; **capitalization of reserves** = issuing free bonus shares to shareholders; **cash reserves** = a company's reserves in cash deposits or bills kept in case of urgent need; ***the company was forced to fall back on its cash reserves***; ***to have to draw on reserves to pay the dividend***; **contingency reserve** *or* **emergency reserves** = money set aside in case it is needed urgently; **reserve for bad debts** = money kept by a company to cover debts which may not be paid; **hidden reserves** *or* **secret reserves** = illegal reserves which are not declared in the company's balance sheet; **sums chargeable to the reserve** = sums which can be debited to a company's reserves; **reserve fund** = profits in a business which have not been paid out as dividend but have been ploughed back into the business **(b) reserve currency** = strong currency used in international finance, held by other countries to support their own weaker currencies; **currency reserves** = foreign money held by a government to support its own currency and to pay its debts; **a country's foreign currency reserves** = a country's reserves in currencies of other countries; ***the UK's gold and dollar reserves fell by $200 million during the quarter*** **(c)** US **Federal Reserve;** *see* FEDERAL **(d) reserve price** = lowest price which a seller will accept (at an auction or when selling securities through a broker); ***the painting was withdrawn when it did not reach its reserve***

residence ['rezɪdəns] *noun* **(a)** house or flat where someone lives; ***he has a country residence where he spends his weekends*** **(b)** act of living or operating officially in a country; **residence permit** = official document allowing a foreigner to live in a country; ***he has applied for a residence permit***; ***she was granted a residence permit for one year***

resident ['rezɪdənt] *noun* person or company living or operating in a country; ***the***

company is resident in France; **non-resident** = person or company that is not officially resident in a country; ***he has a non-resident account with a French bank***; ***she was granted a non-resident visa***

residue ['rezɪdjuː] *noun* money left over; ***after paying various bequests the residue of his estate was split between his children***

residual [rɪ'zɪdjʊəl] *adjective* remaining after everything else has gone; **residual value** = value of an asset after it has been depreciated in the company's accounts

resist [rɪ'zɪst] *verb* to fight against something, not to give in to something; ***the chairman resisted all attempts to make him resign***; ***the company is resisting the takeover bid***

resistance [rɪ'zɪstəns] *noun* showing that people are opposed to something; ***there was a lot of resistance from the shareholders to the new plan***; ***the chairman's proposal met with strong resistance from the banks***; **resistance levels** = price or index level, at which investors feel that the price is too high or too low

> although the FTSE 100 Index recently went through its upper resistance level, he still believes that the London market is in a bear phase and might move down in the short to medium term
>
> *Times*

COMMENT: resistance levels on the Stock Exchange relate to 'sentiment'; if a share is selling at $2.95, and does not rise, it may be that investors see the price of $3.00 as a point above which they feel the share is overvalued; if the price 'breaks through' the $3.00 barrier, then it may continue to rise rapidly, as the resistance level has been broken. The same applies in reverse: if the pound/dollar exchange rate is $1.65, and the pound becomes weaker, the resistance level of $1.60, when broken, may be the sign of a further slide in the pound's value

resolution [rezə'luːʃən] *noun* decision to be reached at a meeting; **to put a resolution to a meeting** = to ask a meeting to vote on a proposal; ***the meeting passed*** *or* ***carried*** *or* ***adopted a resolution to go on strike; the meeting rejected the resolution*** *or* ***the resolution was defeated by ten votes to twenty***

COMMENT: there are two types or resolution which can be put to an AGM: the 'ordinary resolution', usually referring to some general procedural matter, and which requires a simple majority of votes; and the 'special resolution', such as a resolution to change a company's articles of association in some way, which needs 75% of the votes before it can be carried

resolve [rɪ'zɒlv] *verb* to decide to do something; ***the meeting resolved that a dividend should not be paid***

resources [rɪ'sɔːsɪz] *plural noun* **financial resources** = supply of money for something; ***the costs of the London office are a drain on the company's financial resources; the company's financial resources are not strong enough to support the cost of the research programme***; **the cost of the new project is easily within our resources** = we have enough money to pay for the new project

restitution [restɪ'tjuːʃən] *noun* **(a)** giving back (property); ***the court ordered the restitution of assets to the company*** **(b)** compensation or payment for damage or loss **(c)** *(in the EU)* **export restitution** = subsidies to European food exporters

restraint [rɪ'streɪnt] *noun* control; **pay restraint** *or* **wage restraint** = keeping increases in wages under control; **restraint of trade** = (i) situation where a worker is not allowed to use his knowledge in another company if he changes jobs; (ii) attempt by companies to fix prices *or* create monopolies *or* reduce competition, which could affect free trade

restrict [rɪ'strɪkt] *verb* to limit, to impose controls on; ***to restrict credit***; ***we are restricted to twenty staff by the size of our offices***; ***to restrict the flow of trade*** *or* ***to restrict imports***; **to sell into a restricted market** = to sell goods into a market where the supplier has agreed to limit sales to avoid competition; US **restricted security** *see* LETTER SECURITY

restriction [rɪ'strɪkʃən] *noun* limit or controlling; ***import restrictions*** *or* ***restrictions on imports***; **to impose restrictions on imports** *or* **on credit** = to start limiting imports *or* credit; **to lift credit restrictions** = to allow credit to be given freely

restrictive [rɪ'strɪktɪv] *adjective* which limits; **restrictive covenant** = agreement by a borrower not to sell an asset which he has used as collateral for a loan; **restrictive endorsement** = endorsement on a bill of exchange which restricts the use which can be made of it by the person it is endorsed to; **restrictive trade practices** = arrangement between companies to fix prices, to share the market, etc.

restructure [riːˈstrʌktʃə] *verb* to reorganize the financial basis of a company

restructuring [riːˈstrʌktʃərɪŋ] *noun* **(a) the restructuring of a company** = reorganizing the financial basis of a company; **the restructuring of an economy** = reorganizing the basic ways in which an economy is set up **(b)** replacing one type of borrowing by another with a longer maturity date

> restructuring is likely to have an adverse effect on employment
>
> *Investors Chronicle*

> the US rating agency cited the country's deepening recession and the lack of progress in restructuring its banking and industrial sectors
>
> *The Banker*

result [rɪˈzʌlt] **1** *noun* **(a)** profit or loss account for a company at the end of a trading period; ***the company's results for 1998*** **(b)** something which happens because of something else; ***what was the result of the price investigation? the company doubled its sales force with the result that the sales rose by 26%***; **the expansion programme has produced results** = has produced increased sales; **payment by results** = being paid for profits or increased sales **2** *verb* **(a) to result in** = to produce as a result **(b) to result from** = to happen because of something; ***the increase in debt resulted from the expansion programme***

> the company has received the backing of a number of oil companies who are willing to pay for the results of the survey
>
> *Lloyd's List*

> some profit-taking was noted, but underlying sentiment remained firm in a steady stream of strong corporate results
>
> *Financial Times*

retail [ˈriːteɪl] **1** *noun* sale of small quantities of goods to ordinary customers; **retail banking** = normal banking services provided for customers by the main high street banks (as opposed to wholesale banking); **retail dealer** = person who sells to the general public; **retail deposit** = deposit placed by an individual with a bank; **retail fund** = fund sold direct to private investors; **retail investor** = private investor, as opposed to institutional investors; **retail price** = full price paid by a customer in a shop; **retail service provider (RSP)** *US* **retail house** = large stockbroker dealing directly with private retail investors; **retail shop** *or* **retail outlet** = shop which sells goods to the general public; **the retail trade** = all people or businesses selling goods retail; **the goods in stock have a retail value of £1m** = the value of the goods if sold to the public is £1m, before discounts etc., are taken into account **2** *adverb* **he sells retail and buys wholesale** = he buys goods in bulk at a wholesale discount and sells in small quantities to the public **3** *verb* **(a) to retail goods** = to sell goods direct to the public **(b)** to sell for a price; **these items retail at** *or* **for 25p** = the retail price of these items is 25p

> I do not see retail investors overnight becoming big investors in futures and options. There was a lot of direct retail interest before October 1987, but they were badly hurt in the crash
>
> *Financial Weekly*

> statistics from the international stock exchange show that retail, or customer, interest in the equity market has averaged just under £700m daily in recent trading sessions
>
> *Financial Times*

> this is the only retail fund offered by the top-performing institutional money-management firm
>
> *Smart Money*

> private investors dealing outside Sets through one of the large brokers labelled retail service providers (RSPs) might hope to avoid these difficulties
>
> *Investors Chronicle*

retailer [ˈriːteɪlə] *noun* person who runs a retail business, selling goods direct to the public; **retailer number** = number of the retailer, printed at the top of the report slip when depositing credit card payments

retailing [ˈriːteɪlɪŋ] *noun* selling of full price goods to the public; ***from car retailing the company branched out into car leasing***

retail price [ˈriːteɪl ˈpraɪs] *noun* price at which the retailer sells to the final customer

retail price(s) index (RPI) ['ri:teɪl 'praɪs 'ɪndeks] *noun* index showing how prices of retail goods have risen over a period of time

> COMMENT: in the UK, the RPI is calculated on a series of essential goods and services; it includes both VAT and mortgage interest; the US equivalent is the Consumer Price Index

retain [rɪ'teɪn] *verb* **(a)** to keep; ***out of the profits, the company has retained £50,000 as provision against bad debts***; **retained earnings** *or* **retained profit** = amount of profit after tax which a company does not pay out as dividend to the shareholders, but keeps within the company's books; **retained income** = profit not distributed to the shareholders as dividend; ***the balance sheet has £50,000 in retained income*** **(b) to retain a lawyer to act for a company** = to agree with a lawyer that he will act for you (and pay him a fee in advance)

retainer [rɪ'teɪnə] *noun* money paid in advance to someone so that he will work for you, and not for someone else; ***we pay him a retainer of £1,000***

retention [rɪ'tenʃn] *noun* retained earnings, profit which is not paid to the shareholders in the form of dividends, but is kept to be used for future development of the business

retire [rɪ'taɪə] *verb* **(a)** to stop work and take a pension; ***she retired with a £6,000 pension***; ***the founder of the company retired at the age of 85***; ***the shop is owned by a retired policeman*** **(b)** to make a worker stop work and take a pension; ***they decided to retire all staff over 50*** **(c)** to come to the end of an elected term of office; ***the treasurer retires from the council after six years***; ***two retiring directors offer themselves for re-election***

retiral [rɪ'taɪərəl] *noun* US = RETIREMENT

retirement [rɪ'taɪəmənt] *noun* act of retiring from work; **to take early retirement** = to leave work before the usual age; **retirement age** = age at which people retire (in the UK usually 65 for men and 60 for women); **retirement pension** = pension which someone receives when he retires

retrenchment [rɪ'trenʃmənt] *noun* reduction of expenditure or of new plans; ***the company is in for a period of retrenchment***

retroactive [retrəʊ'æktɪv] *adjective* which takes effect from a time in the past; ***retroactive pay rise***; ***they got a pay rise retroactive to last January***

retroactively [retrəʊ'æktɪvli] *adverb* going back to a time in the past

return [rɪ'tɜ:n] **1** *noun* **(a)** profit or income from money invested; ***to bring in a quick return***; ***what is the gross return on this line?***; **return on assets (ROA)** *or* **return on capital employed (ROCE)** *or* **return on equity (ROE)** *or* **return on investment (ROI)** = profit shown as a percentage of the capital or money invested in a business; **rate of return** = amount of interest or dividend produced by an investment, shown as a percentage of the original amount invested **(b)** report; **bank return** = regular report from a bank on its financial position; **official return** = official report; **return date** = date by which a company's annual return has to be made to the Registrar of Companies; **to make a return to the tax office** *or* **to make an income tax return** = to send a statement of income to the tax office; **to fill in a VAT return** = to complete the form showing VAT receipts and expenditure; **nil return** = report showing no sales *or* income or tax etc.; **daily** *or* **weekly** *or* **quarterly sales return** = report of sales made each day, week or quarter **2** *verb* to make a statement; ***to return income of £15,000 to the tax authorities***

> Section 363 of the Companies Act 1985 requires companies to deliver an annual return to the Companies Registration Office. Failure to do so before the end of the period of 28 days after the company's return date could lead to directors and other officers in default being fined up to £2000
>
> *Accountancy*

returns [rɪ'tɜ:nz] *plural noun* **(a)** profits or income from investment; ***the company is looking for quick returns on its investment***; **law of diminishing returns** = general rule that as more factors of production (land, labour and capital) are added to the existing factors, so the amount they produce is proportionately smaller **(b)** unsold goods, especially books, newspapers or magazines sent back to the supplier; *see also* SALES RETURNS

revaluation [ri:væljʊ'eɪʃən] *noun* act of revaluing; ***the balance sheet takes into account the revaluation of the company's properties***; ***the revaluation of the dollar against the franc***

revalue [ri:'vælju:] *verb* to value something again (at a higher value than before); ***the company's properties have been revalued***;

the dollar has been revalued against all world currencies

revenue ['revənju:] *noun* **(a)** money received; ***revenue from advertising*** *or* ***advertising revenue***; ***oil revenues have risen with the rise in the dollar***; **revenue account** = accounting system which records the revenue and expenditure incurred by a company during its normal business; **revenue accounts** = accounts of a business which record money received as sales, commission etc.; **revenue expenditure** = expenditure on purchasing stock (but not on capital items) which is then sold during the current accounting period; **revenue reserves** = retained earnings which are shown in the company's balance sheet as part of the shareholders' funds **(b)** money received by a government in tax; **Inland Revenue** *US* **Internal Revenue Service** = government department which deals with tax; **revenue officer** = person working in the government tax offices

reversal [rɪ'vɜ:səl] *noun* **(a)** change from being profitable to unprofitable; ***the company suffered a reversal in the Far East*** **(b)** sudden change in a share price (either a rise or a fall); ***in the event of a market reversal buyers are rare***

reverse [rɪ'vɜ:s] **1** *adjective* opposite, in the opposite direction; **reverse bid** = bid for a company, where the a target company makes a takeover bid for the company trying to take it over; *US* **reverse mortgage** = arrangement where the owner of a property mortgages it to receive a regular income from the mortgage lender (and not vice versa), based on the equity value of the property; **reverse takeover** = takeover where the company which has been taken over ends up running the company which has bought it **2** *verb* to change a decision to the opposite; ***the committee reversed its decision on import quotas***; **reversing entry** = entry in a set of account which reverses an entry in the preceding accounts

> the trade balance sank $17 billion, reversing last fall's brief improvement
>
> *Fortune*

reversion [rɪ'vɜ:ʃən] *noun* return of property to an original owner; **he has the reversion of the estate** = he will receive the estate when the present lease ends

reversionary [rɪ'vɜ:ʃənəri] *adjective* (property) which passes to another owner on the death of the present one; **reversionary annuity** = annuity paid to someone on the death of another person; **reversionary bonus** = annual bonus on a life assurance policy, declared by the insurer

review [rɪ'vju:] **1** *noun* general examination; ***to conduct a review of distributors***; **financial review** = examination of an organization's finances; **rent review** = increase in rents which is carried out during the term of a lease (most leases allow for rents to be reviewed every three or five years); **wage review** *or* **salary review** = examination of salaries or wages in a company to see if the workers should earn more; **she had a salary review last April** = her salary was examined (and increased) in April **2** *verb* to examine something generally; **to review salaries** = to look at all salaries in a company to decide on increases; ***his salary will be reviewed at the end of the year***; ***the company has decided to review freelance payments in the light of the rising cost of living***; ***according to the lease, the rent is reviewed every five years***; **to review discounts** = to look at discounts offered to decide whether to change them

revise [rɪ'vaɪz] *verb* to change something which has been calculated or planned; ***sales forecasts are revised annually***; ***the chairman is revising his speech to the AGM***

revocable ['revəkəbl] *adjective* which can be revoked; **revocable trust** = trust which can be changed or revoked

revocation [revə'keɪʃn] *noun* action of cancelling something which has previously been agreed; ***the revocation of the bank's licence by the central bank***

revoke [rɪ'vəʊk] *verb* to cancel or to annul; ***to revoke a clause in an agreement***

revolving credit [rɪ'vɒlvɪŋ 'kredɪt] *noun* system where someone can borrow money at any time up to an agreed amount, and continue to borrow while still paying off the original loan (also called 'open-ended credit')

rial [ri'ɑ:l] *noun* currency used in Iran and other Middle Eastern countries, such as Oman and North Yemen; *see also* RIYAL

-rich [rɪtʃ] *suffix* meaning 'which is rich in a certain way'; **oil-rich territory** = territory which has valuable oil-deposits; **asset-rich company** = company which has valuable assets which provide backing for its shares; **cash-rich company** = company which has a large amount of cash

rider ['raɪdə] *noun* additional clause; ***to add a rider to a contract***

RIE = RECOGNIZED INVESTMENT EXCHANGE

riel ['ri:el] *noun* currency used in Kampuchea, the former Cambodia

rig [rɪg] *verb* to arrange for a result to be changed; ***they tried to rig the election of officers***; **to rig the market** = to make share prices go up or down so as to make a profit; **rigging of ballots** *or* **ballot-rigging** = trying to change the result of an election by altering or destroying voting papers (NOTE: **rigging - rigged**)

right [raɪt] **1** *adjective* not left; ***the credits are on the right side of the page*** **2** *noun* **(a)** legal title to something; ***right of renewal of a contract***; ***she has a right to the property***; ***he has no right to the patent***; ***the staff have a right to know how the company is doing***; **foreign rights** = legal title to sell something in a foreign country, such as the right to translate a book into a foreign language; **right to strike** = legal title for workers to stop working if they have a good reason for it; **right of way** = legal title to go across someone's property **(b) rights issue** *US* **rights offering** = giving shareholders the right to buy new shares at a lower price

right-hand ['raɪthænd] *adjective* belonging to the right side; ***the credit side is the right-hand column in the accounts***; ***he keeps the address list in the right-hand drawer of his desk***; **right-hand man** = main assistant

ring [rɪŋ] *noun* **(a)** trading floor on a commodity exchange **(b)** group of people who try to fix prices (especially when buying at an auction) so as not to compete with each other and still make a large profit

ring fence ['rɪŋ 'fens] *verb* **(a)** to separate valuable assets or profitable businesses from others in a group which are unprofitable and may make the whole group collapse **(b)** to identify money from certain sources and only use it in certain areas; ***the grant has been ring-fenced for use in local authority education projects only***; *see also* HYPOTHECATION

ringgit ['rɪŋgɪt] *noun* currency used in Malaysia (also called the 'Malaysian dollar')

rise [raɪz] **1** *noun* **(a)** increase; ***rise in the price of raw materials***; ***oil price rises brought about a recession in world trade***; ***there was a rise in sales of 10%*** *or* ***sales showed a rise of 10%***; ***salaries are increasing to keep up with the rises in the cost of living***; ***the recent rise in interest rates has made mortgages dearer*** **(b)** increase in salary; ***she asked her boss for a rise***; ***he had a 6% rise in January*** (NOTE: American English for this is **raise**) **2** *verb* to move upwards, to become higher; ***prices are rising faster than inflation***; ***interest rates have risen to 15%*** (NOTE: **rising - rose - has risen**)

> the index of industrial production sank 0.2 per cent for the latest month after rising 0.3 per cent in March
>
> *Financial Times*

> the stock rose to over $20 a share, higher than the $18 bid
>
> *Fortune*

> customers' deposit and current accounts also rose to $655.31 million at the end of December
>
> *Hongkong Standard*

> the government reported that production in the nation's factories and mines rose 0.2% in September
>
> *Sunday Times*

risk [rɪsk] *noun* **(a)** possible harm or chance of danger; **to run a risk** = to be likely to suffer harm; **to take a risk** = to do something which may make you lose money or suffer harm; ***he is running the risk of overspending his promotion budget***; ***the company is taking a considerable risk in manufacturing 25m units without doing any market research*** **(b) financial risk** = possibility of losing money; ***there is no financial risk in selling to East European countries on credit***; **risk arbitrage** = buying shares in companies which are likely to be taken over and so rise in price; **risk arbitrageur** = person whose business is risk arbitrage; **risk assets** = assets of a bank which are in securities or bonds which may fall in value; **risk-weighted assets** = assets which include off-balance sheet items for insurance purposes; **risk asset ratio** = proportion of a bank's capital which is in risk assets; **risk capital** = capital for investment which may easily be lost in risky projects, but which can also provide high returns (also called 'venture capital'); **risk management** = managing a company's exposure to risk from its credit terms or exposure to interest rate or exchange rate fluctuations; **risk premium** = extra payment (increased dividend or higher than usual profits) for taking risks; **equity risk premium** = extra return on equities over the return on bonds, because of the risk involved in investing in equities **(c) at owner's risk** = situation where goods shipped or stored are not insured by the transport company or the storage company, and so must be insured by the owner; ***goods left here are at owner's risk***; ***the shipment was sent at owner's risk***

(d) loss or damage against which you are insured; **fire risk** = situation or goods which could start a fire; ***that warehouse full of paper is a fire risk*** **(e) he is a good risk** = it is not likely that the insurance company will have to pay out against claims where he is concerned; **he is a bad risk** = it is very likely that the insurance company will have to pay out against claims where he is concerned

> remember, risk isn't volatility. Risk is the chance that a company's earnings power will erode - either because of a change in the industry or a change in the business that will make the company significantly less profitable in the long term
>
> *Fortune*

risk-adjusted ['rɪskə'dʒʌstɪd] *adjective* calculated after taking risk into account

> the fund has earned Morningstar's highest rating - five star - for its overall risk-adjusted performance
>
> *Smart Money*

risk-based ['rɪskbeɪst] *adjective* calculated against a risk; **risk-based capital** = internationally approved system of calculating a bank's capital value by assessing the risk attached to their assets (cash deposits and gold, for example, have no risk, while loans to Third World countries have a high risk)

risk-free *or* **riskless** ['rɪsk'fri: or 'rɪskləs] *adjective* with no risk involved; ***a risk-free investment***

> there is no risk-free way of taking regular income from your money higher than the rate of inflation and still preserving its value
>
> *Guardian*

> many small investors have also preferred to put their spare cash with risk-free investments such as building societies rather than take chances on the stock market. The returns on a host of risk-free investments have been well into double figures
>
> *Money Observer*

riskiness ['rɪskinəs] *noun* being risky

> faced with a potential downsizing of their operations, banks responded to the less friendly environment by increasing the riskiness of their portfolios
>
> *The Banker*

risky ['rɪski] *adjective* dangerous, which may cause harm; ***he lost all his money is some risky ventures in South America***

rival ['raɪvəl] *noun* person or company that competes in the same market; ***a rival takeover bid***

riyal [ri'ɑ:l] *noun* currency used in Saudi Arabia, Qatar and Yemen

robber ['rɒbə] *noun* person who carries out a robbery

> the design of bank and building society branches is itself acting as a deterrent to armed robbers, as by dispersing customers and staff around the premises for the purposes of non- cash business, rather than standing in orderly queues that can easily be controlled during a robbery
>
> *Financial World*

robbery ['rɒbri] *noun* offence of stealing something from someone using force, or threatening to use force; **armed robbery** = robbery where the robber is armed with a gun

> while the number of armed robberies in financial institutions has declined, offences classed as robbery on the public highway have risen dramatically: many of these offences are actually attacks on security vans collecting and delivering cash
>
> *Financial World*

robust [rə'bʌst] *adjective* strong, able to survive in difficult circumstances

> with a robust domestic economy allowing most banks to show strong results from their retail networks, France could afford to watch the global merger mania gathering pace beyond its borders
>
> *The Banker*

robustness [rə'bʌstnəs] *noun* being strong; **financial robustness** = being in a strong position financially (NOTE: the opposite is **fragility**)

ROCE = RETURN ON CAPITAL EMPLOYED

rock [rɒk] noun **the company is on the rocks** = the company is in great financial difficulties

rock bottom ['rɒk 'bɒtəm] noun **rock-bottom prices** = the lowest prices possible; **sales have reached rock bottom** = sales have reached the lowest point possible

> investment companies took the view that secondhand prices had reached rock bottom and that levels could only go up
>
> *Lloyd's List*

rocket ['rɒkɪt] *verb* to rise fast; ***rocketing prices***; ***prices have rocketed***

ROE = RETURN ON EQUITY

ROI = RETURN ON INVESTMENT

roll [rəʊl] *verb* to make something go forward by turning it over; *US* **rolling account** *or* **rolling settlement** = system where there are no fixed account days, but stock exchange transactions are paid at a fixed period after each transaction has taken place (as opposed to the British system, where an account day is fixed each month); **rolling budget** = budget which moves forward on a regular basis (such as a budget covering a twelve-month period, which moves forward each month); **rolling plan** = plan which runs for a period of time and is updated regularly for the same period

roll over ['rəʊl 'əʊvə] verb **to roll over credit** *or* **a debt** = to make credit available over a continuing period or to allow a debt to stand after the repayment date

> at the IMF in Washington, officials are worried that Japanese and US banks might decline to roll over the principal of loans made in the 1980s to Southeast Asian and other developing countries
>
> *Far Eastern Economic Review*

rollover ['rəʊləʊvə] *noun* extension of credit or of the period of a loan, though not necessarily on the same terms as previously; **rollover credit** = credit in the form of a medium-term loan, covered by a series of short-term loans; **rollover mortgage** = short-term mortgage which is renegotiated with different terms every five years or so

roll up ['rəʊl 'ʌp] *verb* to extend a loan, by adding the interest due to be paid to the capital; **rolled-up coupons** = interest coupons on securities, which are not paid out, but added to the capital value of the security

Romalpa clause [rəʊ'mælpæ 'klɔːz] *noun* clause in a contract, whereby the seller provides that title to the goods does not pass to the buyer until the buyer has paid for them

> COMMENT: called after the case of *Aluminium Industrie Vaassen BV vRomalpa Ltd*

rotation [rəʊ'teɪʃən] *noun* taking turns; **to fill the post of chairman by rotation** = each member of the group is chairman for a period then gives the post to another member; **two directors retire by rotation** = two directors retire because they have been directors longer than any others, but can offer themselves for re-election

Roth [rɒθ] *noun US* **Roth account** *or* **Roth IRA** = individual retirement account in which earnings can be withdrawn tax free at age 591/2provided that they have been invested in the account for more than five years

> COMMENT: one of the attractions of a Roth is that you can continue to invest in it past the age of 70 and you need never withdraw funds from it but pass it on to your heirs as a tax-free annuity

rouble *US* **ruble** ['ruːbl] *noun* currency used in Russia and Belarus

rough [rʌf] *adjective* approximate, not very accurate; **rough calculation** *or* **rough estimate** = approximate answer; ***I made some rough calculations on the back of an envelope***

rough out ['rʌf 'aʊt] *verb* to make a draft, a general plan; ***the finance director roughed out a plan of investment***

round [raʊnd] **1** adjective **in round figures** = not totally accurate, but correct to the nearest 10 or 100 **2** *verb* to make a fractional figure a full figure, by increasing or decreasing; ***some figures have been rounded to the nearest cent***

round down ['raʊnd 'daʊn] *verb* to decrease to the nearest full figure

round-tripping ['raʊnd'trɪpɪŋ] *noun* **(a)** borrowing at one rate of interest and lending the same money short-term at a higher rate (used to borrow on overdraft, when short-term deposit rates are higher) **(b)** *US* buying securities and then selling them quickly

round up ['raʊnd 'ʌp] *verb* to increase to the nearest full figure; ***to round up the figures to the nearest pound***

each cheque can be made out for the local equivalent of £100 rounded up to a convenient figure

Sunday Times

routing ['ru:tɪŋ *US* 'rəutɪŋ] *see* CHECK ROUTING SYMBOL

royalty ['rɔɪəlti] *noun* money paid to an inventor, writer or the owner of land for the right to use his property (usually a certain percentage of sales, or a certain amount per sale); ***oil royalties***; ***he is receiving royalties from his invention***

RPB = RECOGNIZED PROFESSIONAL BODY

RPI ['ɑ: 'pi: 'aɪ] = RETAIL PRICE INDEX

sterling rose yesterday as higher seasonal food prices pushed RPI inflation above its target

Financial Times

RPM ['ɑ: 'pi: 'em] = RESALE PRICE MAINTENANCE

RRP ['ɑ: 'ɑ: 'pi:] = RECOMMENDED RETAIL PRICE

RSP = RETAIL SERVICE PROVIDER

RTGS = REAL-TIME GROSS SETTLEMENT

rubber check ['rʌbə 'tʃek] *noun US* cheque which cannot be cashed because the person writing it does not have enough money in the account to pay it (NOTE: the British equivalent is a **bouncing cheque**)

rubber stamp ['rʌbə 'stæmp] **1** *noun* stamp with rubber letters or figures on it used to stamp the date or a note on a document; ***he stamped the invoice with the rubber stamp 'Paid'*** **2** *verb* to agree to something without discussing it; ***the board simply rubber stamped the agreement***

rule [ru:l] **1** *noun* **(a)** general way of conduct; **as a rule** = usually; ***as a rule, we do not give discounts over 20%***; **company rules** = general way of working in a company; ***it is a company rule that smoking is not allowed in the offices*** **(b) rule of 72** = calculation that an investment will double in value at compound interest after a period shown as 72 divided by the interest percentage (so interest at 10% compound will double the capital invested in 7.2 years) **2** *verb* **(a)** to give an official decision; ***the commission of inquiry ruled that the company was in breach of contract***; ***the judge ruled that the documents had to be deposited with the court*** **(b)** to be in force or to be current; ***prices which are ruling at the moment***

rulebook ['ru:lbʊk] *noun* document which lists the rules by which the members of a self-regulatory organization must operate

ruling ['ru:lɪŋ] **1** *adjective* in operation at the moment, current; ***we will invoice at ruling prices*** **2** *noun* decision; ***the inquiry gave a ruling on the case***; ***according to the ruling of the court, the contract was illegal***

run [rʌn] **1** *noun* **(a)** making a machine work; **a cheque run** = series of cheques processed through a computer; **a computer run** = period of work of a computer; **test run** = trial made on a machine **(b)** rush to buy something; **a run on a bank** = rush by customers to take deposits out of a bank which they think may close down; **a run on the pound** = rush to sell pounds and buy other currencies **2** *verb* **(a)** to be in force; ***the lease runs for twenty years***; ***the lease has only six months to run***; **run to settlement** = futures sale which runs until the actual commodity is delivered **(b)** to amount to; ***the costs ran into thousands of pounds*** **(c)** to work on a machine; ***the computer was running invoices all night*** (NOTE: **running - ran - has run**)

applications for mortgages are running at a high level

Times

runaway inflation ['rʌnəweɪ ɪn'fleɪʃən] *noun* inflation which is at such a high percentage rate that it is almost impossible to reduce (also called 'hyperinflation')

run down ['rʌn 'daʊn] *verb* **(a)** to reduce a quantity gradually; ***to run down stocks*** *or* ***to let stocks run down*** **(b)** to slow down the business activities of a company before it is going to be closed; ***the company is being run down***

run into ['rʌn 'ɪntʊ] *verb* **(a) to run into debt** = to start to have debts **(b)** to amount to; ***costs have run into thousands of pounds***; **he has an income running into six figures** = he earns more than £100,000

running ['rʌnɪŋ] *noun* **(a) running total** = total carried from one column of figures to the next; **running yield** = yield on fixed interest securities, where the interest is shown as a percentage of the price paid **(b) running costs** *or* **running expenses** *or* **costs of running a business** = money spent on the day-to-day cost of keeping a business going

run out of ['rʌn 'aʊt əv] *verb* to have nothing left; to use up all your stock; ***we have run out of headed notepaper***; ***the printer has run out of paper***

run up ['rʌn 'ʌp] *verb* to make costs go up quickly; ***he quickly ran up a bill for £250***

rupee [ru:'pi:] *noun* currency used in India, Mauritius, Nepal, Pakistan and Sri Lanka (NOTE: written **Rs** before the figure: **Rs. 250**)

rupiah [ru'pi:ə] *noun* currency used in Indonesia

Russell index ['rʌsl 'ɪndeks] *noun* any of various indices published by the Russell Company in Tacoma, Washington

> COMMENT: the Russell 3000 Index lists the 3000 largest companies (almost all the companies whose shares are traded in the USA); this index is subdivided into two, the Russell 1000 Index lists the 1000 largest companies in the 3000 Index, and the Russell 2000 Index lists the remainder. There are other indices

> a comparison of their average price/earnings ratio, as measured by the Russell 2000 index, with that of the Standard & Poor's 500-stock index revealed that small caps traded at only a 30% premium
>
> *Smart Money*

> the result has been a strong upward surge in equity prices since mid-January, which has pushed both the Dow Jones Industrial Average and the S&P 500 index to record highs, with the Nasdaq Composite and Russell 2000 not far off record levels as well
>
> *Barron's*

Ss

SA = SOCIETE ANONYME, SOCIEDA ANONIMA

S&L = SAVINGS AND LOAN ASSOCIATION

S&P = STANDARD AND POOR'S

safe [seɪf] **1** *noun* heavy metal box which cannot be opened easily, in which valuable documents, money, etc., can be kept; ***put the documents in the safe***; ***we keep the petty cash in the safe***; **fire-proof safe** = safe which cannot be harmed by fire; **night safe** = safe in the outside wall of a bank, where money and documents can be deposited at night, using a special door; **wall safe** = safe installed in a wall **2** *adjective* **(a)** out of danger; **keep the documents in a safe place** = in a place where they cannot be stolen or destroyed **(b) safe investments** = shares, etc., which are not likely to fall in value

safe deposit ['seɪf dɪ'pɒzɪt] *noun* bank safe where you can leave jewellery or documents

safe deposit box ['seɪf dɪ'pɒzɪt 'bɒks] *noun* small box which you can rent to keep jewellery or documents in a bank's safe

safeguard ['seɪfgɑːd] **1** *noun* action to protect **2** *verb* to protect; ***to safeguard the interests of the shareholders***

safekeeping ['seɪfkiːpɪŋ] *noun* being looked after carefully; ***we put the documents into the bank for safekeeping***

safety [seɪfti] *noun* **(a)** being free from danger or risk; **safety margin** = time or space allowed for something to be safe; **margin of safety** = sales which are above the breakeven point; **to take safety precautions** *or* **safety measures** = to act to make sure something is safe; **safety regulations** = rules to make a place of work safe for the workers **(b) fire safety** = making a place of work safe for the workers in case of fire; **fire safety officer** = person in a company responsible for seeing that the workers are safe if a fire breaks out **(c) for safety** = to make something safe, to be safe; ***put the documents in the cupboard for safety***; ***take a copy of the disk for safety***

salami fraud [sə'lɑːmi 'frɔːd] *noun* fraud where a very small amount of money is removed from each transaction and put into a suspense account (the amounts - 1p or 1c per transaction - are so small that no one notices them, but over a period of time they build up to large sums of money)

salaried ['sælərid] *adjective* earning a salary; ***the company has 250 salaried staff***; **salaried partner** = member of a partnership who is paid a salary

salary [sæləri] *noun* payment for work, made to an employee with a contract of employment, usually in the form of a monthly cheque; ***she got a salary increase in June***; ***the company froze all salaries for a six-month period***; **basic salary** = normal salary without extra payments; **gross salary** = salary before tax is deducted; **net salary** = salary which is left after deducting tax and national insurance contributions; **starting salary** = amount of payment for an employee when starting work; ***he was appointed at a starting salary of £10,000***; **salary cut** = sudden reduction in salary; **salary cheque** = monthly cheque by which an employee is paid; **salary deductions** = money which a company removes from salaries to pay to the government as tax, national insurance contributions, etc.; *US* **salary reduction** = removing money from an employee's salary to put into a pension plan; **salary review** = examination of salaries in a company to see if workers should earn more; **scale of salaries** *or* **salary scale** = list of salaries showing different levels of pay in different jobs in the same company; **the company's salary structure** = organization of salaries in a company, with different rates for different types of job

sale [seɪl] *noun* **(a)** act of selling, act of giving an item or a service in exchange for money, or for the promise that money will be paid; **cash sale** = selling something for cash; **credit card sale** = selling something for credit, using a credit card; **firm sale** = sale which does not allow the purchaser to return the goods; **forced sale** = selling something because a court orders it or because it is the only thing to do to avoid a financial crisis; **sale and lease-back** = situation where a company sells a property to raise cash and then leases it back from the purchaser; **sale or return** = system where the retailer sends goods back if they are not sold, and pays the supplier only for goods sold; ***we have taken 4,000 items on sale or return***; **bill of sale** = document which the seller gives to the buyer to show that a sale has taken place; **conditions of sale** = agreed ways in which a sale takes place (such as discounts and credit terms) **(b) for sale** = ready to be sold; **to offer something for sale** *or* **to put something up for sale** = to announce that something is ready to be sold; ***they put the factory up for sale***; ***his shop is for sale***; ***these items are not for sale to the general public*** **(c) on sale** = ready to be sold in a shop; ***these items are on sale in most chemists*** **(d)** selling of goods at specially low prices; **bargain sale** = sale of all goods in a store at cheap prices; **clearance sale** = sale of items at low prices to get rid of the stock; **fire sale** = (i) sale of fire-damaged goods; (ii) sale of anything at a very low price; **half-price sale** = sale of items at half the usual price

sales [seɪlz] *noun* (i) money received for selling something; (ii) number of items sold; ***sales have risen over the first quarter***; **sales analysis** = examining the reports of sales to see why items have or have not sold well; **sales book** = record of sales; **book sales** = sales as recorded in the sales book; **sales budget** = plan of probable sales; **cost of sales** = all the costs of a product sold, including manufacturing costs and the staff costs of the production department; **sales day book (SDB)** *or* **sales journal** = ledger in which sales are posted with details of customer, invoice, amount and date; **sales department** = section of a company which deals in selling the company's products or services; **domestic sales** *or* **home sales** = sales in the home market; **sales executive** = person in a company in charge of sales; **sales figures** = total sales, or sales broken down by category; **sales force** = group of salesmen; **sales forecast** = calculation of future sales; **forward sales** = sales (of shares, commodities, foreign exchange) for delivery at a later date; **sales invoice** = invoice relating to a sale; **sales journal** = SALES DAY BOOK; **sales ledger** = book in which sales are recorded; **sales ledger clerk** = office worker who deals with the sales ledger; **sales literature** = written information which tries to sell something; ***the bank sent me some sales literature about their new savings accounts***; **sales manager** = person in charge of a sales department; **sales mix** = sales and profitability of a wide range of products sold by a single company; **sales mix profit variance** = differing profitability of different products within a product range; **monthly sales report** = report made showing the number of items sold or the amount of money received for selling stock; ***in the sales reports all the European countries are bracketed together***; **sales return** = report showing sales; **sales returns** = items sold which are returned by the purchaser; **sales returns book (SRB)** = ledger giving details of goods returned by purchasers, including invoice number, credit notes, quantities, etc.; *US* **sales revenue** = income from sales of goods or services; **sales tax** = tax which is paid on each item sold (and is collected when the purchase is made); **sales value** = the amount of money which would be received if something is sold; **sales volume** *or* **volume of sales** = number of units sold; **sales volume profit variance** = difference between the profit on the number of units actually sold and the forecast figure

salesman ['seɪlzmən] *noun* **(a)** man who sells goods or services to members of the public; **door-to-door salesman** = man who goes from one house to the next, asking people to buy something; **insurance salesman** = man who encourages clients to take out insurance policies **(b)** person who represents a company, selling its products or services to retail shops; ***we have six salesmen calling on accounts in central London*** (NOTE: plural is **salesmen**)

salvage ['sælvɪdʒ] **1** *noun* **(a)** saving a ship or a cargo from being destroyed; **salvage money** = payment made by the owner of a ship or a cargo to the person who has saved it; **salvage vessel** = ship which specializes in saving other ships and their cargoes **(b)** goods saved from a wrecked ship, from a fire, etc.; ***a sale of flood salvage items*** **2** *verb* **(a)** to save goods or a ship from being wrecked; ***we are selling off a warehouse full of salvaged goods*** **(b)** to save something from loss; ***the company is trying to salvage its reputation after the managing director was sent to prison for fraud***; ***the receiver managed to salvage something from the collapse of the company***

same [seɪm] *adjective* being or looking exactly alike; **same-day funds** = money which can be withdrawn from an account the same day as it is deposited; **same-store sales** = sales for the same stores over an earlier period; *see also* COMPARABLE, LIKE-FOR-LIKE

---

it led the nation's department stores over the crucial

> Christmas season with an 11.7% increase in same-store sales
>
> *Fortune*

> its consistent double-digit same-store sales growth also proves that it is not just adding revenue by adding new locations
>
> *Fortune*

sample ['sɑ:mpl] **1** *noun* **(a)** specimen, a small part of an item which is used to show what the whole item is like; ***a sample of the cloth*** *or* ***a cloth sample***; **check sample** = sample to be used to see if a whole consignment is acceptable; **free sample** = sample given free to advertise a product **(b)** small group taken to show what a larger group is like; ***we interviewed a sample of potential customers***; **a random sample** = a sample taken without any selection **2** *verb* **(a)** to test or to try something by taking a small amount; ***to sample a product before buying it*** **(b)** to ask a representative group of people questions to find out what the reactions of a much larger group would be; ***they sampled 2,000 people at random to test the new drink***

sampling ['sɑ:mplɪŋ] *noun* **(a)** testing a product by taking a small amount; **acceptance sampling** = testing a small sample of a batch to see if the whole batch is good enough to be accepted **(b)** testing the reactions of a small group of people to find out the reactions of a larger group of consumers

samurai bond ['sæmuraɪ 'bɒnd] *noun* international bond in yen launched on the Japanese market by a non-Japanese corporation; *compare* BULLDOG, SHOGUN, YANKEE

sanction ['sæŋkʃn] noun **economic sanctions** = restrictions on trade with a country in order to influence its political situation or in order to make its government change its policy; ***to impose sanctions on a country*** *or* ***to lift sanctions***

SARL = SOCIETE ANONYME A RESPONSABILITE LIMITEE

save [seɪv] *verb* to keep (money), not to spend (money); ***he is trying to save money by walking to work***; ***she is saving to buy a house***

save-as-you-earn scheme (SAYE) ['seivəzju:'ɜ:n 'ski:m] *noun* scheme where workers can save money regularly by having it deducted automatically from their wages and invested in National Savings

saver [seɪvə] *noun* person who saves money

save up ['seɪv 'ʌp] *verb* to put money aside for a special purpose; ***they are saving up for a holiday in the USA***

savings ['seɪvɪŋz] *plural noun* money saved (i.e., money which is not spent); *GB* **National Savings** = government authority which runs schemes where small investors can invest in government savings certificates, premium bonds, etc.; **savings certificate** *US* **savings bond** = document showing that you have invested money in a government savings scheme (British savings certificates give an interest which is not taxable; in some cases, interest on US savings bonds is also tax exempt); **National Savings Certificates** *or* **NS certificates** = certificates showing that someone has invested in National Savings (the NS issues certificates with stated interest rates and stated maturity dates, usually five or ten years); **savings account** = bank account where you can put money in regularly and which pays interest, often at a higher rate than a deposit account; **savings-related share option scheme** = scheme which allows employees of a company to buy shares with money which they have contributed to a savings scheme

savings and loan (association) (S&L) ['seɪvɪŋz ən 'ləʊn əsəʊsɪ'eɪʃn] *noun* *US* financial association which accepts and pays interest on deposits from investors and lends money to people who are buying property; the loans are in the form of mortgages on the security of the property being bought (NOTE: the S&Ls are also called **thrifts**)

> COMMENT: because of deregulation of interest rates in 1980, many S&Ls found that they were forced to raise interest on deposits to current market rates in order to secure funds, while at the same time they still were charging low fixed-interest rates on the mortgages granted to borrowers. This created considerable problems and many S&Ls had to be rescued by the Federal government

savings bank ['seɪvɪŋz 'bæŋk] *noun* bank where investors can deposit small sums of money and receive interest on it

SAYE ['es 'eɪ 'waɪ 'i:] = SAVE-AS-YOU-EARN

SBA = SMALL BUSINESS ADMINISTRATION

SBF = SOCIETE DES BOURSES FRANCAISES

scale [skeɪl] **1** *noun* **(a)** system which is graded into various levels; **scale of charges** *or*

scale of prices = list showing various prices; **fixed scale of charges** = rate of charging which does not change; **scale of salaries** *or* **salary scale** = list of salaries showing different levels of pay in different jobs in the same company; ***he was appointed at the top end of the salary scale***; **incremental scale** = salary scale with regular annual salary increases **(b) large scale** *or* **small scale** = working with large or small amounts of investment, staff, etc.; **to start in business on a small scale** = to start in business with a small staff, few products, little investment capital; **economies of scale** = making a product more cheaply by manufacturing it or buying it in larger quantities; **diseconomies of scale** = situation where increased production actually increases unit cost; *see note at* DISECONOMIES **2** *verb* **to scale down** *or* **to scale back** = to lower in proportion; **to scale up** = to increase in proportion

> COMMENT: if a share issue is oversubscribed, applications may be scaled down; by doing this, the small investor is protected. So all applications for 1000 shares may receive 300; all applications for 2000 shares may receive 500; applications for 5,000 shares receive 1,000, and applications for more than 5,000 shares will go into a ballot

scalp ['skælp] *verb* to buy or sell to make a quick profit

scalper ['skælpə] *noun* **(a)** person who buys and sells to make a large rapid profit (as by buying and reselling tickets for a popular sporting event, etc.) **(b)** *US* trader who buys and sells the same futures on the same day

scam [skæm] *noun US (informal)* case of fraud

scatter diagram ['skætə 'daɪəgræm] *noun* chart where points are plotted according to two sets of variables to see if a pattern exists

scenario [sɪ'nɑːriəʊ] *noun* way in which a situation may develop

> on the upside scenario, the outlook is reasonably optimistic, bankers say, the worst scenario being that a scheme of arrangement cannot be achieved, resulting in liquidation
>
> *Irish Times*

schedule ['ʃedjuːl *US* 'skedjuːl] *noun* **(a)** timetable, a plan of time drawn up in advance; **to be ahead of schedule** = to be early; **to be on schedule** = to be on time; **to be behind schedule** = to be late; ***the project is on schedule; the building was completed ahead of schedule; I am sorry to say that we are three months behind schedule; the managing director has a busy schedule of appointments; his secretary tried to fit me into his schedule*** **(b)** list (especially additional documents attached to a contract); ***please find enclosed our schedule of charges; schedule of territories to which a contract applies; see the attached schedule*** *or* ***as per the attached schedule*** **(c)** list of interest rates; *GB* **tax schedules** = six types of income as classified for tax; *see also* A, B, C, D, E, F

scheduled ['ʃedjuːld *US* 'skedjuːld] *adjective* listed in a separate schedule

scheme [skiːm] *noun* plan, arrangement, way of working; ***bonus scheme; pension scheme; profit-sharing scheme;*** **scheme of arrangement** = scheme drawn up by an individual to offer ways of paying his debts, and to avoid bankruptcy proceedings

schilling ['ʃɪlɪŋ] *noun* currency used with the euro in Austria

scorched earth policy ['skɔːtʃt 'ɜːθ 'pɒləsi] *noun* way of combating a takeover bid, where the target company sells valuable assets or purchases unattractive assets; *see also* POISON PILL

scout [skaʊt] *noun* person who searches for something, especially someone who looks for promising new members of staff

> top students are lured away in their second or third semester by corporate scouts
>
> *Fortune*

scrap [skræp] *noun* waste material; pieces of metal to be melted down to make new metal ingots; **scrap value** = the value of an asset if sold for scrap

screen [skriːn] **1** *noun* **(a)** flat panel which acts as a protection; **rising screen** = panel which moves upwards to protect a cashier in a bank against robbers **(b)** flat glass surface on which information can be shown; **trading screens** = computer monitors listing stock market prices; ***the screens rapidly turned to red during the morning trading*** **2** *verb* to consider a range of items or people and only select some; **to screen out** = to consider things and remove some their purpose is to assemble portfolios of shares that screen out companies engaged in undesirable activities

Money Observer

screening ['skri:nɪŋ] *noun* considering a range of items or people and only selecting some; *see also* ETHICAL SCREENING

scrip [skrɪp] *noun* security (a share, or the certificate issued to show that someone has been allotted a share); **scrip issue** = issue of shares, where a company transfers money from reserves to share capital and issues free extra shares to the shareholders (the value of the company remains the same, and the total market value of shareholders' shares remains the same, the market price being adjusted to account for the new shares) (NOTE: also called **free issue** *or* **capitalization issue**)

under the rule, brokers who fail to deliver stock within four days of a transaction are to be fined 1% of the transaction value for each day of missing scrip

Far Eastern Economic Review

scripophily [skrɪ'pɒfɪli] *noun* collecting old share certificates and bond certificates as a hobby and investment

SDB = SALES DAY BOOK

Sdn [sen'dɪriən] = SENDIRIAN; *(in Malaysia)* **Sdn berhad** = private limited company

SDRs = SPECIAL DRAWING RIGHTS

seal [si:l] **1** *noun* **(a) common seal** *or* **company's seal** = metal stamp for stamping documents with the name of the company to show they have been approved officially; ***to attach the company's seal to a document***; **contract under seal** = contract which has been legally approved with the seal of the company **(b)** piece of paper, metal or wax attached to close something, so that it can be opened only if the paper, metal or wax is removed or broken; **customs seal** = seal attached by customs office to a box, to show that the contents have not passed through customs **2** *verb* **(a)** to close something tightly; **sealed envelope** = envelope where the back has been stuck down to close it; ***the information was sent in a sealed envelope***; **sealed tenders** = tenders sent in sealed envelopes, which will all be opened at a certain time **(b)** to attach a seal, to stamp something with a seal; ***the customs sealed the shipment***

SEAQ ['si:æk] = STOCK EXCHANGE AUTOMATED QUOTATIONS SYSTEM a computerized information system giving details of current share prices and stock market transactions on the London Stock Exchange: dealers list their offer and bid prices on SEAQ, and transactions are carried out on the basis of the information shown on the screen; transactions are recorded on the SEAQ database in case of future disputes

search [sɜ:tʃ] *noun* examination of records by the lawyer acting for someone who wants to buy a property, to make sure that the vendor has the right to sell it

season ['si:zən] *noun* particular time of year when something happens; **earnings season** = time of year when major companies declare their results for the previous period; ***earnings season will begin in force next week***; *see also* EARNINGS, REPORTING

seasonal ['si:znəl] *adjective* which lasts for a season, which only happens during a particular season; ***seasonal variations in sales patterns***; **seasonal adjustments** = changes made to figures to take account of seasonal variations; **seasonal demand** = demand which exists only during the high season; **seasonal unemployment** = unemployment which rises and falls according to the season

seasoned ['si:zənd] *adjective US* reputable (securities); safe long-term (loan)

seat [si:t] *noun* membership of a stock exchange

did you see the price of a seat on the New York Stock Exchange recently rose to $1.8 million, a new all-time record?

Fortune

SEC ['es 'i: 'si:] = SECURITIES & EXCHANGE COMMISSION

second 1 ['seknd] *adjective* (thing) which comes after the first; **second half-year** = six month period from July to the end of December; **second mortgage** = further mortgage on a property which is already mortgaged; **second quarter** = three month period from April to the end of June; **second round** = new tranche of venture capital raised for a new project after the start-up finance **2** *verb* **(a)** ['seknd] **to second a motion** = to be the first person to support a proposal put forward by someone else **(b)** [sɪ'kɒnd] to lend a member of staff to another company or to a government department, etc., for a fixed period of time; ***he was seconded to the Department of Trade for two years***

secondary ['sekəndri] *adjective* second in importance; **secondary auditor** = auditor for a subsidiary company who has no connection with the primary auditor who audits the accounts of the main company; **secondary banks** = finance companies which provide money for hire-purchase deals; **secondary industry** = industry which uses basic raw materials to make manufactured goods; **secondary market** = market where existing securities are bought and sold again and again, as opposed to a primary market, where new issues are launched; US **secondary mortgage market** = nationwide system organized by various federal mortgage associations for polling mortgages and selling them to investors; **secondary properties** = commercial properties which are not in prime sites and therefore are not as valuable; *compare* PRIMARY

> as things stand, the institutions will not receive anything like enough stock to weight their portfolios and their buying in the secondary market after the issue is expected to push prices higher
>
> *Times*

second-class ['sekndklɑːs] *adjective & adverb* less expensive or less comfortable way of travelling; **second-class mail** = (i) GB less expensive, slower, mail service; (ii) US mail service for sending newspapers and magazines; ***the letter took three days to arrive because he sent it second class***

seconder ['sekəndə] *noun* person who seconds a proposal; ***there was no seconder for the motion so it was not put to the vote***

second half ['seknd 'hɑːf] *noun* period of six months from 1st July to end of December; ***the figures for the second half are up on those for the first part of the year***

secondment [sɪ'kɒndmənt] *noun* being seconded to another job for a period; ***he is on three years' secondment to a US college***

second-ranker ['sekənd 'ræŋkə] *noun* company which occupies the second rank, i.e. not one of the top companies

> pay close attention to the financial pages of the national press each day for pointers on where big investors perceive any value, in particular to the second-rankers in the FTSE 250 index, as well as smaller companies
>
> *Money Observer*

second-tier ['seknd'tɪə] *adjective* not in the first and most important group; **second-tier bank** = bank which is not as large as the main banks in a country; **second-tier market** = secondary market, such as the AIM, where securities which are not listed on the main Stock Exchange can be traded

> while it is a second-tier bank in terms of size and a niche player in the investment banking and securities business, the bank is nonetheless seen as a prized asset, particularly for a potential foreign acquirer
>
> *The Banker*

secret ['siːkrət] *noun & adjective* (something) hidden or not known by many people; ***the MD kept the contract secret from the rest of the board***; ***they signed a secret deal with their main rivals***; **secret reserves** = HIDDEN RESERVES

secretary ['sekrtri] *noun* **(a)** official of a company or society; **company secretary** = person who is responsible for a company's legal and financial affairs; **honorary secretary** = person who keeps the minutes and official documents of a committee or club, but is not paid a salary **(b)** GB member of the government in charge of a department; GB **Chief Secretary to the Treasury** = senior member of the government under the Chancellor of the Exchequer; US **Secretary of the Treasury** *or* **Treasury Secretary** = senior member of the government in charge of financial affairs; *see also* TREASURY

Secretary of State ['sekrtri əv 'steɪt] *noun* **(a)** GB one of several members of the government in charge of departments **(b)** US senior member of the government in charge of foreign affairs

secretariat [sekr'teəriət] *noun* important office and the officials who work in it; ***the United Nations secretariat***

section ['sekʃn] *noun* **(a)** part of something; **legal section** = department in a company dealing with legal matters **(b)** one of the parts of an Act of Parliament

sector ['sektə] *noun* **(a)** part of the economy or the business organization of a country; ***all sectors of the economy suffered from the rise in the exchange rate***; ***technology is a booming sector of the economy***; **public sector** = nationalized industries and public services; *see also* PUBLIC SECTOR BORROWING REQUIREMENT; **private sector** = all companies which are owned by private shareholders, not by the state; ***the expansion is funded completely by the private sector***; ***salaries in the private sector have increased faster than in the public*** **(b)** section of a stock market, listing shares in one types of industry (such as the banking sector)

> government services form a large part of the tertiary or service sector
>
> *Sydney Morning Herald*

> in the dry cargo sector, a total of 956 dry cargo vessels are laid up - 3% of world dry cargo tonnage
>
> *Lloyd's List*

secure [sɪ'kʊə] **1** *adjective* safe, which cannot change; **secure job** = job from which you are not likely to be made redundant; **secure investment** = investment where you are not likely to lose money; **secure socket layer;** *see* SSL; **secure web site** = web site on the internet that encrypts the messages between the visitor and the site to ensure that no hacker or eavesdropper can intercept the information; normally used to provide a secure way of sending credit card or personal information over the internet **2** *verb* **(a) to secure a loan** = to pledge an asset as a security for a loan **(b)** to get (something) safely into your control; ***to secure funds***; ***he secured the backing of an Australian group***

secured [sɪ'kjʊəd] adjective **secured creditor** = person who is owed money by someone, and can legally claim the same amount of the borrower's property if he fails to pay back the money owed; **secured debts** = debts which are guaranteed by assets; **secured loan** = loan which is guaranteed by the borrower giving assets as security

securities [sɪ'kjʊərɪtiz] *plural noun* investments in stocks and shares; certificates to show that someone owns stocks or shares; **gilt-edged securities** *or* **government securities** = investments in British government stock; **listed securities** = shares which can be bought or sold on the Stock Exchange, shares which appear on the official Stock Exchange list; **securities broker** *or* **securities trader** = person whose business is buying and selling stocks and shares; **securities house** = firm which buys and sells securities for clients; **securities markets** = Stock Exchanges, places where stocks and shares can be bought or sold; *US* **Securities and Exchange Commission (SEC)** = the official body which regulates the securities markets in the USA; *GB* **Securities and Futures Authority (SFA)** = self-regulatory organization which regulates the trading in shares and futures, now part of the FSA; *GB* **Securities and Investments Board (SIB)** = formerly the name of the regulatory body which regulates the securities markets in the UK, now the FSA

securitization [sɪkjʊərɪtaɪ'zeɪʃn] *noun* making a loan or mortgage into a tradeable security by issuing a bill of exchange or other negotiable paper in place of the loan

securitize [sɪ'kjʊrɪtaɪz] *verb* to make a loan into a security which can be traded (as in the case of issuing an IOU for a loan)

security [sɪ'kjʊərɪti] *noun* **(a)** stock or share; *see* SECURITIES **(b)** guarantee that someone will repay money borrowed; **to stand security for someone** = to guarantee that if the person does not repay a loan, you will repay it for him; ***to give something as security for a debt***; ***to use a house as security for a loan***; ***the bank lent him £20,000 without security*** **(c) job security** = a worker's feeling that he has a right to keep his job, or that he will never be made redundant; **security of employment** = feeling by a worker that he has the right to keep his job until he retires; **security of tenure** = right to keep a job or rented accommodation, provided that certain conditions are met **(d)** being protected; **security guard** = person who protects an office or factory against burglars; **office security** = protecting an office against theft **(e)** being secret; **security in this office is nil** = nothing can be kept secret in this office; **security printer** = printer who prints paper money, share prospectuses, secret government documents, etc. **(f) social security** = money or help provided by the government to people who need it; ***he lives on social security payments***

seedcorn *or* **seed money** ['si:dkɔ:n *or* 'si:d 'mʌni] *noun* venture capital invested when a new project is starting up (and therefore more risky than secondary finance or mezzanine finance); ***they had their ranch house to operate out of, a used printer and seed money from friends***

segment 1 ['segmənt] *noun* section of a market defined by certain criteria **2** [seg'ment] *verb* to divide a potential market into different segments

segmentation [segmən'teɪʃn] *noun* division of a market or consumers into certain categories according to their buying habits; ***market segmentation will show us ways of getting more variety into our product line***

self- [self] *prefix* referring to oneself

self-employed ['selfɪm'plɔɪd] **1** *adjective* working for yourself and not being on the payroll of a company; ***a self-employed engineer; he worked for a bank for ten years but now is self-employed*** **2** noun **the self-employed** = people who work for themselves

self-financed ['selffaɪ'nænst] adjective **the project is completely self-financed** = the project pays its development costs out of its own revenue, with no subsidies

self-financing ['selffaɪ'nænsɪŋ] **1** *noun* the financing of development costs, purchase of capital assets etc., of a company from its own resources **2** adjective **the company is completely self-financing** = the company finances its development costs, capital assets, etc., from its own resources

self-insurance ['selfɪn'ʃɔːrəns] *noun* insuring against a probable future loss by putting money aside regularly, rather than by taking out an insurance policy

self-made man ['self'meɪd 'mæn] *noun* person who is rich and successful because of his own work, not because he inherited money or position

self-regulating organization = SELF-REGULATORY ORGANIZATION

self-regulation ['selfregjʊ'leɪʃn] *noun* regulation of an industry by itself, through a committee which issues a rulebook and makes sure that members of the industry follow the rules (as in the case of the regulation of the Stock Exchange by the Stock Exchange Council)

self-regulatory ['self'regjʊlətəri] *adjective* (organization) which regulates itself; **Self-Regulatory Organization (SRO)** = organization which regulates the way in which its own members carry on their business, such as the Securities and Futures Authority (SFA)

self-select Pep ['selfsɪ'lekt 'pep] *see* PERSONAL EQUITY PLAN

self-service banking [self'sɜːvɪs 'bæŋkɪŋ] *noun* situation where a bank's customers arrange transactions by themselves, without involving bank staff, for example by using ATMs for cash withdrawals

self-supporting ['selfsə'pɔːtɪŋ] *adjective* which finances itself from its own resources, with no subsidies

sell [sel] **1** *noun* act of selling; **to give a product the hard sell** = to make great efforts to persuade customers to buy it; **he tried to give me the hard sell** = he put a lot of effort into trying to persuade me to buy his product; **soft sell** = persuading people to buy, by encouraging and not forcing them to do so **2** *verb* **(a)** to give goods or services in exchange for money; ***to sell insurance*** *or* ***to sell refrigerators; they tried to sell their house for £100,000***; **to sell forward** = to sell foreign currency, commodities, etc., for delivery at a later date **(b)** to be bought; ***those packs sell for £25 a dozen*** (NOTE: **selling - sold**)

> selling forward, after all, is an admission that you expect your product to be worth less in the future than it is today
>
> *Fortune*

sell-by date ['selbaɪ 'deɪt] *noun* date on a food packet which is the last date on which the food is guaranteed to be good

seller ['selə] *noun* vendor, a person who sells; ***there were few sellers in the market, so prices remained high***; **seller's market** = market where the seller can ask high prices because there is a large demand for the product

selling ['selɪŋ] noun **direct selling** = selling a product direct to the customer without going through a shop; **mail-order selling** = selling by taking orders and supplying a product by post; **selling costs** *or* **selling overhead** = amount of money to be paid for advertising, reps' commissions, etc., involved in selling something; **selling price** = price at which someone is willing to sell; **selling price variance** = difference between the actual selling price and the budgeted selling price

sell off ['sel 'ɒf] *verb* to sell goods quickly to get rid of them

sell out ['sel 'aʊt] *verb* **(a)** to sell all stock; ***to sell out of a product line; we have sold out of that computer game; this item has sold out*** **(b) to sell out** = to sell your business; ***he sold out and retired to the seaside***

sellout ['selaʊt] noun **this item has been a sellout** = all the stock of the item has been sold

sell up ['sel 'ʌp] *verb* to sell a business and all the stock

semi- ['semi] *prefix* half

semiannual ['semi'ænjʊəl] *adjective* (interest) paid every six months

semi-fixed cost *or* **semi-variable cost** ['semi'fɪkst 'kɒst or 'semi'veəriəbl kɒst] *noun* cost which has both fixed and variable parts (the rental of a car may consist of a fixed payment plus a sum which is calculated on the number of miles travelled)

senior ['si:niə] *adjective* **(a)** (sum) which is repayable before others; **senior capital** = capital in the form of secured loans to a company (it is repaid before junior capital, such as shareholders' equity, in the event of liquidation); **senior debts** = debts which must be repaid in preference to other debts (such as a first mortgage over a second mortgage) **(b)** older; more important; (worker) who has been employed longer than another; **senior manager** *or* **senior executive** = manager or director who has a higher rank than others; **senior partner** = most important partner in a firm of solicitors or accountants

seniority [si:i'ɒrɪti] *noun* being older; being an employee of the company longer; **the managers were listed in order of seniority** = the manager who had been an employee the longest was put at the top of the list

sensitive ['sensɪtɪv] *adjective* able to feel something sharply; ***the market is very sensitive to the result of the elections***; **interest-sensitive purchases** = purchases (such as houses or items bought on hire-purchase) which are influenced by interest rates; **price-sensitive product** = product which will sell less if the price is increased

sensitivity analysis *noun* analysis of the effect of a small change in a certain calculation on the final result

sentiment ['sentɪmənt] noun **market sentiment** = general feeling among investors or financial analysts on a stock market

> COMMENT: 'sentiment' (either optimistic or pessimistic) can be influenced by external factors, and affects the prices of shares or the volume of business transacted

separable ['seprəbl] *adjective* which can be separated; **separable net assets** = assets which can be separated from the rest of the assets of a business and sold off

separate ['seprət] *adjective* not together; **separate estate** = property of one of the partners in a partnership, as opposed to the property belonging to the partnership itself

separation [sepə'reɪʃn] *noun US* leaving a job (resigning, retiring, or being fired or made redundant)

sequester *or* **sequestrate** [sɪ'kwestə or 'sekwəstreɪt] *verb* to take and keep (a bank account or property) because a court has ordered it

sequestration [sekwə'streɪʃn] *noun* taking and keeping of property on the order of a court

sequestrator ['sekwə'streɪtə] *noun* person who takes and keeps property on the order of a court

series ['sɪəriz] *noun* group of bonds or savings certificates, issued over a period of time but all bearing the same interest

Serious Fraud Office (SFO) ['sɪəriəs 'frɔ:d 'ɒfɪs] *noun* government department in charge of investigating major fraud in companies

service ['sɜ:vɪs] **1** *noun* **(a)** working for a company, in a shop, etc.; **length of service** = number of years someone has worked; **service agreement** *or* **service contract** = contract between a company and a director showing all conditions of work **(b)** the work of dealing with customers; payment for help for the customer; **the bill includes service** = includes a charge added for the work involved **(c) services** = business of providing help in some form when it is needed (insurance, banking, etc., as opposed to making or selling goods); **answering service** = office which answers the telephone and takes messages for a company; **banking service** = various ways in which a bank can help a customer, such as operating accounts, making transfers, paying standing orders, selling foreign currency, etc.; **basic banking service** = operating ordinary current or deposit accounts for customers; **24-hour service** = help which is available for the whole day; **service bureau** = office which specializes in helping other offices; **service cost centre** *or* **service centre** = section of a company considered as a cost centre, which provides a service to other parts of the company; **service department** = department of a company which does not deal with production or sales (accounts, personnel, etc.); **service industry** = industry which does not make products, but offers a service (such as banking, insurance, transport) **2** verb **to service a debt** = to pay interest on a debt (and also repay the capital at due date); ***the company is having problems in servicing its debts***

service charge ['sɜ:vɪs 'tʃɑ:dʒ] *noun* **(a)** charge added to the bill in a restaurant to pay for service; amount paid by tenants in a block of flats for general cleaning **(b)** *US* charges which a bank makes for carrying out work for a customer (NOTE: the British equivalent is **bank charges**)

session [seʃn] *noun* one of a series of periods during which something usually takes place; **trading session** = one period (usually a day) during which trading takes place on a stock exchange

> statistics from the stock exchange show that customer interest in the equity market has averaged just under £700m in recent trading sessions
>
> *Financial Times*

set [set] **1** *adjective* fixed, which cannot be changed; ***set price*** **2** *verb* to fix or to arrange; ***we have to set a price for the new computer***; ***the price of the calculator has been set low, so as to achieve maximum unit sales***; **the auction set a record for high prices** = the prices at the auction were the highest ever reached (NOTE: **setting - set**)

set against ['set ə'genst] *verb* to balance one group of figures against another group to try to make them cancel each other out; ***to set the costs against the invoice***; ***can you set the expenses against tax?***

set aside ['set ə'saɪd] *verb* to decide not to apply a decision; ***the arbitrator's award was set aside on appeal***

setback ['setbæk] *noun* stopping progress; ***the company suffered a series of setbacks in 1997***; ***the shares had a setback on the Stock Exchange***

> a sharp setback in foreign trade accounted for most of the winter slowdown
>
> *Fortune*

SET Index ['set 'ɪndeks] index of share prices on the Bangkok Stock Exchange

set off ['set 'ɒf] *verb* to use a debt owed by one party to reduce a debt owed to them

Sets ['sets] = STOCK EXCHANGE ELECTRONIC TRADING SYSTEM

settle ['setl] *verb* **(a) to settle an account** = to pay what is owed; **settled account** = arrangement between two parties who agree the accounts between them **(b) to settle a claim** = to agree to pay what is asked for; ***the insurance company refused to settle his claim for storm damage***; **the two parties settled out of court** = the two parties reached an agreement privately without continuing the court case **(c)** to place a property in trust; **settled property** = property which is held in trust

settlement ['setlmənt] *noun* **(a)** (i) payment of an account; (ii) payment for shares bought, delivery of share certificates, etc.; **our basic discount is 20% but we offer an extra 5% for rapid settlement** = we take a further 5% off the price if the customer pays quickly; **settlement in cash** *or* **cash settlement** = payment of an invoice in cash, not by cheque; **settlement date** = date when a payment has to be made; **settlement day** = (i) account day, the day on which shares which have been bought must be paid for (usually a Monday ten days after the end of an account); (ii) *US* day when securities bought actually become the property of the purchaser; *US* **rolling settlement** = payment for shares bought which is carried out a certain number of days after the transaction **(b)** agreement after an argument; **to effect a settlement between two parties** = to bring two parties together to make them agree

settle on ['setl 'ɒn] *verb* to leave property to someone when you die; ***he settled his property on his children***

settlor ['setlə] *noun* person who settles property on someone

set up ['set 'ʌp] *verb* **(a)** to begin (something), to organize (something) new; ***to set up an inquiry*** *or* ***a working party***; **to set up a company** = to start a company legally **(b) to set up in business** = to start a new business; ***he set up in business as an insurance broker***; ***he set himself up as a freelance engineer***

> the concern announced that it had acquired a third large tanker since being set up in 1983
>
> *Lloyd's List*

seven-day money ['sevn'deɪ 'mʌni] *noun* investment in financial instruments which mature in seven days' time

severally ['sevrəli] *adverb* separately, not jointly; **they are jointly and severally liable** = they are liable both as a group and as individuals for the total amount

severance pay ['sevrəns 'peɪ] *noun* money paid as compensation to someone who is losing his job

SFA ['es 'ef 'eɪ] = SECURITES AND FUTURES AUTHORITY

SFO ['es 'ef 'əʊ] = SERIOUS FRAUD OFFICE

shadow director ['ʃædəʊ dɪ'rektə] *noun* person who is not a director of a company, but who tells the directors of the company how to act

shady ['ʃeɪdi] *adjective* not honest; ***a shady deal***; ***he's a shady character***

shake [ʃeɪk] *verb* to surprise or to shock; ***the markets were shaken by the company's results*** (NOTE: **shaking - shook - has shaken**)

shakeout ['ʃeɪkaʊt] *noun* **(a)** reorganization, where some are left, but others go; ***a shakeout in the top management***; ***only three companies were left after the shakeout in the computer market*** **(b)** process of revising prices on a stock market, usually at the end of a sharp rise or fall

> continental stock markets suffered a savage shakeout between mid-July and the first week of October
>
> *Money Observer*

shakeup ['ʃeɪkʌp] *noun* reorganization which is imposed by an outside authority

> non-taxpayers will suffer a drop in income next April thanks to a shakeup in the way share dividends are taxed
>
> *The Times*

shaky ['ʃeɪki] *adjective* not very sure or not very reliable; ***the new issue got off to a shaky start on the market***

share [ʃeə] *noun* **(a) to have a share in** = to take part in or to contribute to; ***to have a share in management decisions***; **market share** *or* **share of the market** = percentage of a total market which the sales of a company cover; ***the company hopes to boost its market share***; ***their share of the market has gone up by 10%*** **(b)** one of many equal parts into which a company's capital is divided (the owners of shares are shareholders or, more formally, 'members'); ***he bought a block of shares in Marks and Spencer***; ***shares fell on the London market***; ***the company offered 1.8m shares on the market***; **'A' shares** = ordinary shares with limited voting rights; **'B' shares** = ordinary shares with special voting rights (often owned by the founder of the company and his family); **bonus share** = extra share given to an existing shareholder; **deferred shares** = shares which receive a dividend only after all other dividends have been paid; **founder's shares** = special shares issued to the person who starts a company; **ordinary shares** = normal shares in a company, which have no special benefits or restrictions; **preference shares** = shares (often with no voting rights) which receive their dividend before all other shares and are repaid first (at face value) if the company goes into liquidation; **share account** = account with a credit union which pays dividends instead of interest; **share allocation** *or* **share allotment** = sharing of a small number of shares among a large number of people who have applied to buy them; **to allot shares** = to give a certain number of shares to people who have applied to buy them; **share capital** = value of the assets of a company held as shares; **share certificate** = document proving that someone owns shares; **share incentive scheme** = incentive scheme which offers employees shares in the company as a reward for work; **share index** = index figure based on the current market price of certain shares on a stock exchange; **share issue** = selling new shares in a company to the public; **share option** = right to buy or sell shares at a certain price at a time in the future; **share premium** = amount to be paid above the nominal value of a share in order to buy it; **share premium account** = part of shareholders' funds in a company, formed of the premium paid for new shares sold above par (the par value of the shares is the nominal capital of the company); **share register** = list of shareholders in a company with their addresses; **share warrant** = document which entitles the holder to some shares in a company (NOTE: American English often used the word **stock** where British English uses **share.** See the note at STOCK)

> falling profitability means falling share prices
>
> *Investors Chronicle*

> the share of blue-collar occupations declined from 48 per cent to 43 per cent
>
> *Sydney Morning Herald*

shareholder [ʃeəhəʊldə] *noun* person who owns shares in a company (formally called a 'member'); ***to call a shareholders' meeting***; **shareholders' equity** = a company's capital which is invested by shareholders, who thus become owners of the company (note that preference shares are not equity capital, since they involve less risk and do not share in the profitability of the company); **shareholders' funds** = the capital and reserves of a company; **majority shareholder** = person who owns more than half the shares in a company; **minority shareholder** = person who owns less than half the shares in a company; ***the solicitor acting on behalf of the minority shareholders*** (NOTE: American English is **stockholder)**

> as of last night the bank's shareholders no longer hold any rights to the bank's shares
>
> *South China Morning Post*

> the company said that its recent issue of 10.5% convertible

```
preference shares at A$8.50 has been oversubscribed, boosting shareholders' funds to A$700 million plus
```

Financial Times

shareholding ['ʃeəhəuldɪŋ] *noun* group of shares in a company owned by one person; **a majority shareholding** = group of shares which are more than half the total; **a minority shareholding** = group of shares which are less than half the total; ***he acquired a minority shareholding in the company***; ***she has sold all her shareholdings***; **dilution of shareholding** = situation where the ordinary share capital of a company has been increased, but without an increase in the assets so that each share is worth less than before (NOTE: American English is **stockholding**)

shareout ['ʃeəaut] *noun* dividing something among many people; ***a shareout of the profits***

sharing ['ʃeərɪŋ] *noun* dividing up; **profit-sharing** = dividing profits among workers; ***the company operates a profit-sharing scheme***; **time-sharing** = (i) owning a property in part, with the right to use it for a period each year; (ii) sharing a computer system with different users using different terminals

shark [ʃɑ:k] noun **loan shark** = person who lends money at a very high interest rate; **shark repellent** = action taken by a company to make itself less attractive to takeover bidders

COMMENT: companies can take various courses of action to make themselves unattractive to raiders. The company's articles can be changed to make it necessary to have more than a simple majority of shares to acquire voting control; directors can be given contracts with golden parachute packages which would be extremely expensive to implement; the company can create vast amounts of debt and give cash to its shareholders as bonus payments

sharp [ʃɑ:k] *adjective* **(a)** sudden; ***sharp rally on the stock market***; ***sharp drop in prices*** **(b) sharp practice** = way of doing business which is not honest, but not illegal

```
a sharp fall in the company's share price can have serious implications for its operations. It could, for example, limit its ability to borrow money
```

Guardian

sharply ['ʃɑ:pli] *adverb* suddenly; ***shares dipped sharply in yesterday's trading***

sheet [ʃi:t] noun **balance sheet** = statement of the financial position of a company at the end of a financial year or at the end of a period; ***the company's balance sheet for 1998***; ***the accountants prepared a balance sheet for the first half-year***

shekel ['ʃekəl] *noun* currency used in Israel

shelf [ʃelf] noun **off-the-shelf company** = company which has already been registered by an accountant or lawyer, and which is ready for sale to someone who wants to set up a new company quickly; *US* **shelf registration** = registration of a corporation with the SEC some time (up to two years is allowed) before it is offered for sale to the public

shell company *US* **shell corporation** ['ʃel 'kʌmpni or kɔ:pə'reɪʃn] *noun* company which does not trade, but exists only as a name with a quotation of the Stock Exchange (shell companies are bought by private companies as a means of obtaining a quotation on the Stock Exchange without having to go through a flotation)

shelter ['ʃeltə] **1** *noun* protected place; **tax shelter** = financial arrangement (such as a pension scheme) where investments can be made without tax **2** *verb* to give someone or something protection

```
if you have a unit trust - which might be sheltered in a Pep - you are probably more than a little confused about the charges
```

The Times

sheriff's sale ['ʃerɪfs 'seɪl] *noun US* public sale of the goods of a person whose property has been seized by the courts because he has defaulted on payments

shilling ['ʃɪlɪŋ] *noun* currency used in Kenya, Somalia, Tanzania and Uganda

shogun bond ['ʃəugən 'bɒnd] *noun* bond issued in Japan by a non-Japanese company in a currency which is not the yen; *compare* SAMURAI BOND

shoot up ['ʃu:t 'ʌp] *verb* to go up fast; ***prices have shot up during the strike*** (NOTE: **shooting - shot**)

shop around ['ʃɒp ə'raund] *verb* to go to various suppliers and compare prices before making a purchase or before placing an order; ***you should shop around before getting your car serviced***; ***he is shopping around for a new computer***; ***it pays to shop around when you are planning to ask for a mortgage***

shopper ['ʃɒpə] *noun* person who buys goods in a shop; ***the store stays open to midnight to cater for late-night shoppers***; **shoppers' charter** = law which protects the rights of shoppers against shopkeepers who are not honest or against manufacturers of defective goods

shopping cart ['ʃɒpɪŋ 'kɑ:t] *noun* feature of a web site that allows a visitor to add products from an electronic catalogue to their electronic shopping basket as they move around the web site; the products are paid for by the visitor when they have finished shopping and either sent by mail-order or delivered electronically

short [ʃɔ:t] **1** *adjective & adverb* **(a)** for a small period of time; **short bill** = bill of exchange payable at short notice; **short credit** = terms which allow the customer only a little time to pay; **in the short term** = in the near future, quite soon; **to borrow short** = to borrow for a short period **(b)** not as much as should be; ***the shipment was three items short***; **when we cashed up we were £10 short** = we had £10 less than we should have had; **to give short weight** = to sell something which is lighter than it should be **(c) to sell short** *or* **to go short** = to agree to sell at a future date something (such as shares) which you do not possess, but which you think you will be able to buy for less before the time comes when you have to sell them; **short position** = situation where an investor sells short (i.e., sells forward shares which he does not own); **short sale** *or* **short selling** *or* **selling short** = arranging to sell something in the future which you do not now own, but which you think you can buy for less than the agreed selling price; ***he admitted that timing is a big factor in short selling***; **short sellers** = people who contract to sell a share in the future, expecting the price to fall so that they can it buy more cheaply before they have to close the sale; **to be short of a stock** = not to have shares which you will need in the future (as opposed to being 'long' of a stock); **to go short** = to sell shares now which you have contracted to purchase at a later date, on the assumption that the market will fall further **2** noun **shorts** = government stocks which mature in less than five years time **3** *verb* to sell short; ***he shorted the stock at $35 and continued to short it as the price moved up***

> how one fund manager returned 57 percent last year - by shorting stocks
>
> *Smart Money*

> the point is not that you should go out and short stocks tomorrow. For reasons that will be clear, shorting is a perilous business not wholly suited to patient investors
>
> *Smart Money*

> in a short sale, an investor or speculator sells borrowed shares in expectation that their price will fall and that the borrowed shares can later be repurchased at a lower price
>
> *Wall Street Journal*

short change ['ʃɔ:t 'tʃeɪnʒ] *verb* to give a customer less change than is right, hoping that he will not notice

short-dated ['ʃɔ:t 'deɪtɪd] adjective **short-dated bills** = bills which are payable within a few days; **short-dated gilts** *or* **gilt-edged securities** = government stocks which mature in less than five years time

shorten ['ʃɔ:tən] *verb* to make shorter; ***to shorten credit terms***

shortfall ['ʃɔ:tfɔ:l] *noun* amount which is missing which would make the total expected sum; ***we had to borrow money to cover the shortfall between expenditure and revenue***

short-range ['ʃɔ:t'reɪnʒ] adjective **short-range forecast** = forecast which covers a period of a few months

short-term ['ʃɔ:ttɜ:m] *adjective* for a short period; ***to place money on short-term deposit***; ***short-term contract***; **on a short-term basis** = for a short period; **short-term debts** = debts which have to be repaid within a few weeks; **short-term forecast** = forecast which covers a period of a few months; **short-term gains** = gains made over a short period (less than 12 months); **short-term loan** = loan which has to be repaid within a few weeks; **short-term paper** = promissory notes, drafts, etc., payable at less than nine months; **short-term security** = security which matures in less than 5 years; **short-term support** = support for a currency in the international market, where the central bank can borrow funds from other central banks for a short period

short-termism ['ʃɔ:t'tɜ:mɪzm] *noun* taking a short-term view of the market, i.e., not planning for a long-term investment

show of hands ['ʃəʊ əv 'hænz] *noun* method of voting (as at an AGM) where members vote on a resolution by raising their hands in the air; *compare* BALLOT

> COMMENT: if it is difficult to decide which side has won in a show of hands, a ballot may be taken

shrink [ʃrɪŋk] *verb* to get smaller; ***the market has shrunk by 20%; the company is having difficulty selling into a shrinking market*** (NOTE: **shrinking - shrank - has shrunk**)

shrinkage ['ʃrɪŋkɪdʒ] *noun* **(a)** amount by which something gets smaller; ***to allow for shrinkage*** **(b)** *(informal)* losses of stock through theft (especially by members of the staff of a shop)

shroff [ʃrɒf] noun *(in the Far East)* (i) accountant; (ii) accounts clerk

SIB = SECURITIES AND INVESTMENTS BOARD

SICAV = SOCIETE D'INVESTISSEMENT A CAPITAL VARIABLE (French unit trust)

side [saɪd] *noun* **(a)** part of something; **credit side** = right-hand side of accounts showing money received; **debit side** = left-hand side of accounts showing money owed or paid to others; *see also* SUPPLY-SIDE ECONOMICS **(b) on the side** = separate from your normal work, and hidden from your employer; ***he works in an accountant's office, but he runs a construction company on the side; her salary is too small to live on, so the family lives on what she can make on the side***

sideline ['saɪdlaɪn] *noun* business which is extra to your normal work; ***he runs a profitable sideline selling postcards to tourists***

sight [saɪt] *noun* seeing; **bill payable at sight** = bill which must be paid when it is presented; **sight bill** *or* **sight draft** = bill of exchange which is payable at sight (i.e., when it is presented for payment); **sight deposit** = bank deposit which can be withdrawn on demand; **sight note** = a demand note, a promissory note which must be paid when it is presented; **to buy something sight unseen** = to buy something without having inspected it

sign [saɪn] *verb* to write your name in a special way on a document to show that you have written it or approved it; ***to sign a letter*** *or* ***a contract*** *or* ***a document*** *or* ***a cheque; the letter is signed by the managing director; the cheque is not valid if it has not been signed by the finance director***

signatory ['sɪgnətri] *noun* person who signs a contract, etc.; ***you have to get the permission of all the signatories to the agreement if you want to change the terms***

signature ['sɪgnətʃə] *noun* name written in a special way by someone; ***a pile of letters waiting for the managing director's signature; he found a pile of cheques on his desk waiting for signature; all the company's cheques need two signatures***

signal ['sɪgnəl] **1** *noun* warning message; ***the Bank of England's move sent signals to the currency markets*** **2** *verb* to send warning messages; ***the resolutions tabled for the AGM signalled the shareholders' lack of confidence in the management of the company***

silent partner ['saɪlənt 'pɑːtnə] *adjective* *US* partner who has a share in the business but does not work in it (NOTE: the British equivalent is a **sleeping partner**)

silver ['sɪlvə] *noun* precious metal traded on commodity markets such as the London Metal Exchange

simple interest ['sɪmpl 'ɪntrəst] *noun* interest calculated on the capital only, and not added to it

single ['sɪŋgl] **1** *adjective* one alone; **single premium policy** = insurance policy where only one premium is paid rather than regular annual premiums; **single-entry bookkeeping** = method of bookkeeping where payments or sales are noted with only one entry; **in single figures** = less than ten; ***sales are down to single figures; inflation is now in single figures;*** **single-figure inflation** = inflation rising at less than 10% per annum; **single-life annuity** = annuity which is paid only to one beneficiary, and stops when he or she dies (as opposed to a 'joint-life annuity'); **the single European market** = the EU considered as one single market, with no tariff barriers between its member states **2** *noun* person who is not married

> eligibility to fund an Education IRA phases out for singles with AGIs of $95,000 to $110,000 and for married couples filing jointly with AGIs of $150,000 to $160,000
>
> *Fortune*

sink [sɪŋk] *verb* **(a)** to go down suddenly; ***prices sank at the news of the closure of the factory*** **(b)** to invest money (into something); ***he sank all his savings into a car-hire business*** (NOTE: **sinking - sank - sunk**)

sinking fund ['sɪnkɪŋ 'fʌnd] *noun* fund built up out of amounts of money put aside regularly to meet a future need, such as the repayment of a loan

sister company ['sɪstə 'kʌmpni] *noun* one of several companies which are part of the same group

SKA Index index of prices on the Zurich Stock Exchange

slam [slæm] *verb US (of a telephone company)* to switch (unlawfully) a customer's telephone service without his consent; ***we suddenly realized we'd been slammed***

slash [slæʃ] *verb* to cut, to reduce sharply; ***to slash prices*** *or* ***credit terms***; ***prices have been slashed in all departments***; ***bank have been forced to slash interest rates***

sleeper ['sli:pə] *noun* share which has not risen in value for some time, but which may suddenly do so in the future

sleeping partner ['sli:pɪŋ 'pɑ:tnə] *adjective* partner who has a share in the business but does not work in it (NOTE: the American equivalent is a **silent partner**)

slide [slaɪd] to move down steadily; ***prices slid after the company reported a loss*** (NOTE: **sliding - slid**)

sliding ['slaɪdɪŋ] *adjective* which rises in steps; **a sliding scale of charges** = list of charges which increase gradually according to value, quantity or time, etc.

slight [slaɪt] *adjective* not very large, not very important; ***there was a slight improvement in the balance of trade***; ***we saw a slight increase in sales in February***

slightly ['slaɪtli] *adverb* not very much; ***sales fell slightly in the second quarter***; ***the Swiss bank is offering slightly better terms***

slip [slɪp] **1** *noun* small piece of paper; **deposit slip** = piece of paper stamped by the cashier to prove that you have paid money into your account; **pay slip** = piece of paper showing the full amount of a worker's pay, and the money deducted as tax, pension and insurance contributions; **paying-in slip** = printed form which is filled in when money is being deposited in a bank; **sales slip** = paper showing that an article was bought at a certain shop **2** *verb* to go down and back; ***profits slipped to £1.5m***; ***shares slipped back at the close*** (NOTE: **slipping - slipped**)

slip-up ['slɪpʌp] *noun* mistake (NOTE: plural is **slip-ups**)

> the active December long gilt contract on the LIFFE slipped to close at 83-12 from the opening 83-24
>
> *Financial Times*

> with long-term fundamentals reasonably sound, the question for brokers is when does cheap become cheap enough? The Bangkok and Taipei exchanges offer lower p/e ratios than Jakarta, but if Jakarta p/e ratios slip to the 16-18 range, foreign investors would pay more attention to it
>
> *Far Eastern Economic Review*

slow [sləʊ] *adjective* not going fast; **slow payers** = companies which pay their bills slowly

slow (down) ['sləʊ 'daʊn] *verb* to stop rising, moving or falling; ***inflation is slowing down***; ***the fall in the exchange rate is slowing down***; ***the management decided to slow down production***

> a general price freeze succeeded in slowing the growth in consumer prices
>
> *Financial Times*

> the fall in short-term rates suggests a slowing economy
>
> *Financial Times*

slowdown ['sləʊdaʊn] *noun* becoming less busy; ***a slowdown in the company's expansion***; **economic slowdown** = general reduction in a country's economic activity

> Consistency would now dictate being prepared to lower rates aggressively in response to a sharp economic slowdown, even though the pound was weak
>
> *The Times*

> analysts believe the sluggishness of retail sales, combined with recent indicators which have shown a steady slowdown in the pace of economic activity, has strengthened the case for a cut of around 1/4percentage point in the Federal Funds rate
>
> *Financial Times*

slump ['slʌmp] **1** *noun* **(a)** rapid fall; ***slump in sales***; ***slump in profits***; ***slump in the value of the pound***; ***the pound's slump on the***

foreign exchange markets **(b)** period of economic collapse with high unemployment and loss of trade; ***we are experiencing slump conditions***; **the Slump** = the world economic crisis of 1929 - 1933 **2** *verb* to fall fast; ***profits have slumped***; ***the pound slumped on the foreign exchange markets***

slush fund ['slʌʃ 'fʌnd] *noun* money kept to one side to give to people as bribes, to persuade them to do what you want

small [smɔ:l] *adjective* not large; **small ads** = short private advertisements in a newspaper (selling small items, asking for jobs, etc.); **small businesses** = little companies with low turnover and few employees; **small businessman** = man who runs a small business; US **Small Business Administration (SBA)** = federal agency which provides finance and advice to small businesses; **small change** = loose coins; **small claims court** = court which deals with disputes over small amounts of money; **action in the small claims court** US **small claims lawsuit** = action by an individual to reclaim a small amount of money through the courts; **the small investor** = person who has a small amount of money to invest; **small shopkeepers** = owners of small shops

small-cap ['smɔ:l 'kæp] *noun & adjective* **small-caps** *or* **small-cap stocks** = (stock) with a small capitalization; *see also* CAP, MEGA-CAP, MICROCAP, MIDCAP

small company ['smɔ:l 'kʌmpni] *noun* company with a turnover of less than £1.4m, with fewer than 50 staff, which is allowed to file modified accounts with Companies House; **small companies** = companies which are quoted on the Stock Exchange, but which have a small capitalization (such companies are considered by some advisers as having better growth potential than the large blue chip companies, though the risk involved is greater)

small-scale ['smɔ:lskeɪl] *adjective* working in a small way, with few staff and not much money; **a small-scale enterprise** = a small business

smart card ['smɑ:t 'kɑ:d] *noun* credit card with a microchip, used for withdrawing money from ATMs, or for purchases at EFTPOS terminals

SMI = stock market index of the Zurich stock exchange in Switzerland

smokestack industries ['sməʊkstæk 'ɪndʌstriz] *noun* heavy industries, such as steel-making

smurf [smɜ:f] *noun* US *(informal)* person who launders money

snake [sneɪk] *noun (informal)* formerly, the group of currencies within the European Exchange Rate Mechanism whose exchange rates were allowed to fluctuate against each other within certain bands or limits

snap up ['snæp 'ʌp] *verb* to buy something quickly; ***to snap up a bargain***; ***he snapped up 15% of the company's shares***

snip [snɪp] noun *(informal)* bargain; ***these laser printers are a snip at £250***

soar [sɔ:] *verb* to go up rapidly; ***food prices soared during the cold weather***; ***share prices soared on the news of the takeover bid*** *or* ***the news of the takeover bid sent share prices soaring***

social ['səʊʃəl] *adjective* referring to society in general; **social costs** = ways in which something will affect people; ***the report examines the social costs of building the factory in the middle of the town***; **social investing** = investing in companies which follow certain moral standards (NOTE: also called **ethical investing**); **social security** = money from contributions paid to the National Insurance provided by the government to people who need it; ***he gets weekly social security payments***; **social security contributions** = regular payments by workers and employers to the National Insurance scheme; **the social system** = the way society is organized

socially responsible funds ['səʊʃəli rɪs'pɒnsəbl 'fʌndz] *noun* US funds which only invest in companies that have a good environmental or employment or social record (NOTE: also called **ethical funds**)

sociedad anonima (SA) *Spanish* Public Limited Company (PLC)

societa per azioni (SpA) *Italian* Public Limited Company (PLC)

société *French* company; **Société anonyme (SA)** = Public Limited Company (PLC); **société anonyme à responsabilité limitée (SARL)** = private limited company (Ltd); **Société d'investissement à capital variable (SICAV)** = unit trust

Société des Bourses Françaises (SBF) company which operates the French stock exchanges and derivatives exchanges

society [sə'saɪəti] *noun* **(a)** way in which people in a country are organized; **consumer society** = type of society where consumers are encouraged to buy goods; **the affluent society** = type of society where most people are rich **(b)** club or group of people with the same interests; **building society** = financial institution which accepts and pays interest on deposits, and lends money to people who are buying property against the security of the property; **cooperative society** = organization where customers and workers are partners and share the profits; **friendly society** = group of people who pay regular subscriptions to a fund which is used to help members who are ill or in financial trouble; **Society for Worldwide Interbank Telecommunications (SWIFT)** = international organization which makes the rapid exchange of payments between banks, stockbrokers, etc., possible on a worldwide scale

socio-economic ['səʊsiəʊi:kə'nɒmɪk] *adjective* referring to social and economic conditions; ***the socio-economic system in capitalist countries***; **socio-economic groups** = groups in society divided according to income and position

soft [sɒft] *adjective* not hard; **soft commodities** = foodstuffs which are traded as commodities (such as rice, coffee, etc.); **soft currency** = currency of a country with a weak economy, which is cheap to buy and difficult to exchange for other currencies; **soft dollars** = rebates given by brokers to money management firms in return for funds' transaction business; **soft landing** = change in economic strategy to counteract inflation, which does not cause unemployment or a fall in the standard of living, and has only minor effects on the bulk of the population; **soft loan** = loan (from a company to an employee or from a government to a new business or to another government) at very low or nil interest; **soft market** = market where there is not enough demand, and where prices fall; **to take the soft option** = to decide to do something which involves least risk, effort or problems; **soft sell** = persuading people to buy by encouraging them, but not forcing them to do so

> after the SEC began trying to rein in soft-dollar abuses, the US Attorney's office was quietly pursuing its own investigation
>
> *Barron's*

> a highly publicized federal investigation into the obscure world of 'soft dollars' has turned into a full-blown inquiry into trading irregularities on the New York Stock Exchange
>
> *Barron's*

> recent months have been quiet for Asian traders of futures contracts in cocoa, palm oil, sugar and coffee, known as 'soft commodities'. The explanation is simple. In contrast to oil, the prices of soft commodities have been flat or declining for most of the year
>
> *Far Eastern Economic Review*

> the so-called 'soft' commissions whereby fund managers can pay commission out of a fund to stockbrokers, and themselves receive back services as a form of rebate of these commissions
>
> *Financial Times Review*

sol [sɒl] *noun* currency used in Peru

sole [səʊl] *adjective* only; **sole agency** = agreement to be the only person to represent a company or to sell a product in a certain area; ***he has the sole agency for Ford cars***; **sole agent** = person who has the sole agency for a product in an area; **sole distributor** = retailer who is the only one in an area who is allowed to sell a certain product; **sole owner** = person who owns a business on his own, with no partners; **sole trader** *US* **sole proprietor** = person who runs a business by himself but has not registered it as a company

solvency ['sɒlvənsi] *noun* being able to pay all debts on due date (NOTE: opposite is **insolvency**)

solvent ['sɒlvənt] *adjective* situation when assets are more than liabilities; ***when he bought the company it was barely solvent*** (NOTE: opposite is **insolvent**)

som [sɒm] currency used in Kyrgystan

sorter/reader ['sɔ:tə'ri:də] *noun* machine in a bank which reads cheques and sorts them automatically

source [sɔ:s] *noun* place where something comes from; ***source of income***; ***you must declare income from all sources to the tax office***; **income which is taxed at source** = where the tax is removed and paid to the government by the employer before the income is paid to the employee; **sources and application of funds statement** = statement in a company's annual accounts, showing where new funds came from during the year, and how they were used

sovereign ['sɒvrɪn] **1** *noun* British gold coin, with a face value of £1 **2** *adjective* referring to an independent country; **sovereign bond** = bond issued by a government; **sovereign risk** = risk that a government may default on its debts (a government cannot be sued if it defaults); **sovereign state** = independent state which governs itself

> the republic is the latest sovereign borrower to be dwngraded by the world's leading rating agencies
>
> *The Banker*

SpA = SOCIETA PER AZIONI

spare [speə] *adjective* extra, not being used; ***he has invested his spare capital in a computer shop***; **to use up spare capacity** = to make use of time or space which has not been fully used

Sparkasse ['ʃpɑːkæsə] *German* savings bank

spec [spek] noun **to buy something on spec** = to buy something as a speculation, without being sure of its value

special ['speʃl] *adjective* different; not normal; referring to one particular thing; ***he offered us special terms***; ***the car is being offered at a special price***; **Special Commissioner** = official appointed by the Treasury to hear cases where a taxpayer is appealing against an income tax assessment; **special deposits** = large sums of money which commercial banks have to deposit with the Bank of England; **special mention assets** = loans made by a bank without the correct documentation; **special notice** = notice of a proposal to be put before a meeting of the shareholders of a company which is made less than 28 days before the meeting; **special resolution** = resolution of the members of a company which is only valid if it is approved by 75% of the votes cast at a meeting (a resolution concerning an important matter, such as a change to the company's articles of association)

special drawing rights (SDRs) ['speʃl 'drɔːɪŋ 'raɪts] *noun* unit of account used by the International Monetary Fund, allocated to each member country for use in loans and other international operations; their value is calculated daily on the weighted values of a group of currencies shown in dollars

specialist ['speʃəlɪst] *noun* **(a)** person or company that deals with one particular type of product or one subject; ***you should go to a specialist in computers*** *or* ***to a computer specialist for advice*** **(b)** *US* trader on the NYSE who deals in certain stocks for his own account, selling to or buying from brokers

specie ['spiːʃi] *plural noun* money in the form of coins

specify ['spesɪfaɪ] *verb* to state clearly what is needed; ***to specify full details of the goods ordered***; ***do not include VAT on the invoice unless specified***

specification [spesɪfɪ'keɪʃn] *noun* detailed information about what is needed or about a product to be supplied; ***to detail the specifications of a computer system***; **job specification** = very detailed description of what is involved in a job; **to work to standard specifications** = to work to specifications which are acceptable anywhere in the industry; **the work is not up to specification** *or* **does not meet our specifications** = the product is not made in the way which was detailed

specimen ['spesɪmən] *noun* thing which is given as a sample; **to give specimen signatures on a bank mandate** = to write the signatures of all people who can sign cheques for an account so that the bank can recognise them

speculate ['spekjuleɪt] *verb* to take a risk in business which you hope will bring you profits; **to speculate on the Stock Exchange** = to buy shares which you hope will rise in value

speculation [spekju'leɪʃn] *noun* deal which it is hoped will produce a profit; ***he bought the company as a speculation***; ***she lost all her money in Stock Exchange speculations***

speculative share ['spekjulətɪv 'ʃeə] *noun* risky share which may go up or down in value; bond with a low credit rating

speculator ['spekjuleɪtə] *noun* person who buys goods, shares or foreign currency in the hope that they will rise in value; ***a property speculator***; ***a currency speculator***; ***a speculator on the Stock Exchange*** *or* ***a Stock Exchange speculator***

spend [spend] *verb* to pay money; ***they spent all their savings on buying the shop***; ***the company spends thousands of pounds on research***

spending [spendɪŋ] *noun* paying money; ***cash spending*** *or* ***credit card spending***; **consumer spending** = spending by consumers; **spending money** = money for ordinary personal expenses; **spending power** = (i) having money to spend on goods; (ii) amount of goods which can be bought for a certain sum of money; ***the spending power of the pound has fallen over the last ten years***; ***the spending power of the student market***

spin [spɪn] *noun* special meaning given to something; **spin control** = giving a special meaning to information; **spin doctor** = person who presents news in such a way that it flatters the person who employs him

> investors who like to follow insider trading really have to watch out for corporate spin control
>
> *Smart Money*

spin off ['spɪn 'ɒf] verb **to spin off a subsidiary company** = to split off part of a large company to form a smaller subsidiary, giving shares in this to the existing shareholders (NOTE: **spinning - span - spun**)

> the world's largest independent oil and gas company was spun off two years ago from its parent
>
> *Far Eastern Economic Review*

spinoff ['spɪnɒf] *noun* **(a)** corporate reorganization in which a subsidiary becomes an independent company **(b)** useful product developed as a secondary product from a main item; ***one of the spinoffs of the research program has been the development of the electric car*** **(c) corporate spinoffs** = small companies which have been split off from larger organizations

> but other times investors appear to underreact, as when they ignore the positive potential of corporate spinoffs
>
> *Smart Money*

> buying new issues is trendy; owning spinoffs is picking up someone else's garbage
>
> *Smart Money*

spiral ['spaɪrəl] **1** *noun* thing which twists round and round getting higher all the time; **the economy is in an inflationary spiral** *or* **wage-price spiral** = the economy is in a situation where price rises encourage higher wage demands which in turn make prices rise **2** *verb* to twist round and round, getting higher all the time; ***a period of spiralling prices***; **spiralling inflation** = inflation where price rises make workers ask for higher wages which then increase prices again (NOTE: British spelling is **spiralling - spiralled** but American spelling is **spiraling - spiraled**)

split [splɪt] **1** *noun* **(a)** dividing up; **share split** = dividing of shares into smaller denominations; **the company is proposing a five for one split** = the company is proposing that each existing share should be divided into five smaller shares (NOTE: the American equivalent is **stock split**) **(b)** lack of agreement; ***a split in the family shareholders*** **2** *verb* **(a) to split shares** = to divide shares into smaller denominations; **the shares were split five for one** = five new shares were given for each existing share held **(b) to split the difference** = to come to an agreement over a price by dividing the difference between the amount the seller is asking and amount the buyer wants to pay and agreeing on a price between the two (NOTE: **splitting - split**) **3** *adjective* which is divided into parts; **split commission** = commission which is divided between brokers or agents; **split payment** = payment which is divided into small units

> COMMENT: a company may decide to split its shares if the share price becomes too 'heavy' (i.e., each share is priced at such a high level that small investors my be put off, and trading in the share is restricted); in the UK, a share price of £10.00 is considered 'heavy', though such prices are common on other stock markets

split trust *or* **split-capital** *or* **split-level investment trust** ['splɪt'kæpɪtl *or* 'splɪtlevəl ɪn'vestmənt 'trʌst] *noun* investment trust with two categories of shares: 'income shares' which receive income from the investments, but do not benefit from the rise in their capital value; and 'capital shares', which increase in value as the value of the investments rises, but do not receive any income

> zeros are one of the classes of share issued by split-capital investment trusts
>
> *Sunday Times*

> all split trusts have a wind-up date. when the underlying assets of the trust are sold off and the proceeds distributed to the various classes of shareholder, according to their entitlements
>
> *Sunday Times*

sponsor ['spɒnsə] **1** *noun* **(a)** organization, such as a merchant bank, which backs a new share issue **(b)** person who pays money to help research or to pay for a business venture; company which pays to help a sport, in return for advertising rights **(c)** company which advertises on TV **2** *verb* **(a)** to pay money to help research or business development; ***a government-sponsored trade exhibition*** **(b)** to pay for a TV programme or sports match, in return for advertising rights; ***the company has sponsored a series of football matches*** **(c)** *US* to play an active part in something, such as a pension plan for employees; ***if you're single and not covered by an employer-sponsored retirement plan***

sponsorship ['spɒnsəʃɪp] *noun* act of sponsoring; ***government sponsorship of overseas selling missions***

spot [spɒt] *noun* price when buying something for immediate delivery; **spot cash** = cash paid for something bought immediately; **spot market** = market for buying commodities or financial instruments for immediate delivery; **spot price** *or* **spot rate** = current price or rate for something which is delivered immediately (also called 'cash price')

> with most of the world's oil now traded on spot markets, Opec's official prices are much less significant than they once were
>
> *Economist*

> the average spot price of Nigerian light crude oil for the month of July was 27.21 dollars per barrel
>
> *Business Times (Lagos)*

spousal ['spaʊzəl] *adjective US* referring to a spouse; **spousal IRA** = IRA set up in the name of a spouse

> if your income is too high for a tax-deductible IRA and your spouse earns little or no income, consider a spousal IRA
>
> *Fortune*

spouse [spaʊz] *noun* the person someone is married to, i.e. their husband or wife; *see also* TRAILING SPOUSE, VIRTUAL SPOUSE

spread [spred] **1** *noun* **(a)** *(in general)* range; **he has a wide spread of investments** *or* **of interests** = he has shares in many different types of companies **(b)** *(banking)* difference between the interest rate a bank pays on deposits and the rate it charges borrowers; *(on the Stock Exchange)* **bid-offer spread** = difference between buying and selling prices (i.e. between the bid and offer prices); *see also* BID, TOUCH **2** *verb* to space out over a period of time; ***to spread payments over several months***; **to spread a risk** = to make the risk of insurance less great by asking other companies to help cover it (NOTE: **spreading - spread)**

> a by-product of the fall-out in stock markets has been a widening of spreads between buying and selling prices on some unit trusts
>
> *Money Observer*

> that's led to erratic swings in share prices and very wide spreads between the buying and selling prices of certain stocks
>
> *Investors Chronicle*

> European fund managers see no need for the bid-offer spread and there have been no howls of protest from the Swiss, French or Germans
>
> *The Times*

> dealers said markets were thin, with gaps between trades and wide spreads between bid and ask prices on the currencies
>
> *Wall Street Journal*

> to ensure an average return you should hold a spread of different shares covering a wide cross-section of the market
>
> *Investors Chronicle*

spreadsheet ['spredʃi:t] *noun* (i) large sheet of paper, laid out in columns, for entering financial data; (ii) computer printout showing a series of columns of figures

square [skweə] *verb* to balance your position by selling futures to balance purchases; **book-squaring** = reducing the dealer's exposure to the market to nil

> before Christmas, dealers reported very little participation in the market, with investors mostly squared away for the year, leaving the market for traders
>
> *Wall Street Journal*

Square Mile ['skweə 'maɪl] *noun* the City (of London), the British financial centre

squeeze [skwi:z] **1** *noun* government control carried out by reducing amounts of money available; **credit squeeze** = period when lending by the banks is restricted by the government; **profit squeeze** = control of the amount of profits which companies can pay out as dividend **2** *verb* to crush or to press; to make smaller; ***to squeeze margins** or **profits** or **credit***; **our margins have been squeezed by the competition** = profits have been reduced because our margins have to be smaller for us to stay competitive

> the real estate boom of the past three years has been based on the availability of easy credit. Today, money is tighter, so property should bear the brunt of the credit squeeze
>
> *Money Observer*

SRB = SALES RETURNS BOOK

SRO = SELF-REGULATORY ORGANIZATION

SSAPs = STATEMENTS OF STANDARD ACCOUNTING PRACTICE

SSI = STANDING SETTLEMENT INSTRUCTIONS

> although the Bank of England recommended that those banks which were amending their SSIs should notify counterparties by 30th September, at least one major European bank sent its SSIs out on 27th October
>
> *The Banker*

SSL SECURE SOCKET LAYER method of providing a safe channel over the internet to allow a user's credit card or personal details to be safely transmitted; ***I only purchase goods from a web site that has SSL security installed: the little key logo on my web browser appears when I am connected to a secure site with SSL***

stability [stə'bɪlɪti] *noun* being steady, not moving up or down; ***price stability***; ***a period of economic stability***; ***the stability of the currency markets***

stabilization [steɪbɪlaɪ'zeɪʃn] *noun* making stable, preventing sudden changes in prices, etc.; **stabilization of the economy** = keeping the economy stable by preventing inflation from rising, cutting high interest rates and excess money supply

stabilize ['steɪbɪlaɪz] *verb* to make steady; **prices have stabilized** = prices have stopped moving up or down; **to have a stabilizing effect on the economy** = to make the economy more stable

stable ['steɪbl] *adjective* steady, not moving up or down; ***stable prices***; ***stable exchange rate***; ***stable currency***; ***stable economy***

staffer ['stɑːfə] *noun* *US* person who is a member of the staff of a company

stag [stæg] **1** *noun* person who subscribes for a large quantity of a new issue of shares hoping to sell them immediately to make a profit **2** verb **to stag an issue** = to buy a new issue of shares not as an investment, but to sell immediately at a profit (NOTE: **stagging - stagged**)

stage [steɪdʒ] *noun* period, one of several points of development; ***the different stages of the production process***; **the contract is still in the drafting stage** = the contract is still being drafted; **in stages** = in different steps; ***the company has agreed to repay the loan in stages***

staged payments ['steɪdʒd 'peɪmənts] *noun* payments made in stages

stagflation [stæg'fleɪʃn] *noun* inflation and stagnation of an economy

stagger ['stægə] *verb* to arrange (holidays, working hours) so that they do not all begin and end at the same time; ***staggered holidays help the tourist industry***; ***we have to stagger the lunch hour so that there is always someone on the switchboard***

stagnant ['stægnənt] *adjective* not active, not increasing; ***turnover was stagnant for the first half of the year***; ***a stagnant economy***

stagnate [stæg'neɪt] *verb* not to increase, not to make progress; ***the economy is stagnating***; ***after six hours the talks were stagnating***

stagnation [stæg'neɪʃn] *noun* not increasing, not making any progress; ***the country entered a period of stagnation***; **economic stagnation** = lack of expansion in the economy

stake [steɪk] **1** *noun* money invested; **to have a stake in a business** = to have money invested in a business; **to acquire a stake in a business** = to buy shares in a business; ***he acquired a 25% stake in the business***; **passive stake** = shareholding where the shareholder takes no active part in running the company **2** verb **to stake money on something** = to risk money on something

> other investments include a large stake in a Chicago-based insurance company, as well as interests in tobacco products and hotels
>
> *Lloyd's List*

stale [steɪl] *adjective* (cheque) which is so old, that the bank will not clear it unless it has been confirmed as correct by the payer (usually cheques which are more than six months old will not be cleared by a bank); **stale bull** = investor who bought shares hoping that they would rise, and now finds that they have not risen and wants to sell them

stamp [stæmp] **1** *noun* **(a)** device for making marks on documents; mark made in this way; ***the invoice has the stamp 'Received with thanks' on it***; ***the customs officer looked at the stamps in his passport***; **date stamp** = stamp with rubber figures which can be moved, used for marking the date on documents; **rubber stamp** = stamp made of hard rubber cut to form words; **stamp pad** = soft pad of cloth with ink on which a stamp is pressed, before marking the paper **(b) postage stamp** = small piece of gummed paper which you buy from a post office and stick on a letter or parcel to pay for the postage **(c) stamp duty** = tax on legal documents (such as the sale or purchase of shares, the conveyance of a property to a new owner) **2** *verb* **(a)** to mark a document with a stamp; ***to stamp an invoice 'Paid'***; ***the documents were stamped by the customs officials*** **(b)** to put a postage stamp on (an envelope, etc.); **stamped addressed envelope** = envelope with your own address written on it and a stamp stuck on it to pay for the return postage; ***send a stamped addressed envelope for a catalogue and price list***

standard ['stændəd] **1** *noun* normal quality or normal conditions which other things are judged against; **standard of living** *or* **living standards** = quality of personal home life (such as amount of food or clothes bought, size of family car, etc.); **gold standard** = linking of the value of a currency to value of a quantity of gold **2** *adjective* normal or usual; **standard agreement** *or* **standard contract** = normal printed contract form; **standard cost** = a future cost which is calculated in advance and against which estimates are measured; **standard direct labour cost** = cost of labour calculated to produce a product according to specification (used to measure estimates); **standard letter** = letter which is sent without any change to various correspondents; **standard rate** = basic rate of income tax which is paid by most taxpayers; **standard risk** = normal risk on a loan which is likely to be repaid on time

Standard and Poor's ['stændəd ən 'pʊəz] American corporation which rates bonds according to the credit-worthiness of the organizations issuing them (its ratings run from AAA to D; any organization with a rating of below BBB is considered doubtful)

> COMMENT: Standard and Poor's also issues several stock market indices: the Standard and Poor's Composite Index (or S&P 500 or Standard & Poor's 500-stock Index) is an index of 500 popular American stocks; other indices are the S&P SmallCap and S&P MidCap

standby ['stænbaɪ] noun **standby arrangements** = plans for what should be done if an emergency happens, especially money held in reserve in the International Monetary Fund for use by a country in financial difficulties; **standby credit** = credit which is available if a company needs it, especially credit guaranteed by a euronote

standing ['stændɪŋ] **1** adjective **standing order** = order written by a customer asking a bank to pay money regularly to an account; ***I pay my subscription by standing order***; **standing settlement instructions (SSIs)** = instructions given by one bank to other banks as to the procedure to be followed when making payments to it **2** *noun* good reputation; ***the financial standing of a company***; **company of good standing** = very reputable company

standstill agreement ['stændstɪl ə'griːmənt] *noun* agreement between a borrower and a lender that it is better to rengotiate the terms of the loan than for the lender to foreclose on the property used as security

start [stɑːt] **1** *noun* beginning; **cold start** = beginning a new business, opening a new shop with no previous turnover to base it on; **house starts** *US* **housing starts** = number of new private houses or flats of which construction has been started during a year **2** *verb* **to start a business from cold** = to begin a new business, with no previous turnover to base it on

starting ['stɑːtɪŋ] *noun* beginning; **starting date** = date on which something starts; **starting salary** = salary for an employee when he starts work with a company

start-up ['stɑːtʌp] *noun* **(a)** action of starting up a new company, or launching a new product (which did not exist before); ***start-up costs are high in manufacturing companies***; **start-up financing** = the first stage in financing a new project, which is followed by several rounds of investment capital as the project gets under way; *see also* SEEDCORN **(b)** new company which has just been set up (NOTE: plural is **start-ups**)

> ranging from start-ups to companies with tens of thousands of employees
>
> *Fortune*

state [steɪt] **1** *noun* **(a)** independent country; semi-independent section of a federal country (such as the USA); *US* **state bank** = commercial bank licensed by the authorities of a state, and not necessarily a member of the Federal Reserve system (as opposed to a 'national bank') **(b)** government of a country; **state enterprise** = company run by the state; ***the bosses of state industries are appointed by the government***; **state ownership** = situation where an industry is nationalized **2** *verb* to say clearly; ***the document states that all revenue has to be declared to the tax office***

> the unions had argued that public sector pay rates had slipped behind rates applying in state and local government areas
>
> *Australian Financial Review*

state-controlled ['steɪtkʌn'trəʊld] *adjective* run by the state; ***state-controlled television***

state-owned ['steɪt'əʊnd] *adjective* owned by the state or by a state

> state-owned banks cut their prime rates a percentage point to 11%
>
> *Wall Street Journal*

statement ['steɪtmənt] *noun* **(a)** saying something clearly; **to make a false statement** = to give wrong details; **statement of expenses** = detailed list of money spent; **statement balance** *or* **balance per statement** = balance in an account on a given date as shown in a bank statement; **bank statement** = written document from a bank showing the balance of an account; **monthly** *or* **quarterly statement** = statement which is sent every month or every quarter by the bank to a customer with an account; **statement of affairs** = financial statement drawn up when a person is insolvent; *see also* FINANCIAL STATEMENT **(b) statement (of account)** = list of invoices and credits and debits sent by a supplier to a customer at the end of each month

Statements of Standard Accounting Practice (SSAPs) rules laid down by the Accounting Standards Board for the preparation of financial statements (similar to the American GAAP)

statistical [stə'tɪstɪkl] *adjective* based on figures; ***statistical analysis***; ***statistical information***; **statistical discrepancy** = amount by which sets of figures differ

statistician [stætɪs'tɪʃn] *noun* person who analyses statistics

statistics [stə'tɪstɪks] *plural noun* study of facts in the form of figures; ***to examine the sales statistics for the previous six months***; ***government trade statistics show an increase in imports***

status ['steɪtəs] *noun* **(a)** importance or position in society; **the chairman's car is a status symbol** = the size of the car shows how important the company is; **loss of status** = becoming less important in a group; **status inquiry** = checking on a customer's credit rating **(b) legal status** = legal position

status quo ['steɪtəs 'kwəʊ] *noun* state of things as they are now; ***the contract does not alter the status quo***

statute ['stætʃu:t] *noun* law made by parliament; **statute book** = list of laws passed by parliament; **statute of limitations** = law which allows only a certain amount of time (a few years) for someone to claim damages or property

statute-barred ['stætʃu:t'bɑ:d] *adjective* (legal action) which cannot be pursued because the time limit for it has expired

statutory ['stætʃutri] *adjective* fixed by law; ***there is a statutory period of probation of thirteen weeks***; **statutory holiday** = holiday which is fixed by law; **statutory regulations** = regulations covering financial dealings which are based on Acts of Parliament, such as the Financial Services Act (as opposed to the rules of self-regulatory organizations which are non-statutory)

stay of execution ['steɪ əv ɪksɪ'kju:ʃn] *noun* temporary stopping of a legal order; ***the court granted the company a two-week stay of execution***

steadily ['stedɪli] *adverb* in a regular or continuous way; ***output increased steadily over the last two quarters***; ***the company has steadily increased its market share***

steadiness ['stedɪnəs] *noun* being firm, not fluctuating; ***the steadiness of the markets is due to the government's intervention***

steady ['stedi] **1** *adjective* continuing in a regular way; ***steady increase in profits***; ***the market stayed steady***; ***there is a steady demand for computers*** **2** *verb* to become firm, to stop fluctuating; ***the markets steadied after last week's fluctuations***; ***prices steadied***

on the commodity markets; ***the government's figures had a steadying influence on the exchange rate***

steep [stiːp] *adjective* very sharp (increase), very high (price); ***a steep increase in interest charges; a steep decline in overseas sales***

step [step] *noun* movement; **in step with** = moving at the same rate as; ***the pound rose in step with the dollar***; **out of step with** = not moving at the same rate as; ***the pound was out of step with other European currencies; wages are out of step with the cost of living***

sterling ['stɜːlɪŋ] *noun* **(a)** standard currency used in the United Kingdom; ***to quote prices in sterling*** *or* ***to quote sterling prices***; **pound sterling** = official term for the British currency; **sterling area** = formerly, area of the world where the pound sterling was the main trading currency; **sterling balances** = a country's trade balances expressed in pounds sterling; **sterling crisis** = fall in the exchange rate of the pound sterling; **sterling index** = index which shows the current value of sterling against a basket of currencies **(b) sterling silver** = official quality of silver articles made and sold (it is 92.5% pure silver)

> it is doubtful that British goods will price themselves back into world markets as long as sterling labour costs continue to rise faster than in competitor countries
>
> *Sunday Times*

stimulate ['stɪmjuleɪt] *verb* to encourage, to make (something) become more active; ***to stimulate the economy; to stimulate trade with the Middle East***

stimulus ['stɪmjuləs] *noun* thing which encourages activity (NOTE: plural is **stimuli**)

stipulate ['stɪpjuleɪt] *verb* to demand that a condition be put into a contract; ***to stipulate that the contract should run for five years; to pay the stipulated charges; the company failed to pay on the date stipulated in the contract; the contract stipulates that the seller pays the buyer's legal costs***

stipulation [stɪpju'leɪʃn] *noun* condition in a contract

stock [stɒk] *noun* **(a)** quantity of goods for sale; **opening stock** = details of stock at the beginning of an accounting period; **closing stock** = details of stock at the end of an accounting period; **stock depreciation** = reduction in value of stock which is held in a warehouse for some time; **stock figures** = details of how many goods are in the warehouse, store etc.; **stock level** = quantity of goods kept in stock; ***we try to keep stock levels low during the summer***; **stock turn** *or* **stock turnround** *or* **stock turnover** = total value of stock sold in a year divided by the average value of goods in stock; **stock valuation** = estimating the value of stock at the end of an accounting period; **to buy a shop with stock at valuation** = to pay for the stock the same amount as its value as estimated by the valuer; **stock in hand** = stock held in a shop or warehouse; **to purchase stock at valuation** = to pay for stock the price it is valued at (NOTE: American English for this is usually **inventory**) **(b)** ownership of a company, divided into shares; **stocks and shares** = shares in ordinary companies; **stock certificate** = document proving that someone owns stock in a company; *US* **stock dividend** = dividend in the form of stock (i.e., a bonus issue of shares); **stock option** = option given to an employee to buy stock of the company at a lower price than the current market price, at some time in the future; **debenture stock** = capital borrowed by a company, using its fixed assets as security; **dollar stocks** = shares in American companies; **government stock** = government securities; **loan stock** = money lent to a company at a fixed rate of interest; **convertible loan stock** = money lent to a company which can be converted into shares at a later date; *US* **common stock** = ordinary shares in a company giving the shareholders the right to vote at meetings and receive a dividend (NOTE: in the UK, the term **stocks** is generally applied to government stocks, and **shares** to shares of commercial companies. In the USA, shares in corporations are usually called **stocks** while government stocks are called **bonds.** In practice, **shares** and **stocks** are interchangeable terms, and this can lead to some confusion)

> US crude oil stocks fell last week by nearly 2.5m barrels
>
> *Financial Times*

> the stock rose to over $20 a share, higher than the $18 bid
>
> *Fortune*

stockbroker ['stɒkbrəʊkə] *noun* person who buys or sells shares for clients; **stockbroker's commission** = payment to a broker for a deal carried out on behalf of a client

stockbroking ['stɒkbrəʊkɪŋ] *noun* trade of dealing in shares for clients; ***a stockbroking firm***

Stock Exchange ['stɒk ɪks'tʃeɪnʒ] *noun* place where stocks and shares are bought and sold; ***he works on the Stock Exchange; shares in the company are traded on the Stock Exchange***; **Stock Exchange Council** = committee which runs the London International Stock Exchange and regulates the way in which its members work; **Stock Exchange listing** = official list of shares which can be bought or sold on the Stock Exchange; **Stock Exchange Automated Quotation system (SEAQ)** = system for showing share prices and transactions on the London Stock Exchange

> the news was favourably received on the Sydney Stock Exchange, where the shares gained 40 cents to A$9.80
>
> *Financial Times*

Stock Exchange Electronic Trading System (Sets) the London Stock Exchange's electronic share trading system in major shares (buyers and sellers are automatically matched by computer)

COMMENT: Sets only applies to electronic share dealing, and not to people who still have paper share certificates to sell. Instead of the previous 'quote-driven' system, Sets is 'order- driven' - i.e., orders to buy or sell are activated immediately and matched via computer. At the moment, Sets is only used for trading in shares of the very largest companies, but it is expected to expand gradually to include companies with smaller capitalization

> only deals worth more than about £4,000 are actually done via Sets - excluding the majority of small investors' transactions
>
> *Investors Chronicle*

> all private investors who trade FTSE 100 stocks - the only shares currently dealt on the electronic order book - are affected by Sets, whatever the size of the deal
>
> *Investors Chronicle*

stockholder ['stɒkhəʊldə] *noun* person who holds shares in a company

stockholding ['stɒkhəʊldɪŋ] *noun* shares in a company held by someone

stock-in-trade ['stɒk'ɪn'treɪd] *noun* goods held by a business for sale

stock jobber ['stɒk 'dʒɒbə] *noun (formerly)* person who bought and sold shares from other traders on the Stock Exchange

stock jobbing ['stɒk 'dʒɒbɪŋ] *noun (formerly)* buying and selling shares from other traders on the Stock Exchange

stock market ['stɒk 'mɑːkɪt] *noun* place where shares are bought and sold (i.e., a Stock Exchange); ***stock market price** or **price on the stock market***; **stock market launch** = selling of shares in a new company on the Stock Exchange; **stock market valuation** = value of shares based on the current market price

stockout ['stɒkaʊt] *noun* situation where an item is out of stock

stockpicking ['stɒkpɪkɪŋ] *noun* selecting shares, making a choice as to which shares to buy (NOTE: the counterpart, deciding how much money to spend on shares, is **asset allocation**)

> the medium-risk portfolio relies more heavily on stockpicking ability
>
> *Investors Chronicle*

stocktaking ['stɒkteɪkɪŋ] *noun* counting of goods in stock at the end of an accounting period; ***the warehouse is closed for the annual stocktaking***; **stocktaking sale** = sale of goods cheaply to clear a warehouse before stocktaking

stop [stɒp] **1** *noun* not supplying; **account on stop** = account which is not supplied because it has not paid its latest invoices; ***to put an account on stop***; **to put a stop on a cheque** = to tell the bank not to pay a cheque which you have written **2** *verb* **(a) to stop an account** = not to supply an account any more on credit because bills have not been paid; **to stop a cheque** = to ask a bank not to pay a cheque you have written; **to stop payments** = not to make any further payments **(b) to stop someone's wages** = to take money out of someone's wages; ***we stopped £25 from his pay because he was late***

stop-go ['stɒp'gəʊ] *noun* economic policy leading to short periods of expansion followed by short periods of squeeze

stop-loss order ['stɒp'lɒs 'ɔːdə] *noun* instruction to a stockbroker to sell a share if the price falls to a certain level (NOTE: the American equivalent is **stop order** or **limit order**)

stoppage ['stɒpɪdʒ] *noun* money take from a worker's wage packet for insurance, tax, etc.

store card ['stɔː 'kɑːd] *noun* credit card issued by a large department store, which can only be used for purchases in that store

straddle ['strædl] *noun* **(a)** spread, the difference between bid and offer price **(b)** buying a put option and a call option at the same time

straight line depreciation ['streɪt 'laɪn dɪpriːʃi'eɪʃn] *noun* depreciation calculated by dividing the cost of an asset by the number of years it is likely to be used

straight bonds *or* **straights** ['streɪt 'bɒndz or streɪts] *noun* normal fixed-interest bonds which can be redeemed at a certain date

Straits Times index ['streɪts 'taɪmz 'ɪndeks] index of prices on the Singapore Stock Exchange

strapped [stræpt] adjective **strapped for cash** *or* **cash-strapped** = short of money

strategist [strætɪdʒɪst] noun **market strategist** = person who plans how to buy and sell on the stock market

> 'It is expensive, but worth the price' argues an independent market strategist
>
> *Barron's*

street [striːt] *noun* **(a)** road in a town; **High Street** = main shopping street in a British town; **the High Street banks** = main British banks which accept deposits from individual customers; **street price** = normal retail price, the price in the shops; ***both sell for $150 (street price), including a headset microphone*** **(b)** US *(informal)* **the Street** = Wall Street; **street name** = nominee name for holding securities

strength [streŋθ] *noun* being strong; ***the underlying strength of the market***; ***the strength of the dollar in Far Eastern finance markets*** (NOTE: the opposite is **weakness**)

strike [straɪk] verb **to strike a bargain with someone** = to come to an agreement; **a deal was struck at £25 a unit** = we agreed the price of £25 a unit; **striking price** *or* **strike price** = (i) price at which a new offer of shares is offered for sale; (ii) price which is calculated as the lowest selling price when selling a new issue of shares by tender (applicants who tendered at a higher price will get shares; those who tendered at a lower price will not) (NOTE: **striking - struck**)

> a call option provides the right to buy stock, while a put option grants the right to sell stock, each at a given 'strike' price
>
> *Wall Street Journal*

strip [strɪp] *noun* **(a)** band of a colour; *see also* MAGNETIC **(b)** *US* action of separating coupons from a bond

stripe [straɪp] *noun see* MAGNETIC

stripper ['strɪpə] noun **asset stripper** = person who buys a company to sell its assets

stripping ['strɪpɪŋ] *noun* **asset stripping** = buying a company in order to sell its assets

strong [strɒŋ] *adjective* with a lot of force or strength; ***a strong demand for the new shares***; ***the company needs a strong chairman***; **strong currency** = currency which is high against other currencies (the opposite is a 'weak currency'); **strong market** = market where prices are moving up; **strong pound** = pound which is high against other currencies

strongbox ['strɒŋbɒks] *noun* safe, a heavy metal box which cannot be opened easily, in which valuable documents, money, etc., can be kept

strongroom ['strɒŋruːm] *noun* special room (in a bank) where valuable documents, money, golds, etc., can be kept

> everybody blames the strong dollar for US trade problems
>
> *Duns Business Month*

> in a world of floating exchange rates the dollar is strong because of capital inflows rather than weak because of the nation's trade deficit
>
> *Duns Business Month*

structural ['strʌktʃərəl] *adjective* referring to a structure; **structural unemployment** = unemployment caused by the changing structure of an industry or the economy

structure ['strʌktʃə] *noun* way in which something is organized; ***the paper gives a diagram of the company's organizational structure***; ***the price structure in the small car market***; ***the career structure within a corporation***; ***the company is reorganizing its discount structure***; **capital structure of a company** = way in which a company's capital is set up; **the company's salary structure** = organization of salaries in a company with different rates of pay for different types of job

stub [stʌb] noun **cheque stub** = piece of paper left in a cheque book after a cheque has been written and taken out

student loan ['stjuːdənt 'ləʊn] *noun* loan made to a student to help him or her through university (the loan is repayable later from earnings)

stuffer ['stʌfə] *noun* piece of advertising material that is put in an envelope for mailing; **statement stuffer** = advertising leaflet enclosed with the monthly bank statement

style [staɪl] *noun* way of doing something; ***managers are expected to stick to a specific style of investing***

sub [sʌb] *noun* **(a)** wages paid in advance **(b)** = SUBSCRIPTION

sub- [sʌb] *prefix* under, less important

sub-account ['sʌbə'kaʊnt] *noun* one of several separate investment accounts on which a variable annuity is based; *see also* ANNUITY

> some companies charge a switching fee if an investor moves from one sub-account to another
>
> *Wall Street Journal*

sub-agency ['sʌb'eɪdʒənsi] *noun* small agency which is part of a large agency

sub-agent ['sʌb'eɪdʒənt] *noun* person who is in charge of a sub-agency

subcontract 1 [sʌb'kɒntrækt] *noun* contract between the main contractor for a whole project and another firm who will do part of the work **2** [sʌbkən'trækt] *verb* to agree with a company that they will do part of the work for a project; ***the electrical work has been subcontracted to Smith Ltd***

subcontractor [sʌbkən'træktə] *noun* company which has a contract to do work for a main contractor

subject to ['sʌbdʒɪkt 'tʊ] *adjective* **(a)** depending on; **the contract is subject to government approval** = the contract will be valid only if it is approved by the government; **agreement** *or* **sale subject to contract** = agreement or sale which is not legal until a proper contract has been signed; **offer subject to availability** = the offer is valid only if the goods are available **(b) these articles are subject to import tax** = import tax has to be paid on these articles

sublease 1 ['sʌbli:s] *noun* lease from a tenant to another tenant **2** [sʌb'li:s] *verb* to lease a leased property from another tenant; ***they subleased a small office in the centre of town***

sublessee [sʌble'si:] *noun* person or company that takes a property on a sublease

sublessor [sʌb'lesə] *noun* tenant who lets a leased property to another tenant

sublet [sʌb'let] *verb* to let a leased property to another tenant; ***we have sublet part of our office to a financial consultancy*** (NOTE: **subletting - sublet)**

subordinated loan [sə'bɔ:dɪneɪtɪd 'ləʊn] *noun* loan which ranks after all other borrowings as regards payment of interest or repayment of capital

subscribe [səb'skraɪb] verb **to subscribe to a share issue** *or* **to subscribe for shares in a company** = to apply for shares in a new company

> the rights issue is to be a one-for-four, at FFr 1,000 a share; it will grant shareholders free warrants to subscribe to further new shares
>
> *Financial Times*

subscriber [səb'skraɪbə] noun **subscriber to a share issue** = person who has applied for shares in a new company

subscription [sʌb'skrɪpʃn] *noun* offering for sale to the public new shares in an existing company, or shares in a new company; **subscription to a new share issue** = offering shares in a new company for sale; **subscription list** = list of subscribers to a new share issue; **the subscription lists close at 10.00 on September 24th** = no new applicants will be allowed to subscribe for the share issue after that date; **subscription price** = price at which new shares in an existing company are offered for sale

subsidiary [səb'sɪdiəri] **1** *adjective* (thing) which is less important; ***they agreed to most of the conditions in the contract but queried one or two subsidiary items***; **subsidiary company** = company which is owned by a parent company **2** *noun* company which is owned by a parent company; ***most of the group profit was contributed by the subsidiaries in the Far East***

subsidize ['sʌbsɪdaɪz] *verb* to help by giving money; ***the government has refused to subsidize the car industry***; **subsidized accommodation** = cheap accommodation which is partly paid for by an employer or a local authority, etc.

> a serious threat lies in the estimated 400,000 tonnes of subsidized beef in EC cold stores
>
> *Australian Financial Review*

subsidy ['sʌbsɪdi] *noun* **(a)** money given to help something which is not profitable; ***the industry exists on government subsidies***; ***the government has increased its subsidy to the car industry*** **(b)** money given by a government to make something cheaper; ***the subsidy on butter*** *or* ***the butter subsidy***

substantial [səb'stænʃl] *adjective* large or important; **to acquire a substantial interest**

in a company = to buy a large number of shares in a company

subtenancy [sʌb'tenənsi] *noun* agreement to sublet a property

subtenant [sʌb'tenənt] *noun* person or company to which a property has been sublet

subtotal ['sʌbtəutl] *noun* total of one section of a complete set of figures

subtract [səb'trækt] *verb* to take away (something) from a total; ***if the profits from the Far Eastern operations are subtracted, you will see that the group has not been profitable in the European market***

sub-underwriter [sʌb'ʌndəraɪtə] *noun* a company which underwrites an issue, taking shares from the main underwriters

subvention [səb'venʃn] *noun* subsidy

succeed [sək'si:d] *verb* **(a)** to do well, to be profitable; ***the company has succeeded best in the overseas markets***; ***his business has succeeded more than he had expected*** **(b)** to do what was planned; ***she succeeded in passing her shorthand test***; ***they succeeded in putting their rivals out of business***

success [sək'ses] *noun* **(a)** doing something well; ***the launch of the new model was a great success***; ***the company has had great success in the Japanese market*** **(b)** doing what was intended; ***we had no success in trying to sell the lease***; ***he has been looking for a job for six months, but with no success***

sucre ['su:kreɪ] *noun* currency used in Ecuador

suitor ['su:tə] *noun* person or company that wants to buy another; **hostile suitor** = person or company making a hostile bid

> the US paint group joins a growing list of hostile suitors that are trying to scupper the increasing number of recommended cross-border takeovers
>
> *Investors Chronicle*

> the company is the latest potential foreign predator to threaten a recommended bid by another foreign suitor
>
> *Investors Chronicle*

sum [sʌm] *noun* **(a)** quantity of money; ***a sum of money was stolen from the personnel office***; ***he lost large sums on the Stock Exchange***; ***she received the sum of £500 in compensation***; **the sum insured** = the largest amount which an insurer will pay under the terms of an insurance; **lump sum** = money paid in one payment, not in several small payments **(b)** total of a series of figures added together

sum ['su:m] *noun* currency used in Uzbekistan

sundry ['sʌndri] *adjective & noun* various; **sundry items** *or* **sundries** = small items which are not listed in detail

sunrise industries ['sʌnraɪz 'ɪndʌstris] *noun* companies in the fields of electronics and other high-tech areas

sunset industries ['sʌnset 'ɪndʌstris] *noun* old-style industries which are being replaced by new technology

superannuation [su:pəænju'eɪʃn] *noun* pension paid to someone who is too old or too ill to work any more; **superannuation plan** *or* **scheme** = pension plan or scheme

supplementary benefit [sʌplɪ'mentəri 'benɪfit] *noun* payments from the government to people with very low incomes

supply [sə'plaɪ] **1** *noun* **(a)** providing something which is needed; **supply price** = price at which something is provided; **supply and demand** = amount of a product which is available and the amount which is wanted by customers; **the law of supply and demand** = general rule that the amount of a product which is available is related to the amount needed by the possible customer **(b) money supply** = amount of money which exists in a country; *see note at* MONEY SUPPLY; **Supply Bill** = Bill for providing money for government requirements; **supply estimates** = UK government expenditure which is voted by Parliament **(c) supply shock** = sudden rise in productivity which gives higher output and profits without inflation

supply side economics [sə'plaɪ'saɪd i:kə'nɒmɪks] *noun* economic theory, that governments should encourage producers and suppliers of goods by cutting taxes, rather than encourage demand by making more money available in the economy

supplier [sə'plaɪə] *noun* person or company that supplies or sells goods or services

support [sə'pɔ:t] **1** *noun* **(a)** giving money to help; ***the government has provided support to the electronics industry***; ***we have no financial support from the banks*** **(b)** agreement or encouragement; ***the chairman has the support of the committee***; **support level** *or* **support point** = level below which a share or a commodity or the stock market will not fall, because of general support from investors; **support price** = price (in the EC) at which a government will buy agricultural produce to stop the price falling **(c) support manager** = manager of the back office of a securities firm **2** *verb* **(a)** to give money to help; ***the government is supporting the electronics industry to the tune of $2m per annum***; ***we hope the banks will support us during the expansion period*** **(b) to support a share price** = to buy shares in order to help the price remain at the current level or even rise

surcharge [sɜ:tʃɑ:dʒ] *noun* extra charge; **import surcharge** = extra duty charged on imported goods, to try to stop them from being imported and to encourage local manufacture

surety ['ʃɔ:ti] *noun* **(a)** person who guarantees that someone will do something; ***to stand surety for someone*** **(b)** deeds or share certificates, etc., deposited as security for a loan

surplus ['sɜ:plʌs] *noun* extra stock, something which is more than is needed; **a budget surplus** = more revenue than was planned for in the budget; **to absorb a surplus** = to take a surplus into a larger amount

surrender [sə'rendə] **1** *noun* giving up of an insurance policy before the contracted date for maturity; **surrender value** = money which an insurer will pay if an insurance policy is given up; **surrender charge** *or* **fee** = charge levied when someone withdraws money invested before the date allowed (this is to deter early withdrawals) **2** verb **to surrender a policy** = to give up an insurance

> this charge usually declines one percentage point a year so that after seven years, a policyholder no longer faces a surrender fee
>
> *Wall Street Journal*

surtax ['sɜ:tæks] *noun* extra tax on high income

surveillance [sɜ:'veɪləns] *noun* careful watch over people or buildings; **surveillance camera** = camera which takes photographs of people in a bank

sushi bond ['su:ʃi 'bɒnd] *noun* bond issued in a foreign currency by a Japanese corporation; *see also* SAMURAI, SHOGUN

suspend [sə'spend] *verb* to stop (something) for a time; ***we have suspended payments while we are waiting for news from our agent***; ***sailings have been suspended until the weather gets better***; ***work on the construction project has been suspended***; ***the management decided to suspend negotiations***

suspense account [sə'spens ə'kaʊnt] *noun* account into which payments are put temporarily when the accountant cannot be sure where they should be entered

suspension [sə'spenʃn] *noun* stopping something for a time; ***suspension of payments***; ***suspension of deliveries***

swap [swɒp] **1** *noun* exchanging one thing for another; **currency swap** = agreement to use a certain currency for payments under a contract in exchange for another currency (the two companies involved each can buy one of the currencies at a more favourable rate than the other); **interest rate swap** = agreement between two companies to exchange borrowings (a company with fixed-interest borrowings might swap them for variable interest borrowings of another company; this is also called 'plain vanilla swap') **2** *verb* to exchange one thing for another

> the simplest and most common type of interest rate swap involves the exchange of a fixed for a variable rate obligation, both denominated in the same currency
>
> *Accountancy*

> the International Finance Corporation, the World Bank's private sector development arm, became the first borrower to swap funds raised in the Portuguese escudo market
>
> *Financial Times*

swaption [swɒpʃn] *noun* option to arrange an interest rate swap at some time in the future

sweetener ['swi:tnə] noun *(informal)* bribe, or anything which makes a deal particularly attractive; **equity sweetener** = incentive to encourage people to lend a company money, in the form of a warrant giving the right to buy shares at a later date and at a certain price (NOTE: the American equivalent is **equity kicker**)

SWIFT = SOCIETY FOR WORLDWIDE INTERBANK FINANCIAL TELECOMMUNICATIONS an organization for sending electronic messages round the world banking system

Swiss franc ['swɪs 'fræŋk] *noun* currency used in Switzerland and Liechtenstein (normally considered a very stable currency)

switch [swɪtʃ] *verb* to change, especially to change investment money from one type of investment to another; ***when war seemed likely, investors switched out of equities into gold***

syndicate 1 [sɪndɪkət] *noun* group of people or companies working together to make money; ***a German finance syndicate***; **arbitrage syndicate** = group of people who together raise the capital to invest in arbitrage deals; **bank syndicate** = group of major international banks which group together to underwrite a massive loan; **underwriting syndicate** = group of underwriters who insure a large risk; **Lloyd's syndicate** = group of underwriters on the Lloyd's insurance market, made up of active underwriters who arrange the business and non-working underwriters (called 'names') who stand surety for any insurance claims which may arise **2** ['sɪndɪkeɪt] *verb* to arrange for a large loan to be underwritten by several international banks

> over the past few weeks, companies raising new loans from international banks have been forced to pay more, and an unusually high number of attempts to syndicate loans among banks has failed
>
> *Financial Times*

synergy ['sɪnədʒi] noun *(of two groups)* producing greater effects by joining forces than by acting separately

system ['sɪstəm] *noun* **(a)** arrangement, organization of things which work together; ***our accounting system has worked well in spite of the large increase in orders***; **decimal system** = system of mathematics based on the number 10; **filing system** = way of putting documents in order for easy reference; **to operate a quota system** = to regulate supplies by fixing quantities which are allowed; ***we arrange our distribution using a quota system - each agent is allowed only a certain number of units*** **(b) computer system** = set of programs, commands, etc., which run a computer; **systems analysis** = using a computer to suggest how a company should work by analyzing the way in which it works at present; **systems analyst** = person who specializes in systems analysis

Tt

tab [tæb] *noun* = *TABULATOR*

table ['teɪbl] **1** *noun* **(a)** list of figures or facts set out in columns; **table of contents** = list of contents in a book; **actuarial tables** = lists showing how long people of certain ages are likely to live **(b) Table A, B, C, D, E** = specimen forms for setting up companies in the Companies Act; *see* A, B, C, D, E **2** *verb* to put items of information on the table before a meeting; ***the report of the finance committee was tabled***; **to table a motion** = (i) to put forward a proposal for discussion by putting details of it on the table at a meeting; (ii) *US* to remove a proposal from discussion indefinitely

tabular ['tæbjʊlə] adjective **in tabular form** = arranged in a table

tabulate ['tæbjuleɪt] *verb* to set out in a table

tabulation [tæbju'leɪʃn] *noun* arrangement of figures in a table

tabulator ['tæbjuleɪtə] *noun* part of a typewriter or computer which sets words or figures automatically in columns

tael [teɪl] *noun* measurement of the weight of gold, used in the Far East (= 1.20oz)

tail [teɪl] *noun US* **(a)** spread between the bid price and the lowest acceptable price on US Treasury bills **(b)** the figures which come after the decimal point (in the quoted price of a bond)

taka ['tækə] *noun* currency used in Bangladesh

take [teɪk] **1** *noun* (i) profit from any sale; (ii) cash received in a shop **2** *verb* **(a)** to receive or to get; **the shop takes £2,000 a week** = the shop receives £2,000 a week in cash sales; **he takes home £250 a week** = his salary, after deductions for tax, etc., is £250 a week **(b)** to do a certain action; **to take action** = to do something; ***you must take immediate action if you want to stop thefts***; **to take the chair** = to be chairman of a meeting; ***in the absence of the chairman his deputy took the chair***; **to take stock** = to count the items in a warehouse; **to take stock of a situation** = to examine the state of things before deciding what to do **(c)** to need (a time or a quantity); ***it took the factory six weeks*** *or* ***the factory took six weeks to clear the backlog of orders***; ***it will take her all morning to do my letters***; ***it took six men and a crane to get the computer into the office*** (NOTE: **taking - took - has taken)**

take away ['teɪk ə'weɪ] *verb* to remove one figure from a total; ***if you take away the home sales, the total turnover is down***

take down ['teɪk 'daʊn] *verb US (of an underwriter)* to receive a share allotment

take-home pay ['teɪk'həʊm 'peɪ] *noun* amount of money received in wages, after tax, etc., has been deducted

take off ['teɪk 'ɒf] *verb* **(a)** to remove or to deduct; ***he took £25 off the price*** **(b)** to start to rise fast; ***sales took off after the TV commercials***

take out ['teɪk 'aʊt] *verb* to remove; **to take out a patent for an invention** = to apply for and receive a patent; **to take out insurance against theft** = to pay a premium to an insurance company, so that if a theft takes place the company will pay compensation

take-out ['teɪkaʊt] *noun* removing capital which you had originally invested in a new company by selling your shares

take over ['teɪk 'əʊvə] *verb* **(a)** to start to do something in place of someone else; ***the new chairman takes over on July 1st***; ***the buyer takes over the company's liabilities***; **the take-over period is always difficult** = the period when one person is taking over work from another is always difficult **(b) to take over a company** = to buy (a business) by acquiring most of its shares; ***the company was taken over by a large multinational***

takeover ['teɪkəʊvə] *noun* buying a controlling interest in a business by buying more than 50% of its shares; **takeover bid** = offer to buy all or most of the shares in a company so as to control it; **to make a takeover bid for a company** = to offer to buy most of the shares in a company; **to withdraw a takeover bid** = to say that you no longer offer to buy the shares in a company; **the**

company rejected the takeover bid = the directors recommended that the shareholders should not accept the offer; ***the disclosure of the takeover bid raised share prices***; *see also* AGREED, CONTESTED, HOSTILE; **Takeover Code** *or* **City Code on Takeovers and Mergers** = code of practice which regulates how takeovers should take place; it is enforced by the Takeover Panel; **Takeover Panel** *or* **Panel on Takeovers and Mergers** = non-statutory body which examines takeovers and applies the City Code on Takeovers and Mergers

take-private ['teɪk'praɪvət] *noun US* arrangement by which a quoted company leaves the Stock Exchange and becomes a privately owned investment; ***the law firm was figuring in six of the seven take-privates last year***; *see also* PUBLIC-TO-PRIVATE

> the 'take-private' has already become a favourite - this is the decision by a quoted company to restore itself to private status because of share price underperformance
>
> *Investors Chronicle*

taker ['teɪkə] *noun* buyer, person who wants to buy (an object for auction, a share, an option, etc.); ***there were no takers for the new shares***

take up ['teɪk 'ʌp] verb **to take up an option** = to accept an option which has been offered and put into action; ***half the rights issue was not taken up by the shareholders***; **take up rate** = percentage of acceptances for a rights issue

takings ['teɪkɪŋz] *plural noun* money received in a shop or a business; ***the week's takings were stolen from the cash desk***

> many takeovers result in the new managers/owners rationalizing the capital of the company through better asset management
>
> *Duns Business Month*

> capital gains are not taxed, but money taken out in profits and dividends is taxed
>
> *Toronto Star*

tala ['tɑːlæ] *noun* currency used in Samoa

tally ['tæli] **1** *noun* note of things counted or recorded; ***to keep a tally of stock movements*** *or* ***of expenses***; **tally clerk** = person whose job is to note quantities of cargo; **tally sheet** = sheet on which quantities are noted **2** *verb* to agree, to be the same; ***the invoices do not tally***; ***the accounts department tried to make the figures tally***

tangible ['tænʒəbl] *adjective* **tangible assets** = assets which are solid (such as machinery, buildings, furniture, jewellery, etc.); **tangible asset value** *US* **tangible net worth** = value of all the assets of a company less its intangible assets (goodwill, patents, etc.); it is shown as a value per share

> the face value of Japan's domestic debt now far exceeds the ability of borrowers to service that debt, due largely to declining corporate profitability and the plunge in the value of Japan's tangible assets - its real estate as well as much of its infrastructure and productive capacity
>
> *The Banker*

TAO = TAXPAYER ASSISTANCE ORDER

tap [tæp] *verb* to get finance by borrowing from investors, lenders, etc.

tap (stock) ['tæp 'stɒk] *noun GB* government stock issued direct to the Bank of England for sale to investors

> COMMENT: government stocks are normally issued in tranches for sale by tender, but small amounts are kept as 'tap stock' for direct sale to investors; the term is applied to any government stocks sold in this way

> the 9% debt, listed on Germany's stock exchanges for the first time in yesterday's session, totals 12bn marks. Five-year notes are sold on a tap basis, sometimes over the course of several months
>
> *Wall Street Journal*

taper *or* **tapering relief** ['teɪpə] *noun* new system of reducing capital gains tax payable when shares are sold, according to the length of time the shares have been held (in the case of shares held for more than 10 years, CGT will be charged on 60% of the capital gains)

> COMMENT: an investor who realises chargeable gains after April 5, 1998, will be subject to tax relief which tapers according to how long he has previously owned the assets. Investors who have owned assets for two years or less from this date will get no tapering relief, while those who have owned assets for 10 years or more will only

have to pay tax on 60 per cent of their chargeable gains. All assets bought before March 17, 1998, will be treated as though they have been owned for exactly one year before April 5, 1998

target ['tɑːgɪt] *noun* thing to aim for; **inflation target** = inflation rate which the government aims to reach at some date in the future; **monetary targets** = figures such as the money supply, PSBR, etc., which are given as targets by the government when setting out its budget for the forthcoming year; **production targets** = amount of units a factory is expected to produce; **sales targets** = amount of sales a representative is expected to achieve; **takeover target** *or* **target company** = company which is the object of a takeover bid; **target market** = market in which a company is planning to sell its goods; **to set targets** = to fix amounts or quantities which workers have to produce or reach; **to meet a target** = to produce the quantity of goods or sales which are expected; **to be on target** = to be heading towards the target that has been set; **to miss a target** = not to produce the amount of goods or sales which are expected; ***they missed the target figure of £2m turnover***

in a normal leveraged buyout the acquirer raises money by borrowing against the assets of the target company

Fortune

the Bank is unlikely to cut interest rates again after the November report showed inflation on target

The Times

Target *or* **TARGET** ['tɑːgɪt] = TRANS-EUROPEAN AUTOMATED REAL-TIME GROSS SETTLEMENT EXPRESS TRANSFER system set up by the European Central Bank to deal with cross-border payments between member states of the EU; *see also* REAL-TIME

target price ['tɑːgɪt 'praɪs] *noun* wholesale price within the EU for certain products, such as wheat, which market management is intended to achieve; it is linked to the intervention price

COMMENT: target prices are set in terms of fixed agricultural units of account, which are converted into different national currencies using adjusted exchange rates known as 'green rates' (in the UK, the 'green pound'). A system of levies on non-EU agricultural imports is used to protect target prices when they are set above the general level of world prices. In addition, the EU has established an internal price support system based on a set of intervention prices set slightly below the target price. If the level of supply is in excess of what is needed to clear the market at the target price, the excess supply is bought by the Community at the intervention price, thereby preventing overproduction from depressing the common price level as would normally happen in a free market

tariff ['tærɪf] *noun* **(a) customs tariffs** = tax to be paid on imported goods; **tariff barriers** = customs duty intended to make imports more expensive; ***to impose tariff barriers on*** *or* ***to lift tariff barriers from a product***; **differential tariffs** = different duties for different types of goods; **General Agreement on Tariffs and Trade (GATT)** = international agreement to try to reduce restrictions in trade between countries (replaced in 1998 by the World Trade Organization) **(b)** rate of charging for electricity, hotel rooms, train tickets, etc.

tax [tæks] **1** *noun* **(a)** money taken by the government or by an official body to pay for government services; **airport tax** = tax added to the price of an air ticket to cover the cost of running an airport; **capital gains tax** = tax on capital gains; **capital transfer tax** = tax on gifts or bequests of money or property; **corporation tax** = tax on profits made by companies; **excess profits tax** = tax on profits which are higher than what is thought to be normal; **income tax** = tax on salaries and wages; **land tax** = tax on the amount of land owned; **sales tax** = tax on the price of goods sold; **turnover tax** = tax on company turnover; **value added tax** = tax on goods and services, added as a percentage to the invoiced sales price **(b) ad valorem tax** = tax calculated according to the value of the goods taxed; **back tax** = tax which is owed; **basic tax** = tax paid at the normal rate; **direct tax** = tax paid directly to the government (such as income tax); **indirect tax** = tax paid to someone who then pays it to the government (such as VAT); **to levy a tax** *or* **to impose a tax** = to make a tax payable; ***the government has imposed a 15% tax on petrol***; **to lift a tax** = to remove a tax; ***the tax on company profits has been lifted***; **exclusive of tax** = not including tax; **tax abatement** = reduction of tax; **tax adjustments** = changes made to tax; **tax adviser** *or* **tax consultant** = person who gives advice on tax problems; **tax allowance** *or* **allowances against tax** = part of income which a person is allowed to earn and not pay tax on; **tax avoidance** = trying (legally) to minimize the amount of tax to be paid; **tax bill** = amount of tax (to be) paid; ***with some easy moves, there's a chance to significantly cut your tax bill***; **in the top tax bracket** = paying the highest level of tax; **tax break** = allowance which can be set off against tax; ***the state offers tax breaks for children and homeowners***; **tax code** = number given to indicate the amount of tax allowances a person has; **tax concession** = allowing less tax to be paid; *US* **tax court** = court which deals with disputes between taxpayers and the Internal Revenue Service (NOTE: the British equivalent is a hearing before the Commissioners of Inland Revenue); **tax credit** = part of a dividend on which the company has already paid tax, so that the shareholder who does not pay tax can reclaim it; **tax deductions** = (i) money removed from a salary to pay tax; (ii) *US* business expenses which can be claimed against tax; **tax deducted at source** = tax which is removed from a salary or interest before the money is paid out; **tax deposit certificate** = certificate showing that a taxpayer has deposited money in advance of a tax payment (the money earns interest while on deposit); **tax evasion** = trying illegally not to pay tax; **tax exemption** = (i) being free from payment of tax; (ii) *US* part of income which a person is allowed to earn and not pay tax on; **tax form** = blank form to be filled in with details of income and allowances and sent to the tax office each year; **tax haven** = country where taxes are low, encouraging companies to set up their main offices there (countries such as the Bahamas are tax havens); **tax holiday** = period when a new company pays no tax; **tax inspector** *or* **inspector of taxes** = official of the Inland Revenue who examines tax returns and decides how much tax someone should pay; **tax loophole** = legal means of not paying tax; **tax relief** = allowing someone not to pay tax on certain parts of his income; **tax return** *or* **tax declaration** = completed tax form, with details of income and allowances which is sent by a taxpayer to the Inland Revenue; **tax shelter** = financial arrangement (such as a pension scheme) where investments can be made without tax; **tax year** = twelve month period on which taxes are calculated (in the UK, 6th April to 5th April of the following year) **2** *verb* to make someone pay a tax, to impose a tax on something; ***the government is proposing to tax businesses at 50%***; ***income is taxed at 25%***; ***luxury items are heavily taxed***

> according to government figures, out of the 120 million individual and corporate returns filed each year, no more than 30,000 end up in tax court
>
> *Smart Money*

> you can project your taxes using dozens of different scenarios, and the program will compute your tax bill
>
> *Smart Money*

> if you recently refinanced your home for a second time, you've probably got a tax break coming
>
> *Smart Money*

> the 1997 Tax Act is chock full of tax breaks for the new year - and it's the perfect time to start capitalizing on them
>
> *Fortune*

taxable ['tæksəbl] *adjective* which can be taxed; **taxable items** = items on which a tax has to be paid; **taxable income** = income on which a person has to pay tax; **taxable supply** = supply of goods which are subject to VAT

taxation [tæk'seɪʃn] *noun* act of taxing; **direct taxation** = taxes (such as income tax) which are paid direct to the government; **indirect taxation** = taxes (such as sales tax) which are not paid direct to the government; **double taxation** = taxing the same income twice; **double taxation agreement** = agreement between two countries that a person living in one country will not be taxed in both countries on the income earned in the other country; **regressive taxation** = system of taxation in which tax gets progressively less as income rises; **graduated taxation** *or* **progressive taxation** = taxation system where tax levels increase as the income is higher

tax-deductible ['tæksdɪ'dʌktəbl] *adjective* which can be deducted from an income before tax is calculated; **these expenses are not tax-deductible** = tax has to be paid on these expenses

tax-deferred ['tæksdɪ'fɜ:d] *adjective* *US* where the payment of federal income tax is put back to a later date; **tax-deferred retirement plan** *or* **savings plan** = savings plan into which a person can regularly put a certain proportion of income, with tax only being payable on retirement

tax-efficient ['tæksɪ'fɪʃənt] *adjective* (investment) which helps avoid tax

zeros are one of the classes of share issued by split-capital investment trusts. They provide a predictable and tax-efficient return, but with a smattering of stock-market risk

Sunday Times

tax-exempt ['tæksɪg'zempt] *adjective* not required to pay tax; (income or goods) which are not subject to tax; **Tax-Exempt Special Savings Account (TESSA)** = account into which money can be placed to earn interest free of tax, provided it is left untouched for five years (the scheme is being phased out)

tax-favored ['tæks'feɪvəd] *adjective US* **tax-favored investment** = investment which offers tax-reducing incentives

unlike other tax-favored investments, it's open to people who earn more than the minimum wage

Fortune

tax-free ['tæks'fri:] *adjective* on which tax does not have to be paid

taxpayer ['tækspeɪə] *noun* person or company that has to pay tax; ***basic taxpayer*** *or* ***taxpayer at the basic rate***; **corporate taxpayers** = companies that pay tax; *US* **taxpayer advocate** = government official whose duty is to adjudicate in cases where ordinary taxpayers complain of treatment by the tax authorities; *US* **Taxpayer Assistance Order (TAO)** = court order allowing a company to recover debts from a taxpayer's salary before tax is paid

within the IRS there's a 'taxpayer advocate' who has extraordinarily broad powers to intervene on behalf of beleaguered taxpayers

Smart Money

the tax advocate has authority to overrule many IRS actions, such as taxpayer levies, repossession and wage garnishing through enforced Taxpayer Assistance Orders (TAOs)

Smart Money

T-bill ['ti:'bɪl] *US (informal)* = TREASURY BILL

T-bond ['ti:'bɒnd] = TREASURY BOND

technical ['teknɪkl] *adjective* **(a)** referring to a particular machine or process; ***the document gives all the technical details on the new computer*** **(b)** referring to influences inside a market (volumes traded, forecasts based on market analysis, etc.), as opposed to external factors, such as oil-price rises, wars, etc.; **technical analysis** = study of the price movements and volumes traded on a stock exchange; **technical correction** = situation where a share price or a currency moves up or down because it was previously too low or too high; **technical decline** = fall in share prices because of technical analysis

market analysts described the falls in the second half of last week as a technical correction

Australian Financial Review

at the end of the day, it was clear the Fed had not loosened the monetary reins, and Fed Funds forged ahead on the back of technical demand

Financial Times

technology stocks *or* **tech stocks** [tek'nɒlədʒi 'stɒks or 'tek 'stɒks] *noun* shares in companies specializing in electronics, communications, etc.

telegraphic transfer [telɪ'græfɪk 'trænsfɜ:] *noun* transfer of money from one account to another by telegraph (used often for sending money abroad, it is quicker but more expensive than sending a draft through the post)

telephone order ['telɪfəʊn 'ɔ:də] *noun* credit card order made by telephone

teller ['telə] *noun* person who takes cash from or who pays cash to customers at a bank

tem [tem] *see* PRO TEM

tenancy [tenənsi] *noun* (i) agreement by which a tenant can occupy a property; (ii) period during which a tenant has an agreement to occupy a property

tenant [tenənt] *noun* person or company that rents a house, flat or office to live or work in; ***the tenant is liable for repairs***; **sitting tenant** = tenant who is living in a house when the freehold or lease is sold

tender ['tendə] **1** *noun* **(a)** offer to do something for a certain price; **to put a project out to tender** *or* **to ask for** *or* **to invite tenders for a project** = to ask contractors to give written estimates for a job; **to put in a tender** *or* **to submit a tender** = to make an estimate for a job; **sealed tenders** = tenders sent in sealed envelopes which will all be opened together at a certain time **(b) to sell shares by tender** = to ask people to offer in writing a price for shares; **tender offer** =

method of selling new securities or bonds by asking investors to make offers for them, and accepting the highest offers **(c) legal tender** = coins or notes which can be legally used to pay a debt (small denominations cannot be used to pay large debts) **2** *verb* **to tender for a contract** = to put forward an estimate of cost for work to be carried out under contract; ***to tender for the construction of a hospital***

tenderer ['tendərə] *noun* person or company that tenders for work; ***the company was the successful tenderer for the project***

tendering ['tendərɪŋ] *noun* act of putting forward an estimate of cost; ***to be successful, you must follow the tendering procedure as laid out in the documents***

tenge ['teŋgə] *noun* currency used in Kazakhstan

tenor ['tenə] *noun* time before a financial instrument matures or before a bill is payable

term [tɜ:m] *noun* **(a)** period of time when something is legally valid; ***the term of a lease***; ***the term of the loan is fifteen years***; ***to have a loan for a term of fifteen years***; ***during his term of office as chairman***; **term account** *or* **term deposit** = money invested for a fixed period at a higher rate of interest; **term assurance** *or* **term insurance** = life assurance which covers a person's life for a period of time (at the end of the period, if the person is still alive he receives nothing from the insurance); ***he took out a ten-year term insurance***; **term loan** = loan for a fixed period of time; **term shares** = type of building society deposit for a fixed period of time at a higher rate of interest; **short-term** = for a period of weeks or months; **long-term** = for a long period of time (over 15 years); **medium-term** *or* **intermediate term** = for a period of one or two years **(b) terms** = conditions, duties which have to be carried out as part of a contract; arrangements which have to be agreed before a contract is valid; ***he refused to agree to some of the terms of the contract***; ***by*** *or* ***under the terms of the contract, the company is responsible for all damage to the property***; ***to negotiate for better terms***; **terms of payment** *or* **payment terms** = conditions for paying something; **terms of sale** = conditions attached to a sale; **terms of trade** = difference between a country's exports and imports; **cash terms** = lower terms which apply if the customer pays cash; **'terms: cash with order'** = terms of sale showing that payment has to be made in cash when the order is placed; **easy terms** = terms which are not difficult to accept, price which is easy to pay; ***the shop is let on very easy terms***; ***to pay for something on easy terms***; **on favourable terms** = on especially good terms; ***the shop is let on very favourable terms***; **trade terms** = special discount for people in the same trade; **in real terms** = actually, really

> the Federal Reserve Board has eased interest rates in the past year, but they are still at historically high levels in real terms
>
> *Sunday Times*

> a flurry of new term accounts mean that savers can earn a top fixed rate of 7.75 per cent (6.20 per cent) on £25,000, with Coventry, fixed for one year. For £10,000 the rate is 7.60 per cent (6.08 per cent)
>
> *Money Observer*

terminal bonus ['tɜ:mɪnəl 'bəʊnəs] *noun* bonus received when an insurance comes to an end

TESSA ['tesə] = TAX-EXEMPT SPECIAL SAVINGS ACCOUNT

thin market ['θɪn 'mɑ:kɪt] *noun* market where there are not many shares available for sale, so the price is distorted (NOTE: the opposite is a **liquid market**); **thin trading** = a day's trading where not many shares are offered for sale, so few bargains are made

> during the summer institutional activity has been very low key. As a result, stock markets have been very thin and that has meant disproportionate share movements
>
> *Money Observer*

third [θɜ:d] *noun* part of something which is divided into three; **to sell everything at one third off** = to sell everything at a discount of 33%; **the company has two thirds of the total market** = the company has 66% of the total market

Third Market ['θɜ:d 'mɑ:kɪt] *see* OVER-THE-COUNTER MARKET

third party ['θɜ:d 'pɑ:ti] *noun* any person other than the two main parties involved in a contract (i.e., in an insurance contract, not the insurance company nor the person who is insured); **third-party insurance** = insurance to cover damage to any person who is not one of the people named in the insurance contract; **the case is in the hands of a third party** =

the case is being dealt with by someone who is not one of the main interested parties

third quarter ['θɔ:d 'kwɔ:tə] *noun* three months' period from 1st July to 30th September

Third World ['θɔ:d 'wɔ:ld] *noun* countries of Africa, Asia and South America which do not have highly developed industries; ***we sell tractors into the Third World*** *or* ***to Third World countries***; ***Third World loans are causing problems to banks in the main developed countries***

Threadneedle Street [θred'ni:dl 'stri:t] street in the City of London where the Bank of England is situated; *see* OLD LADY

3i ['θri: 'aɪ] = INVESTORS IN INDUSTRY finance group owned by the big British High Street banks, providing finance especially to smaller companies

threshold ['θreʃhəʊld] *noun* limit, the point at which something changes; **threshold agreement** = contract which says that if the cost of living goes up by more than a certain amount, pay will go up to match it; **threshold price** = in the EU, the lowest price at which farm produce imported into the EU can be sold; **credit threshold** = limit for credit allowed to a customer; **pay threshold** = point at which pay increases because of a threshold agreement; **tax threshold** = point at which another percentage of tax is payable; ***the government has raised the minimum tax threshold from £6,000 to £6,500***

thrift [θrɪft] *noun* **(a)** saving money by spending carefully **(b)** *US* private local bank, savings and loan association or credit union, which accepts and pays interest on deposits from small investors (NOTE: also called **thrift institutions**)

> the thrift, which had grown from $4.7 million in assets in 1980 to 1.5 billion this year, has ended in liquidation
>
> *Barrons*

thrifty ['θrɪfti] *adjective* careful not to spend too much money

tick [tɪk] **1** *noun* **(a)** *(informal)* credit; ***all the furniture in the house is bought on tick*** **(b)** one step (up or down) in the price of a government bond or of financial futures; *see also* DOWNTICK, UPTICK **(c)** mark on paper to show that something is correct or that something is approved; ***put a tick in the box marked 'R'*** (NOTE: American English for (c) is **check**) **2** *verb* to mark with a sign to show that something is correct; ***tick the box marked 'R' if you require a receipt***

ticker ['tɪkə] *noun US* machine (operated by telegraph) which prints details of share prices and transactions rapidly (formerly printed on paper tape called 'ticker tape', but now shown online on computer terminals); **ticker symbol** = letter used to identify a stock on the ticker tape system

> COMMENT: all securities listed on the US stock exchanges are identified by letter symbols on ticker tape. So shares in Hilton are referred to as HLT, Texaco as TX, Xerox as XRX, etc.

tie [taɪ] *verb* to attach or to link; ***the interest rate is tied to the RPI***; **tied loan** = loan which involves a guarantee by the borrower to buy supplies from the lender (NOTE: **tying - tied**)

tie in ['taɪ 'ɪn] *verb* to link (an insurance policy to a mortgage)

tier [tɪə] *noun* level; **Tier One** = first level of core capital which banks have (covering basic equity capital and disclosed reserves) to conform to the guidelines of the Basle Agreement; **Tier Two** = second level of capital which banks have (this applies to undisclosed debts, provisions against bad debts, etc.) to conform with the guidelines of the Basle Agreement; *see also* SECOND-TIER, TWO-TIER MARKET

> COMMENT: the British stock market is said to have two tiers: the first is the London Stock Exchange, with its listed securities. The second tier (which is linked to the first) is the Alternative Investment Market (AIM) which has less strict criteria for admitting securities, and is often used as a first stage in obtaining a main Stock Exchange quotation

> capital instruments, such as securities with step-ups in interest rates, have been issued with the aim of generating Tier One regulatory capital that is both cost-efficient and can be denominated in non-local currency
>
> *The Banker*

tie up ['taɪ 'ʌp] *verb* to attach or to fasten tightly; to invest money in a certain way, so that it cannot be used for other investments; ***he has £100,000 tied up in long-dated gilts***; ***the company has £250,000 tied up in stock which no one wants to buy***

> a lot of speculator money is said to be tied up in sterling because of the interest-rate differential between US and British rates
>
> *Australian Financial Review*

tie-up ['taɪʌp] *noun* link or connection; ***the company has a tie-up with a German distributor*** (NOTE: plural is **tie-ups**)

tight [taɪt] *adjective* which is controlled, which does not allow any movement; ***the manager has a very tight schedule today - he cannot fit in any more appointments***; ***expenses are kept under tight control***; **tight market** = market where there is only a small spread between bid and offer prices; **tight money** = money which is borrowed at high interest rates because credit is squeezed; **tight money policy** = government policy to restrict money supply

> mortgage money is becoming tighter
>
> *Times*

> a tight monetary policy by the central bank has pushed up interest rates and drawn discretionary funds into bank deposits
>
> *Far Eastern Economic Review*

> the UK economy is at the uncomfortable stage in the cycle where the two years of tight money are having the desired effect on demand
>
> *Sunday Times*

tighten ['taɪtən] *verb* to make (something) tight, to control (something); ***the accounts department is tightening its control over departmental budgets***

> the decision by the government to tighten monetary policy will push the annual inflation rate above the previous high
>
> *Financial Times*

tighten up on ['taɪtən 'ʌp 'ɒn] *verb* to control (something) more; ***the government is tightening up on tax evasion***; ***we must tighten up on the reps' expenses***

till [tɪl] *noun* drawer for keeping cash in a shop; **cash till** = cash register, a machine which shows and adds prices of items bought, with a drawer for keeping the cash received; ***there was not much money in the till at the end of the day***; **till float** = cash put into the cash box at the beginning of the day to allow business to start; **till money** = cash held by banks

time [taɪm] *noun* **(a)** period when something takes place (such as one hour, two days, fifty minutes, etc.); **computer time** = time when a computer is being used (paid for at an hourly rate); **real time** = time when a computer is working on the processing of data while the problem to which the data refers is actually taking place; **time and motion study** = study in an office or factory of how long it takes to do certain jobs and the movements workers have to make to do them; **time and motion expert** = person who analyses time and motion studies and suggests changes in the way work is done **(b)** hours worked; **he is paid time and a half on Sundays** = he is paid the normal rate plus 50% extra when he works on Sundays; **full-time** = working for the whole normal working day; **overtime** = hours worked more than the normal working time; **part-time** = not working for a whole working day **(c)** period before something happens; **time bill** = bill of exchange which is payable at a specific time after acceptance; **time deposit** = deposit of money for a fixed period, during which it cannot be withdrawn; **lead time** = time between placing an order and receiving the goods; **time limit** = period during which something should be done; **to keep within the time limits** *or* **within the time schedule** = to complete work by the time stated

time rate ['taɪm 'reɪt] *noun* rate for work which is calculated as money per hour or per week, and not money for work completed

times ['taɪmz] *preposition* number of times something is multiplied by another; **shares selling at 10 times earnings** = shares selling at a P/E ratio of 10

time scale ['taɪm 'skeɪl] *noun* time which will be taken to complete work; ***our time scale is that all work should be completed by the end of August***; ***he is working to a strict time scale***

time share ['taɪm 'ʃeə] *noun* system where several people each own part of a property (such as a holiday flat), each being able to use it for a certain period each year

time-sharing ['taɪmʃeərɪŋ] *noun* **(a)** = TIME SHARE **(b)** sharing a computer system, with different users using different terminals

timetable ['taɪmteɪbl] *noun* list of appointments or events; **takeover timetable** = time of various events during a takeover bid

COMMENT: the timetable for a takeover bid is regulated by the London Stock Exchange: the formal documents are sent out by the bidding company some days after it has announced that it is making the bid. From the date of sending out the formal documents, the Stock Exchange allows the company 60 days in which to try and persuade as many shareholders as possible to accept the offer. If less than 50% accept, then the bidder can extend the offer, or increase of the offer, or simply let the offer lapse. If another company now makes a rival offer, it too has 60 days to try to gain enough acceptances

tin [tɪn] *noun* valuable metal, formerly traded on commodity markets at an artificially high international price managed by the International Tin Council to protect tin producers from swings in the price

tip [tɪp] **1** *noun* **(a)** money given to someone who has helped you; ***I gave the taxi driver a 10 cent tip***; ***the staff are not allowed to accept tips*** **(b)** advice on something to buy or to do which could be profitable; ***a stock market tip***; ***he gave me a tip about a share which was likely to rise because of a takeover bid***; **tip sheet** = newspaper which gives information about shares which should be bought or sold **2** *verb* **(a)** to give money to someone who has helped you; ***he tipped the receptionist £5*** **(b)** to say that something is likely to happen or that something might be profitable; ***two shares were tipped in the business section of the paper***; ***he is tipped to become the next chairman*** (NOTE: **tipping - tipped)**

title ['taɪtl] *noun* right to own a property; ***she has no title to the property***; ***he has a good title to the property***; **title deeds** = document showing who is the owner of a property

token ['təʊkən] *noun* **(a)** thing which acts as a sign or symbol; **token charge** = small charge which does not cover the real costs; ***a token charge is made for heating***; **token payment** = small payment to show that a payment is being made; **token rent** = very low rent payment to show that a rent is being asked **(b) book token** *or* **flower token** = card bought in a store which is given as a present and which must be exchanged for books or flowers; **gift token** = card bought in a store which is given as a present and which must be exchanged in that store for goods

tolar ['tɒlɑ:] *noun* currency used in Slovenia

toll [təʊl] *noun* payment for using a service (usually a bridge or a ferry); ***we had to cross a toll bridge to get to the island***; ***you have to pay a toll to cross the bridge***

toll call ['təʊl 'kɑ:l] *noun US* long-distance telephone call

toll free ['təʊl 'fri:] *adverb US* without having to pay a charge for a long-distance telephone call; ***to call someone toll free***; ***toll free number***

tombstone ['tu:mstəʊn] noun *(informal)* official announcement in a newspaper showing that a loan or a bond issue has been subscribed, giving details of the banks which have underwritten it

top-hat pension ['tɒphæt 'penʃən] *noun* special extra pension for senior managers

top-slicing ['tɒp'slaɪsɪŋ] *noun* selling part of a holding in a share which is equivalent to the original cost of the investment, leaving another part still held which represents the gain made

a few canny investors acted swiftly to take profits when the market hit an all-time high in July. They either encashed a portion of their Pep portfolio to lock in gains, or indulged in a bit of top-slicing - selling a number of shares in a company that has performed particularly well so that your profit covers the cost of your original investment

Sunday Times

the top-slicing approach means you do not get out of the well-run leading companies entirely

Money Observer

top up ['tɒp 'ʌp] *verb* to add to something to make it more complete; ***he topped up his pension contributions to make sure he received the maximum allowable pension when he retired***

tort [tɔ:t] *noun* harm done to someone or property which can be the basis of a lawsuit

total ['təʊtl] **1** *adjective* complete, with everything added together; ***total amount***; ***total expenditure***; ***total output***; **total income** = all income from all sources; **the cargo was written off as a total loss** = the cargo was so badly damaged that the insurers said it had no value **2** *noun* amount which is complete, with everything added up; ***the total of the charges comes to more than £1,000***; **grand total** = final total made by adding several subtotals **3** *verb* to add up to; ***costs totalling more than £25,000*** (NOTE: British spelling is **totalling - totalled** but American spelling is **totaling - totaled)**

Total Index ['təʊtl 'ɪndeks] index of share prices on the Oslo Stock Exchange

touch [tʌtʃ] *noun* the narrowest spread between the buy and sell prices of a share

tout [taʊt] **1** *noun* person who sells tickets (to games or shows) for more than the price printed on them **2** *verb* **to tout for custom** = to try to attract customers

track [træk] *verb* to follow how something develops, such as one of the stock market indices

> we found out by tracking how deftly the companies handled several simple refinancing questions
>
> *Smart Money*

> tracking the stock market is a good way of providing for the long term, if you're prepared to ride the ups and downs
>
> *Investors Chronicle*

tracker ['trækə] noun **index tracker** *or* **tracker fund** = fund which tracks (i.e. follows closely) one of the stock market indices, such as the Footsie; **tracker PEP** = PEP invested in funds which track a stock market index; **FTSE All-Share tracker** = fund which tracks the FTSE All-Share index

> directing all of their investments into a FTSE All-Share tracker (an index fund) would be not only acceptable but probably very clever. The index fund would probably grow faster than any trust given time
>
> *Money Observer*

> what index trackers do not offer is a means of determining the most vital choice - which mix of markets to invest in. Time spent on this mix does far more for your portfolio's performance than any work choosing fund managers or individual shares
>
> *Money Observer*

> if you still do intend to invest in the long term then it still makes more sense to put money in a cheaper investment vehicle with full exposure to equities like a tracker fund
>
> *Investors Chronicle*

tracking ['trækɪŋ] *noun* following a stock market closely; **tracking unit trust** = trust which follows closely one of the stock market indices; **FTSE 100 index-tracking unit trust** = a unit trust that follows the Footsie 100 index

track record ['træk 'rekəd] *noun* success or failure of a company or salesman in the past; ***he has a good track record as an insurance salesman; the company has no track record in the computer market***

trade [treɪd] **1** *noun* **(a)** business of buying and selling; **export trade** *or* **import trade** = the business of selling to other countries or buying from other countries; **foreign trade** *or* **overseas trade** *or* **external trade** = trade with other countries; **home trade** = trade in the country where a company is based; **trade cycle** = period during which trade expands, then slows down, then expands again; **balance of trade** *or* **trade balance** = international trading position of a country in merchandise, excluding invisible trade; **adverse balance of trade** = situation when a country imports more than it exports; **favourable balance of trade** = situation where a country's exports are larger than its imports; **trade deficit** = difference in value between a country's low exports and higher imports; **trade surplus** = difference in value between a country's high exports and lower imports **(b) to do a good trade in a range of products** = to sell a large number of the range of products; **fair trade** = international business system where countries agree not to charge import duties on certain items imported from their trading partners; **free trade** = system where goods can go from one country to another without any restrictions; **free trade area** = group of countries practising free trade **(c) trade agreement** = international agreement between countries over general terms of trade; **trade barriers** = controls placed by a government to prevent imports coming into the country; **trade bill** = bill of exchange between two companies who are trading partners (it is issued by one company and endorsed by the other); **trade bureau** = office which specializes in commercial enquiries; **to impose trade barriers on** = to restrict the import of certain goods by charging high duty; **trade credit** = credit offered by one company when trading with another; **trade creditors** = companies which are owed money by a company (the amount owed to trade creditors figures in the annual accounts); **trade deficit** *or* **trade gap** = difference in value between a country's high imports and low exports; **trade description** =

description of a product to attract customers *GB*; **Trade Descriptions Act** = act which limits the way in which products can be described so as to protect customers from wrong descriptions made by manufacturers; **trade directory** = book which lists all the businesses and business people in a town; **trade mission** = visit to a country by a group of foreign businessmen to discuss trade; **to ask a company to supply trade references** = to ask a company to give names of traders who can report on the company's financial situation and reputation **(d)** people or companies dealing in the same type of product; **trade association** = group which links together companies in the same trade; **trade counter** = shop in a factory or warehouse where goods are sold to retailers; **trade discount** *or* **trade terms** = reduction in price given to a customer in the same trade; **trade fair** = large exhibition and meeting for advertising and selling a certain type of product; **trade price** = special wholesale price paid by a retailer to the manufacturer or wholesaler **2** *verb* to buy and sell, to carry on a business; ***to trade with another country***; ***to trade on the Stock Exchange***; ***the company has stopped trading***; ***the company trades under the name 'Eeziphitt'***; **traded options** = options to buy or sell shares at a certain price at a certain date in the future, which themselves are bought or sold

> a sharp setback in foreign trade accounted for most of the winter slowdown. The trade balance sank $17 billion
>
> *Fortune*

> at its last traded price, the bank was capitalized around $1.05 billion
>
> *South China Morning Post*

> with most of the world's oil now traded on spot markets, Opec's official prices are much less significant than they once were
>
> *Economist*

trade in ['treɪd 'ɪn] *verb* to give in an old item as part of the payment for a new one; ***the chairman traded in his old Rolls Royce for a new model***

trade-in ['treɪdɪn] *noun* old item (such as a car or washing machine) given as part of the payment for a new one; **trade-in price** = amount allowed by the seller for an old item being traded in for a new one

trademark *or* **trade name** ['treɪdmɑːk *or* 'treɪd 'neɪm] **1** *noun* particular name, design, etc., which has been registered by the manufacturer and which cannot be used by other manufacturers (it is an 'intangible asset') **2** *verb US* to register something as a trademark; ***they trademarked the name after the family dispute***; ***you should trademark the design***

trade-off ['treɪdɒf] *noun* exchanging one thing for another as part of a business deal

trader ['treɪdə] *noun* person who does business by buying and selling; person who buys or sells stocks, shares, options, etc.; **commodity trader** = person whose business is buying and selling commodities; **day trader** = trader who buys and sells the same futures on the same day; **free trader** = person who is in favour of free trade; **insider trader** = person who carries out insider dealing, i.e. illegal buying or selling of shares by staff of a company or other persons who have secret information about the company's plans; **sole trader** = person who runs a business, usually by himself, but has not registered it as a company

trade-weighted index ['treɪd'weɪtɪd 'ɪndeks] *noun* index of the value of a currency calculated against a basket of currencies

> the trade-weighted dollar chart shows there has been a massive devaluation of the dollar since the mid-'80s and the currency is at its all-time low. In terms of purchasing power, it is considerably undervalued
>
> *Financial Weekly*

trading ['treɪdɪŋ] *noun* **(a)** business of buying and selling; **trading account** = account of a company's gross profit; **trading area** = group of countries which trade with each other; **trading company** = company which specializes in buying and selling goods; **adverse trading conditions** = bad conditions for trade; **trading estate** = area of land near a town specially for factories and warehouses; **trading limit** = maximum amount of something which can be traded by a single trader; **trading loss** = situation where a company's receipts are less than its expenditure; **trading partner** = company or country which trades with another; **trading pattern** = general way in which trade is carried on; ***the company's trading pattern shows high export sales in the first quarter and high home sales in the third quarter***; **trading profit** = situation where a company's gross receipts are more than its gross expenditure; **(historical) trading range** = difference between the highest and lowest price for a share or bond over a period of time; **trading stamp** = special stamp given away by a shop, which the customer can collect and exchange later for free goods; **fair trading** = way of doing business which is reasonable and does not harm the customer; *GB* **Office of Fair Trading** = government department which protects consumers against unfair or illegal business **(b)** buying and selling on a Stock Exchange or commodities exchange; **trading for the account** *or* **account trading** = buying shares and selling the same shares during an account, which means that the dealer has only to pay the difference between the price of the shares bought and the price obtained for them when they are sold; **fair trading** = legal trade in shares, the legal buying and selling of shares; **forward trading** = buying or selling commodities forward; **insider trading** = illegal buying or selling of shares by staff of a company who have secret information about the company's plans; **option trading** = buying and selling share options; **trading firm** = stockbroking house; **trading floor** *or* **dealing floor** = (i) area of a broking house where dealing in securities is carried out by phone, using monitors to display current prices and stock exchange transactions; (ii) part of a stock exchange where dealers trade in securities (NOTE: American English for this is also **pit**); **trading post** = position on the trading floor of the New York Stock Exchange, where specialist traders operate

trailing spouse ['treɪlɪŋ 'spaʊs] *noun US* successful working spouse of someone who works abroad (one of the two has to commute at weekends) (NOTE: also called a **virtual spouse**)

trainee [treɪ'ni:] *noun* person who is learning how to do something; ***we employ a trainee accountant to help in the office at peak periods***; ***graduate trainees come to work in the accounts department when they have finished their courses at university***; **management trainee** = young member of staff being trained to be a manager

traineeship [treɪ'ni:ʃɪp] *noun* post of trainee

training ['treɪnɪŋ] *noun* being taught how to do something; ***there is a ten-week training period for new staff***; ***the bank is closed for staff training***; **industrial training** = training of new workers to work in an industry; **management training** = training staff to be managers, by making them study problems and work out solutions to them; **on-the-job training** = training given to workers at their place of work; **off-the-job training** = training given to workers away from their place of work (such as at a college or school); **staff training** = teaching staff better and more profitable ways of working; **training officer** = person who deals with the training of staff; **training unit** = special group of teachers who organize training for companies

tranche [trɑ:nʃ] *noun* one of series of instalments (used when referring to loans to companies, government securities which are issued over a period of time, or money withdrawn by a country from the IMF); ***the second tranche of interest on the loan is now due for payment***

tranchette ['trɑ:nʃət] *noun* small amount of government stock put onto the market for sale to investors

transact [træenz'ækt] verb **to transact business** = to carry out a piece of business

transaction [trænz'ækʃn] noun **business transaction** = piece of business, buying or selling; **cash transaction** = transaction paid for in cash; **a transaction on the Stock Exchange** = purchase or sale of shares on the Stock Exchange; ***the paper publishes a daily list of Stock Exchange transactions***; **foreign exchange transaction** = purchase or sale of foreign currency; **fraudulent transaction** = transaction which aims to cheat someone

transfer 1 ['trænsfɜ:] *noun* moving someone or something to a new place; ***he applied for a transfer to our branch in Scotland***; **transfer of property** *or* **transfer of shares** = moving the ownership of property or shares from one person to another; **airmail transfer** = sending money from one bank to another by airmail; **bank transfer** = moving money from a bank account to another account; **credit transfer** *or* **transfer of funds** = moving money from one account to another; **stock transfer form** = form to be signed by the person transferring shares; **telegraphic transfer** = transfer of money from one account to another by telegraph (used often for sending money abroad, it is quicker but more expensive than sending a draft through the post) **2** [træns'fɜ:] *verb* to move someone or something to a new place; ***the accountant was transferred to our Scottish branch***; ***the sum was transferred to your Madrid account***; ***he transferred his shares to a family trust***; ***she transferred her money to a deposit account***; **transferred charge call** = phone call where the person receiving the call agrees to pay for it (NOTE: **transferring - transferred**)

transferable [træns'fɜːrəbl] *adjective* (document, such as a bearer bond) which can be passed to someone else

transit ['trænzɪt] *noun* movement of goods on the way to a destination; **transit letter** = letter sent with cheques or drafts, listing what is being sent; *see also* ABA TRANSIT NUMBER

translate [trænz'leɪt] *verb* to change into another form

> the normal accounting policy of translating assets and liabilities of overseas subsidiaries into sterling at the exchange rate prevailing at balance sheet date
>
> *Accountancy*

transparency [trænz'peərənsi] *noun* being clear about making decisions and being open to the public about how decisions are reached

> with one currency (the euro) instead of eleven, you are going to see a lot more transparency in prices
>
> *Money Observer*

traveller's cheques *US* **traveler's checks** ['trævləz 'tʃeks] *noun* cheques taken by a traveller which can be cashed in a foreign country

treasurer ['treʒrə] *noun* **(a)** person who looks after the money or finances of a club or society, etc.; **honorary treasurer** = treasurer who does not receive any fee; **treasurer's account** = account of a club or society with a bank **(b)** *US* main financial officer of a company **(c)** *(Australia)* finance minister

treasury ['treʒri] noun **the Treasury** = government department which deals with the country's finance (the term is used in both the UK and the USA; in most other countries this department is called the 'Ministry of Finance'); **treasury bill** = short-term bill of exchange which does not give any interest and is sold by the government at a discount through the central bank (in the UK, their term varies from three to six months; in the USA, they are for 91 or 182 days, or for 52 weeks. In American English they are also called 'Treasuries' or 'T-bills'); **treasury bonds** = long-term bonds issued by the British or American governments; **Treasury notes** = medium-term bonds issued by the US government; **Treasury stocks** = bonds issued by the British government (NOTE: also called **Exchequer stocks**); *US* **Treasury Secretary** = member of the US government in charge of finance (NOTE: the equivalent of the **Finance Minister** in most countries, or of the **Chancellor of the Exchequer** in the UK) *GB* **Chief Secretary to the Treasury** = government minister responsible to the Chancellor of the Exchequer for the control of public expenditure (NOTE: in the USA, this is the responsibility of the Director of the Budget)

Treasuries ['treʒriz] *noun US (informal)* treasury bonds and bills

treble ['trebl] **1** *adverb* three times; ***our borrowings are treble what they were last year*** **2** *verb* to increase three times; ***the company's borrowings have trebled***

trend [trend] *noun* general way things are going; ***a downward trend in investment***; ***we notice a general trend to sell to the student market***; ***the report points to inflationary trends in the economy***; ***an upward trend in sales***; **economic trends** = way in which a country's economy is moving; **market trends** = gradual changes taking place in a market; **trend line** = line on a graph or chart which shows which way a trend is going

> the quality of building design and ease of accessibility will become increasingly important, adding to the trend towards out-of-town office development
>
> *Lloyd's List*

trial ['traɪəl] *noun* **(a)** court case to judge a person accused of a crime; ***he is on trial*** *or* ***is standing trial for embezzlement*** **(b)** test to see if something is correct; **trial balance** = draft calculation of debits and credits to see if they balance

tribunal [traɪ'bjuːnl] *noun* official court which examines special problems and makes judgements; **adjudication tribunal** = group which adjudicates in industrial disputes; **industrial tribunal** = court which can decide in disputes about employment; **rent tribunal** = court which can decide if a rent is too high or low

trigger ['trɪgə] **1** *noun* thing which starts a process; **adjustment trigger** = factor (such as a certain level of interest rates) which triggers an adjustment in exchange rates **2** *verb* to start a process; **trigger point** = point in acquiring shares in a company where the purchaser has to declare an interest or to take certain action

> COMMENT: if an individual or a company buys 5% of a company's shares, this shareholding must be declared to the company. If 15% is acquired it is assumed that a takeover bid will be made, and no

more shares can be acquired for seven days to give the target company time to respond. There is no obligation to make a bid at this stage, but if the holding is increased to 30%, then a takeover bid must be made for the remaining 70%. If 90% of shares are owned, then the owner can purchase all outstanding shares compulsorily. These trigger points are often not crossed, and it is common to see that a company has acquired 14.9% or 29.9% of another company's shares

the recovery is led by significant declines in short-term interest rates, which are forecast to be roughly 250 basis points below their previous peak in the second quarter of 1990. This should trigger a rebound in the housing markets and consumer spending on durables

Toronto Globe & Mail

trillion ['trɪljən] *number* one million millions (NOTE: British English now uses the same meaning as American English; formerly in British English it meant one million million millions, and it is still sometimes used with this meaning; see also the note at BILLION)

if land is assessed at roughly half its current market value, the new tax could yield up to Ø10 trillion annually

Far Eastern Economic Review

triple ['trɪpl] **1** *verb* to multiply three times; ***the company's debts tripled in twelve months; the acquisition of the chain of stores has tripled the group's turnover*** **2** *adjective* three times as much; ***the cost of airfreighting the goods is triple their manufacturing cost***; **triple A rated** = bond or corporation which has the highest credit rating according to Standard & Poor's or Moody's (so called, because the rating is 'AAA')

by issuing preferred shares, which tend to be triple-A rated, management adds permanent capital at a fixed low rate which can be reinvested to achieve higher returns

Barron's

triple witching hour ['trɪpl 'wɪtʃɪŋ 'aʊə] *noun* day when three major types of futures contract fall due at the same time

COMMENT: in the USA, this is the last hour of trading on the third Friday of the months of March, June, September and December, when futures contracts on the Stock Exchange Index, options on these futures contracts, and ordinary stock option contracts all fall due; in the UK, it is a day when euro-options, Footsie options and Footsie futures contracts all expire at the same time. It is normally a day when stock market prices show greater volatility than usual

the spooky sounding Triple Witching Hour cast a nasty spell on the market yesterday as angry dealers complained to the Stock Exchange that the market was in chaos for a short time. Triple Witching occurs when Euro-options, Footsie Options and Footsie futures contracts all expire at the same time. In the recent slack market conditions a lot of money has been made in these 'derivative instruments'

Guardian

triplicate ['trɪplɪkeɪt] noun **in triplicate** = with an original and two copies; ***to print an invoice in triplicate***; **invoicing in triplicate** = preparing three copies of invoices

trophy hunter ['trəʊfi 'hʌntə] *noun* investor who looks for cheap shares

at 354p the shares are trading at about 21 times prospective earnings per share. Not cheap, but not too expensive for trophy hunters

Sunday Business

troubled ['trʌbld] *adjective* in a difficult financial position

troubleshooter ['trʌblʃu:tə] *noun* person whose job is to solve problems in a company

trough [trɒf] *noun* low point (for instance, in an economic cycle); ***the peaks and troughs of the stock market***

troy weight [trɔɪ 'weɪt] *noun* system of measurement of weight used for gold and other metals, such as silver and platinum; **troy ounce** = measurement of weight (= 31.10 grammes) (NOTE: in writing, often shortened to **troy oz.** after figures: **25.2 troy oz.**)

COMMENT: troy weight is divided into grains, pennyweights (24 grains = 1 pennyweight), ounces (20 pennyweights = 1 ounce) and pounds (12 troy ounces = 1 pound). Troy weights are slightly less than their avoirdupois equivalents; the troy pound equals 0.37kg or 0.82lb avoirdupois

true [tru:] *adjective* correct or accurate; **true copy** = exact copy; ***I certify that this is a true copy***; ***certified as a true copy***; **true and fair view** = correct statement of a company's financial position as shown in its accounts and confirmed by the auditors

truncate [trʌŋˈkeɪt] *verb* to operate a simplified banking system by not returning physical cheques to the paying bank

truncation [ˈtrʌŋˈkeɪʃn] *noun* simplified banking system, where actual cheques are not sent to the paying bank, but held in the receiving bank which notifies the paying bank by computer of the details of cheques received

trust [trʌst] **1** *noun* **(a)** being confident that something is correct, will work, etc.; **we took his statement on trust** = we accepted his statement without examining it to see if it was correct **(b)** legal arrangement to pass goods, money or secrets to someone who will look after them well; ***he left his property in trust for his grandchildren***; **he was guilty of a breach of trust** = he did not act correctly or honestly when people expected him to; **he has a position of trust** = his job shows that people believe he will act correctly and honestly **(c)** management of money or property for someone; ***they set up a family trust for their grandchildren***; *US* **trust company** = organization which supervises the financial affairs of private trusts, executes wills, and acts as a bank to a limited number of customers; **trust deed** = document which sets out the details of a private trust; **trust fund** = assets (money, securities, property) held in trust for someone; **investment trust** = company whose shares can be bought on the Stock Exchange and whose business is to make money by buying and selling stocks and shares; **unit trust** = organization which takes money from investors and invests it in stocks and shares for them under a trust deed **(d)** *US* monopoly, a small group of companies which control the supply of a product **2** *verb* **to trust someone with something** = to give something to someone to look after; ***can he be trusted with all that cash?***

trustbusting [ˈtrʌstbʌstɪŋ] *noun US* breaking up monopolies to encourage competition

trustee [trʌˈsti:] *noun* person who has charge of money in trust, person who is responsible for a family trust; ***the trustees of the pension fund***

Truth in Lending Act [ˈtru:θ ɪn ˈlendɪŋ ˈækt] US Act of 1969, which forces lenders to state the full terms of their interest rates to borrowers

tugrik [ˈtu:grɪk] *noun* currency used in the Mongolian Republic

tune [tju:n] *noun* piece of music; **the bank is backing him to the tune of £10,000** = the bank is helping him with a loan of £10,000

turkey [ˈtɜ:ki] noun *(informal)* bad investment; investment which has turned out to be worthless

turn [tɜ:n] *noun* **(a)** movement in a circle, change of direction **(b)** profit or commission; **jobber's turn** = commission earned by a jobber on buying or selling shares **(c) stock turn** = total value of stocks sold in a year divided by the average value of goods in stock; ***the company has a stock turn of 6.7***

turnaround [ˈtɜ:nəraʊnd] *see* TURNROUND

turn down [ˈtɜ:n ˈdaʊn] *verb* to refuse; ***the board turned down their takeover bid***; ***the bank turned down their request for a loan***; ***the application for a licence was turned down***

turnkey operation [ˈtɜ:nki ɒpəˈreɪʃn] *noun* deal where a company takes all responsibility for constructing, fitting and staffing a building (such as a school or hospital or factory) so that it is completely ready for the purchaser to take over

turn over [ˈtɜ:n ˈəʊvə] *verb* **(a)** to have a certain amount of sales; ***we turn over £2,000 a week*** **(b)** to pass something to someone else

> he is turning over his CEO title to one of his teammates, but will remain chairman for a year
>
> *Duns Business Month*

> a 100,000 square foot warehouse can turn its inventory over 18 times a year, more than triple a discounter's turnover
>
> *Duns Business Month*

turnover [ˈtɜ:nəʊvə] *noun* **(a)** *GB* amount of sales of goods or services by a company; ***the company's turnover has increased by 235%***; ***we based our calculations on the forecast turnover*** (NOTE: the American equivalent is **sales volume**) **(b)** number of times something is used or sold in a period (usually one year), expressed as a percentage of a total; **stock turnover** = total value of stock sold in a year divided by the average value of goods held in stock; **turnover of shares** = total value of shares bought and sold on the Stock Exchange during the year (it covers both sales and purchases, so each transaction is counted twice)

turn round ['tɜːn 'raʊnd] *verb* to make (a company) change from making a loss to become profitable; **he turned the company round in less than a year** = he made the company profitable in less than a year

turnround *US* **turnaround** ['tɜːnraʊnd or 'tɜːnəraʊnd] *noun* **(a)** value of goods sold during a year divided by the average value of goods held in stock **(b)** action of emptying a ship, plane, etc., and getting it ready for another commercial journey **(c)** making a company profitable again

> the US now accounts for more than half our world-wide sales; it has made a huge contribution to our earnings turnaround
>
> *Duns Business Month*

24-hour banking ['twentifɔː 'haʊə 'bæŋkɪŋ] banking service provided during the whole day (by cash dispensers in the street, online services, etc.); **24-hour trading** = trading in bonds, securities and currencies during the whole day

> time-zone differences are an attraction for Asian speculators. In Hongkong, it is 5p.m. when the London exchange opens and 9.30 or 10 p.m. when New York starts trading
>
> *Far Eastern Economic Review*

COMMENT: 24-hour trading is now possible because of instant communication to Stock Exchanges in different time zones; the Tokyo Stock Exchange closes about two hours before the London Stock Exchange opens; the New York Stock Exchange opens at the same time as the London one closes

two-tier market ['tuː'tɪə 'mɑːkɪt] *noun* exchange market where two rates apply (usually one for tourists and a commercial rate for businesses)

two-way market ['tuː'weɪ 'mɑːkɪt] *noun* market where there is active buying and selling

tycoon ['taɪkuːn] *noun* important businessman

Uu

UBR = UNIFORM BUSINESS RATE

ultimatum [ʌltɪ'meɪtəm] *noun* statement to a someone that unless he does something within a period of time, action will be taken against him; ***the banks issued an ultimatum to their largest borrowers*** (NOTE: plural is **ultimatums** or **ultimata**)

umbrella organization [ʌm'brelə ɔ:gənaɪ'zeɪʃn] *noun* large organization which includes several smaller ones

unacceptable [ʌnək'septəbl] *adjective* which cannot be accepted; ***the terms of the contract are quite unacceptable***

unaccounted for [ʌnə'kaʊntɪd 'fɔ:] *adjective* lost, without any explanation; ***several thousand units are unaccounted for in the stocktaking***

unanimous [ju:'nænɪməs] *adjective* where everyone votes in the same way; ***there was a unanimous vote against the proposal***; ***they reached unanimous agreement***

unanimously [ju:'nænɪməsli] *adverb* with everyone agreeing; ***the proposals were adopted unanimously***

unaudited [ʌn'ɔ:dɪtɪd] *adjective* which has not been audited; ***unaudited accounts***

unauthorized [ʌn'ɔ:θəraɪzd] *adjective* not permitted; ***unauthorized access to the company's records***; ***the bank charges 26.8% interest on unauthorized overdrafts***; ***no unauthorized persons are allowed into the vaults***; **unauthorized unit trust** = private unit trust operated by a stockbroking firm for its clients

unbalanced [ʌn'bælənst] *adjective* (budget) which does not balance or which is in deficit

unbanked [ʌn'bæŋkt] *adjective* **(a)** (person) who does not have a bank account **(b)** (cheque) which has not been deposited in a bank account

unbundling [ʌn'bʌndlɪŋ] *noun* **(a)** process of separating companies from a conglomerate (the companies were independent in the past, and have been acquired by the conglomerate over a period of time) **(b)** *US* charging separately for each different service provided

uncalled [ʌn'kɔ:ld] *adjective* (capital) which a company is authorized to raise and has been issued but is not fully paid

uncashed [ʌn'kæʃt] *adjective* which has not been cashed; ***uncashed cheques***

unchanged [ʌn'tʃeɪnʒd] *adjective* which has not changed

> the dividend is unchanged at L90 per ordinary share
>
> *Financial Times*

unchecked [ʌn'tʃekt] *adjective* which has not been checked; ***unchecked figures***

uncollected [ʌnkə'lektɪd] *adjective* which has not been collected; ***uncollected subscriptions***; ***uncollected taxes***

unconditional [ʌnkən'dɪʃənl] *adjective* with no conditions; ***unconditional acceptance of the offer by the board***; **the offer went unconditional last Thursday** = the takeover bid was accepted by the majority of the shareholders and therefore the conditions attached to it no longer apply

unconditionally [ʌnkən'dɪʃənli] *adverb* without imposing any conditions; ***the offer was accepted unconditionally by the trade union***

> COMMENT: a takeover bid will become unconditional if more than 50% of shareholders accept it

uncontrollable [ʌnkən'trəʊləbl] *adjective* which cannot be controlled; ***uncontrollable inflation***

uncovered bear [ʌn'kʌvəd] *noun* person who sells stock which he does not hold, hoping to be able to buy stock later at a lower price when he needs to settle

uncrossed cheque ['ʌnkrɒst 'tʃek] *noun* cheque which does not have two lines across it, and can be cashed anywhere (NOTE: also called an **open cheque**)

undated [ʌn'deɪtɪd] *adjective* with no date indicated or written; ***he tried to cash an***

undated cheque; **undated bond** = bond with no maturity date

> COMMENT: the only British government stocks which are undated are the War Loan

under ['ʌndə] *preposition* **(a)** lower than or less than; ***the interest rate is under 10%***; ***under half of the shareholders accepted the offer*** **(b)** controlled by; according to; ***under the terms of the agreement, the goods should be delivered in October***; ***he is acting under rule 23 of the union constitution***

under- ['ʌndə] *prefix* less important than or lower than

underbid [ʌndə'bɪd] *verb* to bid less than someone (NOTE: **underbidding - underbid)**

underbidder [ʌndə'bɪdə] *noun* person who bids less than the person who buys at an auction

undercapitalized [ʌndə'kæpɪtəlaɪzd] *adjective* without enough capital; ***the company is severely undercapitalized***

undercharge [ʌndə'tʃɑ:dʒ] *verb* to ask for too little money; ***he undercharged us by £25***

undercut [ʌndə'kʌt] *verb* to offer something at a lower price than someone else

underemployed [ʌndəɪm'plɔɪd] *adjective* with not enough work; **underemployed capital** = capital which is not producing enough interest

underestimate 1 [ʌndə'estɪmət] *noun* estimate which is less than the actual figure; ***the figure of £50,000 in turnover was a considerable underestimate*** **2** [ʌndə'estɪmeɪt] *verb* to think that something is smaller or not as bad as it really is; ***they underestimated the effects of the strike on their sales***; ***he underestimated the amount of time needed to finish the work***

underlease ['ʌndəli:s] *noun* lease from a tenant to another tenant

underlying inflation rate [ʌndə'laɪɪŋ ɪn'fleɪʃn 'reɪt] *noun* basic inflation rate calculated on a series of prices of consumer items, petrol, gas and electricity, interest rates, etc.

underlying value [ʌndəlaɪɪŋ 'vælju:] noun *(of a company)* basic value of a company, including its assets, goodwill, etc.

> we seek to capitalize on any discrepancies between a company's underlying value and its stock price
>
> *Smart Money*

> in my estimation, the underlying value of the company even now is upwards of $7 a share at a time when shares are trading at 2 3/4
>
> *Barron's*

undermentioned [ʌndə'menʃənd] *adjective* mentioned lower down in a document

underperform [ʌndəpə'fɔ:m] verb **to underperform the market** = to perform worse than the rest of the market; ***the hotel group has underperformed the sector this year***

> he also said that most of his mutual funds would probably underperform the index by 1 to 2 per cent every year
>
> *Money Observer*

underperformance [ʌndəpə'fɔ:məns] *noun* performing worse than the market

> since mid-1989, Australia has been declining again. Because it has had such a long period of underperfomance, it is now not as vulnerable as other markets
>
> *Money Observer*

underrate [ʌndə'reɪt] *verb* to value less highly than should be; ***do not underrate the strength of the competition in the European market***; ***the power of the yen is underrated***

underreact [ʌndəri'ækt] verb *(of market)* not to react strongly enough to a situation; ***the markets underreacted to the oil crisis***

undersell [ʌndə'sel] *verb* to sell more cheaply than; **the company is never undersold** = no other company sells goods as cheaply as this one (NOTE: **underselling - undersold)**

undersigned [ʌndə'saɪnd] *noun* person who has signed a letter; **we, the undersigned** = we, the people who have signed below

underspend [ʌndə'spend] *verb* to spend less; **he has underspent his budget** = he has spent less than was allowed in the budget (NOTE: **underspending - underspent)**

understanding [ʌndə'stændɪŋ] *noun* private agreement; **on the understanding that** = on condition that, provided that; ***we accept the terms of the contract, on the understanding that it has to be ratified by our main board***

understate [ʌndə'steɪt] *verb* to make something seem less than it really is; ***the company accounts understate the real profit***

undersubscribed [ʌndəsəb'skraɪbd] *adjective* (share issue) where applications are not made for all the shares on offer, and part of the issue remains with the underwriters

undertake [ʌndə'teɪk] *verb* to agree to do something; ***to undertake to investigate market irregularities***; ***they have undertaken not to sell into our territory*** (NOTE: **undertaking - undertook - has undertaken**)

undertaking [ʌndə'teɪkɪŋ] *noun* **(a)** a large business **(b)** (legally binding) promise; ***they have given us a written undertaking not to sell their products in competition with ours***; **general undertaking** = undertaking signed by the directors of a company applying for a Stock Exchange listing, promising to work within the regulations of the Stock Exchange

undervaluation [ʌndəvælju'eɪʃn] *noun* being valued at a lower worth than should be

undervalued [ʌndə'vælju:d] *adjective* not valued highly enough; ***the properties are undervalued on the balance sheet***; ***the dollar is undervalued on the foreign exchanges*** (NOTE: the opposite is **overvalued**)

> in terms of purchasing power, the dollar is considerably undervalued, while the US trade deficit is declining month by month
>
> *Financial Weekly*

underwater [ʌndə'wɑ:tə] *adjective* which has lost value; **underwater loan** = loan which is worth less than its book value, as when an item bought with a loan loses its value on the market; **underwater option** = option which has no value

underweight [ʌndə'weɪt] *adjective* **(a)** not heavy enough; **the pack is twenty grams underweight** = the pack weighs twenty grams less than it should **(b)** *(of a portfolio)* with fewer shares in a sector than it should normally have

> for sterling funds committed to Japan, the loss in the third quarter was more than 31 per cent, and over 50 per cent for the year to end-September. Fortunately for most UK funds, they had already gone underweight in Japan
>
> *Financial Times Review*

underwrite [ʌndə'raɪt] *verb* **(a)** to accept responsibility for the purchase of something; **to underwrite a share issue** = to guarantee that a share issue will be sold by agreeing to buy all shares which are not subscribed; ***the issue was underwritten by three underwriting companies*** **(b)** to insure or to cover (a risk); ***to underwrite an insurance policy*** **(c)** to agree to pay for costs; ***the government has underwritten the development costs of the project*** (NOTE: **underwriting - underwrote - has underwritten**)

underwriter ['ʌndəraɪtə] *noun* person or company that underwrites a share issue or an insurance; **Lloyd's underwriter** = member of an insurance group at Lloyd's who accepts to underwrite insurances; **marine underwriter** = person who insures ships and their cargoes

> COMMENT: when a major company flotation or share issue or loan is prepared, a group of companies (such as banks) will form a syndicate to underwrite the action: the syndicate will be organized by the 'lead underwriter' (in the USA called the 'managing underwriter'), together with a group of main underwriters; these in turn will ask others ('sub-underwriters') to share in the underwriting. See also AGREEMENT AMONG UNDERWITERS

underwriting [ʌndə'raɪtɪŋ] *noun* action of guaranteeing to purchase shares in a new issue if no one purchases them; **underwriting fee** = fee paid by a company to the underwriters for guaranteeing the purchase of new shares in that company

undischarged bankrupt [ʌndɪs'tʃɑ:dʒd 'bæŋkrʌpt] *noun* person who has been declared bankrupt and has not been released from that state

undistributed profit [ʌndɪ'strɪbjutɪd 'prɒfɪt] *noun* profit which has not been distributed as dividends to shareholders but is retained in the business

unearned income ['ʌnə:nd 'ɪnkʌm] *noun* money received from interest or dividends, not from salary, wages or profits of your business; *compare* EARNED INCOME

uneconomic [ʌni:kə'nɒmɪk] *adjective* which does not make a commercial profit; **it is an uneconomic proposition** = it will not be commercially profitable; **uneconomic rent** = rent which is not enough to cover costs

unemployed [ʌnɪm'plɔɪd] *adjective* not employed, without any work; **unemployed office workers** = office workers with no jobs; **the unemployed** = the people without any jobs

unemployment [ʌnɪm'plɔɪmənt] *noun* lack of work; **mass unemployment** = unemployment of large numbers of workers; **unemployment benefit** *US* **unemployment**

compensation = payment made to someone who is unemployed

```
tax advantages directed toward small businesses will help create jobs and reduce the unemployment rate
```

Toronto Star

---

unencumbered [ʌnɪnˈkʌmbəd] *adjective* (property) which is not mortgaged

unfair competition [ˈʌnfeə kɒmpɪˈtɪʃn] *noun* trying to do better than another company by using techniques which are not fair, such as importing foreign goods at very low prices or by wrongly criticizing a competitor's products

unfavourable [ˈʌnfeɪvrəbl] *adjective* not favourable; **unfavourable balance of trade** = situation where a country imports more than it exports; **unfavourable exchange rate** = exchange rate which gives an amount of foreign currency for the home currency which is not good for trade; ***the unfavourable exchange rate hit the country's exports***

ungeared [ʌnˈgiːəd] *adjective* with no borrowings

uniform business rate (UBR) [ˈjuːnɪfɔːm ˈbɪznəs ˈreɪt] *noun* tax levied on business property which is the same percentage for the whole country

unincorporated [ʌnɪnˈkɔːpəreɪtɪd] *adjective* business which has not been made into a company (i.e., a partnership or a sole trader)

unissued capital [ʌnˈɪʃuːd ˈkæpɪtəl] *noun* capital which a company is authorized to issue by its articles of association but has not issued as shares

unit [ˈjuːnɪt] *noun* **(a)** single product for sale; **unit cost** = the cost of one item (i.e total product costs divided by the number of units produced); **unit price** = the price of one item **(b)** **monetary unit** *or* **unit of currency** = main item of currency of a country (a dollar, pound, yen, etc.); **unit of account** = standard unit used in financial transactions among members of a group, such as SDRs in the IMF, and the ECU which is used for example, when calculating the EU budget and farm prices) **(c)** single share in a unit trust; **accumulation units** = units in a unit trust, where the dividend is left to accumulate as new units; **income units** = units in a unit trust, where the investor receives dividends in the form of income; **unit-linked insurance** = insurance policy which is linked to the security of units in a unit trust or fund

unitary [ˈjuːnɪtri] adjective *see* REGULATOR

unitize [ˈjuːnɪtaɪz] *verb* to form investments into units which are sold to the public

unit trust [ˈjuːnɪt ˈtrʌst] *noun* organization which takes money from small investors and invests it in stocks and shares for them under a trust deed, the investment being in the form of shares (or units) in the trust

> COMMENT: unit trusts have to be authorized by the Department of Trade and Industry before they can offer units for sale to the public, although unauthorized private unit trusts exist. The US equivalent is the 'mutual fund'

Unitas index [ˈjuːnɪtæs ˈɪndeks] index of prices on the Helsinki Stock Exchange

unlawful [ʌnˈlɔːfʊl] *adjective* against the law, not legal

unlimited [ʌnˈlɪmɪtɪd] *adjective* with no limits; ***the bank offered him unlimited credit***; **unlimited liability** = situation where a sole trader or each partner is responsible for all the firm's debts with no limit to the amount each may have to pay

unlisted [ʌnˈlɪstɪd] adjective **unlisted company** = company whose shares are not listed on the stock exchange; **unlisted securities** = shares which are not listed on the Stock Exchange; **unlisted securities market (USM)** = formerly the market for buying and selling shares which were not listed on the main Stock Exchange, now replaced by the Alternative Investment Market (AIM); *see also* DELIST

unload [ʌnˈləʊd] *verb* **(a)** to take goods off (a ship, etc.); ***the ship is unloading at Hamburg***; ***we need a fork-lift truck to unload the lorry***; ***there are no unloading facilities for container ships*** **(b)** to sell (shares, currency, etc., which the owner does not want or which do not seem attractive); ***we tried to unload our shareholding as soon as the company published its accounts***

unlock [ʌnˈlɒk] verb **to unlock value** = to sell undervalued assets and so increase the value of a company to its shareholders

unpaid [ʌnˈpeɪd] *adjective* not paid; **unpaid balance** = balance of a loan or invoice which still has to be paid after a part payment or instalment payment has been made; **unpaid cheque** = cheque which has been deposited but which is bounced by the bank on which it is written, so the account of the person who should receive is not credited; **unpaid invoices** = invoices which have not been paid

unprofitable [ʌn'prɒfɪtəbl] *adjective* which is not profitable

> the airline has already eliminated a number of unprofitable flights
>
> *Duns Business Month*

unquoted shares [ʌn'kwəʊtɪd 'ʃeəz] *plural noun* shares which have no Stock Exchange quotation

unrealized [ʌn'rɪəlaɪzd] *adjective* not sold to make a profit; **unrealized capital gain** = investment which is showing a profit but has not been sold; **unrealized profit** = profit made when an asset has increased in value but has not been sold (NOTE: also called **paper profit**)

unredeemed pledge [ʌnrɪ'di:md 'pledʒ] *noun* pledge which the borrower has not taken back by paying back his loan

unregistered [ʌn'redʒɪstəd] *adjective* (company) which has not been registered

unsecured [ʌnsɪ'kjʊəd] adjective **unsecured creditor** = creditor who is owed money, but has no security from the debtor for the debt; **unsecured debt** = debt which is not guaranteed by a charge on assets or by any collateral; **unsecured loan** = loan made with no security

unsettled [ʌn'setld] *adjective* which changes often or which is upset; ***the market was unsettled by the news of the failure of the takeover bid***

unstable [ʌn'steɪbl] *adjective* not stable, changing frequently; ***unstable exchange rates***

unsubsidized [ʌn'sʌbsɪdaɪzd] *adjective* with no subsidy

unsuccessful [ʌnsək'sesfʊl] *adjective* not successful; ***an unsuccessful businessman***; ***the project was expensive and unsuccessful***

unsuccessfully [ʌnsək'sesfʊli] *adverb* with no success; ***the company unsuccessfully tried to break into the South American market***

unweighted [ʌn'weɪtɪd] *adjective* without giving any extra value to a certain factor

> an index of shares whose membership is determined by size but where the share price movements are unweighted would resolve the problem of indices exerting influence on the markets
>
> *The Times*

up [ʌp] *adverb & preposition* in a higher position or to a higher position; ***the inflation rate is going up steadily***; ***shares were up slightly at the end of the day***

upcoming [ʌp'kʌmɪŋ] *adjective* which will come in the near future; ***the company is banking on its upcoming new drug to treat strokes***

update [ʌp'deɪt] **1** *noun* information added to something to make it up to date **2** *verb* to revise something so that it is always up to date; ***the figures are updated annually***; **to update a passbook** = to bring a bank passbook up to date, showing entries which have taken place since the last time it was updated (normally done through the computer at the relevant bank, although in some cases it has to be sent to the main office of the bank or building society)

up front ['ʌp 'frʌnt] *adverb* in advance; **money up front** = payment in advance; ***they are asking for £100,000 up front before they will consider the deal***; ***he had to put money up front before he could clinch the deal***

uplift ['ʌplɪft] *noun* increase; ***the contract provides for an annual uplift of charges***

up market ['ʌp 'mɑ:kɪt] **1** *adverb* more expensive, appealing to a wealthy section of the population; **the company has decided to move up market** = the company has decided to start to produce more luxury items **2** *noun* market which is rising; ***how your emerging growth fund performs in a down market is just as important as in an up market*** (NOTE: the opposite is **down market**)

upscale ['ʌpskeɪl] *adjective* upmarket, relatively wealthy

> it is uniquely positioned to please the vast masses who represent Middle America - not too upscale, not too low rent
>
> *Fortune*

upset price ['ʌpset 'praɪs] *noun* lowest price which the seller will accept at an auction

upside ['ʌpsaɪd] noun **upside potential** = possibility for a share to increase in value (NOTE: the opposite is **downside**)

upstream ['ʌpstri:m] *adjective* referring to the operations of a company at the beginning of a process (as drilling for oil as an operation of a petroleum company); *compare* DOWNSTREAM

> even with generous assumptions, the upstream business is probably not worth a great deal

> more than 70p per share at present
>
> *The Times*

upswing ['ʌpswɪŋ] *noun* upward movement of share prices (NOTE: the opposite is **downswing**)

> it helped the young fund take advantage of the market's wild upswings
>
> *Smart Money*

> we pointed out that fund-manager turnover seemed to be on the upswing
>
> *Barron's*

uptick ['ʌptɪk] *noun US* price of a share sold, which is higher than the previous price

up to ['ʌp 'tʊ] *adverb* as far as, as high as; ***we will buy at prices up to £25***

upturn ['ʌptɜ:n] *noun* movement towards higher sales or profits; ***an upturn in the economy***; ***an upturn in the market***

upward ['ʌpwəd] *adjective* towards a higher position; ***an upward movement***

upwards ['ʌpwədz] *adverb* towards a higher position; ***the market moved upwards after the news of the budget***

US *or* **USA** ['ju: 'es or 'ju: 'es 'eɪ] = UNITED STATES (OF AMERICA) **US Treasury bonds** = bonds issued by the US Treasury

use 1 [ju:s] *noun* way in which something can be used; **directions for use** = instructions on how to run a machine; **to make use of something** = to use something; **in use** = being worked; **items for personal use** = items which a person will use for himself, not on behalf of the company; **he has the use of a company car** = he has a company car which he uses privately; **land zoned for industrial use** = land where planning permission has been given to build factories **2** [ju:z] *verb* to take a machine, a company, a process, etc., and work with it; ***we use airmail for all our overseas correspondence***; ***the photocopier is being used all the time***; ***they use freelancers for most of their work***

user ['ju:zə] *noun* person who uses something; **end user** = person who actually uses a product; **user's guide** *or* **handbook** = book showing someone how to use something

user-friendly ['ju:zə'frendli] *adjective* which a user finds easy to work; ***these programs are really user-friendly***

usual ['ju:ʒuəl] *adjective* normal or ordinary; ***our usual terms*** *or* ***usual conditions are thirty days' credit***; ***the usual practice is to have the contract signed by the MD***; ***the usual hours of work are from 9.30 to 5.30***

usury ['ju:ʒəri] *noun* lending money at very high interest

utility [ju:'tɪlɪti] *noun* company that provides an essential service, such as water, gas, electricity, transportation, etc.; **electric utility stocks** = shares in electricity companies

> the stock has barely edged up, but utilities as a group are off about 3% this year
>
> *Barrons*

utilize ['ju:tɪlaɪz] *verb* to use

utilization [ju:tɪlaɪ'zeɪʃn] *noun* making use of something; **capacity utilization** = using something as much as possible

> control permits the manufacturer to react to changing conditions on the plant floor and to keep people and machines at a high level of utilization
>
> *Duns Business Month*

Vv

valorem [və'lɔːrəm] *see* AD VALOREM

valuable ['væljubl] *adjective* which is worth a lot of money; **valuable property** *or* **valuables** = personal items which are worth a lot of money

valuation [vælju'eɪʃn] *noun* estimate of how much something is worth; ***to ask for a valuation of a property before making an offer for it***; **stock valuation** = estimating the value of stock at the end of an accounting period; **to buy a shop with stock at valuation** = to pay for the stock the same amount as its value as estimated by a valuer

value ['væljuː] **1** *noun* amount of money which something is worth; ***he imported goods to the value of £250***; ***the fall in the value of sterling***; ***the valuer put the value of the stock at £25,000***; **good value (for money)** = a bargain, something which is worth the price paid for it; ***that restaurant gives value for money***; ***buy that computer now - it is very good value***; ***holidays in Italy are good value because of the exchange rate***; **to rise in value** = to be worth more; **to fall in value** = to be worth less; **asset value** = value of a company calculated by adding together all its assets; **book value** = value of an asset as recorded in the company's balance sheet; **'sample only - of no commercial value'** = not worth anything if sold; **declared value** = value of goods entered on a customs declaration form; **discounted value** = difference between the face value of a share and its lower market price; **face value** = value written on a coin, banknote or share; **market value** = value of an asset, of a product or of a company, if sold today; **par value** = value written on a share certificate; **portfolio value** = value of a portfolio of shares; **scarcity value** = value of something which is worth a lot because it is rare and there is a large demand for it; **surrender value** = money which an insurer will pay if an insurance policy is given up before maturity date; **value-priced goods** = goods which are good value for money; **value stocks** = shares which provide a good return on investment **2** *verb* to estimate how much money something is worth; ***he valued the stock at £25,000***; ***we are having the jewellery valued for insurance***

> the quant funds we like best mix growth and value stocks
>
> *Smart Money*

value added ['væljuː 'ædɪd] *noun* amount added to the value of a product or service, being the difference between the cost and its sale; **economic value added (EVA)** = difference between a company's profit and the cost of its capital. A company does not have simply to make a profit from its business - it has to make enough profit to cover the cost of its capital, including equity invested by shareholders; **market value added (MVA)** = difference between a company's market value and the amount of its invested capital. MVA reveals how well a company has performed over the long term in using its resources to create value; *see also* VALUE ADDED TAX

> big companies in the US and even its postal service have caught on to EVA for judging an organisation's performance accurately
>
> *Sunday Times*

> in recent years, the twin concepts of market value added (MVA) and economic value added (EVA) have gained popularity as a measure of whether a company has created wealth for shareholders or destroyed it. The system is now widely used by stockbrokers' analysts, fund managers and boards of directors as a tool for assessing management effectiveness
>
> *Sunday Times*

> if it has a positive MVA, that means value is being created for investors. But if the MVA is negative, that means investors' money has been destroyed
>
> *Sunday Times*

Value Added Tax (VAT) ['vælju: 'ædɪd 'tæks] *noun* tax imposed as a percentage of the invoice value of goods and services

> COMMENT: In the UK, VAT is organized by the Customs and Excise Department, and not by the Treasury. It is applied at each stage in the process of making or selling a product or service. Company 'A' charges VAT for their work, which is bought by Company 'B', and pays the VAT collected from 'B' to the Customs and Excise; Company 'B' can reclaim the VAT element in Company 'A''s invoice from the Customs and Excise, but will charge VAT on their work in their invoice to Company 'C'. Each company along the line charges VAT and pays it to the Customs and Excise, but claims back any VAT charged to them. The final consumer pays a price which includes VAT, and which is the final VAT revenue paid to the Customs and Excise

the directive means that the services of stockbrokers and managers of authorized unit trusts are now exempt from VAT; previously they were liable to VAT at the standard rate. Zero-rating for stockbrokers' services is still available as before, but only where the recipient of the service belongs outside the EC

Accountancy

value investing ['vælju: ɪn'vestɪŋ] *noun* basing investment strategy on the value of a company rather than simply on its share price

value investing involves looking beyond many common share price measures, such as earnings per share, instead focusing on issues such as whether a company's sales are growing faster than inflation

Money Observer

value investor ['vælju: ɪn'vestə] *noun* person who buys shares for the value of the company

however, one overall theme characterizes the value investor - the view that investment represents part ownership of a business, not just buying shares

Money Observer

by focusing on companies that are growing in real terms, value investors will not be caught out by the disappearance of inflation

Money Observer

valuer ['væljuə] *noun* person who estimates how much money something is worth

vanilla [və'nɪlə] *see* SWAP

variable ['veəriəbl] **1** *adjective* which changes; **variable costs** = money paid to produce a product which increases with the quantity made (such as wages, raw materials); **variable rate** *or* **floating rate** = rate of interest on a loan which is not fixed, but can change with the current bank interest rates; **variable redemption bond** = bond where the money to be repaid is linked to a variable, such as the price of gold at the time of payment **2** *noun* thing which varies

variance ['veəriəns] *noun* difference; **budget variance** = difference between the cost as estimated for the budget, and the actual cost; **at variance with** = which does not agree with; ***the actual sales are at variance with the sales reported by the reps***; **sales volume profit variance** = difference between the profit on the number of units actually sold and the forecast figure; **sales mix profit variance** = differing profitability of different products within a product range

variation [veəri'eɪʃn] *noun* amount by which something changes; **seasonal variations** = changes which take place because of the seasons; ***seasonal variations in buying patterns***

VAT ['vi: 'eɪ 'ti: or væt] = VALUE ADDED TAX; ***the invoice includes VAT at 17.5%***; ***the government is proposing to increase VAT to 17.5%***; ***some items (such as books) are zero-rated for VAT***; ***he does not charge VAT because he asks for payment in cash***; **VAT declaration** = statement declaring VAT income to the VAT office; **VAT invoicing** = sending of an invoice including VAT; **VAT invoice** = invoice which shows VAT separately; **VAT inspector** = government official who examines VAT returns and checks that VAT is being paid; **VAT office** = government office dealing with the collection of VAT in an area

VATman *or* **vatman** ['vætmæn] *noun* VAT inspector

vatu ['vɑ:tu:] *noun* currency used in Vanuatu

vault [vɒlt] *noun* strongroom in a bank, usually underground, where valuables can be deposited; **vault cash** = cash held by a bank in its vaults, used for day-to-day needs

VC = VENTURE CAPITALIST

VCT = VENTURE CAPITAL TRUST

velocity [və'lɒsɪti] noun **velocity of money** = rate at which money circulates in the economy, usually calculated as the GNP shown as a percentage of the stock of money supply

vending ['vendɪŋ] *noun* selling; **(automatic) vending machine** = machine which provides drinks, cigarettes, etc., when a coin is put in

vendor ['vendɔ:] *noun* **(a)** person who sells (a property); ***the solicitor acting on behalf of the vendor*** **(b)** company selling its shares on a stock market for the first time; **vendor placing** = arranging for an issue of new shares to be bought by institutions, as a means of financing the purchase of another company

venture ['ventʃə] **1** *noun* business or commercial deal which involves a risk; ***he lost money on several import ventures***; ***she has started a new venture - a computer shop***; **joint venture** = very large business project where two or more companies, often from different countries, join together; **venture capital** = capital for investment which may easily be lost in risky projects, but can also provide high returns; **venture capital fund** = fund which invests in finances houses providing venture capital; **venture capitalist (VC)** = finance house or private individual specializing in providing venture capital; **Venture Capital Trust (VCT)** = trust which invests in smaller firms which need capital to grow (money invested in a VCT must remain there for five years, and in return no capital gains are paid on £100,000 worth of VCT shares sold) **2** *verb* to risk (money)

> Venture Capital Trusts are an important plank in bridging the equity gap faced by thousands of smaller companies seeking growth finance
>
> *Evening Standard*

> we have focused the portfolios of all three VCTs on established businesses, with MBOs and MBIs accounting for the majority of investments
>
> *Evening Standard*

> we now have just short of £100m under management - the biggest venture capital trust fund in the UK
>
> *Investors Chronicle*

> several venture capitalists came courting when the company was in line for an institutional buy-out (IBO)
>
> *Evening Standard*

> venture capitalists are turning increasingly to continental Europe for fresh investment opportunities
>
> *Evening Standard*

> along with the stock market boom of the 1980s, the venture capitalists piled more and more funds into the buyout business, backing bigger and bigger deals with ever more extravagant financing structures
>
> *Guardian*

> bids for smaller companies have recently been running at around one a day, with buyers including not only larger UK or US companies but also venture capitalists - who prefer to take underpriced smaller companies private, rather than compete for overpriced unquoted situations
>
> *Money Observer*

verification [verɪfɪ'keɪʃn] *noun* checking if something is correct

verify ['verɪfaɪ] *verb* to check to see if something is correct

vertical ['vɜ:tɪkl] *adjective* upright, straight up or down; **vertical communication** = communication between senior managers via the middle management to the workers; **vertical integration** = joining two businesses together which deal with different stages in the production or sale of a product (as a shoe manufacturer buying a shoe retail chain)

vested interest ['vestɪd 'ɪntrəst] *noun* special interest in keeping an existing state of affairs; **she has a vested interest in keeping the business working** = she wants to keep the business working because she will make more money if it does

vesting day ['vestɪŋ 'deɪ] *noun* day when a formerly nationalized industry becomes owned by its new shareholders

vet [vet] *verb* to examine something carefully; ***all candidates have to be vetted by the managing director***; ***the contract has been sent to the legal department for vetting*** (NOTE: **vetting - vetted**)

viability [vaɪə'bɪlɪti] *noun* being viable, being able to make a profit

viable ['vaɪəbl] *adjective* which can work in practice; **not commercially viable** = not likely to make a profit

videoconference ["vɪdiəʊ'kɒnfərəns] *noun* linking video, audio and computer signals from different locations so that distant people can talk and see each other, as if in the same conference room

> to ensure that his agenda was taken seriously, he asked for special videoconferences to review the divisions' annual long-range forecasts before the scheduled April reviews
>
> *Fortune*

view [vju:] *noun* way of thinking about something; ***the chairman takes the view that credit should never be longer than thirty days***; **to take the long view** = to plan for a long period before your current investment will become profitable; **in view of** = because of; ***in view of the falling exchange rate, we have redrafted our sales forecasts***

viewdata ['vju:deɪtə] *noun* service on TV which gives share prices; some services also allow trading over the phone

virement ['vaɪəmənt] noun *(administration)* transfer of money from one account to another or from one section of a budget to another

virtual credit card ['vɜ:tjuəl 'kredɪt 'kɑ:d] noun *(on the internet)* technology that allows a user to setup a new credit account with a bank on the internet and then use this account number to purchase goods on the internet; this type of credit account can only be used on the internet

virtual spouse ['vɜ:tjuəl 'spaʊs] *noun US* successful working spouse of someone who works abroad (one of the two has to commute at weekends) (NOTE: also called a **trailing spouse**)

virtual tokens ['vɜ:tjuəl 'təʊkənz] noun *(on the internet)* banking technology that allows a user to transfer money from their normal bank to an internet bank and then use this credit to purchase goods on the internet

Visa ['vi:zə] international credit card organization (another is MasterCard)

visible ['vɪzɪbl] *adjective* which can be seen; **visible imports** *or* **exports** *or* **visible trade** = real products which are imported or exported; *compare* INVISIBLE

vivos ['vaɪvəs] noun **gift inter vivos** = present given to another living person

void [vɔɪd] **1** *adjective* not legally valid; **the contract was declared null and void** = the contract was said to be no longer valid **2** verb **to void a contract** = to make a contract invalid

voidable ['vɔɪdəbl] *adjective* (contract) which can be annulled

volatile ['vɒlətaɪl] *adjective* (market or price) which is not stable, but which rises and falls sharply

> blue chip stocks are the least volatile while smaller stocks are the most volatile
>
> *The Times*

> the investment markets appear to have become ever more volatile, with interest rates moving at times to extreme levels, and the stock market veering wildly from boom to slump and back again
>
> *Financial Times Review*

> the FTSE 100 Index ended another volatile session a net 96.3 easier at 6027
>
> *Financial Times*

volatility [vɒlə'tɪlɪti] *noun* being volatile; ***investors are recommended to keep their money in building society accounts because the increasing volatility of the stock market***; **volatility rating** = calculation of how volatile a share is, by calculating how much its performance is different from the normal pattern

volume ['vɒlju:m] *noun* **(a)** quantity of items made or sold; **volume discount** = discount given to a customer who buys a large quantity of goods; **volume of output** = number of items produced **(b)** quantity of shares traded on a stock market; ***average daily volume: 130,000 shares***; **volume of trade** *or* **volume of business** = number of items sold, the number of shares sold on the Stock Exchange during a day's trading; ***the company has maintained the same volume of business in spite of the recession***

> to decide how much of a stock to buy, a program looks at a stock's trading volume
>
> *Smart Money*

> daily trading volumes on the major markets suggest there was no great avalanche of selling;

```
but there was little or no
buying either and, hence, no
support on the downside
```

Financial Times Review

volume of sales *or* **sales volume** ['vɒljuːm əv 'seɪlz] *noun* **(a)** *GB* number of items sold; **low** *or* **high volume of sales** = small or large number of items sold **(b)** *US* amount of money produced by sales (NOTE: the British equivalent is **turnover**)

voluntary ['vɒləntri] *adjective* **(a)** done without being forced; **voluntary liquidation** *or* **voluntary winding up** = situation where a company itself decides it must close and sell its assets; **voluntary redundancy** = situation where the worker asks to be made redundant, usually in return for a large payment **(b)** done without being paid; **voluntary organization** = organization which has no paid staff

voluntarily ['vɒləntrəli] *adverb* without being forced or paid

vostro account ['vɒstrəʊ ə'kaʊnt] *noun* account held by a correspondent bank for a foreign bank; *see also* NOSTRO ACCOUNT

vote [vəʊt] **1** *noun* marking a paper, holding up your hand, etc., to show your opinion, to show who you want to be elected; **to take a vote on a proposal** *or* **to put a proposal to the vote** = to ask people present at a meeting to say if they do or do not agree with the proposal; **casting vote** = vote used by the chairman in the case where the votes for and against a proposal are equal; ***the chairman has the casting vote***; ***he used his casting vote to block the motion***; **postal vote** = election where the voters send in their voting papers by post **2** *verb* to show an opinion by marking a paper or by holding up your hand at a meeting; ***the meeting voted to close the factory***; ***52% of the members voted for Mr Smith as chairman***; **to vote for a proposal** *or* **to vote against a proposal** = to say that you agree or do not agree with a proposal; **two directors were voted off the board at the AGM** = the AGM voted to dismiss two directors; **she was voted on to the committee** = she was elected a member of the committee

voter ['vəʊtə] *noun* person who votes

voting ['vəʊtɪŋ] *noun* act of making a vote; **voting paper** = paper on which the voter puts a cross to show for whom he wants to vote; **voting rights** = rights of shareholders to vote at company meetings; **voting shares** = shares which give the holder the right to vote at company meetings; **non-voting shares** = shares which do not allow the shareholder to vote at company meetings

voucher ['vaʊtʃə] *noun* **(a)** paper which is given instead of money; **cash voucher** = paper which can be exchanged for cash; ***with every £20 of purchases, the customer gets a cash voucher to the value of £2***; **gift voucher** = card, bought in a store, which is given as a present and which must be exchanged in that store for goods; **luncheon voucher** = ticket, given by an employer to a worker, which can be exchanged in a restaurant for food **(b)** written document from an auditor to show that the accounts are correct, that money has really been paid

Ww

wage [weɪdʒ] *noun* money paid (usually in cash each week) to a worker for work done; ***she is earning a good wage** or **good wages in the supermarket***; **basic wage** = normal pay without any extra payments; ***the basic wage is £110 a week, but you can expect to earn more than that with overtime***; **hourly wage** *or* **wage per hour** = amount of money paid for an hour's work; **minimum wage** = lowest hourly wage which a company can legally pay its workers; **wage adjustments** = changes made to wages; **wage claim** = asking for an increase in wages; **wages clerk** = office worker who deals with the pay of other workers; **wage differentials** = differences in salary between workers in similar types of jobs; **wage drift** = difference between wages and money actually earned (the difference being made up by bonus payments, overtime payments, etc.); **wage freeze** *or* **freeze on wages** = period when wages are not allowed to increase; **wage indexation** = linking of increases to the percentage rise in the cost of living; **wage levels** = rates of pay for different types of work; **wage negotiations** = discussions between management and workers about pay; **wage packet** = envelope containing money and pay slip; **wages policy** = government policy on what percentage increases should be paid to workers; **wage-price spiral** = situation where price rises encourage higher wage demands which in turn make prices rise; **wage scale** = list of wages, showing different rates of pay for different jobs in the same company

> COMMENT: the term 'wages' refers to weekly or hourly pay for workers, usually paid in cash. For workers paid by a monthly cheque, the term used is 'salary'

> European economies are being held back by rigid labor markets and wage structures
>
> *Duns Business Month*

> real wages have been held down dramatically: they have risen at an annual rate of only 1% in the last two years
>
> *Sunday Times*

wage-earner ['weɪdʒ'ɜ:nə] *noun* person who earns money in a job

wage-earning ['weɪdʒ'ɜ:nɪŋ] adjective **the wage-earning population** = people who have jobs and earn money

waive [weɪv] *verb* to give up (a right); ***he waived his claim to the estate***; **to waive a payment** = to say that payment is not necessary

waiver ['weɪvə] *noun* giving up (a right); removing the conditions (of a rule); ***if you want to work without a permit, you will have to apply for a waiver***; **waiver clause** = clause in a contract giving the conditions under which the rights in the contract can be given up

wall of money ['wɔ:l əv 'mʌni] *noun* large amount of money ready to be invested on the stock market (especially, money from new investment funds, or foreign investors) (NOTE: similar to the **weight of money**)

wallpaper ['wɔ:lpeɪpə] *noun* shares issued in large numbers during a takeover bid where the purchasing company offers them in exchange for the shares in the company being bought

Wall Street ['wɔ:l 'stri:t] *noun* street in New York where the Stock Exchange is situated; the American financial centre; ***a Wall Street analyst***; ***she writes the Wall Street column in the newspaper*** (NOTE: also simply called **'The Street'**)

> the analyst estimates earning of $1.65 for 1998 and $1.80 for 1999, in line with the Wall Street consensus
>
> *Barron's*

warehouse ['weəhaʊs] *noun* large building where goods are stored; **bonded warehouse** = warehouse where goods are stored until excise duty has been paid; **warehouse capacity** = space available in a warehouse; **price ex warehouse** = price for a product which is to be collected from the manufacturer's or agent's warehouse and so does not include delivery

warehousing ['weəhaʊzɪŋ] *noun* **(a)** act of storing goods; ***warehousing costs are rising rapidly*** **(b)** illegal action where someone buys shares in a company on behalf of another company and holds them in readiness to be surrendered when the second company makes a takeover bid

War Loan ['wɔ: 'ləʊn] *noun* government loan issued in time of war (it is the only undated irredeemable British government stock)

warning ['wɔ:nɪŋ] *noun* notice of possible danger; **health warning** = warning message printed on advertisements for investments, stating that the value of investments can fall as well as rise (this is a legal requirement in the UK)

> the economic crisis in Asia and the strength of sterling remain the favourite excuses offered by UK companies for downbeat trading statements and profit warnings
>
> *Investors Chronicle*

warrant ['wɒrənt] *noun* official document which allows someone to do something; **dividend warrant** = cheque which makes payment of a dividend; **share warrant** = document which says that someone has the right to a number of shares in a company; **warrant holder** = person who holds a warrant for shares; **warrant premium** = premium paid to buy share warrants, above the price of the shares it entitles you to

> warrants give the right to subscribe for ordinary shares at a fixed price and on fixed dates
>
> *Investors Chronicle*

> the rights issue will grant shareholders free warrants to subscribe for further new shares
>
> *Financial Times*

> warrants generally command a premium, which shows how much the share price needs to rise to make the warrants worth exercising. The premium is the percentage amount by which the total acquisition cost (warrant price plus exercise price) exceeds the share price
>
> *Investors Chronicle*

> warrants are also assessed on their gearing, calculated by dividing the share price by the warrant price
>
> *Investors Chronicle*

warrantee [wɒrən'ti:] *noun* person who is given a warranty

warrantor [wɒrən'tɔ:] *noun* person who gives a warranty

warranty ['wɒrənti] *noun* **(a)** guarantee, a legal document which promises that a machine will work properly or that an item is of good quality; ***the car is sold with a twelve-month warranty***; ***the warranty covers spare parts but not labour costs*** **(b)** promise in a contract; **breach of warranty** = failing to do something which is a part of a contract **(c)** statement made by an insured person which declares that the facts stated by him are true

wash sale ['wɒʃ 'seɪl] *noun US* sale and then repurchase of a block of shares (similar to the British 'bed-and-breakfast deal', though in the USA is may also be used as a means of creating fictitious trading volume)

washing ['wɒʃɪŋ] *noun US* selling and buying back the same security, so as to reduce tax liability, or to increase trading volume; *see also* BOND-WASHING

waste [weɪst] *verb* to use more than is needed; ***to waste money*** *or* ***paper*** *or* ***electricity*** *or* ***time***; ***the MD does not like people wasting his time with minor details***; ***we turned off all the heating so as not to waste energy***

wasting asset ['weɪstɪŋ 'æsɪt] *noun* asset which becomes gradually less valuable as time goes by (for example a short lease on a property)

watchdog ['wɒtʃdɒg] *noun* person or group that examines public spending or financial deals, etc.; **the City watchdog** = the Financial Services Authority (FSA), which supervises the financial institutions

watcher ['wɒtʃə] noun **market watcher** = person who follows stock market trends closely

water down ['wɔ:tə 'daʊn] *verb* to make less strong; ***the family's holdings have been watered down by the creation of the new shares***

weak [wi:k] *adjective* not strong, not active; **weak currency** = currency which is trading at a low level against other currencies; **weak market** = share market where prices tend to fall because there are no buyers; **share prices remained weak** = share prices did not rise

weaken ['wi:kn] *verb* to become weak; **the market weakened** = share prices fell

> the Fed started to ease monetary policy months ago as the first stories appeared about weakening demand in manufacturing industry
>
> *Sunday Times*

weakness ['wi:knəs] *noun* being weak (NOTE: the opposite is **strength**)

> indications of weakness in the US economy were contained in figures from the Fed on industrial production
>
> *Financial Times*

wealth tax ['welθ 'tæks] *noun* tax on money, property or investments owned by individual taxpayers

Wechsel ['veχzel] *German word meaning* foreign exchange

weight [weɪt] **1** *noun* **(a)** measurement of how heavy something is; **to sell fruit by weight** = the price is per pound or per kilo of the fruit; **false weight** = weight on a shop scales which is wrong and so cheats customers; **gross weight** = weight of both the container and its contents; **net weight** = weight of goods after deducting the packing material and container; **to give short weight** = to give less than one should; **inspector of weights and measures** = government official who inspects goods sold in shops to see if the quantities and weights are correct; *see also* UNDERWEIGHT **(b) weight of money** = large amount of money ready to be invested on the stock market (especially cash available in pension funds) (NOTE: similar to the **wall of money**) **2** *verb* to give an extra value to a certain factor; **weighted average** = average which is calculated taking several factors into account, giving some more value than others; **weighted index** = index where some important items are given more value than less important ones; **volume-weighted prices** = prices which calculated according to the volume of turnover

> as things stand, the institutions will not receive anything like enough stock to weight their portfolios and their buying in the secondary market after the issue is expected to push prices higher
>
> *The Times*

> the trader makes his profits only to the extent that he can buy more cheaply than the volume-weighted prices
>
> *Barron's*

> weighted indices eliminate the disproportionate influence of movements in the price of small capitalization stocks, but by favouring big shares they replace one distortion with another
>
> *The Times*

> most of the indices prepared by FTSE International are adjusted to attach greater importance or 'weight' to the movements in larger company share prices
>
> *The Times*

weighting ['weɪtɪŋ] *noun* additional salary or wages paid to compensate for living in an expensive part of the country; ***salary plus a London weighting***

wheeler-dealer ['wi:lə'di:lə] *noun* person who lives on money from a series of profitable business deals

whisper ['wɪspə] noun **whisper number** = figure which is mentioned as a rumour

> the analysts and traders work the phones and report hearing an even higher whisper number of $1 a share
>
> *Smart Money*

whistle blower ['wɪsl 'bləʊə] *noun* employee of a company who reports its illegal activities to the authorities

white-collar ['waɪt'kɒlə] *adjective* referring to office workers; **white-collar crime** = crime (especially fraud) committed by office workers, such as computer analysts; **white-collar union** = trade union formed of white-collar workers; **white-collar worker** = worker in an office, not in a factory; **white-collar job** = job in an office

white knight ['waɪt 'naɪt] *noun* person or company that rescues a firm in financial difficulties, especially saving a firm from being taken over by an unacceptable purchaser

White Paper ['waɪt 'peɪpə] *noun GB* report from the government on a particular problem

whizz kid ['wɪz 'kɪd] *noun* person who tries to build up a business empire by frequent purchases of companies financed by bank borrowings or junk bonds

whole-life insurance *or* **policy** [həʊl'laɪf ɪn'ʃuərəns or 'pɒlɪsi] *noun* insurance policy where the insured person pays a fixed premium each year and the insurance company pays a sum when he dies

wholesale ['həʊlseɪl] *noun & adverb* buying goods from manufacturers and selling in large quantities to traders who then sell in smaller quantities to the general public; **wholesale banking** = banking services between merchant banks and other financial institutions (as opposed to 'retail banking'); **wholesale dealer** = person who buys in bulk from manufacturers and sells to retailers; **wholesale market** = interbank money market, where banks and other financial institutions deal with each other; **wholesale price** = price of a product which is wholesale; **Wholesale Price Index** = index showing the rises and falls of wholesale prices of manufactured goods (usually moving about two months before a similar movement takes place on the Retail Price Index); **he buys wholesale and sells retail** = he buys goods in bulk at a wholesale discount and then sells in small quantities to the public

wholesaler ['həʊlseɪlə] *noun* person who buys goods in bulk from manufacturers and sells them to retailers

wholly-owned subsidiary ['həʊliəʊnd sʌb'sɪdiəri] *noun* company which is owned completely by another company

will [wɪl] *noun* legal document where someone says what should happen to his property when he dies; ***according to her will, all her property is left to her children***

> COMMENT: a will should best be drawn up by a solicitor; it can also be written on a form which can be bought from a stationery shop. To be valid, a will must be dated and witnessed by a third party (i.e., by someone who is not mentioned in the will)

windfall ['wɪnfɔːl] *noun* sudden winning of money, sudden profit which is not expected; **windfall profit** = sudden unexpected profit; **windfall (profits) tax** = tax on sudden profits; **windfall wealth** = wealth which comes from a windfall

> Detroit has at times spread its windfall wealth to shareholders through higher dividends
>
> *Fortune*

> 1998 wasn't such a great year for investors seeking cash and share windfalls from demutualizing building societies
>
> *Investors Chronicle*

winding up ['waɪndɪŋ 'ʌp] *noun* liquidation, the closing of a company and selling of its assets; **a compulsory winding up order** = order from a court saying that a company must be wound up; *see also* VOLUNTARY

windmill ['wɪnmɪl] *(informal)* = ACCOMMODATION BILL

window ['wɪndəʊ] *noun* **(a) shop window** = large window in a shop front, where customers can see goods displayed; **window envelope** = envelope with a hole in it covered with plastic like a window, so that the address on the letter inside can be seen; **window shopping** = looking at goods in shop windows, without buying anything **(b)** short period when something is available; **window of opportunity** = short period which allows an action to take place; *US* **discount window** = way in which the Federal Reserve grants loans to a bank by giving advances on the security of Treasury bills which the bank is holding

window dressing ['wɪndəʊ 'dresɪŋ] *noun* **(a)** putting goods on display in a shop window, so that they attract customers **(b)** putting on a display to make a business seem better or more profitable or more efficient than it really is

wind up ['waɪnd 'ʌp] *verb* **(a)** to end (a meeting); ***he wound up the meeting with a vote of thanks to the committee*** **(b) to wind up a company** = to put a company into liquidation; ***the court ordered the company to be wound up*** (NOTE: **winding - wound)**

WIP = WORK IN PROGRESS

wipe off ['waɪp 'ɒf] *verb* to remove completely

> though the crisis has wiped billions of pounds off world stock market values, it has boosted liquidity in the London stock market
>
> *Financial Weekly*

wire transfer ['waɪə 'trænsfə] *noun* telegraphic transfer, the transfer of money from one account to another by telegraph (used often for sending money abroad, it is quicker but more expensive than sending a draft through the post)

witching hour ['wɪtʃɪŋ 'auə] *noun* critical moment on a stock exchange, where several options expire at the same time; **triple**

witching hour = day when three major types of futures contract fall due at the same time; *see also* TRIPLE WITCHING HOUR

withdraw [wɪθ'drɔ:] *verb* **(a)** to take (money) out of an account; ***to withdraw money from the bank** or **from your account; you can withdraw up to £50 from any bank on presentation of a bank card*** **(b)** to take back (an offer); **one of the company's backers has withdrawn** = he stopped supporting the company financially; ***to withdraw a takeover bid; the chairman asked him to withdraw the remarks he has made about the finance director*** (NOTE: **withdrawing - withdrew - has withdrawn)**

withdrawal [wɪθ'drɔ:l] *noun* removing money from an account; **withdrawal without penalty at seven days' notice** = money can be taken out of a deposit account, without losing any interest, provided that seven days' notice has been given; ***to give seven days' notice of withdrawal***; **early withdrawal** = removing money from a term deposit account before due date (usually incurring a penalty)

withholding tax [wɪθ'həʊldɪŋ 'tæks] *noun* (i) tax which takes money away from interest or dividends before they are paid to the investor (usually applied to non- resident investors); (ii) *US* income tax deducted from the paycheck of a worker before he is paid

with profits ['wɪθ 'prɒfits] *adverb* (insurance policy) which guarantees the policyholder a share in the profits of the fund in which the premiums are invested; **with-profit bond** = bond which guarantees a capital return plus the profits which have accumulated during its lifetime

> if you cannot stomach the ups and downs of the stock market, but want a better rate of return than the average bank or building society account, with-profit bonds are a good halfway house between cash and equities
>
> *Sunday Times*

> with-profit holders can also benefit from capital growth in the form of bonuses
>
> *Sunday Times*

won [wɒn] *noun* currency used in North and South Korea

work [wɜ:k] *noun* **(a)** things done using the hands or brain; **casual work** = work where the workers are hired for a short period; **clerical work** = work done in an office; **work in progress (WIP)** = value of goods being manufactured which are not complete at the end of an accounting period **(b)** job, something done to earn money; **work permit** = official document which allows someone who is not a citizen to work in a country

> the control of materials from purchased parts through work in progress to finished goods provides manufacturers with an opportunity to reduce the amount of money tied up in materials
>
> *Duns Business Month*

> the quality of the work environment demanded by employers and employees alike
>
> *Lloyd's List*

worker ['wɜ:kə] *noun* person who is employed; **casual worker** = worker who can be hired for a short period; **clerical worker** = person who works in an office; **factory worker** = person who works in a factory; **worker director** = director of a company who is a representative of the workforce; **worker representation on the board** = having a representative of the workers as a director of the company

workforce ['wɜ:kfɔ:s] *noun* all the workers (in an office or factory)

working ['wɜ:kɪŋ] *adjective* **(a)** which works; **working control of a company** = having enough shares in a company to able to control all its actions (usually, this means 51% of shares); **working partner** = partner who works in a partnership; **working underwriter** = member of a Lloyd's syndicate who actively generates business (as opposed to the 'names' who put up the security) **(b)** referring to work; **working capital** = current assets of a company (cash and stocks) less any liabilities, which a company needs to be able to continue trading (also called 'net current assets'); **working conditions** = general state of the place where people work (if it is hot, noisy, dark, dangerous, etc.); **the normal working week** = the usual number of hours worked per week; ***even though he is a freelance, he works a normal working week***

workload ['wɜ:kləʊd] *noun* amount of work which a person has to do; ***he has difficulty in coping with his heavy workload***

work out ['wɜk 'aʊt] *verb* to calculate; ***he worked out the costs on the back of an envelope; he worked out the discount at***

15%; ***she worked out the discount on her calculator***

works [wɜːks] *noun* factory; ***an industrial works***; ***an engineering works***; **works committee** *or* **works council** = committee of workers and management which discusses the organization of work in a factory; **price ex works** = price not including transport from the manufacturer's factory; **the works manager** = person in charge of a works

work-sharing [ˈwɜːkʃeərɪŋ] *noun* system where two part-timers share one job

workspace [ˈwɜːkspeɪs] *noun* memory, the space available on a computer for temporary work

workstation [ˈwɜːksteɪʃn] *noun* desk with a computer terminal, printer, telephone, etc., where a word-processing operator works

world [wɜːld] *noun* **(a)** the earth; **the world market for steel** = the possible sales of steel in the whole world; **he has world rights to a product** = he has the right to sell the product anywhere in the world **(b)** people in a particular business, people with a special interest; ***the world of big business***; ***the world of publishing*** *or* ***the publishing world***; ***the world of lawyers*** *or* ***the legal world***

---

the EC pays farmers 27 cents a pound for sugar and sells it on the world market for 5 cents

Duns Business Month

---

manufactures and services were the fastest growing sectors of world trade

Australian Financial Review

World Bank [ˈwɜːld ˈbæŋk] *noun* central bank, controlled by the United Nations, whose funds come from the member states of the UN and which lends money to member states (its official title is the International Bank for Reconstruction and Development)

World Trade Organization (WTO) [ˈwɜːld ˈtreɪd ɑːgənaɪˈzeɪʃn] international organization set up with the aim of reducing restrictions in trade between countries (replacing GATT)

worldwide [wɜːldˈwaɪd] *adjective & adverb* everywhere in the world; ***the company has a worldwide network of distributors***; ***worldwide sales*** *or* ***sales worldwide have topped two million units***; ***this make of computer is available worldwide***

worth [wɜːθ] **1** *adjective* having a value or a price; ***do not get it repaired - it is only worth £25***; ***the car is worth £6,000 on the secondhand market***; **he is worth £10m** = his property, investments, etc., would sell for £10m; **what are ten pounds worth in dollars?** = what is the equivalent of £10 in dollars? (NOTE: always follows the verb **to be**) **2** *noun* value; **give me ten pounds' worth of petrol** = give me as much petrol as £10 will buy

worthless [ˈwɜːθləs] *adjective* having no value; ***the cheque is worthless if it is not signed***

wraparound mortgage [ˈræpəraʊnd ˈmɔːgɪdʒ] *noun US* type of second mortgage where the borrower pays interest only to the second lender (who then pays the interest payments on the first mortgage to the first lender)

wreck [rek] **1** *noun* **(a)** ship which has sunk or which has been badly damaged and cannot float; ***they saved the cargo from the wreck***; ***oil poured out of the wreck of the tanker*** **(b)** company which has collapsed; ***he managed to save some of his money from the wreck of the investment trust***; ***investors lost thousands of pounds in the wreck of the investment company*** **2** *verb* to damage badly, to ruin; ***they are trying to salvage the wrecked tanker***; ***the negotiations were wrecked by the unions***

writ [rɪt] *noun* legal document ordering someone to do something or not to do something; ***the court issued a writ to prevent the trade union from going on strike***; **to serve someone with a writ** *or* **to serve a writ on someone** = to give someone a writ officially, so that he has to obey it

write down [ˈraɪt ˈdaʊn] *verb* to note an asset at a lower value than previously; ***the car is written down in the company's books***; **written-down value** = value of an asset in a company's accounts after it has been written down; **write-down allowance** = allowance for the depreciation of an asset over a period of years

writedown [ˈraɪtdaʊn] *noun* noting of an asset at a lower value

---

the holding company has seen its earnings suffer from big writedowns in conjunction with its $1 billion loan portfolio

Duns Business Month

---

write off [ˈraɪt ˈɒf] *verb* (i) to cancel (a debt); (ii) to remove an asset from the accounts as having no value; ***to write off bad debts***; **two cars were written off after the accident** = the insurance company considered that both cars were a total loss; **the cargo was written**

off as a total loss = the cargo was so badly damaged that the insurers said it had no value

> $30 million from usual company borrowings will either be amortized or written off in one sum
>
> *Australian Financial Review*

write-off ['raɪtɒf] *noun* total loss, cancellation of a bad debt, removal of an asset's value in a company's accounts; ***the car was a write-off; to allow for write-offs in the yearly accounts***

write out ['raɪt 'aʊt] *verb* to write in full; ***she wrote out the minutes of the meeting from her notes***; **to write out a cheque** = to write the words and figures on a cheque and then sign it

writer ['raɪtə] *noun* person who writes a cheque; **writer of an option** = person who sells an option

writing ['raɪtɪŋ] *noun* something which has been written; ***to put the agreement in writing; he has difficulty in reading my writing***

WTO = WORLD TRADE ORGANIZATION

Xx Yy Zz

xa (ex-all) *noun* share price where the share is sold without the dividend, rights issue, or any other current issue; **xc (ex-capitalization)** = share price where the share is sold without a recent scrip issue; **xd (ex dividend)** = share price not including the right to receive the current dividend; **xr (ex-rights)** = share price where the share is sold without a recent rights issue

Yankee ['jæŋki:] **Yankee bank** = foreign bank trading in the US

> although most corporate bonds shook off the doom and gloom of Asia to rally nicely in February, a few sectors, like the debt of 'Yankee' banks and insurance companies, stubbornly lagged behind
>
> *Barron's*

Yankee bond ['jæŋki: 'bɒnd] *noun* dollar bond issued in the American market by a non-US company; *compare* BULLDOG, SAMURAI

year [jɜ:] *noun* period of twelve months; **calendar year** = year from January 1st to December 31st; **financial year** = the twelve month period for a firm's accounts; **fiscal year** = twelve month period on which taxes are calculated (in the UK it is April 6th to April 5th of the following year); **year end** = the end of the financial year, when a company's accounts are prepared; ***the accounts department has started work on the year-end accounts***

yearbook ['jɜ:bʊk] *noun* reference book which is published each year with updated or new information

yearling bond ['jɜ:lɪŋ 'bɒnd] *noun* local authority bond which matures in 12 months

yearly ['jɜ:li] *adjective* happening once a year; ***yearly payment***; ***yearly premium of £250***

Yellow Book ['jeləʊ 'bʊk] *noun* publication by the London Stock Exchange which gives details of the regulations covering the listing of companies on the exchange

yen [jen] *noun* money used in Japan (NOTE: usually written as ¥ before a figure: **¥2,700:** say 'two thousand seven hundred yen')

yield [ji:ld] **1** *noun* money produced as a return on an investment, shown as a percentage of the money invested; **current yield** = dividend calculated as a percentage of the price paid per share; ***share with a current yield of 5%***; **dividend yield** = dividend expressed as a percentage of the price of a share; **earnings yield** = money earned in dividends per share as a percentage of the current market price of the share; **effective yield** = actual yield shown as a percentage of the price paid; **fixed yield** = fixed percentage return which does not change; **flat yield** = interest rate as a percentage of the price paid for fixed- interest stock; **gross yield** = profit from investments before tax is deducted; **high yield** = high return on investment; ***a high yield fund***; **income yield** = actual percentage yield of government stocks, the fixed interest being shown as a percentage of the market price; **initial yield** = expected yield on a new unit trust; **interest yield** = yield on a fixed-interest investment; **maturity yield** *US* **yield to maturity** = calculation of the yield on a fixed-interest investment, assuming it is bought at a certain price and held to maturity; **yield curve** = graph showing the yields on different types of investment; **negative yield curve** = situation where the yield on a long-term investment is less than on a short-term investment; **positive yield curve** = situation where the yield on a long-term investment is more than on a short-term investment; **running yield** = yield on fixed interest securities, where the interest is shown as a percentage of the price paid **2** *verb* to produce (as interest or dividend, etc.); ***government stocks which yield a small interest***; ***shares which yield 10%***

> COMMENT: to work out the yield on an investment, take the gross dividend per annum, multiply it by 100 and divide by the price you paid for it: an investment paying a dividend of 20p per share and costing £3.00, is yielding 6.66%

> if you wish to cut your risks you should go for shares with yields higher than average
>
> *Investors Chronicle*

yuan [ju'ɑːn] *noun* currency used in China

zaire [zæ'iːə] *noun* currency used in the Democratic Republic of Congo

zero ['zɪərəʊ] *noun* **(a)** nought, number 0; ***the code for international calls is zero one zero (010)*** **zero inflation** = inflation at 0% **(b)** *(informal)* = ZERO DIVIDEND PREFERENCE SHARE

zero-coupon bond *or* **zero-rated bond** ['zɪərəʊ'kuːpən bɒnd] *noun* bond which carries no interest, but which is issued at a deep discount which provides a capital gain when it is redeemed at face value

zero dividend preference shares (ZDPS) ['zɪərəʊ 'dɪvɪdend 'prefrəns 'ʃeəz] *noun* bonds which pay no dividend, but have a fixed term and a fixed redemption price, which is a little higher than the redemption price on similar gilts though the redemption price is not in fact guaranteed (NOTE: also called **zeros**)

> zero shareholders get no income during the life of the trust
>
> *Sunday Times*

> the institutions have recently begun to realize that zeros are worth buying at their current prices
>
> *Sunday Times*

zero-rated ['zɪərəʊ'reɪtɪd] *adjective* (item) which has a VAT rate of 0%

zero-rating ['zɪərəʊ'reɪtɪŋ] *noun* rating of an item at 0% VAT

zinc [zɪŋk] *noun* metal which is traded on commodity markets, such as the London Metal Exchange

ZIP code ['zɪp 'kəʊd] *noun US* series of numbers used to indicate the area of a town where an address is situated

zloty ['zlɒti or 'zwɒti] *noun* currency used in Poland

zone [zəʊn] **1** *noun* area of a town or country (for administrative purposes); **development zone** *or* **enterprise zone** = area which has been given special help from the government to encourage businesses and factories to set up there; **free trade zone** = area where there are no customs duties **2** *verb* to divide (a town) into different areas for planning purposes; **land zoned for light industrial use** = land where planning permission has been given to build small factories for light industry

SUPPLEMENT

Central Banks

Afghanistan	da Afghanistan Bank, Kabul
Albania	Bank of Albania, Tirana
Algeria	Banque d'Algérie, Algiers
Angola	Banco Nacional de Angola, Luanda
Argentina	Banco Central de la Republica Argentina, Buenos Aires
Armenia	Central Bank of the Republic of Armenia, Yerevan
Australia	Reserve Bank of Australia, Sydney
Austria	Oesterreichische Nationalbank, Vienna
Azerbaijan	National Bank of Azerbaijan, Baku
Bahamas	Central Bank of the Bahamas, Nassau
Bahrain	Bahrain Monetary Agency, Manama
Bangladesh	Central Bank of the People's Republic of Bangladesh, Dhaka
Barbados	Central Bank of Barbados, Bridgetown
Belarus	National Bank of Belarus, Minsk
Belgium	Banque Nationale de Belgique, Brussels
Bermuda	Bermuda Monetary Authority, Hamilton
Bhutan	Royal Monetary Authority, Thimphu
Bolivia	Banco Central de Bolivia, La Paz
Bosnia & Herzegovina	National Bank of Bosnia & Herzegovina, Sarajevo
Botswana	Bank of Botswana, Gaborone
Brazil	Banco Central do Brasil, Brasilia
Brunei	Brunei Currency Board
Bulgaria	Bulgarska Narodna Banka, Sofia
Burundi	Banque de la République du Burundi, Bujumbura
Cambodia	National Bank of Cambodia, Phnom Penh
Cameroon	Banque des Etats de l'Afrique Centrale, Yaoundé
Canada	Bank of Canada, Ottawa
Central African Republic	Banque des Etats de l'Afrique Centrale, Brazzaville
Chad	Banque des Etats de l'Afrique Centrale, N'Djamena
Chile	Banco Central de Chile, Santiago
China	People's Bank of China, Beijing
Colombia	Banco de la Republica de Colombia, Bogota
Congo (Republic of)	Banque des Etats de l'Afrique Centrale, Brazzaville
Congo (Democratic Republic of)	Banque Centrale, Kinshasa
Costa Rica	Banco Central de Costa Rica, San José
Cote d'Ivoire	Banque Centrale des Etats de l'Afrique de l'Ouest, Abidjan
Croatia	Narodna Banka Hrvatske, Zagreb
Cuba	Banco Nacional de Cuba, Havana
Cyprus	Kentrike Trapeza Kyprou, Nicosia
Czech Republic	Czech National Bank, Prague
Denmark	Danmarks Nationalbank, Copenhagen
Dominican Republic	Banco Central de la Republica Dominicana, Santo Domingo
Ecuador	Banco Central del Ecuador, Quito
Egypt	Central Bank of Egypt, Cairo
El Salvador	Banco Central de Reserva de El Salvador, San Salvador
Estonia	Esti Pank, Tallinn
Ethiopia	National Bank of Ethiopia, Addis Ababa
European Union	European Central Bank, Frankfurt
Finland	Suomen Pankki, Helsinki
France	Banque de France, Paris
Gabon	Banque des Etats de l'Afrique Centrale, Libreville

Central Banks - *continued*

The Gambia	Central Bank of the Gambia, Banjul
Georgia	National Bank of the Republic of Georgia, Tbilisi
Germany	Deutsche Bundesbank, Frankfurt
Ghana	Bank of Ghana, Accra
Greece	Trapeza tes Ellados, Athens
Guatemala	Banco de Guatemala, Guatemala City
Guinea	Banque Centrale de la République de Guinée, Conakry
Guinea-Bissau	Banco Nacional de Guiné-Bissau, Bissau
Guyana	Bank of Guyana, Georgetown
Haiti	Banque de la République d'Haïti, Port-au-Prince
Honduras	Banco Central de Honduras, Tegucigalpa
Hungary	Magyar Nemzeti Bank, Budapest
Iceland	Sedlabanki Islands, Reykjavik
India	Reserve Bank of India, Bombay
Indonesia	Bank Indonesia, Jakarta
Iran	Bank Markazi Jomhouri Islami Iran, Teheran
Iraq	Central Bank of Iraq, Baghdad
Ireland	Bank Ceannais na hEireann, Dublin
Israel	Bank of Israel, Jerusalem
Italy	Banca d'Italia, Rome
Jamaica	Bank of Jamaica, Kingston
Japan	Nippon Ginko (Bank of Japan), Tokyo
Jordan	Central Bank of Jordan, Amman
Kazakhstan	National Bank of Kazakhstan, Almaty
Kenya	Central Bank of Kenya, Nairobi
Korea (North)	Central Bank of the Democratic People's Republic of Korea, Pyongyang
Korea (South)	Bank of Korea, Seoul
Kuwait	Central Bank of Kuwait, Kuwait City
Kyrgyzstan	National Bank of the Kyrgyz Republic, Bishkek
Laos	Banque d'Etat de la République Démocratique Populaire Lao, Vientiane
Latvia	Bank of Latvia, Riga
Lebanon	Banque du Liban, Beirut
Lesotho	Central Bank of Lesotho, Maseru
Liberia	National Bank of Liberia, Monrovia
Libya	Central Bank of Libya, Tripoli
Liechtenstein	Liechtensteinische Landesbank
Lithuania	Bank of Lithuania, Vilnius
Luxembourg	Institut Monétaire Luxembourgeois
Macedonia	National Bank of the Republic of Macedonia, Skopje
Madagascar	Banque Centrale de la République Malgache, Antananarivo
Malawi	Reserve Bank of Malawi, Lilongwe
Malaysia	Bank Negara Malaysia, Kuala Lumpur
Mali	Banque Centrale des Etats de l'Afrique de l'Ouest, Bamako
Malta	Central Bank of Malta, Valletta
Mauritania	Banque Centrale de Mauritanie, Nouakchott
Mauritius	Bank of Mauritius, Port Louis
Mexico	Banco de Mexico, Mexico
Moldova	National Bank of Moldova, Chisinau
Mongolia	Central Bank of Mongolia, Ulaan Baatar
Morocco	Banque al-Maghrib, Rabat
Mozambique	Banco de Moçambique, Maputo
Myanmar	Central Bank of Myanmar, Rangoon

Central Banks - *continued*

Namibia	Bank of Namibia, Windhoek
Nepal	Nepal Rastra Bank, Kathmandu
Netherlands	de Nederlandsche Bank, Amsterdam
New Zealand	Reserve Bank of New Zealand, Wellington
Nicaragua	Banco Central de Nicaragua, Managua
Niger	Banque Centrale des Etats de l'Afrique de l'Ouest, Niamey
Nigeria	Central Bank of Nigeria, Lagos
Norway	Norges Bank, Oslo
Oman	Central Bank of Oman
Pakistan	State Bank of Pakistan, Karachi
Panama	Banco Nacional de Panama, Panama
Papua New Guinea	Bank of Papua New Guinea, Port Moresby
Paraguay	Banco Central de Paraguay, Asuncion
Peru	Banco Central de Reserva del Peru, Lima
Philippines	Central Bank of the Philippines, Manila
Poland	Narodowy Bank Polski, Warsaw
Portugal	Banco de Portugal, Lisbon
Qatar	Qatar central Bank
Romania	Banca Nationala, Bucharest
Russia	Central Bank of the Russian Federation, Moscow
Rwanda	Banque Nationale du Rwanda, Kigali
Saudi Arabia	Saudi Arabian Monetary Agency, Riyadh
Senegal	Banque Centrale des Etats de l'Afrique de l'Ouest, Dakar
Seychelles	Central Bank of the Seychelles, Victoria
Sierra Leone	Bank of Sierra Leone, Freetown
Singapore	Monetary Authority of Singapore
Slovakia	National Bank of Slovakia, Bratislava
Slovenia	Banka Slovenia, Ljubljana
Somalia	Central Bank of Somalia, Mogadishu
South Africa	South African Reserve Bank, Pretoria
Spain	Banco de España, Madrid
Sri Lanka	Central Bank of Sri Lanka, Colombo
Sudan	Bank of Sudan, Khartoum
Sweden	Sveriges Riksbank, Stockholm
Switzerland	Schweizerische Nationalbank, Banque Centrale Suisse, Berne
Syria	Central Bank of Syria, Damascus
Taiwan	Central Bank of China, Taipei
Tanzania	Bank of Tanzania, Dar es Salaam
Thailand	Bank of Thailand, Bangkok
Togo	Banque Centrale des Etats de l'Afrique de l'Ouest, Lomé
Tonga	Bank of Tonga, Nuku'alofa
Trinidad and Tobago	Central Bank of Trinidad and Tobago, Port of Spain
Tunisia	Banque Centrale de Tunisie, Tunis
Turkey	Turkiye Cumhuriyet Merkez Bankasi, Ankara
Uganda	Bank of Uganda, Kampala
Ukraine	National Bank of Ukraine, Kiev
United Arab Emirates	Central Bank of the United Arab Emirates, Abu Dhabi
United Kingdom	Bank of England, London
United States of America	Federal Reserve System, Washington
Uruguay	Banco Central del Uruguay, Montevideo
Uzbekistan	Central Bank of Uzbekistan, Tashkent
Venezuela	Banco Central de Venezuela, Caracas
Vietnam	State Bank of Vietnam, Hanoi
Yemen	Central Bank of Yemen, Sana'a

Central Banks - *continued*

Yugoslavia	National Bank of Yugoslavia, Belgrade
Zambia	Bank of Zambia, Lusaka
Zimbabwe	Reserve Bank of Zimbabwe, Harare

World Commodity Markets

Argentina	Bolsa de Cereales, Buenos Aires	grains
Australia	Sydney Futures Exchange	wool, live cattle, gold
Austria	Wiener Börsekammer	timber, textiles, leather
Brazil	Bolsa de Mercadorias de São Paulo	cotton, coffee, soya beans
Canada	Winnipeg Commodity Exchange	grain, gold
France	International Market of Robusta Coffee	coffee
	Cocoa Terminal Market (part of Paris Commodity Exchange)	cocoa beans
	International Market for White Sugar	sugar
Germany	Berliner Produktenöbrse	fodder, flour, grain
	Frankfurter Getreide und Produktenöbrse	fodder, eggs, grain, flour, potatoes, fuel oil
	Niedersächsische Getreide und Produktenöbrse	grain, fodder, flour, fertilizer, potatoes
	Getreide und Warenöbrse Rhein-Ruhr	grain, fodder, flour
	Wormser Getreide und Produktenöbrse	grain, fodder, seeds, fertilizer
Hong Kong	Hong Kong Commodity Exchange	cotton, sugar
India	Tobacco Board, Andhra Pradesh	tobacco
	Coffee Board, Bangalore	coffee
	Central Silk Board, Bombay	silk
	Tea Board of India, Calcutta	tea
	Cardamom Board, Cochin	cardamoms
	Coir Board, Cochin	coir
	Rubber Board, Kerala	rubber

World Commodity Markets - *continued*

Country	Market	Commodities
Italy	Borsa Merci di Bologna	agricultural produce, flour, cereals
	Borsa Merci di Firenze	cereals, fertilizers, flour, vegetable oil, wheat, wine
	Borsa Merci di Padova	alcohol, live cattle, chickens, eggs, fertilizers, fruit, grain, olive oil, timber
	Borsa Merci di Parma	cereals, ham, eggs, flour, pork, potatoes, chickens, tomato concentrate
Japan	Hokkaido Grain Exchange	starch, beans
	Kobe Grain Exchange	grain
	Kobe Raw Silk Exchange	raw silk
	Kobe Rubber Exchange	rubber
	Nagoya Grain Exchange	starch, beans
	Nagoya Textile Exchange	cotton, rayon, wool yarn
	Osaka Grain Exchange	starch, beans
	Osaka Sampin Exchange	cotton, yarn
	Osaka Sugar Exchange	raw sugar, white sugar
	Kanmon Commodity Exchange	starch, beans, sugar
	Tokyo Grain Exchange	starch, beans
	Tokyo Rubber Exchange	rubber
	Tokyo Sugar Exchange	raw sugar, white sugar
	Tokyo Textile Commodities Exchange	cotton yarn, wool yarn
	Tokohashi Dried Cocoon Exchange	silk cocoons
Kenya	Coffee Board of Kenya	coffee
	East African Tea Trade Association	tea
	Kenya Tea Development Authority	tea
Malaysia	Malaysian Rubber Exchange	rubber
	Straits Tin Market, Penang	tin
Netherlands	Egg Terminal Market, Amsterdam	eggs
	Pork Terminal Market	pork
	Potato Terminal Market	potatoes
Norway	Oslo Fur Auctions	fur skins
Singapore	Rubber Association of Singapore	rubber
	Gold Exchange of Singapore	gold

World Commodity Markets - *continued*

United Kingdom	Liverpool Cotton Association	raw cotton
	London Cocoa Terminal Market	cocoa
	London Grain Futures Market	EC barley, EC wheat
	London Metal Exchange	aluminium, copper, lead, silver, nickel, tin, zinc
	London Rubber Terminal Market	rubber
	London Soya Bean Meal Futures Market	soya beans
	London Vegetable Oil Terminal Market	palm oil, soya bean oil
	Coffee Terminal Market	coffee
	Federation of Oils, Seeds and Fats Association	vegetable oil, animal fat, oil seed
	Tea Brokers' Association	tea
	United Terminal Sugar Market	raw sugar, white sugar
	London Jute Association	jute
	London Wool Terminal Market	Australian & New Zealand wool
	Rubber Trade Association	rubber
United States	Mid-American Commodity Exchange	corn, oats, soya beans, wheat, cattle, hogs, gold, silver
	Board of Trade of Kansas City	wheat, grains
	Commodity Exchange, New York	copper, gold, silver, zinc
	New York Cocoa Exchange	cocoa
	New York Mercantile Exchange	butter, beef, potatoes, gold, platinum, palladium, Swiss francs, Deutschmarks, Canadian dollars, pounds, yen
	Chicago Board of Trade	corn, oats, soya bean oil, frozen chickens, wheat, plywood, soya beans, gold, silver, Treasury bonds, Government National Mortgage Association certificates
	Chicago Mercantile Exchange (main market)	cattle, hogs, pork bellies, beef, hams

World Commodity Markets - *continued*

United States *(contd.)*	(International Monetary Market)	pounds, yen, Canadian dollars, Deutschmarks, French francs, guilders, Mexican pesos, Swiss francs, gold, copper, US Treasury bills
	(Associate Mercantile Division)	eggs, timber, frozen turkeys, sorghum, butter, potatoes
	Minneapolis Grain Exchange	wheat, barley, oats, corn, flax seed, rye, soya beans
	Amex Commodities Exchange	financial futures,
	GNMA futures	
	Citrus Associates (NY Exchange)	frozen orange juice
	NY Cocoa Exchange (Rubber)	natural rubber
	NY Coffee and Sugar Exchange	coffee & sugar futures
	NY Cotton Exchange	cotton

Money

In the list of world currencies that follows, words marked (*) usually have no plural: e.g. 1 kyat (one kyat), 200 kyat (two hundred kyat), etc.

Country	*Currency*	*Divided into*	*Abbreviation*
Afghanistan	Afghani*	puli	Af *or* Afs
Albania	Lek*	qindars	Lk
Algeria	Algerian dinar	centimes	DA
Andorra	French franc, Spanish peseta	centimes	
Angola	Kwanza*	lwei	Kzrl
Antigua	East Caribbean dollar	cents	Ecar$ *or* EC$
Argentina	Argentinian peso	australes	
Australia	Australian dollar	cents	A$
Austria	Schilling *or* euro	groschen	Sch *or* ASch
Bahamas	Bahamian dollar	cents	B$
Bahrain	Bahraini dinar	fils	BD
Bangladesh	Taka*	poisha	Tk
Barbados	Barbados dollar	cents	Bd$ *or* BD$
Belarus	Rouble	kopeks	
Belgium	Belgian franc *or* euro	centimes	Bfr *or* Bf *or* FB
Belize	Belize dollar	cents	BZ$
Benin	CFA franc	centimes	CFA Fr
Bermuda	Bermuda dollar	cents	Bda$
Bhutan	Ngultrum*	chetrum	N
Bolivia	Boliviano *or* Bolivian peso	centavos	$b
Bosnia	Marka	para	
Botswana	Pula	thebe	P
Brazil	Real	centavos	R$
Brunei	Brunei dollar	sen	B$
Bulgaria	Lev*	stotinki	Lv
Burkina Faso	CFA franc	centimes	CFA Fr
Burma *(see Myanmar)*			
Burundi	Burundi franc	centimes	Bur Fr *or* FrBr
Cambodia	Riel*	sen	RI
Cameroon	CFA franc	centimes	CFA Fr
Canada	Canadian dollar	cents	Can$ *or* C$
Cape Verde Islands	Escudo Caboverdiano	centavos	CV esc
Cayman Islands	Cayman Island dollar	cents	CayI$
Central African Republic	CFA franc	centimes	CFA Fr
Chad	CFA franc	centimes	CFA Fr
Chile	Chilean peso	centavos	Ch$
China	Yuan* *or* renminbi*	fen	Y
Colombia	Colombian peso	centavos	Col$
Comoros	CFA franc	centimes	CFA Fr
Congo (Republic of)	CFA franc	centimes	CFA Fr
Congo (Democratic Republic of)	Congolese franc	centimes	
Costa Rica	Colón*	centimos	₡
Croatia	Kuna	lipas	
Cuba	Cuban peso	centavos	Cub$
Cyprus	Cyprus pound	cents	£C *or* C£
Czech Republic	Koruna	haleru	K¢

Money - *continued*

Country	*Currency*	*Divided into*	*Abbreviation*
Dahomey *(see Benin)*			
Denmark	Krone	öre	DKr *or* DKK
Djibouti	Djibouti franc	centimes	Dj Fr
Dominica	East Caribbean dollar	cents	EC$
Dominican Republic	Dominican peso	centavos	DR$
Ecuador	Sucre*	centavos	Su
Egypt	Egyptian pound	piastres	£E *or* E£
Eire *(see Irish Republic)*			
El Salvador	Colón*	centavos	ES¢
Equatorial Guinea	CFA franc	centimes	CFA Fr
Estonia	Kroon	sents	
Ethiopia	Birr* *or* Ethiopian dollar	cents	EB
Fiji	Fiji dollar	cents	$F *or* F$
Finland	Marka *or* Markka *or* euro	pennia	MK
France	French franc *or* euro	centimes	Fr *or* F *or* FF
French Guiana	French franc	centimes	Fr *or* F *or* FF
Gabon	CFA franc	centimes	CFA Fr
Gambia, The	Dalasi*	butut	Di
Germany	Mark *or* euro	pfennig	DM
Ghana	Cedi*	pesewas	¢
Georgia	Lari	tetri	
Great Britain *(see United Kingdom)*			
Greece	Drachma	lepta	Dr
Grenada	East Caribbean dollar	cents	Ecar$ *or* EC$
Guatemala	Quetzal	centavos	Q
Guinea	Guinea franc	centimes	
Guinea-Bissau	CFA franc	centimes	CFA Fr
Guyana	Guyana dollar	cents	G$ *or* Guy$
Haiti	Gourde*	centimes	Gde
Holland *(see Netherlands)*			
Honduras	Lempira*	centavos	La
Hong Kong	Hong Kong dollar	cents	HK$
Hungary	Forint	filler	Ft
Iceland	Króna	aurar	Ikr
India	Rupee	paisa	R *or* Re *or* R$
Indonesia	Rupiah*	sen	Rp
Iran	Rial*	dinars	RI
Iraq	Iraqi dinar	fils	ID
Irish Republic	punt *or* Irish Pound *or* euro	pence	IR£
Israel	Shekel	agora	IS
Italy	Lira *or* euro	centesimi	L
Ivory Coast	CFA franc	centimes	CFA Fr
Jamaica	Jamaican dollar	cents	J$
Japan	Yen*	sen	Y *or* ¥
Jordan	Jordanian dinar	fils	JD
Kazakhstan	Tenge		
Kenya	Kenya shilling	cents	KSh *or* Sh
Korea (North)	North Korean won*	chon	NK W
Korea (South)	South Korean won*	jeon	SK W
Kuwait	Kuwaiti dinar	fils	KD

Money - *continued*

Country	*Currency*	*Divided into*	*Abbreviation*
Kyrgystan	Som	tyin	
Laos	Kip*	at	K *or* Kp
Latvia	Lat	santims	
Lebanon	Lebanese pound	piastres	£Leb *or* L£
Lesotho	Loti*	lisente	L
Liberia	Liberian dollar	cents	L$
Libya	Libyan dinar	dirhams	LD
Liechtenstein	Swiss franc	centimes	SFr *or* FS
Lithuania	Lita		
Luxembourg	Luxembourg franc *or* euro	centimes	LFr
Macedonia	Dinar	paras	
Macau	Pataca*	avos	P *or* $
Madeira	Portuguese escudo	centavos	Esc
Malagasy Republic	Malagasy franc	centimes	FMG *or* Mal Fr
Malawi	Kwacha*	tambala	K *or* MK
Malaysia	Ringgit *or* Malaysian Dollar	sen	M$
Maldives	Rufiyaa	laaris	MvRe
Mali	CFA franc	cents	CFA Fr
Malta	Maltese pound *or* lira	cents	£M *or* M£
Mauritania	Ouguiya*	khoums	U
Mauritius	Mauritius rupee	cents	Mau Rs *or* R
Mexico	Peso	centavos	Mex$
Moldova	Leu		
Monaco	French franc	centimes	Fr *or* F *or* FF
Mongolian Republic	Tugrik*	möngös	Tug
Montserrat	East Caribbean dollar	cents	Ecar$ *or* EC$
Morocco	Dirham	centimes	DH
Mozambique	Metical*	centavos	M
Myanmar	Kyat*	pyas	Kt
Namibia	Namibian dollar	cents	
Nauru	Australian dollar	cents	A$
Nepal	Nepalese rupee	paise	NR *or* Nre
Netherlands	Guilder *or* Gudlen *or* Florin *or* euro	cents	HFl *or* DFl *or* Gld *or* Fl
New Hebrides *(see Vanuatu)*			
New Zealand	New Zealand dollar	cents	NZ$
Nicaragua	Córdoba	centavos	C$ *or* C
Niger	CFA franc	centimes	CFA Fr
Nigeria	Naira*	kobo	N *or* ₦
Norway	Krone	o	NKr
Oman	Rial Omani	baizas	RO
Pakistan	Pakistan rupee	paise	R *or* Pak Re
Panama	Balboa	centesimos	Ba
Papua New Guinea	Kina*	toea	Ka *or* K
Paraguay	Guarani*	centimos	G
Peru	Sol	cents	S
Philippines	Philippine peso	centavos	P *or* PP
Poland	Zloty	groszy	Zl
Portugal	Escudo *or* euro	centavos	Esc
Puerto Rico	US dollar	cents	$ *or* US$

Money - *continued*

Country	*Currency*	*Divided into*	*Abbreviation*
Qatar	Qatar Riyal	dirhams	QR
Reunion	CFA franc	centimes	CFA Fr
Romania	Leu*	bani	L *or* l
Russia	Rouble	kopeks	Rub
Rwanda	Rwanda franc	centimes	Rw Fr
St Lucia	East Caribbean dollar	cents	Ecar$ *or* EC$
St Vincent	East Caribbean dollar	cents	Ecar$ *or* EC$
Samoa	Tala	sene	
Saudi Arabia	Saudi riyal *or* rial	halala	SA R
Senegal	CFA franc	centimes	CFA Fr
Seychelles	Seychelles rupee	cents	Sre *or* R
Sierra Leone	Leone	cents	Le
Singapore	Singapore dollar	cents	S$ *or* Sing$
Slovakia	Koruna	haliers	Sk
Slovenia	Tolar	stotin	SIT
Solomon Islands	Solomon Island dollar	cents	SI$
Somalia	Somali shilling	cents	Som Sh *or* So Sh
South Africa	Rand*	cents	R
Spain	Peseta *or* euro	centimos	Pta
Sri Lanka	Sri Lankan rupee	cents	SC Re
Sudan	Sudanese dinar	pounds	SD
Suriname	Suriname guilder	cents	S Gld
Swaziland	Lilangeni*	cents	Li *or* E
Sweden	Krona	örer	SKr
Syria	Syrian pound	piastres	S£
Taiwan	New Taiwan dollar	cents	T$ *or* NT$
Tanzania	Tanzanian shilling	cents	TSh
Thailand	Baht*	satang	Bt
Togo	CFA franc	centimes	CFA Fr
Tonga	Pa'anga	seniti	
Trinidad & Tobago	Trainidad & Tobago dollar	cents	TT$
Tunisia	Tunisian dinar	millimes	TD
Turkey	Turkish lira	kurus	TL
Turkmenistan	Manat	tenesi	
Tuvalu	Australian dollar	cents	$A
Uganda	Uganda Shilling	cents	Ush
Ukraine	Hryvna	kopiykas	
United Arab Emirates	UAE dirham	fils	UAE Dh *or* UD
United Kingdom	Pound sterling	pence	£ *or* £Stg
United States of America	Dollar	cents	$ *or* US$
Uruguay	Uruguayan peso	centesimos	N$
Uzbekistan	Sum	tiyin	
Vanuatu	Vatu	centimes	
Venezuela	Bolívar	centimos	BS
Vietnam	Dong*	xu	D
Virgin Islands	US dollar	cents	US$
Yemen	Riyal	fils	YR
Yugoslavia	Dinar	paras	DN
Zambia	Kwacha*	ngwee	K
Zimbabwe	Zimbabwe dollar	cents	Z$

International Telephone Calls

Country codes (preceded by 00)

Country	Code	Country	Code
Afghanistan	93	Guatemala	502
Albania	355	Guinea	224
Algeria	213	Guinea-Bissau	245
Argentina	54	Guyana	592
Armenia	374	Haiti	509
Australia	61	Honduras	504
Austria	43	Hong Kong	852
Azerbaijan	994	Hungary	36
Bahamas	1 242	Iceland	354
Bahrain	973	India	91
Bangladesh	880	Indonesia	62
Barbados	1 246	Iran	98
Belarus	375	Iraq	964
Belgium	32	Ireland	353
Bolivia	591	Israel	972
Bosnia-Herzegovina	387	Italy	39
Botswana	267	Jamaica	1 809
Brazil	55	Japan	81
Brunei	673	Jordan	962
Bulgaria	359	Kazakhstan	7
Burundi	257	Kenya	254
Cambodia	855	Korea (North)	850
Cameroon	237	Korea (South)	82
Canada	1	Kuwait	965
Central African Republic	236	Kyrgyzstan	7
Chad	235	Laos	856
Chile	56	Latvia	371
China	86	Lebanon	961
Colombia	57	Libya	218
Congo (Republic)	242	Liechtenstein	4175
Congo (Democratic Republic)	243	Lithuania	370
Croatia	385	Luxembourg	352
Cuba	53	Macedonia	389
Cyprus	357	Madagascar	261
Czech Republic	42	Malawi	265
Denmark	45	Malaysia	60
Dominican Republic	1 809	Malta	356
Ecuador	593	Mauritania	222
Egypt	20	Mauritius	230
El Salvador	503	Mexico	52
Estonia	372	Moldova	373
Ethiopia	251	Mongolia	976
Fiji	679	Morocco	212
Finland	358	Mozambique	258
France	33	Myanmar	95
Gabon	241	Namibia	264
Gambia	220	Nepal	977
Georgia	995	Netherlands	31
Germany	49	New Zealand	64
Ghana	233	Nicaragua	505
Greece	30	Niger	227

International Telephone Calls - *continued*

Country codes (preceded by 00)

Nigeria	234
Norway	47
Oman	968
Pakistan	92
Panama	507
Papua New Guinea	675
Paraguay	595
Peru	51
Philippines	63
Poland	48
Portugal	351
Qatar	974
Romania	40
Russia	7
Rwanda	250
Saudi Arabia	966
Senegal	221
Seychelles	248
Sierra Leone	232
Singapore	65
Slovakia	42
Slovenia	386
South Africa	27
Spain	34
Sri Lanka	94
Sudan	249
Suriname	597
Swaziland	268
Sweden	46
Switzerland	41
Syria	963
Taiwan	886
Tajikistan	7
Tanzania	255
Thailand	66
Togo	228
Tonga	676
Trinidad & Tobago	1 809
Tunisia	216
Turkey	90
Turkmenistan	993
Uganda	256
Ukraine	380
United Arab Emirates	971
United Kingdom	44
Uruguay	598
USA	1
Uzbekistan	7
Venezuela	58
Vietnam	84
Yemen	967
Yugoslavia	381
Zambia	260
Zimbabwe	263

Time Zones

Local Time (1200 GMT)

Accra	1200
Addis Ababa	1500
Adelaide	2100
Algiers	1300
Amman	1400
Amsterdam	1300
Ankara	1400
Asuncion	0800
Athens	1400
Baghdad	1500
Bangkok	1900
Beijing	2000
Beirut	1400
Belgrade	1300
Berlin	1300
Berne	1300
Bogota	0700
Bombay	1730
Brasilia	0900
Bratislava	1300
Brussels	1300
Bucharest	1400
Budapest	1300
Buenos Aires	0900
Cairo	1400
Calcutta	1730
Cape Town	1400
Caracas	0800
Chicago	0600
Colombo	1730
Copenhagen	1300
Damascus	1400
Dar es Salaam	1500
Delhi	1730
Dhaka	1800
Dublin	1200
Frankfurt	1300
Geneva	1300
Gibraltar	1300
Hague, The	1300
Harare	1400
Havana	0700
Helsinki	1400
Hong Kong	2000
Istanbul	1400
Jakarta	1900
Jerusalem	1400
Johannesburg	1400
Kampala	1500
Karachi	1700
Kathmandu	1745
Kiev	1400
Kuala Lumpur	2000
Kuwait	1500
Lagos	1300
La Paz	0800
Lima	0700
Lisbon	1300
Ljubljana	1300
London	1200
Los Angeles	0400
Lusaka	1400
Luxembourg	1300
Madeira	1200
Madrid	1300
Malta	1300
Managua	0600
Manila	2000
Mexico	0600
Minsk	1400
Montevideo	1500
Montreal	0700
Moscow	1500
Nairobi	1500
New Delhi	1730
New York	0700
Oslo	1300
Ottawa	0700
Panama	0700
Paris	1300
Perth	2000
Phnom Penh	1900
Port au Prince	0700
Prague	1300
Quebec	0700
Quito	0700
Rabat	1200
Rangoon	1830
Riga	1400
Rio de Janeiro	0900
Riyadh	1500
Rome	1300
St Petersburg	1500
San Francisco	0400
Santiago	0800
Singapore	2000
Sofia	1400
Stockholm	1300
Sydney	2200
Tallinn	1400
Tbilisi	1600
Tehran	1530
Tel Aviv	1400
Tokyo	2100
Toronto	0700
Tripoli	1300
Tunis	1300
Vancouver	0400
Vienna	1300
Vilnius	1400
Warsaw	1300
Washington	0700
Wellington	2400
Zagreb	1300
Zurich	1300

For further details, please tick the titles of interest and return this form to:

Peter Collin Publishing, 1 Cambridge Road, Teddington, TW11 8DT, UK
fax: +44 181 943 1673 tel: +44 181 943 3386 email: info@pcp.co.uk
For full details, visit our web site: http://www.pcp.co.uk

Title	*ISBN*	*Send Details*
English Dictionaries		
English Dictionary for Students	1-901659-06-2	❑
Accounting	0-948549-27-0	❑
Aeronautical	1-901659-10-0	❑
Agriculture, 2nd ed	0-948549-78-5	❑
American Business, 2nd ed	1-901659-22-4	❑
Automobile Engineering	0-948549-66-1	❑
Banking & Finance, 2nd ed	1-901659-30-5	❑
Business, 2nd ed	0-948549-51-3	❑
Computing, 3rd ed	1-901659-04-6	❑
Ecology & Environment, 3ed	0-948549-74-2	❑
Government & Politics, 2ed	0-948549-89-0	❑
Hotel, Tourism, Catering Management	0-948549-40-8	❑
Human Resources & Personnel, 2ed	0-948549-79-3	❑
Information Technology, 2nd ed	0-948549-88-2	❑
Law, 2nd ed	0-948549-33-5	❑
Library & Information Management	0-948549-68-8	❑
Marketing, 2nd ed	0-948549-73-4	❑
Medicine, 2nd ed	0-948549-36-X	❑
Military	1-901659-24-0	❑
Printing & Publishing, 2nd ed	0-948549-99-8	❑
Science & Technology	0-948549-67-X	❑
Vocabulary Workbooks		
Banking & Finance	0-948549-96-3	❑
Business, 2nd ed	1-901659-27-5	❑
Computing	0-948549-58-0	❑
Colloquial English	0-948549-97-1	❑
Hotels, Tourism, Catering	0-948549-75-0	❑
Law, 2nd ed	1-901659-21-6	❑
Medicine	0-948549-59-9	❑
Professional/General		
Astronomy	0-948549-43-2	❑
Economics	0-948549-91-2	❑
Multimedia, 2nd ed	1-901659-01-1	❑
PC & the Internet, 2nd ed	1-901659-12-7	❑
Bradford Crossword Solver, 3rd ed	1-901659-03-8	❑
Bilingual Dictionaries		
French-English/English-French Dictionaries		❑
German-English/English-German Dictionaries		❑
Spanish-English/English-Spanish Dictionaries		❑

Name: ....

Address: ....

....

....Postcode: ....Country: ....